# BIRNBAUM'S

## *Walt Disney World*®

**THE OFFICIAL VACATION GUIDE** **2024** ■

Expert Advice from the Inside Source

**Wendy Lefkon**—EDITORIAL DIRECTOR

**Jill Safro**—EDITOR

**Jessica Ward**—CONTRIBUTING EDITOR

**Jennie Hess**—CONTRIBUTING EDITOR

**Tony Fejeran**—DESIGNER

**Alexandra Mayes Birnbaum**—CONSULTING EDITOR

---

**Stephen Birnbaum**—FOUNDING EDITOR

## DISNEY
### EDITIONS

LOS ANGELES • NEW YORK

# CONTENTS

# WHAT'S NEW?

To spotlight attractions, shows, restaurants, and events that are making (or have recently made) their debut, listings are marked with the icon shown below. Look for it throughout the book. Here are some of the highlights:

*For Steve, who merely made all this possible.*

ISBN 978-1-368-08372-0
FAC-034274-23216

First Edition, September 2023
10 9 8 7 6 5 4 3 2 1
Printed in the United States of America

Other 2024 Birnbaum's Official Disney Guides:
*Disneyland Resort*
*Walt Disney World for Kids*

Visit *www.disneybooks.com*

# A WORD FROM THE EDITOR

For many of us, a visit to Walt Disney World is more than a vacation. It's an escape into fantasy and adventure; a chance to bond with loved ones, make new friends, and experience unabashed optimism and human kindness. It makes us laugh. It inspires us. It encourages us to believe in magic and hope for that "great big beautiful tomorrow." And while dreaming about WDW helped sustain us during the real-world challenges of the recent past, we are beyond thrilled to be planning actual visits to our collective happy place. We're honored to help you do that, too. In fact, Birnbaum has been helping folks navigate Walt Disney World since 1982!

Never before has there been so much incentive to visit (and revisit) the memory-making capital of the world. Magic Kingdom wows guests with its charming mix of classic and contemporary shows and attractions, from Peter Pan's Flight to the thrilling new TRON Lightcycle/Run, plus the return of the rousing pyrotechnic/projection production dubbed Happily Ever After. At the revitalized EPCOT, guests of all ages marvel at the new Journey of Water, inspired by Moana, daredevils spin through space on Guardians of the Galaxy: Cosmic Rewind, and Soarin' Around the World continues to send guests to happy heights. Guests at Disney's Hollywood Studios park can control the *Millennium Falcon* in Star Wars: Galaxy's Edge and be shrunk to the size of a toy in the park's Toy Story Land. And Mickey & Minnie's Runaway Railway transports giddy guests to a wild and wacky cartoon realm. Disney's Animal Kingdom is home to the wildly popular Avatar Flight of Passage, a thriller that lets guests fly on the back of a mountain banshee. The park also boasts the ever-popular Kilimanjaro Safaris and Expedition Everest. And the always dynamic Disney Springs is bursting with eclectic dining, shopping, and entertainment opportunities—including Summer House on the Lake and Drawn to Life, presented by Cirque du Soleil® and Disney.

Of course, that's just the tip of the iceberg, as so much of Walt Disney World (not to mention the real world) has grown and evolved since our last edition. We are privileged and proud to provide readers with our extensively researched, insider look at some of the most cherished attractions, resorts, and eateries on Earth.

When Steve Birnbaum launched this guide, he made it clear what was expected of anyone who worked on it. The book would be meticulously revised each year, leaving no attraction untested, no snack or meal untasted,

PHOTO BY MIKE CARROLL

Editor Jill Safro consults with Mickey and Minnie, the ultimate Disney insiders.

no hotel untried. First-hand experiences like these, accumulated over the years, make this book the most authoritative guide to the World. Our expertise, however, is not achieved by being escorted through back doors of attractions (although we would enjoy that). Instead, we wait in lines with everyone else, always hoping to have a Disney experience like that of any other guest. We also take advantage of WDW's Genie+/Lightning Lane attraction reservation service when budget allows. We'll continue to keep a close eye on it and other aspects of the Disney vacation planning universe—homework we're happy to do for readers like you.

After 52 fun-filled years, Walt's World has vastly expanded—and so has our knowledge of it. On some occasions we've encountered sweltering weather and swelling crowds—times when even the happiest of travelers can turn into Grumpy for a moment or two. Had we known then what we know now, we could have spared ourselves some trying experiences. In one case, a staffer waited more than an hour to take a tour at the Studios. Standing in line with a notebook, she was asked by another guest if there was a quiz at the end. When she explained what she was doing, he expressed surprise to learn that she was waiting with the masses. But that's always been our strategy. We believe the best way to gather useful advice for a Walt Disney World guest is to be one. Over and over again!

## Take Our Advice

We have done our best to keep you from making any tactical mistakes. We realize that even the most meticulous vacation planner needs detailed, accurate, and objective information to prepare a successful itinerary. To achieve that goal, we encourage the sharing of insight and information from Walt Disney World staffers—however, the decision of whether or not to include such information is entirely up to the discretion of this book's editor.

To that end, we have packaged handy bits of advice in the form of sample itineraries and "hot tips" throughout the book. This advice comes directly from the copious notes we've taken during our thousands of days spent in Walt Disney World. We have also used our "Birnbaum's Best" stamp of approval wherever we deemed it appropriate, highlighting favorite attractions and restaurants—the crowd-pleasers we believe stand head, shoulders, and ears above the rest.

You, the reader, benefit from the combination of our many years of experience that, together with our access to insider information, makes this guide unique. We like to think it's indispensable, but we'll let you be the judge of that a few hundred pages from now.

## Credit Where Credit Is Due

Enormous thanks to the teams of dedicated, detail-conscious Walt Disney World cast members from Guest Communications, the Disney Reservation Center, Food & Beverage, Merchandise, Resort Operations, Sports & Recreation, Attractions Operations, Disney Cruise Line, Disney Vacation Club, Marketing, and Disney Parks Synergy.

Kudos to Michelle Olveira for her diligent fact-checking. Immeasurable gratitude also to copy editor extraordinaire Monique Peterson, and to Jennifer Eastwood, Monica Vasquez, Jerry Gonzalez, Marybeth Tregarthen, Chris Ostrander, Kathy Crummey, David Roark, Steven Diaz, Alyce Diamandis, Geoffrey Cook, and Flossie Gillen for their editorial support and production panache.

Hats off to those for whom doing Walt Disney World research is truly a labor of love. The "volunteer" class of 2023 includes the Safro family (Irene, Joy, Hayden Fullerton, and Delaney Irene), the Henning family (Amy, Chris, Avery, Elle, and Reid), Linda Verdon, Trace Schielzo, Jilly Bean Kunkel, Dan Kunkel, Joe D'Agnese, Denise Kiernan, Tina Oliveri, Julia Oliveri, Joseph Oliveri, Bob Cook, Stacey Cook, and Christina Fontana.

Of course, no list of acknowledgments would be complete without mentioning our founding editor, Steve Birnbaum, whose spirit, wisdom, and humor still infuse these pages, as well as Alexandra Mayes Birnbaum, who continues to be a guiding light—to say nothing of being a careful reader of every word.

## The Last Word

Finally, it's important to remember that every worthwhile travel guide is a living enterprise; the book you hold in your hands is our best effort at explaining how to enjoy Walt Disney World at this moment. But its text is in no way etched in stone. Details change often—especially these days! Disney is constantly changing and growing, and in each edition we refine and expand our material to serve your needs even better. For this year's edition, though, this must be the final word.

Have a great visit!
—JILL SAFRO, EDITOR

## DON'T FORGET TO WRITE!

No contribution is of greater value to us in preparing the next edition of this book than your comments on its usefulness and your own experiences at Walt Disney World. We encourage you to email us at **WDI.Birnbaum.Guides@disney.com**, or drop us a note at the address below. Thank you!

**Jill Safro**
**Birnbaum's Walt Disney World 2024**
**Disney Editions**
**77 W. 66th Street**
**3rd Floor/Suite #356**
**New York, NY 10023**

# GETTING READY TO GO

The key to a fabulous vacation at Walt Disney World is advance planning. This remarkably varied complex is too vast and diverse to allow a spontaneous visit to be undertaken with much success—especially when you consider the rapid rate at which the World has expanded and the introduction of Lightning Lanes, a fee-based service that allows visitors to experience shorter wait times. (The work-in-progress service is likely to evolve in 2024—check *disneyworld.com* for

updates.) It does not mean that even the most casual visitors can't have significant fun, but they are bound to have regrets about things they missed because of time pressures or a simple lack of information. The mission of this guide is to eliminate potential frustration while getting the biggest bang for your vacation buck.

What follows, then, is meant to provide a sensible scheme for planning a satisfying Walt Disney World visit, one that will offer the most fun and the least disappointment. But how do you know which of the countless activities will be the most enjoyable for you and your party? Do your homework. The best strategy is to make sure you have a clear idea of all that is available long before you arrive in the Orlando area. All details are subject to change at any time. Visit *disneyworld.com* for updates.

> "To all who come to this happy place: Welcome."
>
> **—Walt Disney**

# When to Go

When talk finally turns to the best time to make a trip to Walt Disney World, Christmas and Easter are often mentioned, as well as the traditional summer vacation period—especially if there are kids in the family. But there is also good reason to avoid these periods, namely the tremendous crowds they attract. And when Disney World is crowded, it can be very crowded, indeed. On the busiest days, visitors may wait in line more than two hours to experience the most popular attractions. That's at least twice as long as during less busy times of the year. Weekends, in general, are quite busy. Sunday night through Wednesday tends to be a bit less so.

Considering seasonal hours, weather, crowd patterns, and Disney resort rates, optimal times to visit Disney are usually mid-January through early February, late April through late May, and September through December (except for Martin Luther King Day weekend, and Thanksgiving and Christmas weeks).

**Hot Tip!** You will never be lonely at Walt Disney World, but you may enjoy a little more elbow room than usual during the months of September and January (with the exceptions of WDW Marathon Weekend and the dates surrounding Martin Luther King Day.)

Note that during some of the less crowded times of the year—particularly during winter—some shows and attractions are closed for renovations. In addition, water parks are often closed for refurbishment during cooler months. Check the (free) My Disney Experience mobile app or website, visit *disneyworld.com*, or call 407-824-4321 for a current schedule.

Early November through December is a festive time of year the world over, and Walt Disney World is no exception. The theme parks are decorated to the nines for the holiday season. (It seems to turn from Halloween to Christmas overnight.) EPCOT holds Christmas concerts, and Magic Kingdom has an enormous twinkling tree on Main Street, U.S.A. Many special events are held during this period, including Mickey's Very Merry Christmas Party in the Magic Kingdom (note that a separate admission ticket is required). The party brings a dusting of "snow" to Main Street, U.S.A. from about 7 P.M. until about midnight for several days a week between mid-November and the first three weeks of December. It also features holiday shows around the park, including

Mickey's Once Upon a Christmastime Parade, plus a unique holiday fireworks show. Select performances from Mickey's Very Merry Christmas Party are also staged in the park during regular hours on the days leading up to, including, and following Christmas. This event often sells out way ahead of time. Get your tickets in advance by using the My Disney Experience website or app, visiting *disneyworld.com*, or calling 407-W-DISNEY (934-7639). Advance purchase prices start at about $149 (same-day purchases are higher). It's usually easier to snag tickets for dates early in the season.

EPCOT celebrates with its International Festival of the Holidays, including the nightly Candlelight Processional, complete with a mass choir, 50-piece orchestra, and a reading of the story of Christmas by a celebrity narrator. Dinner packages are available for some World Show-case restaurants. (They guarantee a table for dinner, plus seating at the popular Candlelight Processional. Without a package, you should arrive at least 90 minutes before showtime.) Not to be left out of the holiday fun, Disney's Hollywood Studios may celebrate with a special-ticket party called Jollywood Nights (first presented in 2023).

Disney Springs gets into the merriment of the season with Christmas trees, twinkling lights, and holly-jolly entertainment—including visits by Saint Nick himself. There are holiday decorations and themes at each WDW resort hotel, too, including a Victorian Christmas at the Grand Floridian, a seaside party at the Yacht & Beach Club, a Cajun holiday at Port Orleans Riverside, and more.

For Walt Disney World hotel reservations, use the My Disney Experience website, visit *disneyworld.com*, or call 407-W-DISNEY (934-7639), your travel agent, or the Walt Disney Travel Company (407-828-8101). Note that special-event tickets are sold separately.

New Year's Eve is a particularly popular date on which to visit Walt Disney World. The theme parks usually offer extended hours—and guests at the Magic Kingdom and EPCOT are treated to extra festive fireworks displays. Many WDW restaurants have special menus, too. For specifics, check *disneyworld.com*.

# Crowd Patterns

## DAY-TO-DAY TRENDS

Weekends tend to be among the most crowded days at Walt Disney World's four theme parks, followed by Mondays, Thursdays, and Fridays. Morning through early afternoon is a bustling time for the theme parks and their popular "E-ticket" attractions. Days that offer Extended Evening Hours tend to be more crowded at their respective theme parks (refer to page 22). When the Florida weather is especially steamy, Disney's water parks tend to pack them in—so be sure to get a very early start if you're headed to Blizzard Beach or Typhoon Lagoon.

When the time comes to plot an itinerary for your Walt Disney World visit, it's helpful to know about crowd patterns beyond the theme parks as well. As a rule, Disney Springs (the dining, shopping, and entertainment district formerly known as Downtown Disney) and the Walt Disney World water parks tend to host their largest throngs on weekends and when the mercury soars. Golfers should note that week-end tee times are typically in the highest demand, while Monday and Tuesday tee times tend to be a bit easier to come by year-round.

## SEASONAL SHIFTS

The chart below indicates the density of crowds in the theme parks throughout the year. Though it's tough to generalize about a property as vast and ever-changing as Walt Disney World—special events (such as the Disney Marathon, Halloween festivities, and EPCOT's International Food & Wine Festival) and package deals can swell theme park attendance during a period typically marked by smaller crowds—the chart highlights historic trends.

Least Crowded means that there will be lines in the parks (there always are!); however, most shows and attractions may be experienced with a bit less waiting than during busier times of the year.

Average Crowds refers to times when there are lots of people around, but lines for shows and attractions are relatively manageable.

Most Crowded reflects times when lines at popular attractions can mean a wait of as much as two to three hours (or more). As a rule, when school is out, the crowds are most definitely in at Walt Disney World.

Note that the chart represents historical trends with regard to crowds at WDW. Patterns are apt to vary.

### LEAST CROWDED

- 2nd week of January through 1st week of February (excluding WDW Marathon Week and Martin Luther King Day Weekend)
- Weeks before and after Labor Day (excluding the holiday weekend itself
- Week after Thanksgiving until the weekend at the start of Christmas week

### AVERAGE CROWDS

- 1st week of January (excluding New Year's Day, which is "Most Crowded")
- 2nd week of February until Presidents' week
- End of February through 2nd week of March
- Last week of April through May
- Period after EPCOT's International Food & Wine Festival ends until the weekend before Thanksgiving

### MOST CROWDED

- All major holidays
- Presidents' week
- WDW Marathon Week and dates of other runDisney events
- 3rd week of March through the 3rd week of April
- Easter week
- June through the 3rd week of August
- Thanksgiving week
- Christmas through New Year's Day
- Any time school's out

# Holidays & Special Events

Special events are staged at Walt Disney World all year long, not only to mark holidays, but also to celebrate other interests. The dates and details that follow are subject to change without notice. For updates about 2024 events, use the My Disney Experience mobile app or website, visit *disneyworld.com*, or call 407-824-4321.

## JANUARY

**Walt Disney World Marathon Weekend** (January 3–7, 2024): Some 26,000 entrants run through the parks and other areas of the World during the 26.2-mile race (January 7). Characters and cast members are on hand for inspiration. Similar hoopla surrounds the half marathon (January 6). The 2-day "Goofy Race and a Half Challenge" usually covers all 4 theme parks and 39.3 miles (January 6 and 7). There is a 10K run (January 4), and a 5K family run, on January 3. (It's okay to walk the 5K, but a 16-minute mile must be maintained.) Runners may opt for the "Dopey Challenge"—all of the aforementioned events within the pacing requirements—and earn a Dopey Challenge finisher medal. Packages are available. Call 407-939-4786 for package details or to book. For marathon weekend event information and schedules, go to *www.rundisney.com*. Registration for this extremely popular event typically opens in the April prior to the January races—and fills up quickly. Rooms are always in high demand. For details on other Walt Disney World running events and/or to sign up for the runDisney newsletter, visit *www.rundisney.com*.

**EPCOT International Festival of the Arts** (January–February): EPCOT itself is a vibrant celebration of culture, cuisine, art, and entertainment. This festival takes those elements to the next level in a special salute to the creative arts. Expect curated art exhibits, live performances—including the crowd-pleasing Disney on Broadway concert series at the America Gardens Theatre—kiosks featuring fanciful artistic nibbles, workshops, lectures, fun photo ops, sidewalk art, and more. For dates and other details about EPCOT's engaging Festival of the Arts,

visit *disneyworld.com/ArtfulEpcot*, use the My Disney Experience app or website, visit *disneyworld.com*, or call 407-939-5277.

## MARCH–JUNE

**Saint Patrick's Day** (March 17): Everyone is Irish on Saint Patrick's Day—especially at Raglan Road's Mighty St. Patrick's Festival at Disney Springs. The family-friendly festivities include music, dancing, dining, and more. (The festivities usually run several days on either side of March 17.) Of course, every day is a celebration of the Emerald Isle at Raglan Road, the Landing's authentic Irish pub. EPCOT's United Kingdom pavilion marks the day with Irish dining, dancing, and pints of Guinness.

**Easter** (March 31, 2024): Most of the Disney parks stay open late during the two weeks straddling Easter Sunday. Mr. and Mrs. Easter Bunny greet guests in the Magic Kingdom. EPCOT hosts an "Egg-stravaganza" hunt—cost is about $6 for a map with stickers (find all the eggs and win a prize). And many of the Disney World resorts offer special Easter-themed fun. Catholic and Protestant services may be offered at the Contemporary resort. Call 407-W-DISNEY for specifics. This is an extremely busy time to visit.

**EPCOT International Flower & Garden Festival** (early March–early July): EPCOT is blooming with elaborate gardens (including more than 30 million fragrant blossoms) and topiary displays, behind-the-scenes tours, and concerts. Pick up a Garden Passport and stamp it as you explore the Outdoor Kitchens throughout the day. The passports are free and may be found at park entrances, at Outdoor Kitchen stations, and at many EPCOT shopping locations. Each Outdoor Kitchen has its own unique stamp.

Another popular element of the Flower and Garden Festival is the Garden Rocks concert series, presented

**Hot Tip!** Disney Springs celebrates Pride Month in June with retail spotlights, unique food and beverage items, and special opportunities for guests to share their pride. And in recognition of Pride, The Walt Disney Company is donating funds to organizations around the planet that support LGBTQ+ communities. To learn more, visit *rainbowdisneycollection.com*.

**Hot Tip!** While Disney Floral and Gifts packed up shop last summer, WDW guests may order in-room cheer via *floridafreshfloral.com*. It's a nice way to add a little magic to an already festive resort room. Details subject to change.

at the America Gardens Theatre near the American Adventure pavilion. Past performers have included the Village People, Rick Springfield, Smash Mouth, Lonestar, and The Spinners. All shows are included with EPCOT admission. Seats are available on a first-come, first-served basis—get there early.

**Mother's Day** (May 12, 2024): Celebrate Mom by treating her to a special Mother's Day meal. Several WDW restaurants—such as Animal Kingdom Lodge's Boma—Flavors of Africa, Olivia's at Disney's Old Key West, Ale & Compass Restaurant at the Yacht Club, and the Contemporary's Steakhouse 71—have been known to offer Mother's Day meals. For details about the 2024 options, use the My Disney Experience mobile app or website, or visit *disneyworld.com*. Note that Walt Disney World resorts are extremely busy on Mother's Day weekend—book early.

**Hot Tip!** Festivities marking The Walt Disney Company's first century—aka Disney 100—are expected to run through early 2024. For details, kindly visit *disneyworld.com*, or use the My Disney Experience mobile app or website. Happy anniversary to The Walt Disney Company!

## JULY–AUGUST

**Fourth of July Celebration:** Double-size fireworks presentations over the Magic Kingdom, EPCOT, and (possibly) Disney's Hollywood Studios make for a colorful night. Disney characters don red, white, and blue finery and greet guests at EPCOT's American Adventure pavilion throughout the day. That pavilion's America Gardens Theatre hosts a patriotic show featuring an expanded cast of the Voices of Liberty. The evening's nighttime spectacular (presented on World Showcase Lagoon) may feature a patriotic finale. This is an exceptionally busy time to visit Walt Disney World.

## AUGUST–NOVEMBER

**EPCOT International Food & Wine Festival** (mid-July–mid-November): EPCOT celebrates the flavors of many different countries (even those not usually represented in World Showcase) through tastings (about $4 to $12 per tapas-style plate), demonstrations from top chefs, the Eat to the Beat concert series, and wine and cooking seminars. It's an extraordinarily satisfying way to wander through the park. It's also insanely popular, so expect lots of company—especially in the evening. For additional details or to make a reservation for a special event (which you should do as far in advance as possible), visit *www.epcotfoodfestival.com*.

**Halloween** (August–October, 2024): The festivities vary a bit from year to year. What follows is a sampling of what to expect:

Fort Wilderness Resort and Campground usually hosts a pumpkin-carving contest and a kids' costume contest, followed by a screening of a spooky movie. It may also offer Halloween-themed wagon rides with storytelling and various surprises along the way. The Magic Kingdom may play host to its Halloween spectacular, **Mickey's Not-So-Scary Halloween Party**, mid-August through October. The special-ticket activities include a parade, fireworks, dancing, appearances by Disney villains (including a Castle Forecourt show called **Hocus Pocus Villain Spelltacular**), trick-or-treating (with free candy!), and a special fireworks presentation. This is an extremely popular—and crowded—Magic Kingdom event. Purchase tickets as far in advance as possible. And don't forget your costume! (For WDW's costume guidelines, visit *disneyworld.com*.) Note that guests with tickets to the Halloween Party may be able to enter the park as early as 4 P.M. (Be sure to ask when you buy your ticket.) As a spooky bonus, **Mickey's Boo-to-You Halloween Parade** makes its way through the Magic Kingdom during the not-so-scary Halloween party. Advance purchase prices range from about $109–$199 for adults, $109–$189 for kids (plus tax; same-day ticket purchases are higher). For details, call 407-827-7200.

**Thanksgiving** (November 28, 2024): All Walt Disney World restaurants are open on Turkey Day, many of them offering Thanksgiving specialties. For updates, call 407-WDW-DINE (939-3463).

**Dapper Day** (Fall and Spring): Dapper Day invites guests to dress up and flaunt their fabulous looks—with a retro-chic, Disney, or contemporary flair—at select WDW parks (and other Disney locales). Usually spread over two days (in the fall and the spring), the remarkably popular group fashion shows are not run nor endorsed by The Walt Disney Company. For current dates and details, visit *https://dapperday.com*.

## NOVEMBER–DECEMBER

**Disney's Magical Holidays:** Decorations and festivities abound in WDW's parks and resorts. The Magic Kingdom park hosts **Mickey's Very Merry Christmas Party** on select nights from early November through the first three weeks of December, complete with snow flurries on Main Street and complimentary cookies and hot cocoa. Entertainment for the special-ticket party includes **Mickey's Once Upon a Christmastime Parade** and a special edition of the fireworks show. Select performances are staged during regular hours just before Christmas. Magic Kingdom may offer a holiday Jungle Cruise, aka the Jingle Cruise. Guests with tickets to the Christmas Party can often enter the Magic Kingdom as early as 4 P.M. Note that the park is densely populated during Mickey's Very Merry Christmas Party. Details are subject to change at any time.

**EPCOT International Festival of the Holidays** (mid-November–late December) may feature the Christmas Candlelight Processional, including a choral concert, plus a well-known celebrity narrator who reads the story of Christmas. The event is included with park admission, but seating is limited and it is exceptionally popular. Arrive at least 90 minutes before showtime, or book a dinner package (which combines dinner at a World Showcase eatery with guaranteed Processional seating). For details, use the My Disney Experience app or website. Holiday kitchens serve sweet and savory treats throughout the holiday season.

Disney Springs gets into the holiday spirit with a cheery mix of twinkling lights, music, a towering tree, and visits from the North Pole's most famous resident. Past years have brought carolers, stilt-walkers, and a lively holiday dance party.

**New Year's Eve Celebration (December 31):** There are extra-spectacular fireworks in the skies above the Magic Kingdom, EPCOT, and (possibly) Disney's Hollywood Studios (though there are no fireworks at all at Animal Kingdom—imagine the stampede!). These parks usually stay open until about 1 A.M. Many of the resort restaurants, as well as the nightspots at Disney Springs, also welcome the new year Disney style.

**Hot Tip!** On dates when Magic Kingdom hosts "special-ticket" events, such as Mickey's Not-So-Scary Halloween Party and Mickey's Very Merry Christmas Party, the park closes early to day guests. (Usually at 6 or 7 P.M., but it could be earlier.)

# Keeping WDW Hours

Since operating hours tend to fluctuate, use the My Disney Experience mobile app or website, or visit *disneyworld.com*, or call 407-824-4321 for updates.

**THEME PARKS:** WDW theme park hours vary seasonally. In May, September, October, parts of November and December, and all of January, the Magic Kingdom is usually open from about 9 A.M. to 8 P.M.; EPCOT is often open from 9 A.M. to 9 P.M. (some attractions may keep different hours), later during peak days/seasons; Disney's Hollywood Studios is open from 9 A.M. until about an hour after sunset; and Animal Kingdom is usually open from 9 A.M. till about 6 or 7 P.M. (or later). The theme parks offer Early Theme Park Entry throughout the week. It's a perk extended to guests staying at Disney-owned and other select resorts and allows them to enter any theme park 30 minutes before it opens to the public. Guests at WDW Deluxe and Deluxe Villa and other select resorts may enjoy extended evening hours on select nights in select theme parks. (See Extra Park Time on page 22.) While "extra magic" time in the parks can be quite satisfying, some shows, shops, attractions, and restaurants do not operate during these periods.

The Magic Kingdom park keeps later hours through summer and other busy periods, including Christmas and Easter weeks. The parks may be open until 1 A.M. on New Year's Eve. Disney's Hollywood Studios often stays open until 10 or 11 P.M. in the summer, too.

**DISNEY SPRINGS—MARKETPLACE, LANDING, AND TOWN CENTER:** Shops are generally open from about 10 A.M. until 11 P.M. Sunday through Thursday; 11:30 P.M. on Friday and Saturday. Restaurant hours vary, with most venues open until at least 11 P.M. or midnight.

**DISNEY SPRINGS, WEST SIDE:** At the AMC cineplex, movies begin as early as 10 A.M. Restaurants are open from about 11:30 A.M. to midnight. Most shops are open from about 10:30 A.M. to 11 P.M. (midnight on Friday and Saturday).

**WATER PARKS:** Disney water parks are usually open from about 10 A.M. to 5 P.M., but extend hours during summer months. Cabanas should be reserved in advance (see Hot Tips on pages 238 and 240).

**WALT DISNEY WORLD PARK TRANSPORTATION:** Bus, boat, Disney Skyliner (airborne gondolas), and monorail service generally begin up to an hour prior to park opening time and continue until about an hour after the parks close. Boats, the Skyliner, and monorails don't always operate for special ticket events.

# Walt Disney World Weather

| | TEMPERATURE AVERAGE | | RAINFALL AVERAGE |
|---|---|---|---|
| | HIGH | LOW | (INCHES) |
| **JANUARY** | 71 | 50 | 2.7 |
| **FEBRUARY** | 73 | 53 | 2.8 |
| **MARCH** | 77 | 57 | 3.8 |
| **APRIL** | 82 | 62 | 2.5 |
| **MAY** | 88 | 68 | 3.3 |
| **JUNE** | 91 | 73 | 8.7 |
| **JULY** | 92 | 76 | 7.1 |
| **AUGUST** | 92 | 76 | 7.8 |
| **SEPTEMBER** | 89 | 74 | 6.0 |
| **OCTOBER** | 84 | 68 | 3.3 |
| **NOVEMBER** | 78 | 60 | 2.4 |
| **DECEMBER** | 72 | 54 | 2.6 |

# How to Get There

## BY CAR

While most visitors to the Orlando area fly in, quite a few choose to drive. If you opt for a road trip, figure on logging no more than 350 to 400 miles a day—a distance that won't wear you down so much that you can't enjoy your journey. It will also help keep your car and its tires healthy. (It's always a good idea to have tires inspected before hitting the open road—flat tires are the most common reason for roadside assistance calls.)

If you plan to navigate with GPS, note Walt Disney World's address in the Hot Tip below. Contact state tourist boards to inquire about free maps, too (yes, they still make maps—the perfect backup system for the GPS!); for a Florida map and guide, call Visit Florida at 888-735-2872, or pick up the latest edition of the *Rand McNally Road Atlas* (available for purchase online and in bookstores).

> **Hot Tip!** Driving to Walt Disney World and in need of an address to plug into the GPS? Look no further: 1180 Seven Seas Drive, Lake Buena Vista, FL 32830. This takes you to the Magic Kingdom area of WDW—follow signs to your final Disney destination.

Reputable automobile clubs offer help with vehicle breakdowns; towing; insurance that covers personal injury, accidents, arrest, bail bond, and lawyers' fees for defense of contested traffic cases; and travel-planning services, including free maps and route mapping. Services vary from one club to the next, and membership fees range widely, from about $50 to $120 a year. (See list at right.)

## RESOURCES FOR ROAD TRIPPERS

There are a variety of reputable national automobile associations to choose from. Among the leading clubs to consider:

- Allstate Motor Club
  Customer Service Center
  800-726-6033
  *www.allstate.com*

- American Automobile Association (AAA)
  407-444-4240 or 800-564-6222
  *www.aaa.com*

- Ford Customer Relationship Center
  800-392-3673

- Geico
  800-207-7847
  *www.geico.com*

- Signature's Nationwide Auto Club
  800-323-2002
  *www.autoclub.com*

Travelers may also check with state tourist boards for free maps. Other map sources are the *Michelin North America Road Atlas* and the *Rand McNally Road Atlas*; they are also sold in many bookstores.

Once you arrive in the Sunshine State, pause for a pit stop at an Official Florida Welcome Center. There you will find specialists on hand to help with travel-planning needs, plus maps, restrooms, picnic tables, and free Florida citrus juice. For details (including operating hours), go to *visitflorida.com* (and click "Welcome Centers" under the "More" tab).

**DID YOU KNOW?**
It's legal to make a right turn at a red light in Florida after coming to a complete stop and yielding to traffic and pedestrians — unless there is a NO TURN ON RED sign. Please pay attention!

## BY AIR

When it comes to airfares, there is no real trick to unearthing the most economical ones: Simply shop around. Call a travel agent, browse the Internet, and keep the following tips in mind:

• Orlando International Airport (MCO) is the closest airport to Walt Disney World. The modern facility has on-site lodging, rental cars, restaurants, and more. For additional information about the airport and its current protocols, visit *orlandoairports.net*. We highly recommend the (free) Orlando International Airport mobile app. It can help you track flights, monitor TSA (Transportation Security Administration) wait times, find local transportation and on-site parking, and more.

**Hot Tip!** If you are flying home via Orlando International Airport (also known as OIA or MCO), allow an extra 60 to 90 minutes to get through airport security. The lines there can be surprisingly long—and you will have to wait your turn, even if it means missing your flight. It is always wise to arrive early.

• With huge waits at regular security lines, having TSA Pre-Check status is well worth the $78 (for a 5-year term). Be sure to apply for it at least 90 days before your trip (and be sure to add your Known Traveler Number to your airline reservation): *tsa.gov/precheck*

• Take advantage of advance-purchase fares (lower rates that apply if a ticket is bought far in advance). And pay attention to what is and isn't included with your ticket —checked bags, overhead space, etc.—The fees add up!

• Plan to fly when most people don't: For most vacation destinations, that usually means leaving the ground on Tuesday or Wednesday.

• Keep in mind that the lowest airfares usually carry a hefty penalty if you have to revise or cancel a ticket.

• Be sure to build the cost of airport transfers or parking into your travel budget.

## BY BUS

Greyhound provides frequent direct service to Orlando and Kissimmee (the latter is closer to Walt Disney World). From either destination, you can take a taxi to your hotel, but first check if your hotel offers shuttle service. For additional information, contact Greyhound at 800-231-2222, or visit *www.greyhound.com*.

## BY TRAIN

Amtrak serves the Orlando, Florida, area twice daily to and from New York City, with stops made along the way. The journey usually takes about 22 hours and costs from about $246 to $355 round-trip, coach. (Book early for lower fares; discounts are often available, so be sure to ask. Passengers over the age of 18 must present valid government-issued photo ID.) If you're staying at a WDW resort, plan to take a cab or shuttle to your hotel. Cars are also available to rent. They are not on-site but are easily reached by shuttle.

For reservations and more train information, call 800-USA-RAIL (872-7245), visit the Amtrak website at *www.amtrak.com*, or contact a travel agent.

## WDW: KNOW BEFORE YOU GO

The information in this chapter is tailored to help you plan, book, and seamlessly modify your Disney vacation dreams. And we've done our best to ensure that it and all other content within this edition of *Birnbaum's Official Guide to Walt Disney World* is as useful, comprehensive, and current as possible. That said, procedures and policies do change now and then—especially these days. So before you begin your trip, be sure to check on the latest Walt Disney World procedural changes and updates at: *disneyworld.disney.go.com/experience-updates/parks*.

## FROM ORLANDO INTERNATIONAL AIRPORT (MCO)*

**BY CAR:** During rush hour, take the airport's South Exit to the Central Florida GreeneWay (Route 417) to Route 536, which leads to Walt Disney World. The tolls run about $3.

For the shortest route, take the North Exit to Route 528, going west toward Tampa. Pick up I-4 west, and go to a WDW exit. Tolls are about $2. The route is usually heavily trafficked, but manageable during non-rush periods of the day. It's busiest on weekday mornings and evenings and any time a theme park is scheduled to open or close.

**BY CAR SERVICE:** Rideshare services Lyft and Uber are both authorized to transport guests to and from Walt Disney World. Be sure to download and familiarize yourself with the app before your trip. Reliable car service is available from Noris Limousines. Expect to pay about $180 for a sedan or an SUV. Limos cost about $380 round-trip for up to 8 people. Reservations are required and cancellations must be made at least 48 hours in advance. Call 407-240-4533, or visit *norislimousines.com.* Prices do not include gratuity and may increase at any time—especially if there is a big jump in prices at the gas pump.

Florida Towncar also offers friendly, direct service to all Disney area resorts. And they offer our readers a special rate, too! Simply mention the Birnbaum Guide when you make the reservation and expect a round-trip flat rate of about $100 for up to 4 passengers (to and from the Orlando International Airport only). That's $15 off the regular price. If you'll need a car seat, request one when you make your reservation. (It will add about $10 to the price.) Call 407-277-5466 (from Florida) or 800-525-7246 (from out of state) at least 24 hours ahead of pickup time, or visit *www.floridatowncar.com.* For an extra $10, the driver will make a 30-minute stop at a grocery store. Quite convenient!

**BY RENTAL CAR:** In the days when Disney's Magical Express was operating (R.I.P. old friend), we shied away from renting a car at Orlando International Airport. The rates are much higher than you'll find away from the airport, plus you need to pay for gas. The good news is that self-parking is free at Walt Disney World–owned-and-operated resorts. The cost for valet parking (available at deluxe resorts and Coronado Springs) is $33 per night. Now that the Magical Express is no more, the rental car option is back on the table. That said, it's by far the priciest choice for shuttling your party between MCO and the House of Mouse. But if your plans include visits to area attractions not within Disney's borders, this may be the right choice for you.

**BY SUNSHINE FLYER:** All aboard! This cheerful and efficient service shuttles guests in buses designed to resemble cars and locomotives from a 1920s passenger train. One-way trips cost about $20 per adult and $11 per child (ages 3 through 12); round-trip transfers run about $39 per adult/$22 per child. You'll find Sunshine Flyer outside Orlando International Airport's Terminal B, Level 1 in the Ground Transportation area between bus bays B5 through B9. For additional information or to make reservations, visit *https://sunshineflyer.com,* or call 321-329-8685.

**BY TAXI:** Metered taxicabs usually cost between $60 and $70 each way, depending on the destination—and the integrity of the driver. (Prices listed at the airport taxi stand are estimates). Some taxis can accommodate up to 9 people (for the price of one). Bell Services can call for a cab at any WDW resort. Note that many drivers do not have SunPass, so it will cost you at least 45 cents a minute while waiting to pay each toll.

**BY MEARS CONNECT:** Having made its debut in early 2022, Mears Connect offers convenient transportation in high-occupancy vehicles. Guests arriving at Orlando International Airport (MCO) can expect luggage handling, convenient airport terminal access, and round-trip service between Walt Disney World area resorts. Mears Connect offers a variety of "enhancements" meant to improve ease of use and provide vehicle options. For additional information, pricing, and to make reservations call 407-423-5566, or visit *www.mearstransportation.com.*

**DISNEY'S MAGICAL EXPRESS:** Disney's Magical Express, the long-running shuttle service between Orlando International Airport (MCO) and Walt Disney World, has been retired—December 31, 2021 marked the end of the road for the Magical Express.

*Note that gratuities are not included in transfer rates. It is customary to tip for good service.*

# Planning Ahead
## Logistics

Organizing a trip properly takes time, but most travelers find the increased enjoyment well worth the effort. The fact is, planning a Disney visit can be a pleasant sort of "armchair" exercise for the whole family. Kids will enjoy their visit to Disney all the more if they, too, are involved in the process. Take it from us, the more information you can gather, the better.

To assist in that effort, we immodestly recommend *Birnbaum's Walt Disney World for Kids*, a colorful look at the World, written for readers ages 7 through 14. For parties aiming to pair a Disney cruise with a WDW visit, the info beginning on page 337 is a good place to start.

**Hot Tip!** So you're using the Birnbaum Guide to plan your trip to Walt Disney World. What are you going to do next? Go to *www.disneyworld.com!* There you can get WDW news and park hours, purchase tickets, make dining reservations, and more. (You can also use the handy-dandy My Disney Experience app or website.)

### INFORMATION SOURCES

For additional information about Walt Disney World, use the My Disney Experience app or website, visit *www.disneyworld.com*, or call 407-W-DISNEY (407-934-7639). Specifics such as park hours, ticket prices, refurbishment schedules, and directions are available through an automated system 24 hours a day. For info by mail, write to: Walt Disney World, P.O. Box 10000, Lake Buena Vista, FL 32830-1000.

Free park guidemaps are available at all four theme parks, just inside the entrance and at Guest Relations locations. Theme Park Tip Boards provide information such as attraction wait times; Disney character appearance, parade, and stage show schedules; and more.

Internet and smartphone users can get details about trip planning, reserve a resort room, order theme park and water park tickets, book (and modify) dining reservations, and get attraction wait times, park operating hours, and special-events descriptions by using the My Disney Experience app or website, or by visiting *disneyworld.com*. Disney Cruise Line vacation packages may be booked at *disneycruise.com*.

For discounts on (non-Disney) area attractions, hotels, and restaurants, contact Visit Orlando at 407-363-5872 and visit *www.visitorlando.com*.

For information about other Central Florida attractions, contact Visit Florida; 888-735-2872 (to request a free visitors guide and map); *www.visitflorida.com*. You can also download area guides from the website.

**On-site Resources:** Those staying at a WDW resort should consider their Lobby Concierge desk a primary resource. Resort guests also receive information via their room's TV. Fort Wilderness campers are advised to stop at the Pioneer Hall Info and Ticket Window, call extension 2788, or touch 11 on a phone near any restroom. (Tablet and smartphone users can access *mydisneyexperience.com* or use the free app.)

### WHAT TO PACK

While there's no formal dress code at Walt Disney World, neat, casual clothing is the rule, with few exceptions. Most notably, jackets are required for men at Victoria & Albert's restaurant in the Grand Floridian resort. Generally speaking, T-shirts and shorts are fine during the day. For evening, slacks, jeans, or Bermuda-length shorts are appropriate. Bathing suits are a must, along with the appropriate attire for any sport you want to pursue. (Tennis, anyone?)

Light sweaters are necessary even in summer—to wear indoors when the air-conditioning gets chilly. From November through March, warmer clothing is a must for evening. Pack for weather extremes so you will be comfy should it become unseasonably warm or cool. Be sure to take hand sanitizer, sunscreen, and bug repellent. Adults must have government-issued photo ID. (Leave selfie sticks at home—they are not permitted in Disney theme or water parks. Also forbidden: weapons of any kind, including toys.) If possible, pack rain gear (a large, light-weight poncho is best). One of the most important items of all? Comfortable walking shoes (two pairs).

**WORDEN'S WISDOM**
When we're not at Walt Disney World, we love to follow others who are via social media. One of our favorite accounts is the Worden family's (@the.worden.fam on Instagram and @thewordenfam on TikTok). We enjoy their content so much that we asked mom Leesa Worden to share some of her WDW tips for this book. Look for her "Worden's Wisdom" wherever you see the Minnie cupcake. And be sure to follow her on social media for more Walt Disney World advice!

Guests staying at the resorts on Hotel Plaza Boulevard may access a tourist-information television station of their own. Some other area hotels also show a version of the programming, usually aiming to provide an overview of all Central Florida attractions.

For Day Visitors: When purchasing one-day admission to a given theme park, guests receive a complimentary guidemap for that park. Ticket holders may receive all four park guides upon request. Extra park guidemaps are available at City Hall (in the Magic Kingdom) and at Guest Relations (in Disney's Hollywood Studios, EPCOT, and Disney's Animal Kingdom), as well as in shops and restaurants throughout the theme parks.

## PACKAGE POINTERS

The sheer number and diversity of packages offering vacations in Central Florida are enough to bewilder even the savviest traveler. Still, such plans are worth exploring. Most offer the convenience of a vacation that's completely organized in advance, and one that will generally cost less than the sum of the same transportation, accommodations, and admission elements purchased separately. In addition, since most package providers purchase blocks of Disney resort rooms, they are an excellent source for securing a room on WDW property when the hotel of your choice is booked solid.

Southwest Vacations (*southwestvacations.com;* 800-243-8372), American Airlines Vacations (800-321-2121;

**Hot Tip!** When purchasing a Walt Disney World vacation package, pay attention to the type of WDW park ticket that's included—and make sure you are able to customize the ticket to meet your needs. See page 21 for more information.

*aavacations.com*), *expedia.com, travelocity.com,* and the Walt Disney Travel Company (407-939-6244 or *disneyworld.com*) all offer packages that may feature WDW on-site hotels, as well as choice off-property accommodations. Some packages may sweeten the deal by including (relatively) lower-cost air transportation.

Vacations and other travel packages may include particular perks and discount offers. For possibilities, check travel websites, or consult a travel agent.

Packages booked via *disneyworld.com* are known as Walt Disney Travel Co. packages, and may include extras such as miniature golf or passes to ESPN Wide World of Sports. For details on how to book packages through *disneyworld.com,* see pages 19–20.

Travel agents may design packages around a specific type of vacation: say, a golf getaway, honeymoon, or family reunion. They may include extra elements such as unlimited tee times or a carriage ride. Still others are tied to an annual event, such as the Walt Disney World Marathon (see Holidays & Special Events on page 10). Air transportation, rental car, travel insurance, or airport transfers can be added to most packages.

**Hot Tip!** New multi-day theme park tickets expire 2 to 14 days after the first day they are used. The "No Expiration" option was discontinued in 2015. Tickets purchased prior to then will be honored at the parks. Email inquiries to *ticket.usage@disneyworld.com.* If you have questions about any ticket purchased in 2016 or later, call Ticket Services: 407-566-4985, Option 4.

The value of a package depends on your party's needs. Before considering options, use this book to help determine which of the accommodations, activities, and attractions most appeal to you. There's genuine value in certain package elements, such as airport transfers. Several packages also include meals with the Disney characters, tennis lessons, golf greens fees, spa treatments, boat rentals, and the like.

Never choose a package that includes elements you don't want or won't have time to enjoy. While extras such as welcoming snacks may sound appealing, their cash value is negligible. Also beware of any packages that tout certain services as selling points that are actually available to *every* Disney guest.

Finally, we highly recommend insuring your trip when purchasing a package, as cancellation fees can be steep and emergencies do happen. Insurance ensures peace of mind (and wallet).

# How to Book a WDW Resort Stay

Have you decided that you would like to stay at one of the Disney–owned-and-operated Walt Disney World resort hotels? Fantastic! We're happy to walk you through the step-by-step process of booking your vacation. First, you'll need to decide if you would like a "room-only" reservation or a vacation package. A package includes theme park tickets, and can include other components, all depending on how much you'd like to customize your Disney vacation. Both types of booking come with the following perks:

• **Theme Park Early Entry Benefit:** Walt Disney World resort guests may enjoy a half hour of early access to any of the four theme parks on most mornings. (For further details, see page 22.)

• **Complimentary use of the Walt Disney World Transportation System:** WDW's vast transportation system includes buses (aka motor coaches), boats, the WDW monorail system, and the Disney Skyliner.

It's important to note that the two reservation types (room-only or package) come with their own unique deposit requirements and cancellation policies. Finally, keep in mind that packages for the Swan, Dolphin, and Four Seasons Orlando, plus Disney Springs area resorts, hotels at Flamingo Crossings, and Bonnet Creek area resorts (hotels that are on WDW property, but are not owned or operated by Disney) can be booked through *disneyworld.com*, but room-only reservations must be booked via each resort's web site or by contacting the hotel directly.

Are you ready to book a WDW resort? You can call 407-949-5277, or follow these steps:

## "ENCHANTING EXTRAS"

Disney offers an ever-changing slate of adventures, tours, and seasonal events, collectively known as the "Enchanting Extras Collection." Options include animal encounters, fishing excursions, art classes, dessert parties, and more. The most widely offered experiences are detailed on the pages of this book. Seasonal offerings, aka "Limited Time Events," and new adventures join the lineup throughout the year. For updates, pricing, or to make reservations for Disney's Enchanting Extras Collection, visit *https://disneyworld.disney.go.com/enchanting-extras -collection/*, or call 407-WDW-PLAY (939-7529).

**Step 1:** Create an account on *disneyworld.com*. This can be done by clicking the link at the very top of the page that says "Sign in or create account." It is best to log in to your account before perusing any room rates or packages.

**Step 2:** Click the tab labeled "Places to Stay" and enter the dates of your vacation and the number of guests. Click "Find Resorts."

**Step 3:** Choose a resort that fits your needs and check for availability. If your heart's set on a particular resort and it's not available for your dates, try adjusting your arrival and departure by a day or two in either direction.

**Step 4:** Choose "Room" or "Package." Know that WDW package prices may automatically pop up with a seven-day park ticket for each member of your party.

Don't worry! You can customize your park tickets on the next page. But first you must select the type of resort room that best fits your needs. (Rates may differ based on date, view, and amenities.) *Annual Passholders should make sure park reservations are available before booking a resort. (As of January 9, 2024, guests using date-based park tickets no longer need park reservations.)*

**Step 5:** If you've chosen a package, you can customize park tickets by choosing the number of days, type of tickets (base tickets or park hoppers), etc. If you've chosen a "room-only" resort reservation, you may need to select "no ticket" to proceed to the checkout page.

**Step 6:** Review your order details very carefully. If you have selected a package, you may now add other extras such as Memory Maker, the Disney Dining Plan (it's back for most of 2024!), and a Travel Protection plan. Once you are finished, proceed to checkout.

**Step 7:** Pay your deposit. For a room-only reservation, the deposit is equal to one-night's stay and the balance is due on your day of arrival. For a package, the deposit is $200 and the balance must be paid *30 days prior to arrival*. Packages may include bonus items such as a free round of mini golf (4 vouchers per package), passes to ESPN Wide World of Sports (4 vouchers per package), and discounts at a number of shopping and dining spots. What if you need to cancel? Packages must be canceled 30 days or more prior to arrival in order to receive a refund of the deposit. Room-only reservations must be canceled at least five days prior to arrival date in order to receive a refund of the deposit.

**Step 8:** Let the countdown begin—you're going to Walt Disney World!

## VIP TOURS

You may have noticed them in the theme parks—those cheery folks in the plaid vests. They are VIP guides, leading guests on customized WDW trips.

The point is to minimize the hassle factor, while maximizing the overall magic component. Though participating in a VIP tour won't necessarily let you cut the line, it may yield some special seating for stage shows and parades. One tour guide can host up to 10 guests at a cost of about $425–$750 per hour. There is a 6-hour minimum per trip. Parties larger than 10 will require a second guide. Make your needs known when you book the tour. Cancellations must be made at least 48 hours in advance to avoid a fee. Call 407-560-4033 for additional VIP tour information or to make a reservation.

## DISNEY DINING PLAN

We are happy to report that after a long hiatus, the Disney Dining plan is back for 2024! The Disney Dining Plan lets guests pre-pay for meals before they arrive at Walt Disney World. While convenient for many, it's not necessarily a money-saver. For details about Dining Plan options (Standard or Quick-Service), use the My Disney Experience mobile app or website, or visit *disneyworld.com*. Consider just how much your travel party can consume before selecting a plan, as some include more sustenance than others. Here's a summary of the standard table-service plan (specifics are subject to change at any time):

Each day of the standard Disney Dining Plan—which costs about $95 a day for adults and $30 for kids (ages 3 to 9), plus tip—is apt to include:

• One table-service meal, including an entrée, dessert (at lunch or dinner), and one beverage.

• One quick-service meal, including an entrée and a beverage.

• One snack, such as ice cream, popcorn, or a medium soft drink at select quick-service spots or snack carts.

• The option of exchanging two table-service meals for one meal at a high-end "Signature" restaurant or a WDW dinner show, such as the Hoop-Dee-Doo Musical Revue.

To sum up: Say your family of four purchases a 5-night package. Together you're entitled to 20 quick-service meals, 20 table-service meals, and 20 snacks. And you are free to use them in any way you want. That is, if you want to skip a meal one day or have 5 meals in a single day, by all means go for it. (Remember there is a finite number of meals allotted.) Usage can be tracked via My Disney Experience, at Guest Relations in the parks and WDW resorts, and by keeping your meal receipts. To redeem a meal credit, present a MagicBand or room key card. Tax is included; gratuities are not. Be sure to tip your servers! Note that guests age 21 and older (with valid I.D.) have the option of ordering an alcoholic beverage (when available).

In addition to traditional table service meals, certain "character dining" experiences are available to Dining Plan participants, as are some Disney Springs locations. Note that children ages 3 through 9 must order from the kids' menu.

To find out which restaurants are participating during your planned visit to Walt Disney World, use the My Disney Experience app or website, visit *disneyworld.com*, or call 407-939-3463.

It's best to purchase a Dining Plan (available starting January 9, 2024) at the same time a Walt Disney World resort stay is booked, though it may be possible to upgrade or add a Dining Plan to an existing reservation. If you purchase a Disney Dining Plan with table-service meals, *you must make reservations for restaurants.* Do so as far ahead as possible! Please check *disneyworld.com* for additional details and updates.

# All About Theme Park Tickets

Buying a park ticket can be very simple. Do you plan on visiting one park on one day? Just pick up a One-Day date-based Ticket. Perhaps you are a frequent visitor and expect to pass through theme park gates dozens of times over the next year. In that case, an Annual Pass is what you're looking for. Now, if your park-going plans lie somewhere in between (and most do), you'll have to be a little more strategic.

When it comes to selecting the perfect type of admission ticket, it pays to do some homework. Study all the options, evaluate your priorities, and make no hasty decisions. For starters, there are several major factors to consider: (1) total number of days you would like to visit theme parks, (2) the actual dates you want to visit the parks, (3) to park-hop or not to park-hop (visit more than one theme park per day), (4) whether you want to pre-pay for "extras" such as the Disney Dining Plan, admission to the WDW water parks, miniature golf courses, the Memory Maker photo package, etc., and (5) dates (if any) on which "Extended Evening Hours" are offered. (This perk is available to guests of select WDW "deluxe" resorts and villas. For details, turn to page 22 and visit *disneyworld.com*.) While some details are apt to change, what follows is meant to help you make wise choices. Keep in mind that most ticket prices are likely to increase this year. For details and pricing updates, use the My Disney Experience mobile app or website, visit *disneyworld.com*, or call 407-824-4321.

**Note:** As of January 9, 2024, theme park reservations are *no longer required* if you purchase a date-based park ticket (anything that's not an Annual Pass). Until then, you should always check for theme park reservation availability *before* purchasing park tickets—or risk being shut out.

## DISNEY THEME PARK TICKETS

**DATE-BASED TICKETS:** Available for 1 to 10 days. Valid for admission to one theme park per day—the Magic Kingdom, EPCOT, Disney's Hollywood Studios, or Disney's Animal Kingdom. The ticket does not allow for park-hopping, but that option may be added. (Guests may customize tickets to fit their vacation needs.) Prices vary, depending on the day of the week and time of year. To get a sense of theme park pricing, see page 25. To see ticket prices during each day of your planned visit to Walt Disney World, go to *disneyworld.com* and study the interactive calendar.

**Expiration:** Date-Based tickets must be used within a certain time period. A 1-day ticket must be used on the specific date for which it was purchased; 2-day tickets must be used within 4 days after the start date; 3-day tickets must be used within 5 days of start date; 4-day tickets must be used within 7 days after start date; 5-day tickets must be used within 8 days of start date; 6-day tickets must be used within 9 days of start date; 7-day tickets must be used within 10 days of start date; 8-day tickets must be used within 12 days of the start date; 9-day tickets must be used within 13 days of the start date; and 10-day tickets must be used within 14 days of start date. Guests who purchase the Park Hopper Plus option get an extra day to use the 2- through 10-day tickets.

The No Expire option was discontinued in February 2015; tickets that were purchased prior to then should be honored at the parks, provided they have the No Expire option. Tickets bought before 2005 are valid, too—they pre-date the No Expire option. For information on how to use older tickets, visit a Walt Disney World ticket booth or call 407-824-4321.

**Hot Tip!** You cannot use a second day's admission to enter a second theme park on the same day you visited another theme park—even if you have days remaining on a multi-day ticket. To do that you must add the Park Hopper option to the ticket or buy a one-day ticket to enter the second park.

## EXTRA PARK TIME

Once upon a time, Walt Disney World offered a service called "E-Ride Nights." Available exclusively to guests staying at Disney-owned-and-operated resorts (plus other select hotels), it allowed for extra park frolicking on designated evenings (for guests with valid park admission used on that particular date). That program morphed into something called "Extra Magic Hours." Similar to E-Ride nights, the extra playtime alternated between morning and evening hours. Fast forward to 2024 and we now have a new chapter in the saga of extended theme park play: "Early Theme Park Entry" and "Extended Evening Hours!"

Introduced as Walt Disney World kicked off its 50th anniversary party in 2021—aka The World's Most Magical Celebration—Early Theme Park Entry gives guests 30 minutes of extra park time, provided they are Disney resort guests or guests of other select hotels, have a theme park reservation (required through January 8, 2024 for guests using date-based park tickets; no reservations required as of January 9), and valid park admission.

Here's how it works: Each day, all four WDW theme parks open their gates 30 minutes early *exclusively* for the aforementioned guests. Again, that's an extra half hour of park time every day at Magic Kingdom, EPCOT, Disney's Hollywood Studios, or Disney's Animal Kingdom, seven days a week. (To reiterate: Early Theme Park entry is available to guests in all WDW resort categories.) Early Theme Park Entry is a bit of a departure from its predecessors, and one that was made with safety and attendance management in mind. Now that all Walt Disney World theme parks are open early every day for WDW resort guests, it's hoped that those happy masses will spread out a bit. That could make for (slightly) smaller crowds and bigger fun. Either way, it's a nice start to a Disney Day.

A second "extra magic" benefit extends to guests registered at a Walt Disney World Deluxe or Deluxe Villa resort only: Extended Evening Hours. This perk allows for extra time in select theme parks on select nights. To participate, WDW Deluxe and Deluxe Villa guests must have a valid date-based ticket for that park, a Park Hopper ticket, or an Annual Pass that isn't blocked out.

For updates, plus additional information about theme park reservations and park-hopping, use the My Disney Experience app or website, or go to *disneyworld.com*. Note that all details are subject to change.

**Park Hopper Option:** This add-on lets guests visit more than one theme park on a single day. The privilege extends through the length of the ticket. It costs about $75 to $85 to add it to a one-day theme park ticket; and about $85 to $95 for all other base tickets (regardless of the number of days on the ticket). Be sure to check operating hours for your planned visit. In our opinion, park-hopping is worthwhile only if the parks are open very late.

**Note:** At press time, guests could begin park-hopping at 2 P.M. In order to "hop" to a second Walt Disney World theme park (until January 9, 2024), you must have already entered your first park with a reservation. As of January 9, 2024, guests using date-based theme park tickets no longer need park reservations—whether they plan to park-hop or not. All details are subject to change at any time. For more park-hopping specifics, use the My Disney Experience mobile app or website, or visit *disneyworld.com*.

**Park Hopper Plus Option:** This add-on covers entry to Blizzard Beach and Typhoon Lagoon water parks, Disney's ESPN Wide World of Sports Complex, miniature golf, or a round of golf at Disney's Oak Trail golf course. For about $95 to $115 extra (depending on the number of days on the ticket), you will get two to ten visits to these spots. The total number of visits depends on the number of days on your base ticket—the more days, the more visits. Details are subject to change.

**Incredi-Pass/Annual Pass:** The Incredi-Pass is a type of Annual Pass available to all guests and offers admission to the four WDW theme parks for a full year with no block-out dates (though a park reservation is required to enter before 2 P.M. on most days and is not a guarantee). It can be used in more than one theme park on the same day (aka park-hopping), and includes use of Walt Disney World's vast transportation system, as well as complimentary standard parking at all four theme parks. Incredi-Passes can be purchased by using the My Disney Experience app or visiting *disneyworld.com*, at the entrance to a Walt Disney World theme park

**Hot Tip!** As of January 9, 2024, guests using date-based admission tickets no longer need a reservation to visit a Walt Disney World theme park! While Annual Passholders do enjoy select no reservations required dates (aka "good-to-go" days), most dates require a park reservation before 2 P.M. As usual, all details are subject to change. For details, go to *disneyworld.com*.

(passes can be renewed there or by mail), at the Ticket Center at Disney Springs, or by calling 407-934-7639. Adults must present a valid, government-issued photo ID for purchase (and may be required for future use of the pass). Annual passes are non-transferable. When offered, expect the cost to be about $1,399 (plus tax) for adults and kids age 3 and up.

All Incredi-Passholders may book up to 5 theme park reservations on a rolling basis (once you use the first one, you can book another). Have the pass *and* a confirmed reservation at a Walt Disney World resort or other select hotel? You can book a park reservation for each day of your stay, plus the aforementioned 5 rolling reservations.

**Hot Tip!** Walt Disney World offers annual passes for Disney Vacation Club (DVC) members and Florida residents. For info, use the My Disney Experience app or website, or call 407-560-7277.

Note that annual passholders may visit the theme parks after 2 P.M. without needing a park reservation, except on Saturdays and Sundays at Magic Kingdom. Incredi-Passbearers qualify for many discounts and benefits, such as reduced rates at select Disney resorts at certain times of year, up to 20-percent off select dining and merchandise, and invitations to special Passholder events. Folks with an Incredi-Pass receive V.I.Passholder Support—a service that can answer questions and explain benefits.

The Incredi-Pass expires one year after first use. A discounted renewal rate may apply if a pass is renewed before it expires. (The old pass must be presented to get a discounted renewal rate.) Passes may be renewed by mail, online, or at a WDW theme park. All details are subject to change.

If you're planning a long visit, or two trips in one year and budget allows, weigh all the options and consider picking up an Incredi-Pass. Guests who take the plunge may opt for the following Annual Pass Add-Ons:

**Water Parks and Sports Option:** For the duration of an annual pass, this add-on includes admission—with no blockout dates—to Typhoon Lagoon and Blizzard Beach water parks, ESPN Wide World of Sports Complex (non-premium events), Disney's Oak Trail golf course, Foot-Golf at Oak Trail, and mini-golf at Fantasia Gardens and Disney's Winter Summerland. The cost is $99, plus tax.

**Photopass Download Option:** For an additional $99, a guest may receive unlimited PhotoPass downloads and discounts on physical merchandise. (For details about Disney's Photopass, see page 143.)

## DECIDING FACTORS

**CHOOSING THE RIGHT TICKET:** Before you make a decision, it helps to map out your vacation. Remember, all tickets start as Base Tickets. They are a bare-bones, admission-to-one-theme-park-at-a-time deal. That's perfect for many folks—especially those planning a relatively short stay. Still, the first step for every potential guest is to decide just how many days they plan to spend in the theme parks. Keep in mind that as days are added, the average price per day goes down. *Unused days expire after the ticket's start date whether activated or not.* (For expiration details, see page 21.) Once the length of stay and the start date are determined, it's time to customize the ticket. If the total number of days is undetermined, err on the side of caution—unused days cannot be refunded. You can, however, add days to a ticket at a park Guest Relations window on the final date of an activated ticket. After that, you'll have to buy a new ticket. Do you want to add the Park-Hopper or Park Hopper Plus Option? Go for it—but remember it'll add to the total price.

**Notes:** Only one person per party needs to have an Annual Pass to net a discount on a WDW resort (when available). This option is great for travelers with flexible schedules, as the discounts do vary, and they are often announced shortly before going into effect.

All ticket prices and structures—including Annual Passes—are subject to change.

**Tickets with Unused Days:** Prior to 2005, WDW park tickets never expired. That is no longer the case. Days remaining on a multi-day admission ticket now expire 2 to 14 days after the ticket's start date (with the exception of Annual Passes). Unused one-day tickets have expiration dates, too.

**Attractions Outside the WDW Theme Parks:** Typhoon Lagoon and Blizzard Beach water park prices are about $69 for a day with no block-out dates and about $64 with block-out dates for adults; $63 for one day with no block-out dates and about $58 with block-out dates for kids (ages 3 to 9). The ESPN Wide World of Sports Complex is about $20 for adults, about $15 for kids (general admission). Admission to the sports complex may be event specific. For details, visit *espnwwos.com*. Prices are apt to rise in 2024.

**Hot Tip!** Value remaining on an expired, unused park ticket may be put toward a new ticket (for use within a year). Details are subject to change. For specifics, call 407-824-4321.

**Hot Tip!** Adults should always carry a government-issued photo ID. You will need it should you have any issues with a MagicBand and to purchase alcoholic beverages while at Walt Disney World.

## MY DISNEY EXPERIENCE

"My Disney Experience" is the all-encompassing moniker attached to the vacation-planning tools managed via the My Disney Experience website or mobile app. It also links ticket cards and MagicBands (wristbands that are linked to various Disney vacation features) and includes (for a fee) the Lightning Lane attraction reservation system (see page 27).

**My Disney Experience App:** A free app, compatible with most Android and Apple iOS smartphones and tablets, My Disney Experience is a tool for reserving tables at Walt Disney World eateries and dinner shows; mobile ordering at many quick service restaurants; purchasing tickets; buying, booking, and tracking Lightning Lane selections for theme park attractions (see page 27); viewing wait times and room charges; tracking Dining Plan entitlements, and more. The app can also be used to open your Walt Disney World–owned-and-operated resort room via a "digital key."

*MyDisneyExperience.com* can be accessed by most personal computers. The site allows for the same advance planning. The My Disney Experience service is free and requires guests to create an account (to which all members of the traveling party should be linked). Note

that kids under age 13 are not permitted to have live, individual accounts. Parents should create and manage a profile for each child (kids' profiles are attached to their parents'). There tends to be a bit of a learning curve, so get started as soon as you can.

After linking a WDW resort reservation or vacation package and tickets to an account, guests may link MagicBands, make and monitor dining reservations, book and track Genie+ times, and load the Memory Maker Photo Package (see page 26). It is important to link all accounts in your traveling party (parties larger than 10 should call 407-939-5277).

All guests may use this service, whether they stay on Disney property or not, provided they can access the website or utilize the app.

Make sure you have the most current version of the My Disney Experience app before heading to WDW. What should you do if you experience glitches with the app while visiting Walt Disney World? First, restart your phone—that often does the trick. If that doesn't work, head to the nearest Guest Services location. The folks there will be happy to help.

**MagicBands:** This wrist accessory can serve as a resort room key and be linked to theme park and water park tickets. Guests can also use it to make purchases throughout WDW (provided the MagicBand is backed up with a credit card and a PIN code has been selected); use it for Disney's PhotoPass (see page 143) and to redeem Lightning Lane access (after booking selections via My Disney Experience); and more. To use it for purchases, tap the Mickey on the band to the Mickey head on the

## LINKING A VACATION IN "MY DISNEY EXPERIENCE"

You've successfully booked a vacation at the Walt Disney World Resort. Awesome and exciting! Now it's time to link your reservation in MyDisneyExperience (MDX) so you can begin vacation planning. (Please keep in mind that Disney-owned hotels, the Swan and Dolphin, and Walt Disney World Good Neighbor Hotels are the only hotels that can be linked through MDX. If you do not plan to stay at one of those properties, you can get set up in MDX using your park tickets.)

There are three avenues by which you can link your vacation in MDX: a room-only reservation, a package (room plus park tickets), or park tickets only. Whichever avenue you choose, make sure to begin by creating a MyDisneyExperience account (if you haven't already done so), logging in, and making a profile for each member of your party. Then return to the MDX home page. To link a room-only

reservation or package, hover over "Resort Hotel" and click "Link a Reservation." You'll need to enter your confirmation number and last name.

To link park tickets, hover over "Park Tickets" and then click "Link Tickets." You'll need to enter the ticket ID numbers and then assign them to members of your party. If you've purchased tickets as part of a package, look for the link on this page that says "Did you purchase your tickets as part of a vacation package? Link Them To Your Account."

Now that your vacation is linked in My Disney Experience, you are primed to book dining reservations (set a reminder for that 60-day window!), "Enchanting Extras" (see page 19), tours and programs (see page 245), and other add-ons such as Memory Maker and Genie+ (see pages 26 and 27).

console. Guests with a confirmed reservation at a WDW–owned-and-operated resort should order MagicBands via their My Disney Experience account (after linking the resort reservation). From there, they'll be redirected to *shopdisney.com*. Note that select MagicBands may be available at a special "pre-arrival" price.

To personalize, simply select a band and add a name. MagicBands that are customized 11 or more days ahead of arrival will be sent to your home. Those personalized within 6 to 10 days of your visit are sent to your resort. MagicBands may be added to a WDW hotel reservation, and special versions may be purchased in the parks, via the My Disney Experience mobile app or website, or

**Hot Tip!** It's possible to purchase MagicBands at the Disney Store at Orlando International Airport. Cast members can help you link them to your My Disney Experience account, too.

*shopdisney.com*. Non-WDW resort guests may purchase MagicBands at WDW parks and at *shopdisney.com*.

The MagicBand is waterproof (but does not float), hypoallergenic, and can be adjusted to fit most wrists. If a band is lost, it can be disabled via the My Disney Experience app (and the website) or with the help of a cast member. MagicBands are non-transferable.

# SAMPLE PARK TICKET PRICES[†]

| Base Ticket* | | 10-Day | 9-Day | 8-Day | 7-Day | 6-Day | 5-Day | 4-Day | 3-Day | 2-Day | 1-Day |
|---|---|---|---|---|---|---|---|---|---|---|---|
| | Ages 10 & Up | $609-$815 ($61-$82/ day) | $594-$801 ($66-$89/ day) | $565-$790 ($71-$99/ day) | $541-$770 ($77-$110/ day) | $514-$751 ($86-$125/ day) | $500-$709 ($100-$142/ day) | $466-$632 ($117-$158/ day) | $344-$496 ($115-$165/ day) | $222-$337 ($111-$169/ day) | $109-$189 |
| | Ages 3-9 | $589-$791 ($60-$79/ day) | $570-$778 ($63-$86/ day) | $548-$768 ($69-$96/ day) | $508-$748 ($73-$107/ day) | $495-$728 ($83-$121/ day) | $485-$687 ($97-$138/ day) | $448-$612 ($112-$153/ day) | $331-$482 ($110-$161/ day) | $213-$327 ($107-$164/ day) | $104-$184 |
| ADD: Park Hopper** | | $85-$95 | $85-$95 | $85-$95 | $85-$95 | $85-$95 | $85-$95 | $85-$95 | $75-$85 | $75-$85 | $75-$85 |
| ADD: Park-Hopper Plus Option*** | | $105-$115 10 visits | $105-$115 9 visits | $105-$115 8 visits | $105-$115 7 visits | $105-$115 6 visits | $105-$115 5 visits | $105-$115 4 visits | $95-$105 3 visits | $95-$105 2 visits | $95-$105 2 visits |
| ADD: Memory Maker **** | | $169/ $199 | $169/ $199 | $169/ $199 | $169/ $199 | $169/ $199 | $169/ $199 | $169/ $199 | $169/ $199 | $169/ $199 | $69 |

---

† These are examples of advance-purchase, Date-Based prices. They do not include tax and have been rounded to the nearest dollar. Prices are lower during non-peak times of year and higher during some holidays. All prices are subject to change.

* Base Ticket admits guest to one theme park each day of use. Park choices are Magic Kingdom, EPCOT, Disney's Hollywood Studios, and Disney's Animal Kingdom.

** Park Hopper Option entitles guest to visit more than one theme park on each day of use. Park choices are any combination of theme parks on each day of use. Price listed is for an adult ticket.

*** Park-Hopper Plus option entitles guest to a specified number

of visits to a choice of entertainment and recreation venues. Choices may include Disney's Blizzard Beach water park, Disney's Typhoon Lagoon water park, and ESPN Wide World of Sports Complex. Price listed is for an adult ticket.

**** Guests who pre-pay for Disney's Memory Maker photo package pay the first price, those who make the purchase within 3 days of their WDW visit pay the second price. If you purchased Memory Maker at the advance purchase price, photos taken within 3 days of the date of purchase will not be included in Memory Maker and must be purchased separately. The Memory Maker Photo package is available to all guests. For details, see page 26.

No personal information is stored on the band—it links to entitlements that were pre-purchased. Remember, you'll need to use a PIN code to make purchases with a MagicBand. And remember: If you lose a band while at WDW, fear not. You can deactivate it via the *My Disney Experience* app, or visit Guest Relations or a WDW resort Lobby Concierge where they'll deactivate it for you.

An enhanced version of this high-tech accessory is also available for purchase by all WDW guests. Dubbed MagicBand+, the souped-up, interactive band features lighting effects, gesture recognition, and more. For details and pricing, visit *shopdisney.com*.

**Note:** MagicBands ordered within 5 days of arrival can't be personalized, nor can such orders be canceled. MagicBands cannot be mailed to all countries.

**MagicMobile Service:** Disney's MagicMobile Service (aka *MagicMobile Pass*) is a handy new feature within the *My Disney Experience* app. With it, many smartphones can act like a (contactless) MagicBand in many ways. It lets you enter WDW theme parks (with valid admission), connect Disney PhotoPass images to your account, charge most purchases to your Disney resort folio during your stay, and more. (New features may be added.) To use it, link your park tickets, hotel reservation, and other pre-purchased entitlements to your *My Disney Experience* account. Then activate the MagicMobile feature, follow the instructions, and you'll be all set. For additional information, go to *disneyworld.disney .go.com/guest-services/magic-mobile*.

**Disney Genie and Genie+:** Built into the *My Disney Experience* mobile app, Disney Genie is like a personalized digital organizer. With it, you can plan and modify a daily WDW itinerary, make dining reservations, get help from a virtual assistant, and more. While Genie service is free, the Genie+ attraction reservation feature comes with a daily fee of about $15 to $40+. The system lets guests choose the next available time to arrive at a variety of attractions and experiences using the Lightning Lane entrance. Note that only one selection can be made at a time and each participating attraction may be accessed just once per day via Genie+ (though guests may re-ride any WDW attraction via the standby line). Note that digital downloads of Photopass attraction photos are included with the purchase of Genie+. For updates and additional information, see page 27, use the *My Disney Experience* mobile app or website, or visit *disneyworld.com*.

**Memory Maker Photo Package:** The Memory Maker package includes all photographs and videos taken in the parks, including those snapped on select attractions and character meal locations for your length of stay. You can view and download the photographs via the *My Disney Experience* app or website, or via the PhotoPass website: *mydisneyphotopass.disney.go.com*. It's possible to customize photos with banners and Disney art, too. At press time, the same-day price was about $199; about $169 if pre-ordered. (We think Memory Maker is usually a worthwhile investment—especially for large parties and those who expect to purchase more than 10 PhotoPass photos. For details, see page 143.)

## PURCHASING TICKETS

Note that all date-based WDW theme park tickets may be purchased in advance—and until January 8, 2024, must be paired with a theme park reservation in order to be used; after that, guests using date-based tickets no longer need park reservations. Tickets are easily ordered via the *My Disney Experience* app or website, *disneyworld.com*, or from a trusted travel agent. Tickets may also be purchased in these ways:

**Tickets by Phone:** All tickets can be purchased by phone; call 407-W-DISNEY (934-7639). Allow at least 15 days for standard delivery; $15 for express delivery (allow 7 days); and $25 for international delivery (allow 12 days). There is no handling fee for pickup at a Walt Disney World Will Call window.

**Tickets Online:** Tickets can be purchased online via the *My Disney Experience* mobile app or website or *www.disneyworld.com*. The fees for delivery are the same as those listed above.

**Tickets by Mail** (Select tickets only): Allow at least three to five weeks for ticket processing, and include a return address. Send a money order (for the total amount due, plus a $4 handling fee), payable to The Walt Disney World Company, to: Walt Disney World, Box 10140, Lake Buena Vista, FL 32830-0030. Attention: Ticket Mail Order.

**Note:** Advance planning is the name of the game when it comes to a Walt Disney World visit. In addition to theme park admission, we recommend purchasing tickets for special events such as Mickey's Not So Scary Halloween Party and Mickey's Very Merry Christmas Party as soon as they become available.

All details are subject to change. For updates, visit *disneyworld.com*, or use the *My Disney Experience* mobile app or website.

# Disney's Lightning Lane Service

Walt Disney World's Fastpass+ attraction reservation service was retired in late 2021. Replacing Fastpass+ entrances for many WDW shows and attractions are "Lightning Lane" entrances. As with Fastpass+, a Lightning Lane selection allows guests to bypass the standby line and experience an attraction with (ideally) an expedited wait time. Unlike Fastpass+, there are two ways to access a Lightning Lane entrance: via Genie+ or Individual Lightning Lane Selection, and each method comes with its own fee and set of participating attractions. (Both are purchased via the Genie portal in the My Disney Experience mobile app. They are not mutually exclusive: you can get both, just one, or neither.) Note that Genie+ may be purchased for a single park or multiple parks (to use the latter, you must have a ticket with park-hopping privileges).

In another departure from the dearly departed Fastpass+ system, Lightning Lane selections are bought and booked on the day they will be used—opening the door for a bit more spontaneity in your Disney day. Note that if you decide to splurge on Genie+, it's best to buy it as early in the day as possible (it can sell out).

**Important note:** Enhancements to Walt Disney World's Lightning Lane service are apt to occur at any time. For updates and information about booking Lightning Lane selections (and other news), use the My Disney Experience mobile app, or visit *disneyworld.com*. Here's how the system worked as this book went to press:

## Genie+ Lightning Lane Service

Genie+ is an add-on feature offered through the My Disney Experience app. (For details about My Disney Experience, see page 24.) For a flat fee of about $15 to $40+ per person, per day, Genie+ allows guests to access theme park shows and attractions via "Lightning Lanes." There are two Genie+ options to choose from: "single park" (good for one park only) and "multiple parks."

Genie+ service is purchased on a day-to-day basis. Be aware that the fee varies based on park, date, and season. So how does it work? First, make sure you've downloaded the (free) My Disney Experience app and linked park tickets (and park reservations for folks using Annual Passes) for each member of your party. At press time, you could purchase Genie+ Lightning Lane service via the app starting at 12:01 A.M. on the day you plan to visit a WDW theme park. At 7 A.M. you may reserve your first Genie+ return time for the day. For information about making advance Lightning Lane selections (if offered), visit *disneyworld.com*.

To redeem your first Genie+ pass, stroll to the Lightning Lane entrance during your one-hour reservation window. Then touch your MagicBand, smartphone (using the MagicMobile feature of the My Disney Experience app), or ticket card to the console. After the light flashes, head in and prepare to zap Zurg at Buzz Lightyear's Space Ranger Spin, go Soarin' around the world, fly the *Millennium Falcon*, or enjoy any of the other roughly 40 attractions included in the program. Once you have redeemed your initial selection (or the arrival window has passed), you can make another selection using the app, up until park closing. It's also possible to make an additional selection if the return window (the time period you select to ride an attraction) is at least 120 minutes from the time you booked the selection. Should you need to modify a Genie+ selection, you can do so via the My Disney Experience app. Each attraction has a limited number of Genie+ selections available per day and they do max out. Sign up for your must-dos as early as possible.

On average, you can expect to enter about 2 to 3 attractions per day with Genie+ (sometimes more) when the first selection is made early in the day, depending on the volume of visitors in the theme parks. While there's no cap on the number of ride reservations you can make (pending availability), you may enter a participating attraction just once per day via the Lightning Lane. Of course, you're free to hit that standby line and re-ride till your heart's content.

Park-hoppers take note: Genie+ (with the multi-park option) hops with you. (At press time, guests were allowed to "hop" to a second theme park starting at 2 P.M., provided that they have tickets with park-hopping privileges.) As the park-hopping hour nears, the Genie+ app feature will include return times that are available at Walt Disney World's other theme parks.

The service aims to provide expedited wait times while spreading guests throughout the WDW theme parks—making traditionally congested areas less so. For folks who prefer to do things on the fly or who find the system a bit daunting (or not worth the splurge), no-fee/no-fuss standby lines will always be available.

**Note:** Disney Genie+ service is available to everyone, pending availability. All details are subject to change. For updates, use the My Disney Experience app or website, or visit *disneyworld.com*.

(Continued on page 28)

(Continued from page 27)

Here's a list of Walt Disney World theme park attractions that offered Genie+ Lightning Lane service as this book went to press. (Note that details are subject to change.):

### GENIE+ ATTRACTIONS IN THE MAGIC KINGDOM*
- Ariel's Grotto
- Big Thunder Mountain Railroad
- Buzz Lightyear's Space Ranger Spin
- Dumbo the Flying Elephant
- Enchanted Tales with Belle
- Festival of Fantasy Parade
- Haunted Mansion
- It's a Small World
- Jungle Cruise
- Mad Tea Party
- Meet Mickey at Town Square Theater
- Mickey's PhilharMagic
- Monsters Inc. Laugh Floor
- Peter Pan's Flight
- Princess Fairytale Hall
- Pirates of the Caribbean
- The Barnstormer
- The Magic Carpets of Aladdin
- The Many Adventures of Winnie the Pooh
- Space Mountain
- Tomorrowland Speedway
- Under the Sea—Journey of The Little Mermaid

### GENIE+ ATTRACTIONS IN EPCOT*
- Disney and Pixar Short Film Festival
- Frozen Ever After
- Journey into Imagination with Figment
- Living with the Land
- Mission: SPACE
- Remy's Ratatouille Adventure
- Soarin' Around the World
- Spaceship Earth
- Test Track
- The Seas with Nemo & Friends
- Turtle Talk with Crush

### GENIE+ ATTRACTIONS IN DISNEY'S HOLLYWOOD STUDIOS*
- Alien Swirling Saucers
- Beauty and the Beast Live on Stage
- Disney Junior Play & Dance!
- For the First Time in Forever: A Frozen Sing-Along Celebration
- Indiana Jones Epic Stunt Spectacular
- Meet Olaf at Celebrity Spotlight

* Attractions may be added or removed at any time. For updates, use the My Disney Experience mobile app or website, or visit *disneyworld.com.*

- Mickey & Minnie's Runaway Railway
- *Millennium Falcon:* Smugglers Run
- Muppet*Vision 3D
- Rock 'n' Roller Coaster Starring Aerosmith
- Slinky Dog Dash
- Star Tours—The Adventures Continue
- The Twilight Zone™ Tower of Terror
- Toy Story Mania!

### GENIE+ ATTRACTIONS IN DISNEY'S ANIMAL KINGDOM*
- The Animation Experience at Conservation Station
- Adventurers Outpost (meet favorite Disney pals)
- Festival of the Lion King
- Dinosaur
- Expedition Everest
- Feathered Friends in Flight!
- Finding Nemo: The Big Blue . . . and Beyond!
- It's Tough to Be a Bug!
- Kali River Rapids
- Kilimanjaro Safaris
- Na'vi River Journey

## Individual Lightning Lane Selection

Lightning Lane access may be purchased for select shows and attractions on an à la carte basis. Each WDW theme park offers a (very) limited number of attractions that can be reserved for a fee. This option lets park-goers select an arrival window for up to 2 attractions per day. Pricing (about $7 to $25+) and availability vary by date, attraction, and park—and may change. For details about reserving Lightning Lanes in advance, visit *disneyworld.com.*

Individual Lightning Lane Selections may be purchased on the day you visit a park. Guests staying at a WDW resort, Shades of Green, Swan, Dolphin, and Swan Reserve may buy theirs starting at 7 A.M. All other guests may make their first purchase as the theme parks open.

At press time, the following attractions had Individual Lightning Lane Selection status: TRON Lightcycle/Run and Seven Dwarfs Mine Train at Magic Kingdom; Guardians of the Galaxy: Cosmic Rewind at EPCOT; Star Wars: Rise of the Resistance at Disney's Hollywood Studios; and Avatar Flight of Passage at Disney's Animal Kingdom. Details are subject to change. *Note that Individual Lightning Lane attractions are not included with Genie+ service.* For updates, use the My Disney Experience mobile app or visit *disneyworld.com.*

Disney's Lightning Lane service is a work-in-progress and will continue to evolve. Expect some attractions to move back and forth between Genie+ and Individual Lighting Lane designation throughout the year.

Bottom line? If budget allows, Genie+ and Individual Lightning Lane Selections can be good ways to cut the time spent in some attraction lines at Walt Disney World—but we are happy to know that traditional standby lines are still available.

# Money-Saving Tips

A Walt Disney World vacation can be an exceptionally expensive undertaking, but it is possible to keep costs down a bit. When budgeting for your trip, keep in mind that WDW prices are comparable to those in a big city. Here are a few tips to help you conserve cash.

## LODGING

• When it comes to saving money on accommodations, timing is truly key. While off-season dates tend to vary depending on the hotel, value season for most Walt Disney World resort hotels generally means January through mid-February, late August through late September, early November, and early December. Weeknights are usually less expensive than weekend nights year-round.

• The Walt Disney World Swan, Dolphin, and Swan Reserve may offer rate specials when other hotels have peak rates. Check *www.swandolphin.com*.

• Consider how much time you will actually spend at the hotel, and don't pay for a place with perks you won't have time to enjoy. Off-property hotels often allow kids to stay free in their parents' rooms, but the cutoff age varies. Be sure to inquire in advance.

**Hot Tip!** It may be comparable in price or a bit cheaper to get a family suite or spread your party out over two rooms in a "value" or "moderate" resort than to have everyone stay in one room at "deluxe" Disney digs.

• When weighing cost-effectiveness of off-property lodging, remember to factor in the time, money, and any inconvenience of the commute between said lodgings, Walt Disney World, and nearby attractions.

• Realize, too, that many advantages of staying on Disney property (tops among them being "Early Entry," which allows guests of WDW–owned-and-operated resorts and other select resorts entry into the theme parks 30 minutes before they open to the public [see page 22], and access to WDW's transportation system) also apply to guests staying in the least expensive rooms in Disney's hotels. The most important hotel monikers for budget-watching Disney fans, All-Star and Pop Century, offer relatively low room rates. Prices at Caribbean Beach and Port Orleans French Quarter & Riverside are slightly higher. Also, note that the only major difference between the least and most expensive rooms in some hotels is often the view.

• The cluster of resorts on Hotel Plaza Boulevard, located near Disney Springs (within Disney's borders), offer rooms starting at about $120 per night. (See page 108.) Good Neighbor hotels in WDW adjacent areas known as Bonnet Creek (see page 116), and Flamingo Crossings offer reasonable rates, too (see page 115). Many throw in free breakfast, to boot.

## GIVE THE BAND A HAND

Attention MagicBand (and MagicBand+) fans: the handy, colorful wrist-wear is reusable! The battery within each standard band has a life expectancy of at least 2 years, while the rechargeable Magicband+ battery endures a bit longer. So if you plan a second (or third) visit to Walt Disney World while your band is still active, you won't have to buy a new one. That should make your wallet happy!

What happens if a MagicBand stops working mid-visit? You can purchase a new one at a WDW shop and have it set up at any Guest Relations location. Or head straight to Guest Relations—with a valid theme park ticket—for a complimentary Admission Card (it may not be as fancy as a MagicBand, but it'll work just fine as a link to your My Disney Experience account).

For more information about MagicBands, see page 24 or visit *disneyworld.com*. Note that MagicBands are no longer free for WDW resort guests, but an advance purchase may net you a discount on some styles of the multi-tasking accessory.

## SATISFYING SUBSTITUTES

Fewer frills doesn't have to mean less fun at Walt Disney World. Here are potential money-saving alternatives to some of WDW's higher-priced treats (details are subject to change):

If you would rather not spring for admission to one of the Disney Springs West Side venues, consider visiting Raglan Road for dinner or drinks with a side of (free) evening entertainment, or taking a trip to Disney's BoardWalk resort. Among other diversions, you will find Jellyrolls (a sing-along dueling pianos bar with a cover of about $18), and Atlantic Dance Hall (a nightclub with no cover charge). Magicians and jugglers may entertain guests on the boardwalk in the evening. A short walk will take you to the Swan hotel, home to the karaoke-friendly Kimonos Lounge and Il Mulino New York Trattoria, where live music may be presented on Friday and Saturday evenings. If you're in the mood for some swingin' jazz (not to mention a fresh-baked Mickey-shaped beignet), swing by Disney's Port Orleans French Quarter Resort and visit Scat Cat's Club—free live music is presented 5 nights a week. Last but not least, there's River Roost at Disney's Port Orleans Riverside resort. There you can catch a cover-free performance of a "playful piano show for all ages," courtesy of an entertainer known as Yeeha Bob Jackson. Use the My Disney Experience mobile app or website, or visit *disneyworld.com* for the performance schedules during your planned visit.

If the Grand Floridian Resort & Spa doesn't quite fit into your budget, consider staying in a Mansion room at Port Orleans Riverside. Southern hospitality replaces Victorian splendor, and though the guestrooms aren't quite as spacious, the air of sophistication makes for a most satisfying stay. And for a relatively sweet deal on a suite, consider the family suites at the vibrant resort known as Disney's Art of Animation. All details are subject to change.

## FOOD

• Disney's Club-Level accommodations, when available, can absorb the cost of some food and drink—the more folks in the room, the better the value.

• Carry snacks and bottled beverages (no glass) that don't require refrigeration and enjoy them picnic style wherever possible.

• Consider lodgings that offer kitchen facilities. The savings on food may be more than the extra accommodations expense. Note that there is a small fridge/beverage cooler in all rooms at WDW–owned-and-operated resorts (no additional charge).

• Staying at a WDW–owned-and-operated resort? We recommend the purchase of a Rapid Fill refillable mug. Each mug costs about $22 (plus tax) and is good for unlimited soft-drink refills at your hotel (coffee, tea, soda pop, and more) for the length of your resort stay. (See page 295.) Note that Rapid Fill Mugs are included with most Disney Dining Plans. Be sure to ask.

• Snack stands are plentiful, but not always handy or cost-efficient. Be sure to pack snacks and refillable water bottles before you arrive.

• Don't plan on three big table-service meals a day. It gets expensive and time consuming (and filling!).

• Save some money by having supplies delivered to your resort. Items such as bottled water, snacks, fresh fruit, and breakfast bars can be enjoyed in the room or out of a backpack. Our list of go-to grocery delivery services includes Amazon Fresh, Walmart+, Instacart, and *gardengrocer.com*. (These companies are authorized to deliver to all Walt Disney World resorts, but are not affiliated with the Walt Disney Company.) Delivery fees may apply.

**WORDEN'S WISDOM**
It rains almost every day from May–October in Florida (and a lot of days after that time, too). Don't let the forecast get you down when you see rain predicted every day! Just bring ponchos, umbrellas, flip flops, and extra clothes to change into if you get wet. Some of our favorite memories are playing in the rain at Disney! (@the.worden.fam on Instagram and @ thewordenfam on TikTok)

**Hot Tip!** To save a little cheddar on Walt Disney World merchandise, dining, bowling, Amphicar tours, Cirque du Soleil, and more, use the coupons at the back of this book. You're welcome!

• The Disney Dining Plan is appealing to guests who enjoy the convenience of pre-paying for all of their vacation meals—but it's no more cost-efficient than paying as you go.

## DISCOUNTS

• Theme Park Annual Passholders may receive discounts on meals, dinner shows, tours, and room rates. (Note that some Annual Passes may not be offered in 2024.)

• Walt Disney World resorts that offer Annual Passholder discounts vary from month to month, and discounted rooms aren't always available for booking very far in advance. It's best to be flexible with travel dates. Annual Passholders may net deals on recreational opportunities, too. For more information, call 407-W-DISNEY (934-7639). Passholders can save 10 to 20 percent at many Walt Disney World eateries. For details, call 407-WDW-DINE (939-3463). Note that Annual Pass structures and discounts are subject to change at any time.

• Discounts on Walt Disney World resort rates and theme park tickets are available to Florida residents, and seasonal promotions occur. Call 407-W-DISNEY (934-7639) for specifics.

• The Swan, Dolphin, Swan Reserve, and some off-property hotels may offer discounts to seniors and the Automobile Association of America (AAA) or AARP members, nurses, and teachers. Some AAA branches provide discounts on park passes, as well as discounts on rooms, and more. Touch base with your local AAA branch for additional information.

• Disney Visa® Cardmembers who pay with their Disney Visa Card enjoy savings on merchandise, dining, and guided tours at Walt Disney World. Cardmembers may use the Disney Visa Card wherever Visa is accepted. Specifics are subject to change. For details, visit *DisneyRewards.com* or *DisneyDebit.com*.

• *www.travelocity.com* has offered a variety of WDW vacation packages. Vacation Outlet occasionally offers Disney Cruise Line packages at a reduced rate; visit *www.vacationoutlet.com* or call 800-825-3633.

• Visit Orlando is an organization that offers handy information and discounted tickets to several area theme parks, shows, restaurants, hotels, and more. To learn about Visit Orlando discount offers and to purchase Walt Disney World park tickets, go to *www.visitorlando.com/offers*.

• Okay, so it's not exactly a discount, but we think that multi-day Date-Based WDW park tickets are worth their weight in gold. The more days you purchase, the lower the cost is per day. (Just don't over-buy days—unused days expire. Extra days can be added as needed, provided the ticket has not yet expired.)

• Visit *disneyworld.disney.go.com/special-offers* to see if any discounts apply for your WDW visit.

## TICKET TAG SYSTEM

As a means of enforcing the non-transferability aspect of all Walt Disney World tickets, Disney has devised a system to trace each ticket to its rightful owner. The procedure is as follows: Touch your MagicBand, ticket, or WDW resort ID (aka "Key to the World" card) to the shiny orb at any theme park entrance. While the machine is crunching the data encrypted on your MagicBand or ticket, gently press the tip of your forefinger onto the glowing gizmo perched beside the orb. Remove your finger and presto! Your MagicBand, ticket card, or resort ID will link to your finger, giving you the green light to enter. All guests over age 3 have to do this every time they use the ticket. Remember to use the same finger every time you enter a park. (It's a good idea to wash your hands after this process.)

# Making a Budget

A stay at Disney's kingdom need not cost a king's ransom (though it certainly can). A well-planned budget can help ensure that money spent at Walt Disney World is money well spent.

Vacation expenses fall into five major categories: (1) transportation (which may include any combination of costs for airfare, airport transfers, train tickets, car rental, gas, parking, tolls, and taxi service); (2) lodging; (3) theme park tickets; (4) meals; and (5) miscellaneous (recreational activities, cover charges, tips, souvenirs, forgotten items, and home expenses such as house-sitting, pet boarding, etc.).

When planning your budget, first consider what level of service suits your needs. Some people prefer to spend fewer days at Disney but stay at a deluxe hotel or dine at pricier restaurants, while others would rather make their money cover a longer vacation that includes a value-priced resort and less-expensive meals. The choice is up to you. Once you've established your spending priorities, determine your price limit. Then make sure you don't exceed it when approximating your expenses — without a ballpark figure to work around, it's easy to get carried away.

## SAMPLE BUDGET

The following is an example of a low- to moderately priced budget designed for a family of four during "peak" season (two adults and two kids planning to stay at Walt Disney World for six nights). Totals do not include transportation expenses or sales tax. Plan your budget accordingly.

## SAMPLE BUDGET*
### Our 6-night Walt Disney World Vacation

**LODGING:**

Disney's Pop Century: about $170–$300 per night (x 6 nights)

Lodging total (before tax) = $1,020–$1,800

**THEME PARK TICKETS:**

Adult 5-day Date-Based Ticket: $500–$709 (x 2 people)

Child 5-day Date-Based Ticket: $485–$687 (x 2 people)

Tickets total (before tax) = $1,970–$2,792

**MEALS:**

(2 inexpensive and one moderate meal per day, plus 1 snack)

Average adult: $110 (x 6 days) (x 2 people)

Average child: $80 (x 6 days) (x 2 people)

Meals total = $2,280

**MISCELLANEOUS:**

Average adult: $65 (x 6 days) (x 2 people)

Average child: $40 (x 6 days) (x 2 people)

Miscellaneous total = $1,260

**VACATION TOTAL** = $6,530–$8,132

Disney may offer discounts on select WDW resort accommodations throughout the year. For details, visit disneyworld.disney.go.com/special-offers.

The WDW resort prices listed here represent average nightly rates for a 6-night stay. Prices do not include tax.

Unsure of how many days you will ultimately spend in the parks? Know that extra days may be added to any Date-Based ticket on or before the ticket's last day. (Upgrade tickets at a Guest Relations window before leaving the theme park on the last day of your ticket.)

Even if you stick to fast food, expect to spend at least $75 per adult and $45 per child, per day.

Careful packing should cut down on miscellaneous expenses, which often include forgotten items such as toothpaste, insect repellent, sunscreen, hand sanitizers, and sunglasses.

* Prices exclude tax and are subject to change. Resort rates fluctuate based on date, season, view, etc. Flexible Date park ticket prices (when offered) are higher. For resort prices during your visit, use the My Disney Experience website or app, or go to disneyworld.com.

# Planning Your Itinerary

When sitting down to plan an itinerary, we've always offered this advice: Start as early as possible! Spontaneity, which can be vastly rewarding in the real world, is not your friend when it comes to planning a Walt Disney World visit. And that advice has never been more valid than it is today. Among the things you'll need to decide on (and book) as soon as possible are: where to stay, what parks you want to visit and on what days, and where to eat (rule to live by: If a restaurant or dining experience accepts reservations, you should make them as far in advance as possible or risk getting shut out). Other Walt Disney World experiences such as fishing excursions, behind-the-scenes tours, Drawn to Life (presented by Cirque du Soleil and Disney), and WDW dinner shows are also quite popular and require a bit of forethought. Here's an idea of what to book when.

**Note:** Details are apt to change from time to time. Check the My Disney Experience app or website or *disneyworld.com* for updates.

## FIRST THINGS FIRST

• Make hotel and transportation arrangements as far ahead as possible. Book via *disneyworld.com* or call 407-W-DISNEY (934-7639). Online check-in is available once the hotel is booked.
• Check park hours for your visit. Closing times will be quite helpful when making evening plans. Create a day-by-day schedule, deciding which area of Walt Disney World to visit on each day of your trip.
• If you plan to use MagicBands (see page 24) during your Walt Disney World visit, order them in advance and link them to your My Disney Experience account before you arrive. (Some bands may be discounted for guests with a confirmed reservation at select Walt Disney World resorts.)

## UP TO 90 DAYS

• If you plan to play golf while at Walt Disney World, you may book a tee time on most WDW golf courses now (see pages 254–255 for details; Disney's Oak Trail golf course may be reserved up to 30 days in advance). Golf lessons may also be reserved now. Call 407-WDW-GOLF (939-4653) for reservations.

## UP TO 60 DAYS

• Double-check park hours for your stay. Hours tend to fluctuate from month to month.
• If you hope to reserve any character meals, know that many are in high demand. We highly recommend setting a reminder for the day your 60-day booking window opens. Many guests get up extremely early in the morning to snag their desired reservation times as soon as they become available on the My Disney Experience mobile app or website. The early bird gets the worm—or, in this case, reservation!
• Use the *Good Meals, Great Times* chapter of this book to choose dining spots. To make reservations, use the My Disney Experience mobile app or website or visit *disneyworld.com/dining*. Parties of 8 or more should call 407-939-3463. Guests with a confirmed reservation at a WDW–owned-and-operated resort may make reservations for up to 10 days of their planned stay. For specifics about dining reservations, see page 311.
• Dinner-show reservations should be secured far in advance. Use the My Disney Experience app or website or visit *disneyworld.com*.
• Specialty cruises (see page 252) may be booked by calling 407-WDW-PLAY (939-7529).
• Fishing excursions (see page 257) may be booked by calling 407-939-2277 or 407-939-7529.
• Tennis lessons (offered at select WDW resorts) may be reserved by calling 321-228-1146.
• Trail-ride reservations should be made in advance. Call 407-939-7529.
• If you'd like to add a behind-the-scenes tour to your trip, now is the time to make a reservation.

## LIGHTNING LANES & VIRTUAL QUEUES

• If you wish to access Walt Disney World theme park shows and attractions via Lightning Lane entrances (with the potential to enjoy expedited wait times), you will need to purchase Genie+ service via the My Disney Experience app or website. You can snag Individual Lightning Lane Selections there, too. (See pages 27–28.) There's no charge to utilize Virtual Queues (offered for select theme park attractions), but you'll need to book them as soon as they become available on the day(s) you plan to visit. Don't forget! For additional information, visit *disneyworld.com*.

# Sample Schedules

Many visitors have a deep desire to cover each and every inch of Walt Disney World in the span of a few short days. While we hesitate to discourage these most ambitious of travelers, we feel the need to enlighten them: Walt Disney World is a staggeringly large place. In fact, it's nearly as big as San Francisco and jam-packed with about as many diversions as you might expect from a city that size. You could spend two full weeks exploring Walt Disney World property and still not have time to do it all. The theme parks alone require every bit of four days just to see the major "E-Ticket" attractions.

What's the best strategy for organizing a Walt Disney World visit? Make a list of the parks, attractions, and activities you most want to see and use it to create an itinerary. Don't forget to allow time for swimming, boating, or relaxing on a lakeside swing.

Assuming you've narrowed your "must-do" list to the barely manageable, we recommend a stay of at least four to five days. This allows for a visit to each of the theme parks and some time to enjoy many of the recreational activities at your resort, not to mention relaxing a bit. You are on vacation, after all. Longer stays can include water parks, Disney Springs, a dinner show, and more. When planning your days (which you should do before leaving home), be sure to take into account theme park operating hours and seasonal temperatures in Central Florida.

The following sample schedules assume that you eat breakfast at your resort (unless otherwise stated) and arrive up to 20 minutes before the official opening time. These schedules, though tirelessly tested and proven successful by Birnbaum's editors, are not carved in stone. Use them as a guide, tailoring the itineraries to suit your family's individual tastes. And use them in conjunction with schedules posted to My Disney Experience or *disneyworld.com* and Tip Boards in the parks.

We have not included specific instructions with regard to Lightning Lane service (Genie+ and Individual Lightning Lane Selections) in our sample itineraries. It's not because we don't use the services. In fact, we recommend using them when theme parks are busy and budget allows for the added expense—but working it into a daily schedule is an inexact science. While many folks choose to take advantage of Genie+ and/or Individual Lightning Lane Selection—especially for the ultra-popular attractions—traditional standby lines are always available. For details about Walt Disney World's Lightning Lane paid reservation services, see page 27. Note that the fee-based Lightning Lane service is expected to morph a bit in 2024.

**Note:** As this book went to press, a handful of Walt Disney World shows, attractions, eateries, and backstage tours and programs were on pause. For updates, use the My Disney Experience mobile app or website, or visit *disneyworld.com*.

# MAGIC KINGDOM
## One-Day Schedule

❈ Begin the day with a stroll down Main Street, U.S.A. You can use the early morning time to shop, relax, and/or have a light breakfast. (If the Main Street Bakery has a daunting wait, consider getting that morning java jolt at Joffrey's Revive in Tomorrowland or Liberty Square's Sleepy Hollow.) Make your way to Cinderella Castle a few minutes before the park's official opening to watch Let the Magic Begin. The "welcome to the park" show features a greeting from Mickey Mouse, musical fanfare, and a special Disney surprise. Next head to Seven Dwarfs Mine Train and/or Big Thunder Mountain Railroad. Then move over to Adventureland for Jungle Cruise, Pirates of the Caribbean, or The Magic Carpets of Aladdin. (If long lines abound, consider the traditionally less-crowded Walt Disney's Enchanted Tiki Room or Swiss Family Treehouse.)

❈ Consider lunching at Liberty Square's Columbia Harbour House or Frontierland's Pecos Bill's Tall Tale Inn.

❈ If time allows, bond with the 999 happy haunts that inhabit the Haunted Mansion before the Festival of Fantasy parade. After watching the peppy processional move on to Fantasyland.

❈ See as much of Fantasyland as possible, including Dumbo the Flying Elephant, It's a Small World, Peter Pan's Flight, Seven Dwarfs Mine Train (if you haven't experienced it yet), and Under the Sea—Journey of The Little Mermaid.

❈ If the timing's right, head to the front of Cinderella Castle for a live stage show (if it's presented on the day you visit Magic Kingdom), or take a relaxing ride on Tomorrowland's PeopleMover.

❈ Haven't seen Tom Sawyer Island, Haunted Mansion, Liberty Square Riverboat, or the Country Bear Jamboree? Go for it!

❈ Visit TRON: Lightcycle/Run, Space Mountain, Buzz Lightyear's Space Ranger Spin, Monsters, Inc. Laugh Floor, and the Tomorrowland Speedway.

❈ Find a spot near the Castle or in the middle of Main Street to view the nightly presentation of the Disney's Happily Ever After fireworks show. (Check a park Tip Board for the schedule.)

❈ If there's time, revisit a favorite attraction (guests are usually able to join the queue right up until closing time).

*(Continued on page 36)*

# MAGIC KINGDOM
## One-Day Schedule
*(Continued from page 35)*

## MAGIC KINGDOM MUSTS:

Here's a list of the attractions that put the magic in the Magic Kingdom:

TRON: Lightcycle/Run

The Haunted Mansion

Big Thunder Mountain Railroad

Pirates of the Caribbean

Peter Pan's Flight

It's a Small World

Space Mountain

Buzz Lightyear's Space Ranger Spin

The Many Adventures of Winnie the Pooh

Seven Dwarfs Mine Train

Under the Sea—Journey of The Little Mermaid

Tiana's Bayou Adventure (expected to open by late 2024 or early 2025)

## IF YOU HAVE YOUNG CHILDREN:

• Head directly to Fantasyland (walk right through the Castle if you can) and visit It's a Small World, Peter Pan, The Many Adventures of Winnie the Pooh, Under the Sea—Journey of The Little Mermaid, and Dumbo the Flying Elephant. Meet Ariel in her grotto and cool off at the Casey Jr. Splash 'N' Soak Station (spray zone).

• Stop for a spin in a teacup or a ride the Prince Charming Carrousel on the way to Frontierland. Sing along with Big Al and the gang at the Country Bear Jamboree.

• Check the schedule for the stage show at Cinderella Castle on Main Street, U.S.A.

• Line up for the afternoon parade about 30 minutes early. Or skip the parade, finish up Fantasyland, and take a magic carpet ride in Adventureland. If it's hot (and your tot has swim diapers), visit the camel near the magic carpets. It spits cool water!

• Most little ones enjoy visiting Tom Sawyer Island and Monsters, Inc. Laugh Floor.

## LINE BUSTERS:

Even when the park is packed, there are some attractions with shorter or faster-moving lines. Among them are Tomorrowland Transit Authority PeopleMover, Hall of Presidents, The Enchanted Tiki Room, Carousel of Progress, Mickey's PhilharMagic, Country Bear Jamboree, and Tom Sawyer Island.

## LIGHTNING LANE SERVICE*:

A substantial number of Magic Kingdom attractions may be reserved via the My Disney Experience app. At a cost of about $15–$40+ per person, per day, Genie+ allows guests to bypass the traditional standby line and utilize the (ideally) faster-moving Lightning Lane for select shows and attractions. A second way to access the Lightning Lane is to purchase an Individual Lightning Lane Selection to a (very) select number of attractions (limited to 2 per person, per day). For a comprehensive listing of Genie+ and Individual Lightning Lane attractions and procedures, visit *disneyworld.com*, or use the My Disney Experience app or website (see page 27 for details).

Lightning Lane service is offered at all Walt Disney World theme parks. Note that, unlike the defunct Fastpass+ advance reservation system, Lightning Lane passes (Genie+ and Individual Lightning Lane Attraction Selections) come with additional fees.

* Details are subject to change at any time. For updates, use the My Disney Experience mobile app or website.

# EPCOT
## One-Day Schedule

- Plan to arrive early, as EPCOT guests may be admitted a bit before the posted opening time. If you enter from the park's front entrance, make a beeline for Test Track and Soarin' Around the World. If you enter via World Showcase's International Gateway, consider starting with France's Remy's Ratatouille Adventure or Frozen Ever After in Norway before hitting Test Track. Guests with no health or motion sickness issues should experience the out-of-this-world adventure known as Guardians of the Galaxy: Cosmic Rewind (which may require using a Virtual Queue) and the "highly intense" version of Mission: SPACE Orange Mission. Otherwise, ride Mission: SPACE Green Mission—the gentler, non-spinning version.

- Frozen Ever After, in the Norway pavilion, is a wildly popular attraction—get there as early as possible.

- Enjoy lunch at Space 220 (reservations are a must), Sunshine Seasons in The Land, Connections Eatery, Coral Reef Restaurant, or La Cantina de San Angel.

- After exploring The Land, take time to screen the Disney and Pixar Short Film Festival in the Imagination pavilion. Afterward, visit ImageWorks, a small, high-tech playground. Kids love it—almost as much as they do the enthralling Leap Frog Fountains in the front of the pavilion and Journey of Water–Inspired by Moana. Follow it up with The Seas with Nemo & Friends.

- If you're up for some pin trading (or shopping), stop by the collector pin shop near Spaceship Earth. Cast members displaying pins are always willing to swap any Disney pin for another Disney pin.

- The line for Spaceship Earth should have dwindled by now. Head to the giant geosphere to experience an intriguing journey through time. Check out the nearby Dreamers Point (if it's open) when you're done.

- Make your way back to World Showcase by early evening and start your world tour at Canada. Proceed counterclockwise around the lagoon. Don't miss Remy's Ratatouille Adventure in the France pavilion. And take in as much live entertainment as you can—World Showcase has a lot to offer!

- After dinner, scope out a spot to watch the nighttime spectacular. (There are good viewing locations all around World Showcase Lagoon.) Return to your spot about 30 to 40 minutes before the show.

**TIMING TIP:** If you have a World Showcase restaurant reservation, allow 30 to 45 minutes to get there from the front gate. Taking a FriendShip water taxi can save some time, but it isn't much faster than brisk walking.

*(Continued on page 38)*

# EPCOT
## One-Day Schedule

*(Continued from page 37)*

## EPCOT ESSENTIALS:

There is a lot to see and do at Disney's discovery park. Don't leave EPCOT without investigating these outstanding attractions:

Soarin' Around the World

Frozen Ever After

Test Track

Spaceship Earth

Turtle Talk with Crush

Disney & Pixar Short Film Festival

Living with the Land

Nighttime Spectacular

The American Adventure show

Mission: SPACE

Remy's Ratatouille Adventure

Guardians of the Galaxy: Cosmic Rewind

## IF YOU HAVE YOUNG CHILDREN:

• Begin the day by visiting with Disney characters and exploring The Seas with Nemo & Friends. Then head over to the Imagination! pavilion to ride Journey Into Imagination with Figment and visit the ImageWorks play zone. Be sure to check out the nearby Journey of Water, too.

• At World Showcase, ride Remy's Ratatouille Adventure in France. Then head to Norway's Frozen Ever After attraction. Afterward, hit Mexico's boat ride: Gran Fiesta Tour Starring The Three Caballeros.

• Visit the Kidcot Fun Stop in each country. Don't miss the koi pond in Japan and Germany's tiny village.

• If the weather is warm, let little ones splash in the interactive fountain on the pathway joining World Celebration with World Showcase or the spray zone in front of Test Track.

## LINE BUSTERS:

Tired of long lines? Head to Disney & Pixar Short Film Festival in Imagination!, or the movies in China, Canada, and France (*Impressions de France* and the *Beauty and the Beast* Sing-Along). The Spaceship Earth line thins out in the afternoon, as do the lines for the attraction inside The Seas with Nemo & Friends and Gran Fiesta Tour Starring The Three Caballeros in the Mexico pavilion.

## LIGHTNING LANE SERVICE*:

A number of EPCOT attractions may be reserved via the My Disney Experience app. At a cost of about $15–$40+ per person, per day, Genie+ allows guests to bypass the traditional standby line and utilize the (ideally) faster-moving Lightning Lane for select shows and attractions. A second way to access a Lightning Lane is to purchase an Individual Lightning Lane Selection to a (very) select number of attractions (limited to 2 per person, per day). For a current listing of Genie+ and Individual Lightning Lane attractions and procedures, use the My Disney Experience mobile app (refer to page 27 for details).

Lightning Lane service is offered at all Walt Disney World theme parks. Note that, unlike the retired Fastpass+ advance reservation system, Lightning Lane selections (Genie+ and Individual Lightning Lane Attraction) come with additional fees.

* Details are subject to change at any time. For updates, use the My Disney Experience mobile app or website.

# DISNEY'S HOLLYWOOD STUDIOS
## One-Day Schedule

- Some attractions open later in the morning; check a park Tip Board for exact times. Also, many shows run on a schedule (e.g., For the First Time in Forever: A Frozen Sing-Along Celebration, and Beauty and the Beast—Live on Stage). If you purchase Genie+ Lightning Lane service via the My Disney Experience app (see page 27 for details), make your first selection as soon as possible. And arrive early—wait times build quickly in these parts.

- This park has a very popular land known as Star Wars: Galaxy's Edge. Get there early to ride the area's duo of crowd-pleasers—Star Wars: Rise of the Resistance and Millennium Falcon: Smugglers Run.

- All Toy Story Land attractions are exceptionally popular, but Slinky Dog Dash is the megastar of the colorful play zone. Arrive as early as you can.

- Daredevils should make Rock 'n' Roller Coaster a priority, followed by some eye-opening drops at The Twilight Zone™ Tower of Terror.

- Experience Mickey & Minnie's Runaway Railway! The wild whirl through a cartoon realm is fun for all, but is an especially high priority for younger guests.

- If Beauty and the Beast is playing soon, grab a seat. Otherwise, plan to come back later and instead catch a short film at the Mickey Shorts Theater.

- Pause for lunch at 50's Prime Time Café or Sci-Fi Dine-In Theater (with a reservation), Woody's Lunch Box, Sunset Ranch Market, or ABC Commissary.

- See Muppet*Vision 3-D, Star Tours—The Adventures Continue, and the Indiana Jones Epic Stunt Spectacular. Take tots to Disney Junior Play and Dance!

- If you missed Beauty and the Beast—Live on Stage, go now, and if you haven't hit it yet, be sure to experience Tower of Terror.

- If Fantasmic! is being presented, you want to get a spot in line at least 50 minutes before showtime. Note that if you choose to skip Fantasmic!, plan to exit the park before the last performance breaks. If you do stay for the show, know that you can meander through select shops while the throngs exit.

- If you haven't already hit Mickey & Minnie's Runaway Railway—the park's giggle-inducing trip through a cartoon realm—do so now!

- Are Disney Movie Magic and The Wonderful World of Animation happening tonight? If so, make a point of catching these spirited projection displays.

*(Continued on page 40)*

# DISNEY'S HOLLYWOOD STUDIOS
## One-Day Schedule
*(Continued from page 39)*

## STUDIOS STANDOUTS:

When you visit Disney's Hollywood Studios, be sure to catch as many of the following attractions as possible:

Mickey & Minnie's Runaway Railway

*Millennium Falcon:* Smugglers Run

Rock 'n' Roller Coaster Starring Aerosmith

Star Wars: Rise of the Resistance

Alien Swirling Saucers

Toy Story Mania!

Slinky Dog Dash

Fantasmic!

Muppet*Vision 3-D

The Twilight Zone™ Tower of Terror

Beauty and the Beast—Live on Stage

Star Tours—The Adventures Continue

## LIGHTNING LANE SERVICE*:

A number of attractions may be reserved via Disney's Genie+ service. At a cost of about $15–$40+ per person, per day, Genie+ allows guests to bypass the traditional standby line and utilize the (ideally) faster-moving Lightning Lane for select shows and attractions. A second way to access the Lightning Lane is to purchase an Individual Lightning Lane Selection to a (very) select number of attractions (limited to 2 per person, per day). For a current listing of Genie+ and Individual Lightning Lane attractions and procedures, use the My Disney Experience mobile app (refer to page 27 for details).

   Note that, unlike Walt Disney World's recently retired Fastpass+ advance reservation system, Lightning Lane passes (Genie+ and Individual Attraction Selections) come with additional fees.

* Details are subject to change at any time. For updates, visit *MyDisneyExperience.com.*

## LINE BUSTERS:

When lines abound at Disney's Hollywood Studios, we suggest visiting the following: Indiana Jones Epic Stunt Spectacular (the theater fits about 2,000 guests at a time); Muppet*Vision 3-D; For the First Time in Forever: A Frozen Sing-Along Celebration (this indoor theater also has a high capacity); Lightning McQueen's Racing Academy; and Star Wars Launch Bay.

## IF YOU HAVE YOUNG CHILDREN:

• Begin with Mickey & Minnie's Runaway Railway, followed by Toy Story Mania! (if your child is old enough to wear 3-D glasses). Next up: Alien Swirling Saucers. After that, head to Muppet*Vision 3-D. (If your tot is too young to wear 3-D glasses, bypass the Muppets and go to the Mickey Shorts Theatre for a classic Mickey Mouse cartoon and/or a visit with Anna and Elsa at For the First Time in Forever.

• Stop for lunch before heading to Sunset Boulevard for Beauty and the Beast—Live on Stage (be sure to check the performance schedule before you arrive). Zoom on over to Lightning McQueen's Racing Academy, but skip Fantasmic!—parts of the show tend to spook wee ones.

• Join the fun at Disney Junior Play and Dance! and catch up with Disney characters at Animation Courtyard and Commissary Lane.

# DISNEY'S ANIMAL KINGDOM
## One-Day Schedule

- Guests who arrive prior to park opening may wait for the "rope drop" after passing through The Oasis. Many shows run on a schedule, so check for times throughout the day. If you want to experience Kilimanjaro Safaris or Expedition Everest without a big wait, arrive as early as you can. Check the schedules for Festival of the Lion King, Feathered Friends in Flight, and the new Finding Nemo: The Big Blue . . . and Beyond show. Note that if you choose to buy Lightning Lane service (Genie+ and/or Individual Lightning Lane Selection) to bypass standby lanes for select shows and attractions, you can do so via the My Disney Experience app (for details, see page 27).

- As you enter the park, pass through the Oasis and go to Pandora—The World of Avatar. Daredevils should make a beeline for Avatar Flight of Passage. If the line for Na'vi River Journey is on the manageable side, go for it. If not, make your way over to Asia.

- In Asia, tackle Expedition Everest, ride Kali River Rapids (if you don't mind getting soaked), then visit tigers and Komodo dragons at the Maharajah Jungle Trek and see Feathered Friends in Flight!

- Plan to arrive at The Festival of the Lion King theater at least 45 minutes prior to your preferred showtime. If possible, mingle with Mickey and Minnie (at the Adventurers Outpost) before seeing Festival of the Lion King.

- Stop at Yak & Yeti, Harambe Market, Flame Tree Barbecue, or Nomad Lounge (inside Tiffins Restaurant) for lunch. Then board the Wildlife Express train to Rafiki's Planet Watch and visit the Affection Section petting farm. Be sure to collect Wilderness Explorer badges along the way.

- After experiencing Africa's Kilimanjaro Safaris, take a relaxing hike on the animal-laden Gorilla Falls Exploration Trail.

- Make your way to DinoLand, stopping to take in It's Tough to Be a Bug! along the way. After riding Dinosaur, head to the Finding Nemo stage show. Take young kids to play in The Boneyard before leaving the area.

- Revisit favorite attractions. If you postponed the drenching Kali River Rapids, now is a good time to fit it in.

- When the sun sets, watch the Tree of Life "awaken"—as colorful images are projected onto the mighty baobab tree, while music envelops the area. (Each awakening vignette lasts about ten minutes and can be seen from the front and back of the Tree of Life when the park is open late.)

*(Continued on page 42)*

# DISNEY'S ANIMAL KINGDOM
## One-Day Schedule

*(Continued from page 41)*

## ANIMAL KINGDOM ACES:

An abbreviated visit to Disney's Animal Kingdom park is enough to make anybody growl. The following shows and attractions are sure to soothe the savage beast, er, guest:

Avatar Flight of Passage

Finding Nemo: The Big Blue . . . and Beyond!

Kali River Rapids

Kilimanjaro Safaris

Gorilla Falls Exploration Trail

Donald's Dino-Bash!

Expedition Everest

Dinosaur

Maharajah Jungle Trek

Festival of the Lion King

Feathered Friends in Flight

It's Tough to Be a Bug!

Winged Encounters—The Kingdom Takes Flight

## LIGHTNING LANE SERVICE*:

A number of attractions may be reserved via Disney's Genie+ service. At a cost of about $15–$40+ per person, per day, Genie+ allows guests to bypass the traditional standby line and use the (ideally) faster-moving Lightning Lane for select attractions. A second way to access the Lightning Lane is to purchase an Individual Lightning Lane Selection to a (very) select number of attractions (limited to 2 per person, per day). For a current listing of all Genie+ and Individual Lightning Lane attractions, use the My Disney Experience mobile app (refer to page 27 for details).

Lightning Lane service is offered at all Walt Disney World theme parks. Note that, unlike the retired Fastpass+ advance reservation system, Lightning Lane access (Genie+ and Individual Lightning Lane Attraction Selections) comes with additional fees.

## LINE BUSTERS:

When herds of guests mob Disney's Animal Kingdom shows and attractions, there are a few places to escape the stampede: The Oasis, Gorilla Falls Exploration Trail, Maharajah Jungle Trek, Discovery Island Trails, The Boneyard playground, and Rafiki's Planet Watch. (You will need to take the Wildlife Express train to reach Rafiki's Planet Watch—it's the only way to get there.)

## IF YOU HAVE YOUNG CHILDREN:

• Explore the Oasis on your way into the park. As you cross the bridge to Discovery Island, stop at the Wilderness Explorer Headquarters and get started collecting badges. Then go to the Adventurers Outpost to meet Mickey and Minnie.

• Stop by the Tree of Life to discover all of the animal carvings in its trunk. (Note that the show inside the tree, It's Tough to Be a Bug!, is very intense and may frighten young children.)

• Take a lunch break at Pizzafari or Restaurantosaurus. Be sure to explore The Boneyard area, see Feathered Friends in Flight, and ride TriceraTop Spin.

• In Asia, go to the Maharajah Jungle Trek and catch a performance of Finding Nemo: The Big Blue . . . and Beyond. Ride Africa's Kilimanjaro Safaris. See the Gorilla Falls Exploration Trail. Then take the Wildlife Express train to Rafiki's Planet Watch.

* Details are subject to change at any time. Use the My Disney Experience app or visit *MyDisneyExperience.com* for updates.

# MAGIC KINGDOM
## Half-Day Schedule

### MORNING/AFTERNOON*

- Arrive early—Main Street may open before the rest of the park. Use the time to shop, nosh, and catch the park's welcoming show. Where to go next? It's a big decision. Know that the area you postpone may have long lines by the time you get there. We usually like to start in Adventureland—but if you arrive at park opening (or earlier), consider kicking off the day with Tomorrowland's TRON: Lightcycle/Run.

- Bond with buccaneers at Pirates of the Caribbean before making a beeline for Frontierland's Big Thunder Mountain Railroad. (Note that Tiana's Bayou Adventure is expected to be open by late 2024 or early 2025.)

- Visit The Haunted Mansion, and then (if you plan on staying through the afternoon) grab a spot for the afternoon parade, The Festival of Fantasy.

- Watch the Festival of Fantasy parade (and wave hello to Anna and Elsa!) in Frontierland. Or skip the processional and head to Peter Pan's Flight, Seven Dwarfs Mine Train, The Many Adventures of Winnie the Pooh, It's a Small World, and Under the Sea—Journey of The Little Mermaid.

- Go to Tomorrowland to ride TRON (if you haven't done it, yet) and Space Mountain. Follow them up with Buzz Lightyear's Space Ranger Spin. Take youngsters for a relaxing trip on the PeopleMover (but warn them that there will be several moments of total darkness).

### HALF DAY WITH YOUNG KIDS

Start at Main Street's Town Square Theater. See Mickey inside. If it's close to parade time, grab a spot on the curb. After exploring Fantasyland, consider the Country Bear Jamboree. Watch Mickey's Royal Friendship Faire at Cinderella Castle. Soar on a magic carpet in Adventureland, then head to Tomorrowland for Tomorrowland Speedway and Buzz Lightyear's Space Ranger Spin. Cap off the day with a viewing of Happily Ever After, the Magic Kingdom's nightly extravaganza.

### AFTERNOON/EVENING*

- Check the My Disney Experience website or mobile app for the day's entertainment schedule. Try to catch Mickey's Magical Friendship Faire stage show (at Cinderella Castle). And be sure to see the Festival of Fantasy parade. (Warn little ones about a pending appearance by a fire-breathing dragon.)

- Explore Town Square Theater. If the wait to meet Mickey Mouse is more than 45 minutes, consider coming back in the evening.

- Start in Adventureland. Ride the Jungle Cruise and Pirates of the Caribbean.

- Head to Frontierland. Make it a priority to ride Big Thunder Mountain Railroad. Then see the Country Bears or Tom Sawyer Island (note that the island closes at dusk).

- Hit the best of Fantasyland, including It's a Small World, Seven Dwarfs Mine Train, Peter Pan, Journey of The Little Mermaid, and The Many Adventures of Winnie the Pooh.

- Be sure to take in Haunted Mansion and any Liberty Square area attractions on your list.

- Now it's time for Tomorrowland. Go to Space Mountain, TRON: Lightcycle/Run, and/or Buzz Lightyear's Space Ranger Spin.

- Catch Once Upon a Time—a festive light show that's projected onto Cinderella Castle. And don't miss Happily Ever After, the park's beloved fireworks spectacular.

- If there's time, revisit a favorite attraction, do a little shopping, or grab a snack and take a break as the masses file out of the park for the night.

* For details on where to meet and mingle with favorite Disney characters, see page 147.

# EPCOT
## Half-Day Schedule

### MORNING/AFTERNOON

- Head directly to Guardians of the Galaxy: Cosmic Rewind (if it offers a standby line), or Norway's Frozen Ever After, followed by Test Track and Soarin' Around the World (this requires a bit of legwork, but it's worth hitting the big draws as early as you can). If you're up for the "intense" Mission: SPACE voyage to Mars, go for it. (We prefer the "less intense," non-spinning version of the attraction, also known as The Green Mission.)

- Visit The Seas with Nemo & Friends, Imagination!, Journey of Water–Inspired by Moana, and Spaceship Earth before moving on to World Showcase. (Save Spaceship Earth for later in the morning, after the wait time goes down a bit.) When hunger calls, stop for lunch. See the countries that interest you most, making sure to catch Remy's Ratatouille Adventure in France and Norway's Frozen Ever After attraction (if you haven't already), the show inside The American Adventure, and Mexico's Gran Fiesta Tour Starring the Three Caballeros.

### SEE THE CHARACTERS*

China (Mulan)

Entrance Plaza (Pluto and Goofy)

France (Belle and Aurora)

Germany (Snow White)

Imagination! (Mickey Mouse, Joy, and Vanellope)

Mexico (Donald Duck)

Morocco (Jasmine)

Norway (Anna and Elsa, in the Royal Sommerhus)

World Discovery (Daisy Duck)

United Kingdom (Mary Poppins and Alice in Wonderland)

World Showcase Gazebo (Minnie Mouse)

*Characters and locations are subject to change.

### AFTERNOON/EVENING

- If you don't have reservations and would like to try for dinner at a table-service restaurant, use the My Disney Experience app or stop by Guest Relations to check for any walk-up availability. If not, consider dining at the nearby BoardWalk resort (it's a short stroll or FriendShip ride away). Note that reservations are necessary for most locations.

- See as much of World Discovery and World Nature as possible before heading to World Showcase. (All sections of the park generally stay open until about 9 P.M., but some attractions may close at 7 P.M.)

- Spend the evening touring World Showcase. Keep an eye on the clock so you can secure a good spot around the lagoon to take in the park's nighttime spectacular. There are excellent viewing locations all around World Showcase lagoon.

- Avoid the crush of exiting crowds by browsing the wares in the new Creations Shop near Test Track.

### HALF DAY WITH YOUNG KIDS

Begin with a visit to Norway's Frozen Ever After and/or Remy's Ratatouille Adventure, then The Seas with Nemo & Friends pavilion (enjoy a journey in a clam-mobile, see Turtle Talk with Crush, and romp at Bruce's Sub House). Follow it with a visit to Spaceship Earth. If your child is old enough to wear 3-D glasses, take in at least the first film in Imagination's Disney & Pixar Short Film Festival. (It's a blast!) Visit the Kidcot Fun Stops throughout the park and stop by the mini village in Germany. If time allows, take in Journey Into Imagination with Figment and ImageWorks in the Imagination pavilion (if they are operating during your visit to the park).

# DISNEY'S HOLLYWOOD STUDIOS
## Half-Day Schedule

## MORNING/AFTERNOON

- Kick-start the day with a visit to the park's newest land—Star Wars: Galaxy's Edge.

- Make a beeline for Slinky Dog Dash, followed by Toy Story Mania!, and trips to Rock 'n' Roller Coaster and Tower of Terror (don't ride them on a full stomach). From there, head over to Mickey & Minnie's Runaway Railway, and Muppet*Vision 3-D or Star Tours—The Adventures Continue.

- Say hi to the mice at Mickey & Minnie starring in Red Carpet Dreams.

- See Beauty and the Beast—Live on Stage (the theater is on Sunset Boulevard) or For the First Time in Forever: A Frozen Sing-Along Celebration (on Hollywood Boulevard).

- For a quick bite, stop at The Backlot Express, Woody's Lunch Box, or Sunset Ranch Market.

## SEE THE CHARACTERS*

Celebrity Spotlight near Commissary Lane (Olaf)

Hollywood Boulevard at opening time (characters vary)

Animation Courtyard (Pluto and Disney Junior friends such as Fancy Nancy, Doc McStuffins, and Vampirina)

Brown Derby Lawn (Chip and Dale)

Commissary Lane (Minnie and Mickey)

Hollywood Boulevard (Donald and Daisy)

Pixar Place (Mr. and Mrs. Incredible, Frozone, Edna Mode, and Sulley)

Star Wars: Galaxy's Edge (Chewbacca, BB-8, Rey, First Order Stormtroopers, Kylo Ren, and more)

Toy Story Land (Jessie, Buzz, Woody)

*Characters are subject to change.

## AFTERNOON/EVENING

- Daredevils should begin with Tower of Terror and Rock 'n' Roller Coaster.

- Pop over to Toy Story Land and visit Slinky Dog Dash, Toy Story Mania!, and Alien Swirling Saucers.

- Take a spin on Mickey & Minnie's Runaway Railway and see Beauty and the Beast—Live on Stage.

- Explore planet Batuu in Star Wars: Galaxy's Edge.

- Take in Star Tours, Muppet*Vision 3-D, For the First Time in Forever—A Frozen Sing-Along Celebration, and *Vacation Fun* at the Mickey Shorts Theater.

- See the Indiana Jones Epic Stunt Spectacular show, then jump in line for Fantasmic! Or skip Fantasmic! and revisit favorite shows and attractions. Try to catch the Wonderful World of Animation show at the Chinese Theatre on Hollywood Boulevard. (If Fantasmic! has two performances, the second is usually less crowded.)

## HALF DAY WITH YOUNG KIDS

Start with Toy Story Land attractions: Alien Swirling Saucers and Toy Story Mania! (if your child is old enough to wear 3-D glasses), followed by Mickey & Minnie's Runaway Railway, For the First Time in Forever—A Frozen Sing-Along Celebration, Disney Junior Play and Dance!, the Mickey Shorts Theater, Beauty & the Beast—Live on Stage, and Lightning McQueen's Racing Academy. Meet Disney Junior pals in Animation Courtyard. Skip Fantasmic!—it's just too intense (and a bit long) for most tykes.

# DISNEY'S ANIMAL KINGDOM
## Half-Day Schedule

### MORNING/AFTERNOON

🐭 Go directly to Pandora—The World of Avatar to ride Flight of Passage. Then head to Asia to ride the thrilling Expedition Everest and the soaking Kali River Rapids, and hike the Maharajah Jungle Trek.

🐭 Experience Feathered Friends in Flight on the way to the Kilimanjaro Safaris attraction and the Gorilla Falls Exploration Trail.

🐭 Check a Times Guide to see when the Festival of the Lion King show is playing today. Plan to arrive up to 45 minutes before showtime.

🐭 Finish up with a performance of Finding Nemo: The Big Blue . . . and Beyond!, Dinosaur, and It's Tough to Be a Bug!—though the last two are too intense for most tots. Take young adventurers to The Boneyard playground instead.

### SEE THE CHARACTERS*

At press time, some traditional Disney-style character meet-and-greets were on "temporary pause" at Animal Kingdom. While they are expected to return, there are still opportunities to see popular pals as they cruise along the park's Discovery River. Mickey and Minnie greet folks in person at the Adventurers Outpost on Discovery Island. Moana mingles on Discovery Island, too. You may find Donald, Daisy, Chip, and Dale in DinoLand U.S.A. Kevin likes to wander around Discovery Island. Daisy, Goofy, and Mickey join Donald for meals at Tusker House (reservations required). Other characters, such as Pocahontas and Meeko, Russell and Dug, and Rafiki and Timon may wave to guests from flotillas on the Discovery River. For updates, use the My Disney Experience app, visit *disneyworld.com*, or ask at a Guest Relations location inside the park.

*Details and characters are subject to change.

### AFTER LUNCH

🐭 Check the My Disney Experience app for the Festival of the Lion King schedule. Arrive up to 45 minutes before showtime. Then visit Mickey and Minnie at the Adventurers Outpost on Discovery Island. Be sure to soar on a mountain banshee at Flight of Passage in Pandora—The World of Avatar.

🐭 Head to the Kilimanjaro Safaris ride. Then hike the scenic Gorilla Falls Exploration Trail and take the Wildlife Express train to Rafiki's Planet Watch.

🐭 Ride Expedition Everest and Kali River Rapids, and experience the Maharajah Jungle Trek. Try to catch Feathered Friends in Flight, too (the first performance takes place in the late morning).

🐭 Wander the Discovery Island Trails before pausing to take in It's Tough to Be a Bug!

🐭 Before indulging in dinner, dodge dastardly dinos on Dinosaur.

🐭 If the park is open after dark, watch the Tree of Life awaken (the short-but-sweet show can be seen from the front and the back of the tree). Or use the time to revisit favorite shows and attractions.

### HALF DAY WITH YOUNG KIDS

Scope out animal life in The Oasis before stopping at the Wilderness Explorer Headquarters on the bridge to Discovery Island. Then head over to the Adventurers Outpost to meet Mickey and Minnie, followed by a visit to DinoLand U.S.A. Explore The Boneyard playground area and swirl on TriceraTop Spin. Enjoy the Kilimanjaro Safaris in Africa. If time allows, take the train to Rafiki's Planet Watch, where kids can bond with live animals (mostly goats). A bird show known as Feathered Friends in Flight captivates park guests of all ages.

# Making the Most of Longer Visits

Longer stays allow the chance to sample more of the World's myriad offerings. Spend another day in the one park you most enjoyed. Lounge by the pool, go biking, or play some tennis or golf. Shop till you drop at Disney Springs. Cool off at one of Disney's innovative water parks. Enjoy a meal at a Walt Disney World resort hotel, and try a special dinner at Victoria & Albert's in the Grand Floridian or at the Contemporary's delightful California Grill. Sample the restaurants at Disney Springs or spend an evening exploring the BoardWalk. Take a

golf, tennis, or archery lesson. Go fishing or horseback riding. Visit a relaxing day spa. See a movie. Enjoy a picnic on the beach. Participate in a behind-the-scenes program. Play a round or two of miniature golf. Visit Tri-Circle D Ranch at Fort Wilderness. Catch a game at the ESPN Wide World of Sports Complex. Enjoy the many activities offered by your Walt Disney World resort. Or just sit back and chill. For even more ideas, refer to our *Sports & Recreation*; *Everything Else in the World*; and *Good Meals, Great Times* chapters.

## HOW TO SAVE A RAINY DAY

Florida rain showers come and go with such regularity that you could almost set your watch by them, especially during summer months. They're usually brief, though torrential. Of course, there are times when gray clouds linger longer. Here are some ways to make the most of a soggy day:

• See a movie (or two!) on one of AMC Theatres' many screens at Disney Springs. (See page 231 for details.)

• Head for an arcade—many WDW resorts have one. Games are appropriate for guests of all ages. (The arcades at Art of Animation and Contemporary are larger than most.)

• Don your rain gear and go to EPCOT. The engaging pavilions house a bounty of sheltered diversions. Rain ponchos are sold throughout WDW for about $12 each. (Keep in mind that crowds at all of

the parks tend to dwindle a bit during inclement weather—as do the lines for popular attractions.)

• On soggy days, the Magic Kingdom may offer a splashy character parade in lieu of its usual afternoon processional. If the Rainy Day Cavalcade is offered during your visit, be sure to catch it. And feel free to sing and splash along.

• Swap your shoes for alley-friendly footwear and pound some pins at Splitsville—a bodacious bowling zone located at Disney Springs West Side. They serve food and drinks, too. (See page 232 for details.)

# Customized Travel Tips
## Traveling with Children

Tell kids that a Walt Disney World vacation is in the works and the response is apt to be overwhelming! Our guide *Birnbaum's Walt Disney World for Kids 2024*, written for kids ages 7 and up, can be a useful resource for getting them involved in the planning from the outset. Filled with information about the World from a child's perspective, it can be used as a reference before and during the trip, a place to collect character autographs, and a post-trip souvenir keepsake.

Walt Disney World ranks among the most appealing spots on Earth for families with kids. Keep in mind, however, that a child under age 14 must be accompanied by a guest age 14 or older to enter the theme parks and kids under age 7 must be accompanied by a person over age 14 to board theme park attractions; kids under 10 must be accompanied by an adult at the water parks.

**Child Care:** In-hotel-room child-care service can be summoned to all Disney-owned resorts (fees apply). The service is available 24/7, though it is not provided by Disney. A company called Kid's Nite Out offers one-to-one babysitting in your Walt Disney World Resort hotel room for kids ages 6 weeks to 18 years. Arts and crafts, reading, and playing games are among the activities offered. For pricing and to make a reservation with Kid's Nite Out, visit *kidsniteout.com*, call 800-696-8105, or inquire at your resort's Lobby Concierge. You can also arrange for a childcare expert to accompany your family during visits to Disney theme parks, providing assistance when needed. Another company, Super Sitters, offers similar services. To reach them, visit *supersittersincfl.com*, or call 407-382-2558. While authorized to operate within Walt Disney World, neither Kid's Nite Out nor Super Sitters is affiliated with nor endorsed by the Walt Disney Company.

## PARENTAL PERK

Families with babies or small children should know about the "rider switch" policy (aka "baby swap") at the theme parks. At attractions with age or height restrictions, a parent who waits nearby with a young child while the other parent enjoys the attraction can go right on soon after the first parent comes off. Be sure to ask the attendants at the attraction's entrance. They will tell you how to proceed.

**Children's Activity Centers:** Camp Dolphin operates daily from 4 P.M. to 11 P.M. and accepts kids ages 5 to 12. There are three payment packages, depending on the time that your child will attend the camp: early evening (4 P.M. to 8 P.M.; $65 per child), late evening (8 P.M. to 11 P.M.; $50 per child) or full evening (4 P.M. to 11 P.M.; $85 for the first child and $65 for each additional child). The package includes supervised arts & crafts, movie screenings, board games, themed activities, and more. A meal is included with the early evening session and a snack is included for late evening. For more information, visit *www.swandolphin.com*, or call 407-934-4000. Four Seasons Orlando offers a free Kids Camp for kids ages 4 through 12. For specifics, call 407-313-7777, or go to *www.fourseasons.com/orlando*.

**Baby Care Centers:** Located in all theme parks, these centers are for parents with young children. They are not meant as day care. All kids must be accompanied by a parent or guardian. There are rocking chairs and comfy couches in feeding rooms for nursing mothers and screenings of Disney films for kids. Centers have facilities for changing diapers, preparing formula, warming bottles, and washing bottles. Diapers, bottles, formula, pacifiers, and baby food are among the supplies for sale. Baby Care Center locations are listed on all theme park guidemaps. There are changing tables in most women's, many men's, and all family restrooms.

**Lost Children:** Disney employees (also known as cast members) will know what to do if a child starts to call for his or her parents. If your child wanders off, tell the nearest cast member and stop at the Baby Care Center or City Hall in the Magic Kingdom (on Main Street, U.S.A.); at Guest Relations or the Baby Care Center in EPCOT; at Guest Relations in Disney's Hollywood Studios; or at Guest Relations in Animal Kingdom. A computerized system allows for a detailed description of the child and the child's status, helping to reunite families quickly. It helps if your child has your mobile telephone number, too. In emergencies, an all-points bulletin can be put out among Disney cast members. The Guest Relations staff at each park can help, too.

Prepare youngsters for the possibility of an accidental separation. Direct your kids to contact the nearest park worker (someone wearing a costume and a name tag) and ask for help.

**Refrigerators:** For parents of young children, an in-room fridge is not a luxury, it's a necessity. Accommodations at all WDW–owned-and-operated resorts come equipped with a small fridge/beverage cooler. Many Disney Vacation Club Villas accommodations are equipped with full-size refrigerators.

**Baby Food:** Many parents choose to ship a box of food and baby supplies to their resort before they leave home. (Note that there is a $6 fee for any package or mail that goes through a WDW resort Front Desk.) It is possible to purchase baby food at most Disney resorts, but the selection is small. For a wider variety of foodstuffs to choose from, consider a trip to Publix at 7880 Winter Garden Vineland Road. (To get a resort's address for the GPS, inquire at the Front Desk. You will need it for the return trip.)

Target and Walmart, as well as several nearby stores, are also within a reasonable driving distance. If you need a ride, be sure to hire an authorized service for the trip (Lyft, Uber, Minnie Van, and taxis are all possibilities. If you need a cab, ask a resort staffer for help.) Another good option is *gardengrocer.com*. The company is authorized to deliver to most Disney-area hotels and stock a wide variety of items, including many organic, gluten-free, and kosher selections.

**Bed Rails:** If you would like bed rails for a child, it's best to request them in advance (and confirm before you leave home). Call 407-934-7639 and ask that they be added to your Walt Disney World resort reservation. Note that bed rails may be used on standard-size beds, but not smaller pull-down beds.

**Cribs:** Some Walt Disney World resort rooms come with a small, portable playpen-like crib. Look for it in the closet. If it's not there, call to have one sent to your room. They're free, but somewhat flimsy.

**Diapers:** Each Disney resort has at least one shop in which to pick up diapers. If you're brand loyal, pack your own. (Consider shipping diapers to your resort so you don't have to pack them and know that a $6 fee will be charged for each package handled by the Front Desk.) Be sure to throw extra swim diapers into your bag each morning. You never know when you'll run into an interactive fountain on Disney property. They're

**Hot Tip!** Walt Disney World is stroller central. Make yours easier to spot in sprawling stroller parking zones by adorning it with a colorful sign, scarf, balloon, or flag—or all of the above. You'll be happy you did.

## TIPS FOR TOTS

Walt Disney World is as toddler-friendly as it gets. Here are a few pointers to make it even more so:

• Familiarize your child with Disney characters before your WDW trip. That way they'll be more likely to enjoy meeting them and less likely to be frightened by them.

• Disney resort rooms are designed with little ones in mind, but we recommend packing baby-proofing items such as outlet plugs and doorknob covers or locks.

• Fireworks (and thunder) can scare little ones silly—and the booms can hurt sensitive ears. We recommend you pack noise-canceling headphones. If your tot is spooked by loud noises, be prepared to make a hasty exit once the booms begin. Disney's Hollywood Studios' Fantasmic! show also tends to terrify tots.

• Be sure to bring snacks when you head out for the day. It's tough to find toddler-friendly nibbles once you leave your resort.

• You will be asked to collapse your stroller before boarding a Walt Disney World resort bus or boat—but not on the monorail or Disney Skyliner.

• Don't forget sunscreen that's sensitive to toddler skin. Pack a hat for an infant.

• Bring a small, familiar toy from home and keep it with you at all times. (Don't take a favorite—you don't want to lose a treasure.)

• Don't underestimate the play value of a good splash. Take time to relax and enjoy the invaluable amenity that is the Walt Disney World resort pool. Of course, swim diapers are a must.

• Remember that your child may enter Disney parks without a ticket (aka free of charge) until his or her third birthday.

• Pack a thermometer and your go-to baby-friendly analgesic—just in case.

necessary for pool use, too. Guests using cloth diapers should note that most WDW resorts offer credit-card-operated washers, dryers, and detergent dispensers.

**RESORT FUN:** Many Disney resort hotels have playgrounds and kid-friendly pools (complete with supervised pool parties and life jackets to borrow), plus nightly campfires and screenings of Disney films—all included with the resort reservation. Other resort activities are offered for a fee. For details, see page 106.

**STROLLERS:** All four theme parks offer stroller rentals, available for $15 for one day and $13 each day of a Length of Stay (multi-day visit) rental. (If you'll need a stroller for several days, a Length of Stay rental ticket is the way to go.) Disney Springs rents single strollers for about $15 a day, plus a $100 refundable deposit (with a valid credit card). Guests may rent strollers from Sundries, near the Disney Springs bus depot. Double strollers cost $31 for one day and $27 per day of a multi-day rental. Strollers are not available for rent at either of the Walt Disney World water parks. Walt Disney World strollers are made of hard plastic and are not ideal for babies. They are

If you have a baby, you'll need a stroller for your visit. Although they may be rented at Walt Disney World, consider bringing one from home. It'll save you money and the hassle of getting one each time you visit a park. Plus, there's the convenience of using it everywhere you go. (Disney rents strollers at the theme parks and Disney Springs, but they're made of uncomfortable hard plastic and can't leave the place from which they are rented.)

If you'd like to come and go with a more comfy set of wheels, consider Disney's featured provider ScooterBug. They are authorized to deliver strollers and ECVs to WDW resorts: *scooterbug.com/orlando*. Another company of note is Magic Strollers. Conveniently located between WDW and the Orlando International Airport (MCO), the strollers and the service are top notch: *www.magicstrollers.com*; 866-866-6177. For more information, turn to page 70.

designed to accommodate children who weigh up to 50 pounds. A limited number of infant-friendly single strollers may be available. Length of Stay rentals must be paid for in full at the time of first rental. Put your receipt in a safe, dry place—that's what you will need to show to get a stroller on the remaining days of your stay. That receipt will also come in handy should your stroller go missing (it happens). Simply present it at the nearest stroller rental location and you will receive a replacement stroller.

Strollers are not permitted inside attractions (they should be parked in designated stroller parking zones) and cannot be removed from the park in which they are rented. It's very important to park in a stroller zone. Otherwise, your stroller will likely be re-parked by a cast member in the nearest designated stroller spot.

If you rent a stroller in the morning and plan to hop to another theme park on the same day, just present the receipt for a replacement at the second park. Strollers should be returned to a rental location before leaving a Disney theme park.

**Notes:** You will be asked to remove your child and fold the stroller before boarding Disney World buses and boats. There's no folding necessary when boarding the monorail or the Skyliner. (For information about the Disney Skyliner, turn to page 67.)

You may take your own stroller to Walt Disney World theme parks, but wagons are not permitted. Strollers can be no larger than 31 inches wide and 52 inches long. No exceptions.

## TIPS FOR TEENS

When it comes to teens at Disney World, *The Little Mermaid's* Ariel has plenty of company. Of course, be they of the fish or human variety, teenage guests have special needs all their own. Here are some tips from our Walt Disney World teen experts:

• Try to get along with your brothers and sisters—even if it isn't always easy. Don't bug them to do the things you want to do all the time. Try to do things they want to do, too.

• Pack a hat or a visor. Why? It's much easier to throw a hat on than waste time doing your hair—plus it keeps the sun out of your eyes.

• One of the coolest things for teens to do is an evening at a theme park (especially when the park is open late!). Another good nighttime activity is to explore Disney Springs. And don't forget about relaxing at the hotel pool.

• Have some of your own money on hand. If it's your hard-earned cash, you probably won't spend it as quickly as you would your Mom's or Dad's!

• Attention, parents! Try to include your teens in planning the trip. If they get a say during planning, they will be much happier when they arrive at Walt Disney World. Also, don't make them get up at 6 A.M. every day. Try to give them a day or two to wake up late and lounge around the resort or visit a water park.

# Traveling without Children

Walt Disney World has become a very popular destination for adults traveling without kids, appealing to singles, couples, and empty-nesters alike. And Disney has responded to the growing demand with an ever-growing entertainment and dining selection for big kids without youngsters in tow. Just add mouse ears.

## COUPLES

There is a place for lovebirds at Walt Disney World. Actually, there are many spots in Walt's World that are perfectly suited to those with romantic intentions (provided, of course, that privacy is not a prerequisite!).

• Grown-ups love to roam the parks unencumbered by little ones and strollers. The Magic Kingdom's carousel-and-castle combo invokes enchantment in true fairy-tale tradition. EPCOT's World Showcase has the aura of a whirlwind tour (and the inspiration for a future trip?), with countries as intriguing and far-reaching as Japan and Morocco. Disney's Hollywood Studios conjures romance, adventure, and movie-style thrills. And what could be more enjoyable than sharing a safari through Disney's Animal Kingdom?

By day, there is romance in the theme parks for couples who are already inclined to hold hands; by night, the parks sparkle with an intensity that inspires sudden mushiness in those who never considered themselves the type, and that's before the fireworks.

## THE MOST ROMANTIC PLACES IN THE WORLD

### WDW RESORTS
- Animal Kingdom Lodge
- BoardWalk Resort
- Contemporary
- Grand Floridian
- Polynesian Village
- Port Orleans Riverside
- Wilderness Lodge

### WDW RESTAURANTS
- The Boathouse
- Cinderella's Royal Table
- Cítricos
- Enzo's Hideaway
- Flying Fish
- Jiko—The Cooking Place
- Le Cellier Steakhouse
- Monsieur Paul
- Narcoossee's
- Paddlefish
- Sanaa
- Victoria & Albert's

### WDW LOUNGES
- Belle Vue Lounge at BoardWalk
- The Boathouse (dock seating) at Disney Springs
- Cítricos Lounge at the Grand Floridian resort
- Il Mulino New York Trattoria Lounge at the Swan
- The Edison in Disney Springs
- Nomad Lounge at Disney's Animal Kingdom
- Rooftop lounge at Disney Springs' Paddlefish

### WDW THEME PARK SPOTS
- All of EPCOT's World Showcase
- Happily Ever After fireworks presentation at the Magic Kingdom
- Nighttime spectacular at EPCOT

• As Disney's themed resorts go about transporting guests to various times and places, they make quite a few passes through settings straight out of everyone's favorite fantasy escape textbook—from the Victorian charms of the Grand Floridian to the exotic island getaway that is the Polynesian Village resort. You won't find a more inspirational backdrop than that at the rustic Wilderness Lodge, marked by geysers and steamy hot springs, and a grand stone fireplace. At the nostalgic BoardWalk resort, surrey bikes are available to rent for romantic rides along the waterfront. And a peaceful stroll around Crescent Lake is a lovely way to cap off a Disney day.

• The myriad of recreational activities that couples may enjoy at Walt Disney World includes tennis, fishing, golf, ballooning, carriage rides, couples treatments at one of several on-property spas, and more.

## OLDER TRAVELERS

Disney World can sometimes be challenging for older travelers. And the heat, particularly in summer, can be hard to take. But with the proper planning and precautions, it's just as delightful for older visitors as for kids.

• Make special requests when you reserve your room. For example, if a member of your party requires a wheelchair-accessible room or grab bars in the bath—ask for them, and confirm requests before arrival.

• For slower times, visit the parks Monday through Wednesday. (Thursdays through Sundays tend to attract lots of locals.)

## VACATION INSURANCE

No one books a vacation expecting to cancel it at the last minute—yet sometimes life intervenes and it's simply unavoidable. So it may be worth working travel insurance into your vacation budget (we do). It may include coverage for trip cancellation and interruption, travel delay, loss of baggage, medical expenses, and more. Be sure to ask about travel insurance when you reserve your trip. You'll be glad you did.

• The Florida sun tends to be brutal year-round. Stay hydrated and always wear sun protection (don't forget hands and feet).

• Try to eat early or late to avoid the big mealtime crowds. In the Magic Kingdom, select restaurants such as the Jungle Skipper Canteen and Columbia Harbour House. Or take the monorail to the peaceful Polynesian Village, Contemporary, or Grand Floridian resorts, where there are plenty of pleasant dining options (be sure to check ahead to find out which places serve lunch). In EPCOT, the Coral Reef restaurant and La Hacienda are pleasant spots. At Disney's Hollywood Studios park, the Hollywood Brown Derby offers a relaxing meal, as does Mama Melrose's Ristorante Italiano.

• If you need to store medicine, know that a beverage cooler or mini fridge is included with the room at all WDW–owned-and-operated resort hotels. (Check with your resort to make sure it's cool enough to safely store medication.) All park First Aid Stations are equipped to store medicine, too. (No charge.)

• Don't underestimate distances at EPCOT or Animal Kingdom; you may need to walk more than three miles in a day in each of these parks. Wear comfortable shoes and remember to take breaks.

**Hot Tip!** Even the fittest of seniors may want to avoid some of Walt Disney World's more physically challenging attractions. Do heed all warning signs posted at the entrances to thrill rides and consider steering clear of high-activity-level experiences such as the Magic Kingdom's Swiss Family Treehouse (seemingly endless stairs!), and the Maharajah Jungle Trek and Gorilla Falls Exploration Trail at Disney's Animal Kingdom (lots of walking and few places to rest).

• Pace yourself. It's smart to head back to your hotel for a swim or a nap in the afternoon and then return to the parks later on. The hotels connected by monorail are particularly convenient for this.

• Many Orlando-area hotels and attractions offer discounts to seniors and AARP members. Contact the Official Visitor Information Center (407-363-5872) for additional information.

• Be sure to pack extra doses of any medication—in case of travel delays or other reasons for an extended visit. Pack contact info for your doctors and copies of all prescriptions, too. It pays to be prepared.

## SOLO TRAVELERS

Those who travel alone (be it for business or just for fun) can have as memorable a time here as they would anywhere else.

• Solo travelers with extra time should consider taking a behind-the-scenes tour.

• Many of the finer restaurants now have counters at which to eat—perfect for chatting with other diners.

• Sometimes, being a solo traveler can mean shorter wait times at attractions. Test Track is among those with "single rider" lines.

• Other opportunities for unencumbered travelers include balloon rides (at Disney Springs), horseback riding (at Fort Wilderness), taking a spin in a pontoon boat at a Disney resort, enjoying an early morning bass fishing excursion (407-939-2277 or 407-939-7529), and watching a game (at ESPN Wide World of Sports). Call 407-939-7529.

• Disney Springs' lounges and restaurants can be fertile meeting places. (Sports fans find its City Works Pour House & Eatery most enjoyable.) The BoardWalk resort is another lively destination. And sushi lovers fit right in at the California Grill sushi bar (in the lounge area of the popular eatery).

• The bars/lounges at most WDW resort hotels are relaxed and inviting. (Geyser Point Bar & Grill at Wilderness Lodge scores points for relaxation, while Ale & Compass at Yacht Club ranks high on the conviviality chart.) The same animated atmosphere prevails at the Tune-In Lounge in the 50's Prime Time Cafe at Disney's Hollywood Studios and at the Rose & Crown Pub (in the U.K. pavilion at Epcot's World Showcase).

## IMPORTANT TELEPHONE NUMBERS

**AdventHealth Celebration Hospital:** 407-303-4000

**Annual Passholder Assistance:** 407-939-7277

**Behind-the-Scenes Tours:** 407-WDW-TOUR (939-8687)

**Central Reservations:** 407-W-DISNEY (934-7639)

**Dining Reservations & Info:** 407-WDW-DINE (939-3463)

**Disability Services:** 407-560-2547

**Dr. P. Phillips Hospital:** 407-351-8500

**Disney PhotoPass:** 407-560-4300

**Emergency:** 911

**ESPN Wide World of Sports Complex:** 407-939-1500

**Existing Tickets:** 407-934-7639

**Golf Reservations:** 407-WDW-GOLF (939-4653)

**Goofy:** Unlisted

**My Disney Experience and MagicBands:** 407-939-4357

**New Tickets:** 407-939-7679

**Recreation and Tours:** 407-WDW-PLAY (939-7529)

**Theme Park Information:** 407-939-2273

**Walt Disney Travel Company:** 407-828-8101

**Walt Disney World Information:** 407-824-4321

# Tips for International Travelers

Visitors from outside the U.S. need not feel like strangers in a strange land when they arrive at Walt Disney World—even if they speak a language other than English. Helpful information is available in many languages. These tips may also be useful:

• International guests without pre-arranged transportation to Walt Disney World can use a car-sharing service (Lyft or Uber) or go to the airport taxi stand. The cost of a taxi ride from Orlando International Airport (MCO) to a Disney hotel is usually about $65, but may be higher. A 10- to 20-percent gratuity is suitable for good service. For guests planning to use a car-sharing service, download the mobile app and create an account before you leave home.

• A valid passport or government-issued photo ID is required to check in at a Walt Disney World resort hotel.

• Free park guidemaps can be found in Spanish, French, German, Portuguese, and Japanese at the entrance to all Walt Disney World theme parks, as well as at Guest Relations locations.

• Free translation services are available at all four theme parks and include a translation device called Ears to the World, Disney's Show Translator. The units are lightweight headsets that use wireless technology to provide synchronized narration at several theme park attractions. They are available in French, German, Japanese, Portuguese, and Spanish. There is no charge to use a translation device, but a $25 (refundable) deposit is required to borrow one.

• Several Disney resort hotels offer services for their international guests. Ask about them when making hotel reservations.

• When making your reservations through 407-WDW-DINE (939-3463) or WDW-PLAY (939-7529), ask to speak with a foreign-language host or hostess.

• Most Disney restaurants offer menus in various languages. Some even have picture menus.

• Guests must be at least 21 years old to consume alcoholic beverages in the state of Florida.

• Foreign currency exchange is offered at Guest Relations in the four Disney theme parks.

• Disney's MagicBands can act as a charge card (as well as a room key). Most purchases made at Walt Disney World can be billed to a credit card that is linked to an active MagicBand or resort ID.

• Many Disney employees are fluent in more than one language. Languages spoken (in addition to English) are noted on employee name tags.

• Guests traveling long distances and through time zones should conserve their energy. It might be wise to relax by the pool on the day of arrival, instead of trying to fit in a full day at a theme park — it's never beneficial to start a vacation exhausted!

• Phone cards for international calls are sold at some Walt Disney World shops and in many WDW resorts. Inquire at Guest Relations.

## TELEPHONE DOS AND DON'TS

It's common for hotels to assess a massive surcharge for phone calls, and Disney is no exception. To avoid big bills, use your mobile phone, and keep these tips in mind for the hotel phone:

• A direct-dialed, long-distance call will set you back the cost of the call at the AT&T operator-assisted day rate, plus a 65 percent surcharge! The rate applies to both domestic and international long-distance. Applicable taxes are included.
• Prepaid phone cards are available for purchase in most WDW resort lobbies.
• There is no extra fee for a guest to make credit card, prepaid phone card, or any type of operator-assisted call from a resort-room telephone.
• There's no charge to call an 800 number from a WDW resort room.
• There's no charge to call from room to room within a Disney resort—but there may be a charge to call between resorts.
• Check with your mobile-phone carrier to avoid tallying up "roaming" charges. And switch your phone from roaming to Wi-Fi whenever possible.
• All Walt Disney World-owned-and-operated resorts support mobile computing via laptop and tablet. Wi-Fi service is free.

# Travelers with Disabilities

Disney tends to get high marks from travelers with disabilities because of attention paid to special needs. For more information, call 407-560-2547, or email *disability.services@disneyparks.com*. Here is an overview of services.

**GETTING AROUND:** Designated parking is available for guests throughout Walt Disney World (a valid disability parking placard is required). From the Transportation and Ticket Center (TTC), the Magic Kingdom is accessible by ferry or by monorail. All monorail stations are accessible to wheelchairs. Ramps can be lengthy and a bit steep, but manageable.

**Wheelchairs:** Guests who use wheelchairs may bring their own to Walt Disney World. They also have the option of renting one at a theme park or from a local vendor. Wheelchairs may be rented in theme parks for $12 per day ($10 per day with a Length of Stay rental). In the Magic Kingdom, they are available at the Stroller and Wheelchair Rental, inside the entrance. EPCOT's rental areas are inside the main entrance and at the International Gateway entrance. Oscar's Super Service rents wheelchairs at the Studios. At Disney's Animal Kingdom park, wheelchairs may be rented at Garden Gate Gifts Stroller Rental area.

**Hot Tip!** The theme park disability parking areas can be quite a distance from the wheelchair rental locations. If you require assistance, seek out a courtesy wheelchair to get you to the park's front entrance.

If you plan to visit Disney parks for several days, consider getting a multi-day wheelchair rental. Known as a Length of Stay rental, it comes at a $2-per-day discount. You'll pay for the entire stay when you first visit a theme park. Simply show your receipt to the attendant the next time you visit a rental location to receive a new wheelchair.

Disney water parks have a small number of wheelchairs and Electric Conveyance Vehicles (ECVs) on hand. Wheelchairs cost $12 per day, while ECVs rent for $50 a day. Both require a $100 refundable deposit. Disney Springs rents wheelchairs for $12 a day, plus a $100 refundable deposit, from Sundries (located near the bus depot). ECVs are available there for $50 per day with a $100 (refundable)

**Hot Tip!** Service animals are welcome at most locations in WDW theme parks and resorts. At Walt Disney World Resort, a service animal is a dog or miniature horse that is trained to do work or perform tasks for, and to assist, an individual with a disability. For additional information, please email Disability Services at *disability.services@ disneyparks.com*, or call 407-560-2547.

deposit. Wheelchairs at ESPN Wide World of Sports complex run $12 per day with a $100 refundable deposit. Walt Disney World Resorts with zero-depth-entry pools may have a small number of wheelchairs available to assist guests entering the pools.

**Electric Conveyance Vehicles (ECVs):** Electric Conveyance Vehicles (ECVs) are available for rent in all WDW theme parks. They cost about $50 a day, plus a $20 refundable deposit. They usually sell out early. A word of advice: Practice makes perfect. So before you head into a thicket of park guests, take it for a test drive — and please do not exceed the velocity of an average pedestrian.

Equipment rented at a park cannot leave that park. If you will need to use it for the whole trip, consider calling a company that rents standard and electric wheelchairs, as well as scooters. Keep in mind that you'll have to transport the wheelchair or scooter from your resort to your daily destinations. (Monorails and buses are equipped to accommodate, but some boats are not.) Companies from which to rent include ScootAround (*scootaround.com*; 888-441-7575) and Walker Mobility (*walkermobility.com*; 407-518-6000). Pickup and delivery (often for free or with a small surcharge) are available at all hotels in the WDW area (not just those on Disney property). In our opinion, guests are often better off renting from a local vendor or bringing their own equipment. The quality is generally better, and you don't have to worry about availability. Note that with the exception of ScooterBug (see page 70), guests must be present for delivery and pick-up from all other vendors. The Walt Disney Company is not affiliated with, nor does it endorse, any of these companies.

There are designated areas for guests using wheelchairs to view the fireworks/nighttime spectaculars at Magic Kingdom and EPCOT, and to watch parades in the Magic Kingdom. Check a park guidemap for current locations.

**Accessibility:** It's relatively easy to get around the parks by wheelchair and scooter. Most WDW attractions are accessible to guests who can be lifted from chairs with help from a member of their party, and some can accommodate guests who must remain in the wheelchair. Consult each park's Guide for Guests with Disabilities (for a free set, write to Walt Disney World Guest Correspondence, P.O. Box 10000, Lake Buena Vista, FL 32830) for details about access, or check with the ride host or hostess. At the water parks, life jackets are available for all guests.

Most Disney hotels have accommodations suitable for guests with disabilities, including roll-in showers. Other features—which vary, based on the resort—include accessible bathrooms, bed accessories, strobe-light smoke detectors, in-room Text Typewriters (aka TTYs), and more. At least 7 WDW resort hotels offer zero-depth-entry pools. For help selecting a resort, ask for the Special Reservations Department when you contact Walt Disney World Central Reservations (Voice: 407-939-7807; TTY: 407-824-4321).

 **Hot Tip!** First aid locations (in the theme parks, water parks, and resort hotels) let guests store and use their own portable medical equipment, such as nebulizers, at their facilities.

### RESOURCES:

**Visual Disabilities:** Guests can get a handheld device that verbally describes each park as well as many attractions. Each requires a $25 refundable deposit. Portable tactile maps may be borrowed from Guest Relations in each theme park (with a refundable deposit). Braille guides, Braille menus at most restaurants, and Braille maps are also available.

**Hearing Disabilities:** Sign Language interpretation for select live shows is offered on a rotating basis. For the schedule, use My Disney Experience, or go to a WDW Guest Relations location. For details, visit *disneyworld.disney.go.com/guest-services/hearing -disabilities-services,* or call 407-824-4321 at least two weeks ahead of time.

Assistive-listening devices that amplify attraction audio are available at the Magic Kingdom's City Hall and at Guest Relations in EPCOT, Animal Kingdom, and Disney's Hollywood Studios. A $25 refundable deposit is required.

Disney's Handheld Devices feature Handheld Captioning, a portable captioning system which displays

 **Hot Tip!** What happens if your Electric Conveyance Vehicle breaks down? If you rented it at a Disney park, notify a nearby employee and a replacement will be delivered to you. If it's your own, contact Guest Relations for assistance. For units rented from outside companies, please contact the rental provider.

on-screen text at select theaters and attractions. They are available from Guest Relations at all theme parks. There is a fully refundable $25 daily deposit for use.

**Booking the Trip:** These organizations specialize in assisting disabled travelers (and are not affiliated with The Walt Disney Company):
• The Society for Accessible Travel & Hospitality; 212-447-7284; *sath.org.*
• TravelAble Vacations (*travelablevacations.com;* 855-500-3440) will work with you to personalize a Disney vacation targeted to your accessibility needs.
• Guide Me Away (*guidemeaway.com;* 888-532-5575) plans accessible vacations and has team members with disabilities with whom you can speak.

**Motor Vehicles:** Mobility Works (877-275-4915; *mobilityworks.com*) rents wheelchair-accessible vans and offers pickup and delivery for Orlando International Airport (MCO) and most Walt Disney World–area hotels. Side- and rear-entry ramps are available, as are hand-controlled vans.

**Medical Equipment Rental:** AdventHealth (407-939-7480; *wondermeetswellness.com*) provides medical equipment delivery, as well as 24/7 virtual care, onsite urgent care, prescription delivery, and more.

Brevard Medical Equipment rents everything from walkers and bathroom safety items to portable oxygen, lift chairs, and sleep apnea systems. The company offers rentals for cruises, too. (321-455-0195; *brevardmedicalequip.com*)

## ATTRACTION ACCESS

Most park attractions are accessible to guests who are able to get out of their wheelchairs (with or without assistance). And a growing number have queues that can be navigated in a wheelchair. When that's the case, guests are urged to do so. If a wheelchair cannot be accommodated in the queue area, ask an attendant to direct you to an auxiliary entrance. Such entrances are intended for guests using wheelchairs or with service animals. For specifics on this policy, guests should visit a Guest Relations location.

# WDW Weddings & Honeymoons

Believe it or not, Walt Disney World is one of the most popular honeymoon destinations in the United States. Why the appeal? The resorts offer romantic stretches of white-sand beaches for evening strolls, fine restaurants, and a host of recreational activities to rival almost any other destination. Add to that the fantasy of the Magic Kingdom, the wonder of EPCOT, the glamour of Disney's Hollywood Studios, and the majesty of Animal Kingdom—plus Disney Springs and BoardWalk nightlife, water parks, and the nearby Disney Cruise Line—and it's not hard to see why Walt Disney World is tops with newlyweds.

After years of fending for themselves, folks looking to honeymoon here now have help at hand. A variety of options caters to newly married couples, as well as blended families joining together for the first time. For additional information, visit *disneyweddings.com/honeymoons*, or call toll-free: 877-566-0969.

## MY DISNEY EXPERIENCE

My Disney Experience has been described as "a whole new way to plan and share your Walt Disney World vacation." Prospective visitors may go to *MyDisneyExperience.com* or use the free app. After setting up a profile, guests can use My Disney Experience to book many elements of a Walt Disney World vacation—including restaurant reservations and Genie+ and Individual Lightning Lane selections for many theme park attractions (see page 27 for details)—and even track the arrival times for buses at Walt Disney World. For additional information, see pages 24-27.

## HONEYMOON REGISTRY

Launched, appropriately, on Valentine's Day, the honeymoon registry is a service for happy couples planning a Disney honeymoon. Gifts include theme park tickets, resort accommodations, carriage rides, spa treatments, and more. For more information or to sign up for the (free) Disney Honeymoon Registry, visit *disney.honeymoonwishes.com*, or call 800-801-3493 during regular business hours.

Over the years, the folks at Walt Disney World have received oodles of requests from couples wanting to get married at one of the theme parks. They responded by creating Disney's Fairy Tale Weddings and have been making wedding dreams come true for more than 25 years. Happy couples can tie the knot in fairy-tale ceremonies at some theme parks, as well as many other spots around Walt Disney World.

The Yacht & Beach Club, BoardWalk, Polynesian Village, and Port Orleans Riverside resorts host their share of weddings each year. The elegant Wedding Pavilion, on the grounds of the Grand Floridian Resort and Spa, offers a Victorian-style indoor setting with a prime view of Cinderella Castle and the Seven Seas Lagoon. The pavilion, which overflows with romantic ambiance, has seating for approximately 250 guests. Couples can fill their wedding albums with photos taken at Picture Point, under a trellis of climbing white roses, with the faraway castle in the background.

Weddings range from elegant affairs, with no hint of Disneyana, to lavish ceremonies in which the bride arrives in Cinderella's horse-drawn Crystal Coach and Mickey Mouse and Minnie Mouse are among the guests at the wedding reception.

At Franck's Bridal Studio, Disney wedding experts work with couples to customize each affair. Among the services offered are cakes, photography, flowers, and entertainment. They can help secure accommodations, rehearsal dinners, bachelor and bachelorette parties, and more. Feel free to stop by during your next WDW visit. F.Y.I.: Franck's was named for the character portrayed by Martin Short in the Disney film *Father of the Bride*.

For more information about planning a Walt Disney World wedding or honeymoon packages, call 321-939-4610, or visit *www.disneyweddings.com*.

# Fingertip Reference Guide

### BARBERS AND SALONS

One of the most amusing places to get a haircut is the Magic Kingdom's old-fashioned Harmony Barber Shop. It's located beside the Car Barn in the Town Square section of Main Street, U.S.A. The cost for a cut starts at about $21 for adults and $20 for kids. (Pricing does not include gratuity, which must be presented in cash.) Treat tots to a special "my first haircut" experience for about $28. Fancy a beard trim? Head here with at least $8 in your pocket. Operating hours are usually 9 A.M. to 5 P.M. daily. Walk-ins may be accommodated on a first-come, first-served basis. For details and to make reservations, use the My Disney Experience mobile app or website, or visit *disneyworld.com*.

Haircuts, coloring, manicures, and other services may be offered at Ship Shape at the Yacht & Beach Club (407-939-7727), Mandara Spa at the Dolphin (407-934-4772), the salon at Four Seasons Orlando (407-313-7777), and the Casa de Belleza at Coronado Springs (407-939-7727).

### BUSINESS SERVICES

Disney provides a range of services for those who simply must mix business with pleasure. Copiers, fax machines (also found at Guest Relations in the theme parks), and FedEx materials may be available at the Lobby Concierge or Business Center at many Walt Disney World resorts.

The Contemporary, Grand Floridian, Animal Kingdom Lodge, Yacht & Beach Club, Swan, Dolphin, Swan Reserve, and Coronado Springs resorts can also provide computers and printers. There is a video-conferencing center near Disney Springs. For additional information about Walt Disney World business services (including whether or not they'll be offered during your stay), call 407-827-2000.

### CAMERA NEEDS

Disney's PhotoPass photographers will happily snap shots of you with their cameras (for details, see page 143) or with your camera or mobile phone. Note that selfie sticks are not allowed in WDW theme parks or water parks. If you plan to use a camera, be sure to take extra charged batteries and memory cards— just in case.

### CAR CARE

There are three Speedway gas stations (with convenience stores) at Walt Disney World, all open 24/7. One is at 1475 Buena Vista Drive across from Disney Springs; another is near the Magic Kingdom Auto Plaza at 1000 Car Care Drive. The 300 East Buena Vista Drive location also has a car wash.

Breakdowns happen, but they don't spell disaster. All Disney roads are patrolled by police and security officers who can call for help. If you need a tow or other services, call the Walt Disney World Car Care Center (407-824-0976). The service is available to all Disney resort guests. Located in the Magic Kingdom Auto Plaza, the Car Care Center offers full mechanical services and free towing on Disney property, Monday through Friday, 7 A.M. to 7 P.M.; Saturdays 7 A.M. to 4 P.M.; Sundays 8 A.M. to 3 P.M. For off-property car care and assistance, all guests can rely on Riker's Roadside Services (*rikerstowingorlando.com*; 407-855-7776; ) for vehicle towing, Riker's Automotive & Tire (407-238-9800; *rikersauto.com*) for repairs, or AAA (provided you are an active AAA member).

### HEALTH & SAFETY PROTOCOLS

Disney is committed to health and safety. Face coverings are optional for guests in indoor and outdoor locations. However, face coverings are not permitted while experiencing water slides or in water at pools and water parks. Details are subject to change.

### DRINKING LAWS

In Florida, the legal drinking age is 21. Minors may accompany their parents to Disney lounges and bars, but might not be allowed to sit at the bar itself. Magic Kingdom table-service eateries serve alcohol at lunch and dinner. Alcoholic beverages are served throughout the other theme parks and Disney Springs.

Spirits are sold in at least one retail location at most Walt Disney World resorts.

## LOCKERS

Lockers can be found in the following theme park locations: to the right, just inside the Magic Kingdom entrance; beside Spaceship Earth (to the right, as you enter) in EPCOT; near Oscar's Super Service at the Studios; and inside the entrance (to the left) at Animal Kingdom. Lockers are available at the Transportation and Ticket Center (TTC), too.

All parks have small (12.5 by 10 by 17-inch) and large lockers (15.5 by 13 by 17-inch). Cost is about $10 per day for small lockers and $12 for large ones. EPCOT and Magic Kingdom also offer jumbo lockers. The super-size storage compartments measure 17 by 22 by 26 inches and cost $15 per day. Items may not be stored overnight. Lockers are cleaned out after the park closes. Locker rentals are not transferable from theme park to theme park. Plan accordingly.

## LOST & FOUND

The extensive indexing system maintained by Walt Disney World's Lost & Found department is impressive, especially when a treasured possession goes missing, whether it's false teeth or a teddy bear. (Both have been found; the dentures were never claimed.)

If you lose something, immediately report it to one of these Lost & Found locations: City Hall in Magic Kingdom, Guest Relations at EPCOT, Disney's Hollywood Studios, and Animal Kingdom park entrance, or the Lobby Concierge at any Walt Disney World resort. At Fort Wilderness Resort & Campground, dial 7-2726 from any comfort station telephone; from outside the campground, phone 407-824-2726 between the hours of 8:30 A.M. and 5 P.M. Eastern time.

Items that go missing in a Disney theme park may be claimed on the day of the loss at the park's Lost & Found. After your visit to Walt Disney World, you may realize that you left an item behind. In that case, visit *disneyworld.disney.go.com/guest-services/lost-and-found*.

Nobody begins the day expecting to lose something. But trust us, it pays to plan ahead. Put your name and contact info on your valuables, especially phones and cameras. Disney does a good job of tracking lost items, but it's a lot easier to locate a labeled smartphone out of the heap of battery-drained look-alikes than it is to find the one with the "blue case."

Once you've submitted a form, you will receive an email with your lost item claim number. The Lost & Found team will continue to look for your item and provide an email update. For additional Lost & Found info, visit the aforementioned website.

We highly recommend attaching contact information to all valuables.

## MAIL

Postage stamps are sold at all WDW resorts; at World of Disney at Disney Springs; at the Newsstand shop in the Magic Kingdom; and at shops near the lockers in EPCOT, Disney's Hollywood Studios, and Animal Kingdom.

The old-fashioned mailboxes in Disney parks are not official United States Post Office mailboxes, but postcards and letters (with postage) can be sent from them. Postmarks will read "Lake Buena Vista," not "Walt Disney World."

Don't mail anything that's in any way time-sensitive—it takes a whole lot longer for mail to reach its destination when sent from here.

Mail may be addressed to WDW guests in care of their hotel. It should clearly feature the word "Guest" on the front and the intended recipient's arrival date. Note that a $6 per package handling fee will apply to all packages received through the Front Desk or delivered to a Walt Disney World resort hotel room.

## MEDICAL MATTERS

Travelers with chronic health issues are advised to carry copies of all prescriptions and get names of local doctors from hometown physicians. Disney is equipped to deal with minor medical issues. In the Magic Kingdom, next to the Crystal Palace restaurant, there is a First Aid Center staffed by a registered nurse; there is another such facility at EPCOT in the Odyssey Center complex. At Disney's Hollywood Studios, the First Aid Center is inside Guest Relations at the main entrance. Animal Kingdom's First Aid Center is on Discovery Island near Creature Comforts. *In the case of a medical emergency, call 911 and alert the nearest employee*. Paramedics will arrive as promptly as possible.

Walt Disney World resort hotel guests and theme park day guests staying at other area hotels have

access to nearby services providing medical attention. AdventHealth Centra Care Walk-In Urgent Care (*www.centracare.org*), owned and operated by AdventHealth, has 20 locations in the Walt Disney World area, most near pharmacies and with X-ray facilities. Guests in need of additional care will be transported to the hospital when necessary.

The main Centra Care facility is at 12500 South Apopka Vineland Road (407-934-2273; very close to Disney Springs and Hotel Plaza Boulevard) and is open 24 hours a day, seven days a week. The Centra Care Walk-In facility at 8014 Conroy-Windermere Road (407-291-8975; near the resorts at Universal Studios Orlando) is open 8 A.M. to 8 P.M. weekdays and 8 A.M. to 5 P.M. on weekends. One location in Kissimmee is at 8201 W. Irlo Bronson Highway (407-465-0846). It's open from 8 A.M. to 8 P.M. weekdays and 8 A.M. to 5 P.M. weekends.

For minor medical matters, guests may access doctors and health care providers 24/7 by using the Adventhealth mobile app. (We recommend downloading the app before you leave home.)

Transportation to Centra Care Urgent Care is complimentary for Walt Disney World Resort Guests, and can be arranged through First Aid or Resort Front Desk Cast Members, or by calling Advent-Health at (407) 939-7480. Waits in clinics can be lengthy, but drivers can call ahead to learn which has the shortest wait. The most common maladies reported by Walt Disney World guests? Sunburn, blisters, fevers, earaches, and injuries from falls. Please be careful!

**For Diabetics:** All Disney parks and resorts can provide refrigeration services for insulin. WDW–owned-and-operated resort accommodations have beverage coolers, and small refrigerators may be rented at most other resorts for a small fee. The fee may be waived for folks who need the fridge to store medicine, but a doctor's note may be required. (For information about renting medical equipment, turn to page 56.)

**Prescriptions:** Turner Drugs (407-828-8125) delivers medications to many Orlando-area resorts, including those on Disney property.

### MONEY

Cash, traveler's checks, American Express, Master-Card, Visa, Discover Card, Diner's Club, JCB Card, and Disney gift cards are accepted as payment for most WDW charges.

Guests staying at a WDW–owned-and-operated resort enjoy a purchasing perk: Provide a major credit card at check-in and a MagicBand or hotel ID may be used to cover most expenses incurred at Walt Disney World. (They may be used to make purchases until midnight after you check out.)

**ATMs:** Automated teller machines are scattered throughout WDW. There are several in each theme park, plus at the Transportation & Ticket Center (TTC). Most WDW resorts have ATMs; the Fort Wilderness ATM is at Pioneer Hall. There are 5 at Disney Springs. Most bank and credit cards are accepted; fees range from about $2 to $3 (free for Chase Bank customers).

**Note:** It's always a good idea to notify your bank that you will be using your debit (or credit) card while on vacation. That should keep fraud protection software from freezing your account when you use it outside your home banking zone.

**Banking:** Truist, in Celebration, Florida (approximately four miles from Disney Springs), offers a variety of services. Guests can get cash advances; receive incoming wire transfers (for a fee); and cash, replace, or purchase American Express traveler's checks. Fees may apply. This branch is open from 9 A.M. to 5 P.M. Monday through Thursday; 9 A.M. until 6 P.M. Fridays; and 9 A.M. to 1 P.M. on Saturdays; the drive-through follows the same schedule. It's on Celebration Water Tower Place, 74 Blake Boulevard, Celebration, FL; 407-964-3333.

**Foreign Currency Exchange:** An individual may exchange up to $50 in foreign currency each day at Guest Relations locations in the theme parks, and up to $500 at the Concierge desk at Disney–owned-and-operated resorts.

### PETS AT WDW

No pets (other than trained service animals) are permtted in the theme parks, Disney Springs, or the water parks. Of course, that's no reason to leave Fifi or Fido at home—especially when you can treat them to a pampered getaway at the Best

Friends Pet Resort, a sprawling luxury facility (please don't call it a kennel!) complete with cat condos, doggy suites, and special accommodations for "pocket pets," including birds and hamsters. Cats or dogs from shared households may share quarters, but cats and dogs are not allowed to cohabitate (for obvious reasons).

The modern facility, which is the only dedicated place where guests may board animals at Walt Disney World, provides a full range of hospitality services, including day care (boarding in suites), grooming services, and doggy day camp (group sessions where the pups play games and frolic with other dogs under the supervision of a trained animal counselor).

Best Friends Pet Resort is located at 2510 Bonnet Creek Parkway, across from Disney's Port Orleans resort. Its services are available to everyone, but guests staying at WDW resorts net slight discounts. Indoor boarding (which includes two walks) costs $49 per day; indoor/outdoor boarding (with two walks) runs $52 a day; vacation villas (one walk, play group, flat-screen TV, webcam, and a private patio) cost $107, and VIP luxury suites (two walks, two play groups, TV, webcam, and private patio) cost $133 each day.

To prevent separation anxiety, guests are encouraged to visit pets during regular operating hours. Though hours vary, Best Friends is generally open from about one hour before the earliest theme park opening to about one hour or so after the latest park closing. The center's not open to the public 24 hours, but it is staffed around the clock (great for guests who experience travel delays or emergencies). There are certified veterinary technicians on staff, and all associates are trained in animal first aid. For directions, additional information about services, or to make reservations, visit *www.bestfriendspetcare.com*, or call 407-209-3126.

Be sure to bring your pet's certificate of vaccinations, as Florida law requires proof of immunization for animals involved in biting incidents. Elderly pets must be in good health with bladder and bowel control, and be mobile. Pack a familiar blanket or toy, too. And never leave your pet in the car—it's extremely dangerous and it's against the law.

**Note:** Certain pets are permitted at some campsites at Walt Disney World's Fort Wilderness Resort & Campground. For specifics, call 407-824-2900.

**Outside Walt Disney World:** For information about pet-friendly Orlando-area hotels, call Visit Orlando: 407-363-5872.

## RELIGIOUS SERVICES

Though religious services are occasionally offered on Disney property, regular services are available at local houses of worship.

**Catholic:** The closest Catholic church is Mary, Queen of the Universe Shrine, 2½ miles southeast of Lake Buena Vista, at 8300 Vineland Ave. It seats 2,000 people. For mass times and details, visit *www.maryqueenoftheuniverse.org*, or call 407-239-6600.

**Jewish:** Reform services are held at the Congregation of Reform Judaism (928 Malone Dr., Orlando; 407-645-0444; *www.crjorlando.org*), by Winter Park, approximately 20 miles from Walt Disney World's borders. Conservative services are held at Temple Ohalei Rivka, aka the Southwest Orlando Jewish Congregation (11200 South Apopka Vineland Road; 407-239-5444; *www.sojc.org*), approximately two miles from Disney Springs.

**Muslim:** Prayer takes place five times a day at the Islamic Center of Orlando, 11543 Ruby Lake Rd.; 407-238-2700; *www.icorlando.org*.

**Protestant:** Services are offered at the Community Presbyterian Church, 511 Celebration Ave., Celebration, FL; 407-566-1633; *www.commpres.org*.

## SHOPPING FOR NECESSITIES

At least one shop in every WDW resort stocks a small selection of toiletries. In addition to fuel, each of WDW's Speedway locations offers a convenience store; *www.speedway.com*. Over-the-counter health aids, plus other useful items, may be available at the Emporium in the Magic Kingdom park; they are kept behind the counter, so ask for what you want (you may be redirected to another location).

In EPCOT, a selection of sundries is sold in at least one shop. At Disney's Hollywood Studios, stop by

Crossroads of the World. At Animal Kingdom, get the bare necessities at Island Mercantile.

Local supermarkets include Publix (7880 Winter Garden Vineland Road) and Target (4795 W. Irlo Bronson Memorial Highway). Speedway gas stations have stores with grocery items and sundries. It's also convenient to have groceries delivered. (WDW resort rooms are equipped with small beverage coolers). Place your order with a delivery service (Amazon Fresh, Instacart, *gardengrocer.com*, etc.) and set the address as your Disney resort. (Make sure your name is listed as the order recipient.) Bell Services will store your groceries until you pick them up (or have them delivered for a fee of about $6.) Note that the aforementioned companies are not affiliated with or endorsed by the Walt Disney Company.

### SMOKING

Smoking (including e-cigarettes/vaping) is prohibited in all indoor and outdoor spaces at Walt Disney World, unless designated as "smoking areas." Eateries are smoke-free, as are bars and lounges. WDW resort rooms (and balconies) are also smoke-free zones. A $250–$500 cleaning fee will be added to the bill for guests who smoke in their room or on the balcony. Tobacco products are not sold in the parks. Guests older than age 21 may buy tobacco products at some resorts and Disney Springs venues (with government-issued photo ID). It is a statewide tobacco smoking policy, so if you leave Disney property, the same rules apply. If you have questions about WDW's smoking policy, ask a cast member or visit *disneyworld.disney .go.com/guest-services/designated-smoking-areas*. Do note that smoking marijuana is not permitted anywhere on Walt Disney World property.

### TELEPHONE CALLS

Every time a local phone call is placed from a Central Florida landline, callers must dial the area code and seven-digit number.

## LOST ADULTS

Occasionally, traveling companions get separated in the crush of the crowds, or someone may fail to show up at a meeting spot. When this happens, it's good to know that messages can be left for phone-free or battery-drained fellow travelers at Guest Relations in any of the Disney parks. (For lost children, notify a cast member.)

**Hot Tip!** The point of a WDW visit is to escape the real world—silence mobile phones and stick to texting when possible. If you have to make a call, kindly do so by the nearest public phone station. And *PLEASE* do not use a mobile phone while experiencing Walt Disney World shows or attractions. Otherwise, the noise and the light will disrupt the magic for you and those around you.

Rates charged by non-Disney resorts can vary a lot (for all calls). Ask about rates and fees before making calls beyond your resort. See page 54 for telephone tips.

### THEME PARK RESERVATIONS

Guests using date-based tickets are required to make park reservations through January 8, 2024. After that, no reservations are necessary! However, park reservations *are* required for Annual Passholders on most days before 2 P.M. (Reservation-free days for Annual Passholders are called "good-to-go" days.) To make reservations and learn more about good-to-go days, use the My Disney Experience app or website. Please visit *disneyworld.com* for updates and additional information. Details are subject to change.

### TIPPING

Tips are no less valued at Walt Disney World resorts than at any other hotel—$1 to $3 per bag is appropriate for lugging luggage; $2 to $4 per person, per night for housekeeping services (be sure to include a note to avoid confusion). Gratuities of 15 to 20 percent (excluding tax) are customary at full-service restaurants. (If the service is exceptional or otherwise, adjust accordingly.) Gratuity is included in the room-service bill at all WDW resorts and some off-property hotels. Meals that are prepaid with the Disney Dining Plan (except for the Hoop-Dee-Doo Musical Review dinner show; see page 316) do not include gratuity—please tip your servers.

Give cab drivers at least a 15 percent tip for good service. Baggage handlers at train stations and airports and bus drivers expect about $1 to $3 per bag.

### WILDLIFE

Florida is home to a vast array of fauna, including alligators, snakes, manatees, armadillos, owls, and more. Never feed wild animals. Doing so alters their natural behavior and is often against the law.

# TRANSPORTATION & ACCOMMODATIONS

The popularity of Walt Disney World has made the region around Orlando one of the world's major tourism and commercial centers, and transportation sources—from a state of the art airport to an efficient network of highways—bring happy visitors to the area by the millions.

There's no doubt that getting to and around the Walt Disney World region can be confusing. The only more perplexing dilemma may be choosing the best accommodations for your group from the huge assortment of resort hotels and motels.

The accommodations owned and operated by Disney itself range from futuristic towers to rustic-looking cabins tucked deep in piney woods. In between are resorts that evoke striking images of Africa, the South Pacific, historic Florida, early Atlantic City, the Pacific Northwest, New England, the Caribbean, New Orleans, Spain, and the

sports, movie, and music worlds, plus a sprawling, well-maintained campground. And that list doesn't include the many villas or the studios and one-, two-, and three bedroom "homes" that can be rented or "purchased" through a special vacation-ownership system (aka Disney Vacation Club). What follows should help travelers sort out the broad range of lodging options within the borders of Walt Disney World. Regardless of where you plan to stay, we offer this important piece of advice: Book your room as far in advance as possible. You'll be glad you did.

> "My business is making people, especially children, happy."
> —Walt Disney

# Getting Oriented

The Central Florida city of Orlando is the municipality with which Walt Disney World is most closely associated. Disney World, however, is located in a far smaller community called Lake Buena Vista, Florida. It's about 15 miles from Orlando's business center. All of Walt Disney World's hotels and restaurants are located within the borders of Lake Buena Vista.

**ORLANDO-AREA HIGHWAYS:** The most important traffic artery in Orlando is I-4, which runs diagonally through the area from southwest to northeast, cutting through the southern half of WDW. It then angles on toward Orlando and Winter Park, ending near Daytona Beach at I-95, which runs north and south along the Atlantic coast.

**Hot Tip!** Parking lots are cleverly labeled throughout Walt Disney World. Yet many drivers still misplace their vehicles. Avoid being dopey: Always snap a photo or jot down your parking location!

All the city's other important highways intersect I-4, and each has a name as well as a number. From south to north, they include U.S. 192 (aka Irlo Bronson Memorial Highway), which takes an east-west course that crosses the Walt Disney World entrance road and leads into downtown Kissimmee on the east; S.R. 528, aka the Beachline Expressway (formerly the Beeline), which shoots eastward from I-4; S.R. 435 (aka Kirkman Road), which runs north and south and intersects International Drive, where many motels catering to Walt Disney World visitors are located; U.S. 17-92-441 (aka Orange Blossom Trail), which runs north and south, paralleling Kirkman Road on the east; and S.R. 50 (aka Colonial Drive), which runs east and west. S.R. 429 (aka the Western Expressway), leads to a Walt Disney World entrance near the Coronado Springs resort (exit 8).

**WALT DISNEY WORLD EXITS:** The nearly 40-square-mile tract that is Walt Disney World is roughly rectangular. I-4 runs through its southern half from southwest to northeast. Major Walt Disney World destinations can be reached by taking the I-4 exits suggested in the paragraphs that follow; off the highway, clear signage makes it easy for visitors to get anywhere in the World.

This road is congested more often than not. Keep in mind that construction work and special events will often require rerouting of traffic patterns on I-4:

• **EXIT 64A**, marked "192/Magic Kingdom," leads to the Magic Kingdom, Fort Wilderness, and Palm and Magnolia golf courses, as well as the Grand Floridian Resort & Spa, Polynesian Village, Contemporary, and Wilderness Lodge resorts.

• **EXIT 65** leads to Disney's Hollywood Studios; ESPN Wide World of Sports Complex; Disney's Animal Kingdom theme park; Blizzard Beach; Art of Animation; Coronado Springs; All-Star Music, All-Star Sports, and All-Star Movies; Pop Century; and Disney's Animal Kingdom Lodge.

• **EXIT 67**, marked "EPCOT/Disney Springs," leads to EPCOT, Typhoon Lagoon, Disney Springs, Lake Buena Vista golf course, Disney's Saratoga Springs Resort & Spa, the BoardWalk, Caribbean Beach, Riviera, Swan, Dolphin, Swan Reserve, Yacht and Beach Club, Port Orleans Riverside and French Quarter, and Disney's Old Key West resorts.

• **EXIT 68**, marked "S.R. 535/Lake Buena Vista," is the best route to the resorts on Hotel Plaza Boulevard (aka the Disney Springs resort area). It can also serve as an alternate route to EPCOT and Disney Springs.

**Hot Tip!** The cost to valet park a vehicle at deluxe WDW-owned-and-operated resorts, plus Coronado Springs is $33 per day (not including gratuity). Self-parking at all Walt Disney World-owned-and-operated resorts is free!

# WDW Transportation

Walt Disney World transportation is extensive, with boats, buses, the monorail, and the Disney Skyliner (airborne gondolas that debuted in 2019) all doing their part to shuttle guests around.

One of the system's hubs is called the Transportation and Ticket Center (TTC) and is located near the Magic Kingdom. Monorail, bus, and ferry service connect the TTC to points throughout the World. Day visitors must park (or be dropped off) here before taking a monorail or ferry to the Magic Kingdom. (Most Walt Disney World resort guests can bypass the TTC via direct buses to and from their respective resorts.)

The monorail runs along a circular route near the Magic Kingdom theme park, making stops at the TTC,

Polynesian Village, Grand Floridian, Magic Kingdom, and Contemporary. A separate monorail route connects the TTC to EPCOT. Bus service is the cornerstone of the WDW transportation system. Buses usually operate starting one hour before park opening time until about an hour after closing; bus stops are clearly marked. Travel times vary, depending on the route.

Although Walt Disney World resort guests are provided with complimentary transportation to all sites on-property, that transportation is not always direct. Build in extra time for travel, especially if you have dining reservations or a Lightning Lane selection. Also, know that traveling between resorts usually requires at least one transfer. From several WDW locales, water

## SHOULD YOU RENT A CAR?

If you plan to spend all of your time on Walt Disney World turf, you can probably spare yourself the car-rental expense. Ride-sharing, towncar, taxi, and shuttle service from the airport to all area hotels is available around the clock. Within Walt Disney World's borders, an exhaustive network of transportation brings guests from point to point (if not always immediately or directly). Most area hotels offer their own bus service to and from the Disney theme parks (inquire in advance about schedules and costs, if any). Note that baby strollers must be collapsed before boarding Disney bus and water taxi transportation.

For those planning to resort-hop within Walt Disney World or any attractions outside Walt's world, taxis and services such as Lyft, Minnie Van, and Uber can often do the trick. A rental car is an option, too. It is easy (but pricey) to rent a car at the airport: National (800-227-7368), Alamo (800-327-9633), Avis (800-331-1212), Budget (800-527-0700), or Dollar (800-800-4000)—

but note that the rates are much higher than at other locations due to hefty airport fees. For day (or multi-day) trips, consider renting from Alamo, Enterprise, or National at the Disney Car Care Center (407-824-3470; free shuttle service is available from select Disney resorts) or one of the rental agencies that have desks at the resorts on Hotel Plaza Boulevard, or simply inquire about car rental at the Front Desk of your resort. It is free to self-park a vehicle at a Walt Disney World resort hotel—but there is a daily fee for valet parking. Keep in mind that area traffic can be brutal—always build in extra time to reach your final destination, especially if you have a restaurant reservation.

taxis usher guests to Magic Kingdom, EPCOT, Disney's Hollywood Studios, Disney Springs, or between resorts. Boats depart every 20 to 25 minutes. Walt Disney World buses generally run in intervals of 20 to 50 minutes (or more)—please plan accordingly. The Disney Skyliner connects Pop Century, Art of Animation, Caribbean Beach, and Riviera resorts with EPCOT and Disney's Hollywood Studios. What follows is a rundown of the components that make up the vast Walt Disney World Transportation System.

**MINNIE VAN SERVICE:** Polka-dotted, 6-passenger "Minnie" vans whisk guests around Walt Disney World—provided they have activated the Lyft app on a smart device. Simply open the app from anywhere within Walt Disney World Resort to access the service, request a ride, and pay for the trip. Cars are usually minutes away. Prices vary based on distance traveled from pick-up location to requested destination within Walt Disney World Resort. You will see the total cost and pay for the service through the Lyft app. Note that Minnie Van rates are generally higher than trips of equal distance provided by Lyft, Uber, or taxi.

Each Disney cast member–driven car is equipped with 2 car seats, and specially outfitted vehicles may be requested for folks who use wheelchairs or Electric Conveyance Vehicles (ECVs). Once the Minnie Van service is selected, the Lyft app will offer the estimated arrival time for the vehicle.

Minnie Van service is offered at Walt Disney World between 6:30 A.M. and 12:30 A.M. daily. Service to and from Orlando International Airport (MCO) was not offered at press time. For updates, use the My Disney Experience app or website, or visit *disneyworld.com*.

**THE MONORAIL:** The WDW monorail system has two main loops, which converge at the Transportation and Ticket Center (TTC). One loop connects the TTC with the Magic Kingdom, plus the Polynesian Village, Grand Floridian, and Contemporary resorts. (The Magic Kingdom is the third stop on the resort track and the first stop on the express track.) Another loop links EPCOT with the TTC. Monorails run from about 7 A.M. until about one hour after park closing. Strollers don't have to be collapsed to board the monorail.

**Timing Tips:** It can take 5 to 10 minutes to travel between stops on the Magic Kingdom resort loop, making for a grand circle total of 25 to 50 minutes. However, there are times of day when trains are taxed with greater volume than usual, causing delays at the station and on the beam. If there's an alternate form

of transportation available at busy times of day (bus, boat, your feet, etc.), consider taking it. Otherwise, plan ahead and anticipate delays. Monorails may not run during special ticket events. For the schedule, ask at any WDW resort Front Desk or theme park Guest Relations location.

## WDW TRANSPORTATION TIPS

- Most WDW buses are equipped with wheelchair lifts. Such buses have a blue emblem on the windshield and rear door.
- When using the WDW transportation system to get from a resort to a theme park, or from one park to another, allow an extra 45 minutes (or more) to get to your destination.
- The interval between the arrivals of Disney buses is about 25 to 50 minutes (possibly more, possibly less).
- Be forewarned: It takes a long time to travel by bus from resort to resort. Plan on a trip of up to 100 minutes and at least one transfer (at a theme park or at Disney Springs).
- It's possible to rent a car from any Walt Disney World–owned-and-operated resort (plus many others). For details, inquire at the Lobby Concierge desk, or contact the Front Desk.
- Monorails usually begin service about 30 minutes before the earliest theme park opening time and run until about one hour after the latest park closing time (and they don't always run during special ticket events and extended park hours).
- There is no direct transportation between Disney's BoardWalk and most WDW resorts. You must travel to Disney Springs or a park and transfer to the appropriate bus (or take the Disney Skyliner [to EPCOT's International Gateway], a car-sharing service, or a taxi). That said, it's easy to stroll over to the Swan, Dolphin, Swan Reserve, Yacht Club, and Beach Club resorts.
- Try to avoid vacating a theme park or water park just as it closes. Instead, plan to linger a bit in a shop, or grab a seat and watch the crowds crawl toward their respective buses, boats, airborne gondolas, cars, and monorails.
- The Disney Skyliner may temporarily cease operation due to inclement weather. Should that happen, alternate transportation will be provided.
- Keep in mind that the most obvious method of transportation may not turn out to be the quickest. For example, it is often much faster to walk to the Magic Kingdom from the Contemporary resort than it is to take the monorail. (The same can be said for the Grand Floridian and the Polynesian Village resort hotels—especially at park opening or closing time.)
- Guests staying at a WDW-owned-and-operated resort receive complimentary, standard self-parking at all WDW theme parks. Details are subject to change.

**CAR SERVICE:** Ride-sharing services Lyft and Uber may transport guests throughout Walt Disney World—as does the Minnie Van service (see page 66 for details). For assistance with taxis, go to a Bell Services desk. To reserve a Minnie Van, download the Lyft mobile app. (Disney's Minnie Van works with the Lyft app, but is operated by Disney cast members.)

**DISNEY WATER TRANSPORTATION:** FriendShip water taxis connect Disney's Hollywood Studios with the Swan, Dolphin, Yacht, Beach, and BoardWalk resorts, and EPCOT's International Gateway entrance. FriendShips also traverse EPCOT's World Showcase Lagoon.

Water taxis also connect the Magic Kingdom park with the Grand Floridian, Polynesian, Wilderness Lodge, and Fort Wilderness resorts. Ferry boats transport guests between the Transportation and Ticket Center and the Magic Kingdom. The Sassagoula Express ferries guests to Disney Springs from Port Orleans (French Quarter and Riverside), Old Key West, and Saratoga Springs resorts. Most routes run on 10- to 25-minute intervals. Hours of operation vary based on weather conditions. No luggage or alcohol is permitted. All strollers must be folded and stowed out of the aisle.

**WORDEN'S WISDOM**
Strollers aren't just for babies and toddlers! We bought a gently used jogging stroller and call it our "Disney stroller." We only use it for Disney trips! Walking miles a day for a week straight can be hard on little kids and a stroller ride can be a nice break. You can rent strollers, too! (@the.worden.fam on Instagram and @thewordenfam on TikTok)

**TAXI SERVICE:** Authorized taxis (run by Mears Transportation) are available for about $4.20 for the first mile, $2.40 per extra mile (407-422-2222). Payment may be made with a credit card or cash. Make sure you stick with authorized taxis. Unauthorized services may charge outrageous, unregulated rates. Inquire at the Bell Services desk at your resort's front entrance. They'll direct you to an authorized taxi or order one on your behalf. (Pay attention to the route the driver takes—we've been subjected to "the scenic route" on several occasions.)

**DISNEY SKYLINER:** This grand airborne gondola system connects Disney's Hollywood Studios and EPCOT's International Gateway entrance with four Walt Disney World resort hotels: Disney's Art of Animation, Pop Century, Caribbean Beach, and the Riviera. Many of the colorful cars are adorned with Disney character illustrations and all provide a scenic, free-of-charge way to travel among the aforementioned properties. Many gondolas can accommodate guests using wheelchairs. The units use cross ventilation to maintain air flow (not traditional A.C.). For details about the high-flying Disney Skyliner, use the My Disney Experience mobile app or website, or visit *www.disneyworld.com.*

**DISNEY BUS TRANSPORTATION:** Motor coaches can get you just about anywhere you need to go on Disney property. Bus service from most WDW resort hotels begins about 45 minutes prior to park opening and ends an hour prior to park closing. Return service to the hotels ends one hour after park closing. At press time, bus service to Disney Springs from Walt Disney World resort hotels started up as Disney Springs opened for the day, while return service to Walt Disney World hotels was offered until about an hour after Disney Springs closed each night. Some routes require you to transfer buses. Wonder when the next bus will arrive at your resort? Open the My Disney Experience app to view your resort reservation and tap "See Bus Times." Details are subject to change.

**Note:** No alcohol or luggage of any type is permitted on Disney buses. All strollers must be folded (prior to boarding the bus) and kept out of the aisle.

# WDW Accommodations

With a myriad of resorts in the Orlando area to choose from, it's definitely a challenge to select a hotel. Here's a bit of advice.

**Weigh the Options:** First decide whether to stay on or off Disney property. Many opt for a Walt Disney World resort because the conveniences and perks that are offered to resort guests are appealing (see page 69). Given that, there are still two major factors that tend to lure guests to non-Disney hotels both on and off WDW property: vacation budget and itinerary.

Travelers on a tight budget may find off-property options that are quite reasonable. However, Disney offers rooms as low as about $150–$250 per night (depending on hotel and date), so choose off-property accommodations only if the price difference is substantial. WDW room rates are based on double occupancy. Additional adult guests may result in an increase in the rate. There is no charge for kids age 17 or younger.

Guests who will spend only part of their trip exploring Disney may also prefer an off-property hotel—one that's closer to the other area attractions on their itinerary.

There's also the issue of what one considers deluxe. Disney–owned-and-operated "deluxe" resorts tend to provide more amenities and services than their "moderate" and "value" counterparts, but they do not always rival comparably priced digs in the outside world.

**Deciding Factors:** Once the on- or off-property decision has been made, it's time to look at hotels. The big differences among Walt Disney World accommodations are in the proximity to theme parks, size of the rooms and bathrooms, level of service, dining and transportation options, recreational facilities, views, landscaping, extended evening hours at select theme parks for select resort guests, and, of course, the all-important *cost*. Resorts within Disney's borders fall into two categories: owned-and-operated by Disney and Good Neighbor properties (for more about Good Neighbor resorts, see page 114.)

Consider how much time you'll spend in the room, whether you'd like to return to the hotel during the day, and if you will have time to use all the amenities that are included. Parties with five or more members have an additional concern: how best to accommodate their group. It may be comparable in price (possibly even lower) to reserve two value-priced rooms or a family suite (at All-Star Music or Art of Animation) instead of one luxe Disney hotel room.

**Ask the Right Questions:** Once a hotel that meets all basic criteria is selected, it's best to do some further research to avoid surprises at check-in.

For example, ask about any possible hidden costs, like fees for shuttle service to and from Walt Disney World destinations or taxes that may not be included in the quoted price. Though most off-property hotels offer transportation to Disney, price, trip frequency, and the number of buses vary. Find out the exact schedule and the number of stops made. Ask where the bus picks up and drops off, too. Try to avoid those that stop in the middle of busy parking lots.

Some hotels advertise a misleading proximity to Disney. While a hotel may be a short distance from the border, the commute to the parks may be considerable. Get specifics.

**Reserve a Room:** Found the perfect hotel for your vacation needs? Book it before someone else does, and don't forget to ask about any special discounts, seasonal promotions, and cancellation policies.

## A ROOM WITH A VIEW

There's a lot to be said for throwing back the curtains and gazing at a breathtaking view, provided you have the time to appreciate it and your view is within your price range. The following is a breakdown of the various "views" you may be offered at Walt Disney World resorts. It will help you choose the best category for your budget.

Although the categories vary, depending on resort type, the "standard" view room is always the lowest rate available: Details are subject to change at any time.

### Value Resorts
Standard or Preferred = Location specific.
   The view can be parking lot, pool, garden, or anything else.
### Moderate Resorts
Standard View = Landscaping or parking lot
Water View = Pool, marina, lake, river, fountain
### Deluxe Resorts
Resort View = Landscaping or parking lot
Water View = Pool, lake, lagoon, fountain, or other water
Savanna View = Animal pastures
   (at Disney's Animal Kingdom Lodge only)
Theme Park View = View of Magic Kingdom

# Walt Disney World Resorts

Walt Disney World resort hotels fall into two categories: Disney–owned-and-operated and non-Disney–owned resorts. Of all the WDW properties, the Swan, Dolphin, Swan Reserve, Four Seasons Orlando, and the resorts on Hotel Plaza Boulevard don't belong to Disney. Services and benefits in these resorts are slightly modified (see pages 91, 108, and 113).

**On-Property Perks:** The WDW Resort Guest Early Entry benefit, which allows 30 extra minutes in any theme park for all guests registered at a Disney-operated resort on most mornings (with valid admission); Theme Park Extended Evening Hours, available only to Walt Disney World Deluxe and Deluxe Villa resort guests (see page 22); free self-parking, unlimited use of Disney's transportation system; the convenience of charging most purchases to the hotel bill; plus nightly campfires and Movies Under the Stars. Guests staying at a Disney–owned-and-operated resort (and other select resorts) can reserve Individual Lightning Lane Selections (fees apply; see page 27) starting at 7 A.M. Details may change at any time. Check *disneyworld.com* for updates.

**Room Amenities:** Disney resort hotel rooms all come with a small safe, shampoo, phone with voice mail, a flat-screen TV, and free (occasionally spotty) Wi-Fi. There is a hair dryer, iron (with board), small (unstocked) beverage cooler/mini fridge (in all WDW–owned-and-operated resorts regardless of their category), and a coffeemaker (with coffee, sugar, and powdered creamer) in most rooms. Guest laundry facilities and dry cleaning, are offered in most resorts (for a fee).

## RESORT PRIMER

**Payment Methods:** WDW hotel bills and deposits may be paid by credit card, gift cards, traveler's checks, money order, cash, or personal check. Checks must bear the guest's name and address, be drawn on a United States bank, and be accompanied by proper photo ID (a valid driver's license or government-issued passport will do the trick).

**Room Deposit Requirements:** When booked as a "room-only" resort reservation, a deposit equal to one night's lodging (or campsite rental) is required at the

### ONLINE CHECK-IN

Are you planning a stay at a Disney-owned-and-operated resort? If so, you can take advantage of Disney's online check-in service. Meant to streamline the check-in experience, the virtual service is available in advance of and up through arrival day.

How does one check in via the Internet? It's easy. Simply visit *www.disneyworld.com*, or the My Disney Experience app or website. Checking in online does not mean you can check in early—unless, of course, there is a room available (a happy surprise that has been known to happen). When your room is ready, you'll receive the number via text.

Online check-in expedites the arrival experience by getting the pesky paperwork out of the way prior to arrival. Before you log on, know that you'll be asked to provide the following: the credit card that will be used for room charges, mobile number, address, arrival time, and room-location requests (but know that special requests are subject to availability).

With all that info already in the system, guests just need to get to the resort, wait for a text with the room number, and open the door with a MagicBand or mobile phone by tapping Unlock Door via the My Disney Experience app. Of course, friendly Front Desk folks are on hand to answer all questions and offer guidance should you need it.

time that a reservation is made. Reservations are automatically canceled if deposits are not received by the 14-day deadline. (See pages 19–20 for details about how to book a resort hotel room, deposit requirements, and cancellation policies.) Packages booked through *disneyworld.com* (aka The Walt Disney Travel Company) require a $200 deposit. Ask about the cancellation policy when you book your room.

When booking by telephone, guests may pay the deposit with a major credit card. Those who wish to use another payment method may do so by mailing it with the payment stub that comes with the reservation confirmation. Call to confirm that your payment was received.

**Cancellation Policy:** With the exception of Disney Resort Hotel packages, deposits for resort stays will be fully refunded if the reservation is canceled at least five days before the scheduled arrival. Vacation packages must be canceled at least 30 days ahead to get a refund on the deposit.

**Hot Tip!** The following WDW resorts can accommodate up to 5 guests in a standard room: Grand Floridian, Contemporary, Polynesian Village, Yacht & Beach Club, BoardWalk, Port Orleans Riverside, and Caribbean Beach. Fort Wilderness Cabins sleep 6. Note that Moderate resort rooms feature a child-size, pull-down bed.

**Parking Fees:** Overnight self-parking is free of charge at all Walt Disney World–owned-and-operated resort hotels. The nightly fee to valet park a vehicle at a Disney resort is $33.

**Check-in and Checkout:** The relatively early checkout time (11 A.M. at all Walt Disney World–owned-and-operated lodgings) and the late check-in times (3 P.M. in most hotels and campsites, 4 P.M. at Disney Vacation Club [DVC] accommodations) often come as a bit of a surprise. Guests who arrive before check-in time can

## STROLLER RENTALS

ScooterBug, Walt Disney World's featured provider, supplies prams for guests to rent in the theme parks and at Disney Springs. If you'd like to travel to and from these destinations with a stroller, you will need to have one delivered to your resort. For details, pricing info, and to reserve a ScooterBug buggy, go to *scooterbug.com/orlando* or call 800-726-8284.

If you'll have a car during your WDW visit, you may consider renting from Magic Strollers. Brought to you by the folks behind Owner's Locker (above, right), the company offers models from the popular Baby Jogger City Mini and Summit series. While strollers can be delivered to many area hotels (including the Swan, Dolphin, Swan Reserve, Four Seasons, and resorts on Hotel Plaza Boulevard), they can't be sent to WDW-owned-and-operated resorts. Fortunately, strollers are available for pick-up at the Magic Stroller Warehouse (a short drive from Walt Disney World). As a bonus, rentals via the Magic Stroller Warehouse net guests a 25-percent discount. For a price quote, go to *www.magicstrollers.com* and plug in your rental dates. We highly recommend purchasing the insurance, too. For a flat fee of $25, you're covered for any damage or theft that may occur during the time you have custody of the stroller. For additional information or to make a reservation, visit *www.magicstrollers.com*, or call 866-866-6177.

PHOTO BY AMY HENNING

## STASH YOUR STUFF

If you count yourself among the merry multitudes who travel to Walt Disney World at least once a year, a system called "Owner's Locker" was devised with you in mind. Simply put, it lets you stash your vacation gear in a private purple locker in the WDW area and have it delivered to you each time you visit the Mouse. That means you'll have less to check at the airport (the locker is great for storing liquids and "must-check" items) and lighten your load overall. Say goodbye to lugging items such as sunscreen, baby supplies, cooking items, rain gear, non-perishable snacks, first aid supplies, toys, DVDs, rainy-day activities, and much more.

It's called Owner's Locker because customers are given their own industrial-strength, secure storage bin when they join the program. Expect to pay about $105 a year for the Value Plan ($30 for each round-trip visit). The Moderate Plan costs $125 per year (including one round-trip visit a year; $30 for each extra visit), or about $225 a year for the Deluxe Plan, which allows for unlimited round-trip visits at no additional charge. There is a one-time locker purchase fee upon joining Owner's Locker (and for adding new lockers).

How does it work? As soon as you plan your WDW trip, schedule a round-trip delivery via *www.ownerslocker.com*. Your locker will make its way from a climate-controlled storage facility to your resort before check-in time. Call the Bell Services desk and expect the purple chest to arrive in minutes (don't forget to tip accordingly). Owner's Locker service is available at all Disney resorts and many other area hotels (though the business is neither owned nor endorsed by the Walt Disney Company). For additional information or to join Owner's Locker, call 800-431-6588, or visit *www.ownerslocker.com*.

pre-register, store luggage at Bell Services (without a fee), and head to the parks or relax by the resort pool.

**MagicBands:** Walt Disney World resort guests may pre-order MagicBands via *mydisneyexperience.com* or purchase them at a merchandise location at WDW. When linked with a valid WDW resort reservation the bands (which double as room keys; guests who check in without MagicBands will be issued Key to the World cards for hotel room access) entitle guests to use of Disney transportation (through the last day of their stay) and charging privileges (if linked to a major credit card) to cover most purchases at Walt Disney World. You'll be asked to program a personal pin code at check-in. Should you use your MagicBand to make a purchase at WDW, you will use that pin code to complete the

For Walt Disney World resort rates and to make reservations, visit *disneyworld.com*, or call 407-939-1936. For rates at the Four Seasons resort at Walt Disney World, call 800-267-3046, or visit *www.fourseasons.com/orlando*. For the Walt Disney World Swan, Dolphin, and Swan Reserve, visit *www.swandolphin.com*, or call 888-828-8850. For the properties on Hotel Plaza Boulevard (near Disney Springs), visit *disneyspringshotels.com*.

transaction. Disney resort guests may pre-order Magic-Bands at pre-arrival prices via *mydisneyexperience.com*. For more on MagicBands, see page 24.

**Note:** Charges that are incurred on a MagicBand or hotel ID after checkout will be reflected in a revised bill, which may be requested at the resort's Front Desk or sent via email. Swan, Dolphin, and Swan Reserve guests may use their resort IDs for charges in those hotels only.

**Walt Disney World Resort Rates:** One key factor in determining WDW hotel pricing is resort category. Disney has three main categories for its resort hotels: Deluxe, Moderate, and Value (refer to the Category Conundrum sidebar for details). Deluxe digs cost the most, value resort rooms the least, and moderates fall somewhere in between. When it comes to Walt Disney World accommodations rates, the calendar is another key factor. Traditionally, prices are higher during peak times of year (weekends, holidays, summer, school vacations, etc.) and a bit lower during times surrounding holidays and when school is in session. Many resorts offer lower rates on some weeknights year-round.

Rates within a Walt Disney World resort vary based on the room's view and the type of accommodation—studio, villa, suites, campsite, etc. Would you like to enjoy a deluxe resort's Club Level service? It will add to the nightly rate of your accommodations, but could lower your daily dining budget. Some resorts may offer rooms with an extra layer of Disney magic. (Rates for specially themed rooms tend to run a bit higher than for traditionally appointed rooms.)

For additional information and pricing details or to make a Disney resort reservation, call 407-934-7639, or visit *www.disneyworld.com*.

## CATEGORY CONUNDRUM

Value vs. Moderate vs. Deluxe—which resort category is best for you? Categories reflect the price of a room, the style of the accommodation, and level of service.

• Deluxe properties (the most expensive) are defined by their larger, practically appointed rooms, multiple restaurants, and such amenities as spa services. This category generally includes Disney Vacation Club properties. One invaluable perk that comes with staying at a WDW Deluxe or Deluxe Villa resort is theme park Extended Evening Hours (see page 22).

• Moderate properties (which are in WDW's middle range, price-wise) feature comfortably sized rooms, full-service restaurants and food courts, and bellhop luggage service.

• The Fort Wilderness Camping category covers campsites, but not Wilderness Cabins (which fall into the Disney Vacation Club/Deluxe category).

• Value properties (the least expensive resort category) offer fewer frills and smaller quarters. Meals are offered at food courts. Recreation and transportation options tend to be somewhat limited at these resorts.

**Hot Tip!** On weekends and when peak rates are in effect at Walt Disney World-owned-and-operated resort hotels, rates at the Swan, Dolphin, and Swan Reserve are often much lower. Conversely, Swan and Dolphin tend to have their highest rates on business days and during traditional convention times of year.

# WALT DISNEY WORLD RESORT FINDER

| NAME & LOCATION | SETTING/THEME | FAVORED BY | ROMANTIC HIDEAWAYS |
|---|---|---|---|
| **Animal Kingdom Lodge***  Animal Kingdom Resort Area  (page 102) | African wildlife preserve | Animal lovers—nearly every room affords a view of wandering wildlife  Art aficionados—authentic African artwork abounds  Disney Vacation Club members | Private balconies by moonlight  Sunset lounge overlooking the savanna |
| **BoardWalk Inn & Villas***  EPCOT Resort Area  (page 94) | Turn-of-the-20th-century Atlantic City | Night owls—the entertainment options are numerous and right in the backyard  EPCOT lovers, who will appreciate the short commute  Disney Vacation Club members | Moonlight strolls along the boardwalk  A special fireworks cruise |
| **Contemporary***  Magic Kingdom Resort Area  (page 78) | Retro-futuristic exterior, thoroughly modern interior | Families—the monorail whisks through it, and the Magic Kingdom is a short walk away  Professionals, who can take advantage of the hotel's many business services  Disney Vacation Club members | The rooftop lookout (available exclusively to patrons of California Grill), which helps make up for the resort's otherwise less-than-romantic atmosphere |
| **Disney's Riviera***  EPCOT Resort Area  (page 88) | A celebration of the grandeur of Europe | Fireworks fans—a rooftop restaurant offers prime views of theme park pyrotechnics  Admirers of the Disney Skyliner. (The airborne gondola system stops nearby.)  Disney Vacation Club members | Topolino's Terrace late in the day  Peaceful strolls around the nearby Barefoot Bay |
| **Grand Floridian Resort & Spa***  Magic Kingdom Resort Area  (page 82) | Victorian seaside resort | Honeymooners—who will love spending much of their vacation basking in the resort's unebbing romantic atmosphere  Magic Kingdom and monorail fans  Disney Vacation Club members | Meticulously manicured gardens  The Grand Lobby for a drink at the Enchanted Rose lounge |

* Animal Kingdom Lodge, Beach Club, BoardWalk, Contemporary, Grand Floridian, Old Key West, Polynesian, Riviera, Saratoga Springs, and Wilderness Lodge have Disney Vacation Club accommodations.

| KIDS ADORE | DINING TIP | RESORT CATEGORY & AMENITIES | |
|---|---|---|---|
| The kopje, a rocky outcropping from which to spy on critters<br><br>Animal-watching<br><br>Lobby activities | Sample the exotic eats and atmosphere of Sanaa while savoring the sights of the savanna. | | |
| The 200-foot waterslide at the main pool<br><br>The live entertainment on the boardwalk at night<br><br>Board games in the Belle Vue Lounge (available for use throughout the day) | Sip a smoothie or a frozen margarita from Boardwalk Joe's Marvelous Margaritas while strolling the boards. 🐭<br><br>There is a new spot to grab a quick breakfast! Located just off the lobby, Carousel Coffee offers a variety of light bites, caffeinated beverages, and more. | Theme Park Extended Evening Hours (see page 22)<br><br>Full-service restaurants and fast-food spots<br><br>Luggage service<br><br>Valet parking ($33 a night)<br><br>Swimming pools<br><br>Beaches on which to stroll and build sandcastles (except for Animal Kingdom Lodge)<br><br>On-site kids' activities<br><br>Most rooms sleep five guests<br><br>Monorail, bus, boat, or Skyliner transport to all parks<br><br>Movies Under the Stars (outdoor screenings of classic Disney films) | **DELUXE** |
| The "party" held every 45 minutes at Chef Mickey's fabulously fun character meals<br><br>Watching the monorail whoosh through the resort<br><br>Boat rides from the marina | Reserve California Grill for a time that's likely to coincide with the Magic Kingdom's fireworks show—or eat early and come back for the show with your receipt in hand. The view is amazing. 🐭 | | |
| The S'il Vous Play interactive water play area. Inspired by the grand public fountains of Europe, the splash zone features a ballet of friendly *Fantasia* characters.<br><br>Having breakfast with Disney pals at Topolino's Terrace—Flavors of the Riviera | Topolino's Terrace offers bird's-eye views of EPCOT's nighttime spectacular. Check the schedule for the day you plan to dine here and book a table accordingly.<br><br>Le Petit Café morphs from a coffee bar into a wine bar every afternoon. 🐭 | | |
| Nightly marshmallow roasts and alfresco Disney films<br><br>Zero-depth-entry pool and a Mad Hatter-themed splash zone<br><br>Watching Happily Ever After (Magic Kingdom fireworks spectacular) from the shores of the Seven Seas Lagoon. | Guests of Cítrico's Lounge may enjoy an array of international wines and cocktails and/or dine on anything from the restaurant's menu—including the sensational sweet corn bisque. | | |

🐭 These resorts host character meals.

# WALT DISNEY WORLD RESORT FINDER

| NAME & LOCATION | SETTING/THEME | FAVORED BY | ROMANTIC HIDEAWAYS |
|---|---|---|---|
| **Polynesian Village\***<br><br>Magic Kingdom Resort Area<br><br>(page 80) | South Pacific | Romantics—fireworks views and lush, tropical setting may make you swoon<br><br>Vacationers looking for a hotel with a real resort feel<br><br>Magic Kingdom and monorail fans<br><br>Disney Vacation Club members | Beach swings for two<br><br>Tropical, torch-lit evening strolls |
| **Swan, Dolphin, & Swan Reserve**<br><br>EPCOT Resort Area<br><br>(page 91) | Beachfront whimsy | Guests who want many of the Disney perks but not necessarily the Disney hotel<br><br>Bargain hunters—when WDW resorts are "peak," these resorts may offer discounts | A peaceful area beside the grotto pool waterfall |
| **Wilderness Lodge\***<br><br>Magic Kingdom Resort Area<br><br>(page 84) | America's grandest national parks | Sweethearts—love is always in the air at this resort<br><br>Winter visitors—the warm, cozy atmosphere is even more inviting when the many fireplaces are roaring<br><br>Disney Vacation Club members | Steamy, bubbling "hot springs" whirlpools<br><br>The cozy alcoves hidden on each floor of the main building |
| **Yacht & Beach Club\***<br><br>EPCOT Resort Area<br><br>(page 89) | Martha's Vineyard and Nantucket Island | Ambitious guests—those who plan to see and do everything Disney has to offer will like the central location<br><br>EPCOT fans, who enjoy the proximity of Disney's discovery park<br><br>Disney Vacation Club members | The Yacht Club's peaceful gazebo<br><br>Secluded hot tubs<br><br>The beach—perfect for strolling hand in hand |
| **Old Key West\***<br><br>Disney Springs Resort Area<br><br>(page 100) | Key West | Guests looking for a homey, village atmosphere<br><br>Disney Vacation Club members<br><br>Those who appreciate roomy rooms | Private garden tubs—they come with all accommodations but the studios |
| **Saratoga Springs Resort & Spa\***<br><br>Disney Springs Resort Area<br><br>(page 99) | Historic Saratoga Springs, New York | Peace seekers—the atmosphere is meant to soothe<br><br>Disney Vacation Club members<br><br>Space seekers. The accommodations are a bit more spacious than at other WDW resorts. | Pretty gardens and meandering pathways<br><br>Private garden tubs—they come with all accommodations but the studios |

\* Animal Kingdom Lodge, Beach Club, BoardWalk, Contemporary, Grand Floridian, Old Key West, Polynesian, Riviera, Saratoga Springs, and Wilderness Lodge have Disney Vacation Club accommodations.

| KIDS ADORE | DINING TIP | RESORT CATEGORY & AMENITIES | |
|---|---|---|---|
| The 142-foot water slide- and waterfall-endowed lava pool, plus a tiki-themed splash zone | The sushi served at Kona Cafe is second to none. Order it (and other menu items) to go and have a poolside picnic. (Place your Mobile Order with the My Disney Experience app.) 🐭 | | **DELUXE** |
| The swan-shaped pedal boats<br><br>The giant swan and dolphin statues perched atop their respective resorts<br><br>A grotto pool complete with waterfall and winding waterslide | The Swan's Kimonos Lounge serves sushi with a side of karaoke. 🐭 | Theme Park Extended Evening Hours (see page 22)<br><br>Full-service restaurants and fast-food spots<br><br>Luggage service<br><br>Valet parking ($33 a night)<br><br>Swimming pools<br><br>Beaches on which to stroll and build sandcastles<br><br>On-site kids' activities | |
| Totem poles, an erupting geyser, and oodles of Hidden Mickeys to search for | Storybook Dining at Artist Point offers guests an exclusive chance to meet the Queen from *Snow White and the Seven Dwarfs*. (Snow White, Dopey, and Grumpy are there, too!)<br><br>Savor morning coffee from a fireside rocking chair. 🐭 | Most rooms sleep five guests<br><br>Monorail, bus, boat, or Skyliner transport to all parks<br><br>Movies Under the Stars (outdoor screenings of classic Disney films) | |
| Stormalong Bay—the sprawling sand-bottomed, three-acre pool, with a waterslide and a neat shipwreck on which to play | Cape May Cafe's bountiful nighttime buffet has many a surf-and-turf fan lining up for more. 🐭 | ———<br><br>Specifics may differ for the Swan, Dolphin, and Swan Reserve | |
| Crafts and games offered at Community Hall<br><br>The pool's sandcastle slide and poolside activities | Olivia's pleases all palates with a nice mix of pastas and fresh fish. Shrimp fritters are a yummy way to start a meal. | Kitchens or kitchenettes, full-service restaurants, fast food spots<br><br>Luggage service<br><br>Swimming pools and on-site recreation such as bike rentals<br><br>Front-door parking<br><br>Villas sleep 4-12 | **DELUXE VILLA RESORTS (DVC) †** |
| The kids-only water-spray area near the pool<br><br>Kid-oriented activities offered at Community Hall | Turf Club is a low-profile, local dining room.<br><br>Disney Springs and its tempting array of eateries is just across the lake—and easily accessed by a walking path or water taxi. | Bus transport to all parks<br><br>Washers and dryers<br><br>Boat to Disney Springs<br><br>Movies Under the Stars (outdoor screenings of Disney films)<br><br>Theme Park Extended Evening Hours (see page 22) | |

🐭 These resorts host character meals.

# WALT DISNEY WORLD RESORT FINDER

| NAME & LOCATION | SETTING/THEME | FAVORED BY | ROMANTIC HIDEAWAYS |
|---|---|---|---|
| **Caribbean Beach**<br><br>EPCOT Resort Area<br><br>(page 87) | Tropical islands | Families—the colorful design, themed pool, and beach setting make this hotel ideal for families<br><br>Skyliner fans! The resort's station is the main hub of the Disney Skyliner, with all 3 lines departing and arriving there. | Aruba beach—the hotel's longest, most secluded stretch of sand |
| **Coronado Springs**<br><br>Animal Kingdom Resort Area<br><br>(page 104) | A celebration of Mexican, Spanish, and South American cultures | Conventioneers—which means more business services (and a health club), higher food prices, and slightly less family entertainment than at the other moderate resorts at WDW | The waterfront in the peaceful Casitas area<br><br>Secluded corners of Cafe Rix<br><br>The delightful Dahlia Lounge |
| **Port Orleans French Quarter & Riverside**<br><br>Disney Springs Resort Area (pages 97-98) | New Orleans French Quarter and Southern ambience, respectively | Lovebirds on a budget—the Riverside decor is like many of Disney's deluxe hotels, as is the romance factor, but the price is considerably less<br><br>Big Easy fans. The French Quarter provides a peaceful, urban environment | Any room in Magnolia Bend's stately mansions<br><br>The peaceful gardens scattered about the Riverside quarters |
| **All-Star Movies, Music, & Sports**<br><br>Animal Kingdom Resort Area<br><br>(page 101) | Larger-than-life fun | Penny savers of all ages—these resorts offer fun, colorful theming, plus most of the WDW perks at a much lower price than at most other Disney resorts<br><br>Space cravers—who adore the family suites at All-Star Music | All-Star Music's Jazz and Broadway areas |
| **Art of Animation**<br><br>ESPN Wide World of Sports Area<br><br>(page 106) | Classic and colorful Disney animation | Extended families and families with babies—it's great to have the extra sleeping area that comes with the family suites | The Drop Off pool bar is a sweet spot for a (quasi) quiet evening interlude |
| **Pop Century**<br><br>ESPN Wide World of Sports Area<br><br>(page 105) | American pop culture | Budget watchers and nostalgia buffs—this sprawling resort celebrates pop history with bright colors and big icons<br><br>Young athletes and their families—ESPN Wide World of Sports is located nearby | Sipping specialty cocktails poolside |
| **Fort Wilderness Cabins** and Campground**<br><br>Magic Kingdom Resort Area (page 85) | Rustic woods | Seasoned RV enthusiasts—Disney's hookups are considered top-notch<br><br>Families—who appreciate the modern amenities of the cabins, which fit six and fall into Walt Disney World's DVC "deluxe" resort category | Horse-drawn carriage rides<br><br>The Fort Wilderness beach—perfect for viewing the Electrical Water Pageant on Bay Lake |

** As part of the Disney Vacation Club, newly refurbished Wilderness Cabins fall under WDW's Deluxe resort category.

| KIDS ADORE | DINING TIP | RESORT CATEGORY & AMENITIES | |
|---|---|---|---|
| The fortress pool and Caribbean Cay Island<br><br>The coconut postcards sold at the Calypso Trading Post (real coconuts!) | Spyglass Grill and Banana Cabana raise the bar for poolside quick-service eateries.<br><br>At quick-service Centertown Market, guests pick up meals from walk-up windows after their buzzer goes off. | Restaurant and food court<br><br>Luggage service<br><br>Swimming pools with slides<br><br>On-site recreation, such as bike rentals<br><br>Movies Under the Stars (outdoor screenings of Disney films)<br><br>Rooms sleep four to five guests<br><br>Bus or Skyliner transport to all parks | **MODERATE** |
| The Dig Site—which encompasses the resort's playground, whirlpool, and main pool with its Mayan temple waterslide | To start the day in a pleasant way, consider breakfast at Rix Sports Bar & Grill. For a quicker start to the day, head over to El Mercado de Coronado or the grab-and-go area of Cafe Rix or Barcelona Lounge. | | |
| The pool, fishing hole, and play area at the Riverside's Ol' Man Island. And the "Royal Guest Rooms" rock!<br><br>The French Quarter's Doubloon Lagoon—a sea-serpent-themed family pool | Sample the fresh beignets from Scat Cat's Club-Cafe. You'll think you're in The Big Easy. | | |
| Awe-inspiring, super-size icons—the movie and sports themes score the highest points<br><br>Extra-large arcades<br><br>Organized pool games and on-site activities for kids and families | Pick up a pizza at the pickup window in the food court and have a pizza party by the pool. | Food court<br><br>Luggage service<br><br>Swimming pools<br><br>Movies Under the Stars (outdoor screenings of Disney films)<br><br>Bus or Skyliner transport to all parks | **VALUE** |
| The Righteous Reef soft-surface squirt zone<br><br>Super-size icons from *Finding Nemo*, *Cars*, *The Lion King*, and *The Little Mermaid* | Dine in one of the loveliest food courts Disney has to offer: Landscape of Flavors. Indulge in tandoori chicken, seared salmon, bacon cheddar cheeseburgers, "super" slices of pizza, and sesame chicken stir-fry. | | |
| The state-of-the-art arcade<br><br>Wildly oversize cell phones, yo-yos, bowling pins, and more<br><br>The interactive dance parties held in the lobby each afternoon. Do "The Hustle!" | Petals pool bar serves some of the World's most refreshing liquid treats: the non-alcoholic strawberry smoothie and the raspberry "Lava" smoothie. | | |
| Pony rides, wagon rides, and campfire marshmallow roasts with Chip and Dale | Join the nightly campfire circle, roast marshmallows, and rub elbows with Disney's famous chipmunk duo.<br><br>Pioneer Hall is home to the Hoop-Dee-Doo Musical Revue, a perennially popular dinner show | Recipient of perfect ratings from *Trailer Life* and *Woodall's* magazines<br><br>Bus transport to all parks<br><br>Water transportation to Magic Kingdom | **FT. WILDERNESS** |

# Magic Kingdom

## Contemporary & Bay Lake Tower

Watching the monorail trains disappear into the Contemporary's 15-story A-frame tower never fails to impress. The sleek trains look like long spaceships docking as they glide inside the resort.

Passengers, for their part, are impressed by the cavernous lobby, with its tiers of balconies and, at its center, the soaring 90-foot-high, floor-to-ceiling tile mural depicting scenes from the Southwest. (Look carefully and you may spot the five-legged goat.)

This imposing structure has 656 rooms in its main tower and adjacent garden wing, plus those in Bay Lake Tower—open to all guests (not just Disney Vacation Club members). There are shops, a snack bar, restaurants, lounges, a marina, health club, and more. The pool area incorporates two hot tubs and a waterslide. The convention center offers business services. One of the resort's most notable features is its 15th-floor observation deck. From here, guests dining at the resort's California Grill can enjoy a bird's-eye view of the Magic Kingdom park. Another huge bonus: a walking path to the Magic Kingdom (it's about a 6-to-12-minute stroll away; the path extends to the Grand Floridian and Polynesian Village).

A Club-Level package is available for guests who stay in the hotel's 14th-floor suites. Club-Level amenities include express check-in and checkout, complimentary breakfast, snacks and beverages (including spirits) throughout the day, plus evening appetizers and desserts. The 12th floor also provides guests with Club-Level privileges. The phone number for the Contemporary is 407-824-1000.

**ROOMS:** Contemporary rooms were completely (and dramatically) refurbished in 2021 and boast a sleek and contemporary design with clever-but-subtle nods to *The Incredibles*. (The supers' uniforms actually adorn the back of the closet. No capes!) Standard rooms are evenly apportioned among the main tower and garden building (aka the garden wing). Rooms located in the tower have balconies, and offer (magnificent) views of Bay Lake or the Magic Kingdom. Dreaming of waking up with a view of Cinderella Castle? Make sure to book the theme park view category, request an odd number room, and keep your fingers crossed! Most rooms can

PHOTO BY JILL SAFRO

accommodate 5 guests (plus a child under 3). Typical units have a daybed and two queen-size beds; some have a king-size bed and a daybed. And every room has a flat-screen TV. Note that many of the bathrooms have a shower-only option. If you require a traditional tub, make your needs known when you book your room.

Connecting rooms may be requested, though not guaranteed. Suites, consisting of a living room and one or two bedrooms, can sleep 4 to 12 people. Amenities include iron (with board), hair dryer, shampoo and conditioner, and coffeemaker (complete with coffee and sweetened, powdered creamer).

The monorail may be heard from lower rooms in the main tower. For maximum quiet, request a higher floor or stay in the adjacent garden wing. Of course, all rooms get serenaded by the nightly fireworks at the nearby Magic Kingdom park.

The 15-story Bay Lake Tower, a Disney Vacation Club (DVC) property that sits next to the Contemporary and is connected by a covered walkway, mimics the color scheme and strong horizontal lines of its neighbor. The tower's crescent shape hugs a lakeside pool.

Studios sleep up to four and offer a kitchenette, queen-size bed, and double sleeper sofa. Sleeping up to five, the one-bedroom villas have full kitchens, two bathrooms, a king-size bed in the master bedroom and queen sleeper sofa, and a sleeper chair in the living room. Two-bedroom villas sleep up to nine, and the two-story grand villas sleep up to 12. All room configurations feature a flat-screen TV and free Wi-Fi.

**WHERE TO EAT:** The Contemporary offers a diverse array of restaurants and snack spots. (Room service was on pause at press time, but may return.)

**California Grill:** On the 15th floor. The specialty is California fare—flatbreads, grilled meats, seafood, and market vegetables. An extra-special treat: the dramatic, panoramic view of the Magic Kingdom park's fireworks for dining guests. Check-in is on the second floor.

**Chef Mickey's:** Mickey and his pals host meals at this fourth-floor institution. The hearty breakfast features Mickey-shaped waffles as well as traditional items. Dinner offers carved meats, daily specials, and a variety of entrées, plus desserts.

**Contempo Cafe:** A quick-service spot with high-quality, freshly prepared fare (there's a grab-and-go selection, too), this snack bar is on the fourth floor.

**Steakhouse 71:** The space formerly occupied by The Wave . . . of American Flavors is now home to a stellar steak-oriented eatery. It serves three meals a day.

**WHERE TO DRINK:** The Contemporary is home to some of the World's most inviting lounges.

**California Grill Lounge:** There's a tiny bar on the resort's 15th floor, within the California Grill. The restaurant's enormous picture windows provide a dramatic backdrop for sipping California wines and other drinks and nibbling appetizers. Seating is extremely limited.

**Contemporary Grounds:** This sleek lobby coffee bar serves cappuccino, espresso, latte, and other coffee drinks, plus smoothies, pastries, and snacks.

**Outer Rim:** On the fourth-floor concourse, overlooking Bay Lake, the Outer Rim serves beer, wine, cocktails, and specialty drinks.

**Sand Bar and Cove Bar:** These poolside spots offer drinks and light snacks.

**Steakhouse 71 Lounge:** Stop here for a full bar and a selection of savory snacks.

**WHAT TO DO:** Volleyball nets may be set up on the beach. Fishing excursions may be arranged (refer to the *Sports & Recreation* chapter for details). A resort entertainment schedule is available at the Front Desk.

**Arcade:** The Game Station, a spacious arcade, can be found on the resort's fourth floor.

**Bass Fishing:** See page 257.

**Boating:** Pontoon boats may be rented at the Boat Nook by the resort's marina.

**Campfire:** Campfires and marshmallow roasts take place every evening, weather permitting. Afterward, everyone is treated to an alfresco screening of a Disney film—aka "Movies Under the Stars."

**Health Club:** The third-floor Olympiad Fitness Center has strength machines, bikes (regular and recumbent),

**Hot Tip!** Guests staying in rooms with a park view may gaze upon the Magic Kingdom and its fireworks presentations. The nighttime viewing experience may be enhanced by tuning the in-room TV to channel 105—it plays the soundtrack to Happily Ever After.

sauna, treadmills, and lockers. Equipment use is free to Contemporary guests.

**Jogging:** A nearly one-mile jogging path loops around Bay Lake Tower and the resort's Garden Wing.

**Shopping:** The cavernous fourth-floor concourse is home to three shops. Fantasia sells plush toys, games, accessories, clothing for kids, and more. Fantasia Market proffers books, snacks, soft drinks, and liquor. Bay View Gifts (BVG) carries Disney character merchandise and apparel for all ages, items with the Contemporary resort logo, jewelry, and kitchenware. Fresh-baked goods and candy are also available.

**Swimming:** In addition to a round, lakeside pool, the free-form pool features a 17-foot-high slide, a small squirt zone, and a whirlpool or two. Life jackets may be borrowed. Organized pool games are offered on most days. Private cabanas can be rented at Bay Lake pool. For pricing and reservations, call 407-939-7529 between 7 A.M. and 11 P.M. Eastern time.

**Tennis and Pickleball:** The Contemporary resort's lone court is adjacent to Bay Lake Tower. There is no charge to play. Equipment may be borrowed from Community Hall or Boat Nook Marina.

**Yoga:** A 30-minute gentle yoga class has been offered on select mornings. Space is limited to 15 Contemporary resort guests. Kids must be accompanied by an adult. Details are subject to change. For details, inquire at the resort's Lobby Concierge.

**TRANSPORTATION:** The Contemporary resort is connected to the Transportation and Ticket Center (TTC) and the Magic Kingdom by monorail. From the TTC, EPCOT can usually be reached by transferring to another monorail. Buses transport guests to Disney's Hollywood Studios, Animal Kingdom, Blizzard Beach, Typhoon Lagoon, and Disney Springs. (A transfer may be required for the water parks.) Watercraft transport guests to the Magic Kingdom park. Guests may also stroll over to the nearby Magic Kingdom (it takes about 6 to 12 minutes). The pedestrian path extends to the Grand Floridian, Polynesian Village, and the TTC.

PHOTO BY JILL SAFRO

# Polynesian Village

The Polynesian Village resort is as close an approximation of the real thing as Walt Disney World's designers could create. The vegetation is lush, and the architecture summons the tropics. The mood is set by a cavernous lobby that features open areas and sweeping vistas of the Seven Seas Lagoon. The structure in which it is housed, the Great Ceremonial House, is the central building in the Polynesian Village. The Front Desk, shops, and most of the restaurants are located here. Flanking the Ceremonial House on either side are 11 two- and three-story village longhouses named for various Pacific islands. The Bora Bora Bungalows on the Seven Seas Lagoon are part of the Disney Vacation Club accommodations at the resort. The monorail stops at this hotel, making it a convenient place to stay; in fact, it's just a short monorail ride to the Magic Kingdom theme park.

**Hot Tip!** The Polynesian Village is in the midst of a growth spurt. When the pixie dust finally settles (likely by late 2024), the resort will have a brand-new DVC (Disney Vacation Club) tower. Details are subject to change. For updates, visit *disneyworld.com*.

Club-Level service offers such amenities as express check-in; continental breakfast; snacks and drinks every afternoon; cocktails, hors d'oeuvres, and desserts in the evening; and a lounge with a prime view of the Seven Seas Lagoon and Cinderella Castle (and the nightly fireworks display). Club-Level rooms and suites are located in the Tonga and Hawaii buildings. The phone number for the Polynesian Village is 407-824-2000.

**ROOMS:** Many of the recently refurbished rooms—which feature festive *Moana* touches—have balconies, and most have a view of the gardens, Seven Seas Lagoon, or one of the resort's swimming pools. Many guest rooms have two queen-size beds and a daybed, and can sleep five guests (plus a child under the age of 3). Adjoining rooms may be requested (but are not guaranteed). The Polynesian's suites—located in the Tonga building—can accommodate four to nine guests. Some have a king-size bed in the bedroom and one queen-size bed in the parlor. Amenities include a flat-screen TV, free Wi-Fi, coffeemaker (with coffee), hair dryer, and a small refrigerator/beverage cooler. In addition to the establishments listed on these pages, snacks and soft drinks are available via vending machines.

**WHERE TO EAT:** The Polynesian has a nice selection of eateries at which to dine:

**Capt. Cook's:** On the lobby level of the Great Ceremonial House, this lively quick-service spot is good for light fare throughout the day. In addition to packaged salads and sandwiches, there are items such as pastries and fresh fruit, plus a made-to-order section, too. This is the place to head when you wish to fill your refillable resort mug. (For a one-time purchase fee, you are entitled to unlimited soft-drink refills at all WDW resort Rapid Fill locations for the length of your stay.)

**Kona Cafe:** A family eatery on the second floor of the Great Ceremonial House, Kona Cafe serves lunch and dinner with an Asian flair (including sumptuous sushi), while the breakfast menu is filled with traditional American selections.

**Kona Island:** This island is a coffee bar featuring fresh-brewed Kona coffee (including specialty drinks), plus pastries, fruit, and breakfast sandwiches. In the evening, this casual corner offers sushi (California rolls and spicy tuna rolls), plus a selection of treats including cupcakes, chocolate-covered strawberries, and chocolate-covered bacon (yes, you read that right).

**Oasis Grill:** Set beside the Oasis pool and available exclusively to Polynesian resort guests, the Grill serves up items such as cheeseburgers, fish tacos, chicken avocado wraps, and more. Note that guests must use a MagicBand or room key to access this area.

**DID YOU KNOW?**
The white sand on the beaches near the Polynesian and Grand Floridian resorts and along the Seven Seas Lagoon actually came from the bottom of Bay Lake, located behind Disney's Contemporary resort.

PHOTO BY JILL SAFRO

**'Ohana:** On the second floor of the Great Ceremonial House, 'Ohana serves family-style dinners roasted over a fire pit. Character friends (including Lilo and Stitch) host breakfast each morning.

**Pineapple Lanai:** The Poly is a happy place for fans of the chilly treat known as Dole Whip (frozen, non-dairy pineapple dessert). It's served (plain, as a float, or with vanilla soft-serve) at this kiosk near the Lava pool.

**WHERE TO DRINK:** As might be expected, both the drink offerings and the settings in which they are served are as tropical as they come. Guests may sip at the following:

**Barefoot Bar:** Adjacent to the Lava Pool, this watering hole is open seasonally.

**Oasis Bar:** An alfresco lounge, Oasis offers beer, wine, sangria, specialty cocktails (we dig the Frosty Pineapple), and drinks sans alcohol. The Oasis Bar is available exclusively to Polynesian resort guests.

**Tambu Lounge:** There's a tropical air about this lounge near 'Ohana. There's a full bar, but we go straight for the creamy, frozen piña coladas (available with or without alcohol).

**Trader Sam's Grog Grotto:** The spirited first-floor lounge is next to Captain Cook's snack bar. Sam's is a delightful Disney lounge offering tropical drinks and small plates in a richly themed locale. There is indoor and outdoor seating, with the outdoor patio tables much easier to snag than the bar stools inside.

**F.Y.I.:** Trader Sam currently operates the Gift Shop, er, "Lost & Found" in the Magic Kingdom's Jungle Cruise attraction. (Yeah, be sure not to leave anything behind after you enjoy that attraction.)

**WHAT TO DO:** A wide range of activities is available at the Polynesian, including a jogging path. Guided fishing excursions can also be arranged. A resort entertainment schedule is available at the Front Desk.

**Bass Fishing:** Refer to page 257 or call 407-WDW-FISH (939-3474).

**Boating:** Fireworks cruises are available. Pontoon boats may be rented at the nearby Contemporary resort's marina.

**Shopping:** BouTiki is the go-to place for resort-wear, souvenirs, sweet treats, and more. Moana Mercantile sells Disney souvenirs, toys, magazines, and fashions. It's also stocked with food, spirits, soft drinks, snacks, and other fixings for an impromptu party.

**Swimming:** There are two pools here: the Oasis, an unguarded, zero-depth-entry pool near the Samoa, Niue, Hawaii, Tokelau, and Rarotonga buildings; and the larger free-form Lava pool, near the marina. The latter is complete with slide and zero-depth-entry. There is also the Kiki Tiki Splash area (an aquatic playground for little ones, located near the Lava pool), a hot tub with views of Cinderella Castle, and an expanded poolside deck. A limited number of wheelchairs are available to borrow for use in the pool. The beaches are strictly for sunbathing, sandcastle-building, afternoon snoozing, and fireworks viewing (no swimming allowed).

**TRANSPORTATION:** The Polynesian Village is on the monorail line to the Magic Kingdom and the Transportation and Ticket Center (TTC). It's also possible to get to the TTC on foot (it takes 5 to 10 minutes). From the TTC, EPCOT may be reached by transferring to the EPCOT monorail. (If the EPCOT monorail is not operating, buses are provided.) Buses transport guests to Disney's Hollywood Studios, Disney's Animal Kingdom, Blizzard Beach, Typhoon Lagoon, and Disney Springs. (A transfer may be required for the water parks.) Water taxis ferry guests to the Magic Kingdom park. Guests may reach the Grand Floridian, Magic Kingdom, and Contemporary by the monorail or via lakeside walking path.

PHOTO BY JILL SAFRO

# Grand Floridian Resort & Spa

At the turn of the 20th century, Standard Oil magnate Henry M. Flagler saw the realization of his dream: The railroad he had built to "civilize" Florida had spawned along its right-of-way an empire of grand hotels, lavish estates, prominent families, and opulent lifestyles. High society blossomed in the winter months, as the likes of John D. Rockefeller and Teddy Roosevelt checked into the Royal Poinciana in Palm Beach, enjoying the sea breezes from the oceanside suites.

Unfortunately, the grand hotel was lost to a fire, and Florida's golden era faded with the Depression. But nearly a century after Flagler first made Florida a fashionable resort destination, Walt Disney World opened its "grand" hotel—a 668-room Victorian structure with gabled roofs and carved moldings—on 40 acres of Seven Seas Lagoon shorefront, between the Magic Kingdom park and the Polynesian Village resort.

Like its late-19th-century predecessors, the Grand Floridian resort boasts abundant verandahs, intricate latticework, turrets, towers, and red-shingle roofs. And yet it offers all the advantages of modern living, including monorail service. With five restaurants, multiple lounges, four shops, a convention center, two pools, a kids' splash zone, a marina, and full-service health club and spa, the Grand Floridian is not only a grand hotel but also a complete resort. There's a handy walking path connecting the resort with the Magic Kingdom, too.

The main building houses the Grand Lobby, a palatial space soaring five stories to a ceiling of stained-glass domes and glittering chandeliers. Palms and an aviary decorate the sitting area; an open-cage elevator carries guests to the shops and restaurants on the second floor. The turn-of-the-20th-century theme is everywhere, from the employees' costumes to the restaurants, room decor, and the lobby piano music. The phone number for the Grand Floridian resort is 407-824-3000.

**ROOMS:** The rooms are filled with charm, decorated as they might have been a century ago—with elegant light fixtures and marble-topped sinks. In-room amenities include hair dryer, beverage cooler, TV, nightly turn-down service (available upon request), coffeemaker (with coffee and sweetened non-dairy creamer), and free Wi-Fi service.

The main building houses Club-Level rooms and suites; lodge buildings, each four and five stories high, contain standard rooms, slightly smaller "attic" chambers, and suites. Villas, located in a building near the Beach Pool, are available to rent when not occupied by Disney Vacation Club members.

Most rooms measure more than 400 square feet and include two queen-size beds, plus a daybed, to accommodate up to five people. Many rooms have a terrace. Suites include a parlor, plus one, two, or three bedrooms; there are queen-size beds in the bedrooms.

On the third floor, the Club-Level desks offer such services as reservations and information. The fourth floor features a quiet seating area where continental breakfast and evening refreshments are served.

**WHERE TO EAT:** Most restaurants and lounges are in the main building. In-room dining is offered, too.

**Cítricos:** The largest of the hotel's restaurants serves market-fresh local cuisine. It's open for dinner only. Several items are available in the lounge, too. (Order from the bartender.)

**Gasparilla Island Grill:** This reliable snack bar offers sandwiches, salads, flatbreads, and more.

**Grand Floridian Cafe:** Its verandah-like feel makes this a relaxing place for a simple sit-down meal. All meals are served. There is limited outdoor seating.

**Narcoossee's:** This sophisticated eatery has a prime shoreline location. The seasonal menu includes sustainable seafood paired with award-winning wines.

**1900 Park Fare:** A buffet restaurant decorated with carousel horses, plants, and Big Bertha, the carnival

## DID YOU KNOW?

Movie buffs may find the Grand Floridian resort strangely familiar. Its design is based, in part, on that of the Hotel Del Coronado in California. Scenes from the classic film *Some Like It Hot* were shot there.

organ. Characters have hosted meals here. This eatery was closed for refurbishment at press time. All details are subject to change. For updates, visit *disneyworld.com*.

**Victoria & Albert's:** An upscale eatery named after the former queen and prince consort of England, this spot serves a (pricey) fixed-price menu (to guests ages 10 and up). Reservations are a must.

**WHERE TO DRINK:** The lounges here can be lovely escapes. Cítricos and Narcoossee's both have bars, complete with a full menu for dining. Drinks (bought from any bar) may also be enjoyed in the Grand's majestic lobby.

**Cítricos:** Proof that good things do indeed come in small packages (8 bar stools and 4 tables), this lounge has a great wine list, specialty coffees, and full menu.

**Enchanted Rose:** There's an elegant *Beauty and the Beast*–inspired watering-hole in the space formerly occupied by Mizner's Lounge. Indoor and outdoor seating is available, as is a full bar, and a small bites menu featuring caviar, truffle fries, and more.

**Garden View Tea Room:** This pretty spot offers a view of the hotel's lush, landscaped garden and pool area. Afternoon tea is served (as are finger sandwiches and small desserts). This spot was "on pause" at press time.

**Narcoossee's:** Located in the heart of the restaurant, this lounge offers an extensive wine list and craft beer selection, plus a lounge menu.

**Pool Bars:** These two bars (known as Courtyard and Beaches) feature a variety of beverages, while Beaches also serves lunch and dinner.

**WHAT TO DO:** The Grand Floridian Resort & Spa offers many of the recreational facilities of a traditional beach resort. Fishing excursions may be arranged (refer to the *Sports & Recreation* chapter for details). The resort's entertainment schedule is available at the Front Desk.

**Arcade:** The pocket-sized Arcadia Games is adjacent to the Gasparilla Island Grill (near the marina).

**Basketball:** Hoops may be shot on a half-court near the health club. Registered Grand Floridian guests may borrow basketballs on a first-come, first-served basis.

**Bass Fishing:** See page 257.

**Boating:** Pontoon boats are available for rent (at the Captain's Shipyard Marina). Each boat can accommodate up to 10 guests. Drivers must be at least 18 years of age. The cost is $45 per half hour. To rent a pontoon boat, you will have to present a valid driver's license. Reservations are not required. Smoking is not permitted on the boat. All guests younger than age 12 must wear (provided) life jackets.

**Campfire:** Resort guests are invited to gather around the fire and roast marshmallows (the marshmallows are free and s'mores kits start at about $5). Afterward, everyone is treated to a screening of a Disney film—aka "Movies Under the Stars." Both events may be canceled due to inclement weather.

**Golf:** This resort is near Disney's Magnolia, Palm, and Oak Trail golf courses. Call 407-WDW-GOLF (939-4653), or visit *www.disneyworldgolf.com* for information or to reserve tee times.

**Health Club:** The modern exercise facility, adjacent to The Grand Floridian Spa, is outfitted with an array of fitness equipment.

**Salons:** The Bibbidi Bobbidi Boutique offers royal makeovers for young guests. Kids can choose a hairstyle then add makeup, nail color, and accessories—even a Disney costume. This spot was "on pause" at press time.

**Shopping:** On the first floor of the main building is Curiouser Clothiers (resort-wear and swimwear), and Sandy Cove, for gifts, sundries, and home decor. One level up is M. Mouse Mercantile (Disney merchandise) and Basin White (soaps and bath supplies).

**Spa:** A pleasant pampering palace, The Grand Floridian Spa offers soothing packages—and a lovely relaxation room to enjoy before and after your appointment.

Treatment hours are usually 9 A.M. to 6 P.M. daily. Prices start at about $175 for a 50-minute massage and about $70 for a 20-minute facial. For more information, or to schedule an appointment, visit *disneyworld.com/spas*. Details are subject to change.

**Swimming:** There are two large pools at the Grand. Both feature zero-depth-entry, and the Beach Pool also has waterfalls and a 181-foot slide. There's an *Alice in Wonderland* splash zone for little ones. Kids get giddy when the Mad Hatter's mammoth hat tips over, dumping massive amounts of water onto bathers below.

**TRANSPORTATION:** The Grand Floridian is connected to the Transportation and Ticket Center (TTC) and Magic Kingdom by monorail. From the TTC, EPCOT is reached by transferring to another monorail. (If the EPCOT monorail isn't operating, buses are provided.) Buses transport guests to Disney's Hollywood Studios, Animal Kingdom, Blizzard Beach, Typhoon Lagoon, and Disney Springs. (A transfer may be required to reach the water parks.) Watercraft travel to the Magic Kingdom. There is a walking path to Magic Kingdom, Contemporary resort, Polynesian Village, and the TTC. (It comes in very handy when lines abound at the monorail station.)

# Wilderness Lodge, Villas, & Cabins

This resort artfully recalls the spirit of the early American West and the feeling of the National Park Service lodges built during the early 1900s. These grand structures architecturally unified the elements of wilderness parks, kept harmony with nature, and incorporated the culture of Native Americans. The Wilderness Lodge artfully recaptures this rustic charm.

The resort is located between the Contemporary and Fort Wilderness on Bay Lake. The majestic lobby is an eight-story, log-structured building. Massive bundled log columns support a series of trusses, while two Pacific Northwest totem poles soar 55 feet into the air. Four levels of corridors surround the lobby, providing access to guestrooms, sitting nooks, and terraces. The mono-rail does not stop here. Club-level service is available on the top floor of the Lodge. There are villas here, too: Boulder Ridge Villas and Copper Creek Villas & Cabins (Copper Creek joined the Disney Vacation Club family in 2017). The telephone number for the Wilderness Lodge is 407-824-3200.

**ROOMS:** All of the Lodge's 740 beautifully refurbished guestrooms have two queen-size beds or one king-size bed and a balcony. Bathrooms have separate vanity areas with double sinks. Guestroom walls are bright and feature an outdoorsy motif. Subtle odes to Disney wildlife complete the theme. Rooms include a steamer,

PHOTO BY JILL SAFRO

hair dryer, coffeemaker (with coffee and sweetened non-dairy creamer), mini refrigerator, free Wi-Fi, and flat-screen TV.

The 181 Boulder Ridge villas are housed in a five-story building adjoining the main Lodge. This tribute to turn-of-the-20th-century design is also one of the two Disney Vacation Club (DVC) properties at this resort. The style of the villas building was inspired by the natural grandeur of Rocky Mountain geyser country. At Copper Creek (the other DVC property), guests may choose from studios, 1-, 2-, and 3-bedroom villas, and lakeside cabins.

Each studio has a queen-size bed, a double sleeper sofa, and a kitchenette with microwave, coffeemaker (with coffee), and mini refrigerator. (Boulder Ridge villas have a pull-down bed, too.) Villas sleep 4 to 12 guests and have dining areas, kitchens, an iron (with board) laundry facilities, master baths with bubble-jet tubs, and DVD players. They include a king-size bed in the master bedroom, a living room with a queen sleeper sofa, and either two queen-size beds or a queen-size bed and a double sleeper sofa in the extra bedrooms.

Each of the 26 waterfront Cascade Cabins features two bedrooms (and sleeps up to 8 guests), two bath-rooms, large dining and living room spaces, floor-to-ceiling windows, exposed wooden beams, and an interior-exterior stone-hearth fireplace.

Villas and cabins are available to all guests when not occupied by Disney Vacation Club members.

**WHERE TO EAT:** The Northwest theme is carried out with flair in the hotel's eateries. Room service was on pause at press time, but is expected to return.

**Artist Point:** Decorated with art representing painters who first chronicled the Northwest landscape, this spot features "Storybook Dining"—a prix-fixe dinner hosted by Snow White, Dopey, Grumpy, and the evil Queen. (It's the only place at WDW to meet her highness.)

**Geyser Point Bar & Grill:** With its cedar beams and natural stone, this rustic, open-air waterside spot invites guests to pair small plates with beverages from the Pacific Northwest. It's a delightful spot.

**Roaring Fork:** Quick service food and light snacks are available at this cozy snack bar. This is also the site of the resort's "refillable mug" station. (For details, see page 287.) Roaring Fork's operating hours are usually about 7 A.M. until 11 P.M.

**Whispering Canyon Cafe:** A boisterous, family-style restaurant with skillets and shenanigans offers top-notch all-day dining.

**WHERE TO DRINK:** Two pleasant spots are available.

**Geyser Point Bar & Grill:** Geyser Point is a waterside retreat with a full bar featuring an array of beer, wine, cocktails, and soft drinks—and an excellent fireworks vantage point is just steps away.

**Territory Lounge:** This low-key lounge honors the survey parties who led the move westward. Specialty drinks, wine, beer, and snacks are served.

**WHAT TO DO:** The resort offers many recreational activities. Teton Boat & Bike Rental is in the Colonel's Cabin by the lake. Fishing excursions may be arranged (refer to the *Sports & Recreation* chapter for details). Note that some WDW resort activities were on pause at press time, but are expected to return.

**Arcade:** The Buttons and Bells Arcade has about 30 different games to enjoy.

**Bass Fishing:** See page 257.

**Biking:** Bicycles may be rented at the nearby Fort Wilderness Resort & Campground (at the Bike Barn) for scenic rides around the resort.

**Carolwood Pacific Room:** A fireplace and railroad memorabilia add atmosphere to this relaxing room, equipped with comfy seating, tables, and games. It is located in the Wilderness Lodge Villas building.

**Campfire:** Resort guests are invited to gather round the campfire (on select nights) and roast marshmallows. (Marshmallows are complimentary for Wilderness Lodge guests; s'mores kits start at about $5.) Afterward, everyone is treated to a screening of a Disney film—aka "Movies Under the Stars." You'll find the movie lawn between the marina and Geyser Point Bar & Grill. For the week's movie screening schedule, check with the resort's Front Desk.

**Health Club:** The only thing rustic about the Sturdy Branches health club is the structure it's housed in. Open from 6 A.M. to at least 9 P.M. daily, it features modern equipment, a sauna, and more.

**Salon by the Springs:** In the market for a manicure, pedicure, hair styling, or other spa services? Spring to this salon! It's open daily from 9 A.M. to 5 P.M., and reservations can be made by calling 407-WDW-SPAS.

**Shopping:** Wilderness Lodge Mercantile stocks basic necessities and sundries, as well as a line of clothing with the Wilderness Lodge logo and Disney character merchandise. There is a small selection of grocery items, too. The mercantile is usually open until about 10:30 P.M.

**Swimming:** The zero-depth-entry Boulder Ridge Cove pool appears as if it were carved from a natural rock-scape. A beach, a kiddie pool, two whirlpools, and a geyser complete the design. Fire Rock Geyser erupts on the hour from early morning until 10 P.M. Most kids enjoy the splash zone.

**TRANSPORTATION:** Boats (aka water taxis) usually ferry guests to the Magic Kingdom, Contemporary, and Fort Wilderness. Buses transport folks to Magic Kingdom, EPCOT, Fort Wilderness, Disney's Hollywood Studios, Disney's Animal Kingdom, Blizzard Beach, Typhoon Lagoon, and Disney Springs. (A bus transfer may be required for the water parks.)

# Fort Wilderness Resort & Campground

The very existence of this canal-crossed expanse—with more than 750 acres of cypress and pine—always surprises visitors who come to Walt Disney World expecting to find nothing more than theme parks.

Tucked among the campsites are hundreds of Wilderness Cabins for rent, complete with housekeeping service. The cost is comparable to that of some of the more expensive rooms at Disney resorts, but each sleeps up to 6 guests and offers about 500 square feet of space. The phone number for the Fort Wilderness resort and campground is 407-824-2900.

**CAMPSITES:** Fort Wilderness has 843 traditional sites. They feature electricity hookups (30/50-amp), water, sanitary disposal, complimentary Wi-Fi, and cable TV. Partial-hookup campsites supply electricity, water, and cable TV only. All campsites feature a paved driveway pad, picnic table, and charcoal grill. Most loops have at least one air-conditioned comfort station complete with restrooms, private showers, ice machine, phones,

PHOTO BY JILL SAFRO

free Wi-Fi, and a laundry room. A site allows for occupancy by up to ten. Each site has room for one car, plus the camping vehicle. Other cars may be parked in the main lot at Fort Wilderness.

The various campground areas are designated by numbers. The 100–500 loops are closest to the beach, the Settlement Trading Post, and Pioneer Hall. The 1500–1900 loops are far away from the beach, but close to the active Meadows area. The 2000 loop is farthest from the beach and many other Fort Wilderness activities, but is quieter and more private than all other loops. Premium campsites are big-rig friendly and are wider and deeper to accommodate large vehicles. Pets are welcome at all campsites for a nightly charge of $5. They can frolic at Waggin' Tails Dog Park, the "off leash" pet play area.

### THE CABINS AT DISNEY'S FORT WILDERNESS RESORT:

These newly re-imagined woodland dwellings offer a lovely, natural escape. Falling into WDW's "deluxe" resort category, the Disney Vacation Club (DVC) cabins are decorated with wilderness accents. Each stand-alone cabin offers spacious accommodations, sleeping up to six adults and features a bedroom, bathroom, living room, full kitchen, and private patio. A select number of cabins are dog-friendly (for a fee). This "fresh take" on the traditional cabin experience was a work-in-progress as this book went to press. For updates and additional information, visit *disneyworld.com*.

**Notes:** No extra camping equipment allowed; all guests must be accommodated in a cabin.

**WHERE TO EAT:** There are several eateries here, but many folks opt to cook their own meals. A small selection of supplies is sold at the Meadow Trading Post and the Settlement Trading Post. Inquire about nearby grocery stores when you check in, or use an authorized delivery service such as *gardengrocer.com* (fees apply).

**The Chuck Wagon:** Dinner vittles are sold from a nifty retro camper.

**Meadow Snack Bar:** Among the offerings available at this poolside snack spot: pizza, garden salad, BBQ pulled-pork sandwiches, hot dogs, chips, ice cream, soft drinks, and spirited beverages.

**P&J's Southern Takeout:** This take-away venue offers hearty fare throughout the day: breakfast platters, pizza, ribs, fried chicken, burgers, salads, and more. You can chow down at nearby tables or take the grub to go.

**Trail's End Marketplace:** This re-imagined Pioneer Hall spot serves satisfying quick-service fare for breakfast, lunch, and dinner.

**WHERE TO DRINK:** Cocktails, soft drinks, and pub grub are served at Crockett's Tavern in Pioneer Hall.

**WHAT TO DO:** There are plenty of free activities from which to choose, including two pools (the Meadow Swimmin' pool has an aquatic play zone for tots and a slide), tennis, pickleball, Movies Under the Stars, and campfire sing-alongs (complete with appearances by Chip and Dale, plus marshmallows and s'mores kits for a fee). Guests can enjoy wagon, pony, bike, and carriage rides, plus fishing, canoeing, kayaking, archery, and more (fees apply). For specifics, go to *disneyworld.com* and refer to the *Everything Else in the World* and *Sports & Recreation* chapters, and inquire at the Fort Wilderness check-in desk. Pioneer Hall is home to a perennially popular dinner show known as the Hoop-Dee-Doo Musical Revue (see page 318 for details.)

**TRANSPORTATION:** Buses circulating at 15- to 40-minute intervals provide transportation within the campground, while buses and boats connect Fort Wilderness Resort & Campground to the rest of the World. The Magic Kingdom park is best reached via watercraft that depart from the marina. Buses to Wilderness Lodge leave from the Settlement stop only. Buses to EPCOT, Disney's Animal Kingdom, Disney's Hollywood Studios, Blizzard Beach, Typhoon Lagoon, and Disney Springs depart from the Outpost stop. (A transfer may be required to reach a Disney water park.)

Electric golf carts may be rented outside the Reception Outpost as an alternative means of getting around within the campground. Call 407-824-2742 to reserve a cart. Available to Fort Wilderness guests exclusively, golf carts rent for about $74 per night (including tax). They're available for pickup starting at 1 p.m., and should be returned by 11 a.m. on the return date. Guests must be at least 18 years old to rent a golf cart, and at least 16 (with a valid driver's license) to drive one.

PHOTO BY JILL SAFRO

# EPCOT Area

## Caribbean Beach

This vibrant, tropical hotel—which is southeast of EPCOT and near Disney's Hollywood Studios—offers an idyllic island-style getaway. Introduced to the World in 1988, Caribbean Beach continues to be a favorite among WDW visitors. The resort is composed of brightly colored buildings surrounding the 45-acre Barefoot Bay.

A village consists of a cluster of two-story buildings, a guest laundry, and a lakefront stretch of beach. Old Port Royale acts as a "port of entry," providing a tropical atmosphere for guests to check in, access lobby concierge services, shop, dine, and relax. Stone walls, pirates' cannons, and lush landscapes add to the resort's immersive atmosphere.

The lakeside recreation area includes a pool with waterfalls and a slide; the Barefoot Bay Bike Works, where bicycles may be rented; and a 1.2-mile promenade around the lake that's perfect for biking, walking, or jogging. Kids love it here. The phone number for the Caribbean Beach resort is 407-934-3400.

**ROOMS:** Rooms are located in two-story buildings in the island villages. A typical 340-square-foot room has two queen beds, and most sleep up to four. Some rooms can sleep up to five (with a fold-down bunk-size bed). The rooms here are a bit larger than standard rooms at Disney's other moderate resorts. Rooms are decorated in tones softer than the colors on the exteriors. Each one has a small fridge/beverage cooler, coffeemaker (with coffee), and free Wi-Fi. A note for the budget-conscious: Rooms are identical in terms of size and

**Hot Tip!** If you hope to take part in Early Entry at a WDW theme park (see page 22 for details), build in extra time for the morning commute. Lines for the Skyliner—and all other modes of Disney transportation—can be rather lengthy at the start (and end) of the day.

comfort, but rates differ depending on location, view, and theming. Note that there are no elevators—guests use stairs to access rooms on the second floor.

**WHERE TO EAT:** Guests may dine at Sebastian's Bistro, Centertown Market, and Spyglass Grill. The Banana Cabana poolside lounge offers first-rate fare, too.

**Banana Cabana:** A cheery lounge with a solid menu, Banana Cabana offers pull-apart rolls, chile con queso, jerk chicken sandwiches, cheeseburgers, salad with grilled shrimp, and pineapple-coconut bread pudding.

**Centertown Market:** The indoor market sells freshly prepared quick-service meals with Caribbean influences. There is a grab-and-go section, too.

**Sebastian's Bistro:** A pleasant waterside locale, Sebastian's Bistro serves family-style dinner with Latin and Caribbean flair.

**Spyglass Grill:** A seasonal, walk-up counter near the Trinidad pool, Spyglass serves three meals a day—which may be enjoyed on a patio overlooking Barefoot Bay.

**WHERE TO DRINK:** Soft drinks and cocktails may be purchased at all resort dining spots, but the best bet for bending elbows is Banana Cabana—an open-air oasis offering luscious libations, satisfying small bites, and menu items from the nearby Sebastian's Bistro.

**Hot Tip!** Portable playpen-like cribs that accommodate one child under age 3 are available at all Disney resorts. Ask about them when you call to reserve your room. They're free. (If you'd like to request bed rails for your little one, refer to page 49 of the *Getting Ready to Go* chapter of this book. They're free, too.)

**WHAT TO DO:** Barefoot Bay provides many a recreational opportunity. Fishing excursions take place on the lake, while biking, walking, and jogging may happen around it. An entertainment schedule is available at the Front Desk. Details are subject to change.

**Biking:** Bicycles may be rented at Barefoot Bay Bike Works. Rides may take guests around the resort's scenic 45-acre lake known as Barefoot Bay.

**Fishing:** Guided fishing excursions are offered on Barefoot Bay. Call 407-WDW-FISH (939-3474) for additional info and to make a reservation.

**Playground:** There is a small playground to explore.

**Shopping:** Calypso Trading Post carries a selection of Disney merchandise, swimwear, sundries, and snacks.

**Swimming:** Each village has its own pool, and the main pool, dubbed Fuentes del Morro, conjures up images of high-seas pirate adventures. It has two slides, one whirlpool spa, and a splash zone for children under 48 inches tall. Youngsters simply adore it.

**TRANSPORTATION:** Buses go to Magic Kingdom, Animal Kingdom, Blizzard Beach, Typhoon Lagoon, and Disney Springs. The Disney Skyliner whisks guests to EPCOT and Disney's Hollywood Studios. (A transfer may be required to reach the water parks.) If the Skyliner is not operating (due to inclement weather), alternate transportation will be provided. (See page 67 for Skyliner details.) Getting around within the resort is done via "Internal Resort Shuttle" buses.

## Disney's Riviera Resort

Walt and Lillian Disney marveled at the majesty of Europe and the Mediterranean coastline—and this resort pays tribute to their travels and the region that inspired them. It's a compelling blend of Disney artistry and the sights, sounds, tastes, and heritage of the sun-drenched Riviera.

Disney's Riviera Resort is the 15th Disney Vacation Club (DVC) property, and its rooms are available to all guests (not just members of the Disney Vacation Club). The resort made its grand debut in fall 2019. For more information, use the My Disney Experience website or mobile app, or visit *disneyworld.com*.

**Villas:** All of the 489 units have balconies or a patio, and most have a view of landscapes or pools. Amenities include a flat-screen TV, free Wi-Fi, coffeemaker (with coffee), hair dryer, and a small fridge. Deluxe studios sleep up to 5 guests and feature a kitchenette; one- and two-bedroom villas have full kitchens with a dining space that opens to a living area; an en-suite luxury bath; and a laundry area with a washer and dryer.

**WHERE TO EAT AND DRINK:** There's also a nice selection of eateries at which to dine or pick up sustenance to enjoy in your room:

**Bar Riva:** Visit this open-air pool bar with seaside decor for snacks, drinks, and views of the pool.

**Le Petit Café:** Coffee bar by day, wine bar by night, this elegant French patisserie specializes in beverages and casual bites throughout the day.

**Primo Piatto:** With a modern design and a traditional feel, this quick-service spot offers family-friendly fare.

**Topolino's Terrace:** A rooftop retreat with French and Italian influences, Topolino's serves breakfast with Disney characters and (character-free) dinner daily.

**F.Y.I.:** Topolino is what Mickey answers to in Italy.

**WHAT TO DO:** Riviera guests may partake in many recreational activities, including bocce ball, poolside activities, and arts & crafts in the Eventi Room.

**Health Club:** Guests may work out in a modern facility known as The Athlétique Fitness Center.

**Shopping:** The resort's retail outlet, La Boutique, offers Disney souvenirs and fashions, and features an Art on Demand kiosk (which sells prints from Riviera's custom art collection). It also stocks assorted spirits, soft drinks, snacks, and other grocery items.

**Swimming:** There are two pools here: the tranquil Beau Soleil leisure pool; and the Riviera pool, which features a winding stone turret water slide. The S'il Vous Play splash zone is ideal for little ones.

**TRANSPORTATION:** Buses go to Magic Kingdom, Animal Kingdom, Blizzard Beach, Typhoon Lagoon, and Disney Springs. (A transfer may be required for the water parks.) The Disney Skyliner whisks guests to EPCOT and Disney's Hollywood Studios.

# Yacht & Beach Club, and Beach Club Villas

The New England seaside exists at Walt Disney World in the form of the Yacht & Beach Club, and the Beach Club Villas. Situated near EPCOT's International Gateway entrance (aka EPCOT's back door), the resorts are set around the 25-acre Crescent Lake. The adjacent properties, designed by noted architect Robert A. M. Stern, share most facilities—including a pool area, a convention center offering business services, and transportation options.

The Yacht Club's design evokes images of the New England seashore hotels of the 1880s. Guests enter the five-story gray clapboard building along a wooden-planked bridge. The spartan guestrooms feature blue curtains; walls, furniture, and accents in shades of brown and beige; and faux wood floors throughout (no carpet). A lighthouse on the pier serves as a beacon to welcome guests back to the hotel from WDW attractions. To contact the Yacht Club, call 407-934-7000.

Distance from the ocean is irrelevant over at the sand-and-surf-focused Beach Club resort. There's a sandy volleyball court and beachside swings on the white-sand shore of Crescent Lake. Guests are met by hosts and hostesses dressed in colorful beach resort costumes of the 1870s. The phone number for the Beach Club resort is 407-934-8000.

**ROOMS:** The Beach Club's rooms are amply sized and a bit more modern than the resort's overall motif. Yacht Club rooms are also roomy, if a bit more austere. Most rooms feature two queen beds or one king bed (higher than the beds in most WDW resort rooms), and many have a daybed (a couch that converts to a single bed). Most of the suites have a king-size bed, and may have two queen beds, and/or a sleeper sofa or a fold down single bed. In the bathrooms, there is a separate vanity with double sinks. Each room has an iron (with board), hair dryer, free Wi-Fi, mini fridge, coffeemaker (with coffee, sugar, and sweetened non-dairy creamer), and a safe. Club-Level rooms (with exclusive access to a room with a concierge, snacks, and drinks) are available.

A five-story building beside the Beach Club is home to 177 two-bedroom equivalents. The villas are available to all guests, subject to availability. Each studio has a queen-size bed, a double sleeper sofa, and a fold-down

bunk-size bed, plus a kitchenette with a microwave, coffeemaker, and mini fridge, as well as a flat-screen TV and DVD player. Larger villas sleep 4 to 8 guests, and all have a dining area, kitchen, laundry room, and a master bath with whirlpool tub. They include a king-size bed in the master bedroom, living room with queen sleeper sofa, and either two queen-size beds or a queen-size bed and a double sleeper sofa. Yacht Club guests may have up to two dogs stay in their room for an extra $75 per night. (Note that dogs—with the exception of service animals—are not permitted at the Beach Club.)

**WHERE TO EAT:** The themes of yachting and the sea play a role in the eateries found at their respective resorts.

**Ale & Compass Restaurant:** The lighthouse-themed eatery serves three meals a day. It's at the Yacht Club, just off the lobby (next to Ale & Compass Lounge).

**Beach Club Marketplace:** Stop here for hot and cold breakfast items such as scrambled eggs, Mickey waffles, pastries, and croissants, as well as soup, salads, sandwiches, and snacks. Rapid Fill (refillable) mugs may be purchased and filled here, too.

**Beaches and Cream Soda Shop:** An old-fashioned spot with massive appeal, this classic soda fountain doles out frosty shakes, malts, and varied ice cream sundaes. Burgers and sandwiches are served as well. The crowd-pleasing happy place is located near the Stormalong Bay pool/mini water park.

**Cape May Cafe:** A buffet featuring flavors of the New England coast is presented nightly. The bountiful feast features shrimp, clams, and mussels, plus steak, chicken, salad, and more. Breakfast is hosted by Minnie Mouse and several of her Disney pals.

**Hurricane Hanna's Waterside Bar & Grill:** Sandwiches, seafood rolls, salads, burgers, and snacks are served here. A full bar is offered and poolside beverage service is available. If you buy a refillable resort mug, this is one spot to top it off during your stay. (This spot keeps shorter hours than other refill locations.)

**Market at Ale & Compass:** An upscale snack bar, the Market offers freshly prepared selections for breakfast, lunch, and dinner. Breakfast items include Mickey-shaped waffles; breakfast sandwiches; oatmeal; and sticky buns. Lunch and dinner feature paninis (grilled chicken, veggie, or Italian), soup, and more. There is a grab-and-go area with snack items to choose from. Rapid Fill mugs may be purchased and filled here.

**Yachtsman Steakhouse:** Select cuts of aged beef are the specialty of the house. Fresh seafood, pasta, and poultry are also offered.

**WHERE TO DRINK:** The lounges in the Yacht and Beach Club resorts offer a variety of specialty drinks and snacks in relaxing seaside-themed settings.

**Ale & Compass Lounge:** This Yacht Club locale features a full bar, plus a small bites menu. Revelers may imbibe from about 4 P.M. until about 11 P.M. The popular watering hole can be quite cacophonous.

**Crew's Cup:** A cozy lounge, Crew's Cup is the place to try local beer and brews shipped from the world's seaports—as well as spirits, soft drinks, and appetizers. It's next door to Yachtsman Steakhouse.

**Martha's Vineyard:** This relatively quiet lounge at the Beach Club offers selections from American and international vineyards, served by the glass or bottle, as well as a full bar and appetizers.

**WHAT TO DO:** There is enough to do here to fill a vacation. A lakeside sand volleyball court stands near the Beach Club. Equipment can be borrowed from the Front Desk (no charge). Pontoon boats may be rented at the marina. Ask about the resort recreation schedule at the Front Desk—they've got activities for kids of all ages. (Fees may apply.) Surrey bikes may be rented at the nearby BoardWalk resort.

Fantasia Gardens Mini Golf complex is close by, and guided fishing excursions may be arranged (see *Sports & Recreation*). And last but not least, the BoardWalk entertainment district is a short walk around the lake.

**Boating:** Pontoon boats are available for rent from the Bayside Marina (shared by the Yacht and Beach Club resort hotels).

**Campfire:** Resort guests are invited to gather round the campfire (on select nights) and roast marshmallows. (Marshmallows are free for Yacht or Beach Club guests; s'mores kits start at about $5.) Afterward, everyone is treated to a screening of a Disney film. The campfire may be canceled due to inclement weather.

**Health Club:** The Ship Shape health club has strength and cardio machines and is open around the clock to BoardWalk resort guests age 14 and older. (Use your MagicBand or hotel room key card to gain access to the Ship Shape heath club.)

**Salon:** The Ship Shape salon (which was on pause at press time) sits between the Yacht Club and the Beach Club, poolside. It traditionally offers a line of hair care services; call 407-939-7727.

**Shopping:** At the Yacht Club, Market at Ale & Compass is an all-purpose shop stocked with character merch and sundries. At the Beach Club, the Beach Club Marketplace has a similar selection.

**Swimming:** Between the marina and the beach is the centerpiece of the dual resort—Stormalong Bay, a 3-acre pool area that's a mini water park. There is a lagoon for relaxed swimming, and another with currents, jets, and sand-bottomed areas. Several whirlpools are scattered throughout the area. Next to the main pool is a shipwreck, complete with waterslide. There's one unguarded pool and whirlpool at the far end of each hotel. There's an unguarded pool by the Beach Club Villas. The beach is nice for sunbathing, but swimming is not permitted.

**Tennis and Pickleball:** There is one lighted court on the Yacht Club side of the property. Equipment is available at the Yacht Club Front Desk.

**TRANSPORTATION:** Guests travel to EPCOT and Disney's Hollywood Studios via FriendShip water taxis or walkways. (It takes about 5 to 7 minutes to walk to EPCOT and about 20 to hoof it to Disney's Hollywood Studios.) It's also possible to get to the Studios via the Disney Skyliner (the station is near EPCOT's International Gateway). Buses go to Magic Kingdom, Animal Kingdom, Disney Springs, Typhoon Lagoon, and Blizzard Beach.

# Swan, Dolphin & Swan Reserve

These three resorts, situated near the shores of Crescent Lake, can easily be distinguished by the 47-foot swan and 56-foot dolphin statues that top the Swan and Dolphin, respectively, and the unique angled rooftop of the new Swan Reserve (a sleek, boutique hotel). The waterfalls, rows of palm trees, and beachfront location all reflect the tropical Florida landscape that was the original inspiration for their design by noted architect Michael Graves. The late master's unique style is represented in the turquoise waves on the colored facade of the Swan's 12-story main building and two 7-story wings, as well as in the Dolphin's exterior mural, which features a bodacious banana-leaf pattern. The soaring 27-story triangular tower at the center of the Dolphin is flanked by four 9-story guestroom wings.

**Hot Tip!** The Swan, Dolphin, and Swan Reserve resort hotels may offer seasonal promotions throughout the year. For information and/or to make a reservation, call 888-828-8850, or visit *swandolphin.com*.

PHOTO BY JILL SAFRO

The sleek addition to the resort, the 14-story Swan Reserve, opened in 2021 and plays off the water theming in its design both inside and out. The trio of resorts share extensive convention facilities, many recreational options, and a host of eateries. The hotels are operated by Marriott but are treated as Walt Disney World resorts; guests here enjoy most WDW resort benefits, most notably access to Early Theme Park Entry and a 7 A.M. head start to book Individual Lightning Lane Selections each day. (To use the paid attraction reservation service, create an account via the My Disney Experience app or website, link your hotel confirmation number and the last name on the reservation, and make your purchase via the app.) One difference of note: Guests can't use their room keys to charge purchases on Disney property, with the exception of within the Walt Disney World Swan, Dolphin, and Swan Reserve resorts themselves.

The telephone number for the resorts is 407-934-4000. Reservations for all three resorts may be made by visiting *www.swandolphin.com*, at *www.facebook.com/swananddolphin*, or by calling 888-828-8850.

**ROOMS:** All rooms have a fresh look, with soothing hues of white, blue, and gray, plus sleek, modern furniture. Amenities include weekday newspaper delivery, digital safes, mini fridge, coffeemaker (with tea and Starbucks coffee), irons and boards, two dual-line phones (with free, unlimited local and long-distance service), two bottles of water per day, and enhanced high-speed, wireless Internet access. Rooms equipped for guests with disabilities are available. Valet parking is $42 per day (plus tax); self-parking costs about $32 a day.

There are 349 rooms and 151 suites at the Walt Disney World Swan Reserve. There are 756 rooms and 55 suites at the Swan, each with one king-size or two queen-size "Westin Heavenly Beds." At the Dolphin, the 1,514 rooms (including 112 suites) feature two double beds or one king-size "Heavenly" bed. Swan rooms also include a vanity and dressing area.

## MEETINGS AND CONVENTIONS

Convention centers at Walt Disney World range from about 20,000 to 300,000 square feet. The Dolphin's is the largest at 360,000 square feet. The Contemporary has 3 ballrooms and a spacious pre-function area with lots of natural light. The center at the Yacht & Beach Club is reminiscent of a grand turn-of-the-century New England town-meeting hall. The Grand Floridian Resort and Spa has a lavish center with silk brocade walls. BoardWalk offers a smaller conference area with a lakeside gazebo for outdoor events. And Coronado Springs, the first moderately priced Disney resort to offer convention facilities, has one of the largest hotel ballrooms in the U.S.

Among the unique services available to Disney conventioneers is the use of Disney characters and performers for events. Special events can even be held in the parks. Resort business centers have clerical staffs and computers, in addition to faxing and photocopying equipment. (These services are available to all resort guests.)

Those interested in scheduling a convention should call 321-939-7129 (for WDW-owned-and-operated resorts) or 407-934-4290 (Swan, Dolphin, and Swan Reserve). Organizers are advised to book six months in advance, especially for large groups.

**WHERE TO EAT:** In addition to many restaurant choices, in-room dining is offered.

**Amare:** The complex's newest signature restaurant, located at the Swan Reserve, serves casual upscale Mediterranean-inspired cuisine three meals a day.

**Cabana Bar & Beach Club:** This poolside eatery near the Dolphin serves burgers, grilled chicken sandwiches, flatbreads, and more. The bar serves specialty drinks.

**The Fountain:** Homemade ice cream is the star at this Dolphin spot. Sundaes, shakes, and burgers are served.

**Rosa Mexicano:** The Dolphin's newest eatery offers a fresh take on authentic Mexican cuisine.

**Fuel:** The chic Dolphin snack bar invites guests to fuel up with specialty coffees, baked goods, sandwiches, salads, beverages, frozen yogurt, and other snacks.

**Garden Grove:** This Swan eatery features a park-like atmosphere—complete with a giant, lifelike tree in the center of the dining room. For additional information, visit *swandolphin.com*.

**Grounds:** Located off the lobby of the Swan Reserve, Grounds specializes in coffee, smoothies, sandwiches, and grab-and-go selections.

**Il Mulino New York Trattoria:** The highly acclaimed Italian restaurant is located on the first floor of the Swan. The setting, which is somewhat reminiscent of an old-world trattoria, is relaxed yet vibrant. Features such as Piatti per il Tavolo (family-style dining) and wood-fired pizzas complement Il Mulino New York's family-friendly Walt Disney World locale.

**Picabu:** This Dolphin cafeteria/store can be found on the resort's first floor. The convenience store section sells snacks and sundries. It serves Starbucks coffee, too.

**Shula's:** An upscale celebration of two American favorites: steak and professional football. It's a bit

PHOTO BY JILL SAFRO

pricey, but the steaks are superb and the side orders are big enough to share. There is a children's menu (chicken, cheeseburgers, etc.). The (enforced) dress code at Shula's is business casual.

**Splash Pool Bar and Grill:** A casual, poolside cafe near the Swan serving specialty sandwiches and snacks. A full-service bar is also located here.

**Tangerine:** A Swan Reserve poolside spot, Tangerine serves signature drinks along with casual fare: flatbreads, salads, burgers, sandwiches, and (refreshing) tangerine-flavored ice pops.

PHOTO BY JILL SAFRO

**Todd English's bluezoo:** This eatery features coastal cuisine, beef, and chicken dishes with international and domestic influences.

**WHERE TO DRINK:** It's easy to find a nice sipping spot in this neck of the woods.

**Java:** This lobby spot at the Swan offers a java jolt for early birds on the go. Enjoy specialty coffees, light breakfast items, soft drinks, and fresh pastries.

**Kimonos:** The Asian decor makes this Swan lounge an inviting place for sake, sushi, and other Japanese selections. Karaoke is a house specialty. This place is generally hopping a bit later than most other Walt Disney World resort lounges.

**Phins:** A snazzy Dolphin lobby lounge featuring beer, wine, and specialty drinks.

**Shula's Steak House Lounge:** Settle into a comfy chair and sip a drink in this small-but-swanky lounge adjacent to Shula's dining room.

**Tangerine:** Savor poolside sips and savory snacks at this Swan Reserve spot.

**WHAT TO DO:** The Swan, Dolphin, and Swan Reserve share many recreation options. Volleyball nets and hammocks may be set up on the beach. Guests may play pool, table tennis, and giant chess near the pool. The Fantasia Gardens Mini Golf complex and BoardWalk are nearby. Disney's Hollywood Studios is a FriendShip water taxi ride (or about a 20-minute walk) away. (It takes about 10 minutes to travel by boat.)

**Arcade:** A room with video games, air hockey, and more is located near Picabu on the first floor of the Dolphin. Fees apply.

**Boating:** Watercraft are available from a dock near the pool area (weather permitting). The swan-shaped paddle boats may be borrowed for free by guests of the Swan or Dolphin. Simply present a valid resort ID and an attendant will escort you to your fine feathered float. Life jackets should be worn by all passengers.

## THE SWAN RESERVE

The Walt Disney World Swan Reserve is a 14-story Marriott Autograph Collection Hotel with views of nearby Crescent Lake. Like its sister hotels the Swan and Dolphin, the Swan Reserve is treated as a Walt Disney World resort with many resort amenities and benefits; most notably, access to Early Theme Park Entry. The Reserve offers 349 rooms and 151 suites that can accommodate families of 6 to 10. The hotel exterior sparkles with colors and hues of water, evoking a sense of serenity that's carried inside to guest rooms with shades of white, blue, and gray.

Amenities include a safe, mini refrigerator, single serve coffee maker (with tea and coffee), clock radio with dual USB charging stations, large-screen HDTV, iron (with board), complimentary telephone service, pillow-top mattresses, high-speed wireless Internet service, and several premium streaming channels. Guest rooms feature one king or two queen beds. Floor-to-ceiling windows offer stunning views of resort surroundings.

Just a short walk from EPCOT and Disney's Hollywood Studios, Swan Reserve has a stylish lounge for cocktails and light dinner fare, a Mediterranean restaurant serving three meals daily, a coffee bar, and a poolside restaurant serving lunch and dinner. It shares extensive convention facilities plus recreational and dining options with the Swan and Dolphin. The direct hotel line is 407-934-3000. Reserve at *swandolphin.com* or by calling 888-828-8850.

**Children's Program:** Camp Dolphin welcomes kids (potty-trained) ages 5 through 12 and has supervised activities from 4 P.M. until 11 P.M. There are three payment packages, depending on what time your kid(s) attend: Early Evening (4 P.M. to 8 P.M., $65 per child); Late Evening (8 P.M. to 11 P.M., $50 per child), or Full Evening (4 P.M. to 11 p.m., $85 for the first child, $65 for each additional child.) Camp Dolphin space is limited, so book early. Reservations are required.

**Health Clubs:** There is a fitness center near the pool area at the Dolphin and a smaller health club near Splash Terrace at the Swan.

**Playground:** A sandy play area with swings and jungle gyms is near the grotto pool.

**Shopping:** Disney Cabanas, located in the Swan lobby, sells character merchandise and sundries. There are two shops at the Dolphin: Accents offers resort-wear for men and women and the Cabana Beach Hut offers "pool-fun" essentials. And the convenience store within Picabu sells grocery items and sundries.

**Spa and Salon:** The Mandara Spa (at the Dolphin) offers full-service body treatments, plus hairstyling, manicures, pedicures, and more.

**Swimming:** There are two lap pools, a themed grotto pool with slides, and a kiddie pool between the Swan and Dolphin. Several whirlpools are scattered about the recreation area. The Swan Reserve has an additional pool for guests to enjoy. Life jackets may be borrowed (no charge). Be sure to keep a close eye on your little splashers at all times.

Swan, Dolphin, and Swan Reserve guests receive $30 off one Mandara Spa treatment of $200 or more for each night of their stay. For further info, go to *swandolphin.com*, or call 407-934-4772. Details are subject to change without notice.

**TRANSPORTATION:** Guests may travel to EPCOT and Disney's Hollywood Studios via water taxis or walkway. (It takes about 10 minutes to walk to EPCOT's back entrance—where there is a Disney Skyliner station—and about 20 minutes to reach the Studios. Water taxis don't move much faster—and they make multiple stops—so allow plenty of time to reach either destination.) Buses go directly to Animal Kingdom, Disney Springs, and the Transportation and Ticket Center. (To reach Magic Kingdom, guests transfer to a monorail or ferry boat at the TTC.)

# BoardWalk Inn & Villas

The enchantment of a bygone era is recaptured at the BoardWalk. The resort combines a waterside entertainment complex with deluxe hotel accommodations and vacation villas. Dining, recreation, shopping, and entertainment venues line the boardwalk, and sparkling lights trim the buildings. The ambience continues throughout, with detailed architecture featuring colorful facades, flagged turrets, and striped awnings, all reminiscent of the turn of the 20th century. BoardWalk resort guests may walk or take a water taxi to EPCOT's International Gateway entrance and Disney's Hollywood Studios. The telephone number for BoardWalk Inn & Villas is 407-939-5100.

**ROOMS:** Accommodations here evoke the charm of early Eastern-seaboard inns. Most have private balconies or patios. The BoardWalk Inn has 372 deluxe rooms.

Guestrooms at the inn sleep up to five, and feature two queen-size beds (or one king-size bed) and a single, sleeper couch. Romantic two-story garden suites each have a private garden enclosed by a white picket fence. They sleep two and have a living room on the first floor and a king-size bed in the unenclosed bedroom loft. The inn also has Club-Level rooms and suites.

The 282 two-bedroom equivalents are collectively called BoardWalk Villas. These are Disney Vacation Club villas, available to everyone when not occupied by members. Each studio has a queen-size bed and double sleeper sofa, plus a kitchenette with microwave, coffeemaker, and small refrigerator/beverage cooler. Larger (one-, two-, and three-bedroom) villas sleep 4

to 12 people, and feature dining areas, fully equipped kitchens, laundry facilities, master baths with whirlpool tubs, and TV with DVD player. They also include a king-size bed in the master bedroom, a living room with a queen sleeper sofa, and a queen-size bed, plus a double sleeper sofa in any additional bedrooms. All rooms have an iron and board, hair dryer, and free Wi-Fi.

**WHERE TO EAT:** This resort boasts a wealth of dining and snacking options. A variety of vendors along the boardwalk tempt with funnel cakes, corn dogs, pizza, stuffed pretzels, specialty coffees, cocktails, and more.

**BoardWalk Ice Cream:** Cool off with cups, cones (cake or sugar), and creatively crafted sundaes at this cheery dessert destination.

**Big River Grille & Brewing Works:** This working brewpub features a full menu, complemented by fresh specialty ales. Guests may observe the brewmaster through floor-to-ceiling glass walls.

**BoardWalk Deli:** A Northeastern-style deli, this space has sandwiches, fresh-baked breads, and bakery items. It's also the resort's refillable mug station (see page 295).

**BoardWalk Pizza Window:** This handy walk-up window sells pizza by the slice, side salads, and mini cannolis. It's open for lunch and dinner (until about 11 P.M.).

**BoardWalk Carts:** Stands along the boards offer snacks such as hot dogs, cheese-stuffed pretzels, nachos, wings, chili fries, and more.

**Carousel Coffee:** This bright, if spartan spot, is a great place to get morning coffee and pastries, and light snacks throughout the afternoon. You'll find it on the resort's second floor, just off the lobby.

**The Cake Bake Shop:** A sweet addition to the Board-Walk dining scene, this spot offers sweet and savory eats, along with afternoon tea service, in an elegant-yet-casual atmosphere.

**Flying Fish:** The Fish features a show kitchen, and its upscale menu emphasizes expertly prepared seafood, steak, and fresh seasonal items. As a Disney Dining Plan Signature Restaurant, Flying Fish requires two credits per meal, per person.

**Trattoria al Forno:** An Italian eatery, Trattoria features old-world favorites for the whole family. The morning meal is a character affair.

**WHERE TO DRINK:** Guests have a multitude of options right in their backyard.

**AbracadaBAR:** This enclave proffers potent potables and alcohol-free elixirs in an escapist environment. You will find it next to Flying Fish.

**Atlantic Dance Hall:** This waterfront nightclub is an elegantly designed dance spot. You must be at least 21 to enter. There's usually no cover charge, but there are exceptions for special events.

**Belle Vue Lounge:** Listen to old-time tunes on antique radios in this lounge near the lobby. In addition to beer, wine, and specialty drinks, there's a full bar.

**Jellyrolls:** Dueling pianos provide entertainment in a casual warehouse atmosphere. The cover charge is about $18 nightly (subject to change). You must be at least 21 to enter. Note that this place cranks the A.C. year-round.

**Leaping Horse Libations:** The carousel-themed pool bar at Luna Park serves a variety of cocktails, as well as soft drinks, sandwiches, and snacks.

**WHAT TO DO:** The three-quarter-mile pathway encircling Crescent Lake provides a ready venue for walkers and joggers. Guests may rent boats from the Yacht & Beach

## RESORT ROUNDUP

What's the best place to stay at Walt Disney World? It's a tough question—and one that Birnbaum editors are asked all the time. The answer? Well, it depends. Do you have a favorite park? What's your price range? Will a sea serpent's tongue that doubles as a pool slide make your day? All factors to consider. Here are our favorites in each of WDW's categories:

 **DELUXE**

**BoardWalk:** In addition to a picturesque setting, this resort is all about location. For starters, you can walk to EPCOT (and the Studios if you're feeling ambitious). Of course, you can always take a water taxi. You're a stone's throw from the more serene Yacht & Beach Club resorts, but get to enjoy the bustling excitement of the BoardWalk entertainment district. Strolls around Crescent Lake are soothing for the soul. Excellent dining options abound. The festive pool area is fun for all ages. And the Skyliner is a short walk away. In our opinion, BoardWalk is as Disney as it gets.

*Honorable mentions: Contemporary, Grand Floridian, and Polynesian Village*

 **MODERATE**

**Port Orleans Riverside:** One need not be an old-timey gazillionaire to live like one. Many of the guest buildings at this resort were designed to resemble sprawling historic mansions. There's a table-service restaurant and a cozy lounge (which may offer entertainment). The food court has a certain Southern charm. Kids enjoy dropping their hooks in the fishing hole (catch-and-release) and splashing in the free-form pool on Ol' Man Island. Pretty gardens and a relatively reasonable price add to the appeal.

*Honorable mention: Caribbean Beach Resort*

 **VALUE**

**Art of Animation:** This colorful WDW Value property has some of the boldest theming around and a top-notch food court—but what sets it apart is the splashy Big Blue Pool. The family suites, which fall under Disney's Moderate resort category, are a good value (during most times of year). We're particularly fond of the *Cars*-themed accommodations, but all areas get a happy thumbs-up. And having two bathrooms (in the suites) is a valuable bonus for most traveling parties. The resort is part of the Disney Skyliner transportation system, too.

*Honorable mention: All-Star Movies*

Club's Bayside Marina. The Fantasia Gardens Miniature Golf complex is nearby. At the resort, Ferris W. Eahlers Community Hall lends and rents equipment for recreational pursuits and hosts rainy day activities. Fishing excursions can be arranged. A resort entertainment schedule is available at the resort's Front Desk.

**Arcade:** Side Show Games Arcade has a small selection of interactive games.

**Surrey Biking:** A (strenuous) trip around Crescent Lake on a pedal-powered surrey bike (a canopied quadracycle) is also offered on the boardwalk. Bikes, which accommodate 2 or 4 people, rent for about $21.

**Health Club:** Muscles & Bustles health club has steam rooms, modern exercise machines, and circuit-training equipment. The health club is open 24 hours a day for BoardWalk resort guests.

**Midway Games:** This area on the BoardWalk's Wild-Wood Landing features games of luck and skill similar to those found along traditional boardwalks. There is a charge to play.

**Shopping:** The Screen Door General Store on the boardwalk is the source for basic necessities. It also stocks apparel, character merchandise, a small selection of groceries, dry goods, snacks, and beverages. Thimbles & Threads, also on the boardwalk, carries apparel for men and women. Wyland Galleries features marine and environmental art.

**Swimming:** The resort's swimming area, aka Luna Park, has a pool with a 200-foot slide, "Keister Coaster,"

patterned after a wooden roller coaster. BoardWalk has two unguarded pools. There are three whirlpool spas, one in each pool area.

**Tennis and Pickleball:** This resort sports two courts (with lights). Borrow equipment at Community Hall.

**TRANSPORTATION:** Guests travel to EPCOT and Disney's Hollywood Studios via boats or walkways. (It takes about 10 minutes to walk to International Gateway, EPCOT's back entrance and home to a Disney Skyliner station. The stroll to Disney's Hollywood Studios takes about 20 minutes. It's possible to travel to the Studios via the Skyliner, too.) Buses transport guests to the Magic Kingdom, Animal Kingdom, Typhoon Lagoon, Blizzard Beach, and Disney Springs. (A transfer may be required for the water parks.)

## DISNEY VACATION CLUB

Disney Vacation Club (DVC) grants members the convenience of flexible vacations from year to year, with the ability to choose when and where to visit, how long to stay, and the type of accommodation. It starts with the purchase of a real estate interest in a DVC property. For a one-time purchase price and annual dues, members can enjoy vacation stays at Aulani Resort & Spa (in Oahu, Hawaii); Bay Lake Tower at Contemporary resort, Animal Kingdom Villas, The Villas at Disney's Grand Floridian Resort & Spa, Old Key West Resort, Beach Club Villas, BoardWalk Villas, the Boulder Ridge Villas and Copper Creek Villas & Cascade Cabins at Disney's Wilderness Lodge (note that the Boulder Ridge Villas and the Copper Creek Villas & Cascade Cabins are separate DVC properties), The Cabins at Fort Wilderness Resort, Saratoga Springs Resort & Spa, the Polynesian Villas & Bungalows, and the Riviera resort at WDW; Disney's Vero Beach Resort in Florida; Disney's Hilton Head Island Resort in South Carolina; the Villas at Disney's Grand Californian Resort & Spa and the Disneyland Hotel's Discovery Tower in California; plus access to other destinations around the globe. Through Member Getaways, DVC members may also elect to stay at their choice of more than 500 resorts around the globe, including most Disney-owned-and-operated resorts and the Disney Cruise Line.

Disney's Vero Beach Resort is a two-hour drive from Walt Disney World. It has villa-type accommodations that are comparable to those at Disney's Old Key West Resort—with lush surroundings, the beach, and local sights. The close proximity makes it easy to tack a beach vacation onto a WDW visit.

Disney Vacation Club information centers may be found at each of the Walt Disney World resort hotels and theme parks. For additional information, call 800-800-9100, or visit *www.disneyvacationclub.com*.

# Disney Springs Area

## Port Orleans French Quarter

This 1,008-room resort invites comparisons to the historic French Quarter of New Orleans.

Starting at the entrance gate, with its wrought-iron portal and overgrown landscape, the appeal of the Delta City surrounds arriving guests. The entry drive leads to the heart of the "city," which is Port Orleans Square. The central building was based on a turn-of-the-20th-century mint. The Mint houses check-in facilities, a shop, food court, and an arcade. To reach Port Orleans French Quarter, call 407-934-5000. Details are subject to change.

**ROOMS:** The guestrooms are located in seven 3-story buildings (with elevators). Most rooms have two queen beds; some king-size beds are available. The rooms are a bit smaller than the standard rooms at the more expensive Walt Disney World hotels, but they are comfortable for a family of four. Buildings are brightly colored and have wrought-iron railings of varying designs. Connecting rooms may be requested but can't be guaranteed. The least expensive rooms overlook gardens or parking areas, and the most expensive rooms offer water views. All rooms have a coffeemaker (with coffee), mini fridge/beverage cooler, and free Wi-Fi.

**WHERE TO EAT:** A counter-service food court has several dining options. Disney Springs, and its plethora of eateries, is accessible by boat or bus.

**Sassagoula Floatworks & Food Factory:** A variety of specialty foods is available in this festive food court, including gumbo, jambalaya, burgers, pizza, ice cream, and assorted baked goods.

**Scat Cat's Club–Cafe:** Swing by between 7 A.M. and 11 P.M. for coffee drinks and treats such as Mickey-shaped beignets. On select evenings, the adjacent Scat Cat's Lounge features live jazz music.

**WHERE TO DRINK:** Scat Cat's Club Lounge is open nightly (and offers live jazz music Wednesday through Sunday nights), and Mardi Grogs pool bar serves a variety of cocktails, as well as soft drinks. Of course, there's always Disney Springs—a short boat (or bus) ride away. F.Y.I.: The boat service is known as the Sassagoula River Cruise.

PHOTO BY JILL SAFRO

**WHAT TO DO:** A themed pool is the highlight of the recreational opportunities here.

**Arcade:** South Quarter Games is located at Port Orleans Square. The arcade has a selection of state-of-the-art interactive games.

**Biking:** Bicycles and surrey bikes are available for rent at Port Orleans Riverside.

**Carriage Rides:** Refer to page 243 for details about horse-drawn carriage rides.

**Fishing:** Two-hour guided fishing excursions are available (*see Sports & Recreation*).

**Shopping:** Jackson Square Gifts & Desires, located at Port Orleans Square, features Disney character merchandise, clothing bearing the Port Orleans resort logo, and assorted sundries.

**Swimming:** A pool dubbed Doubloon Lagoon was built around a bright blue sea serpent. The waterslide is the mythical creature's tongue—kids love it. There's a whirlpool spa, too. Port Orleans French Quarter guests are also invited to swim in the pool at Ol' Man Island at Port Orleans Riverside.

**TRANSPORTATION:** Buses transport guests to the Magic Kingdom, EPCOT, Disney's Hollywood Studios, Animal Kingdom, Typhoon Lagoon, Blizzard Beach, and Disney Springs. (A transfer may be required for the water parks.) Small water taxis transport guests along the Sassagoula River to Disney Springs, too.

PHOTO BY JILL SAFRO

# Port Orleans Riverside

Here, the city feel of the French Quarter gives way to the rural South. The resort is divided into "parishes." Closest to the "city," guestrooms are found in Mansion homes; farther upriver are the Bayou guestrooms, with a more rustic feel. The phone number for the Port Orleans Riverside resort is 407-934-6000.

**ROOMS:** The 2,047 Mansion and Bayou rooms are of the same size, and most have two queen beds (some king-size beds are available); nearly 950 of the Bayou rooms have a bunk-size bed (recommended for kids under 9) as well. The Magnolia Bend Mansion rooms are in elegant manor homes with stately columns and grand staircases. The Bayou rooms are in rustic, weathered-wood buildings that are tucked among flora native to the area. Although all of the buildings have two to three floors, only the Magnolia Bend Mansions have elevators.

The Bayou guestrooms surround Ol' Man Island, a 3½-acre recreational area with a big pool, playground, and fishing hole. Decorative touches include wood floors, lantern lights, and a washboard sink. The closet space is not enclosed. The rooms are a bit small, but they can accommodate 4 to 5 guests (when the fifth guest is a small child). Rooms have a coffeemaker (with coffee), mini fridge/beverage cooler, and Wi-Fi (free).

More than 450 Riverside rooms invite guests to live like royalty. These "Royal Guest Rooms" have special touches inspired by several of Disney's animated classics (all featuring royalty of some sort), ornately decorated beds with fiber-optic special effects, artwork featuring Princess Tiana and other Disney royals, and more. If you want the royal treatment while residing at Port Orleans Riverside, make your wishes known when you book the room. Note that the rates for these rooms run higher than for standard rooms.

**WHERE TO EAT:** The hotel has a table service restaurant, food court, and pool bar.

**Boatwright's Dining Hall:** This 200-seat table-service eatery, located next to Riverside Mill, serves Cajun specialties and American fare for dinner. Reservations are recommended.

**Riverside Mill:** This food court resembles an old-timey cotton mill with a working waterwheel that powers the cotton press inside. The counter-service establishment offers all sorts of choices. The basic selections are available for breakfast. Lunch and dinner bring pizza, pasta, burgers, sandwiches, salads, soup, fries, pastries and other snacks, plus beer, wine, specialty coffees, and soft drinks. If you purchase a refillable resort mug, the Riverside Mill is where you'll do the refilling.

**WHERE TO DRINK:** Two lounges possess an enticing degree of charm.

**Muddy Rivers:** The poolside bar serves beer, wine, cocktails, soft drinks, sandwiches, salads, and snacks.

**River Roost:** Situated in a room designed as a cotton exchange, this lounge features a full bar and creative pub grub (including Mardi Gras fritters, and spinach and artichoke dip with cornbread crostini)—and lively performances from Yeeha Bob Wednesday through Saturday nights.

**WHAT TO DO:** A wealth of activities is offered at Ol' Man Island—a recreation center featuring a pool, whirlpool, wading pool, fountains, and a playground.

**Arcade:** The Medicine Show Arcade features a small selection of games.

**Biking:** Bicycles may be rented by the hour or the day.

**Carriage Rides:** Horse-drawn carriages take guests for 25-minute rides throughout the resort grounds. Carriages hold up to 4 adults or 2 adults and 3 small kids. Each trip departs from the Port Orleans Riverside marina. For reservations, visit *disneyworld.com*.

**Fishing:** Two-hour guided fishing excursions are available (turn to *Sports & Recreation* for details). It's also possible to drop a line at the Fishin' Hole on Ol' Man Island. Catch-and-release only.

**Playground:** An elaborate play area is located on Ol' Man Island next to the pool.

**Shopping:** Fulton's General Store sells Disney character merchandise, clothing, and sundries.

**Swimming:** In addition to the main pool and kiddie pool at Ol' Man Island, there are five unguarded pools (aka "quiet pools") at the resort. Guests may also swim in the Port Orleans French Quarter pool.

**TRANSPORTATION:** Buses go from Port Orleans Riverside to Magic Kingdom, EPCOT, Disney's Hollywood Studios, Animal Kingdom, Typhoon Lagoon, Blizzard Beach, and Disney Springs. Small water taxis ferry guests to and from Disney Springs. A walking path connects this resort with Port Orleans French Quarter.

# Saratoga Springs Resort & Spa

Just across the lake from the hustle and bustle of Disney Springs (reachable by bus, boat, or walkway), this DVC (Disney Vacation Club) resort is a calm complement to its nearest neighbor. Disney's Saratoga Springs Resort & Spa aspires to recapture the heyday of upstate New York country retreats of the late 1800s. The resort covers 65 acres—with some rooms nearly a mile from the main building. To contact Saratoga Springs, call 407-827-1100.

**ROOMS:** There are studios and villas with one, two, and three bedrooms. A studio is a room with a queen bed, a double-size pull-down bed, bathroom, kitchenette, microwave, and coffeemaker. All units have a porch or a balcony, access to laundry facilities, and free Wi-Fi.

One-bedroom villas have a king-size bed in the master bedroom, plus queen- and twin-size pull-down beds. The one bathroom has a deep-soak garden tub (with water jets). The full kitchen has a fridge, stove, toaster, microwave, coffeemaker, dinnerware, and dishwasher. Each unit has its own washer and dryer.

Two-bedroom villas at Saratoga Springs feature an additional bath and bedroom, with two queen beds or one queen and a double pull-down bed. The three-bedroom Grand Villa has similar features to the two-bedroom models, but is about twice the size and has four bathrooms (and no pull-down bed).

The resort's Treehouse Villas, elevated on pedestals and designed to blend into the woodsy environment, offer serene views of the surrounding treetops. Each "cabin-casual" villa has a full kitchen, TVs, three bedrooms, and two bathrooms, and sleeps up to nine.

**WHERE TO EAT:** There are three eateries here and dozens across the lake. BBQ areas are available to resort guests.

**The Artist's Palette:** Ostensibly set in a converted artist's loft, this spot offers all meals. Among the selections are salads, sandwiches, thin-crust pizzas, and baked goods.

**The Paddock Grill:** Set beside the Paddock pool, this walk-up window serves three meals a day.

**Turf Club Bar & Grill:** Dinner is served in this spot with a horse-racing motif. Patio dining is available.

**Groceries:** Grocery pick-up is available from the market section of The Artist's Palette. If you have a car, ask for directions to a nearby grocery store.

**WHERE TO DRINK:** In addition to local bars, guests may imbibe at nearby Disney Springs (accessible by Sassagoula River Cruise ferries or on foot).

**Backstretch Bar:** A seasonal, poolside drinkery.

**On the Rocks:** A poolside oasis with a full bar.

**The Paddock Grill:** This grill doubles as a bar. Handy!

**Turf Club Bar & Grill**: This spot serves a variety of beverages, plus snacks.

**WHAT TO DO:** Guests may rent bicycles, play basketball, swim, walk, swat tennis balls, shoot pool, and more. Be sure to pick up a resort entertainment schedule at the Front Desk.

**Arcade:** Expect to find the usual bells and whistles at Win, Place, or Show.

**Biking:** Bicycles may be rented from Horsing Around Rentals. (Kids under age 17 must wear bike helmets.)

**Golf:** The resort is adjacent to the Lake Buena Vista course. (Non-metal spikes are required.)

**Health Club:** This spot features strength and cardio machines and weight-lifting equipment.

**Playground:** There are two playgrounds and a splash zone at which little ones may frolic.

**Shopping:** The Artist's Palette stocks a nice variety of souvenirs and sundries.

**Spa:** The local spa traditionally offers massage therapy, manicures, facials, aromatherapy, and more. It was "on pause" at press time, but may re-open at any time. Check *disneyworld.com* for updates.

**Swimming:** High Rock Spring cascades down rugged rock work and feeds into a large free-form (heated) zero-depth-entry pool. The splash zone has a waterslide, two whirlpools, and a play area for kids. There are four unguarded pools, too.

**Tennis:** Two clay courts are available on a first-come, first-served basis from 9 A.M. to 10 P.M. Equipment may be borrowed from Horsing Around Rentals.

**TRANSPORTATION:** Buses go from the resort to all theme and water parks. (A transfer may be required for the water parks.) Boats ferry guests to Disney Springs (it's about 10 to 25 minutes on foot). The internal bus makes 7 stops throughout the Saratoga Springs resort. Buses arrive every 20 to 60 minutes (or more).

PHOTO BY JILL SAFRO

# Disney's Old Key West Resort

Escape to the spirit of the Florida Keys. Disney's Old Key West Resort is the original Disney Vacation Club property, but villas not occupied by members are available for nightly rental. It has the laid-back feel of a resort community and all the amenities that go with resort life. The homey, modern accommodations have lots of space and the convenience of kitchen facilities, making the resort nice for longer stays. The telephone number for Old Key West is 407-827-7700.

**VILLAS:** A studio consists of a large room with two queen-size beds, a table and chairs, a small fridge, free Wi-Fi, microwave, and sink. Bathrooms are spacious. Each of the one-bedroom villas has a king-size bed in the master bedroom and a queen-size sleeper sofa and a sleeper chair in the living room; the master bath has a whirlpool tub, sink, and shower.

The two-bedroom villa features a king-size bed in the master bedroom, two queen-size beds in the second bedroom, living room with queen-size sleeper sofa and TV with blu-ray player, free Wi-Fi, dining room, and a kitchen with a fridge, dishwasher, toaster, coffeemaker, plates, flatware, cooking utensils, and more.

The master bathroom is divided into two rooms with an extra-large whirlpool tub and a sink in one and an oversize shower, sink and vanity, and toilet in the other. There is a porch or balcony off the living room and bedroom, and ceiling fans in each room. The configuration of the two-story, three-bedroom Grand Villas is similar to that of the two-bedroom models, but adds a third bedroom with two double beds. As for capacity, studios sleep 4 and one-bedroom villas sleep 5 people; two-bedroom villas sleep 9 guests, and the two-story, three-bedroom villas accommodate 12.

**WHERE TO EAT:** In addition to the table-service restaurant known as Olivia's Cafe, there are grills and picnic tables. (Pick up supplies at Conch Flats General Store.)

**Good's Food to Go:** The perfect place to pick up breakfast sandwiches, Mickey waffles, and breakfast platters in the morning. Burgers, chicken strips, sandwiches, salads, ice cream, pastries, and other snacks are offered later in the day. Soft drinks, cold-brew coffee, cocktails, and (more than a dozen) beers are served.

**Olivia's Cafe:** This full-service restaurant serves Key West favorites, plus more traditional American fare, for brunch (from 7:30 A.M. to 2 P.M.) and dinner. Menus change seasonally. Reservations are recommended.

**WHERE TO DRINK:** The watering holes at Old Key West are as laid-back as they come.

**Gurgling Suitcase:** This tiny bar serves specialty drinks, wine, beer, soft drinks, plus lunch and dinner items.

**Turtle Shack:** This seasonal, poolside destination serves drinks, salads, sandwiches, and light snacks.

**WHAT TO DO:** At Conch Flats Community Hall, table tennis, board games, a large-screen TV, blu-ray rentals, and planned activities are offered. There are basketball, shuffleboard, and volleyball courts, and equipment is available at Hank's Rent 'N Return. Pick up a resort entertainment schedule at the Front Desk.

**Arcades:** O.K.W. boasts two arcades: Electric Eel Game Room and Flying Fish Game Room.

**Biking:** Bikes and surrey bikes may be rented from Hank's Rent 'N Return.

**Health Club:** The Fitness Center offers a nice variety of exercise equipment.

**Playground:** There are three kids' play areas located throughout the resort.

**Shopping:** Conch Flats General Store has groceries, character merch, sundries, and more.

**Swimming:** The main, guarded pool is located behind the Hospitality House. It features a 125-foot waterslide inside what appears to be a giant sandcastle. There is a whirlpool, a kiddie pool, and a sandy play area nearby. The resort has three unguarded pools.

**Tennis and Pickleball:** There are two lighted courts by the main pool, plus a third on Old Turtle Pond Road.

**TRANSPORTATION:** Buses go to the theme parks, water parks, and Disney Springs. (A transfer may be required for the water parks, depending on the season.) Build in a bit of extra time for bus travel. Water taxis also make the trip between the resort and Disney Springs.

# Animal Kingdom Area

## All-Star Movies, Music, & Sports

The All-Star resorts are among the most vividly themed at Walt Disney World. Each resort has 1,500 to 1,920 rooms housed in ten buildings devoted to five Disney movies, types of music, or sports.

The All-Star Movies resort celebrates Disney films: *Toy Story*, *The Mighty Ducks*, *Fantasia*, *101 Dalmatians*, and *The Love Bug*. Resort buildings are adorned with such icons as 40-foot Dalmatians and wildly oversize versions of Buzz Lightyear and Woody.

At the All-Star Music resort, Broadway, country, jazz, rock, and calypso are the themes. A walk-through, neon-lit jukebox; a three-story pair of cowboy boots; and a theater marquee are among the oversize icons.

Sports fans will find themselves in a world of tennis, baseball, football, surfing, or basketball at the All-Star Sports resort. Larger-than-life football helmets, surf-boards, tennis balls, basketball hoops, and baseball bats adorn the buildings.

As value resorts, the three All-Star properties offer relatively few frills, but the service and whimsical atmosphere are pure Disney.

Guests check in at Cinema Hall for All-Star Movies, Melody Hall for All-Star Music, or Stadium Hall for All-Star Sports. To reach All-Star Movies, call 407-939-7000; to phone All-Star Music, call 407-939-6000; to contact All-Star Sports, call 407-939-5000.

**ROOMS:** The guestrooms, measuring 260 square feet, are rather small compared with those at Port Orleans, which are 314 square feet. Most guestrooms have two

queen beds, a vanity area with a sink, a bathroom, free Wi-Fi, a small dresser, and a small table with chairs.

All-Star Music has 216 Family Suites. Each one sleeps up to six and has two bathrooms, a primary bedroom with a queen bed, a second bedroom with 2 queen beds (including a pull down queen bed that doubles as a dining table), Wi-Fi, and a kitchenette with mini fridge, sink, microwave, and coffeemaker (with coffee).

**WHERE TO EAT:** There are three food courts—World Premiere in Cinema Hall, Intermission in Melody Hall, and End Zone in Stadium Hall. Each features a bakery, grab-and-go items, and stations geared to pizza, pasta, salads, and burgers. The food courts feature seating areas with beverage bars.

**WHERE TO DRINK:** The convivial Silver Screen Spirits, Singing Spirits, and Grandstand Spirits pool bars serve drinks throughout the day and evening.

**WHAT TO DO:** Guests may swim in any of the All-Star resort pools. They may rent boating equipment at any Walt Disney World resort marina. Inquire about the recreation schedule at the Front Desk.

**Arcades:** Each of the All-Star resort hotels has its own arcade filled with classic and modern games.

**Playground:** A small playground can be found in each hotel's courtyard area.

**Shopping:** Maestro Mickey's in Melody Hall, Sport Goofy's Gifts and Sundries in Stadium Hall, and Donald's Double Feature in Cinema Hall each feature character merchandise, hats, shirts, pins, books, character items, snacks, and sundries.

**Swimming:** Each hotel has two pools and a kiddie pool. The main pool at All-Star Movies has a *Fantasia* theme (look for Sorcerer Mickey). The smaller Duck Pond Pool is based on *The Mighty Ducks*. At the All-Star Music resort, the Calypso Pool is in the form of a giant guitar, while the Piano Pool bears a striking resemblance to a grand piano. At All-Star Sports, Surfboard Bay has an ocean motif. The smaller Grand Slam Pool pays tribute to our national pastime.

**TRANSPORTATION:** Buses make pickups at the All-Star Resorts' Cinema Hall, Melody Hall, and Stadium Hall for trips to each of the theme parks, water parks, and Disney Springs.

# Disney's Animal Kingdom Lodge & Villas

At first glance, Disney's Animal Kingdom Lodge evokes images of a sleepy, little thatched-roof game lodge in the wilds of southern Africa. Upon closer examination, however, it's clear that the only things sleepy or little about this place are the small creatures that live in its shadow. Those animals, along with their more sizable cousins, inhabit acres of meticulously re-created African savanna that practically surround the resort. Birds and all manner of hoofed animals, including giraffes, zebras, and Thomson's gazelles, call the wildlife reserve home. With the freedom to wander within a dozen or so yards of the lodge itself, these enthralling critters allow guests to go on safari without leaving their balconies.

The resort is located about one mile from Disney's Animal Kingdom park (which is accessible by bus). The lobby is a huge, high-ceilinged room, richly appointed with colorful African artwork and artifacts. The biggest draw here is the four-story observation window overlooking the savanna. It's one of many portals through which to gaze upon wildlife.

Like the African game lodges on which it is based, Disney's Animal Kingdom Lodge was constructed using a semicircular design. From overhead, it looks a bit like a horseshoe. This allows for maximum animal-viewing potential. Indeed, a large number of the resort's guestrooms have direct views of the savanna areas. Be sure to specify your viewing preference when you book a room. The telephone number for Disney's Animal Kingdom Lodge is 407-938-3000.

**ROOMS:** The 972 rooms, which are notably smaller than those at other deluxe Disney resorts, feature dark-wood furniture, sand-colored walls, and laminated wood flooring. Deluxe rooms are a tad more spacious than their standard counterparts. Most rooms have two queen beds (some king beds are available) and sleep up to four people. All rooms have balconies. Suites include a parlor, plus one or two bedrooms; there are king-size or queen-size beds in the bedrooms. Bathrooms have a separate vanity area with double

PHOTO BY MIKE CARROLL

**Hot Tip!** Balloons are not allowed in outdoor areas (including balconies) at Disney's Animal Kingdom Lodge and Kidani Village—it's a safety issue for the animals.

sink. Rooms have hair dryer, free Wi-Fi, clothing steamer, and small fridge/beverage cooler. Club-Level service (aka "concierge") is available.

The Villas are located in Jambo House and in the Kidani Village, an area that features thatched-roof, hewn-timber homes. Also included in this village are a pool, modern fitness center, shop, table-service restaurant, and more. As with all Disney Vacation Club resort hotels, the villa homes are available to all guests when not being used by members. For information on this member of the Disney Vacation Club family, call 800-800-9100, or visit *www.disneyvacationclub.com*.

**WHERE TO EAT:** In addition to its eateries, Maji pool bar, Victoria Falls, and Sanaa Lounge serve tasty fare.

**Boma—Flavors of Africa:** Boma is modeled after a bustling African marketplace. The restaurant boasts many types of cuisine in what chefs describe as a "global fusion" style. Served buffet style, the cuisine is a marvelous mix of French, Malaysian, Indian, Chinese, and English.

**Jiko—The Cooking Place:** The colors of sunset are the backdrop for this reliable restaurant. Wines are from South Africa.

**The Mara:** A high-quality quick-service eatery, The Mara offers made-to-order flatbreads, South African veggie bowls, BBQ pork sandwiches, and salads, plus kid-pleasers such as burgers and chicken nuggets.

**Sanaa:** This Kidani Village star features African- and Indian-inspired cuisine.

**WHERE TO DRINK:** The lounges here are rustic and inviting. Some even offer the opportunity to sip beverages while observing wildlife. Note that Jambo House and Kidani Village are connected by bus service.

**Cape Town Lounge and Wine Bar:** Located inside Jiko—The Cooking Place, this spot features a selection of fine wines from South Africa.

**Maji and Uzima Springs:** These poolside bars serve specialty and traditional drinks.

**Sanaa:** A 24-seat lounge, inspired by African spice markets, is within the restaurant of the same name.

**Victoria Falls:** Set alongside a soothing waterfall, this mezzanine-level lounge offers appetizers, South African wines, beer, and assorted cocktails.

**WHAT TO DO:** Spying on African wildlife is the main event in these parts. However, if you can manage to pry yourself away from those hoofed exhibitionists for a bit, there are plenty of other diversions available—including tennis, basketball, shuffleboard, and a BBQ pavilion. Note that guests are welcome to partake in recreational activities offered at other Disney resort hotels, too. An Animal Kingdom Lodge entertainment schedule is available at the Front Desk (at Jambo House and Kidani Village).

**Arcades:** Pumbaa's Fun & Games and Safari So Good are both stocked with the latest games.

**Health Clubs:** The Zahanati Fitness Center, at Jambo House, has modern exercise equipment and a sauna. Kidani Village's Survival of the Fittest also offers state-of-the-art exercise equipment.

**Playground:** The Hakuna Matata playground is situated near the Uzima pool.

**Shopping:** The Zawadi Marketplace stocks Africa-themed gifts, Disney-character merchandise, clothing with the Animal Kingdom Lodge logo, and sundries. Johari Treasures tempts shoppers at Kidani Village.

**Swimming:** The resort's main pool, Uzima, is meant to resemble a watering hole. More impressive than the size of the zero-depth-entry pool, however, is the view from the pool deck. There is a kids' pool and two whirlpools nearby. Kidani Village is home to an additional swimming pool (Samawati Springs) and to Uwanja Camp, a watery playground.

**Tennis and Pickleball:** There are two courts at Kidani Village available to all Animal Kingdom Lodge guests.

**TRANSPORTATION:** Buses go to the Magic Kingdom (a 25- to 35-minute ride), EPCOT, Disney's Hollywood Studios, Animal Kingdom, Typhoon Lagoon, Blizzard Beach (a transfer may be required for the water parks), and Disney Springs. Buses arrive every 25 to 60 minutes.

# Coronado Springs

An oasis set on the shore of Lago Dorado, the resort celebrates the spirit of Spanish, Mexican, and South American explorers, artists, writers, and architects. There is a blend of classic influences, Disney touches, and modern comforts. The 2,400 rooms are found in four guest areas that stretch around Lago Dorado, a 22-acre lake. The striking 15-story Gran Destino Tower features a two-story lobby and a scenic rooftop eatery.

It can take 5 minutes or more to walk to the farthest rooms. (Many guests opt to use the bus that makes a loop around the resort.) There is an upscale food court and elaborately themed table service eateries. A convention center offers access to business services. The telephone number for Coronado Springs is 407-939-1000.

**ROOMS:** Standard rooms are a bit smaller than those at Disney's deluxe hotels, but adequate for up to four; each has two queen beds (some king-size beds are available). The sleek rooms are awash in shades of brown with the occasional splash of color and feature faux wood floors. Amenities include a coffeemaker, tiny fridge, mini safe, hair dryer, and free Wi-Fi. In the Casitas area, where many suites are located, terra-cotta guest buildings occupy a city-like landscape. In the pueblo-style Ranchos, scattered along a dry streambed, rooms have a rustic feel. Cabanas, located along the rocky palm-lined beach, reflect the casual feel of their namesake. There are Club-Level rooms in Gran Destino Tower.

**WHERE TO EAT:** In addition to four full-service restaurants and a food court, several resort lounges serve satisfying fare throughout the day.

**Cafe Rix:** A quick-service eatery, Rix has offerings for breakfast, lunch, and dinner.

**Maya Grill:** Open for dinner, Maya offers seafood, steak, and authentic Mexican dishes.

**El Mercado de Coronado:** This nontraditional food court feels like a cheery, open-air market.

**Rix Sports Bar & Grill:** This table-service spot serves three meals a day, and is in the main building.

**Three Bridges Bar & Grill:** Choose one of three bridges to reach this happy place built in the middle of Lago Dorado. Beer, wine, sangria, Spanish specialty coffees, and cocktails are served here, as is a full menu of solid sustenance with a Spanish flair.

**Toledo—Tapas, Steak, & Seafood:** Perched on the top of Gran Destino Tower, Toledo serves Latin-inspired cuisine and bird's-eye views of WDW.

**WHERE TO DRINK:** There are currently five places at which to wet your whistle at Coronado Springs.

**Barcelona Lounge:** This Gran Destino Tower lobby locale is a coffee house by day and artisanal cocktail bar by night.

**Dahlia Lounge:** Perched on the top of Gran Destino Tower, this vibrant zone serves beer, wine, cocktails, and small plates.

**Laguna Bar:** A lagoonside lounge outside the lobby, this spot serves drinks daily.

**Rix Sports Bar & Grill:** This spot offers a full bar, plus substantial grub.

**Siestas Cantina:** In the Dig Site area, this pool bar lets swimmers and archaeologists enjoy drinks and light fare (three meals a day).

**WHAT TO DO:** The resort has volleyball, a short nature trail, and other recreational diversions.

**Arcade:** Iguana Arcade is in the Dig Site area.

**Biking:** Rent bikes and surrey bikes at La Marina. Details are subject to change.

**La Vida Health Club—Massage, Salon & Fitness:** The fitness center offers strength and cardio equipment 24/7. Spa services such as massage and custom facials are available. And the salon provides hair-care services, beard and mustache trims, plus manicures and pedicures. Hours are usually about 6 A.M. until 9 P.M. To make an appointment, call 407-939-7727.

**Playground:** The Explorer's Playground, part of the Dig Site area, includes a sandbox, complete with Mayan carvings waiting to be excavated.

**Shopping:** Panchito's Gifts & Sundries is where to find souvenir items with a Southwestern flavor, Disney-themed merchandise, and necessities.

**Swimming:** The main pool is in the Dig Site recreation area. It surrounds a 50-foot Mayan pyramid and has a 123-foot waterslide. There's a 22-person hot tub (the largest one at WDW) and toddler pool in the Dig Site, too. The resort offers 3 unguarded pools.

**TRANSPORTATION:** Buses go to Magic Kingdom, EPCOT, Disney's Hollywood Studios, Disney's Animal Kingdom, Typhoon Lagoon, Blizzard Beach, and Disney Springs. (A transfer may be required for the water parks.)

# ESPN Wide World of Sports Area

## Pop Century

What do you get when you mix decades of American pop culture with a Disney resort? Pop Century! Like the All-Star resorts, Pop Century is a vivid celebration of Americana. The 2,880-room resort represents the second half of the twentieth century. The colorful resort's larger-than-life "time capsules" commemorate the toys, fads, dance crazes, and catchphrases that swept the nation from the 1950s through the 1990s. It's groovy . . . you dig?

As a Walt Disney World value resort, the Pop Century property offers few frills, but the service is good, the atmosphere's colorful, and the transportation is efficient. There's even a peaceful lake to stroll around on temperate days. (It's shared by Pop's next-door neighbor, Disney's Art of Animation resort.) Guests check in at Classic Hall, which also features a food and merchandise location, large arcade, and guest services desk. To contact Disney's Pop Century resort, call 407-938-4000.

**ROOMS:** Guestrooms measure 260 square feet (a bit smaller than Port Orleans' rooms, which are about 314 square feet). Each room has either a queen bed and a pull-down queen bed or one king bed, a vanity area with a sink, a bathroom, a small dresser, a table with chairs, a beverage station with a fridge, and free Wi-Fi.

**WHERE TO EAT:** The food court features a bakery and a convenience market, plus several stands geared to pizza, pasta, burgers, and more. Items of note: POP'ing pimento burgers, shrimp and grits, seared salmon, braised beef, honey BBQ pork sandwich, Greek salad with shrimp, and "POP goes bananas" cupcakes.

**WHERE TO DRINK:** Liquid refreshments are served at Petals, a bar located near the Hippy Dippy pool.

**WHAT TO DO:** Guests may swim in any of the Pop Century resort pools and enjoy a 1.4-mile walk or run around Hourglass Lake. Ask about the resort entertainment schedule at the Front Desk.

**Arcade:** Revisit classic video games or discover some new ones at Fast Forward arcade.

**Playground:** There is one soft-surface playground.

**Shopping:** The Everything Pop shop has a selection of toys, clothes, character merch, sundries, and snacks.

**Swimming:** The hotel has three pools (shaped like a bowling pin, computer, and a flower), plus a kiddie pool. (The Flower Power pool has flower-shaped water jets!)

**TRANSPORTATION:** Buses stop at Classic Hall for trips to Magic Kingdom and Animal Kingdom, plus Blizzard Beach, Typhoon Lagoon, and Disney Springs. (A transfer may be required for the water parks.) The Skyliner stops here, too. (The station is shared with Disney's Art of Animation resort.) The Skyliner stops at Hourglass Lake Station and flies to Disney's Hollywood Studios and EPCOT International Gateway. For details, see page 67 and visit *www.mydisneyexperience.com.*

# Disney's Art of Animation

The Walt Disney World resort landscape boasts a bright burst of color thanks to this vivid celebration of Disney animation. A crowd-pleasing Value resort, Disney's Art of Animation made its debut in 2012.

Pop Century's next-door neighbor (the two resorts share access to Hourglass Lake and the nearly 1.4-mile jogging path that surrounds it), Art of Animation sports colossal figures from classic animated films. It also has three themed pools, playgrounds, festive courtyards, a sizable arcade (one of the best at WDW), and a splash zone featuring everyone's favorite clownfish, Nemo. The resort also offers free Wi-Fi, laundry facilities, and dry cleaning (fees apply for the last two services).

## WDW RESORT FUN

Walt Disney World resort hotels are famous for their immersive theming and enviable proximity to the theme parks, but they can also be playgrounds in and of themselves. Recreation and relaxation opportunities abound, and many of them are complimentary for registered WDW resort guests. Here is a sampling of the possibilities:

- Sunrise yoga
- Games and dance parties at the pool
- Resort tours (i.e., "Jambo House Art Tour" at Animal Kingdom Lodge and "Wonders of the Lodge Art & Architecture Tour" at Wilderness Lodge)
- Trivia challenges
- Evening campfires (marshmallow roasting optional)
- Disney Movies Under the Stars
- Arts & crafts (fees may apply)

Activities vary from resort to resort (and month to month) and may be canceled due to inclement weather. For the lineup during your stay, request a Recreation Calendar when you check in.

**ROOMS:** The 864 standard rooms, which are housed in *The Little Mermaid*–themed buildings, sleep up to 4 and come with the usual amenities afforded to Walt Disney World's Value resorts (refer to pages 76–77 for details). Each measures 277 square feet and has a queen bed and a pull-down queen bed (some rooms have one king bed only), a vanity area with a sink, a bathroom with a tub or shower, a small dresser, a table with chairs, and free Wi-Fi. The 1,120 festive family suites (considered Moderate by Disney), which are themed to *Cars*, *Finding Nemo*, and *The Lion King*, feature 3 separate sleeping areas, accommodate up to 6 guests, and come with 2 TVs, a queen-size bed, double-size pull-down bed, and sleeper sofa. Each 565-square-foot suite has a living room, 2 bathrooms, and a kitchenette (with a small fridge/beverage cooler, microwave, and coffeemaker).

**WHERE TO EAT:** The brilliantly hued Landscape of Flavors food court features cooking stations serving burgers, chicken, sandwiches, pizza, pasta, and more. There are also sweet treats such as cookies, muffins, pastries, and cupcakes. It's open for breakfast, lunch, and dinner. There is a varied grab-and-go selection, too. Guests are welcome to pop over to the nearby Pop Century for a bite or a drink.

**WHERE TO DRINK:** The Drop Off bar is a full-service watering hole located near the Big Blue Pool.

**WHAT TO DO:** Guests may swim in any of the three Art of Animation resort pools, walk or jog around Hourglass Lake, play in the Pixel Play Arcade, and enjoy poolside activities such as bingo, trivia, dance parties, relays, and more.

**Arcade:** Pixel Play Arcade is in Animation Hall, across from Landscape of Flavors. You'll need to purchase a game card to play. Available to all WDW resort guests, the arcade is open round the clock. Boasting a wide variety of gaming diversions, Pixel Play is one of the best arcades at Walt Disney World.

**Jogging and Walking:** The resort is encircled by a scenic trail that's 1.38 miles long.

**Playground:** The Righteous Reef playground can be found in the middle of the Finding Nemo courtyard.

**Shopping:** The cheery Ink and Paint Shop stocks books, pins, character merchandise, Art of Animation resort–themed souvenirs, sundries, snacks, and more.

**Swimming:** The hotel has three pools: Flippin' Fins, Cozy Cone, and the ever-popular Big Blue Pool, plus a *Finding Nemo*–themed splash zone known as The Schoolyard Sprayground.

**TRANSPORTATION:** Buses stop at Animation Hall for trips to WDW theme parks, water parks, and Disney Springs. (A transfer may be required for the water parks.) The Disney Skyliner stops here, too. It connects guests with EPCOT, Disney's Hollywood Studios, Caribbean Beach resort, and the Riviera resort. For Disney Skyliner details, turn to page 67.

## CLUB-LEVEL DIGS

When selecting a Walt Disney World resort you'll find there is a lot to consider: proximity to the parks, recreational opportunities, restaurants, budget, and more. While there is a plethora of possibilities under that "more" umbrella, one of most enticing temptations is known as Club Level. It's a special room category offered at Coronado Springs (in Gran Destino Tower) and most of Disney's Deluxe resort hotels, including Animal Kingdom Lodge, Beach Club, BoardWalk, Grand Floridian, Contemporary, Polynesian Village, Saratoga Springs, Wilderness Lodge, and Yacht Club. Prices vary, but for (at least) an extra $150 to $300+ per night, Club Level provides a bevy of benefits. Among them: personalized check-in; turn-down service; itinerary planning assistance; personalized daily itineraries; access to the Club-Level lounge; newspapers in the aforementioned lounge; and more.

While specifics vary a bit from resort to resort, all Club-Level lounges serve early-morning coffee and tea, continental breakfast, afternoon snacks, dinnertime appetizers, and evening desserts and cordials. Soft drinks and alcoholic beverages are included. The offerings are more ample at some resorts (Board-Walk, Grand Floridian, and Contemporary spring to mind), but all usually have something for everyone in the party to enjoy. Board-Walk, Contemporary, and Polynesian Village offer fireworks views, too—with the Contemporary and Polynesian providing the most dramatic fireworks-viewing vistas.

With the exception of Grand Floridian and Contemporary (which have two lounges each), there is one Club-Level lounge at every participating resort. These pleasant rooms have a homey feel and are yours to enjoy until midnight of the day you check out of the resort.

Bottom line? Disney's Club-Level digs definitely fall into the "super splurge" category of vacation indulgences—certainly worth considering if budget allows. And depending on the size of your party and the amount of time you spend bonding with your resort, you may even save a few bucks. Note that details are subject to change. (Some Club-Level service was on pause at press time, but is expected to return.) For additional information, check the My Disney Experience mobile app or website or call 407-939-7777. All details are subject to change.

# Resorts near Disney Springs

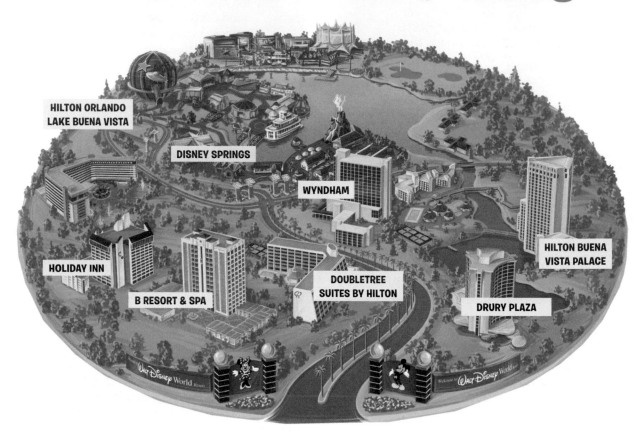

These hotels—DoubleTree Suites by Hilton, Wyndham, B Resort & Spa, Hilton Buena Vista Palace, Hilton Orlando Lake Buena Vista, Holiday Inn, and Drury Plaza Hotel Orlando—though inside WDW boundaries, are neither owned nor operated by Disney. However, a few have been here since 1971 or soon thereafter (under different names), accommodating Mickey enthusiasts from the get-go. The hotels are not Disney-themed, though some may offer meals hosted by Disney characters, many have Disney shops, and all boast Disney's "official" hotel status. For details, visit *disneyspringshotels.com*.

Often referred to as Disney Springs Resort Area Hotels, they line the mile-long Hotel Plaza Boulevard. The Hilton Buena Vista Palace and Wyndham are across from the Disney Springs Marketplace. The other four properties are about a 10- to 25- minute stroll away. Privileges of staying in one of these hotels may include:

• Guests who link their reservation to a valid park ticket via the *My Disney Experience* app or website may be able to enjoy Walt Disney World's "Resort Guest Early Entry" benefit in 2024. *We recommend checking with your hotel of choice to be sure*. All details are subject to change.

• Handy pedestrian bridges connect Hotel Plaza Blvd. with Disney Springs Marketplace at Disney Springs.

• Flexibility to book tickets for both on- and, in most cases, off–Walt Disney World property attractions.

• Preferred access to Disney golf courses.

• A "Passport to Savings" coupon book with discounts on dining, shopping, and entertainment.

• Advanced reservations for Disney restaurants.

• Shuttle service to the four theme parks (fees may apply). Be sure to allow extra time for travel. Note that buses load and unload in the middle of the parking lot at some of the parks.

Guests staying in the resorts on Hotel Plaza Boulevard have to pay to park at Disney theme parks ($25–$50) and they can't charge purchases made at Walt Disney World shops and restaurants with a resort ID—though they can buy MagicBands to link with tickets and make

Lightning Lane assignments via the My Disney Experience mobile app or website, or *disneyworld.com*.

At press time, Hotel Plaza Boulevard resort guests could book Individual Lightning Lane Attraction Selections (via WDW's à la carte attraction reservation system) starting at theme park opening times, along with all other guests. (See page 27 for details. Fees apply.) Specifics may change at any time. Check with the hotel itself or visit *mydisneyexperience.com* for updates.

To reserve a Disney Springs Area/Hotel Plaza Boulevard resort, go to *disneyspringshotels.com*, call the resort directly, or contact Walt Disney World Central Reservations (407-934-7639). These resorts are included in several Walt Disney Travel Company packages.

All of the following hotels offer accommodations for travelers with disabilities. To get to Hotel Plaza Boulevard from I-4, take Exit 68. For more information, visit *disneyspringshotels.com*. All details subject to change.

**Hot Tip!** Many of the resorts on Hotel Plaza Boulevard (in the Disney Springs Resort Area) offer discounts for seniors, members of the military, AAA members, and more. To learn about these discounts and other special offers, visit *disneyspringshotels.com/special-offers*.

**DOUBLETREE SUITES BY HILTON:** The only all-suite hotel in the Disney Springs area, the DoubleTree Suites by Hilton has a stellar staff, homey atmosphere, and low-slung facade reminiscent of WDW's Contemporary hotel. Upon check-in, guests receive the hotel chain's signature warm chocolate chip cookies. Each of the 229 roomy suites (625 square feet) has a separate living and sleeping room. Every living room features a sofa sleeper, a wet bar area with a small refrigerator, coffee-maker, and microwave, safe, and a small dining/work area. The one-bedroom suites sleep up to six people with either two queen beds or one king bed. Two bedroom suites are available.

Recreational facilities include a heated pool and whirlpool as well as a splash pad and playground for kids. For athletes, there is a fitness center, two lighted tennis courts, and a jogging trail. EverGreen Cafe offers a full breakfast buffet, plus lunch and dinner. The Reef Pool Side serves light meals and tropical poolside drinks. EverGreen Lounge serves beverages nightly. A lobby market provides snacks, drinks, and groceries. There is a Disney shop, too.

Rates range from $128 to $674. Self-parking costs $22 per day. The daily resort fee is $23 and includes additional amenities (inquire with the hotel). Double-Tree Suites by Hilton Disney Springs, 2305 Hotel Plaza Blvd., Lake Buena Vista, FL 32830; 407-934-1000 or 800-222-8733; *www.hilton.com*.

**WYNDHAM:** With a cheerful Bermuda-themed lobby, the Wyndham offers two distinct lodging opportunities: A 19-story tower with 232 rooms is known as Wyndham Lake Buena Vista, while the Wyndham Garden section features 394 rooms spread over two 5-story buildings. (Make your preference known when you make your reservation.) At Wyndham Lake Buena Vista, most rooms have two double beds, though 77 king-bed rooms are available. "Disney view rooms" overlook Disney Springs

PHOTO BY JILL SAFRO

and have distant views of theme park fireworks. At Wyndham Garden, rooms have two double beds or one king bed with standard, courtyard, pool, or lake view. All accommodations include a mini fridge, coffeemaker, premium Wi-Fi, TV, plush bedding, a safe, hair dryer, and iron (with board). Guests net a discount at many of the shops and eateries at nearby Disney Springs—safely and easily accessible via pedestrian bridge. The hotel provides scheduled shuttle transportation to all four WDW theme parks, too.

Extensive recreational facilities include an exercise room, a sand volleyball court, and a basketball court. The impressive Oasis Aquatic Playground features a heated pool with zero-depth-entry, interactive features such as water cannons, and a hot tub. There's a health club, arcade, and business center, too.

LakeView Restaurant (on the mezzanine level) serves a full American breakfast buffet daily. Sundial, which is open 'round the clock, has light fare and grab and go items. Joffrey's Coffee Shop offers pastries, hot breakfast sandwiches, and barista service. For craft brews, wine, cocktails, light bites, and soft drinks, head to the Eclipse Lounge or the poolside Oasis Restaurant and Bar.

Rates range from about $119 to $309 year-round. There is an additional daily resort fee of $34 for other amenities, plus a $28-per-day parking fee. Valet parking costs $28 per day. Wyndham, 1850 Hotel Plaza Blvd., Lake Buena Vista, FL 32830; 407-828-4444 (Wyndham Lake Buena Vista); 407-842-6644 for Wyndham Garden; *www.wyndhamlakebuenavista.com*.

**HILTON ORLANDO LAKE BUENA VISTA:** This hotel gets high marks for its 23 well-groomed acres, laid-back ambience,

PHOTO BY JILL SAFRO

pool area, and upscale shops. The 814 non-smoking rooms are outfitted with two queen or one king bed (suites are available for larger parties) and have mini-bars, voicemail, safes, and high-speed Internet access.

In addition to its two heated pools, whirlpool, and children's pool, the resort has a round-the-clock video arcade. There is a business center, too.

Among the resort's lineup of restaurants and lounges, Benihana Steakhouse and Sushi serves Japanese favorites (dinner only), plus entertainment; Covington Mill serves breakfast and lunch; for updates about restaurants at this hotel, go to *www.hiltonorlandoresort.com*. The menu at Rum Largo Poolside Bar and Cafe includes burgers, sandwiches, salads, and tropical beverages alfresco; Mainstreet Market is part deli, part country store (proudly serving Starbucks coffee). For light meals, snacks, or drinks, drop in at John Ts lounge. There is an Avis car rental location on the premises. And the popular Disney Springs shopping, dining, and entertainment district is a 5- to 10-minute walk away, across a handy pedestrian footbridge.

Recreational facilities include a fitness room and a large game room. Rates range from about $174 to $331; suites range from about $305 to $489. Self-parking costs $25 per day; valet parking costs $35 per day. There is a $35 per day resort fee. Hilton, 1751 Hotel Plaza Blvd., Lake Buena Vista, FL 32830; 407-827-4000 or 800-782-4414; *www.hiltonorlandoresort.com*.

**HOLIDAY INN:** This family-friendly hotel features 323 non-smoking rooms that have either one king or two queen beds. Some may be available with views of nearby Disney Springs. Guestrooms are decorated with modern touches and include a flat-screen TV with DirecTV, coffeemaker (with coffee), microwave, mini refrigerator, safe, and hair dryer. Bathrooms have granite countertops and feature Dove products. Free high-speed Wi-Fi is available in all guestrooms and restaurants, as well as in the lobby.

The Palm Breezes Restaurant, located in the atrium, serves three meals a day (kids age 11 and under eat free). Palm Breezes has a grab-and-go section and a bar. There is a zero-depth-entry heated swimming pool, a whirlpool spa, poolside sundeck, 24-hour fitness center, and a 24-hour game room. Laundry services are offered (fees apply). Parking charges apply for self and valet parking. There is an additional daily resort fee.

Rates range from approximately $109 to $272. Holiday Inn; 1805 Hotel Plaza Blvd., Lake Buena

Vista, FL 32830; 407-828-8888 or 888-465-4329; *www.hiorlando.com.*

**B RESORT & SPA:** A glitzy resident of Hotel Plaza Boulevard, B Resort & Spa pulls out all the modern stops in its 394 guestrooms and suites. Amenities include 47-inch high-def flat-screen TVs, bunk beds (in select rooms), in-room safe, beverage cooler, coffeemaker, iron (with board), and modern work station. Select rooms have sleeper sofas. Kitchenettes are available in the suites. Free wireless Internet service is available to all guests. The Kids' Zone has movie screenings and arcade games.

Resort guests may enjoy the outdoor, heated infinity-edge saltwater pool with interactive water features, the B Indulged full-service spa, and the 24-hour B Active fitness center. The American Kitchen Bar & Grill features "farm-to-table dining" and presents a salad bar on the back of a 1950s cherry-red Ford pickup truck that sits in the center of the restaurant. The Bar at American Kitchen, which offers happy hour from 5 P.M. to 7 P.M. daily, is open until midnight. The Pick-Up is a casual one-stop shop and ice cream parlor just off the lobby. It serves quick breakfasts, snacks, beverages, and, of course, ice cream. The hotel provides complimentary shuttle service to WDW theme parks (aka "B on the Move"). Details are subject to change.

Room and suite rates range from about $130 to $629. Self-parking is $24 per day; valet parking is about $30 per day. B Resort, 1905 Hotel Plaza Blvd., Lake Buena Vista, FL 32830. For information or to make reservations, visit *www.bresortlbv.com*, or call 407-828-2828 or 888-662-4683.

**HILTON BUENA VISTA PALACE:** The tallest hotel in the Disney Springs area and the largest of the resorts based at Hotel Plaza Boulevard (it's actually near the intersection of Hotel Plaza Boulevard and Buena Vista

## SHADES OF GREEN

Shades of Green is a recreational retreat for active and retired military personnel and their families, members of the reserves and the National Guard, and U.S. Department of Defense employees. This 586-room resort is near the Grand Floridian but is not linked with the monorail system.

The resort features two tennis courts, two pools, a small health club, restaurant, bar and lounge, gift shop, arcade, laundry facilities, and free transportation around WDW.

Room rates are based on military or civilian grade. Select multi-day tickets are offered at a discount. The property's three golf courses—the Palm, the Magnolia, and Oak Trail—are open to all Walt Disney World guests (see *Sports & Recreation* for details). All other activities are for hotel guests and their families only.

The phone number for the Shades of Green resort is 407-824-3400; *www.shadesofgreen.org.*

PHOTO BY JILL SAFRO

**Hot Tip!** The Hilton Buena Vista Palace is just a 5-minute walk from the Marketplace at Disney Springs. It is directly across the street, safely and easily accessed by an elevated pedestrian bridge. The bridge, which may be accessed by stairs or elevator, is stroller and wheelchair accessible.

Drive) is a cluster of towers set on 27 acres. The resort, which is also known as Hilton Orlando Buena Vista Palace, is quickly (and safely) connected to Disney Springs via pedestrian bridge.

Each of the 1,011 rooms has two queen beds or one king, a coffeemaker, 50-inch flat-screen TV, Wi-Fi, ceiling fan, and weekday newspaper in the lobby. Most rooms have a balcony or patio. In addition, there are 103 one- and two-bedroom suites and two-story penthouses with microwaves. Twin/queen sofa beds are in suites and rooms with king beds. Guestrooms have a small safe and mini fridge. Children's videos may be rented for in-room viewing.

The hotel also provides exclusive tee times to Walt Disney World golf courses, baggage storage, and a coin-operated guest laundry. Dining spots include the lakeside Letterpress restaurant, which serves brunch from 7 A.M. to 2 P.M. daily. Citrus 28 Grab N Go, open from 6 A.M. until midnight, features freshly prepared light meals, gourmet sandwiches, and snacks, plus drinks (including Starbucks coffee), free Wi-Fi, and a casual seating area; Sunnies Lobby Lounge offers appetizers, snacks, and cocktails from 4 P.M. until 11 P.M.; Shades Pool Bar & Restaurant serves burgers, fries, wraps, soft drinks, and libations; and the seasonal Blue Sports Bar offers liquid refreshments.

The resort's impressive recreation zone features a zero-depth-entry pool with lazy river Float Lagoon, a pool designated for grown-ups, and poolside food and beverage service. Pool cabanas may be rented. There's a 24-hour fitness center that includes accessible equipment for guests with disabilities.

Rates for most Buena Vista Palace rooms are generally about $190 and up per night (no charge for kids under 18); suites, which sleep four to eight, are $433 and up. Rollaway beds cost $35 per night; cribs are free. Hilton Buena Vista Palace, 1900 Buena Vista Dr., Lake Buena Vista, FL 32830; 407-827-2727 or 855-605-0316; *www.buenavistapalace.com*.

**DRURY PLAZA HOTEL ORLANDO:** The 604-room Drury Plaza Hotel is an exciting new addition to the Hotel Plaza Boulevard resort family. Queen and king rooms offer either two queen beds or one king and a small seating area. Two-room suites feature either two queens or one king bedroom separated by a door from the living area, which includes a pull-out queen sofa sleeper. Specialty guestrooms can include a terrace or views of the Magic Kingdom nightly fireworks show, Happily Ever After (a bit distant, but still enjoyable). Amenities include free Wi-Fi, 55-inch TV, coffeemaker, microwave, mini fridge, iron with board, in-room safe, and hair-dryer. A full hot breakfast is included each morning. (It's served on the hotel's second floor from 6:30 A.M. to 9:30 A.M. on weekdays and 7 A.M. to 10 A.M. on weekend mornings).

The Drury has a large saltwater pool, whirlpool, and splash pad (with water cannons!), as well as the Level Up Arcade. Dining options include the Kitchen + Bar and Restaurant in the lobby area, which offers drinks and light fare (plus lovely views of the lake) and Lakeside Bar & Grill, which can be found near the pool and serves appetizers, sandwiches, wraps, and drinks. Market Place is an area that sells Starbucks coffee, beer and wine, grab-and-go food and beverage items, and frozen treats. Pizza Hut Express (located inside the Market Place) has pizza, pasta, breadsticks, drinks, and more. And every day from 5:30 P.M. till 7 P.M., it's "Kickback" time on the second floor! That's when guests may enjoy dinnertime snacks and cold drinks at no additional charge. The menu varies from day to day, but guests may enjoy selections such as hot dogs, chili, pasta, salads, soups, sliders, meatballs, and chips with salsa and nacho cheese.

The hotel offers complimentary shuttle service to (and from) all four Walt Disney World theme parks. Parking is $25 a day (plus tax). Rates range from about $145 to $275. Drury Plaza Hotel Orlando, 2000 Hotel Plaza Blvd., Lake Buena Vista, FL 32830; 407-560-6111; *druryplazahotelorlando.com*.

# Four Seasons Orlando

Located on Dream Tree Boulevard (near Disney's Fort Wilderness Resort and Campground), this resort took up residence at Walt Disney World in 2014. The 443-room luxury property boasts more than 26 lakeside acres, as well as a multitude of recreational diversions and high convenience for Disney guests. Spanish Revival architecture reflects Florida's Golden Age mansions and is surrounded by a vibrant array of foliage. There is a business center, plus meeting space. Four Seasons Orlando resort is an AAA Five-Diamond award winner. For info or to make reservations, call 800-267-3046 or visit *www.fourseasons.com/orlando*.

**ROOMS:** All rooms have furnished balconies, one king or two queen beds, twice-daily housekeeping service, newspaper, 24-hour room service, and high speed Internet and standard Wi-Fi. Rooms also come with a safe, coffeemaker (with coffee), Bose bluetooth speakers, TV, and minibar. Accommodations feature marble bathrooms with double sinks and soaking tub, hair dryer, makeup mirrors, and a TV in the mirror. Hypoallergenic bedding is available on request. Cribs may be requested (no charge), as can high chairs, bottles, and toddler toys. Babysitting services may be arranged for an hourly fee (reservations must be made at least 2 weeks in advance).

The non-smoking resort has many rooms that are accessible for guests with disabilities. Make your needs known when you book the room.

Suites have king beds, two bathrooms, and a living area with a queen sleeper sofa. To book a room, call 800-267-3046. For suites (including Royal Suite, which can connect up to 9 bedrooms, and the Presidential Suite, which can connect up to 4), call 407-313-6734.

There's an on-site Disney Planning Center. When it comes to WDW privileges, the resort is similar to the Swan and Dolphin resorts. Among the perks:

• Guests who link their reservation to a valid park ticket via the My Disney Experience app or website can enjoy Walt Disney World's "Resort Guest Early Entry" benefit (see page 22).

• Disney characters may visit Ravello for the "Good Morning Breakfast" on Thursdays and Saturdays year-round (and on Tuesdays during school breaks and major holidays). Details are subject to change.

• Complimentary transportation to the four WDW theme parks may be provided by a Four Seasons luxury motor coach. (There are on-site vehicles to rent, too.)

At press time, Four Seasons Orlando guests could book Individual Lightning Lane Selections starting at theme park opening times, along with all other guests. (See page 27 for details on the system that allows folks to reserve same-day return times for select attractions. Fees apply.) Details are subject to change. For updates, check the My Disney Experience app or website.

**WHERE TO EAT:** There are 5 full-service eateries, a coffee bar, and 24-hour room service. Reservations are recommended for Capa and Ravello (call 407-313-6161).

**Capa:** This Michelin Star Spanish-style steakhouse specializes in prime cuts, tapas (small plates), and local seafood such as freshly shucked oysters. There is indoor and outdoor seating at this rooftop spot. The lofty perch also offers views of Happily Ever After, the Magic Kingdom's nightly fireworks spectacular.

**Lickety-Split:** Located just off the lobby, this is the perfect place for gourmet coffees and quick bites. All-day selections include sandwiches, salads, wraps, fruit cups, yogurt parfaits, gelato, and spirited drinks.

**PB&G:** Think fresh salads, grilled fish tacos, popcorn shrimp, burgers, spicy tuna poke, and crab cake sandwiches at this open-air eatery, located poolside (all seating is alfresco). Be sure to save room for a decadent dessert. Kids can choose a hot dog, mac & cheese, pizza, grilled cheese, turkey sandwich, or grilled fish.

**Plancha:** Located at the Tranquilo golf course, this lakeside restaurant serves a mix of American clubhouse favorites and Cuban-inspired dishes and drinks. Happy hour features appetizers, cocktails, and imported cigars. Brunch is offered on Sundays.

**Ravello:** In addition to regionally influenced specialties, this Michelin-starred restaurant serves pizza and house-made pasta. Two private dining rooms are available. Ravello is open for breakfast and dinner.

**WHERE TO DRINK:** Guests may quench their thirst and enjoy nibbles at a duo of lovely (and lively) lounges.

**Lobby Bar:** Drinks mix well with the appetizers, entrées, and desserts at this lounge.

**Capa Bar:** As you sip a beverage on the patio, you may also enjoy the Magic Kingdom's fireworks.

**WHAT TO DO:** The Explorer Island play province could be enjoyed for days on end. In addition to a swimmer's paradise, the island boasts volleyball and basketball courts, Ping-Pong, and more.

**Children's Program:** The resort's complimentary "Kids for All Seasons" program is open daily to youngsters ages 4 to 12. Check with the hotel for hours. Trained staffers supervise and entertain kids throughout the day. Little ones under the age of 4 are welcome to participate if accompanied by a guardian.

**Fun and Games:** The Mansion is a family-focused hangout with outdoor activities. The Hideout has video games, basketball hoops, and beach volleyball.

**Golf:** Golfers may argue that the resort's crowning glory is the Tranquilo course at Four Seasons Golf and Sports Club Orlando. The Tom Fazio–designed, 18-hole, 6,968-yard, par 71 course is a certified Audubon sanctuary with opportunities to view wildlife between swings. Amenities include a pro shop, golf instruction, driving range, putting green, club rental, and a restaurant. The course is exclusively available to hotel guests and members (fees apply). To reserve tee times, call 407-313-7777.

**Health Club:** The Fitness Center has cardio equipment and weights. Fitness classes are offered. Trainers are on hand, too (for a fee).

**Movies:** The resort presents alfresco films on select nights at the "dive-in" movie screen.

**Spa:** The Spa at Four Seasons evokes the peace and natural beauty of Florida's Everglades. The Zen zone features 18 treatment rooms, which include 6 couples suites (one of which is a bungalow for private retreats). The Salon offers hair-styling, manicures, pedicures, and more. There are packages for kids, too. For an appointment, visit *www.fourseasons.com/orlando/spa*.

**Swimming:** The resort's swimming areas are part of an enormous splashy play zone known as Explorer Island. The 5-acre pool complex features a zero-depth-entry pool and toddler slide, interactive splash zone, two water slides, and a lazy river. Plus there's a pool designated for the 21-and-over set. Cabanas are available for a fee.

**Tennis:** The resort sports three Har-Tru tennis courts for play and instruction (fees apply to both activities).

**Weddings:** From the rehearsal dinner to the ceremony, reception, and honeymoon, Four Seasons can accommodate wishes for most occasions. Call 407-313-6745, or visit *www.fourseasons.com/orlando/weddings*.

**TRANSPORTATION:** A complimentary bus goes to the Transportation and Ticket Center (TTC) every 30 minutes or longer (from there, guests take a ferry or monorail to the Magic Kingdom); buses go to EPCOT, Disney's Hollywood Studios, and Animal Kingdom once every hour. The resort staff recommends using a car service as the most efficient means of getting around Disney property and for traveling to and from the airport.

## GOOD NEIGHBOR HOTELS

With more than 450 hotels (and counting!), choosing Orlando-area accommodations can be a tad intimidating. Thanks to Disney's Good Neighbor policy, it doesn't have to be. In addition to the 30+ resorts within Walt Disney World's borders there's a subset of nearby hotels that are held to Disney's standards of service and excellence. Collectively known as Disney's Good Neighbor Hotels, each is expected to offer "value, convenience, and quality to every Central Florida visitor." In addition to Disney's coveted stamp of approval, every Good Neighbor property is AAA-approved, has a Guest Services desk to assist with Disney vacation planning and ticket purchases, and is comfortable, convenient, and relatively close to Walt Disney World.

Good Neighbor hotels include standard, premium, and suite accommodations, and are located within 2 to 14 miles of the House of Mouse. They range in price from value to deluxe, with many offering free breakfast, shuttles to Disney theme parks (fees may apply), and more than a few are pet-friendly.

You can book à la carte (room only) Good Neighbor digs by contacting the hotel itself, or reserve a vacation package via The Walt Disney Travel Company. (Packages include accommodations and theme park tickets, with pricing based on party size and travel dates.) For additional information about the Good Neighbor Hotel program, a complete listing of participating hotels, or to book a WDW Good Neighbor Hotel vacation package, visit *https://disneyworld.disney.go.com/resorts/more/*.

Two additional clusters of hotels also enjoy special status vis-à-vis Disney's certification: The Bonnet Creek Area "Official" Resorts and Flamingo Crossings Area "Gateway" Resorts. The properties under these banners share the qualities of Disney's Good Neighbor Hotels, as well as boasting enviable proximity to Walt Disney World itself. (See pages 115–117 for details.)

# Bonnet Creek Area Resorts

Bonnet Creek is a 70-acre development that borders Walt Disney World and is surrounded by a nature preserve. It's also home to a trio of Disney's "Official" hotels. As of October 1, 2022, guests of Signia by Hilton and Waldorf Astoria may enjoy Disney's Early Entry perk and may enter any WDW theme park (with valid admission *and* a park reservation) 30 minutes early each day. Each offers complimentary shuttle service to and from all four Disney theme parks and Disney Springs. For more information, or to purchase a vacation package, visit *disneyworld.disney.go.com/resorts/more/#/bonnetcreek-area/*, or call 407-939-5277. For accommodations-only reservations, contact the hotel itself. All details are subject to change.

**SIGNIA BY HILTON ORLANDO BONNET CREEK:** The Signia hotel offers deluxe guest rooms in marble and warm wood tones with either a king-size bed or two queen beds, a sitting area, and a workspace (with convenient outlets). Room views are of the pool, nature preserve, golf course, or Disney theme park. One- and two-bedroom suites are available. Amenities include a 55-inch television, in-room coffee and tea, premium bath and shower supplies, a safe suitable for laptop computers, iron (with board), mini-fridge, and Wi-Fi.

The family-friendly pool area has a lagoon-style pool, a lazy river, pool slide, and private cabanas. There is a 24-hour fitness center and a nearby spa.

There are 12 dining options, shared with its sister property, the Waldorf Astoria Orlando (see below). In-room dining is available from 6 A.M. until 11 P.M.

Room rates range from about $289 to $560, plus a $45 daily resort fee. On-site, self-parking also costs $48 per day. Signia by Hilton Orlando Bonnet Creek, 14100 Bonnet Creek Resort Lane, Orlando, FL 32821; 407-597-3600; *www.signiabyhiltonbonnetcreek.com*.

**WALDORF ASTORIA ORLANDO:** This hotel shares land with its sister property, the Signia by Hilton Orlando Bonnet Creek, mentioned above. The upscale hotel offers deluxe guest rooms with high-end furnishings and amenities. Rooms have either a king-size bed or two queen beds, a sitting area, and a spacious workspace. Bathrooms are outfitted with an Italian marble bath with glass shower, soaking tub, and luxury bath amenities. One-and two-bedroom suites are available, many with views of a golf course and nature preserve.

Amenities include a 55-inch TV, in-room coffee and tea, a safe (big enough for a laptop), bathrobes (to borrow), iron with board, mini-fridge, and Wi-Fi.

There are a dozen dining options, including the casual Harvest Bistro (which offers American comfort food), Aquamarine (drinks, burgers, and other poolside fare), Myth lobby bar, Oscar's Brasserie (breakfast), and three signature dining destinations: Zeta Asia, Bull and Bear, and La Luce. In-room dining is available from 6 A.M. to 11 P.M.

The swimming area has a zero-depth-entry pool and a hot tub. Private cabanas are available (fees apply). Guests at this resort may also enjoy the pool at the nearby Signia by Hilton Orlando Bonnet Creek. The Waldorf-Astoria 18-hole world championship golf course is on the premises (fees apply). There is a kids club and a 24-hour fitness center.

Rates range from about $609 to $1,436 per night, plus a daily resort fee of $45. Valet parking costs $48 per day. Waldorf Astoria Orlando FL, 14200 Bonnet Creek Resort Lane, Orlando, FL 32821; 407-597-5500; *www.waldorfastoriaorlando.com*.

**WYNDHAM GRAND ORLANDO RESORT BONNET CREEK:** Set on 62 acres, surrounded by woodland and a lake with jogging trails, the Wyndham's 400-room property offers deluxe rooms with either one king or two queen beds, and some rooms have bunk beds. Accommodations have Mediterranean-style furniture, contemporary accents, and modern amenities—including a 55-inch TV, coffeemaker, quartz countertops, safe, fridge, and iron (with board). Some rooms have balconies.

The resort features five pools, two lazy rivers, and a mini-golf course. The 5,700-square-foot Blue Harmony Spa offers full- and half-day spa packages.

Dining options include the upscale Deep Blu Seafood Grille & Sushi, Bar 1521, Back Bay Bar and Grill (which overlooks the 10-acre lake), the family-friendly Tesoro Cove (which serves a hot breakfast buffet), and The Barista (serving Starbucks coffee).

Room rates range from about $289 to $560, plus a $38 daily resort fee. Self-parking costs $29 per day; valet parking costs $38 per day. The hotel offers complimentary, scheduled shuttle service to area attractions. Wyndham Grand Orlando Resort Bonnet Creek, 14651 Chelonia Parkway, Orlando, FL 32821; 407-390-2300; *www.wyndhamgrandorlando.com*.

# Flamingo Crossings Area Resorts

Flamingo Crossings is the moniker attached to a new commercial district located by the western edge of Walt Disney World property. The expansive area was designed around a retail village and features a variety of casual dining spots and several of Walt Disney World's official "Gateway Hotels." For more information or to book a travel package, go to *disneyworld.disney.go.com/resorts/more/#/flamingo-crossings-area,* call 407-939-5277 (between 7 A.M. and 11 P.M. Eastern time), or contact the hotel itself.

## SUITE HOTELS

**FAIRFIELD INN & SUITES BY MARRIOTT ORLANDO:** With 228 rooms and 48 suites, Fairfield can easily accommodate parties of varying sizes. Basic studio rooms feature either one king (which sleeps 2), or two queen beds (which accommodates 4). Suites offer either one king or two queen beds and a sofa bed (the former suite setup sleeps up to 4, the latter 6). There is room for one crib, too.

Crisp, minimalist décor throughout the hotel has shades of blue, white, and various earth tones. Each unit is equipped with a mini fridge, 55-inch TV, iron (with board), and a microwave. The hotel offers free high-speed Wi-Fi in all rooms and public areas, plus a business center and laundry facilities (fees apply).

The Fairfield's heated resort-style pool is accompanied by a splash pad. The poolside Flying Flamingo serves up appetizers and light fare. There are batting cages, one basketball court, and a soccer field, as well as a fitness center.

This hotel also offers free self-parking and complimentary breakfast daily (bonus)! There is no shuttle service to Walt Disney World destinations, but car services and taxis serve the area (fees apply). Room rates range from about $160 to $277. Fairfield Inn & Suites Orlando, 631 Flagler Ave., Winter Garden, FL 34787; 407-993-9200; *www.marriott.com.*

**RESIDENCE INN BY MARRIOTT:** This sleek property offers 224 spacious studio, one- and two-bedroom suites in shades of beige and brown. All accommodations have separate living and sleeping areas (and have room for one crib), plus a fully equipped kitchen. Each unit is equipped with a mini fridge, 55-inch LCD TV, iron (with board), and hair dryer. Free high-speed Wi-Fi is available in all rooms and public areas. There is a business center and laundry facilities (fees apply).

Days here begin with the best kind of breakfast: complimentary! In addition to the hot breakfast, dining options include a lobby bar (for drinks and appetizers) and Featherstone's—a poolside locale with offerings such as tropical drinks and hot food items.

There is a heated swimming pool and a cozy area with comfy seating around a fire pit. There are batting cages, a basketball court, plus a fitness center.

There is no shuttle service to Walt Disney World or other destinations, but car services and taxis serve the area (fees apply). Room rates range from about $186 to $324. On-site parking is free of charge. Pets are accepted for a fee. Residence Inn by Marriott, 2111 Flagler Avenue, Winter Garden, FL 34787; 407-993-3233; *www.marriott.com.*

**TOWNEPLACE SUITES BY MARRIOTT ORLANDO:** Designed to feel homey, the hotel offers 250 well-appointed suites. All feature either two queen or one king bed, sofa beds, fully equipped kitchens, living area, smart TV, free high-speed Wi-Fi, and a customizable closet system (with room for one crib). Some suites have views of Walt Disney World fireworks. Complimentary hot and cold buffet breakfast is included. Handy items such as slow cookers, blenders, and board games may be borrowed throughout your stay.

In addition to the free breakfast, paid dining options include Flamingo's Bar & Grille for indoor and outdoor casual dining featuring burgers, sandwiches, and pizza. Flamingo's Coffee Bar features Starbucks coffee. The hotel also has a mini-market for snacks and sundries.

Among the assorted amenities this hotel shares with the neighboring SpringHill Suites are a resort-style swimming pool, game room, 24-hour fitness center, picnic pavilion, and outdoor grills.

Rates range from about $125 to $293. Pets are permitted (for a fee). On-site self-parking is free. Round-trip shuttle service to Walt Disney World costs about $5 (plus tax) per person, per trip. Car services and taxis serve the area, too (fees apply). TownePlace Suites Orlando, 13295 Hartzog Rd., Winter Garden, Florida 34787; 407-507-1300; *www.marriott.com*.

**HOMEWOOD SUITES BY HILTON:** Offering upscale accommodations, this 229-room hotel features studio suites in neutral tones with one king bed, or one-bedroom suites with either two queen beds or one king. All have a full kitchen with stove top, microwave, coffeemaker, dishwasher, and full-sized fridge. All units come with a 42-inch TV, easy-to-program alarm clock, dining table, and more. There's free Wi-Fi in all rooms and common areas. The hot, daily breakfast buffet is complimentary, too.

Recreational facilities are shared with its next-door neighbor, Home2 Suites by Hilton. The outdoor pool area boasts a large water slide and a kiddie pool. There's a fitness center and sports courts (including a basketball court, soccer field, and batting cage), as well as an on-site laundry. This is a pet-friendly hotel (fees apply). A shuttle provides transportation to and from select theme parks (for a fee). Guests enjoy sips and snacks at the lobby bar and The Bent Bill pool bar.

Rates range from about $118 to about $259 per night. On-site self-parking is free. Homewood Suites by Hilton, 411 Flagler Ave., Winter Garden, Florida, 34787; 407-993-3011; *www.hilton.com*.

## MODERATE HOTELS

**SPRINGHILL SUITES BY MARRIOTT ORLANDO:** This 248-suite hotel features suites in teal and golden tones that have either two queen or one king bed and a sofa bed, a desk, a spacious closet, and smart TV. All suites have a mini-fridge, microwave, coffeemaker, and free high-speed Wi-Fi. Some suites have views of Walt Disney World fireworks. Breakfast is complimentary.

Among the amenities shared with SpringHill Suites are a resort-style pool, game room, 24-hour fitness center, picnic pavilion, table tennis, practice field, and outdoor grills.

Dining options include Flamingo's Bar & Grille for indoor and outdoor casual dining. (The full-service spot offers burgers, sandwiches, and pizza.) Flamingo's Coffee Bar brews Starbucks coffee. The hotel features a mini-market for snacks and sundries, too.

Pets are not allowed at this hotel. Room rates range from about $125 to $232. On-site self-parking is available free of charge. Round-trip shuttle service to Walt Disney World costs about $5 (plus tax) per person, per trip. SpringHill Suites Orlando, 13279 Hartzog Rd., Winter Garden, Florida 34787; 407-507-1200; *www.marriott.com*.

**HOME2 SUITES BY HILTON ORLANDO:** A 272-unit hotel, Home2 Suites is a nice choice for an extended-stay. Its selection of spacious, modern suites include those of the studio, 1-bedroom, and 2-bedroom variety. Studios have either one king bed or two queen-size beds; 1-bedroom suites feature one king bed; and 2-bedroom suites have one queen and one king. All suites have sofa beds and sport a southwestern feel in hues of burnt oranges, blues, deep plums, and earth tones. Confirmed connected rooms are a possibility (based on availability).

Accommodations feature two 40-inch TVs, and a kitchen with a microwave, coffeemaker, dishwasher, and a full-sized fridge. (Induction burner cooktops are available from the front desk.) There are outdoor grills, too. Other amenities include a hair dryer, iron (with board), and a radio alarm clock. Free Wi-Fi is available in-room and in the lobby. There is a complimentary breakfast buffet, plus a lobby bar, and a pool bar.

Recreational facilities are shared with its neighbor, Homewood Suites by Hilton. There's a pool area with a waterslide and kiddie pool; a fitness center; and sports courts (including basketball and soccer). The hotel is pet-friendly (fees apply). Shuttles provide transportation to and from select theme parks (for a fee).

Rates range from about $140 to $312. On-site self-parking (in an attached garage) is free. Home2 Suites by Hilton, 341 Flagler Ave, Winter Garden, Florida, 34787; 407-993-3999; *www.hilton.com*.

# Where in the World?

All of the photos on this page were taken at Walt Disney World resorts! Do you know where? We challenge you to find all the spots where these images were shot and snap a (non-flash) photo for yourself as you discover each one. Happy hunting! (For locations, turn to page 364.)

# MAGIC KINGDOM

The Magic Kingdom is the most enchanting part of the World. Few who visit it are disappointed, and even the most blasé travelers manage a smile. The sight of the soaring spires of Cinderella Castle, the gleaming woodwork of the Main Street shops, and the crescendo of music that follows the parades never fail to have an effect. Even when the crowds are large and the weather is hot, a visitor who has toured this wonderland dozens of times can still look around and think how satisfying this place is for the spirit.

What makes the Magic Kingdom truly timeless is its combination of the classic and the futuristic. Both childhood favorites and space-age concepts have a home here. Every "land" has a theme, carried through from the costumes worn by the hosts and hostesses and the food served in the restaurants to the merchandise sold in the shops, and even the design of the trash cans. Thousands of details contribute to the overall effect, and recognizing these touches makes any visit more enjoyable.

But the delight most guests experience upon first glimpse of the Magic Kingdom can disappear when disorientation sets in. There are so many bends to every pathway, so many sights and sounds clamoring for attention, it's too easy to wander aimlessly and miss the best the Magic Kingdom has to offer. So we earnestly suggest that you study this chapter before the start of your visit.

> "Here you leave today—and visit the worlds of yesterday, tomorrow, and fantasy."
>
> **—Walt Disney**

# MAGIC KINGDOM

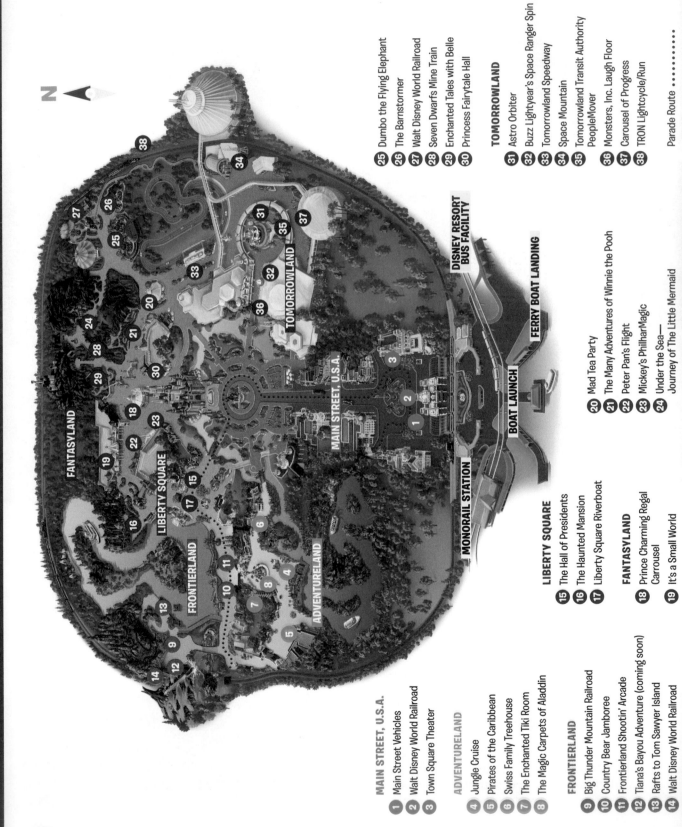

N

**MAIN STREET, U.S.A.**
1  Main Street Vehicles
2  Walt Disney World Railroad
3  Town Square Theater

**ADVENTURELAND**
4  Jungle Cruise
5  Pirates of the Caribbean
6  Swiss Family Treehouse
7  The Enchanted Tiki Room
8  The Magic Carpets of Aladdin

**FRONTIERLAND**
9   Big Thunder Mountain Railroad
10  Country Bear Jamboree
11  Frontierland Shootin' Arcade
12  Tiana's Bayou Adventure (coming soon)
13  Rafts to Tom Sawyer Island
14  Walt Disney World Railroad

**LIBERTY SQUARE**
15  The Hall of Presidents
16  The Haunted Mansion
17  Liberty Square Riverboat

**FANTASYLAND**
18  Prince Charming Regal Carrousel
19  It's a Small World
20  Mad Tea Party
21  The Many Adventures of Winnie the Pooh
22  Peter Pan's Flight
23  Mickey's PhilharMagic
24  Under the Sea—Journey of The Little Mermaid
25  Dumbo the Flying Elephant
26  The Barnstormer
27  Walt Disney World Railroad
28  Seven Dwarfs Mine Train
29  Enchanted Tales with Belle
30  Princess Fairytale Hall

**TOMORROWLAND**
31  Astro Orbiter
32  Buzz Lightyear's Space Ranger Spin
33  Tomorrowland Speedway
34  Space Mountain
35  Tomorrowland Transit Authority PeopleMover
36  Monsters, Inc. Laugh Floor
37  Carousel of Progress
38  TRON Lightcycle/Run

Parade Route ••••••••

DISNEY RESORT BUS FACILITY
MONORAIL STATION
BOAT LAUNCH
FERRY BOAT LANDING

# Getting Oriented

When you visit Walt Disney World's original theme park, it's vital to know the lay of the "lands." The Magic Kingdom has six themed lands — Main Street, U.S.A.; Adventureland; Frontierland; Liberty Square; Fantasyland (including the Storybook Circus neighborhood); and Tomorrowland. Main Street, U.S.A., begins at Town Square, located just inside the park gates, and runs directly to Cinderella Castle. The area in front of the castle is known as the Central Plaza or the Hub. Bridges over the waterways here serve as passages to each of the park's themed lands.

As you enter the Hub, the first bridge on your left goes to Adventureland; the next, to Liberty Square and Frontierland. On your right, the first bridge heads to Tomorrowland; the second bridge, to Fantasyland. The end points of the pathways leading to the lands are linked by a street that's roughly circular, so that the layout of the park resembles a wheel.

Complimentary park guidemaps are available at the entrance, at City Hall in Town Square, and at some shops. You will find them to be valuable navigational and scheduling resources.

## HOW TO GET THERE

Take Exit 64B off I-4. Continue about four miles to the Auto Plaza and park; walk or take a tram to the main entrance complex, known as the Transportation and Ticket Center (TTC). Choose a ten-minute ferry ride or a slightly shorter trip by monorail for the last leg of an anticipation-filled journey.

By WDW Transportation: From Grand Floridian and Polynesian Village: monorail, boat, or pedestrian walkway. From Contemporary: monorail or walkway. (It's roughly a 7- to 12-minute stroll, depending on the pace.) From EPCOT: monorail to the Transportation and Ticket Center (TTC), then transfer to the Magic Kingdom monorail or ferry boat. (If the monorail isn't operating, bus transportation will be available.) From Disney's Animal Kingdom and Disney's Hollywood Studios: bus. From the resorts on Hotel Plaza Boulevard: bus to the TTC, then transfer to a monorail or ferry. From Fort Wilderness Resort & Campground: boat (aka water taxi) or bus. From Wilderness Lodge: boat or bus. From Disney Springs: bus to any WDW resort and transfer to the Magic Kingdom–bound bus (or the monorail). From all other Walt Disney World resorts: buses (aka motor coach).

## PARKING

All-day car parking at Magic Kingdom starts at $25 for day visitors (free for Walt Disney World resort guests with a valid resort ID or an annual pass; trucks, trailers, and RVs cost more; preferred parking starts at $45–$50). Bear left after passing through the Auto Plaza; attendants will direct you into a lot. Several preferred lots are within walking distance of the Transportation and Ticket Center; all others are served by trams.

Note the section and aisle in which you park. (Write it down and use the Car Locater feature in the My Disney Experience mobile app.) Keep the receipt—it allows for re-entry to the parking area throughout the day, plus parking at WDW's other theme parks.

## HOURS

The Magic Kingdom park is generally open from about 9 A.M. to about 9 P.M. However, during busy seasons, it's open later. It's best to arrive up to an hour before opening time. Guests may be allowed to wander about Main Street, U.S.A., before the rest of the park opens for the day. It's possible to shop and grab breakfast before Let the Magic Begin—the live Castle stage show that kicks off each day.

Note that on select days, Magic Kingdom may offer after-hours "special ticket" events such as Mickey's Not So Scary Halloween Party, Mickey's Very Merry Christmas Party, and more. The park tends to be a bit more crowded on such days, so plan accordingly.

## GETTING AROUND

Horseless carriages, horse-drawn trolleys, and a fire engine have taken turns offering one-way trips up and down Main Street, U.S.A. (during non-peak hours) for more than half a century. Walt Disney World Railroad steam trains have made a 20-minute loop of the park, stopping to pick up and drop off passengers at stations at Main Street, U.S.A., Frontierland, and the Storybook Circus area of Fantasyland. You can expect to do quite a bit of walking during a Magic Kingdom visit—wear comfy shoes.

# Park Primer

### BABY FACILITIES

The best place in the Magic Kingdom to take care of little ones' needs is the Baby Care Center. This cheery site, equipped with changing tables and facilities for nursing mothers, is next to the Crystal Palace eatery. Disposable diapers are for sale at the Baby Care Center (if possible, bring your own—the packages are small and a tad on the pricey side). All park restrooms are equipped with changing facilities.

### DISABILITY INFORMATION

Most shops and restaurants, and many attractions, are accessible to guests using wheelchairs. Additional services are available for guests with visual or hearing disabilities. The (free) Guide for Guests with Disabilities provides an overview of services, including transportation, parking, and attraction access. You can get one at the park entrance or at City Hall on Main Street. For more information, see the "Travelers with Disabilities" section of the *Getting Ready to Go* chapter.

### FERRY VERSUS MONORAIL

For guests arriving by car or bus, it's necessary to decide whether to travel to the Magic Kingdom by ferry or monorail. The monorail usually makes the trip from the Transportation and Ticket Center (aka TTC) in about 7 to 10 minutes, while the ferry takes about 10. On busy days, the ferry may get you there faster (long lines can form at the monorail, and most people don't make the short walk to the ferry landing). Guests who use wheelchairs should note that while the monorail platforms are accessible, the ramp leading to the boarding area is a bit on the steep side, prompting many guests to opt for the ferry.

### FIRST AID

Licensed care providers tend minor medical problems at the First Aid Center during regular park hours. If

you have medicine that requires refrigeration, the Center will store it for you. (Medication must be in its original container and clearly labeled.) Containers can be provided for the safe disposal of hypodermic needles. If you have other special needs or concerns, please contact Disability Services at *disability.services @disneyparks.com*, or 407-560-2547.

The park's First Aid Center is between the Crystal Palace and Casey's Corner restaurants, just off Main Street. ***For a medical emergency, call 911 from any phone and alert a cast member (park worker).***

### INFORMATION

City Hall, just inside the park entrance, serves as the Magic Kingdom's information headquarters. Guest Relations reps can answer questions and help with MagicBands. Park guidemaps are also available there. Should you have any problems with a park ticket or a question about the number of unused days left on your ticket, City Hall is a good place to go. Another go-to source for park information such as parade times, show schedules, character appearances, restaurant availability, and attraction standby wait times is the My Disney Experience app or website.

### LOCKERS

Unattended lockers are located just inside the park entrance, all the way to the right. Standard lockers cost $10 per day; large lockers run $12 per day; and jumbo lockers cost $15 per day. Park-hoppers take note: Locker rental is not transferable from park to park—if you hop from Magic Kingdom to another Disney theme park, you'll need to rent another locker at your new destination.

### LOST & FOUND

While in the park, report lost items at City Hall on Main Street and/or complete a form at *disneyworld .disney.go.com/guest-services/lost-and-found*. After your visit, go to the aforementioned website.

### LOST CHILDREN

Report lost youngsters at City Hall or the Baby Care Center, and alert the nearest Disney employee to the problem. To expedite reunions, supply kids with a copy of your mobile number before you visit the park.

**Hot Tip!** Some shows and attractions keep shorter hours than the Magic Kingdom itself (e.g., The Enchanted Tiki Room, Country Bear Jamboree, and Tom Sawyer Island). To make sure you catch your favorites, check a Tip Board in the park or use the (free) My Disney Experience app.

## MONEY MATTERS

Magic Kingdom park has several automated teller machines (ATMs): at City Hall on Main Street, U.S.A.; near the Frontier Shootin' Arcade; by the Space Mountain exit; and near Pinocchio Village Haus. Most types of foreign currency can be exchanged at City Hall on Main Street, U.S.A. (amounts are limited).

Credit cards (American Express, Visa, MasterCard, JCB, Discover Card, and Diner's Club) are accepted as payment for admission, merchandise, and at most dining locations. Disney gift cards are accepted at most places, as are MagicBands and resort ID cards held by guests registered at select Walt Disney World resorts (backed up with a major credit card).

## PARK RULES

To ensure a comfortable, safe, and enjoyable experience for all, visitors are asked to comply with all Park Rules, signs, and instructions including:

- All bags are subject to inspection.
- Guests are subject to screening via wand and/or metal detector.
- Proper attire is required.
- Smoking (including e-cigarettes and vaping) is not permitted in any Disney park. Marijuana smoking and Marijuana-enriched products are prohibited.
- Selfie sticks are not permitted in Disney parks.
- All weapons (including toys) are prohibited.

For additional information and a complete listing of Disney Park Rules, visit Guest Relations, or go to *disneyworld.com/ParkRules*.

## SAME-DAY RE-ENTRY

Wear your MagicBand if you used it for admission or retain your ticket if you leave the Magic Kingdom and plan to return to it later the same day.

## SECURITY CHECK

All guests entering the Magic Kingdom are subject to a thorough security check, including metal detector screening. In addition, backpacks, parcels, handbags, etc., may be searched by security personnel before guests may pass through the entrance.

## STROLLERS & WHEELCHAIRS

Wheelchair Rental, located just inside the entrance, all the way to the right, offers wheelchairs (some oversized) and Electric Conveyance Vehicles (ECVs). Strollers are available under the Main Street Train Station. The cost for single strollers is $15 per day

 **Hot Tip!** Will you need a stroller during your visit? Consider bringing one from home. It will save you money, and can be used all over WDW. (Walt Disney World strollers may not be removed from the parks in which they are rented.) Chances are your baby buggy is a lot more comfy than the ones in the theme parks, too—they are made of hard plastic. If your stroller is too cumbersome for travel, you may want to invest in a lightweight, inexpensive "umbrella"-style pram, or renting from ScooterBug (the company authorized to deliver to and from all Walt Disney World resorts).

($13 per day with a multi-day rental); double strollers cost $31 per day ($27 a day with a multi-day rental); wheelchairs are $12 per day, $10 with a multi-day rental; $50 per day for ECVs, plus a $20 refundable deposit. Quantities are limited. Be sure to hold on to your receipt (and store it in a safe, dry place); it can be used on the same day for a replacement stroller or wheelchair at any of the theme parks. Multi-day rentals, called Length of Stay tickets, net you a bit of a discount on the daily price.

To keep your stroller from getting lost in a sea of clones, personalize it with an item such a colorful sign or ribbon. Never leave valuables in an unattended stroller. Always park in designated areas. (Unattended baby buggies will be relocated to the nearest stroller lot.) Note that wagons (of any kind) are not permitted in Disney parks.

## ADMISSION PRICES

Restricted to use only in the Magic Kingdom. Prices are for Date-Based tickets. (At press time, sales of Flexible Date tickets were on pause, but they may return.) Prices exclude tax and are likely to rise in the coming year.

| | ADULT | CHILD** |
|---|---|---|
| ONE-DAY BASE TICKET* | $109 - $159 | $104 - $154 |

* 1-Day tickets are valid only on the selected date. This is the cost of a 1-day/1-park-only ticket. Terms are subject to change. For details and updates, visit *disneyworld.disney.go.com/admission/tickets*.

** 3 through 9 years of age; children under age 3 free (no ticket required)

# Main Street, U.S.A.

Stepping onto Main Street, U.S.A., feels a little like jumping through a time portal. Welcome to turn-of-the-twentieth century America! Double-decker buses and horse-drawn trolleys are the transportation mode of choice, peppy patriotic music underscores the bustle of merry, moving masses, and the tantalizing aroma of fresh-baked goodies perfumes the air.

A rose-colored retrospective? Maybe. But this is Disney's version of a small-town Main Street—and the charm of this nostalgic land is lost on no one. With an old-fashioned train station at one end and a fairy tale castle at the other, Main Street, U.S.A., whisks you from reality to fantasy in a few short blocks.

All of the addresses here feature fresh coats of paint, curlicued gingerbread moldings, and pretty details. Add to that the baskets of hanging plants and gaslights, and Main Street, U.S.A., becomes a true showplace—both in the bright light of high noon and after nightfall, when the tiny lights edging all of the rooflines are flicked on.

The street represents an idealized American town. Although such a town never really existed, many claim to have served as the inspiration for it. Chances are Walt Disney got the idea from Marceline, Missouri, the tiny rural town that was his boyhood home.

Most of the structures along the thoroughfare are given over to shops, and each one looks a bit different. Inside and out, maintenance and housekeeping are superb. White-suited sanitation workers patrol the street to pick up litter and quickly shovel up any evidence of the horses that pull the trolley cars from Town Square to the Hub. As in the rest of the Magic Kingdom, the pavement here is washed down every night with hoses. Diligent workers focus on the details:

PHOTO BY JILL SAFRO

from maintaining the little white lights around the roofs to making sure all the woodwork stays meticulously painted. The horse-shaped, cast-iron hitching posts are repainted several times a year—and totally scraped down each time. The result of these efforts is a gleaming Main Street in a town we would all love to call home!

The "attractions" along Main Street, U.S.A., are relatively minor compared to the really big deals such as Tomorrowland's Space Mountain or Peter Pan's Flight in Fantasyland. But each and every shop has its own quota of merchandise that is meant as much for show as for sale. It's almost as entertaining to watch the cooks stir up gooey batches of fudge or peanut brittle at the Main Street Confectionery as it is to actually savor a sample. The shop windows, particularly at the Emporium, are worth a look.

Once you start to meander along Main Street, be sure to notice all of the names embossed on the second-story windows. Above the Uptown Jewelers store (by the Confectionery) is that of Walt Disney's nephew, Roy E. Disney. And you will see Walt's name above the ice cream parlor. Other names emblazoned on Main Street windows are those of people closely connected with The Walt Disney Company.

> **Hot Tip!**
>
> Attention, early birds: M.K. guests (with valid park admission media) are welcome to visit Main Street, U.S.A., before the posted Magic Kingdom opening time. You can spend about 30 to 45 minutes moseying along the nostalgic thoroughfare, grabbing some breakfast, shopping for souvenirs, and enjoying some old-timey ambience. As posted park opening time nears, head to the Cinderella Castle forecourt stage for a brief welcome show known as Let the Magic Begin (refer to page 146 for details about the short-but-sweet kickoff to the day).

**Hot Tip!** Kids under the age of 14 must be accompanied by someone age 14 or older when visiting any Walt Disney World theme park or water park.

**WALT DISNEY WORLD RAILROAD:** The best introduction to the Magic Kingdom is the 1½-mile journey on this rail line, which is as much a must for the first-time visitor as it is for railroad buffs. It offers an excellent orientation as it passes by most of the park's major lands. This beloved Magic Kingdom institution was dormant for a few years, as Imagineers built a new *TRON*-themed attraction in

Tomorrowland (for details about TRON Lightcycle/ Run, see page 140)—but we're delighted to share that it's now chugging through the park in all of its glory!

Walt Disney himself was a railroad aficionado. During the early years of television, viewers watched films of him circling his own backyard in a one-eighth-scale train, the *Lilly Belle* (named for his wife).

The Walt Disney World Railroad also has a *Lilly Belle* among its quartet of meticulously restored, narrow-gauge trains—originally built between 1916 and 1928. The others are named *Roy O. Disney*, *Walter E. Disney*, and *Roger E. Broggie* (a Disney Imagineer who shared Walt's enthusiasm for antique trains). All of them were built in the U.S. around the turn of the 20th century and later taken to Mexico to haul freight in the Yucatán, where Disney scouts found them in 1969. Brought north once again, they were completely overhauled, and even the smallest of parts were reworked or replaced.

PHOTO BY JILL SAFRO

**MAIN STREET VEHICLES:** A number of vehicles can be seen traveling up and down Main Street, U.S.A.— horseless carriages and jitneys patterned after turn-of-the-twentieth-century vehicles; a spiffy scarlet fire engine; and a troop of trolleys drawn by Belgians and Percherons, two strong breeds of horse that once pulled plows in Europe. These mighty animals—weighing in at about a ton each and shod with plastic (easier on their hooves)—pull the trolley the length of Main Street about two dozen times during each of their working days. Between shifts, they can be seen resting inside Main Street's Car Barn. Feel free to stop at the entrance to wave hello. At day's end, the horses go home to their barn at WDW's Fort Wilderness.

**Hot Tip!** Guests staying at the Contemporary, Grand Floridian, and Polynesian resorts can walk to and from the Magic Kingdom's front gate. The trip takes about 7 to 20 minutes. (The Polynesian is the farthest from the park, so allow extra time if that's your starting point— just in case.) The walkways are quite handy when there are long lines for the monorail or water taxis.

**Note:** The Main Street Vehicles generally operate during early daytime hours on off-peak days. Details are subject to change.

**TOWN SQUARE THEATER:** Elaborately themed as a Victorian-era theater, this is a wonderful place to meet and mingle with Mickey Mouse. Of course, this being a *magic* kingdom, Mickey has a few tricks up his sleeve. Yep, in addition to all his other skills, the Mouse is a master magician. Who knew? Note that this is strictly a "backstage" experience, as Mickey's magic show is still in the rehearsal stage. The wait here can be long—that Mickey is one popular mouse!

**Hot Tip!** Tuesday and Wednesday tend to be the least crowded days at the Magic Kingdom.

# Adventureland

Adventureland seems to have even more atmosphere than the park's other lands. That may be due to its neat separation from the rest of the Magic Kingdom by the bridge over Main Street on one end and by a gallery-like structure (where it merges with Frontierland) on the other, or, possibly, it's because of the abundance of lush landscaping.

A centrally located attraction, The Magic Carpets of Aladdin, sets the tone for this corner of the Kingdom. Surrounded by tropical splendor, the area has the look and feel of a bustling marketplace—the likes of which one might stumble upon in Agrabah.

As guests stroll away from Main Street, they may hear the sound of beating drums, squawks of parrots, and the regular boom of a cannon. Paces quicken. The wonders soon to be encountered do not disappoint.

## CALLING ALL PIRATES!

Captain Jack Sparrow needs your help. He knows there's treasure to be found and enemies to fight in Adventureland (yeah, that means you, Captain Barbossa!), but Captain Jack can't do it alone. So he's recruiting Magic Kingdom guests to join his pirate posse. That's where you come in!

The interactive quest, dubbed "A Pirate's Adventure—Treasures of the Seven Seas," begins at The Crow's Nest, near the Pirates of the Caribbean attraction. That's where potential pirates use a MagicBand or talisman (which activates magical effects throughout the land) and a mission map. There are five missions in all, some of which involve dodging blow darts and cannon fire. It's free to play (how's that for a hidden gem?!), and the maps and talisman are yours to keep.

**SWISS FAMILY TREEHOUSE:** This is everybody's idea of a dream treehouse, with its many levels and comforts—patchwork quilts, mahogany furniture, candles stuck in abalone shells, even running water in every room. Based on the wondrous banyan-tree home in Disney's 1960 rendition of the classic story *Swiss Family Robinson*, it rarely fails to intrigue. It's easy to understand why, when given the chance to leave the island (several adventures later), all but one member of the Robinson family chose to stay on. The only modern convenience the Robinsons need? An elevator! Expect to burn off a few calories climbing up and down the stairs. Be sure to enjoy the view of the park from the treetop.

The Spanish moss draping the branches is real; the tree—unofficially dubbed *Disneyodendron eximus*, a genus that is translated roughly as "out-of-the-ordinary Disney tree"—was constructed by the WDW props department. Some stats: Its concrete roots poke 42 feet into the ground, about 300,000 lifelike polyethylene leaves "grow" on the tree's 1,400 branches, and there are 116 stairs to climb from beginning to end. Keep that in mind before you commit to this breezy tour.

**JUNGLE CRUISE:** Inspired in part by the 1955 documentary *The African Lion* and the classic film *The African Queen*, the 10-minute adventure is one of the crowning achievements of Magic Kingdom landscape artists for the way it takes guests through surroundings as diverse as a Southeast Asian jungle, the Nile Valley, and an Amazon rainforest. Along the way, passengers encounter zebras, giraffes, lions, mischievous monkeys, and more (all of the Audio-Animatronics variety); they also see elephants bathing and tour a temple—while listening to an amusing, if occasionally corny, spiel delivered by the skipper. (Bet you didn't know that Schweitzer Falls was named after the famous doctor Albert . . . Falls.)

**Hot Tip!** The Jungle Cruise has a dedicated entrance for guests who use wheelchairs. When the accessible boat arrives, cast members will put a ramp in place. Folks who can transfer may park their wheelchair in an area near the attraction's exit.

This beloved, classic attraction was refreshed by Disney Imagineers a few years back. Expect to see an increased (and mischievous) wildlife presence, surprise scenarios, and, of course, a ton of tomfoolery. It's popular with guests of all ages.

**F.Y.I.:** Jungle Navigation Co. Ltd., the company that runs the cruises in these parts, is owned by longtime Adventureland resident Alberta Falls—Albert Falls's great granddaughter.

**WALT DISNEY'S ENCHANTED TIKI ROOM:** Welcome to a tropical (and blissfully air-conditioned) paradise. After a pre-show greeting courtesy of talented toucans known as Clyde and Claude, guests stroll into the legendary Tiki Room. Here, fine-feathered legends José, Michael, Pierre, and Fritz take center stage—as they did when the attraction first opened at Disneyland in 1963. Cherished for its historical significance (the Tiki Birds starred in the original Audio-Animatronics attraction), the show has evolved a bit over time.

The performance features the aforementioned avian friends, plus some 200 additional birds, flowers, and tiki statues singing up a tropical storm. Let's all sing like the birdies sing!

**THE MAGIC CARPETS OF ALADDIN:** Adventureland's high-flying attraction is conveniently located in the Agrabah-themed center of the action. It features not one, but 16 carpets that soar through the air in a fashion similar to those airborne elephants over in Fantasyland. Each flying carpet accommodates four guests at a time. Depending on where you sit, you may control the carpet's movement (vertical controls are in the front row; tilting forward/backward are in the back row). Be prepared to dodge the occasional stream of liquid, courtesy of an expectorating camel.

**BIRNBAUM'S ★BEST★ PIRATES OF THE CARIBBEAN:** Quite simply, this attraction is one of the very best of the *Magic Kingdom* park's classic adventures. The beloved ten-minute cruise originated in Disneyland and was added to Walt Disney World's Magic Kingdom (in slightly revised form) due to popular demand. Here, guests board a small boat and set sail for a series of scenes showing a pirate raid on a Caribbean island town, dodging cannon fire and weathering one small, though legitimate, watery dip along the way (warn young kids). There are singing donkeys, plastered pigs, and marauding miscreants; the observant may note a few familiar rapscallion residents. Beloved scallywag Captain Jack Sparrow has dropped anchor here, as has his nefarious nemesis, Captain Barbossa. And there's a new pirate in town! Following an extensive ride refurbishment a few years back, the famous redhead (and longtime resident of the attraction) has joined forces with the local marauders and hopes to help the townspeople "unload" their valuables at the Mercado Auction.

While it may not be the World's most politically correct attraction, the rendition of "Yo Ho, Yo Ho, a Pirate's Life for Me"—the catchy theme song—makes the somewhat unsavory scenario into something that comes across as good fun.

And, yes, this is the attraction that inspired the series of *Pirates of the Caribbean* movies—which, in turn, inspired the attraction.

# Frontierland

With the Rivers of America lapping at its borders and Big Thunder Mountain rising in the distance, this re-creation of the American Frontier encompasses the area from the Mississippi River to the Southwest, from the 1770s to the 1880s. In these parts, the shops, eateries, and attractions have unpainted barn siding or stone or clapboard walls, and there are several wooden sidewalks of the sort Marshal Matt Dillon used to stride along. The Walt Disney World Railroad has a station here.

**FRONTIERLAND SHOOTIN' ARCADE:** This modest arcade is set in an 1850s town in the Southwest Territory. Positions overlook Boothill, a town complete with bank, jail, hotel, and cemetery.

Genuine Hawkins .54-caliber buffalo rifles have been refitted, and when the infrared beam strikes any of the targets, an interesting result is triggered. Struck tombstones rise, sink, spin, or change their epitaphs; hit a cloud and a ghost rider gallops across the sky; a bullseye on a gravedigger's shovel causes a skull to pop out of the grave.

**Note:** There's no additional charge to play at the Frontierland Shootin' Arcade. (It used to cost a dollar.)

**COUNTRY BEAR JAMBOREE:** The Country Bears may never make it to the Grand Ole Opry, but they don't seem to mind. Disney's brood of banjo-strummin' bruins has been playing to packed houses in Grizzly

Hall for more than half a century. Judging by all the toe tappin' and hand clappin' that accompany most of the performances, this classic show remains a quaint, countrified crowd-pleaser. As for the few folks who aren't charmed by the backwoods ballads and down-home humor, well, they just have to grin and bear it.

As guests are settling into their seats (all of which provide a decent view of the show), Buff, Max, and Melvin are beginning to grumble. Despite their status as permanent fixtures in the theater, the mounted animal heads would rather not "hang around all day" waiting for the show to get going. The 11-minute revue opens with a rousing ditty by the Five Bear Rugs. The wheels set in motion, the remaining songs come fast and furious. Together, they capture the spirit of a music genre that has a tendency to celebrate and lampoon itself at the same time.

For example, Bunny, Bubbles, and Beulah bemoan "All the Guys That Turn Me On Turn Me Down"; Henry, the easygoing emcee who sports a coonskin cap (still attached to the 'coon), belts out "The Ballad of Davy Crockett"; and Big Al, the oversize tone-deaf fan favorite, croons "Blood on the Saddle," much to the delight of the giggle-prone audience.

**Timing Tip:** This attraction typically opens at about 11 A.M., even when the rest of Magic Kingdom opens earlier in the day.

**TOM SAWYER ISLAND:** This tranquil patch of land in the middle of the Rivers of America has hills to scramble up, a working windmill, Harper's Mill, with an owl in the rafters and a perpetually creaky waterwheel; and a few pitch-black caves. To reach the island, guests take a raft across the river. (It's the only way to get there and back.)

Pleasant paths wind this way and that, and it's easy to get disoriented. Keep an eye out for mounted maps scattered about the island.

There are two cool bridges to discover here — a suspension bridge and a barrel bridge, which floats atop some lashed-together wooden barrels. When one person bounces, everybody lurches — and all but the most chickenhearted laugh. Both bridges are easy to miss, so be sure to keep your eyes peeled.

Across the suspension bridge is Fort Langhorn. Poke around and you should discover a twisting and slightly scary escape tunnel. Walk along the pathway on the banks of the Rivers of America and you'll find your way back to the bridges.

The whole island seems as rugged as backwoods Missouri and, probably as a result, it actually feels a lot more remote than it is—enough to be able to provide some welcome respite from the park bustle.

One particularly pleasant way to relax here is at a waterside table. Aunt Polly hasn't sold snacks for some time, but you're encouraged to bring your own if you'd like to enjoy a nosh in this lovely setting. Restrooms are beside the main raft landing and inside Fort Langhorn.

**Timing Tip:** This attraction closes at dusk.

**BIRNBAUM'S** ★**BEST**★ **TIANA'S BAYOU ADVENTURE:** Originally known as Splash Mountain, this newly re-imagined crowd-pleaser is set to celebrate Mardi Gras in jubilant fashion—thanks to a splashy new *Princess and the Frog* make-over. The theme (and name) may be new, but rest assured Splash fans: the thrills of the classic Splash Mountain experience endure. This **NEW** Frontierland adventure is expected to be open by late 2024 (possibly a bit later—or earlier!)

**Hot Tip!** If you would like to get soaked on Tiana's Bayou Adventure, sit on the right side of the log/attraction vehicle. That side is notorious for receiving the biggest splash. (Though nobody leaves this ride dry!)

In this 11-minute ride, guests board hollowed-out logs and drift on a whimsical waterborne journey through bayous (where glowing fireflies light up the night sky), down waterfalls, and over the top of a super-steep spillway into an $H_2O$-filled splash zone five stories below. Along the way, they join Princess Tiana and jazz-loving alligator Louis as they prepare a special celebration for the people of New Orleans. Throughout the journey, the sounds of zydeco music fill the air, courtesy of a band of cuddly critters—including an otter, raccoon, beaver, and a turtle playing cleverly hand-crafted instruments. (FYI: Zydeco is a blend of rhythm and blues that was born in Louisiana.)

It is a bit terrifying at the top, but once back on the ground, it seems most riders just can't wait for another trip—even though they may get drenched. (Water-wary guests are sometimes seen wearing rain ponchos on this attraction. On the other hand, if you want to get soaked, try to sit up front or on the right; seats in the back receive a smaller splash.)

By the second or third time around, it's possible to relax a bit, enjoy the interior scenes, and take in the spectacular views of the Magic Kingdom from the top of the mountain. At this point, you may even manage to keep your eyes open for the duration of the final fall—or at least part of it.

**Notes:** You must be at least 40 inches tall to ride Tiana's Bayou Adventure. The final drop may be too scary for some kids (and grown-ups!). There's a small play area for parents to tend to tykes while older kids ride. If you would like to absorb as little precipitation as possible, sit on the left side of the log—just know that no seat is entirely splash free. Details are subject to change. For updates, use the *My Disney Experience* mobile app or website, or visit *disneyworld.com*.

**Hot Tip!** If you find yourself in the Big Thunder Mountain Railroad area of Frontierland during a parade and would like to make a hasty(ish) exit from Frontierland or the park itself, look no further than the Walt Disney World Railroad Station. Accessed via stairs (or ramp) near Tiana's Bayou Adventure, the railroad will whisk you to Fantasyland's Storybook Circus (home of Dumbo and the Barnstormer) and then to Main Street, U.S.A.

**BIRNBAUM'S ★BEST★ BIG THUNDER MOUNTAIN RAILROAD:** It's certainly not hard to spot Big Thunder Mountain, the lone red rock formation this side of the Mississippi. Even newcomers to the Magic Kingdom will be able to distinguish this park landmark from its mountainous counterpart—Space Mountain—because Big Thunder resembles an actual mountain range. The beloved attraction's designers took Utah's Monument Valley as inspiration, and the resemblance is quite remarkable.

According to Disney legend, the 2.5-acre mountain is chock-full of gold—and the owner of the Big Thunder Mining Co., one Barnabas Bullion, is mighty eager to get his hands on it. But according to the local residents, Big Thunder Mountain is very protective of its gold—and foolish folks who attempt to mine its riches are doomed to failure. Sure enough, the mountain has been plagued by mysterious forces and natural disasters ever since old Barnabas set up shop.

After passing through an interactive queue area, guests are advised to remove their hats and glasses, "'cause this here's the wildest ride in the wilderness!" Do heed the warning, but don't despair. The ride, though thrilling,

is relatively tame, so you can relax a bit and take in the sights. (Passengers seated near the caboose experience more turbulence than those seated closer to the front of the speedy mine train.)

A bleating billy goat atop a peak, a family of possums hanging overhead, and a dark cavern full of bats, not to mention chickens, donkeys, and washed-up miners, can be spotted along the way. Be sure to keep an eye out for the flooded-but-not-quite-sunken saloon—it's easy to miss the first time around.

A continuous string of curves and dips around Big Thunder's pinnacles and caverns is sure to please thrill-seekers of all ages, but the adrenaline surge is caused by more than just the speed of the trip. The added sound of a rickety track, a steam whistle that blows right before the train accelerates into a curve, and an earthquake all compound the passengers' anticipation, making this classic attraction one of the Magic Kingdom's most popular.

**Notes:** You must be at least 40 inches tall and free of motion sickness, back and neck problems, and other health issues to ride Big Thunder Mountain Railroad. Seats in the front of the train provide a less wild ride than those toward the caboose. Expectant mothers should not ride Big Thunder Mountain Railroad.

**Timing Tip:** Plan to visit early in the morning, during a parade, or just before closing time. This attraction may not operate during inclement weather.

# Liberty Square

The transition between Frontierland on one side and Fantasyland on the other is so smooth that it's hard to say just when you arrive at Liberty Square, yet ultimately, there's no mistaking the location. The small buildings are clapboard or brick and topped with weather vanes; the decorative moldings are Federal or Georgian in style; the glass is sometimes wavy; and there are flower boxes in shop windows. The square is home to two of the Magic Kingdom's most famous attractions—The Haunted Mansion and The Hall of Presidents. There's also a rather convincing replica of the Liberty Bell, a Christmas shop, and a living, more-than-a-century-old "Liberty Tree."

**THE HALL OF PRESIDENTS:** The attraction has evolved a bit since making its debut back in 1971. The current version is an epic theatrical production that brings the story of the American presidency to life. The show, which takes place in a 700-seat theater, pays tribute to the ordinary people who have risen to the nation's highest office and led Americans through extraordinary circumstances. The action begins with a stirring, original film—developed by a Pulitzer Prize–winning historian—which adroitly relays the dramatic story of the United States of America. At the film's end, a curtain rises to reveal (an Audio-Animatronics version of) each and every person who has served as president of the United States of America.

The patriotic production explores America's enduring origins, the framing of the United States Constitution, and the hard-fought struggles along the way—such as the American Revolution and the Civil War.

With the addition of Joe Biden, all 46 U.S. presidents are represented. Observant guests may note that there are only 45 Audio-Animatronics figures on the stage.

### Did You Know?

Liberty Square's aura of authenticity is enhanced by its duo of landmark look-alikes. The park's Liberty Tree, a more than 130-year-old oak (replanted from another area of WDW property in 1971) represents the original Liberty Tree in Boston, Massachusetts. (It's where the Sons of Liberty gathered in the months building up to the Boston Tea Party.) Each night, the tree is illuminated with 13 lanterns—one for each of the nation's original 13 colonies. Disney's Liberty Bell is no less impressive. Made for the Magic Kingdom in 1989, it's a dead ringer for the real deal. In fact, it was cast from the same mold that created the original bell that hangs in Philadelphia.

No, Disney Imagineers did not misplace a POTUS. Grover Cleveland served two non-consecutive terms, so he is the 22nd and 24th U.S. president.

Displays in the pre-show area give guests a chance to gaze upon bits of Americana, such as painted eggs from a White House Easter egg hunt and dresses from former first ladies (exhibit items will be swapped out from time to time).

**LIBERTY SQUARE RIVERBOAT:** Based in the park's Liberty Square and built in dry dock at Walt Disney World, the *Liberty Belle* is a genuine steamboat. Its boiler turns water into steam, which is then piped to the engine, which drives the paddle wheel that propels the boat. It's not the real deal in one key respect, however: It moves through the nine-foot-deep Rivers of America on an underwater rail.

The pleasant ride, with narration by an actor playing Mark Twain, is a good way to beat the heat on steamy afternoons. En route, a variety of on-shore props creates a sort of Wild West effect: moose, deer, a log cabin, and the like. The tour is completed within 17 minutes.

**Note:** This peaceful aquatic attraction usually opens about an hour or so after the park itself and shuts down earlier than most *Magic Kingdom* attractions.

PHOTO BY JILL SAFRO

**BIRNBAUM'S**
**★BEST★**

**THE HAUNTED MANSION:** This extra eerie, eight-minute experience is among the Magic Kingdom's most enjoyable. However, guests who expect to be scared silly when they enter the big old house, modeled after those built in New York's Hudson River Valley in the eighteenth century, will be just a tad unfulfilled. This haunted house steers clear of anything too terrifying, and a good-spirited voice-over keeps the mood light. Still, some of the scenes, as well as the darkness, may be too much for some tykes.

Once you're inside the portrait hall, entered after passing through the front doors, you'll be asked to step to the dead center of the room. It is also where you will meet your "Ghost Host" and learn how he met his demise. As the space begins to stretch it's fun to speculate: Is the ceiling moving up, or is the floor dropping?

The spooky journey through the mansion takes place in a Doom Buggy. The attraction is full of tricks and treats for the eyes; just when you think you've seen it all, there's something new: staircases to nowhere, bats' eyes on the wallpaper, a terrified cemetery watchman and his mangy mutt, and the image of a creepy lady in a floating crystal ball (aka Madame Leota).

One of the biggest jobs of the maintenance crews here is not cleaning up, but keeping things dirty. The manse is littered with some 200 trunks, chairs, dress forms, harps, rugs, and knickknacks and requires a lot of dust. Cobwebs are bought in liquid form and strung up by a secret process.

When waiting to enter, take time to enjoy the interactive queue area. And on the way out, take a moment to pay your respects at the pet cemetery. Mr. Toad, we hardly knew you. Sniff, sniff.

# Fantasyland

Walt Disney called this a "timeless land of enchantment," and his successors termed it "the happiest land of all" — and it is, for many. It is also the home of a number of rides that are particularly well liked by kids of all ages. Head here for the quintessential Disney theme park experience.

**CINDERELLA CASTLE:** Just as Mickey stands for all the merriment in Walt Disney World, this storybook castle represents the hopes and dreams of childhood — a time in life when anything is possible and dreams really do come true.

Rising to a height of 189 feet (and sporting 27 turrets), Walt Disney World's Cinderella Castle is more than twice the height of Disneyland's Sleeping Beauty Castle.

For inspiration, Disney Imagineers looked to the palaces of author Charles Perrault's France, still showplaces of Europe. The design took the form of a romanticized composite of such courts as Fontainebleau, Versailles, and famed chateaux of the Loire Valley. Of course, they also turned to the original designs for the fairy-tale castle in Disney's 1950 classic, *Cinderella.*

Unlike real European castles, Cinderella's is made of steel and fiberglass; in lieu of dungeons, it has service tunnels. However, like other fabled castles, it's protected by a moat. And from any vantage point, Cinderella Castle looks as if it came straight from the land of make-believe.

**Mosaic Murals:** The elaborate murals beneath the castle's archway rank among the true wonders of the World. They tell the story of the little cinder girl and one of childhood's happiest happily-ever-afters, using a million bits of glass in some 500 different colors, plus real silver and 14-karat gold.

**Cinderella Wishing Well:** This pleasant alcove, nestled along a path to Tomorrowland, is a nice spot from which to gaze at the castle. Any coins tossed into the water are donated to children's charities. Don't forget to make a wish as you part with your penny.

**PRINCE CHARMING REGAL CARROUSEL:** Not everything in the Magic Kingdom is a Disney version of the real article. This carrousel, discovered at the now-defunct

Olympic Park in Maplewood, New Jersey, was built back in 1917 (technically making it the oldest attraction in the park). That was the end of the golden century of carousel building, which began around 1825. During the Disney refurbishment, many of the original horses were replaced with horses made of fiberglass. No two of the 90 horses are exactly alike. Can you spot what's believed to be Cinderella's trusty steed? Hint: It's the only equine with a golden ribbon on its tail!

**ARIEL'S GROTTO:** The Little Mermaid (Ariel) spends most of each day greeting guests in her Fantasyland grotto. Ariel loves to chat, pose for photos, and sign autographs. Details are subject to change.

**FAIRYTALE GARDEN:** This charming alcove is tucked beside Cinderella Castle. Several times each day, Mirabel (the fan-favorite from *Encanto*) stops by to visit with park guests. Details are subject to change.

**MICKEY'S PHILHARMAGIC:** Mickey Mouse and a panoply of his pals (including Donald, Simba, and Ariel) strut their musical stuff in this 3-D production.

The show is a lively amalgam of music, effects, and animation—including a brand-new scene based on the film *Coco*. Of course, this being Fantasyland, the film is by no means ordinary. It's colorful, crisp, and to the delight of many a goggle-wearing guest, three-dimensional. The spirited presentation unfolds on a 150-foot wide canvas. Special surprises take place off-screen, too.

There are moments of darkness during the show. If you're unsure as to whether your child might find this (or any attraction) unsettling, express your concern to an attendant. They'll help you make the right decision. All guests must wear 3-D glasses to enjoy the show.

**BIRNBAUM'S ★BEST★ PETER PAN'S FLIGHT:** "Come on, everybody, here we go!" So says Peter Pan at the start of this nonstop flight to Never Land. The 3-minute adventure, which takes you soaring in a pirate ship, fancifully retells the story of Peter Pan—a boy with a knack for flying and an immunity to maturity. The effects in this Fantasyland attraction are simple, but enchanting.

The journey starts in the Darling family nursery—which siblings Wendy, Michael, and John quickly abandon to follow Peter Pan on a trip to his homeland. As in Disney's animated feature, one of the most beautiful scenes—and one that makes this attraction a treat for grown-ups as well as smaller folk—is the

sight of nighttime London, dark blue and speckled with twinkling lights. Keep your eyes peeled for Big Ben and Tower Bridge. It's lovely.

By the time you spot your first mermaid, you're deep in the heart of Never Land. Alas, something is terribly wrong—Captain Hook and his buccaneer buddies have taken the Darling kids captive. It's all really a trap for Peter (Hook is still peeved at Pan for serving his hand to a crocodile). Does everyone live happily ever after? We'll never tell.

**PRINCESS FAIRYTALE HALL:** Practice your curtsy as you approach this hall—once inside expect to meet regal folks such as Cinderella, Elena of Avalor, Rapunzel, and Tiana. Characters vary. This renowned royal residence fills the space formerly occupied by the Snow White's Scary Adventures attraction. All details are subject to change. For updates, check *disneyworld.com*.

**BIRNBAUM'S ★BEST★ IT'S A SMALL WORLD:** *Hola! Guten Tag! Hello!* No matter what language you speak, what you look like, or where you live, you still have a lot in common with folks the

PHOTO BY JILL SAFRO

**Hot Tip!** Many Fantasyland attractions are dark, and, in some cases, special effects may be too intense for tots and some small children. However, they all tend to love It's a Small World and The Many Adventures of Winnie the Pooh. Nothing scary about that!

world over (including an especially high tolerance for a singsong melody that persistently reminds us that it's a small world after all). That's the cheerful message driving this pleasant 10-minute boat trip around the world.

Originally created for New York's 1964–65 World's Fair, the classic attraction is an oldie but goodie (and it is exceptionally popular with young kids and those who prefer calm theme park experiences). The boat moves at slightly swifter than a snail's pace, drifting past hundreds of colorfully costumed dolls from around the world—all of whom know all the words to the ride's famously infectious theme song (written by Disney Legends, the Sherman Brothers).

A showcase of diversity, the attraction is a simple celebration of human similarities. It's also a relaxing alternative to many of the Magic Kingdom's higher-tech, longer-line attractions.

PHOTO BY JILL SAFRO

**DUMBO THE FLYING ELEPHANT:** This is purely and simply a kiddie ride, though children of all ages have admitted to loving it.

A beloved symbol of Fantasyland, the ride relocated to the Storybook Circus neighborhood and doubled in size—but rest assured, the Dumbo experience remains the same. Consider stopping here early in the morning,

or during a parade, when the line—which is often prohibitively long—thins a bit. Inspired by the 1941 Disney film classic *Dumbo*, the high-flying ride lasts an enjoyable two minutes.

**Note:** Guests in Dumbo's standby line are free to frolic in a covered play zone while they wait for a text to tell them it's time to ride. The line for Dumbo the Flying Elephant tends to dwindle later in the day, especially when the Magic Kingdom keeps long hours.

**THE BARNSTORMER:** At this miniature roller coaster attraction, guests follow the same fluky flight path taken by the daredevil pilot formally known as the Great Goofini (aka Goofy). Don't let the size fool you: This one-minute ride proves that big thrills do indeed come in small packages.

Although guests of all ages enjoy this wild ride, they must be at least 35 inches tall to enter. The flight may be too turbulent for some. And please, resist the urge to snack before riding.

**CASEY JR. SPLASH 'N' SOAK STATION:** The famous locomotive Casey Jr. invites Magic Kingdom guests to cool off in this colorful splash zone, conveniently located beside Fantasyland's train station. Be sure to dress tykes in swim diapers.

**MAD TEA PARTY:** The fanciful theme of this 2-minute ride—in a group of oversize teacups that whirl and spin wildly—was inspired by a scene in the Disney Studios' 1951 animated production of *Alice in Wonderland*. During the sequence in question, the Mad Hatter hosts a tea party for his un-birthday.

level. Along the way, they join Ariel, Flounder, and all of their aquatic acquaintances, and enjoy major musical movements and pivotal plot points from the classic animated feature. It's fun for the whole family.

Unlike many rides in Fantasyland, this is not just for younger kids; the 5-to-20-something crowd seems to like it best. Keep in mind that when the cups stop spinning, your head may continue to do so. Skip this ride if you suffer from motion sickness or if you have recently enjoyed a meal or a snack. And don't miss the woozy mouse that pops out of the teapot at the center of the platform—he ignored our advice.

**THE MANY ADVENTURES OF WINNIE THE POOH:** Everyone's favorite honey-lovin' cub treats Magic Kingdom guests to wild and whimsical 3½-minute tours of his home turf—the Hundred Acre Wood.

The attraction features a most unlikely method of transportation: honey pots! They whisk (and bounce) guests through the pages of a giant storybook and into the Hundred Acre Wood, where the weather's most blustery. The wind is really ruffling the feathers of one of the locals. Sight gags abound, from a bubble-blowing Heffalump (hey, this is Fantasyland) to a treacherous flood that threatens to sweep Tigger, Piglet, and the rest of the gang away. When Pooh saves the day, it's time to celebrate—and everyone is invited to the party.

Like other Fantasyland attractions, parts of this one take place in the dark. Some young children may find it a bit unsettling. That said, most little ones dig Pooh's interactive queue area. While waiting to ride or for others to do so, youngsters can bang on big vegetable "drums," play tug-of-war with a gopher, and scrawl their names in a flowing wall of honey.

**UNDER THE SEA—JOURNEY OF THE LITTLE MERMAID:** In the Magic Kingdom's first attraction to feature everyone's favorite Disney mermaid, guests are invited to board continuously moving clam-mobiles and embark on a happy voyage above and below sea

**BIRNBAUM'S ★BEST★** **SEVEN DWARFS MINE TRAIN:** Heigh-ho, heigh-ho! A roller coaster is whimsically transporting guests on a happy musical journey through the workplace of the Seven Dwarfs—the mine where a million diamonds shine. The ride vehicles sway back and forth a bit as they zoom along the track, so folks with motion sickness or other health issues should sit this one out. Intensity-wise, the family-friendly attraction fits somewhere between the park's Barnstormer roller coaster (page 135) and Big Thunder Mountain Railroad (page 130). The queue has a few interactive surprises, too. This 2½-minute attraction is extremely popular. Guests must be at least 38 inches tall to ride Seven Dwarfs Mine Train.

**ENCHANTED TALES WITH BELLE:** This clever mix of show and character encounter is one of those "you have to see it to believe it" experiences. Located in Maurice's exquisitely detailed cottage, the 30-minute experience includes Audio-Animatronics versions of Lumiere and Madame Wardrobe, plus an audience-participation performance by Belle in Beast's library. There are lots of parts to play—be sure to volunteer!

# Tomorrowland

The original Tomorrowland attempted a serious look at the future. But as Disney planners discovered, it isn't easy to portray a future that persists in becoming the present. So the old Tomorrowland has given way to a friendlier, space-age town whose neighborhood atmosphere is more in keeping with the other lands in the Magic Kingdom. This is the future that never was, the fantasy world imagined by the science-fiction writers and movie-makers of the 1920s and '30s. It's a land of sky-piercing beacons and glistening metal, where shiny robots do the work, whisper-quiet cars glide along an elevated highway, and even time travel is possible.

**BIRNBAUM'S** **BUZZ LIGHTYEAR'S SPACE RANGER SPIN:**
**★BEST★** The Evil Emperor Zurg is up to no good. As soon as he gathers enough batteries to power his ultimate weapon of destruction — KERPLOOEY! — it's curtains for the toy universe as we know it. It's up to that Space Ranger extraordinaire Buzz Lightyear and his trusty Junior Space Rangers (that means you) to save the day.

So goes the story line of Tomorrowland's video-game-inspired spin through toyland. The adventure is experienced from a toy's point of view. Guests begin their 4½-minute tour of duty as Space Rangers at Star Command Action Center. This is where Buzz gives his team a briefing on the mission that lies ahead. Then

it's off to the Launch Bay to board the ride vehicles. The ships feature dual laser cannons, glowing lights, and a piloting joystick.

Once Junior Space Rangers blast off, they find themselves surrounded by Zurg's robots, who are mercilessly ripping batteries from toys. As Rangers fire at targets, beams of light fill the air. For every target hit, you will be rewarded with sound effects and points. The points are accumulated throughout the journey and tallied automatically. Although the vehicles follow a rigid "flight" path (they're on a track), the joystick allows riders to maneuver the spaceships, turning from side to side or spinning in circles while taking aim at their intended targets.

To up your score at Buzz Lightyear's Space Ranger Spin, keep the trigger depressed at all times. Also, be sure to aim for moving or distant targets—they provide some of the biggest point payoffs. The target on top of the volcano is quite valuable, and the one beneath Emperor Zurg will net you a whopping 100,000 points every time you zap it!

When the star cruiser arrives at Zurg's spaceship, it's showdown time. Will good prevail over evil? Or has time run out for the toy universe? And will you score enough points to be a Galactic Hero (999,999)? Most people improve their scores with a little practice. Note that the seat on the left side of the ride vehicle tends to have better access to the high-point-yielding targets in the first room.

**MONSTERS, INC. LAUGH FLOOR:** That Mike Wazowski is one enterprising eyeball. It seems the fuzzy fellow from Monsters, Inc. has opened a comedy club. Why? Well, it turns out his hometown is experiencing a bit of an energy crisis. Mike's clever plan is to tap into a decidedly alternative (not to mention free) fuel source to provide power for Monstropolis . . . laughter. But where can he possibly gather enough giggles to fuel an entire city? In a 400-seat theater in Tomorrowland, that's where. To accomplish his ambitious goal, monster of ceremonies Mike has recruited a couple of cornball comedians. Their job is to make you laugh yourself silly. And they are not too proud to resort to slapstick while doing so.

Guests are encouraged to text a joke while waiting in the queue, so come prepared. (Standard text messaging rates apply.)

**TOMORROWLAND TRANSIT AUTHORITY PEOPLEMOVER:** Boarded near Astro Orbiter, these open-air trains (known to Disney purists as the WEDway) move at a speed of about seven miles per hour along almost a mile of track, beside or through most of the attractions in Tomorrowland. They are operated by a linear induction motor system that has no moving parts, uses little power, and emits no pollution.

The breezy excursion through Tomorrowland takes about ten minutes. There's usually less than a 15-minute wait to board (though lines can build up quite a bit on very busy days). It's one of our favorites. However, moments of darkness (as the train passes through Space Mountain) may be a bit unsettling for some little ones. Warn them before you climb aboard.

**ASTRO ORBITOR:** Here, passengers fly for two minutes in machine-age rockets designed to look more like oversize Buck Rogers toys than twenty-first-century space shuttles. Riders are surrounded by vibrantly colored, whirling planets as they are treated to an astronaut's-eye view of Tomorrowland.

**TOMORROWLAND SPEEDWAY:** Little motorcars that burn up the tracks at this attraction provide quite a bit of the background noise in Tomorrowland. Young kids especially enjoy the not-especially-speedy, herky-jerky driving experience.

The vehicles have rack-and-pinion steering and disc brakes, but unlike most cars, they run along a track. Yet even expert drivers have trouble keeping them going

in a straight line. (Resist the urge to panic when you notice the lack of a brake pedal—when you take your foot off the gas, the racecar comes to a quick, if not screeching, halt.) The one-lap tour of Tomorrowland takes about four minutes.

**Notes:** You must be at least 32 inches tall to ride, 54 inches tall to drive the car by yourself. Guests who are at least 32 inches tall may drive if accompanied by someone 54 inches or taller. Bumping may occur. Bypass this speedway if you have neck issues, back issues, or other health concerns. If you're pregnant, you are advised to sit this one out.

**BIRNBAUM'S ★BEST★ SPACE MOUNTAIN:** This classic "E-ticket" attraction, which blasted onto the *Magic Kingdom* scene in 1975 (and was completely refurbished in 2009), is a can't-miss crowd-pleaser for throngs of thrill-seekers. Rising to a height of more than 180 feet, this gleaming steel-and-concrete cone houses an attraction that most people call a roller coaster. The ride takes place in an outer-space-like darkness that gets inkier and scarier as the journey progresses. The rockets that roar through this blackness attain a maximum speed of just over 28 miles per hour—but somehow it feels a whole lot faster.

The Space Mountain experience is wild enough to send glasses, purses, wallets, and even an occasional set of false teeth plummeting to the bottom of the track, so be sure to find a safe place for your possessions before the ride starts. It's also turbulent enough to upset the stomachs of those so unwise as to ride it

PHOTO BY JILL SAFRO

immediately after eating. (Those who change their minds at the last minute have access to a "chicken" exit. Ask a ride attendant for directions to the door.)

**Notes:** Guests must be at least 44 inches tall and in good health and free from heart conditions, motion sickness, back or neck problems, or any other physical limitations to ride. Expectant mothers should skip the trip. Children under age 7 must be accompanied by a guest age 14 or older.

**BIRNBAUM'S** **★BEST★** **NEW** **TRON LIGHTCYCLE/RUN:** A retro-futuristic thriller, TRON Lightcycle/Run delivers a brief-but-exhilarating race through "the Grid." The high-speed coaster experience kicks off with a powerful launch and propels riders into various twists and turns on a dramatic race through the digital frontier. The goal is to surge beyond fierce opponents in an attempt to cross eight energy gates and secure victory for your team! Guests experience the out-of-this-world adventure while aboard a zippy neon train of two-wheeled light-cycles. (The ride vehicles are not ideal for all heights and builds. It's best to jump aboard a test seat at the

attraction's entrance before jumping into the queue.) Lightcycles reach a maximum speed of about 60 mph as they zoom both inside and out! The illuminated outdoor canopy is exceptionally lovely after dark—ride by day and night if possible. (You can stroll beneath the canopy without experiencing the attraction, too.)

**Notes:** For guests who are unable to enjoy the motor-bike-style vehicles, there is (very) limited traditional roller coaster–style seating. Just ask.

TRON Lightcycle/Run features sudden turns, sharp drops and stops, and moments of darkness. As with other high-energy theme park attractions, it's best to refrain from eating just before riding. To ride, guests must be at least 38 inches tall and in good health and free from heart conditions, motion sickness, back or neck problems, claustrophobia, or any other physical limitations. Expectant moms should pass on this one. Loose articles must be stored in a nearby locker (no charge) or with a non-riding member of your party. Finally, if you plan to wear a dress to the park, be sure to add bike shorts to your ensemble. You'll be glad you did.

**WALT DISNEY'S CAROUSEL OF PROGRESS:** First seen at New York's 1964–1965 World's Fair and moved here in 1975, this 20-minute experience showcases the evolution of the American family and how much life changed—and ostensibly progressed—with the introduction of electricity. The hook here is that as a scene ends, the audience moves to the next one—not unlike being on a carousel (hence the name of the attraction). This is a wonderful place to escape the crowds and heat, not to mention take a much-needed load off weary feet.

# Shopping

No one travels to the Magic Kingdom exclusively to shop. But as many a visitor has learned, shopping is one of the most enjoyable pastimes here.

The Magic Kingdom's many boutiques and stores may stock more than just Disneyana. Along with the more predictable items in Main Street shops, it's possible to discover cookbooks, glassware, and dishes; pirate hats, designer handbags, 14-karat gold charms, and filigreed costume jewelry. In Adventureland, shops may boast items imported from the exotic regions the area represents. Throughout the park, stores generally have a healthy supply of Disney character-themed merchandise, plus items that complement the themes of the various lands and the attractions that occupy them.

In some shops, you can watch people at work: a candy maker hand-dipping caramel apples in the Main Street Confectionery, a glassblower crafting wares in Main Street's Crystal Arts, etc.

We recommend shopping in the early afternoon, rather than at day's end, when shops are most crowded. However, keep in mind that some Main Street shops stay open about a half hour after park closing, in case you need any last-minute gifts on the way out. Most purchases may be shipped to your home (fees apply).

Finally, as with other offerings at Walt Disney World, some of the shops and experiences described on these pages were suspended at press time. Will they all be operating this year? We sure hope so! For updates, use the My Disney Experience app or website.

## MAIN STREET, U.S.A.

**THE ART OF DISNEY:** Tucked inside the Main Street Cinema, the small shop showcases Disney-inspired fine art and collectibles, books, puzzles, and more. If you're lucky, there will be a Disney artist on hand to personalize a sketch just for you. Searching for collector pins? They got 'em. You can watch classic Mickey Mouse cartoons here, too.

**BOX OFFICE GIFTS:** Housed in Main Street U.S.A.'s Town Square Theater, this is the place to buy mouse ears and have them monogrammed, and to shop for straw hats, caps, pins, and other headgear previously offered at The Chapeau shop (R.I.P., The Chapeau: 1971–2021). It's also the place to view and pick up PhotoPass photos, purchase a Disney camera strap, and procure pins and MagicBand paraphernalia.

**CURTAIN CALL COLLECTIBLES:** After visiting with Mickey Mouse at the Town Square Theater, guests meander through this souvenir shop. Said souvenirs include clothing and collectibles featuring assorted Disney characters, including the Big Cheese himself.

**CRYSTAL ARTS:** Cut-glass bowls, vases, glasses, and plates glitter in the cases of this crystal-chandeliered emporium. It has a lovely selection of miniature Disney characters meticulously crafted from glass. An engraver or a glassblower is often at work. There's a fireplace, too. Stop here to watch craftspeople mold shields and carve metal—impressive!

**DISNEY CLOTHIERS:** This shop offers clothing for young guests, including shirts and sleepwear, all of which incorporates Disney characters. Look for accessories, bags, and trendy trinkets.

## WHERE TO EAT IN THE MAGIC KINGDOM

A complete listing of all Magic Kingdom eateries—full-service restaurants, fast-food eateries, and snack shops—can be found in the *Good Meals, Great Times* chapter. Refer to the Magic Kingdom section, beginning on page 262.

**EMPORIUM:** Framed by a two-story-high portico, the Magic Kingdom's largest gift shop stocks stuffed animals and toys, T-shirts, kitchen items, home decor, hats, mugs, and much more.

The cash registers always seem to be busy, especially in the late afternoon hours and just before park closing time. Nearby lockers make for convenient storage of purchases. (Fees apply.)

**Hot Tip!** Your Walt Disney World shopping spree does not have to end when your vacation does. Simply visit *shopdisney.com*. The site stocks items from the parks, plus many other Disney-themed treasures. Select items may come with a discount for Disney Rewards Visa cardholders, Disney Vacation Club members, and Annual Passholders. (Details are subject to change.)

You may choose to begin your Magic Kingdom day by shopping here, as Main Street usually opens before the rest of the park does. If you do, remember to take advantage of the aforementioned lockers (fees apply). Home delivery is offered, too (fees apply). And make a point of peering into the Emporium's windows, which usually feature elaborate displays ranging from seasonal themes to character tableaux.

**Note:** Package pickup and resort delivery were on pause at press time, but may return.

**HARMONY BARBER SHOP:** Situated next door to the Main Street Car Barn, the quaint, old-fashioned setting for this working shop (with occasional appearances by a harmonizing quartet) merits a peek even if you have no need for a trim. When operating, it's usually open from about 9 A.M. to 5 P.M. daily. This is a popular spot for a child's first haircut, but they serve older kids and grown-ups, too (haircuts and beard trims). Walk-ins may be accepted (though there may be a wait). For pricing specifics and to make a reservation, use the My Disney Experience app or website, or visit *disneyworld.com*. Note that a gratuity is not included with the price and must be presented in cash. Just a heads up.

**MAIN STREET FASHION AND APPAREL:** Character-related gifts and apparel are the hallmarks of this section of the Emporium shop. The area also stocks golf shirts, bags, hats, sweatshirts, and accessories. You'll find it next to Casey's Corner.

**MAIN STREET CONFECTIONERY:** Tasty treats are sold in this old-fashioned, newly expanded, pink-and-white paradise. It's a delight at any time of day, but more so when the cooks in the shop's glass-walled kitchen dip apples in caramel or roll out freshly made crispie treats. Then the candy sends up clouds of aroma that you could swear were being fanned out onto the street. There's fresh-made fudge, chocolate-dipped strawberries, and candy-coated marshmallows, along with jelly beans and many other confections that'll satisfy any sweet tooth.

**NEWSSTAND:** No news is sold in the Magic Kingdom—even at its trusty newsstand, which is near the park entrance. (It's to the left, just inside the gate.) The stand sells character items and souvenirs. (It may not be open in all of 2024.)

## LET IT RAIN

The show doesn't stop just because of a little storm. Instead, shops throughout the Magic Kingdom sell plastic ponchos and umbrellas to help keep guests dry. (If there is lightning in the area, some attractions will temporarily cease operation. Safety first.) If you're lucky, you may even catch a performance of the Magic Kingdom's Rainy Day Cavalcade!

## DISNEY'S PHOTOPASS

As you wander the theme parks, Disney cast members will be happy to snap your picture—just ask! After mugging for the camera, you will be asked to scan your MagicBand (see page 24) or a PhotoPass card. It will link all such photographs together for viewing on the Internet. You can ogle and email the low-res images for free for up to 45 days after they are taken. High res digital images and high-quality prints of various sizes are for sale. To buy or peruse photos, visit *mydisneyphotopass.com* or use your My Disney Experience account. All Walt Disney World theme parks have spots for photo viewing/purchasing. Check a (complimentary) park guidemap for locations. Individual photo downloads start at about $17, while the unlimited Memory Maker Package runs about $169 if purchased in advance. (This is a bit of a splurge, but a very convenient way to get quality shots of your whole party.) Say cheese!

**THE SHADOW BOX:** Watching Rubio Artist Co. silhouette cutters snip black paper into likenesses of park guests is one of Main Street's more fascinating diversions. The speed at which they work is astounding. It's a unique keepsake you'll treasure for years to come. The Shadow Box is at the corner of Main and Center streets.

**UPTOWN JEWELERS:** Designed to resemble a turn-of-the-twentieth-century collectibles shop, this spiffy store specializes in jewelry, watches, handbags, scarves, purses, wallets, shoes, garments, and accessories from The Disney Dress Shop, and other gifts. Note that the Uptown Jewelers store is home to the Disney Parks/PANDORA Jewelry Collection.

**WHEELCHAIR AND ECV RENTAL:** Guests may rent strollers at a spot under the Main Street Train Station. Wheelchairs and Electric Conveyance Vehicles (ECVs) are offered at a separate location, directly across from the Newsstand, just inside the park entrance. (The supply of ECVs is limited—get there early.) All rentals are offered on a first-come, first-served basis. Hold on to the receipt—it will get you a replacement stroller or wheelchair should yours disappear during the day or if you "hop" to another theme park. Note that any equipment rented at this location cannot be taken out of the Magic Kingdom.

## ADVENTURELAND

**AGRABAH BAZAAR:** Stop here to find clothing and accessories covered with animal prints and images, toys and clothing with a safari theme, and more. The bazaar may also stock souvenirs and snacks themed to Disney pals. It may not be open in all of 2024.

**BWANA BOB'S:** In addition to tropically themed jewelry, Bob peddles bags, hats, pins, sunglasses, and more.

**ISLAND SUPPLY:** This small tropical shop features a large selection of sunglasses and sunglass accessories.

**PLAZA DEL SOL CARIBE BAZAAR:** Ahoy there, mateys! A swashbuckler's delight, the joint adjoining the Pirates of the Caribbean sells stuff celebrating both the attraction and the feature films of the same name. It also stocks other pirate booty, including Jolly Roger flags, rings, dolls, pirate costumes, themed hats, and eye patches. If that's not enough treasure for you, check out the candy and snacks. This is one of our favorite Walt Disney World shops.

## FRONTIERLAND

**BIG AL'S:** Named for perhaps the most popular (and least talented) member of the Country Bears, this riverfront locale is known for its selection of headwear, including Davy Crockett-style caps.

PHOTO BY JILL SAFRO

**FRONTIER TRADING POST:** This is a popular place to shop for collector pins and associated accoutrements. Since it has the largest selection of pins in the park, they might want to rename this the Pin Trading Post. The Trading Post also has a small selection of Western-themed shirts, plus hats, decorative rocks, and MagicBands.

**PRAIRIE OUTPOST & SUPPLY:** Though "on pause" at press time, this turn-of-the-twentieth-century general store is known for candy (including a wall of jelly beans), coffee, cookies, pastries, jellies, and kitchen accessories.

## LIBERTY SQUARE

**LIBERTY SQUARE PORTRAIT GALLERY:** Guests may have their portraits or caricatures drawn in this open-air studio in the middle of Liberty Square.

**MEMENTO MORI:** Welcome, foolish mortals—to a spooky and spectacular shop dedicated to all things Haunted Mansion. Here you may find anything from gargoyle candle holders and hourglasses to "Ghost Host" gear and hitchhiking ghost figurines.

**YE OLDE CHRISTMAS SHOPPE:** A wide variety of festive Yuletide items, including decorative Disney-themed gifts and ornaments (many of which can be personalized), is available year-round. Look for items such as stockings, tree toppers, and Christmas cards.

## FANTASYLAND

**BIBBIDI BOBBIDI BOUTIQUE:** This spirited salon offers young guests the opportunity to be transformed into princesses and knights. Magical makeovers are usually available from  about 8 A.M. to about 7 P.M. Prices vary. Magic Kingdom admission is required to visit this boutique. (There is an a additional Bibbidi Bobbidi Boutique location at Disney Springs. While there is no admission fee for Disney Springs, there is a charge for services at both boutique locations.) For pricing or to make a reservation, call 407-939-7895. Photo packages are offered, too. Reservations are strongly recommended for this popular boutique.

**BIG TOP SOUVENIRS:** A not-so-hidden gem, Big Top is joyfully themed and full of energy. Step inside the tent and discover Disney merchandise galore. At the center of the tent is Big Top Treats—a circus-themed confectionery dispensing caramel corn, cupcakes, cookies, crispie treats, caramel apples, cotton candy, and other sweet treats. Yum.

**BONJOUR VILLAGE GIFTS:** Visit this small Fantasyland boutique if you're looking to augment your Disney princess doll collection. Also on hand: housewares, clothing, bags, collectibles, and a small selection of merchandise with a *Beauty and the Beast* theme.

**FANTASY FAIRE:** Set beside the Mickey's PhilharMagic attraction, this faire focuses on Disney-themed head-wear, plus shirts, bags, and toys.

**HUNDRED ACRE GOODS:** Located at the exit of The Many Adventures of Winnie the Pooh attraction, this small shop is stuffed with wares featuring friends from the Hundred Acre Wood (among other places). Among the items Pooh Bear proffers are toys, hats, shirts, baby clothing, snacks, and bottled soft drinks.

**SIR MICKEY'S:** Expect to find Disney princess-themed clothing and souvenir items in this shop with a design based on *The Brave Little Tailor*, the cartoon in which Mickey defeats a fearsome giant to win the heart of Princess Minnie. (It was one of the most elaborate and expensive Mickey Mouse cartoons ever made.) Mouse ears may be purchased and monogrammed here.

## TOMORROWLAND

**TOMORROWLAND LAUNCH DEPOT:** The cavernous space **NEW** previously occupied by the Tomorrowland Light & Power Co. (between Space Mountain and the TRON Lightcycle/Run attraction) has been re-themed and restocked. The shelves in this futuristic shop are currently brimming with all things *TRON*-related: including reflective shirts, jackets, hats, and other apparel for the whole family, lots of items that light up (clocks, water bottles, bags, and more), customizable identity chips (which let guests "enter the grid" and personalize a variety of high-tech goodies), plus a selection of grab-and-go snacks and drinks.

**STAR TRADERS:** This is one of the better places to visit for festive, Disney-themed items: plush toys, hats, shirts, candy, etc. Sunglasses and sun-care products are also sold. The Tomorrowland Transit Authority PeopleMover passes through here, too. (To catch a glimpse of it, just look up!)

# Entertainment

In this most magical corner of the World, a slate of live performances ranks among the more serendipitous discoveries. The Magic Kingdom's entertainment mix includes dazzling high-tech shows and old-fashioned numbers alike.

Details will change during the year, but the following is a good indication of this theme park's entertainment repertoire. Check a Magic Kingdom Tip Board, use the My Disney Experience mobile app or website, or visit *disneyworld.com* for the current lineup and showtimes during your visit.

**CASEY'S CORNER PIANIST:** A peppy pianist tickles the ivories of a snow-white upright, just outside Casey's Corner on Main Street, U.S.A. Twenty-minute performances take place throughout the day.

**DAPPER DANS:** You just might encounter a barbershop quartet while strolling down Main Street. Conspicuously clad in straw hats and striped vests, the ever-so jovial Dapper Dans tap-dance and let one-liners fly during their short, four-part-harmony performances. Each show runs about 20 minutes.

**BIRNBAUM'S ★BEST★ HAPPILY EVER AFTER:** It's back! This beloved nighttime spectacular, on hiatus during Walt Disney World's 50th anniversary celebration, made its joyful return last spring. A dynamite, pyrotechnic/digital projection extravaganza, Happily Ever After is presented most evenings when Magic Kingdom park stays open after dark. The jubilant spectacle takes place on and above Cinderella Castle and Main Street, U.S.A. Showtimes

vary—check a park Tip Board or the (free) My Disney Experience app or website for specifics. The action is ideally viewed from Main Street, U.S.A. (which is part of the show!), but can be seen from many perspectives throughout the park. The show is typically presented nightly, rain or shine, but it may be canceled due to inclement weather. Details are subject to change.

**FAIRYTALE GARDEN:** Mirabel from *Encanto* greets guests in this nook beside Cinderella Castle each day (on the right side when facing the Castle from Main Street). Check a park Tip Board for specifics.

**FLAG RETREAT:** At about 5 P.M. each afternoon (check the *My Disney Experience app*), patriotic music fills the air as a color guard marches to Town Square, on Main Street, U.S.A., and takes down the American flag.

**BIRNBAUM'S** ★**BEST**★ **FESTIVAL OF FANTASY PARADE:** A cheerful, musical celebration of Disney Animation, this parade traditionally wends its way down Main Street once a day. The festival focuses on Disney friends who frequent Fantasyland. Kids love to wave to favorite characters—especially Elsa, Tiana, and other Disney royals. The elaborate parade floats are impressive to behold.

The Festival of Fantasy parade highlights the classic tales of *Tangled*, *The Little Mermaid*, *Sleeping Beauty*, *Pinocchio*, *Brave*, *Dumbo*, and more.

**HOEDOWN HAPPENING:** Every now and then a happy hoedown happens near the Grizzly Hall (home of the Country Bear Jamboree). The interactive hootenanny is presented by talented Frontierland cast members—who may be joined by character friends such as the Country Bears. The cheerful display usually wraps up with the Hokey Pokey. Do join in! The seemingly spontaneous party isn't always listed with the park's daily entertainment offerings—so be sure to ask a local worker about the next possible performance.

**MICKEY'S MAGICAL FRIENDSHIP FAIRE:** Mickey and his band of merrymakers are hosting a joyous festival in front of Cinderella Castle, and they are welcoming friends old and new—including you!

Goofy has invited folks from *The Princess and the Frog*; Donald Duck's guests include friends he met at the Snuggly Duckling in the Land of the Enchanted Woods; and Daisy Duck introduces her guests Rapunzel and Flynn Ryder. Mickey has a very special surprise for *Frozen* fans: He traveled all the way to The Land of Mystic Mountains to invite Olaf, Anna, and Elsa (who brings along a little of her trademark icy magic). Festivities include lively dancing, special effects, and memorable music—including an original song. The show is presented daily (but may be canceled due to inclement weather). We recommend viewing this show just before or just after a parade (when parades are offered, of course).

Note that this show replaced Mickey's Royal Friendship Faire and made its debut in early 2022. For updates, check *disneyworld.com* or use the My Disney Experience mobile app or website.

**LET THE MAGIC BEGIN:** The Magic Kingdom park kicks off each morning with a whimsical welcome ceremony. The brief-but-enjoyable show invites guests to gather 'round the Castle forecourt. Mickey Mouse and his pals soon take the stage to greet eager parkgoers. And faster than you can say "Bibbidi bobbidi boo!"—the Magic Kingdom's day has officially begun! Guests who plan to see this show may enter the park up to an hour before the scheduled opening time.

**MAIN STREET PHILHARMONIC:** Clad in bright red and white, Walt Disney World's merry marching band serenades park guests with old-school marches, big-band standards, and classic Disney ditties. Each perky performance lasts about 20 minutes. For showtimes, check the My Disney Experience mobile app.

## HOLIDAY HAPPENINGS

It's a rare holiday that passes quietly at Disney's Magic Kingdom. During certain holidays, the park breaks curfew, staying open late and stepping up its nighttime entertainment. On these festive occasions, special performances of parades and the fireworks are often in store. For updates use the My Disney Experience app or website, or visit *disneyworld.com*.

**EASTER:** Easter is a delightful, though quite busy, time to visit the park. Mr. and Mrs. Easter Bunny may be on hand to help guests celebrate the occasion.

**FOURTH OF JULY:** The busiest day of the summer— and with good reason: There's usually a double-size fireworks extravaganza that lights up the skies above Cinderella Castle and the Seven Seas Lagoon. 'Tis a thrilling spectacle. Arrive at the Magic Kingdom as early as possible for this packed, patriotic occasion.

**HALLOWEEN:** This most spooky of holidays is celebrated on (many) select nights from August through October with a special-ticket event: Mickey's Not-So-Scary Halloween Party. The park closes a bit early on such nights. (Guests with party tickets can remain in M.K.) Expect characters in costume, creepy music and effects, and trick-or-treating throughout the park. In years past, Mickey's Boo-to-You Halloween Parade was featured, as was a special fireworks show. Special entertainment may include performances by the Cadaver Dans (a decidedly dressed down version of the park's beloved barbershop quartet). For details and to order tickets, use the My Disney Experience mobile app or website, visit *disneyworld.com/halloween*, or call 407-939-5277.

**CHRISTMAS:** A towering Christmas tree goes up in Main Street's Town Square, and the entire Magic Kingdom is decked out as only Disney can do it.

On select nights in November and December, WDW's original park hosts a special-admission celebration long known as Mickey's Very Merry Christmas Party. (The number of tickets is limited and this event tends to sell out quickly.) The festivities, complete with hot cocoa, cookies, and snow flurries on Main Street, U.S.A., may include a running (or two) of Mickey's Once Upon a Christmastime Parade, holiday shows, and a special fireworks show. Disney characters are on hand, too.

Mickey's Very Merry Christmas party is a popular (and enjoyable) event. Purchase tickets way ahead of time. And don't forget to don your holiday apparel; *www.disneyworld.com/christmasparty*. On dates when the Christmas Party is offered, the park closes early to day guests. Plan accordingly.

**NEW YEAR'S EVE:** It has always been true that on December 31 the throngs flock here in massive numbers. Expect a dazzling fireworks display (which may also be offered on December 30) and oodles of happy holiday decorations. There's often plenty of nip in the air as the evening goes on—dress in layers.

## WHERE TO FIND THE CHARACTERS AT THE MAGIC KINGDOM

Traditionally, Mickey and his Disney pals make appearances at the park throughout the day. In addition to shows and cavalcades, you can often see him in Town Square Theater. Mirabel meets with guests in Fairytale Garden (next to Cinderella Castle). Alice and her Wonderland friends may appear near the Mad Tea Party. Pooh and Tigger have been known to frequent Fantasyland. Disney royals such as Rapunzel, Tiana, and Elena visit Princess Fairytale Hall. You may find Goofy, Donald, Daisy, and Minnie at Pete's Silly Sideshow. Peter Pan likes to hang out near his Fantasyland attraction. Ariel enjoys greeting folks in her Fantasyland grotto. Snow White and Mulan have appeared on the porch at the Town Square Theater. Belle meets guests following performances of Enchanted Tales with Belle. And Anna and Elsa wave to guests from a float in the Festival of Fantasy parade. Park eateries such as Cinderella's Royal Table and the Crystal Palace offer opportunities to mingle with Disney pals, too. (See page 312.) For updates, visit *disneyworld.com*. Details are subject to change.

# Hot Tips

- Get to the Magic Kingdom about a half hour before the park is scheduled to open—guests may get a sneak peek at Main Street, U.S.A., before the rest of the park starts up for the day.

- On most mornings, Mickey Mouse and his pals welcome guests to the park in Let the Magic Begin, a ceremony offered 5 minutes before the Magic Kingdom's posted opening time.

- If you're driving to the Magic Kingdom, start very early. Most visitors arrive between 9:30 A.M. and 11:30 A.M., and the adjoining roads and parking lots are jammed.

- No matter what mode of travel you choose, allow extra time to reach the park entrance. Area traffic and security checks can cause delays—especially during peak times of day.

- For the best fireworks view, stand on Main Street, U.S.A., between Town Square and Casey's Corner. If you don't mind missing the projections on Main Street, know that the fireworks can be seen from vantage points throughout the park.

- All Walt Disney World theme parks and water parks offer free Wi-Fi, but charging stations are rare. We recommend you bring a battery pack from home or buy a portable phone charging system from an in-park kiosk for about $30.

- The Main Street plaza gardens are a lovely place for a picnic (on the lawn). Don't forget sun protection.

- On super soggy afternoons, the Magic Kingdom's usual parade may not be presented. Instead, guests may be treated to the short-but-very-sweet Rainy Day Character Cavalcade. Catch it if you can!

- Travel light. The fewer bags you have, the faster you will pass through the security check-point.

- Avoid the inevitable mealtime rush hours by eating early or late: before 11:30 A.M. or after 2 P.M., and before 5 P.M. or after 8 o'clock in the evening.

- Table-service restaurants are in high demand in the Magic Kingdom. Book yours as early as possible. (And if you can't use a reservation, be sure to cancel it to avoid fees.)

- At busy times in the park, take in these (usually) less-packed attractions: The Country Bear Jamboree, The Enchanted Tiki Room, Walt Disney's Carousel of Progress, and the Hall of Presidents.

- Use a smartphone to check all attraction wait times via the My Disney Experience app (which may be downloaded for free).

- If your party decides to split up, set a meeting place and time. Avoid regrouping in front of Cinderella Castle, since this area can become quite congested.

- You can usually get in line for an attraction right up until the minute the park closes.

- Jazz up the time spent waiting in line with Play Disney Parks—a free mobile app that entertains with attraction-themed fun, interactive in-park adventures, trivia, and other diversions.

- Park guests have the right to "chicken out" at any time while waiting in line. In other words, should you or a member of your party have second thoughts about soaring on Space Mountain, visiting with the grinning ghosts of the Haunted Mansion, or braving another attraction, simply inform an attendant and you will be discreetly whisked out a special exit.

- If you have rented a stroller, plan to return it just before the nightly fireworks presentation. That way, after the show, you can make a beeline for your pillow rather than stand in a line to return the stroller.

- Some of the merchandise found in the shops at Walt Disney World may be purchased with the Shop Disney Parks app and at *shopdisney.com*.

- If the park closes early on the day you plan to visit, consider booking dinner at a Magic Kingdom area resort (Contemporary, Grand Floridian, Polynesian Village, or Wilderness Lodge). But keep in mind that transportation to and from the Magic Kingdom and its parking lot only runs for approximately one hour after the park closes. Plan accordingly.

- At press time, TRON: Lightcycle/Run and Seven Dwarfs Mine Train were available via Individual Lightning Lane selection (fees apply). For updates, use the My Disney Experience app or website, or visit *disneyworld.com*.

# Hidden Mickeys

Disney Imagineers have hidden Mickey's image all over Walt Disney World. Some are easier to track down than others. Here are some of the most popular "Hidden Mickeys" at the Magic Kingdom. How many can you find? Check the box when you spot each one!

☐ **PIRATES OF THE CARIBBEAN:** As you enter the ride's main building and get on the standby line (the queue on the left), keep your eyes peeled for four large cabinets hanging on both sides of the wall (you will pass a set of smaller ones on the right before reaching these). The locks on the cabinets form Hidden Mickeys.

☐ **BIG THUNDER MOUNTAIN RAILROAD:** At the very end of the ride and after the train slows down, look to your right to find two sets of gear shifts laying on the ground. The second set forms a Hidden Mickey, although you may notice that the dimensions are not quite proportional (Mickey's ears are significantly smaller than his "head").

☐ **THE HAUNTED MANSION:** In the ghostly party scene, look at the bottom left corner of the banquet table for a Hidden Mickey made of two saucers and a plate. (This Hidden Mickey is easily replicated at home!)

☐ **CAROUSEL OF PROGRESS:** In the Christmas scene, look to the far left for nutcrackers lined up on top of the fireplace. The nutcracker farthest to the left is a Mickey nutcracker. Also in this scene, look for a Mickey plush toy in a box under the Christmas tree and a special pepper grinder on the kitchen counter (it's best seen from seats on the right side of the revolving theater).

☐ **BUZZ LIGHTYEAR'S SPACE RANGER SPIN:** Once you enter the ride's interior queue, look for a poster on the right called "Planets of the Galactic Alliance" and locate a planet called "Pollost Prime." One of the continents forms a Mickey profile. Keep your eyes peeled during the attraction's last room and you will see this same planet on the left side.

☐ **MICKEY'S PHILHARMAGIC GIFT SHOP:** Take a look at the ledge that surrounds this shop. Spot the metal music stands and you've found some Hidden Mickeys!

☐ **UNDER THE SEA–JOURNEY OF THE LITTLE MERMAID:** When your ride vehicle enters the scene where everyone's favorite crab sings "Under the Sea," you may spot several purple corals that collectively form Mr. Mouse's head. (Hint: Two are on the floor and one is on a wall.)

☐ **IT'S A SMALL WORLD:** Don't rush into the queue, because the wait time sign forms a Hidden Mickey if you tilt your head to the left. Once on the ride, pay close attention while in the Africa room and search for purple leaves hanging from the ceiling that form several Hidden Mickeys. (Hint: You will find them by the giraffes.)

☐ **THE MAGIC CARPETS OF ALADDIN:** You'll feel like a pro once you find this small but very cool Hidden Mickey. First find the Agrabah Bazaar shop (across from the Magic Carpets of Aladdin exit) and find the pole with a thick blue stripe at the bottom. Take about three steps toward the attraction and look down to find a charm in the cement with a Hidden Mickey in the center.

☐ **TOMOROWLAND TRANSIT AUTHORITY PEOPLE-MOVER:** Toward the end of the ride, you'll glide past a futuristic woman getting her hair done. That fashionable future-dweller has a Hidden Mickey on her belt buckle. (Hint: She's on the right side of the ride vehicle's forward motion.)

☐ **SWISS FAMILY TREEHOUSE:** As you make the trek up (and down) the treehouse stairs, take a good look at the tree's giant trunk. What is cleverly camouflaged by moss and bark? A subtle-but-familiar silhouette.

☐ **TORTUGA TAVERN:** Peek in this Adventureland eatery's window and you will see three candles that line up to form a Hidden Mickey.

*Specifics may change during 2024.*

# Where in the World?

All of the photos on this page were taken at the Magic Kingdom. Do you know where? We challenge you to find all the spots where these images were shot and safely snap a (non-flash) photo for yourself as you discover each one. Happy hunting! (For locations, turn to page 364.)

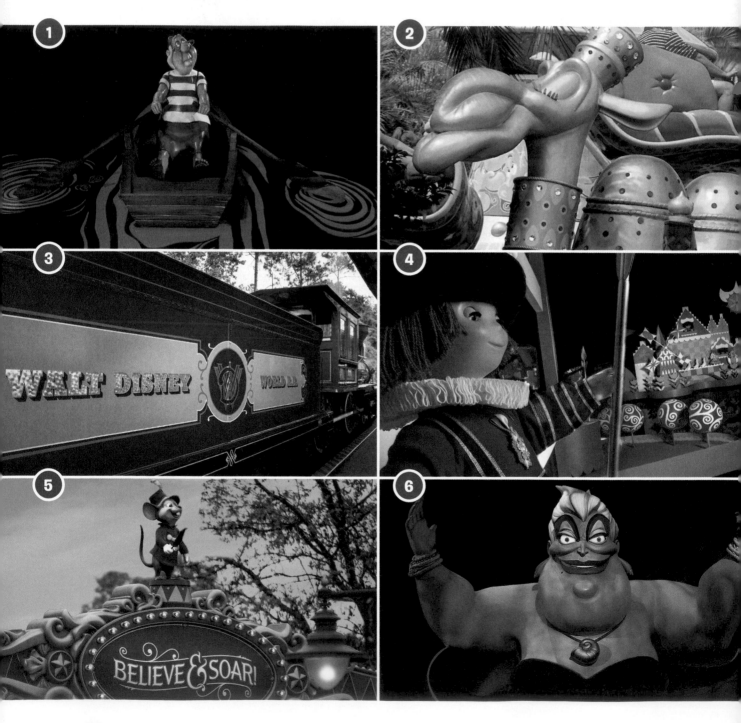

# EPCOT

Imagine a place with an entertainment inventory that includes both a rich sampling of world cultures and a fun, enlightening journey to the technological frontier. You now have an inkling of the eye-opening and mind-broadening potential of EPCOT — a happy place that has evolved most imaginatively since the day it opened.

Walt Disney suggested the idea way back in 1966: "EPCOT will be an experimental prototype community of tomorrow that will take its cue from the new ideas and technologies that are emerging from the creative center of American industry." It would never be completed, he said, but would "always be introducing and testing and demonstrating new materials and systems." On October 1, 1982, Walt Disney's dream became a reality. The park consists of four areas of exploration: World Celebration, World Discovery, World Nature, and World Showcase. The initial trio examines ideas in science, technology, and other topics in ways that make them downright irresistible. The last celebrates the diversity of the world's peoples, portraying a stunning array of nations, with extraordinary devotion to detail. Test Track puts guests on the thrilling inside track of the fast-paced world of automobile design. A re-imagined Soarin' — known as Soarin' Around the World — delivers the breathtaking sensation of flight. And favorites such as Spaceship Earth, Turtle Talk with Crush, and Frozen Ever After continue to ignite the imaginative forces within us all. In keeping with the ever-evolving tradition, EPCOT guests will be treated to enhancements for years to come.

Think of EPCOT as Disney's playground for curious, thoughtful, and adventurous guests of all ages. The experiences it delivers — all of them wonders of the real world — continue to amaze, educate, inspire, and (of course) entertain.

> "It's kind of fun to do the impossible."
> —**Walt Disney**

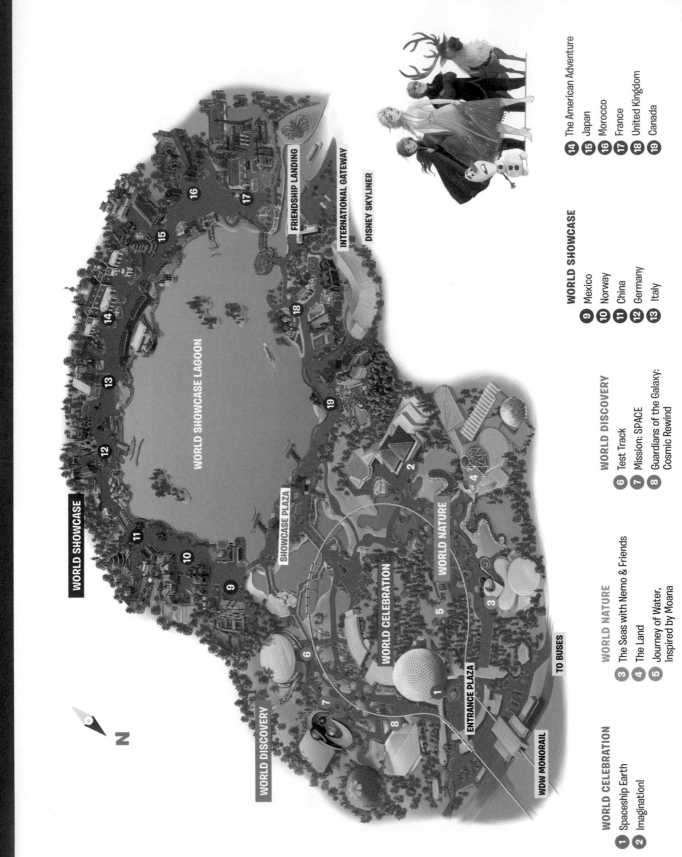

# EPCOT

WORLD SHOWCASE LAGOON

WORLD SHOWCASE

FRIENDSHIP LANDING

INTERNATIONAL GATEWAY

DISNEY SKYLINER

SHOWCASE PLAZA

WORLD DISCOVERY

WORLD CELEBRATION

WORLD NATURE

ENTRANCE PLAZA

TO BUSES

WDW MONORAIL

**WORLD CELEBRATION**

**1** Spaceship Earth
**2** Imagination!

**WORLD NATURE**

**3** The Seas with Nemo & Friends
**4** The Land
**5** Journey of Water,
Inspired by Moana

**WORLD DISCOVERY**

**6** Test Track
**7** Mission: SPACE
**8** Guardians of the Galaxy:
Cosmic Rewind

**WORLD SHOWCASE**

**9** Mexico
**10** Norway
**11** China
**12** Germany
**13** Italy

**14** The American Adventure
**15** Japan
**16** Morocco
**17** France
**18** United Kingdom
**19** Canada

# Getting Oriented

Triple the Magic Kingdom park and you have an idea of the size of EPCOT. As for layout, it's shaped a bit like an hourglass. The pavilions of World Celebration, World Nature, and World Discovery fill the northern bulb, while the international potpourri known as World Showcase occupies the southern bulb. World Celebration is anchored on the north by the imposing silver geosphere dubbed Spaceship Earth, with World Discovery and World Nature filling out the region formerly known as Future World.

As you pass through EPCOT's main Entrance Plaza, Spaceship Earth looms ahead. Pathways curve around the 180-foot-tall geosphere, depositing guests throughout the park. Test Track, Mission: SPACE, and Guardians of the Galaxy: Cosmic Rewind flank Spaceship Earth on the east, while Imagination!, The Land, and The Seas with Nemo & Friends lie to the west.

In World Showcase, the international pavilions are arranged around World Showcase Lagoon, with The American Adventure on the lake's southernmost shore. Several paths stretch from the park's north end (which includes EPCOT's main entrance) to World Showcase Promenade, a 1.2-mile thoroughfare that wraps around the lagoon, winding past each International pavilion in the process.

### HOW TO GET THERE

Take Exit 67 off I-4. Continue along to the EPCOT Auto Plaza; if you park in a distant parking lot, take a tram to the entrance (if the service is offered).

**By WDW Transportation:** From the Grand Floridian, Contemporary, and Polynesian Village: hotel monorail to the Transportation and Ticket Center (TTC), then switch to the TTC-EPCOT monorail or bus. From Magic Kingdom: express monorail or resort monorail to the TTC, then switch to the TTC-EPCOT monorail. From Disney Springs: bus to any resort, then transfer to an EPCOT bus or boat. From Disney's Hollywood Studios: Disney Skyliner, water taxi, or bus. From Disney's Animal Kingdom, all other WDW resorts, Four Seasons resort, and the resorts on Hotel Plaza Boulevard: buses or Disney Skyliner.

International Gateway (EPCOT's "back door"), provides access to the park via World Showcase. Located between the France and U.K. pavilions, it may be reached via walkways and FriendShip water taxis from BoardWalk, Yacht & Beach Club, Swan and Dolphin, and Disney's Hollywood Studios. The Disney Skyliner connects International Gateway with the Studios, plus Caribbean Beach, Art of Animation, Pop Century, and Riviera resorts. International Gateway has a Guest Relations location, too.

### PARKING

All-day car parking at EPCOT starts at $25 for day visitors (standard parking is free to WDW resort guests and most annual passholders; trucks, trailers, and RVs cost more; preferred parking is $45–$50). Trams, which provide transportation between distant lots and EPCOT's main entrance, were "on pause" at press time. Be sure to note the section and aisle in which you park. Parking receipts allow for re-entry here (and other Disney parks) throughout the day.

### HOURS

EPCOT's hours are usually about 9 A.M. to 9 P.M. During certain holiday periods and summer months, hours are extended. It's best to arrive a bit early. For updates, use the My Disney Experience app or website, or visit *disneyworld.com*.

### GETTING AROUND

Water taxis, called FriendShips, ferry guests across World Showcase Lagoon. It's not much quicker than walking, but it's a nice way to rest weary feet. The only other way to traverse this vast area is on foot. Note that FriendShip boats do not operate during EPCOT's nighttime spectacular.

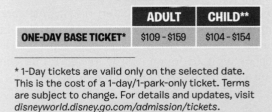

## ADMISSION PRICES

Restricted to use only in EPCOT. Prices are for Date-Based tickets. Prices exclude tax and are likely to rise in 2024 (they always do!).

|  | ADULT | CHILD** |
|---|---|---|
| **ONE-DAY BASE TICKET*** | $109 – $159 | $104 – $154 |

* 1-Day tickets are valid only on the selected date. This is the cost of a 1-day/1-park-only ticket. Terms are subject to change. For details and updates, visit *disneyworld.disney.go.com/admission/tickets*.

** 3 through 9 years of age; children under age 3 free (no ticket required)

# Park Primer

### BABY FACILITIES

There are changing tables, a feeding area with high chairs, a kitchen with a microwave and sink, and comfy facilities for nursing mothers at the Baby Care Center, located between Test Track and the Mexico pavilion. Disposable diapers may be kept behind the counter at some EPCOT shops.

### DISABILITY INFORMATION

Nearly all of EPCOT is accessible to guests using wheelchairs. Parking for guests with disabilities is available. Additional services are available for guests with visual and hearing disabilities. The complimentary Guide for Guests with Disabilities is offered at the park entrances and at Guest Relations. For more information, visit *disneyworld.com* and refer to the *Getting Ready to Go* chapter of this book.

### CAMERA NEEDS

The World Traveler shop (at International Gateway) and the Pin Traders–Camera Center (near Spaceship Earth) stock some batteries. Memory cards are not sold at WDW. It's best to bring other camera necessities from home. Selfie sticks are not permitted inside any Disney theme or water park.

### FIRST AID

Minor medical problems are handled at the First Aid Center, between Test Track and the Mexico pavilion. *In case of emergency, tell an employee and call 911.*

### INFORMATION

Guest Relations, which has locations at the main Entrance Plaza, in World Celebration, and at International Gateway, has guidemaps and a helpful staff.

### LOST CHILDREN

If you lose track of a child, alert the nearest park employee ASAP. A member of your party should remain in the area where you became separated, as kids are typically found nearby. (Be sure kids have your mobile number handy at all times.)

### LOCKERS

Lockers are found near Spaceship Earth and at the International Gateway entrance. Cost is $10–$15 for unlimited use throughout the day (in EPCOT only).

### LOST & FOUND

Report lost belongings to a Guest Relations location and complete a report at *disneyworld.disney.go.com/guest-services/lost-and-found.*

### MONEY MATTERS

There are automated teller machines (ATMs) at the main entrance, on the path between World Celebration and World Showcase, and at The American Adventure pavilion. Some foreign currency may be exchanged at Guest Relations. Major credit cards (American Express, JCB, Discover, Visa, Diner's Club, and MasterCard), and Disney gift cards are accepted throughout WDW. MagicBands and Walt Disney World resort IDs are accepted at most EPCOT locations (if they're backed up with a major credit card).

### SAME-DAY RE-ENTRY

Be sure to wear your MagicBand (if you used it for admission to the park) or retain your ticket if you plan to return to EPCOT later the same day.

### SECURITY CHECK

Guests entering WDW theme parks are subject to a thorough security check. All bags will be checked by security personnel before guests may enter. A metal detector screens guests. Weapons (including toys) are prohibited. For details and a complete listing of Disney Park Rules, visit a Guest Relations location, or go to *www.disneyworld.com/ParkRules.*

### STROLLERS & WHEELCHAIRS

Strollers, wheelchairs, and ECVs (Electric Conveyance Vehicles) may be rented at both EPCOT entrances. Cost is $15 for single strollers, $31 for doubles, and $12 for wheelchairs. A Length of Stay rental yields a $2-per-day discount for a single, $4-per-day for a double. It costs $50 a day for an ECV, plus a $20 deposit. Quantities are limited. The receipt can be used that same day to get a replacement at any WDW theme park. If you bring your own stroller, it can't be larger than 31 inches wide and 52 inches long.

# World Celebration

A mere listing of the basic themes covered by the pavilions at EPCOT — including agriculture, the ocean, the land, car design, communication, imagination, technology, and space — tends to sound a tad academic. But when these intriguing topics are presented with a special flair, they become part of an experience that ranks among Disney's most entertaining.

Some of these subjects are explored in the course of lively and unusual "adventures," involving a whole arsenal of motion pictures, special effects, and Audio-Animatronics figures so lifelike that it is hard to remain unmoved. The basic elements are also appealing in their own right, from the palm-tree-dotted Entrance Plaza (which has been thoroughly refurbished) to the path under Spaceship Earth, the many-faceted "geosphere" that has become the universal symbol of EPCOT.

The park is so vast that it's hard to know what to do first. Many guests stop at Spaceship Earth (in World Celebration) on their way into the park. As a result, they end up spending more time waiting in line than they need to. A wise alternative is to save Spaceship Earth for later in the day (when the lines inevitably thin out), and head for World Discovery or World Nature. Take in Frozen Ever After and Remy's Ratatouille Adventure (at World Showcase) and as many Nature and Discovery attractions as time allows. Refer to page 37 for a more detailed version of this EPCOT touring plan.

**Hot Tip!** If you've got small children in your party, be sure to do Frozen Ever After and Remy's Ratatouille Adventure in World Showcase, Journey of Water, Inspired by Moana, and The Seas with Nemo & Friends in World Nature, and the Imagination! pavilion in World Celebration (little ones simply adore the Leapfrog Fountains outside Imagination!). And don't miss the Kidcot Fun Stop craft areas in the 11 countries of World Showcase.

## DREAMERS POINT

**NEW** Among Walt Disney's dreams for EPCOT were that it be dedicated to the happiness of the people who go there and that the Experimental Prototype Community of Tomorrow "always be in a state of becoming." Those dreams have certainly been fulfilled by Imagineers as EPCOT has grown and evolved throughout the years. And now guests can dream along with Walt at a new statue that celebrates the legacy of the original dreamer. You'll find it near the exit to Spaceship Earth. And remember: When you dream with Walt, you have to dream big!

Another strategy — one that requires quite a bit of extra walking, but can help skirt a long line or two — is to explore World Showcase early in the day, while many guests interact with attractions in the rest of the park. Then, in the late afternoon — when many folks have migrated to World Showcase — return to the area formerly known as Future World. Although long lines can be found during peak seasons at Soarin' Around the World, Mission: SPACE (both versions), Guardians of the Galaxy: Cosmic Rewind, Spaceship Earth, Frozen Ever After, and Test Track throughout most of the late morning and afternoon, it's often a bit less hectic from late afternoon until park closing time. But don't forget to make it back to World Showcase Lagoon in time to see the park's explosive nighttime spectacular. There are excellent viewing locations throughout the World Showcase promenade. Get there early to stake out your preferred turf.

# SPACESHIP EARTH

As it looms impressively just above the Earth, this great, faceted silver structure looks a little bit like a spaceship ready to blast off. It appears large from a distance, and it seems even more immense when viewed from directly underneath. It's no surprise that some visitors simply stop beneath it and gawk.

The show inside, which explores the continuing quest by human beings to create the future, remains one of EPCOT's most compelling—if slower moving—attractions. It's an intriguing, narrated journey through time. It also has an interactive element that's a real hoot.

A common misconception about Spaceship Earth is that it is a geodesic dome. Not so. It is a *geosphere*. A geodesic dome is only half a sphere, while Spaceship Earth is almost completely round. Known to many simply as "the Ball," Spaceship Earth is a sight to behold.

Noted science-fiction writer Ray Bradbury, together with a team of consultants from the Smithsonian Institution, the Los Angeles area's prestigious Huntington Library, the University of Southern California, and (among others) the University of Chicago, collaborated with Disney in developing this memorable 14-minute journey. It begins in an inky-black time tunnel, complete with a musty smell that suggests the dust of ages, and continues through history from the days of Cro-Magnons (30,000 or 40,000 years ago) to humans in the future.

**Hot Tip!** The line for Spaceship Earth is usually quite long during the early morning hours and relatively short in the late afternoon and evening.

Every scene is executed in exquisite detail. The symbols on the wall of the Egyptian temple really are hieroglyphics, and the content of the letter being dictated by the pharaoh was excerpted from a missive actually received by an agent of a ruler of the period. Later on you'll catch a glimpse of a 1970s' mainframe computer room and a garage scene depicting the creation of the personal computer.

All of these sights are enough to keep heads turning as the "time machines" wend their way upward. The most dazzling scene is saved for the ride's finale, when the audience is placed in outer space—with a prime view of our beautiful, blue planet, aka Spaceship Earth. The journey winds down with a custom look at your own future, courtesy of a nifty touch screen in the ride vehicle.

The post-show area—Project Tomorrow—features several interactive areas all emphasizing technology and its influence on daily life. Themes include medicine, power, and accident avoidance.

### DID YOU KNOW?

Spaceship Earth weighs 16 million pounds! Its silver outer "skin" is made up of 11,324 aluminum and plastic-alloy triangles. And rainwater never falls off the sphere—it's channeled into the ball and surreptitiously funneled away.

**CLUB COOL:** Adjacent to the Creations Shop, this cool club is Coca-Cola's complimentary International Tasting Station. After quenching your thirst, courtesy of the Coca-Cola Company, you may choose to do a bit of shopping. There's plenty of Coke-themed merchandise to peruse here, as well as a handy "Coke"-tail bar with beverages, floats, and other treats (fees apply for merch and items from the bar). Note that two of the sample flavors tend to be acquired tastes . . . just a heads-up!

**CREATIONS SHOP:** A dynamic shopping destination, Creations embodies the spirit and tradition of EPCOT. In addition to its status as a bustling emporium, the bright and airy space is a showcase for artists who've created unique odes to Mickey Mouse. The wares are meant to "extend Disney storytelling" and let guests bring a bit of it home. To that end, there's an extensive selection of Disney merchandise. Creations Shop, which opened in 2021, replaced MouseGear as this park's flagship shop. It usually stays open about a half hour later than the rest of EPCOT.

# IMAGINATION!

The oddly shaped glass pyramids that house the park's Imagination! pavilion are quite a striking sight to behold. They certainly set the stage for the atypical experiences inside. One of the major attractions is Journey Into Imagination with Figment, a slow-moving tour of the Imagination Institute. Also located here is the Disney and Pixar Short Film Festival.

Another pavilion highlight is the set of classic, quirky fountains outside — the Jellyfish Fountains, which spurt streams of water that spread out at the top, looking for an instant like their namesake sea creature, and the Leap Frog Fountains, which send out smooth streams of water that arc from one garden plot to another in the most astonishing fashion. Kids love 'em.

**BIRNBAUM'S** **DISNEY AND PIXAR SHORT FILM FESTIVAL:**
**★BEST★** Head over to the Magic Eye Theater to enter the bright and imaginative world of three animated shorts. Though films are subject to change, the one that is expected to play throughout 2024 is *Get a Horse*. It stars everyone's favorite mouse as he, Minnie, and their pals Horace Horsecollar and Clarabelle Cow delight in a manic, musical wagon ride. It combines with two other films to make for a most merry movie experience. Each of the animated shorts is presented in 3-D (pick up your glasses on the way into the theater) and features entertaining "4-D" effects. This unexpectedly delightful attraction has appeal for guests of all ages, provided they are mature enough to wear 3-D glasses. (It's also a very nice way to enjoy some restorative air-conditioning!) For updates on the short films set to be screened during your trip to EPCOT, visit *disneyworld.com* or use the My Disney Experience website or mobile app.

**JOURNEY INTO IMAGINATION WITH FIGMENT:** Figment, the beloved purple dragon with the orange wings and yellow eyes, is on hand to guide guests on an imaginative quest. The intended goal? To figure out, once and for all, the best way to capture the human imagination. No easy task.

The journey takes place inside the Imagination Institute, where guests are invited to tour the institute's various labs, such as the Sight Lab, the Sound Lab, and the Smell Lab. All in all, it's a tame experience, save for the occasional blast of air or flashing lights. The disappearing butterfly is a true highlight.

Nostalgia buffs, take note: The classic song "One Little Spark," which made its debut with the original version of this ride (in 1983), underscores the current version of the show.

**IMAGEWORKS:** It's a rare tot-aged ImageWorks visitor who doesn't experience at least some of the emotion felt by the little one who cried when her parents tried to whisk her away from the interactive play area. There used to be more to explore, but it's still worth a visit.

There's a small shop with a large selection of Figment-themed souvenirs. Nestled near the exit of ImageWorks Labs, the store also proffers hats, T-shirts, toys, snacks, and other Disney wares.

# World Nature

## THE SEAS WITH NEMO & FRIENDS

Welcome to one of the largest facilities ever dedicated to humanity's relationship with the ocean. The pavilion was designed by Disney Imagineers, in cooperation with oceanographic experts and scientists.

Though it enjoys the distinction of being one of the park's classic pavilions (it made its splashy debut in 1986), what used to be known as The Living Seas is as fresh as ever — thanks in part to a familiar clownfish called Nemo and some of his aquatic acquaintances.

Once inside, guests can find the animated critters' real-life counterparts, including clownfish, blue tangs, sharks, and puffer fish.

The pavilion also features a Nemo-themed ride, a nifty interactive encounter with an animated turtle, and an engaging post-show area. Little ones enjoy Bruce's Sub House — a hands-on/fins-on play area that celebrates the ocean's toothiest residents. From there, take a look at a simulated Caribbean coral reef environment. For many, the crowning jewel of this pavilion is the simple-but-spectacular Turtle Talk with Crush. This pavilion is an excellent destination for big and little kids alike.

**SEA BASE ALPHA SHOP:** All visitors to the Seas pavilion filter though this shop on their way back to EPCOT's World Nature zone — and many stop to peruse the wares. In addition to many a *Finding Nemo*–themed souvenir, this area celebrates other colorful creatures of the sea — in the form of shirts, hats, and plush toys.

**BRUCE'S SUB HOUSE:** Explore this small adventure zone within Sea Base Alpha and you just may learn a thing or two about Bruce (from *Finding Nemo*) and his fellow sharks. There are several hands-on activities (including a chance to learn what shark skin feels like), exhibits such as Bruce's scrapbook, and fishy photo ops. You can also test your undersea expertise by taking quizzes crafted by Nemo's teacher, Mr. Ray. Good luck!

### WHERE TO EAT IN EPCOT

A complete listing of EPCOT eateries—full-service restaurants, fast-food spots, and snack shops—can be found in the *Good Meals, Great Times* chapter of this book. Refer to the EPCOT section, beginning on page 270.

## JOURNEY OF WATER, INSPIRED BY MOANA

**NEW** Water is the star of the show at this lush new nature trail, which takes its inspiration from the film *Moana*. While guests meander the pretty pathways, they can witness water come to life as it leaps and flows around them. Just like Moana's pal the ocean, the water here has a personality of its own. As they explore, guests learn about water's endless journey around the globe and why the natural water cycle is important for our planet. So if you want to be in-the-know about $H_2O$, now you know where to go! Journey of Water, Inspired by Moana made its splashy debut last year.

**THE SEAS WITH NEMO & FRIENDS ATTRACTION:** Imagineered in the style of classic Disney family attractions, this undersea adventure is fun for everyone. In it, guests climb aboard a clam-mobile and enter a colorful coral reef. It seems Nemo has wandered off yet again, and his teacher, Mr. Ray, needs help finding him. So keep your eyes peeled!

**Hot Tip!** Many of Walt Disney World's moving attractions—such as Spaceship Earth—can be slowed down to make the boarding process easier for guests with physical limitations and guests who can transfer from a wheelchair (with assistance from someone in their party). Ask a cast member as you enter the attraction.

This ride feels like a little bit of the Magic Kingdom's Fantasyland swam off to EPCOT. The colorful mixture of animated and authentic sea life makes for a nicely layered experience. There's a bit of suspense involved—including several moments of darkness, an appearance by Bruce the shark, and a stressful jellyfish encounter—but rest assured, it all ends happily.

**BIRNBAUM'S ★BEST★ TURTLE TALK WITH CRUSH:** If ever there was a Disney attraction that left park guests smiling and asking, "How do they do that?!"—this is it. The concept seems to be simple enough—a 10-minute, animated show featuring the surfer-dude sea turtle from *Finding Nemo*. The amazing part? The cartoon critter interacts with the audience.

In doing so, he imparts turtle-y wisdom, answers guests' questions, and cracks more than a few jokes. You have to see it to believe it. To do that, you will have to wait your turn—it's popular with guests of all ages. Oh, and Dory, Hank, Bailey, Destiny, Marlin, and Squirt have been known to pop in for a visit, too. Note that kids are encouraged to sit on the floor in front of the big screen. There are benches to accommodate the rest of Crush's guests. The typical guest reaction to this show? It's totally awesome, dude!

**CORAL REEF AQUARIUM:** The man-made reef exists in an enormous tank that holds about six million gallons of salt water and more than 50 species of sea life. Among the 4,000 or so inhabitants are turtles, angelfish, sharks, dolphins, and diamond rays. It's worth it to stop by when breakfast or lunch is served. The feeding frenzy is fun to watch.

Guests sometimes get to see scuba divers testing and demonstrating diving gear and monitoring equipment as they carry on training programs with dolphins.

The Caribbean Coral Reef aquarium is also home to two rescued manatees. Each of these weighty, wondrous creatures gobbles up nearly 100 heads of lettuce per day. They're a sight to behold.

## UNDER THE SEA

A pair of behind-the-scenes EPCOT tours offers guests a closer look at life in The Seas with Nemo & Friends' underwater environs: DiveQuest gives certified scuba divers the opportunity to explore one of the world's largest aquariums. And Dolphins in Depth offers guests the opportunity to learn about dolphin behavior as they closely observe researchers and trainers interacting with dolphins. Reservations for either of the aforementioned adventures can be made via *disneyworld.com*, or by calling 407-WDW-TOUR (939-8687). For additional information about these programs, turn to page 246 of the *Everything Else in the World* chapter and visit *disneyworld.com*.

# THE LAND

Occupying six acres, this enormous skylighted pavilion examines the nature of one of everybody's favorite topics — food. It also gives guests a chance to soar above the clouds in a celebration of flight. A boat ride explores farming in the past and future. Narration gives visitors the chance to learn about the experimental agricultural techniques practiced in the pavilion.

**TIMING TIP:** The Land pavilion's Soarin' Around the World is an exceptionally popular attraction. It's best to visit very early in the morning or grab a Genie+ Lightning Lane selection if possible. (Fees apply for Lightning Lane service. See page 27 for details.)

**LIVING WITH THE LAND:** The Land pavilion's 13½-minute boat ride through meticulously re-created natural locales opens with a dramatic storm scene. Guests sail through tropical rainforests, prairie grain fields, and a family farm. As the boat passes through each realistic setting, recorded narration offers commentary on humanity's ongoing struggle to cultivate and live in harmony with the land. Note the details that make each setting so convincing, such as sand gently blowing over the desert and light flickering from the television in the farmhouse window.

In the next segment, guests enter a plant research laboratory and solarium. Here, our planet's major food crops are being grown in research projects, along with rare new crops that may someday help meet Earth's ever-growing dietary needs.

Also of interest are the experiments being conducted to explore the practice of farming fish, and a desert farm area, where plants get nutrients through a drip irrigation system that delivers just the right amount of water — important in a dry climate.

As unreal as some may appear, all of the plants on view in the experimental greenhouses are living. In contrast, those in the biomes (the ecological communities viewed from the boat ride) were made in Disney studios out of lightweight plastic that simulates the cellulose found in real trees. The trunks and branches were molded from live specimens; the sycamore in the farmhouse's front yard, for example, duplicates one that stands outside a Burbank, California, car wash. Thousands of polyethylene leaves were snapped on.

**Hot Tip!** Got a rumbly in your tumbly? Head for Sunshine Seasons in The Land pavilion. There is a variety of counter-service and grab-and-go selections—apt to appease even the pickiest of eaters. (It's located on pavilion's lower level.)

Note that all of the greenhouse flora is quite real — please resist the urge to touch plants or the sand in which they live.

**BIRNBAUM'S ★BEST★** **SOARIN' AROUND THE WORLD:** Up, up, and away! On this high-flying EPCOT ride (it is one of the most popular attractions in all of Walt Disney World), you will be suspended in a hang-glider-type vehicle up to 45 feet in the air, above a giant IMAX projection dome, and treated to an aerial tour of awe-inspiring landscapes and treasured landmarks. Soarin' has been delighting park guests with its wraparound glory since 2005 — but these days, instead of hovering over just one state (California), park visitors are treated to a much broader aerial tour of the planet.

Soarin' Around the World showcases some of the world's most glorious sights: The Great Wall of China, the plains of Africa, the oceans of Fiji, the Grand Canyon, Egyptian pyramids, and much more. With the wind

in your hair and your legs dangling in the breeze, the hang glider feels so real that you may even be tempted to pull up your feet for fear of tapping the rooftops and landscapes below.

The joyful journey takes about 6 minutes and employs synchronized wind currents, scent machines, and a rousing musical score set to a film that wraps 180 degrees around you. The re-imagined version of this attraction touched down in 2016. It features a high-tech digital screen and projection system and is a hit with guests of all ages.

**Note:** You must be at least 40 inches tall and free of back problems, heart conditions, motion sickness, and other physical limitations to ride. It's much calmer than traditional "thrill" rides, but the sensation of flight is quite realistic. If you're afraid of heights, sit this one out. (Should you discover that you're afraid of heights mid-ride, closing your eyes may help.) Place loose items (including flip-flops) in the pouch under your seat or on the floor in front of you — and be sure to collect them at the end of the flight.

**AWESOME PLANET:** A moving cinematic experience plays continuously at The Land's Harvest Theater. *Awesome Planet* is a visual exploration of the beauty, diversity, and dynamic story of the astonishing orb that we all call home.

The film is the result of a collaboration between Disney Imagineers and the Disney Conservation Fund. Enhanced with in-theater effects (including wind, water, and scents), it tells the story of life on our planet — and why it is so important for us to take care of it. The 10-minute movie runs continuously throughout the day.

# World Discovery

**Note:** Kids who are less than 7 years old must be accompanied by a guest over the age of 14; guests under 40 inches cannot ride; passengers must be free of back problems, heart conditions, motion sickness, and other physical limitations. Pregnant women are advised to sit this one out.

## TEST TRACK

**BIRNBAUM'S ★BEST★** Fasten your safety belt, please! This high-octane destination puts guests through the creative and somewhat frenetic motions of automobile design and testing. The experience starts with guests designing a vehicle in the attraction's high-tech pre-show area. What's most important to you in a car: efficiency, power, responsiveness, or capability? Use a touch screen to design a car with your priorities in mind, then take your virtual "Sim Car" over to the Sim Track and give it a test drive. (They easily could have dubbed this pavilion Sim Track—a Test Track by any other name would be just as cool.)

The 4-minute ride is similar to the original version of Test Track—there's lots of zigging and zagging on the front end, followed by a dramatic near-miss with a big noisy truck. Along the way, you will learn how well your car did in each of the categories featured in the design stage. Finally, a long straightaway feeds into a series of banked turns and another straight shot that sends vehicles rocketing around the pavilion at top speed (up to 65 mph!). The computer-controlled, six-seater vehicles are equipped with video and audio, but no steering wheels or brake pedals. After all is said and done, guests have the opportunity to create a 15-second commercial for their new car and send the video to a friend via email.

**Hot Tip!** If you don't mind splitting up your party, head for the "single rider" line at Test Track. It's generally shorter than the standby line.

## GUARDIANS OF THE GALAXY: COSMIC REWIND

**BIRNBAUM'S ★BEST★** Welcome, Terrans! (That's what folks native to the planet Xandar call Earthlings.) You have been invited—by none other than Nova-Prime Irani Rael—to witness an interstellar demonstration. The innovators at Nova Corps have developed a piece of technology called a Cosmic Generator. It can create jump points (tunnels connecting two places) within the fabric of space. The Xandarians, who are quite eager to show off their nifty new technology, have decided to teleport EPCOT guests to a Nova spaceship to see it in action.

At first, all goes smoothly. Then, all of a sudden, CODE RED! The Cosmic Generator's stolen by a colossal alien who creates a jump point to the dawn of time. His intent? To alter the course of humanity *forever*. Oh, and he plans to do it right away. Of course, Irani Rael alerts the Guardians of the Galaxy—but they're too far away to arrive in time. So it's up to *you* to help save the day! (Thanks to some quick calculations by Rocket the Raccoon, you have the power to do so.)

What follows is a rollicking, rock-'n'-roll-fueled, roller coaster ride. Featuring a backwards launch (the first ever on a Disney coaster), plenty of twists and turns, and ride vehicles that rotate a full 360 degrees, this thrilling trip through space can be intense. And the mix of enormous projection screens and an otherwise pitch-black environment is disorienting for sensitive equilibriums. It's best not to ride on a full stomach.

You must be at least 42 inches tall to experience this attraction, and free from high blood pressure; heart, back, and neck problems; motion sickness; and other physical limitations. Pregnant guests should not ride. At press time, this was designated an "Individual Lightning Lane" attraction (see page 28). Details may change. For updates on ways to access this smile-inducing thriller, go to *disneyworld.com*. This ride rocks!

# MISSION: SPACE

Think you've got "the right stuff"? Well, this is your chance to prove it. EPCOT's out-of-this-world attraction has a bold mission—to give you a chance to feel the excitement and extreme intensity of space travel without ever leaving the planet.

There are two ways to experience this attraction: the "highly intense" Orange Mission to Mars, and the "less intense" Green Mission around Earth. The original Mission: SPACE attraction provides a galaxy of thrills for many brave and sturdy theme park guests. The adventure begins with a white-knuckle blast-off of a spacecraft (which has snug seating for four) on an important mission to Mars. The sustained G-force during the launch is intended to be most realistic. Once en route, expect a rather strange, spectacular sensation. It's not quite weightlessness, but according to astronauts who've felt the real thing, it's pretty darn close. (So much so that it also tends to duplicate the not-so-spectacular sensation of space sickness. In fact, Mission: SPACE has the dubious distinction of being the first attraction in theme park history to be equipped with motion-sickness bags.)

Throughout the journey, you're expected to work with your fellow crew members (assuming the roles of navigator, captain, engineer, and pilot) to accomplish the mission. For the "highly intense" version, we recommend ignoring this call to duty and keeping your eyes glued directly to the screen. This will allow you to sit back and enjoy the ride and decidedly downsize the dizziness factor.

The highly intense version of this attraction has been known to wreak havoc on the equilibrium. To cut the chances of losing your lunch, keep your eyes open at all times and fixed on the screen in front of you. You may be tempted to tilt your head or shut your eyes. Don't. (We promise you will arrive safely on Mars whether you fulfill your astronaut duty or not.)

Bottom line? Most guests who don't get queasy on the "highly intense" Orange Mission tend to rave about it. For us, well, we admit we prefer the ride's gentler version—aka the Green Mission. It's intended for those who would rather not spin. The experience is a bit different on "Mission: SPACE-lite," but it gives everyone a chance to travel through space without getting woozy. The effects may be toned down, but they are still quite extraordinary. We completely enjoy the "less intense" mission around our home planet.

**Note:** Guests must be at least 40 inches tall for the (less intense) Mission: SPACE Green Mission. For the Orange Mission, guests must be at least 44 inches tall and free of back and heart problems, motion sickness, and any other physical limitations. Pregnant women must skip the trip, as should anyone with claustrophobic tendencies. And don't eat just before riding!

## DID YOU KNOW?
Nearly 12 percent of Walt Disney World—enough land to cover nearly 3,000 football fields—is devoted to gardens and maintained landscapes. That's 4,000 acres worth of beauty!

# EPCOT Adventures

EPCOT offers an intriguing collection of unusual adventures. Experiences range from a walking greenhouse tour to an up-close encounter with majestic sea creatures. The following programs were offered at press time and others may be added. For details, (plus pricing updates and reservations), call 407-WDW-TOUR (939-8687), or go to *disneyworld.com*. All details (including prices) are subject to change.

**BEHIND THE SEEDS:** An opportunity for guests of most ages to get a closer look at the greenhouses and fish farm that are the heart of The Land pavilion at EPCOT. During the tour, guests will have close encounters with insects and plants. A skilled guide shares knowledge of hydroponics growing systems and crops from around the planet. Expect to be on your feet for the full hour (give or take) of this experience. Cost is about $35 per person. The minimum age to participate is three, but this tour is best enjoyed by sturdy adults and older kids.

**Hot Tip!** EPCOT is much bigger than it seems, so allow lots of time to get from place to place. (It can take more than a half hour to walk from Spaceship Earth to The American Adventure.) Keep this in mind if you have a restaurant reservation or hope to snag a nice viewing location along the World Showcase promenade for the park's nighttime spectacular. Note that FriendShip water taxis (boats that ferry folks across the lagoon) don't operate during the show or for periods before and after the show.

## DISNEY'S DUCKTALES WORLD SHOWCASE ADVENTURE

**NEW** Calling all treasure hunters! There are seven priceless "Lost Magic Treasures" hidden throughout World Showcase—and you can join Scrooge McDuck on his quest to find them before they fall into the wrong hands! To team up with Mr. McDuck, you'll need a smart device and the (free) Play Disney Parks app. As you play, you'll visit World Showcase pavilions, solve mysteries, and outsmart villains along the way. The game is based on *DuckTales,* but one need not be familiar with the show to enjoy this international adventure. Treasures are hidden in the following World Showcase pavilions: United Kingdom, Canada, France, Japan, Germany, China, and Norway. We wish you the best on the righteous quest!

Reservations for the tour may be made in advance by using the My Disney Experience app or website, or via *disneyworld.com*. Same-day reservations and walk-ins may be available on a limited basis. (Check at the tour desk on the lower level of The Land pavilion—near the left side of the entrance to the Soarin' Around the World attraction.) Theme park admission is required, but is not included with the tour price.

**DIVEQUEST:** The highlight of the 2-hour program is a 40-minute underwater adventure—complete with sharks, turtles, rays, and other fish—in The Seas with Nemo & Friends aquarium. Participants must show proof of current scuba certification and be at least 10 years old. The cost is about $219 per person. Guests ages 10 through 15 must dive with a parent or guardian. Gear is provided. EPCOT admission is neither required nor included in the price of the tour.

**DOLPHINS IN DEPTH:** This 2-hour EPCOT program (about 30 minutes takes place in the water) teaches guests about dolphin behavior as they interact with the social sea creatures and observe researchers and trainers working with them. Cost is about $199 per person. Guests must be at least 48 inches tall to participate. Kids under the age of 18 must be accompanied by a paying adult. EPCOT park admission is not required or included. Wet suits are provided; you must wear your own swimsuit (underneath the wet suit).

PHOTO BY JILL SAFRO

# World Showcase

Noble sentiments about humanity and the fellowship of nations, which have motivated so many World's Fairs in the past, also inhabit World Showcase. But make no mistake about it: This region of EPCOT is unlike any previous international exposition.

The group of pavilions that encircles World Showcase Lagoon (a body of water that is the size of several football fields, with a perimeter of about 1.2 miles) demonstrates Disney conceptions about participating countries in remarkably realistic, consistently entertaining styles. You won't find the real Germany here—rather, the country's essence, much as a traveler returning from a visit might remember what he or she saw in the actual Deutschland.

Shops, restaurants, and attractions are housed in a group of structures that is an artful pastiche of all the elements that give that nation's countryside and towns their distinctive flavor. Although occasional liberties have been taken when scale and proportion required them, careful research governed the design of every nook and cranny.

Equally impressive is the cuisine. With no fewer than 15 upscale eateries to choose from, it's no wonder some guests here do nothing but nosh. (That is especially true during EPCOT's popular International Food & Wine Festival, a time when dozens more nations contribute to an already fortified international menu. See page 11 for additional information.)

In World Showcase shops, many of the wares represent the country in whose pavilion they are sold. Skilled craftspeople are occasionally on hand to demonstrate their arts. Thanks to special cultural-exchange programs and recruiting efforts, many World Showcase staffers usually hail from the countries the pavilions represent.

Traditionally, a diverse lineup of entertainment has ensured that all visitors experience more than a little culture. World Showcase entertainment is as authentic as the Disney casting directors can make it, with international performers commonly featured and new festivities always in the works.

Pavilions are described in the order in which they are encountered while moving counterclockwise around World Showcase Lagoon after crossing the bridge from World Celebration. Details are subject to change.

**Hot Tip!** Guests may enter World Showcase via the International Gateway entrance (aka EPCOT's back door) as much as a half hour prior to the park's official opening time—allowing plenty of time to reach favorite attractions in this and other EPCOT neighborhoods.

# CANADA

Celebrating the many beauties of the U.S.A.'s neighbor to the north, the area devoted to the Western Hemisphere's largest nation is complete with its own mountain, waterfall, rushing stream, rocky canyon, mine, and splendid garden massed with flowers. There's even a totem pole, a trading post, and an elaborate, mansard-roofed hotel similar to ones built by Canadian railroad companies as they pushed west around the turn of the twentieth century. All this is imaginatively arranged somewhat like a split-level house, with the section representing French Canada on top, and another devoted to the mountains alongside it and below. From a distance, the Hôtel du Canada, the main building here, looks like little more than a bump on the landscape — as does EPCOT's single Canadian Rocky Mountain. But viewed up close, they both seem to tower as high as the genuine article.

The gardens were inspired by the Butchart Gardens, on Vancouver Island, British Columbia, a famous park created on the site of a limestone quarry. The hotel is modeled, in part, after Ottawa's Victorian-style Château Laurier. Musical entertainment takes place at the Mill Stage, a theater on the World Showcase Promenade (on the United Kingdom side of the pavilion).

PHOTO BY JILL SAFRO

## PLAY DISNEY PARKS APP

Disney Imagineers have designed an app meant to enhance a visit to any Walt Disney World theme park. The (free) software adds a layer of fun to waiting in line, plus a whole lot more. Loaded with games, the Play Disney Parks app invites guests to hone their theme park trivia smarts, earn rewards for visiting certain locales, and even interact with the park itself. (It uses Bluetooth to trigger in-park special effects.)

The app offers adventures for all four Disney theme parks. For example, EPCOT guests take the Soarin' Challenge (travel game), while folks at Magic Kingdom design spaceships at (where else?) Space Mountain. An ideal place to use it is at Star Wars: Galaxy's Edge in Disney's Hollywood Studios, where all signs are written in Aurebesh (the native language of the planet Batuu). The Play Disney Parks app is an Aurebesh to English translator! It also helps Studios' guests discover hidden treasures and hack into droids.

The Play Disney Parks app is not part of the My Disney Experience app (it's a separate download). Message, data, and roaming rates may apply. As with all apps, this one can drain a smartphone battery quickly. Travel with (charged) back-up battery packs.

**CANADA FAR AND WIDE:** Step into the Circle-Vision 360 film, *Canada Far and Wide*, and find yourself surrounded by the breathtaking sights and sounds of this northern nation. Of course, you won't be alone — Canadian actors Catherine O'Hara and Eugene Levy act as your guides, taking guests through prairies, plains, snowfields, rivers, rocky mountainsides, and beyond. Humor and hockey are included. The motion picture provides a you-are-there feeling that makes all of this spectacular scenery still more memorable. Be warned that you'll have to stand for the show, as there are no seats in this theater. *Canada Far and Wide* operates on a seasonal basis.

**NORTHWEST MERCANTILE:** Found to the left of the pavilion's plaza, this spot features a variety of Canada-themed items such as shirts, attire celebrating Canadian sports, plush animals, maple-flavored snacks, tiny totem poles, pajamas, plus other souvenirs and collectibles. Skeins of rope, tin scoops, lanterns, and antique ice skates hanging from the long beams above set the mood, together with the structure itself. After a visit to the Mercantile, you can peruse a preponderance of products from the United States' northerly neighbor at a cluster of carts on the World Showcase promenade.

PHOTO BY JILL SAFRO

# UNITED KINGDOM

In the space of only a few hundred feet, visitors to this pavilion stroll from an elegant London square to the edge of a canal in the rural countryside — via a bustling urban English street framed by buildings that constitute a veritable rhapsody of historic architectural styles. But one scene leads to the next so smoothly that nothing ever seems amiss. Do note the meticulous attention to detail: the half-timbered High Street structure that leans a bit, and the hand-painted "smoke" stains that make the chimneys look as if they have been there for centuries. When a thatched roof is required, it's right where it should be — though the roof may be made of plastic broom bristles because fire regulations prohibit the real thing. Off to the side is a pair of scarlet phone booths identical to those that used to be found around the United Kingdom. And there are eight architectural styles characteristic of actual streetscapes, from English Tudor to Georgian and Victorian.

There is no major attraction in this pavilion; instead, it features a selection of quaint shops and The Rose & Crown — a popular restaurant and pub that serves a selection of beers and ales that would be the toast of any "local" in London itself. Live entertainment is usually offered here at EPCOT's version of the United Kingdom, including rock concerts courtesy of a cover band called Command Performance, and cheerful visits by Mary Poppins and Alice from *Alice in Wonderland*.

**THE CROWN & CREST:** This shop looks like a backdrop for a child's fantasy of the days of King Arthur, with its high rafters decked out with bright banners, fireplace (and crossed swords above), and wrought-iron chandelier. Souvenirs featuring the Union Jack are the stock-in-trade at this emporium adjoining the Sportsman's Shoppe. Name histories and family crests are also sold, as are chess sets, swords, shields, and knights in shining armor. There are also items that pay tribute to rock bands of the U.K., plus British apparel and accessories.

**SPORTSMAN'S SHOPPE:** Ramble on over to the Sportsman's Shoppe for clothing and accessories centered on uniquely British sports and locales. There's also a sizable selection of shirts and souvenirs featuring the Rose & Crown Pub (the U.K. pavilion's local watering hole), plus a line of Guinness Stout merchandise (think glasses, shirts, coasters, bottle openers, etc.). Don't miss the tartan map on the wall opposite The Crown & Crest; it identifies plaids from Glen Burn and Gordon to Langtree and St. Lawrence. The shop's facade resembles a stately stone manor built during the last half of the sixteenth century.

**THE TEA CADDY:** Fitted out with heavy wooden beams and a broad fireplace to resemble the Stratford-upon-Avon cottage of William Shakespeare's wife, Anne Hathaway, this shop stocks English teas, both loose and in bags, in a variety of flavors. Other items include teapots, china, jewelry, biscuits, and candy.

PHOTO BY JILL SAFRO

**Hot Tip!** A lovely place from which to view the park's nighttime spectaular is the patio area at the Rose & Crown Pub in the United Kingdom pavilion. Try to snag one of the few lagoonside tables—in the self-serve sitting area—at least 45 minutes before showtime. If you miss out on a seat, grab a pint (from the kiosk on the promenade) and enjoy the standing-room view.

**THE TOY SOLDIER:** There's a selection of items here celebrating films such as *Peter Pan*, *Alice in Wonderland*, *Mary Poppins*, and the gang from the Hundred Acre Wood: Pooh, Piglet, Eeyore, and Tigger, too.

**THE QUEEN'S TABLE:** This shop is one of the loveliest in all of EPCOT. That is particularly true of the store's elegant Adams Room, embellished with elaborate moldings and a crystal chandelier. The refined setting is a fitting background for the handbags, jewelry, and other fragrant items that are available.

Don't neglect to inspect small, serene Britannia Square outside the shop farthest from the promenade. But for its diminutive size and the Florida climate, it feels a bit like London itself.

## INTERNATIONAL GATEWAY

Known to many as EPCOT's back door, International Gateway is between the United Kingdom and France pavilions. There's a ticket window and Guest Relations location just outside the gate. (Yes, it's possible to enter and exit the park here.) Note that guests are subject to a thorough security screening. All bags are screened here and guests must pass through a metal detector before they may enter the theme park. The International Gateway area is also home to:

**DISNEY SKYLINER STATION:** Walt Disney World's popular airborne gondola system connects EPCOT with Disney's Hollywood Studios theme park, and Caribbean Beach, Pop Century, Art of Animation, and Riviera resorts. The Disney Skyliner (see page 67) is the newest addition to Walt Disney World's vast transportation network.

**FRIENDSHIP LANDING:** Disney's water taxis, known as FriendShip boats, ferry guests to the Yacht & Beach Club, BoardWalk, and the Swan and Dolphin resorts, and to Disney's Hollywood Studios (the last stop before the boat returns to the resorts and back to EPCOT). The FriendShip dock is just outside the International Gateway entrance. It's possible to walk to all of the aforementioned destinations, too. (It takes about 25 to 35 minutes to stroll to the Studios, depending on your strolling pace.)

**STROLLER AND WHEELCHAIR RENTAL:** International Gateway offers strollers and wheelchairs to guests entering EPCOT via the park's "back door." Hold on to your rental receipt; it can be used for a same-day replacement in all WDW theme parks (should you park-hop and/or leave EPCOT and return later on same day). It's possible to get a replacement stroller here. There's a limited number of ECVs available for rent, too.

**WORLD TRAVELER:** Snacks, EPCOT souvenirs, Disney fashions, backpacks, character merchandise, and a package pickup depot are located at this handy spot near "EPCOT's back door." Note that WDW's package pickup service was on pause at press time, but may return. (When it's offered, the handy service allows guests to send in-park purchases to a package pickup location for retrieval later in the day.)

## FRANCE

Nine buildings here have mansard roofs and casement windows so Gallic in appearance that you may expect to see a Bohemian poet looking down from above. A canal-like offshoot of the lagoon seems like the Seine itself; the footbridge that spans it recalls the old Pont

PHOTO BY JILL SAFRO

des Arts. There's a kiosk like those that punctuate the streets of Paris and a bakery whose heavenly rich aromas announce its presence long before it's visible.

Elegant shops sell perfumes, wine, and other items. Their roofs are fashioned with real copper or slate, and the cabinetry is finely crafted. Galerie des Halles — the iron-and-glass-ceilinged market that Paris once counted as one of its most beloved institutions — lives again.

An interesting background note: The main entrance to the pavilion recalls the architecture of Paris, most of which was built during the Belle Epoque ("beautiful age"), the last decades of the nineteenth century.

Note that Aurora (of *Sleeping Beauty* fame) has been known to mingle with guests in this pavilion.

**BEAUTY AND THE BEAST SING-ALONG:** There's something here that wasn't here before: a sing-along in the France pavilion's Palais du Cinéma! The interactive experience was created by Disney legend Don Hahn, who produced both the animated and live-action versions of *Beauty and the Beast*. The show, which runs during the day, is enjoyed by the young and the young at heart.

Before entering the theater, be sure to note the gallery cases in the wait area. They pay tribute to the costumes, music, and artwork that brought French literature to life through cinema, theater, ballet, and opera.

**BIRNBAUM'S**  **IMPRESSIONS DE FRANCE:** Shown in the Palais du Cinéma, a quaint little theater that's not unlike the one at Fontainebleau, this enchanting 18-minute film takes viewers on a thoroughly charming trip through France. It's presented during evening hours.

The film shows off a tree-dotted estate, fields and vineyards at harvest time, a flower market and a pastry shop, a glacier, and a harbor full of squawking gulls. Viewers visit the Eiffel Tower; Versailles and its gilt Hall of Mirrors (just outside Paris); Mont Saint Michel; the French Alps; and Cannes, the star-studded resort city on the Mediterranean coast. All this is even more appealing thanks to a superb soundtrack, consisting almost entirely of the music of French classical composers.

Though not a Circle-Vision 360 film like the movies shown at China and Canada, the wide screen adds yet another dimension to the viewing experience. The France film used only five cameras, and it is shown on five large projection surfaces — 200 degrees around.

**F.Y.I.:** *Impressions de France* is recognized by the *Guinness World Records* as the longest-running daily screened film in the world.

**BIRNBAUM'S** **REMY'S RATATOUILLE ADVENTURE:** EPCOT's France pavilion has a famous tenant . . . Remy the rat! Yep, there's a new rodent in town. The namesake vermin/chef from Disney's *Ratatouille* is the star of this whimsical, family-friendly 3D experience.

As you enter Gusteau's Restaurant, the not-so-coincidental setting for this culinary caper, you are immediately shrunk to the size of a rat. Then climb aboard a rat-mobile and you're off! Throughout the adventure, you'll follow Remy as he romps on the roof and scampers through the dining room, kitchen, and walls — much to the chagrin of a cheesed Chef Skinner. There are lots of twists, turns, and silly surprises along the way. In fact, it may take multiple visits to catch all the

delicious details. The kooky (or is that cook-y?) escapade culminates with a pop-in at a rousing, rats-only dinner party. *Bon appétit!*

Remy's Ratatouille Adventure is fun for all ages, but some very young children may be spooked by moments of near darkness and/or by being pursued by the scowly Skinner. The ride experience is gentle enough for most EPCOT visitors, but it does combine motion with 3D animation. Just a heads-up.

**LA SIGNATURE:** Aka Guerlain Paris, this boutique features Guerlain cosmetics and fragrances.

**L' ESPRIT DE LA PROVENCE:** Adjoining Les Vins de France, this lovely shop offers French housewares, including kitchen accessories, soaps, and cookbooks. There's a nice selection of *Ratatouille* themed items, too.

**SOUVENIRS DE FRANCE:** Everything from Eiffel Tower statuettes to Impressionist-style prints is offered at this location near the exit of the cinema. Bags, flags, T-shirts, and berets are among the offerings. The area is based on Paris's now-demolished Les Halles, the city's old fruit and vegetable market. This space is also home of a wildly popular bakeshop: Les Halles Boulangerie & Patisserie.

**LES VINS DE FRANCE:** Selections in this rustic wine shop range from the relatively inexpensive to the pricey, from

**Hot Tip!** Resist the urge to fit all of the World Show-case movies into a single day, especially if you're traveling with young children.

*vin ordinaire* going for several dollars to upward of $99 for a rare vintage. Wine tastings are held here to sample the offerings (for a fee). Champagne, beer, and superb spirited slushes are also sold (the latter may be served from a kiosk on World Showcase Promenade). Among the wares, expect to find wine glasses with a World Showcase theme, bottle openers and toppers, aprons, and candy. Toward the back of the shop you will find soaps and sachets.

**PLUME ET PALETTE:** One of the loveliest shops in World Showcase, this Art Nouveau–inspired location is home to Christian Dior fragrances, along with beautiful scarves and unique apparel collections.

# MOROCCO

Nine tons of tile were handmade, hand cut, and shipped from Morocco to EPCOT to create this World Showcase pavilion. To capture the unique quality of this North African nation's architecture, Moroccan artisans came to EPCOT to practice the mosaic art that has been a part

of their homeland for thousands of years. Koutoubia Minaret, a meticulously detailed replica of the famous prayer tower in Marrakesh, stands guard at the entrance. A courtyard with a fountain at the center leads to the medina (Old City). Between the traditional alleyways and the more modern sections are the pointed arches and swirling patterns of the Bab Boujeloud gate, a replica of the one that stands in the city of Fez. An ancient working waterwheel irrigates the gardens, and the motifs repeated throughout the buildings include carved plaster and wood, tile, and brass. Spice Road

Table, located right on the lagoon, is an ideal spot to catch a breeze off the water while sipping a pomegranate mimosa or other cocktail and sampling Moroccan small plates. Live entertainment may be presented on World Showcase Promenade. Jasmine drops by to say hello to guests, too.

**SOUK AL MAGREB:** This waterside enclave located on the World Showcase promenade spills over with hand-crafted keepsakes and authentic apparel and accessories. Also featured: assorted toys, costumes, and clothing themed to Disney's *Aladdin*.

# JAPAN

Serenity rules in Japan. Except, of course, when the pavilion resounds with traditional music performed by a drum-playing duo or group.

The landscaping, designed in accordance with traditional symbolic and aesthetic values, contributes to the pavilion's peaceful mood. Rocks, which in Japan represent the enduring nature of the Earth, were brought from North Carolina and Georgia (since boulders are scarce in the Sunshine State). Water, symbolizing the sea (which the people of Japan consider a life source), is abundant; the Japan pavilion garden has a stream and pools inhabited by koi (fish). Evergreen trees, which in Japan are symbols of eternal life, are here in force.

Disney horticulturists created this very Japanese landscape using few plants native to that country because the climate there is so different from that of Florida. Among the few trees here native to Japan are the sago, near the courtyard entrance to the Katsura Grill; the two Japanese maple trees, identifiable by their small leaves, not far away (near the first stairway from the promenade on the left side of the courtyard as you face it); and the prickly monkey-puzzle trees, near the walkway to the promenade, on The American Adventure side of the pagoda. Needle-sharp thorns make the latter the only species of tree that monkeys are unable to climb.

The pagoda was modeled after an eighth-century structure located in the Horyuji Temple, in Nara, Japan. The striking torii gate hugging the shore of World

PHOTO BY JILL SAFRO

Showcase Lagoon derives from the design of the one at the Itsukushima shrine in Hiroshima Bay.

**BIJUTSU-KAN GALLERY:** Housing an ever-changing cultural display, this small gallery has offered, among other exhibitions, the Kitahara Collection of Tin Toys, featuring toys produced between 1880 and 1970. Most recently, the exhibit "Kawaii—Japan's Cute Culture" was featured here.

**MITSUKOSHI MERCHANDISE STORE:** There are kimonos, T-shirts bearing Japanese characters, fine jewelry, and a selection of bowls and vases meant for flower arranging for sale at this spacious store set up by Mitsukoshi—a four-centuries-old retail firm.

The shop features a wall of sake selections (and a small sake bar), plus chopsticks, bonsai, jewelry, china, paper fans, and origami products. There is also a bounty of toys, bags, snacks, and teas. You can even buy an oyster and discover a pearl! The pleasant atmosphere and wide variety of merchandise make this destination a rewarding experience for the casual browser and the serious shopper alike. The building's design was inspired by the Gosho Imperial Palace, which was constructed in Kyoto in 794 A.D.

**DID YOU KNOW?**
The five stories of the Japanese pagoda symbolize earth, water, fire, wind, and sky.

# THE AMERICAN ADVENTURE

**BIRNBAUM'S ★BEST★** When it came to creating The American Adventure pavilion, the centerpiece of EPCOT's World Showcase neighborhood, Disney Imagineers were given relatively free rein. So the 110,000 bricks of the imposing Colonial-style structure that houses a stirring show, BBQ restaurant, and shop are the real thing—patiently crafted by hand from soft Georgia clay.

The show inside stands out because of its wonderfully evocative settings, its detailed sets, and the 35 impressive Audio-Animatronics players, some of the most lifelike ever created by the Disney organization. A stirring a cappella vocal group called Voices of Liberty periodically serenades guests in the American Adventure building's grand rotunda. By all means, catch one of their patriotic performances.

**THE AMERICAN ADVENTURE SHOW:** One of the most ambitious EPCOT attractions, this 26-minute presentation celebrates the American spirit from the nation's birth. Beginning with the arrival of the pilgrims at Plymouth Rock and their harsh first winter on the western shore of the Atlantic, the Audio-Animatronics narrators—a lifelike Ben Franklin and a thoroughly convincing Mark Twain—recall significant people and events in American history: the Boston Tea Party, George Washington and the grueling winter at Valley Forge, the influential abolitionist Frederick Douglass, the celebrated nineteenth-century Nez Perce chief Joseph, and many more. The Philadelphia Centennial Exposition is remembered, along with women's rights campaigner Susan B. Anthony, telephone inventor Alexander Graham Bell, and the steel giant and philanthropist Andrew Carnegie. Naturalist John Muir converses onstage with Teddy Roosevelt. Charles Lindbergh, Rosie the Riveter, Jackie Robinson, and Walt Disney are represented. So are John Wayne, Lucille Ball, Margaret Mead, John F. Kennedy, Martin Luther King Jr., and Billie Jean King.

The idea is to recall episodes in history, positive and negative, that contributed to the growth of the spirit of America, by engendering "a new burst of creativity" (in the designers' words) "or a better understanding of ourselves as partners in the American experience."

To learn how each of the many featured historical figures spoke during his or her lifetime, researchers contacted historians and cultural institutions—the Philadelphia Historical Commission, the State Historical Society of Missouri, the Department of the Navy's Ships Historical Branch, and others. When recordings were not available, educated guesses were made:

PHOTO BY JILL SAFRO

Alexander Graham Bell's voice was created on the basis of contemporary comments about his voice's clarity, expressiveness, and crisp articulation, combined with the fact that his father taught elocution. A highlight of the show is the majestic music played by the Philadelphia Symphony Orchestra. The inspirational "Golden Dreams" finale was updated in 2018, as was the sound system.

Before the show begins, be sure to read the inspirational quotes that line the walls of Disney's Independence Hall—Jane Addams, Charles Lindbergh, Herman Melville, Althea Gibson, and Walter Elias Disney are among the notable Americans who are quoted.

**Hot Tip!** The Voices of Liberty, a stellar eight-member a cappella vocal group, serenades guests in the American Adventure pavilion's main rotunda several times a day. Their last performance tends to be around 4 P.M. Each show runs about 15 minutes. Catch it if you can!

**AMERICAN HERITAGE GALLERY:** Inside the pavilion (on the right side of the grand lobby as you enter), is one of six art galleries at EPCOT. Its current exhibit, "Creating Tradition: Innovation and Change in American Indian Art," celebrates historical and contemporary American Indian art and cultures. It showcases 89 objects, representing 40 tribal nations from seven North American regions. Visitors to the exhibit hear native languages and blended contemporary music styles, experiencing first-hand how American Indian art is both ancient and timeless. Details are subject to change.

**ART OF DISNEY:** Stop by this cheery shop to peruse an assortment of Disney collectibles. The store showcases a variety of art inspired by Disney animation and theme parks. There is a collection of unique pieces by acclaimed artists, including prints, sculptures, and figurines.

**THE AMERICA GARDENS THEATRE:** An ever-changing slate of entertainment is presented in this lakeside amphitheater in front of The American Adventure pavilion. Concert series such as Eat to the Beat, Garden Rocks, and Disney on Broadway have taken place on this stage, too (during EPCOT's International Food & Wine Festival, International Festival of the Arts, and Flower & Garden Festival)—as has the Candlelight Processional, which is traditionally offered during the holiday season. Showtimes are posted at the theater. For current offerings, use the My Disney Experience mobile app or website, or visit *disneyworld.com*.

PHOTO BY JILL SAFRO

# ITALY

The arches and cutout motifs that adorn the World Showcase reproduction of the Doge's Palace in Venice are just the more obvious examples of the attention to detail lavished on the structures in this relatively small pavilion. The angel perched atop the scaled-down campanile was sculpted on the model of the original, right down to the curls on the back of its head. It was then covered with real gold leaf, despite the fact that it was destined to perch almost 100 feet in the air.

The other statues in the complex, including the sea god Neptune presiding over a fountain, are similarly exact. And the pavilion even has an island like Venice's own, its seawall appropriately stained with age, plus moorings that look like barber poles, with several Venetian gondolas tied to them. St. Mark the Evangelist is also remembered, together with the lion that is the saint's companion and Venice's guardian. These can be seen atop the two massive columns that flank the small arched footbridge that connects the island to the mainland. The only deviation from Venetian reality is the alteration of the site of the Doge's Palace in reference to the real St. Mark's Square.

The quaint pavilion is equally interesting from a horticultural point of view. The island boasts kumquat trees and citrus plants typical of the Mediterranean. The tall, narrow trees that stand like dark columns are Italian cypresses, which are common in their native country. And the plant climbing a trellis beside the fountain is an honest-to-goodness grape vine.

**ENOTECA CASTELLO:** This shop on the edge of the piazza features a selection of red and white Italian wines. Wine tasting is offered, too (for about $8–$15). It's possible to purchase an ice cold Italian beer, too. *Salute!*

**IL BEL CRISTALLO:** There is a veritable *abbondanza* of Italian fragrances, shirts, and accessories, plus purses, wallets, and bags in this shop (just off the promenade on the Germany side of the piazza).

**LA BOTTEGA ITALIANA:** Stop here for items such as wine glasses, wine accessories, Italian snacks, aprons, plates, cookbooks, bags, dish towels, oven mitts, glassware, hats, shirts, flags, key chains, and plush toys.

**LA GEMMA ELEGANTE:** This shop boasts an assortment of handcrafted Venetian masks (which range in price from about $30 to $500), plus a selection of items featuring Topolino and Topolina (that's how Mickey and Minnie are known in Italy)—bowls, plates, shirts, skirts, mugs, pillows, and more.

PHOTO BY JILL SAFRO

# GERMANY

There are no villages in Germany quite like this one. Inspired by various towns in the Rhine region, Bavaria, and the German north, it boasts structures reminiscent of those found in urban enclaves as diverse as Frankfurt, Freiburg, and Rothenburg. There are stair-stepped rooflines and towers, balconies and arcaded walkways, and so much overall charm that the scene seems to come straight out of a fairy tale. The beer hall to the rear is almost as lively as those at Munich's famed Oktoberfest. The shops, which offer a range of merchandise from wine and sweets to ceramics and cuckoo clocks, teddy bears, steins, and freshly prepared caramel treats are so tempting that it's nearly impossible to leave the area empty-handed. And as an added bonus, Snow White makes appearances by the local wishing well.

The elements that constitute the Germany pavilion are described here as they would be encountered while walking clockwise around the cobblestone-paved plaza. The plaza is known as St. Georgsplatz, after the statue at its center. St. George, the patron saint of soldiers, is depicted with a dragon that legend says he slew during a pilgrimage to the Middle East.

Try to time your World Showcase peregrinations to take you to the Germany pavilion on the hour, when the handsome, specially designed glockenspiel at the plaza's rear can be heard chiming in a melody composed specifically for the pavilion.

**Note:** Some of Germany's shops were temporarily unavailable at press time, but are expected to return.

**DAS KAUFHAUS:** A two-story structure, with an exterior that is patterned after a merchants' hall known as the Kaufhaus (located in the German town of Freiburg im Breisgau), stocks souvenirs and holiday merchandise.

**F.Y.I.:** In English, Das Kafhaus means "big store."

**DER TEDDYBÄR:** Adjacent to the Volkskunst shop, this toy store was "on pause" at press time. Fret not, toy collectors—most of Der Teddybär's wares are available at the nearby Volkunst shop. All details are subject to change. For updates, visit *disneyworld.com*.

**KARAMELL-KÜCHE:** This caramel kitchen tempts with housemade sweet treats made from buttery caramel. Many items are made fresh on-site. Fan favorites—this spot has a fervid following—have included caramel-filled chocolate chip cookies, crunchy apples enveloped in caramel, chocolate or vanilla cupcakes topped with

rich vanilla icing with a gooey dab of caramel on top, caramel corn, packaged Werther's candies, and much more. Don't come here on an empty stomach—you could go bankrupt.

**KUNSTARBEIT IN KRISTALL:** This shop to the left of the Biergarten features Austrian and crystal jewelry (including tiaras), beer mugs, wine glasses in traditional German tints of green and amber, and crystal decanters. Glassware may be etched on the spot.

**STEIN HAUS:** The "house" is actually a quaint little shop that celebrates *bier*, featuring steins, mugs, shirts, and collectibles. *Prost!*

**VOLKSKUNST:** An aesthetically appealing establishment, Volkskunst is filled with a burgher's bounty of toys and other playthings. An impressive selection of plush toys extends beyond the teddy bear bonanza: look for lions, penguins, pigs, pandas, and more. It stocks bears of the gummy kind, too. And if you're in the market for an authentic cuckoo clock, look no farther! This is also the place to find a beer stein, merch featuring *Snow White and the Seven Dwarfs*, and other whimsical wares.

**WEINKELLER:** Germany's local wine shop, situated near the rear of St. Georgsplatz, offers about 50 varieties of German wine. Wine tastings are held here daily (for a fee). The selection includes vintages meant for everyday consumption, plus some fine estate wines. These are white (with a few exceptions), because white wine constitutes the bulk of Germany's vinicultural output. (Only about 20 percent of German wine bottlings are red.) Bottles of wine and liqueur, glasses, cheese plates, and candy are sold, too. The setting itself is charming—low-ceilinged and quite cozy.

PHOTO BY JILL SAFRO

## VILLAGE TRADERS

Located between the Germany and China pavilions, this open-air shop sports a selection of handcrafted gift items from Africa, India, Spain, and Australia. Browse through such souvenirs as wind chimes, handbags, musical instruments, jewelry, bowls, hats, and shirts. Details are subject to change at any time. For Village Traders updates, use the My Disney Experience app or website, or visit *disneyworld.com*.

**DIE WEIHNACHTS ECKE:** This shop sets a visitor's mind to thoughts of Christmas—even on the steamiest days of summer. Ornaments, decorations, and gifts made by various German companies line the merry shelves.

One particular item of note is the pickle ornament. Pickle ornaments are considered a special Christmas tree decoration by many families in Germany. Historically, it is always the last ornament hung on the tree, with a parent hiding it among the other ornaments. Kids gleefully search for it—and the one who finds it gets a special little present from St. Nicholas, left for the most observant child. Can you find the pickle ornament on each tree in the shop? It's not easy!

# CHINA

Dominated by the Disney version of Beijing's Temple of Heaven and announced by banners that proclaim good wishes to passersby (the Chinese characters translate to: "May good fortune follow you on your path through life" and "May virtue be your neighbor"), this pavilion conveys a level of serenity that offers an appealing contrast to the hearty merriment of the bordering Germany and the gaiety of nearby Mexico. Part of this quiet environment is the by-product of the soothing, traditional Chinese music. The gardens also make a major contribution. They are full of rosebushes native to China, and there is a century-old mulberry tree (to the left of the main walkway into the pavilion), with a pomegranate tree and a wiggly-looking Florida native known as a water oak nearby.

The number of stones in the floor of this pavilion's main structure is not random; the center stone is surrounded by nine stones because nine is considered a lucky number in China. Around the edge of the outer room rise 12 columns—because 12 is the number of months in the year and the number of years in a full cycle of the Chinese calendar. Be sure to stand on the round stone in the center of the room: Every whisper is amplified.

A spacious emporium is devoted to wares from China, and two eateries add to the overall atmosphere. However, all this is secondary to the motion picture shown inside the Temple of Heaven—a Circle-Vision 360 film that is one of the most diverting World Showcase attractions. Keep in mind that this movie is a standing-room-only viewing experience.

**REFLECTIONS OF CHINA:** This cinematic presentation shows the beauties of a land that few EPCOT visitors have seen firsthand—and does it so vividly that it's possible to see the film twice and still not fully absorb all the wonderful sights.

A Circle-Vision 360 movie, *Reflections of China* is presented in a theater-in-the-round. Filmmakers used a total of nine cameras to capture cultural and scenic images that wrap completely around the audience. The majestic tour includes some rural stops, plus visits to cities such as Hong Kong, Macau, Beijing, and Shanghai.

The movie includes footage of many landmarks, such as the 2,400-year-old Great Wall and Tiananmen Square, as well as some newer cultural developments. Overall, it showcases the majesty of this ancient country and highlights some of the more dramatic changes that have taken place over time. Note that the theater has no seats. Rest weary feet before you enter!

**HOUSE OF GOOD FORTUNE:** This vast emporium, located off the narrow, charming Street of Good Fortune, offers a huge assortment of merchandise—lanterns, hats, wine, beer, fine jewelry, silk robes, shoes (including sandals and flip-flops), prints, porcelain items, tea sets, candles, neckties, Buddha statues, chess sets, (non-prescription) reading glasses, and much more. Kids adore the huge variety of panda-themed plush toys. Handheld fans may be personalized on the spot.

**HOUSE OF WHISPERING WILLOWS:** When exiting the movie theater, be sure to stop by the House of Whispering Willows, an exhibit of ancient Chinese art and artifacts. Changed periodically, it invariably includes fine pieces from well-known collections.

# NORWAY

Set between Mexico and China is Norway, a pavilion added to the World Showcase mix in 1988. Built in conjunction with Norwegian companies, the pavilion celebrates the rich history, folklore, and culture of one of the Western world's oldest countries.

The cobblestone town square is an architectural showcase of the styles of such Norwegian towns as Bergen, Alesund, and Oslo. There's also a Norwegian castle fashioned after Akershus, a 14th-century fortress still standing along Oslo's harbor; the castle here houses the Akershus restaurant. Few can resist walking into the bakery for a taste of its treats. In a show of modernity, a statue of Norway's legendary marathoner Grete Waitz stands behind the bakery. Shops stock handicrafts and folk items: hand-knit woolens, wood carvings, and glass and metal artwork.

*Frozen* fans can also visit Arendelle, in the popular attraction Frozen Ever After. And for those guests who would like to meet Anna and Elsa of *Frozen* fame — great news: They're here!

**ROYAL SOMMERHUS—MEET ANNA & ELSA:** Attention all *Frozen* fans! Royal sisters Anna and Elsa cordially invite you to visit them at their cozy summer cabin (aka Royal Sommerhus).

**F.Y.I.:** Arendelle, the fictional queendom in which the royal siblings reside, is said to be in Norway. But you already knew that, right?!

**BIRNBAUM'S**
**★BEST** **FROZEN EVER AFTER:** Be prepared to let it go as you are whisked off to the icy queendom of Arendelle in this enchanting boat ride. The snowy adventure celebrates the story from the film *Frozen* and the characters that are near

and dear to just about everybody's heart: Anna, Elsa, Olaf, Kristoff, and Sven — plus the Snowgies from the *Frozen Fever* animated short. The crowd-pleasing attraction, which replaced Maelstrom, immerses guests in favorite moments and music from the film. Frozen Ever After can have exceptionally daunting waits — head here as soon as it opens for the day.

**THE FJORDING:** Here you should find a nice variety of Norwegian gifts. Sweaters, active wear, high-quality winter wear, Viking helmets, trolls, toys, fragrances, and candy are among the varied selection of wares at The Fjording. The back room offers all things *Frozen*. Would you like to pose for a photo with a giant troll? You have come to the right place! Guests over age 21 may also pick up a bottle of Glogg — a traditional drink popular in Scandinavia.

**STAVE CHURCH GALLERY:** Inside the wooden stave church, there is an exhibit that explores Norwegian culture. It's interesting (and sad) to note that only about 30 stave churches remain in Norway today.

PHOTO BY JILL SAFRO

# MEXICO

The lush tangle of tropical vegetation surrounding the great pyramid that encloses this pavilion and the Mexican restaurant on the edge of World Showcase Lagoon provides only the barest suggestion of the immersive and charming area inside.

Dominated by a re-creation of a quaint plaza at dusk, the pyramid's interior is rimmed by balconied, tile-roofed, colonial-style structures. Crowding a fountain area is a marketplace selling handicrafts, and to the left is a shop stocked with other handsome wares. On the right is a hopping cocktail spot known as La Cava del Tequila. To the rear, the San Angel Inn serves authentic fare. And behind it, a waterborne attraction features a whirlwind Mexican tour.

Take a look at the cultural exhibit inside the pyramid entrance on the way in. Note that the building was inspired by Meso-American structures dating from the third century A.D. Afterward, take a duck break — Donald Duck greets guests next to the Mexico pavilion throughout the day. And enjoy some traditional Mexican folk music, courtesy of Mariachi Cobre.

### GRAN FIESTA TOUR STARRING THE THREE CABALLEROS:

Big news: The Three Caballeros (Donald Duck, Panchito, and José Carioca) are reuniting for a big show in Mexico City! Unfortunately, the ever mischievous Donald Duck has gone missing in Mexico — and guests join Panchito and José in the quest to find him. In doing so, you will be treated to a whirlwind (slow-moving) boat tour of the country. It's a cheery montage of film, props, and Audio-Animatronics figures.

Trivia buffs should note that the Audio-Animatronics versions of the Three Caballeros that appear in the finale made their original Disney World debut in 1971. They were a part of the Magic Kingdom's original Mickey Mouse Revue in the Fantasyland Theater — and remained there until 1980 (when the show left Walt Disney World for Tokyo Disneyland).

**EL RANCHITO DEL NORTE:** Located on World Showcase Promenade, this spot features gifts and souvenirs.

**LA PRINCESSA DE CRISTAL:** Presented by Arribas Brothers and located next to the entrance to the Gran Fiesta Tour Starring the Three Caballeros attraction, this alcove offers crystal tiaras, character figurines, rings, bracelets, necklaces, and glass slippers. If your timing's right, you may get to watch glass blown by an in-house artisan.

**LA TIENDA ENCANTATA:** Visit this cheery store inside the pyramid and you'll discover Oaxacan wood carvings and merchandise with a *Coco* theme.

**PLAZA DE LOS AMIGOS:** Brightly colored artwork, baskets, sombreros, decorative parrots, musical instruments, and pottery make this mercado (market) at the plaza's center as bright and almost as lively as one in Mexico itself. Brilliantly hued piñatas figure strongly in the scenery here. Authentic pre-Columbian figures are on display. Other items that may be available include spices, hot sauce, salsa, liquors, cocktail accessories, and candy. The plaza is also a fitting space in which to peruse items themed to the film *Coco* and the Mexican holiday known as *Dia de los Muertos* (Day of the Dead).

# SHOWCASE PLAZA

**DISNEY TRADERS:** A shop carrying fashions for the whole family, accessories, plush dolls, and toys.

**PORT OF ENTRY:** Merchandise combining the charm of classic Disney characters and EPCOT themes is the primary stock-in-trade. Sundries are also sold. It may offer food and wine-related items, too.

# Entertainment

EPCOT traditionally presents a dynamic array of live performances each day, making it very important to consult a schedule when you arrive. For details, use the *My Disney Experience* mobile app or website, go to *disneyworld.com*, or inquire at one of EPCOT's Guest Relations locations. Current showtimes may be listed on park Tip Boards, too.

**AMERICA GARDENS THEATRE:** The lagoon-side venue at The American Adventure pavilion hosts an ever-changing program of live entertainment, such as the always popular Garden Rocks, Disney on Broadway, and Eat to the Beat concert series. The beloved EPCOT Candlelight Processional is presented on this stage during the winter holiday season.

**COMMUNICORE HALL:** Across the plaza from Creations Shop, you'll find a sleek new multi-use venue known as CommuniCore Hall. Okay, you may **NEW** not find it right away—it was being built as this book went to press. But when the pixie dust settles, the hall will host everything from musical performances and art displays to cooking demonstrations, and more. Mickey and friends will greet guests here, too.

**JAMMITORS:** When they're not tidying up the park, these jolly janitors drum up fun with the most unlikely of musical instruments: trash cans! Each rhythmic jam lasts about 10 minutes.

**KIDCOT FUN STOPS:** There is an activity area in each of the countries of World Showcase. These spots invite kids to collect activity cards at EPCOT's international pavilions. Youngster-friendly activities include games and crafts.

**BIRNBAUM'S ★BEST★ NIGHTTIME SPECTACULAR:** When the curtain closed on Harmonious in 2023, an old favorite moved back into the World Showcase lagoon: EPCOT Forever. The rousing, temporary, nighttime spectacular—which mixes lasers, fireworks, special effects, kites, and classic EPCOT music is expected to yield its aquatic terrain to an exciting new show in 2024.

The crowd-pleasing EPCOT spectacular is visible from anywhere along the World Showcase promenade and takes place nightly. (Though it may be postponed due to inclement weather.) It is usually presented at park closing time. Details are subject to change. For updates, use the *My Disney Experience* mobile app or website, or visit *disneyworld.com*.

**WORLD SHOWCASE PERFORMERS:** It's all but impossible to complete a circuit of EPCOT's World Showcase without catching a performance while en route. Keep an eye on the schedule and be sure to take in entertainment at each pavilion, often performed by folks from the country represented. Among the possibilities: a legendary mariachi band known as Mariachi Cobre, an Italian juggler, Japanese drummers, an American a cappella group, a British rock band, and more.

## Holiday Happenings

During Easter week, the Fourth of July, Thanksgiving, Christmas week, and New Year's Eve, EPCOT usually offers extended hours and presents extra entertainment to celebrate the respective occasion.

**CHRISTMAS:** The park is exceptionally festive throughout the holiday season. EPCOT's International Festival of the Holidays is an international yuletide extravaganza. It usually features the joyous holiday traditions of all 11 World Showcase nations, complete with musical performances, seasonal food and drink, and decorations galore. Of course, the 2024 holiday celebration should include the park's extremely popular candlelight choral processional.

The Candlelight Processional, a stirring presentation of traditional holiday songs, includes a reading of the Christmas story by a celebrity narrator. This is an exceptionally popular event. (See page 12 for details.)

# Hot Tips

- On your way into the park, pick up a free guidemap. (You can use the one on page 152 to help you navigate, too!)

- Use the My Disney Experience mobile app or website, visit *disneyworld.com,* or check an in-park Tip Board for EPCOT's entertainment schedule for the day.

- Wait times for EPCOT attractions tend to be the longest at midday and shortest in the early evening.

- During peak seasons, preferred reservation times at EPCOT's table-service restaurants book quickly—make reservations as far in advance as possible. However, some tables may be available on a first-come, first-served basis (with a wait). Plan to arrive at least 15 minutes ahead of your reservation time—and be prepared to wait for a bit.

- Youngsters can collect activity cards in each of the eleven countries represented in EPCOT's World Showcase. Stop at a Kidcot Fun Stop to pick 'em up. Crafts are a possibility, too.

- Interactive fountain areas at EPCOT provide guests of all ages with a chance to cool off. Pack waterproof diapers for little ones who will undoubtedly spend time splashing in the water.

- If you plan to stay until park closing and are traveling by WDW bus, take your time getting to the depot—the wait will be longer than usual as EPCOT's day comes to an end. Wait out the exodus at the Creations shop or relax on a bench as the masses stroll by.

- Allow extra time to explore the post-shows at Spaceship Earth, Journey into Imagination with Figment, and Mission: SPACE—especially if you have little ones in tow.

- EPCOT is a good park to "hop" to from another park (provided your ticket has the hopper option). It's often open until at least 9 P.M.

- FriendShip water taxis are unlikely to transport you across World Showcase Lagoon any faster than a brisk walk, but they are a foot-friendly way to make the half-mile-plus journey.

- For a dynamite view of EPCOT's nighttime extravaganza, book dinner at Mexico's La Hacienda de San Angel up to an hour before showtime.

- Fancy a sweet sip of an International Coca-Cola drink? You're in luck! EPCOT's beloved Club Cool tasting station/shopping spot offers free samples throughout the day. Located next to the Creations Shop, Club Cool features a selection of new and classic, fizzy flavors—some tastier than others.

- The Disney Skyliner has a station at EPCOT's International Gateway entrance (aka the "back door"). It's in World Showcase, between the France and the United Kingdom pavilions.

## WHERE TO FIND THE CHARACTERS AT EPCOT

The original EPCOT Character Spot has closed, but it has a worthy successor in the new Communicore Hall. Guests can head there to meet Mickey and his friends throughout the day. Goofy and Minnie may appear near the park's main entrance. The Gazebo on World Showcase Promenade (by Mexico) is a good place to spot Disney pals (possibly Pluto), while Figment, Joy, and Vanellope von Schweetz spend time at the Imagination! pavilion. Disney princesses host meals at Norway's Akershus Royal Banquet Hall. Chip and Dale mingle with diners at the Garden Grill in The Land pavilion. Queens Anna and Elsa hang out at Norway's Sommerhus. Snow White visits Germany (near the wishing well). Mary Poppins and Alice grace the United Kingdom with their presence. Jasmine mingles in Morocco. Donald Duck says hello to guests in Mexico. Belle and Aurora greet folks in France. And Mulan visits China. Note that all details are subject to change at any time. For updates and character appearance schedules, check the My Disney Experience mobile app or website, or visit *disneyworld.com.*

# Hidden Mickeys

**These are some of the most popular "Hidden Mickeys" at EPCOT. How many can you find? Check the square when you spot each one!**

☐ **MISSION: SPACE:** When your ship lands on Mars, you may spy a Mickey on a rooftop to the right of the landing strip. (It's made of satellite dishes.)

☐ After you exit the ride and enter the gift shop, look up in the center of the room to find a side profile of Mickey painted on the ceiling.

☐ **MEXICO:** Toward the end of the Gran Fiesta Tour boat ride, you'll see a barge on your left. On that barge is a Hidden Mickey made of strategically arranged bongo drums.

 ☐ **LIVING WITH THE LAND:** As you walk through the ride queue, try to locate three bubbles on the large mural that come together to form a Hidden Mickey. (Hint: It's near the middle of the mural.)

☐ About halfway through the attraction, you may notice a water hose carefully coiled into the shape of Mickey Mouse's noggin.

 ☐ **SOARIN' AROUND THE WORLD:** As you soar over Utah's Monument Valley, keep an eye out for a trio of hot air balloons that briefly converge to form an H.M.

☐ As the ride comes to a finish, note pyrotechnic bursts that strategically line up with Spaceship Earth.

 ☐ **THE AMERICAN ADVENTURE PAVILION:** Look for a painting of early American settlers crossing a river with covered wagons. One of the wagon-pulling oxen has a Mickey near its left front leg.

 ☐ Another painting features workers constructing a building. Check out the tops of the beams behind the construction team. They form a classic Hidden Mickey! (The painting is on the first floor, on the right, and toward the back of the rotunda.)

 ☐ **FRANCE:** Head to Monsieur Paul to find swirly shaped Mickey Mouse heads on the marquee at the entrance, as well as atop the eatery's menu display.

☐ Before stepping inside Les Vins de France, look up at the columns on each side of the entrance. The columns have Mickey-inspired shapes on them!

☐ While visiting EPCOT's France pavilion, pay close attention to the wedding party scene in the *Impressions de France* film—there is a Hidden Mickey on a second-floor window!

☐ **CANADA:** It's easy to locate the totem poles in this pavilion—but it's a bit more challenging to find the Hidden Mickey on the left one.

☐ **THE SEAS WITH NEMO & FRIENDS:** In the play zone known as Bruce's Cub House, look for two large posters—one titled "Did You Know?" and the other titled "Bruce's Shark World" (they are on opposite sides of the room). Each has an oyster in the lower right-hand corner that contains a Mickey-shaped pearl. If you pay attention at the shark tank, you'll be rewarded with a Hidden Mickey sighting (or two). The Mouse's head appears on the bottom of the tank, shaped by some strategically positioned rocks.

☐ **JOURNEY INTO IMAGINATION WITH FIGMENT:** About halfway through the ride and as you move through Figment's house, look up in the bathroom. Figment's commode forms a Hidden Mickey with two red circles on the ground next to it.

☐ **SPACESHIP EARTH:** In the Renaissance scene, look quickly to your left to find the first painter standing in front of a table (his back is to you). On the top left of the table, three white-paint circles form a classic Hidden Mickey.

☐ Later on, keep your eyes open for a Hidden "W.D.I." (the abbreviation for Walt Disney Imagineering) on the microphone of the radio broadcaster (on the left side of the ride vehicle's forward motion).

☐ **GERMANY:** Look up to spot three armor-wearing fellows festooning a facade to the right of the big clock in St. Georgsplatz. The suit closest to the glockenspiel sports an H.M.

☐ **JAPAN:** Finding the koi pond here is easy—but can you find the Hidden Mickey in the pond? And no, it is not a Mickey-shaped fish!

*Specifics may change during 2024.*

# Where in the World

All of the photos on this page were taken at EPCOT. Do you know where? We challenge you to find all the spots where these images were shot and snap a (non-flash) photo for yourself as you discover each one. Happy hunting! (For locations, turn to page 364.)

# DISNEY'S HOLLYWOOD STUDIOS

Disney's Hollywood Studios has been described as "the Hollywood that never was and always will be." A bit hokey, perhaps—but also true. Enter the gates and the mosaic of flashy neon, chromed Art Deco, streamlined architecture, and swinging musical soundtrack plunges you into the Hollywood of the 1940s. A nostalgic view of the movie-making capital has been combined with a variety of current TV- and movie-themed attractions and a delightful selection of eateries to create this Walt Disney World enclave. The combined result is an entertainment lineup worthy of a rave review.

Since opening in 1989, the park has continued to grow and evolve. The bright and cheery Toy Story Land made its debut in 2018, and an immersive adventure zone known as Star Wars: Galaxy's Edge blasted onto the scene soon after. While visiting the distant planet of Batuu, intrepid park visitors can take the controls of

the legendary *Millennium Falcon* starship and join an epic battle in the Studios' wildly popular thriller—Star Wars: Rise of the Resistance.

The park's collection of shows and attractions boasts such classic crowd-pleasers as *The Twilight Zone*™ Tower of Terror, the rollicking Rock 'n' Roller Coaster, the zany Toy Story Mania!, and an explosive struggle between good and evil in Fantasmic! Each adds a new dimension to the Hollywood term "action."

> "The motion picture has become a necessity of life."
>
> **—Walt Disney**

# DISNEY'S HOLLYWOOD STUDIOS

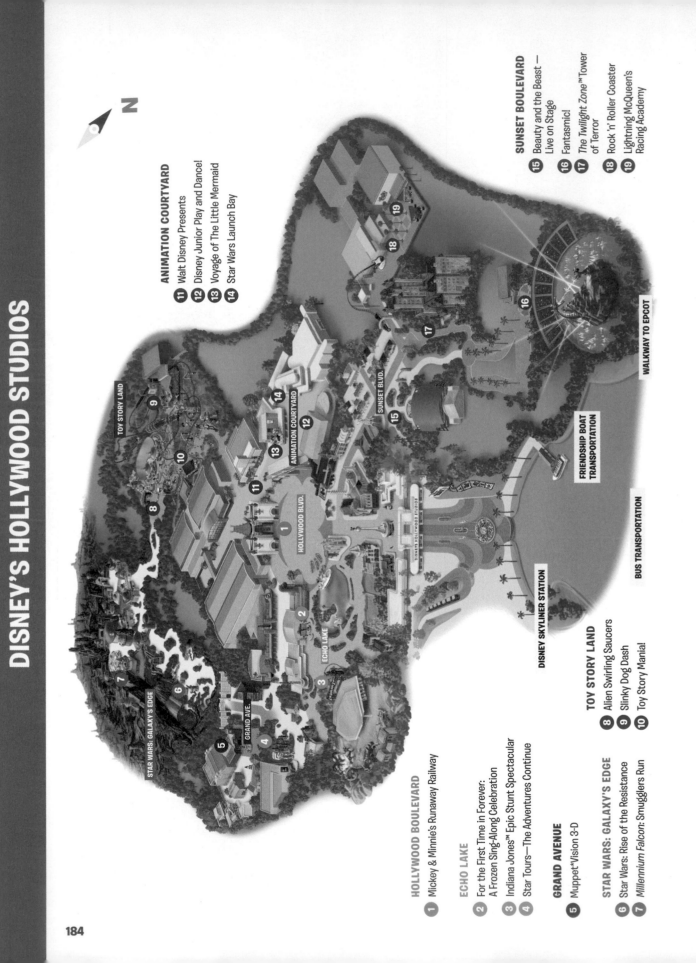

**HOLLYWOOD BOULEVARD**

1. Mickey & Minnie's Runaway Railway

**ECHO LAKE**

2. For the First Time in Forever:
A Frozen Sing-Along Celebration
3. Indiana Jones™ Epic Stunt Spectacular
4. Star Tours—The Adventures Continue

**GRAND AVENUE**

5. Muppet*Vision 3-D

**STAR WARS: GALAXY'S EDGE**

6. Star Wars: Rise of the Resistance
7. Millennium Falcon: Smugglers Run

**TOY STORY LAND**

8. Alien Swirling Saucers
9. Slinky Dog Dash
10. Toy Story Mania!

**ANIMATION COURTYARD**

11. Walt Disney Presents
12. Disney Junior Play and Dance!
13. Voyage of The Little Mermaid
14. Star Wars Launch Bay

**SUNSET BOULEVARD**

15. Beauty and the Beast — Live on Stage
16. Fantasmic!
17. The Twilight Zone™ Tower of Terror
18. Rock 'n' Roller Coaster
19. Lightning McQueen's Racing Academy

# Getting Oriented

Disney's Hollywood Studios has a layout with no distinctive shape or main thoroughfare. As such, the park can be a bit of a challenge to navigate. Study a guidemap as you enter.

The park entrance deposits guests on the shop-lined Hollywood Boulevard. This avenue leads to an ornate replica of the Hollywood landmark Grauman's Chinese Theatre. Walking along the Boulevard, you'll come to Hollywood Junction. Here, the palm-tree-dotted Sunset Boulevard branches off to the right.

Meander to the far end of Sunset Boulevard and you will reach the Hollywood Hills amphitheater, home of Fantasmic!, Rock 'n' Roller Coaster, and *The Twilight Zone*™ Tower of Terror. The charming street is also graced with several shopping venues, the Sunset Ranch Market, and the Theater of the Stars Amphitheater, where Beauty and the Beast — Live on Stage is presented.

Stand in the Center Stage area, facing the Chinese Theatre, and you will notice an archway just off to your right. This leads to Animation Courtyard, home to Disney Junior Play and Dance! and Star Wars Launch Bay. Nearby Toy Story Land is home to Toy Story Mania!, Slinky Dog Dash, and Alien Swirling Saucers. If you turn left off Hollywood Boulevard, you're on course for Echo Lake attractions such as Indiana Jones Epic Stunt Spectacular and Star Tours — The Adventures Continue. Beyond Star Tours there are two more themed zones: Grand Avenue, home to Muppet*Vision 3-D, and a futuristic realm known as Star Wars: Galaxy's Edge.

## HOW TO GET THERE

By car, take Exit 65 off I-4. Continue for about a mile to the parking area. Walk or take a tram to the entrance (if tram service is offered).

**By WDW Transportation:** From Swan, Dolphin, Yacht & Beach Club, and BoardWalk resorts: boat or walkway. From Fort Wilderness: bus from the Outpost stop. From EPCOT: boat, bus, or the Disney Skyliner. From Caribbean Beach, Pop Century, Art of Animation, and Riviera resorts: Disney Skyliner or bus. From Magic Kingdom, Animal Kingdom, all other WDW resorts, and the resorts on Hotel Plaza Boulevard: bus only. From Disney Springs: bus to any WDW resort and transfer to a bus, or boat, or the Disney Skyliner.

## PARKING

All-day parking starts at $25 for day visitors (standard parking is free to Walt Disney World resort guests and annual passholders; $45–$50 for preferred parking). When operating, trams provide transportation from the parking area to the park entrance and back. Do note the section and the aisle in which you park. The ticket allows for re-entry to the Studio's parking area (and at other WDW theme parks) all day long.

## HOURS

Park hours are usually about 9 A.M. until about 9 P.M. During some holiday periods and summer months, park hours may be extended. It's best to arrive before the posted opening time — guests tend to line up early and it can take a bit of time to clear the gates. Depending on the season, some shows don't open until late morning. Others may close before the rest of the park does. All details are subject to change.

## ADMISSION PRICES

Restricted to use only in Disney's Hollywood Studios. Prices are for Date-Based tickets. Rates for Flexible Date tickets (when offered) are higher. Prices exclude tax and are likely to rise in 2024.

| | ADULT | CHILD** |
|---|---|---|
| **ONE-DAY BASE TICKET*** | $109 - $179 | $104 - $174 |

* 1-Day tickets are valid only on the selected date. This is the cost of a 1-day/1-park-only ticket. Terms are subject to change. For details and updates, visit *disneyworld.com/tickets*.

** 3 through 9 years of age; children under age 3 free (no ticket required)

# Park Primer

### BABY FACILITIES

Changing tables and pleasant facilities for nursing mothers can be found at the Baby Care Center at Guest Relations near the park entrance.

### DISABILITY INFORMATION

Most Walt Disney World attractions, restaurants, shops, and shows are accessible to guests who use wheelchairs. Additional services are available for guests with visual or hearing disabilities. Stop by the park's Guest Relations location when you arrive. For a detailed overview of the various services offered, including transportation, parking, attraction access, and more, pick up a complimentary copy of the Guide for Guests with Disabilities. For more information, refer to the *Getting Ready to Go* chapter of this book and visit *disneyworld.com*.

### FIRST AID

Minor medical problems can be handled at the First Aid Center, next to Guest Relations near the park entrance (on Hollywood Boulevard). *For medical emergencies, alert a cast member and call 911.*

### INFORMATION

Guest Relations, just inside the park entrance (on the left), has guidemaps and an ever-resourceful staff. For details and to make dining arrangements for park eateries, visit *disneyworld.com*, use the My Disney Experience mobile app or website, or call 407-939-3463.

### LOCKERS

Lockers, found by Oscar's Super Service, just inside the main entrance, cost about $12 per day for large lockers, and $10 a day for small ones for use all day (at Disney's Hollywood Studios only). Payments are made at a self-service kiosk (via cash [U.S. currency only] or major credit card; guests paying with Magic-Bands, MagicMobile, or a Disney gift card should visit the Crossroads of the World kiosk).

### LOST CHILDREN

If you become separated from a child, alert a cast member to the problem. To expedite reunions, supply your youngster(s) with your mobile phone number before you head to the park.

### LOST & FOUND

Report a lost item to Guest Relations, just inside the theme park's entrance, or fill out a lost item report at *disneyworld.com/LostandFound*.

### MONEY MATTERS

There is an automated teller machine (ATM) at the intersection of Hollywood and Sunset boulevards. In addition to U.S. currency, major credit cards (Visa, American Express, Discover, MasterCard, JCB, and Diner's Club), Disney gift cards, MagicBands, and Walt Disney World resort key cards are accepted for payment at most park locations. (WDW resort key cards and MagicBands must be backed up with a major credit card.)

### SAME-DAY RE-ENTRY

Be sure to wear your MagicBand (if you used it for admission), use Disney MagicMobile (see page 26), or retain your ticket if you plan to return to the park later the same day.

### SECURITY CHECK

Guests entering Walt Disney World theme parks are subject to a thorough security check. All bags will be screened by security personnel before guests may enter the park. All weapons (including the toy variety) are prohibited. For additional information and a complete listing of Walt Disney World Park Rules, visit a WDW Guest Relations location or go to *disneyworld.com/ParkRules*.

### STROLLERS & WHEELCHAIRS

Strollers, wheelchairs, and Electric Conveyance Vehicles (ECVs) may be rented from Oscar's Super Service, inside the park entrance on the right. The cost for strollers is about $15; about $12 for wheelchairs. A double stroller costs $31. A Length of Stay rental ticket saves wheelchair and single stroller renters $2 a day, and double strollers $4 a day. Cost for ECVs is $50, plus a $20 refundable deposit. Hold on to the receipt — it can be used on the same day for a replacement at any Walt Disney World theme park. Quantities are limited (especially for ECVs).

# Sunset Boulevard

Disney's Hollywood Studios has a brand of attractions altogether unique. Some allow you to step into the world of your favorite movie, others let you relive your favorite screen moments. Others go so far as to allow guests to gain a bit of showbiz experience along with gaining a bit of insight. Still others present popular characters and stories in new forms—from rousing stage shows to bona fide thrill rides.

Unlike the twisty path of the California street, Disney's version of Sunset Boulevard is a straightaway that lets guests make a beeline for some of the park's biggest thrills. Those thrills include Rock 'n' Roller Coaster, Fantasmic!, and Tower of Terror.

## The Twilight Zone™ Tower of Terror

**BIRNBAUM'S ★BEST** The Hollywood Tower Hotel is the creepy home of a spectacular thrill ride. On the facade of the 199-foot-tall building hangs a sparking electric sign. As the legend goes, a bolt of lightning struck the building on Halloween night in 1939. An entire guest wing disappeared, along with an elevator carrying five people.

The line for the ride runs through the lobby, where dusty furniture, cobwebs, and old newspapers add to the eerie atmosphere. As guests enter the library, they see a TV brought to life by a bolt of lightning. Rod Serling invites them to enter The Twilight Zone.

Guests are led toward the boiler room to enter the ride elevator. (This is your last chance to change your mind about riding—ask a ride attendant to point you toward the "chicken exit.") Once you take a seat in the elevator, the doors close and the car begins its ascent. At the first stop, the doors open and guests peek down a corridor. Among the effects is a ghostly visit by the hotel guests who vanished. The doors close and you continue the trip skyward.

At the next stop, you will enter another dimension, a combination of sights and sounds reminiscent of the classic television series *The Twilight Zone*. In fact, Disney Imagineers watched each of the 156 original *Twilight Zone* episodes at least twice for inspiration. This part of the ride is a somewhat disorienting experience, in part because the elevator moves horizontally.

What happens next depends entirely upon the whim of Disney Imagineers, who have programmed the attraction so that the drop sequence is chillingly random. At the top (approximately 157 feet up), passengers can look out at the Studios below. Once the doors shut, you plummet 13 stories. The drop only lasts about two seconds, but it seems a whole lot longer.

Just when you think it's over, the elevator launches skyward, barely stopping before it plunges again. And again. As you exit, Rod Serling claims this is the kind of thing "they don't tell you about in any guidebook." It's been our privilege to prove him wrong.

From the time you are seated, the trip takes about five minutes. Note that you must be at least 40 inches tall to ride Tower of Terror. It is not recommended for pregnant women, people with heart conditions or with back or neck problems. Though thrilling (and scary), the drops are surprisingly smooth. Still, if you'd rather not experience the sensation of being a human yo-yo, sit this one out.

PHOTO BY JILL SAFRO

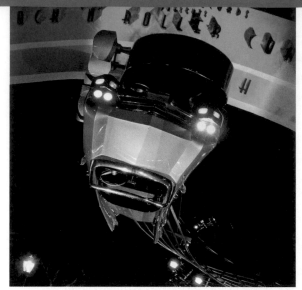

## Rock 'n' Roller Coaster Starring Aerosmith

**BIRNBAUM'S ★BEST★** Hang on—one of the fastest coasters in Walt Disney World history is guaranteed to rock your world. Rock 'n' Roller Coaster is ideally suited for those who consider the Tower of Terror just a little on the tame side.

The indoor attraction reaches a speed of nearly 60 miles per hour—in 2.8 seconds flat. The feeling is not unlike that of sitting in a supersonic jet as it blasts off the deck of an aircraft carrier. Other twists include two rollover loops and a corkscrew—marking the first time Disney has turned guests upside down on American soil. Each ride covers a half mile of track and lasts a memorable (if harrowing) 1 minute, 22 seconds.

The ride's premise is this: The rock band Aerosmith has cut their recording session short because they are late for a concert. As they rush out, they offer you a backstage pass to the show. The only thing standing between you and the big show is a classically chaotic Los Angeles freeway.

In an effort to get to the show on time, you will zip through the nighttime Los Angeles streets in a super stretch limo. The ride vehicles (designed to resemble limousines) are all equipped with a high-tech sound

**Hot Tip!** You will need to stop at a locker (near the park entrance) before you ride Rock 'n' Roller Coaster—there's no place to store loose articles in the ride vehicles (and they WILL fall out!).

system (five speakers per seat make for a mega-decibel ride), and the remainder of the high-speed journey features rockin' synchronized sound—adding a rather dramatic dimension to the roller coaster experience most daredevils have come to expect. Each limo-train is equipped with 120 speakers and features a different Aerosmith song—all of which were custom-recorded for the WDW attraction.

You must be free of back, neck, and heart problems to experience this topsy-turvy tour. Expectant mothers should sit this one out. Guests must be at least 48 inches tall to ride Rock 'n' Roller Coaster.

## Beauty and the Beast— Live on Stage

**BIRNBAUM'S ★BEST★** Several times each day, Belle, Beast, Gaston, Lumiere, Mrs. Potts, and the rest of the cast of the classic Disney film *Beauty and the Beast* come to life at the 1,500-seat Theater of the Stars, near Tower of Terror, on Sunset Boulevard.

The 30-minute live show is as entertaining as they come. The staging is just right, and the music's simply addictive as it traces the classic tale—from Belle's dissatisfaction with her life in a small provincial town to the climactic battle between the staff of the Beast's castle and Gaston and the townspeople. Lumiere and friends perform the song "Be Our Guest" with a delightful display of dancing flatware. Latecomers can often find seats in the bleachers (in the back of the theater). Some scenes (especially when Gaston leads an angry brigade to hunt down the Beast) can be intense for some young children. The show is presented daily. Check a park Tip Board or the My Disney Experience mobile app for the performance schedule.

PHOTO BY JILL SAFRO

# Lightning McQueen's Racing Academy

Get ready to start your engines and learn what it takes to be a racing champ from Lightning McQueen himself. The Piston Cup legend doles out dramatic Driver's Ed wisdom at his Racing Academy throughout the day. He kicks off each session by sharing some tricks of the trade via state-of-the-art simulator and a wraparound screen. Things don't always go smoothly, but his pals from Radiator Springs are on hand to help him navigate the bumps in the road and get back on course. Will he emerge victorious? Zoom on over to find out. After the show, everyone gets to meet and pose for photos with Cruz Ramirez (that's Cruz in the picture on the right).

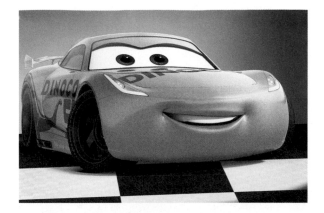

The approximately 10-minute show—which made its debut in 2019—is most popular with young *Cars* fans. It takes place inside Sunset Showcase, a theater that neighbors the Rock 'n' Roller Coaster attraction.

## TRIP THE LIGHT FANTASMIC!

**BIRNBAUM'S ★BEST★** Fantasmic!, a lavish musical production, plays most nights at the Hollywood Hills Amphitheater on Sunset Boulevard. A dramatic mix of fireworks, fountains, lasers, and Disney characters, it invites guests to take a peek into the dream (and nightmare) world of Mickey Mouse.

Though similar to its Disneyland counterpart, half of this 30-minute production is original. The action follows Mickey through a series of dreams. In the first, he appears at the base of a mountain, shoots fireworks from his fingertips, and conducts an orchestra of colorful fountains. (Guests seated up front may get spritzed.) Soon, poor Mickey is plagued by nightmares as Disney villains take over his dreams. (This aspect has been known to scare small children.) In the end, the Mouse and his pals prevail (of course!).

Seating begins about 90 minutes before the show starts, though some guests line up even earlier. Arrive as early as your schedule allows. Check a park Tip Board or the My Disney Experience app or website for showtimes.

We recommend sitting toward the back—the view is good and it's easier to get out after the show. There is standing room, too. After the finale, plan to sit for a bit. It can take 20 to 30 minutes for the crowd to exit the theater.

**Timing Tip:** The show is presented on most nights. For the performance schedule, check the My Disney Experience mobile app or website, or check *disneyworld.com*. On evenings when Fantasmic! is presented twice, see the later show. Afterward, as other guests exit the park, take time to browse the shops that keep their doors open after hours.

# Animation Courtyard

PHOTO BY JILL SAFRO

Disney's Hollywood Studios park pays tribute to the art of animation with Disney Junior Play and Dance!, The Voyage of The Little Mermaid, and a celebration of animation pioneer Walt Disney in an exhibit known as Walt Disney Presents.

## Voyage of The Little Mermaid

One of Disney's Hollywood Studios' most popular attractions for young guests, this is a 17-minute live musical production, adapted from the Disney animated classic *The Little Mermaid*. The show is presented in a theater with an underwater feel. In it, many of the film's beloved animated characters, such as Flounder and Sebastian, are brought to life by puppeteers. The show opens with a lively rendition of "Under the Sea," then animated clips from the movie are shown as human performers join the puppets on stage.

Ariel is the star and performs songs from the film. Prince Eric makes an appearance, and an enormous Ursula glides across the stage to steal Ariel's voice. Of course, as in the movie, the happy ending prevails. The story line is a little bit disjointed, hopping from scene to scene, and some of the signature songs are missing. However, most viewers are familiar with the film, so this choppiness doesn't detract much from the show.

There are lots of special effects, including cascading water, lasers, and a thunderstorm that may be somewhat frightening for some very young children. Note that many effects are best enjoyed from the middle to the rear of the theater. All audience members get spritzed with water—don't wear your finest attire.

This theater is a nice place in which to take a break, with performances traditionally presented throughout the day. Check the My Disney Experience app to see if the show will be offered during your visit to Disney's Hollywood Studios. If so, plan to arrive approximately 15 to 30 minutes before the scheduled start time.

**Note:** On pause at press time, this attraction may not operate in 2024. For updates, visit *disneyworld.com*.

## Disney Junior Play and Dance!

A jolly celebration of Disney Junior, this live show is most popular with very young guests—who are always the most enthusiastic members of the audience. The performance space holds large crowds of (mostly tiny) people at a time. Seating is minimal, but there's plenty of room to sprawl out on the carpeted floor. All guests are invited to sing, dance, catch bubbles, and laugh themselves silly during the interactive dance party. Disney Junior favorites such as Doc McStuffins, Timon, Vampirina—and, of course, Mickey Mouse—join the party, too. The show is usually presented daily and lasts about 10 minutes.

## Star Wars Launch Bay

Guests who don't get their fill of the Force in the land known as Star Wars: Galaxy's Edge can get their fix here—Star Wars Launch Bay offers an immersive atmosphere in which to experience both the light and dark sides. Housed in the space once occupied by The Magic of Disney Animation, Launch Bay features props and movie memorabilia (some genuine, some convincing replicas) celebrating Star Wars and the re-awakened Force. It's also where guests may meet friends and foes such as Chewbacca, BB-8, and Darth Vader.

Note that details are subject to change. For updates, use the My Disney Experience mobile app or website, or check *disneyworld.com*.

## Walt Disney Presents

You can follow Walt Disney from "Mickey Mouse to the Magic Kingdoms" in this multi-media exhibit near the path to Toy Story Land. Among the treasures included in this tribute to the man behind the mouse are young Walt's second-grade school desk, the original Audio-Animatronics Abraham Lincoln from the 1964 New York World's Fair, *Mickey Mouse Club* props, Jungle Cruise and Spaceship Earth models, original costumes from Disney films and television shows, and more. A small movie theater may screen previews of upcoming Disney films. Character greetings are occasionally offered here, too. This attraction was previously known as Walt Disney: One Man's Dream. All details are subject to change at any time. For updates and character appearance schedules, use the My Disney Experience mobile app or website, or check *disneyworld.com*.

PHOTO BY JILL SAFRO

# Toy Story Land

PHOTO BY JILL SAFRO

Toy Story Land is a cheerful, toy-centric zone located just beyond the park's Animation Courtyard region. It lets guests of all ages experience the world from a toy's point of view. This joyfully elaborate version of Andy's backyard features three different attractions for honorary toys to enjoy: Slinky Dog Dash, Alien Swirling Saucers, and Toy Story Mania. To Toy Story Land—and beyond!

## Slinky Dog Dash

Welcome to Andy's backyard—the site of a very special (and popular!) roller coaster. Yep, Andy has successfully assembled his Mega Coaster Kit, complete with Slinky Dog

**BIRNBAUM'S ★BEST★**

PHOTO BY JILL SAFRO

ride vehicles. The only things missing are action figures to ride 'em. That's where *you* come in!

Channel your inner toy and climb aboard Slinky's back to enjoy a zippy trip through Toy Story Land. The family-friendly ride is tamer (and smoother) than the park's Rock 'n' Roller Coaster, but it offers big thrills, including dramatic drops and bouncy hops.

Guests must be at least 38 inches tall to ride. Skip this ride if you are pregnant, or suffer from motion sickness or other health issues. Intensity-wise, Slinky Dog Dash is similar to the Magic Kingdom's Seven Dwarfs Mine Train. It's thrilling without being overwhelming (for most visitors).

**Notes:** Get there as early in the morning as possible, and, if budget allows, reserve a Genie+ Lightning Lane selection. (Fees apply for Lightning Lane service. See page 27 and visit *disneyworld.com* for specifics.)

PHOTO BY JILL SAFRO

## Alien Swirling Saucers

The Little Green Men were beyond delighted when Andy opened the playset he won at the Pizza Planet—it came with a set of flying saucers! Our alien friends have powered up said saucers and are ready to take you for a ride. So jump inside a rocket-shaped toy and hang on. The aliens may not be very good pilots, but don't worry—the ride vehicles never leave the ground. However, they do swirl beneath "The Claw" while a peppy, intergalactic soundtrack fills the air around the action.

Guests must be at least 32 inches tall and free of motion sickness to take this silly, spinning saucer trip. Don't ride on a full stomach.

## Toy Story Mania!

**BIRNBAUM'S ★BEST★** This engaging *Toy Story* experience is an energetic, interactive toy box tour with a twist: Guests wear 3-D glasses as they take aim at animated targets with toy cannons. The adventure is about as high-tech as they come, yet rooted in classic midway games of skill. As points are scored, expect effusive encouragement from a cast of cheerleaders—*Toy Story*'s Woody, Buzz, Hamm, Rex, Trixie, and, of course, the Green Army Men.

Fans of the Magic Kingdom's Buzz Lightyear's Space Ranger Spin will no doubt delight in this adventure, which takes the experience of an interactive attraction

> **Hot Tip!** Don't sweat the accuracy number in Toy Story Mania!—it's meaningless. Fire as fast and furiously as possible. That way, you'll hit more targets in less time! And if you've ridden before, you can skip the practice round and save your arm strength for the targets that count.

into a whole new dimension. As far as skill level goes, there is something for just about everyone to enjoy at Toy Story Mania!—from first-timers to the most seasoned of gamers.

The herky-jerky motion of this ride (as the vehicles move from scene to scene) may be a bit too much for folks with sensitive backs, motion sickness, or other health issues. If motion makes you woozy, consider skipping Toy Story Mania.

# Grand Avenue

A brief stroll down Grand Avenue deposits guests at Grand Park—the site of the Muppet-ational attraction known as Muppet✱Vision 3-D—complete with its glorious finale called "A Salute to All Nations, but Mostly America."

Waldo, the "Spirit of 3-D." Among the highlights is Miss Piggy's solo, which Bean Bunny turns into quite a fiasco. Sam Eagle's grand finale leads to trouble as a veritable war breaks out, culminating with a cannon blast to the screen, courtesy of everyone's favorite Swedish Chef.

Including the pre-show, expect to spend about 29 minutes with Kermit and crew at Muppet✱Vision 3-D. Shows run continuously throughout the day. Note that guests must wear 3-D glasses to enjoy this attraction. If your little one is too young to keep the glasses on, skip this Muppet encounter.

## Muppet✱Vision 3-D

**BIRNBAUM'S ★BEST★** Known as one of the most entertaining shows at Disney's Hollywood Studios, this 3-D (though some describe it as 4-D) movie is quite remarkable. A funny 12-minute pre-show gives clues about what's to come. Once inside the theater, many will notice that it looks just like the one from Jim Henson's classic TV series *The Muppet Show*. Even the two curmudgeonly fellows, Statler and Waldorf, are seated up in the house-right balcony, bantering and offering their typically critical (and somewhat crotchety) commentary on the show.

The elaborate production comes directly from Muppet Labs, presided over by Dr. Bunsen Honeydew—and his long-suffering assistant, Beaker—and introduces

# Echo Lake

Once you spot a dinosaur noshing on some seaweed, you know you've entered the Echo Lake region of Disney's Hollywood Studios. In addition to Dinosaur Gertie's Ice Cream of Extinction, this zone offers guests the chance to learn about moviemaking effects, to fly with C-3PO, and to sing along with Anna and Elsa.

## For the First Time in Forever: A Frozen Sing-Along Celebration

Have you ever heard of a song called "Let It Go"? Yes, we thought so. But have you ever had the privilege of singing it with Queen Elsa herself? Now's your chance! In fact, most of the *Frozen* gang is on hand for a spirited audience-participation sing-along.

Presented in the Hyperion Theater, the 30-minute show features a retelling of the *Frozen* story, courtesy of a duo of Arendelle storytellers. It includes clips from the beloved film (presented on a ginormous screen) and live appearances by Anna, Kristoff, and (eventually) Elsa. Guests of all ages are encouraged to sing along with a few *Frozen* ditties. Don't know all the words? Just follow the bouncing snowflake.

This celebration is popular with *Frozen* fans of all ages. Check the performance schedule and plan to arrive a bit before your desired showtime. Oh, and don't wear your finest clothing—you *will* get snowed on!

## Indiana Jones™ Epic Stunt Spectacular

Earthquakes, fiery explosions, and other dramatic events give guests insight into the science of movie stunts and effects at this 2,000-seat amphitheater. Stunt people re-create scenes from Indiana Jones films and demonstrate the skills required to keep audiences on the edge of their seats. But the 30-minute show isn't all flying leaps. Guests also see how the elaborate stunts are pulled off—safely—while the crew and an assistant director explain what goes on both in front of and behind the camera.

> **Hot Tip!** Outside of the Indiana Jones show, there's a sign that says, DO NOT PULL THE ROPE. Ignore it and pull that rope! You'll be glad you did.

In one segment, a dramatic scene from *Raiders of the Lost Ark* is staged. A 12-foot-tall rolling boulder chases a Harrison Ford look-alike out of the temple. The flames are so intense that the audience can feel the heat. The crew then dismantles the set, revealing the remarkable lightness of movie props, as assistants roll the ball uphill for the next show. The explosive action continues and leads to a desert finale in which the hero and his sweetheart make a death-defying escape.

There are moments during this show when audience members might wonder if something has actually gone

PHOTO BY JILL SAFRO

wrong. But by revealing tricks of the trade, the directors and stars show that what appears to be dangerous is actually a safe, controlled bit of movie magic.

Audience participation is always a possibility. Note that this outdoor show is subject to cancellation due to inclement weather. For additional information, visit *disneyworld.com*, or use the (free) My Disney Experience mobile app or website.

PHOTO BY JESSIE WARD

## Star Tours— The Adventures Continue

**BIRNBAUM'S ★BEST★** Inspired by George Lucas's blockbuster series of beloved Star Wars films, this classic Studios attraction—which first opened in 1989—is still going strong. The current Star Tours experience touched down in 2011, complete with a revised storyline. The 3-D experience offers guests the chance to ride in (modified) StarSpeeders (which happen to be the exact same type of flight simulator used by some military and commercial airlines to train new pilots).

A galaxy of trouble awaits Jedi wannabes, but fear not—the Force will be with you. The best part? There

**DID YOU KNOW?**

When Star Tours made its original WDW debut, it did so in grand style. On hand for the official grand opening fesivities were legendary performers Mark Hamill and Carrie Fisher—and Star Wars creator, George Lucas!

are nearly 70 different adventures, so multiple visits yield multiple surprises—all of which involve scenes from various films from the Star Wars saga.

This is a rather turbulent space flight—seat belts are a definite requirement. Passengers must be free of back problems, heart conditions, motion sickness, and other physical limitations to ride. Guests under 40 inches tall and kids younger than 3 may not ride. Pregnant guests must skip this one. To all who ride: Fasten your seat belt and may the Force be with you. Details are subject to change at any time.

## Mickey Shorts Theater

Settle into Mickey's shorts (the seats in the theater resemble those famous red trousers—complete with yellow buttons) and get ready for some not-so-serious vacation fun. The revelry comes by way of a one-of-a-kind cartoon short that highlights some of Mickey and Minnie's favorite vacation memories, plus a few new ones to boot. The super-silly show features original animation, plus clips from classic Mickey shorts such as *Croissant de Triomphe*, *Panda-monium*, *Yodelburg*, *Dumb Luck*, *Couples Sweaters*, and *Potatoland*.

This attraction, officially dubbed *Vacation Fun— An Original Animated Short with Mickey & Minnie*, runs for about 15 minutes. It's enjoyed by guests of all ages, and is a great way to cool off and rest up for even more vacation fun at the Studios. After the credits roll, guests vacate the theater via a room filled with fanciful photo ops.

You'll find the Mickey Shorts Theater next to For the First Time in Forever: A Frozen Sing-Along Celebration. Shows run continuously, but may finish up before the park closes for the day. Check a park Tip Board or the My Disney Experience app or website for the schedule.

PHOTO BY JILL SAFRO

# Hollywood Boulevard

One of the park's (and Hollywood's) main drags, this boulevard is dotted with Art Deco–style shops bursting with treasures. The pleasant thoroughfare is bookended by the park's main entrance and an elaborate replica of Grauman's Chinese Theatre—home to the popular giggle-inducing attraction known as Mickey & Minnie's Runaway Railway.

## Wonderful World of Animation

A celebration of Disney's legendary story-telling history, this nightly show is a stirring tribute to 100 magical years of Disney and Pixar animation.

The festivities are appropriately bookended by the mouse who started it all, Mickey himself. In between on-screen appearances by the Big Cheese, guests are taken on a colorful journey through a myriad of memorable moments—and themes such as magic, family, adventure, romance, and friendship—from *Sleeping Beauty*, *Aladdin*, *Frozen*, *Cinderella*, *The Lion King*, *The Incredibles*, *Beauty and the Beast*, *Wreck-It Ralph*, *Coco*, *Toy Story 4*, and more.

The state-of-the-art projection display fittingly uses the facade of the park's Chinese Theatre as its silver screen. (The structure is a full-scale replica of Grauman's Chinese Theatre, a landmark Hollywood movie palace.) The 12-minute spectacle is presented rain or shine and is best viewed from Hollywood Boulevard, close to and facing the Chinese Theatre. With nods to the vast library from Disney and Pixar Animation Studios' long legacy, Wonderful World of Animation is an apt way to wrap up a day at Disney's Hollywood Studios. Details are subject to change.

## Mickey & Minnie's Runaway Railway

**BIRNBAUM'S ★BEST** Enter a wild and wacky cartoon realm via Mickey & Minnie's Runaway Railway—a fanciful, family-friendly attraction that chugged its way into Disney's Hollywood Studios (and our hearts) in early 2020. Housed inside the replica of Grauman's Chinese Theatre, the "2.5-D" (no glasses required) adventure begins with the premiere of a new cartoon that guests watch in the pre-show area. In it, Mickey and Minnie are preparing for a picnic. When a train driven by Goofy pulls up beside them, it's all aboard for everyone! Thanks to a bit of movie magic, guests are invited to step into the action and enter the zany, unpredictable world of a Mickey Mouse cartoon short. The train zigs and zags through nine scenes, while a happy tune underscores the jolly journey. ("Nothing Can Stop Us Now" is a gift that keeps on giving—you will be humming the optimistic earworm long after the ride comes to an end).

In addition to dozens (possibly hundreds?) of Hidden Mickeys, this delightful experience features a bounty of Easter eggs for eagle-eyed Disney fans—including the number 1928 (the year our beloved Mickey Mouse entered the world) and a poster featuring *The Great Moving Ride* (a tribute to the previous tenant of this space—The Great Movie Ride).

Mickey & Minnie's Runaway Railway is suitable—and enjoyable—for guests of all ages. The experience can be a bit herky-jerky (especially when the ride vehicle weathers a cyclone). Folks with back or neck issues may want to skip the trip.

# Star Wars: Galaxy's Edge

**Hot Tip!** Park guests can take a Galaxy's Edge visit to a whole new level with Star Wars Datapad. Part of the (free) Play Disney Parks app, Datapad lets you hack into droids, translate signs, take on odd jobs, and even choose a side as travelers vie for control of Black Spire Outpost. Choose wisely. And may the Force be with you.

There's a dramatic adventure zone deep in the heart of the park—Star Wars: Galaxy's Edge. The land is set on the planet Batuu, a remote outpost on the far reaches of the galaxy. As the story goes, Batuu was once a busy crossroads along the old sub-light-speed trade routes. Now, thanks to the rise of hyperspace travel, Batuu has pretty much fallen off the radar. It's far from deserted, however. In fact, the largest settlement on the planet, Black Spire Outpost, has become quite the haven for folks who prefer to fly under the radar: smugglers, rogue traders, and space-traveling adventurers. It's also a prime spot for those trying to avoid the ruthless First Order.

In addition to otherworldly shops and snack spots, you'll find *Millennium Falcon: Smugglers Run* and *Star Wars: Rise of the Resistance*. Each attraction invites guests to live out their own Star Wars adventures.

## *Millennium Falcon:*
## *Smugglers Run*

Are you eager to jump into hyperspace on the "fastest hunk of junk in the galaxy"? Here's your chance to take the controls of Han Solo's beloved bucket of bolts, the one and only *Millennium Falcon!*

It seems Hondo Ohnaka is running a "legitimate business" out of a spaceport and he needs extra flight crews to make some special runs for him—provided they don't ask too many questions. That's where you come in.

Before entering the cockpit of the legendary starship, you and five fellow crew members are assigned a role. There are three jobs (pilot, gunner, and engineer) and a common goal: complete the mission without banging up the ship. At the end of the thrilling (and bumpy) flight, your crew will receive a point total—and a few choice words from Hondo.

Guests must be at least 38 inches tall to experience this attraction and be free of motion sickness and other health issues. Expectant mothers should skip the jarring *Millennium Falcon:* Smugglers Run.

## Star Wars: Rise of
## the Resistance

**BIRNBAUM'S ★BEST★** What happens when Star Wars heroes and villains end up on the same planet? A *massive* battle breaks out!

In one of the most ambitious adventures ever created by Disney Imagineering, this immersive attraction places you in the middle of an epic battle between the First Order and the Resistance—including a tense face-off with the infamous Kylo Ren.

The journey takes guests aboard a full-size transport shuttle and a Star Destroyer. It's a thrilling and harrowing adventure—and not for the faint of heart. To ride, guests should be free of health issues and at least 40 inches tall. Expectant mothers are advised to skip this one. Rise of the Resistance is an insanely popular experience—get there as early as possible, or secure entry via the Lightning Lane. (Fees apply. See page 27 for details.)

# Shopping

PHOTO BY JILL SAFRO

The Studios is bursting with treasures just waiting to be discovered. The following descriptions should give you a good sense of what to expect. Note that some spots were temporarily unavailable at press time, but they're expected to return soon.

## HOLLYWOOD BOULEVARD

**CELEBRITY 5 & 10:** Modeled after a 1940s Woolworth's, this shop carries housewares such as pillows, blankets, dish towels, teapots, pitchers, aprons, mugs, magnets, and a selection of glassware.

**COVER STORY:** A small area located just through The Darkroom, this is the place to pick up Disney souvenirs such as hats, pins, and autograph books.

**CROSSROADS OF THE WORLD:** Smack in the middle of the entrance plaza, this Hollywood Boulevard landmark serves as a lofty lookout point for Mickey Mouse. The kiosk deals mostly in pins, but has souvenirs, sunscreen, bug spray, hand sanitizer, sundries, and hats, plus park guidemaps. This is also the place to stop if you would like to rent a nearby locker using a gift card or Magic-Band. (Lockers are next to Oscar's Super Service.)

**THE DARKROOM:** The Art Deco facade of this shop sports a gigantic camera, so it's easy to spot. Given that, one would expect it to sell camera stuff, but it's focused on MagicBands, pins, and phone accessories.

**KEYSTONE CLOTHIERS:** A myriad of Marvel- and Star Wars-themed merch lines shelves of Keystone Clothiers.

**MICKEY'S OF HOLLYWOOD:** M.O.H. is *the* place to find Disney character shirts, hats, plush toys, magnets, bags, books, slippers, beach towels, sunglasses, snack items, MagicBands, Mickey ears, pins, Disney's Hollywood Studios keepsakes, and much more.

**MOVIELAND MEMORABILIA:** This kiosk, located just to the left of the Studios' main entrance, stocks shoes, bags, stuffed toys, hats, sunglasses, key chains, and other souvenirs. Movieland Memorabilia is accessible from both inside and outside the park entrance.

PHOTO BY JILL SAFRO

**OSCAR'S SUPER SERVICE:** In addition to renting strollers and wheelchairs, Oscar stocks strollers for purchase, plus packaged snacks, sundries, soft drinks, bags, hats, and other souvenir items.

**SID CAHUENGA'S ONE-OF-A-KIND ANTIQUES AND CURIOS:** Swing by Sid's to peek at the shots snapped by the park's Photopass photographers throughout the day.

PHOTO BY JILL SAFRO

See something you like and you can purchase it on the spot. Of course, you can always peruse now and buy later via *disneyworld.com/photopass*.

## SUNSET BOULEVARD

**BEVERLY SUNSET:** This cheery locale is Pixar Central. Pop in to peruse items such as plush toys, action figures, shirts, headbands (with aliens, Slinky Dog, and other familiar characters), pins, and games.

**LEGENDS OF HOLLYWOOD:** Modeled after the Academy Theater, which was built in Inglewood, California, in 1939, this store offers a selection of PANDORA jewelry and Disney-themed fashion merchandise.

PHOTO BY JILL SAFRO

**MOUSE ABOUT TOWN:** An excellent source for clothing featuring Mickey Mouse. Expect to find items such as hats, shirts, jackets, socks, and assorted accessories.

**ONCE UPON A TIME:** This little shop's exterior replicates the Carthay Circle Theatre in Hollywood, where *Snow White and the Seven Dwarfs* made its debut in 1937. The emporium offers children's apparel, plush toys, accessories, and a selection of souvenirs with decidedly Disney touches.

**REEL VOGUE:** Spin your big-screen dreams from reel to real in this elegant emporium of Tinseltown treasures: toys, gifts, games, snacks.

**ROCK AROUND THE SHOP:** If you conquer Rock 'n' Roller Coaster, you've earned the right to shop here. (You can also enter via the exit, should you opt out of the ride.) Look for music-related items, plus shirts, hats, and other rockin' memorabilia.

**SUNSET CLUB COUTURE:** A sophisticated selection of fashion accessories (hats, headbands, purses, backpacks, footwear, etc.), plus a selection of family apparel with a Mickey or Minnie theme is sold here.

**SUNSET RANCH PINS AND SOUVENIRS:** This shop carries Disney collector pins, plus plush character toys, souvenirs, cards, and assorted sundries.

**TOWER GIFTS:** Inside the Hollywood Tower Hotel, near the Tower of Terror exit, this spot specializes in Hollywood Tower Hotel merchandise—shirts, towels, robes, Front Desk bells, glasses, bellhop hats, handbags, and Tower of Terror Jenga. They stock collector pins, too. The shop is a good place to wait for the rest of your party should you decide to skip the trip to *The Twilight Zone*™ via the Tower of Terror.

## WHERE TO EAT IN DISNEY'S HOLLYWOOD STUDIOS

A complete listing of eateries at the Studios theme park— full-service restaurants, quick-service eateries, and snack shops—can be found in the *Good Meals, Great Times* chapter. See the Disney's Hollywood Studios section, beginning on page 280.

## DISNEY MOVIE MAGIC

A spirited homage to "a Hollywood that never was, and always will be," this sparingly presented show celebrates more than 80 years of (mostly) Disney cinema classics. Expect to see a myriad of memorable movies from *Mary Poppins* to *Guardians of the Galaxy*. (A sequence featuring Disney's epic adventure, *Mulan*, was added in 2021.)

The cutting-edge projection display fittingly uses the facade of the park's iconic Chinese Theatre as its silver screen. (The structure is a full-scale replica of Grauman's Chinese Theatre, a landmark Hollywood movie palace and home of a popular attraction known as Mickey & Minnie's Runaway Railway.)

The nighttime show, which runs for approximately ten minutes, is best viewed from Hollywood Boulevard (facing the Chinese Theatre, of course). Get there early—and don't forget the popcorn! Will the show be presented during your visit? Check a park Tip Board, use the My Disney Experience mobile app or website, or visit *disneyworld.com*.

## BEYOND THE BOULEVARDS

**LAUNCH BAY CARGO:** Located in Star Wars Launch Bay, Cargo offers Star Wars–themed collectibles. It has memorabilia, replica costumes and props, plus books and toys, and more.

**THE DISNEY STUDIO STORE:** Expect to find T-shirts, hats, toys, and accessories inspired by Disney films at this Animation Courtyard shop.

**FROZEN FRACTALS:** This open-air shop specializes in items featuring friends from Arendelle.

**INDIANA JONES ADVENTURE OUTPOST:** Parked next to Indiana Jones Epic Stunt Spectacular, the outpost—when operating—is the place to discover adventure clothing and items emblazoned with the Indy insignia.

**JESSIE'S TRADING POST:** Guess what Andy discovered in the attic? A nifty Jessie's Trading Post play set! He set it up in Toy Story Land and now it's stocked with a selection of toys and souvenirs.

**IT'S A WONDERFUL SHOP:** Spot the snowman out front and you've found this perpetual Yuletide celebration. Ornaments, stockings, and nutcrackers are sold all year long. (The shop was "on pause" at press time.)

**STAGE 1 COMPANY STORE:** Stage 1, which was on pause at press time, usually sells toys, shirts, and other merchandise featuring the Muppets and Disney pals.

**TATOOINE TRADERS:** A bustling shop near the Star Tours exit, Tatooine Traders has souvenirs themed to Star Wars, as well as the Star Tours attraction.

## STAR WARS: GALAXY'S EDGE

**BLACK SPIRE OUTFITTERS:** Guests who wish to blend in on Batuu can suit up at this boutique. Costumes representing the light and dark side of the Force are available for guests of all ages.

**CREATURE STALL:** Stop here to adopt an other-worldly pet. Lifelike creatures from which to choose include tentacle-beast rathtars, cooing baby tauntauns, tongue-lashing worrts, and growling puffer pigs.

**DOK-ONDAR'S DEN OF ANTIQUITIES:** The ever-mysterious Dok-Ondar has stuffed this shop with everything from jewelry and ancient tools to rare kyber crystals, statues, and (very) high-end lightsabers.

**DROID DEPOT:** If you have dreamed of owning your own astromech droid, dream no more: the depot has mini droids waiting for you to customize. There are two basic models: an R (like R2-D2 or R5-D4) or a BB unit (the ball-droid style similar to BB-8 and the evil BB-9E). Once you choose your droid pieces (as they roll by on a nifty conveyor belt), you can put them together in the assembly area. Then head over to the chip station to select a personality circuit. Last but not least, bring your droid to life at the activation center. Extra customization is available (for a fee). Reservations can be made (up to 2 weeks in advance) via *disneyworld.com*.

**SAVI'S LIGHTSABERS:** The First Order would not allow the manufacture of lightsabers—so Savi took that task underground. Head here to build your own high-end lightsaber. Colors include Sith red, Jedi blue and green, and Mace Windu purple. Choose wisely. Reservations can be made (up to 2 weeks in advance) via *disneyworld.com*.

**TOYDARIAN TOYMAKER:** A rather enterprising Toydarian (a species introduced in *Star Wars: The Phantom Menace*) has opened a street market in Star Wars: Galaxy's Edge. Inside, you will discover a trove of Toydarian goodies, including handcrafted-style toys ostensibly created by local artisans of Batuu.

# Entertainment

In this theme park, it's almost always showtime. The following list is a good sample of the Studios' stage presence. For updates on the entertainment offerings at Disney's Hollywood Studios use the My Disney Experience app or website, or visit *disneyworld.com*.

**DISNEY MOVIE MAGIC:** Gather 'round the Chinese Theatre to watch this 10-minute celebration of Disney films. At press time, the show was offered on a very limited basis.

**FANTASMIC!:** What does Mickey Mouse dream about? Find out at Fantasmic! The dynamic nighttime show mixes music, fireworks, light and water effects, and a bit of Disney magic. Watch as Mickey drifts off to sleep and dreams he is the mighty Sorcerer's Apprentice—only to have Disney villains flip the script and turn his happy dream into a nightmare. Don't worry. Mickey is a very imaginative fellow (even while asleep), and good ultimately triumphs over evil. The show is presented in an amphitheater just off Sunset Boulevard. It's quite popular—get there early to snag a seat.

**Notes:** Fantasmic! is an outdoor show and may be canceled due to inclement weather. Guests seated in the front rows may get a little wet. Just a heads up.

PHOTO BY JILL SAFRO

**GREEN ARMY DRUM CORPS:** Andy's army marches through the backyard several times a day, playing dramatic drum sequences as they do so. Ten-hut!

**WONDERFUL WORLD OF ANIMATION:** An action-packed projection show takes guests on a journey through 100 years of Disney and Pixar animation. The show uses the Chinese Theatre facade as its screen—line up early to get a good view. Wonderful World of Animation is presented nightly. Details are subject to change.

## WHERE TO FIND THE CHARACTERS AT DISNEY'S HOLLYWOOD STUDIOS

There are plenty of opportunities to see Disney pals at this park. You will find Disney Junior characters (Vampirina, Fancy Nancy, and Doc McStuffins) in the Animation Court-yard area. Say hi to Max in his Powerline suit on Grand Ave. Jessie, Woody, and Buzz visit Toy Story Land. Mickey mingles with park-goers at "Mickey and Minnie Starring in Red Carpet Dreams." Of course, Minnie appears at that location, too. Chip and Dale may enjoy a picnic near the Brown Derby restaurant. Donald, Daisy, and Goofy may appear near the park entrance. Olaf can be found chilling at the Celebrity Spotlight location. Disney characters visit the Hollywood & Vine restaurant, too. (Disney Junior characters are on hand for breakfast; Minnie, Mickey, Goofy, and Pluto host lunch and dinner.) Star Wars friends (and foes) hang out at Star Wars Launch Bay and Star Wars: Galaxy's Edge. Who else may you encounter in this park? Frozone, Edna Mode, Mr. and Mrs. Incredible, Cruz Ramirez, and more. Details are subject to change. For updates, visit *disneyworld.com*.

## Hot Tips

- Fantasmic! is presented on most nights. When will it be offered during your visit? Check an in-park Tip Board or use the My Disney Experience mobile app to find out. Know that the show may be canceled due to inclement weather.

- Guests may bypass select standby lines with Lightning Lane Service. Fees apply; see page 27 for details.

- Resist the urge to eat just before riding the Tower of Terror, Rock 'n' Roller Coaster, *Millennium Falcon:* Smugglers Run, Star Wars: Rise of the Resistance, Slinky Dog Dash, Star Tours—The Adventures Continue, or Toy Story Mania!.

- Some attractions keep shorter hours than the park itself. Check a park Tip Board or the My Disney Experience mobile app for schedules.

- Wanna meet a snowman? Disney's Hollywood Studios is the only WDW park in which Olaf greets guests. He hangs out at Celebrity Spotlight.

- All Walt Disney World theme parks and water parks offer free Wi-Fi, but charging stations are rare. We recommend you bring a battery pack from home or buy a portable phone charging system from an in-park kiosk for about $30.

- For a table-service meal, make an advance reservation for any of these eateries: Roundup Rodeo BBQ, 50's Prime Time Cafe, Sci-Fi Dine-In Theater, Mama Melrose's Ristorante Italiano, Hollywood Brown Derby, or Hollywood & Vine. For details, refer to the *Good Meals, Great Times* chapter.

- Some shops on Hollywood Boulevard are open about 30 minutes past park closing time.

- Your little one may love The Muppets, but if the tyke isn't ready to wear the glasses necessary to enjoy Muppet✳Vision 3-D, skip the attraction.

- There is a FriendShip water taxi link between Disney's Hollywood Studios and EPCOT. The boat docks to the left as you exit the Studios. You may also get to EPCOT via the Disney Skyliner gondola system. It's possible to get there on foot, too. (It takes approximately 20 to 30 minutes to walk to EPCOT, depending on your pace.) All other Disney theme parks and water parks may be reached by complimentary Disney Motor Coach (aka bus).

- Every so often, the wait time for *Twilight Zone™* Tower of Terror is listed as 13 minutes. Should that happen while you're in the park, make a beeline for the popular ride—"13 minutes" is (spooky) code for virtually no wait.

- The waits for Rock 'n' Roller Coaster, the *Twilight Zone™* Tower of Terror, Mickey & Minnie's Runaway Railway, Star Tours—The Adventures Continue, and some of the attractions in Toy Story Land tend to diminish as the day wears on.

- Check an in-park Tip Board, use the My Disney Experience app, or visit *disneyworld.com* for wait times, character appearance schedules, and updates about park offerings.

- Many attractions and shows stop admitting guests prior to the park's closing time (and some don't open until a few hours after the park does). Check a park Tip Board for schedules. Attractions that you may enter up until the very last minute include *The Twilight Zone™* Tower of Terror, Rock 'n' Roller Coaster, Slinky Dog Dash, Toy Story Mania!, and Star Tours—The Adventures Continue.

- Fantasmic! is a perpetually popular nighttime spectacular. Plan to arrive at the Fantasmic! entrance at least one hour before showtime—or risk arriving to a full house.

- If you skip Fantasmic!, plan to exit the park before the show ends. That way, you'll avoid the bottleneck at the exit. If you choose to enjoy the show, know that it can take about 20 to 30 minutes for the Fantasmic! audience to vacate the theater.

- If you lose your nerve just prior to boarding Tower of Terror or Rock 'n' Roller Coaster, fear not: both attractions offer a last-minute egress opportunity (aka the "chicken exit"). Ironically, the chicken exit at Tower of Terror comes in the form of an elevator. Rest assured that the escape elevator is fully functional.

- There are 3 different ways to access Rock 'n' Roller Coaster and *Millennium Falcon:* Smuggler's Run: Standby, Single Rider, and Lightning Lane (see page 27). Groups of more than one are welcome to jump on the Single Rider line at any time. Doing so may result in less wait time than the standby line, but members of the party will be split up. Note that Single Rider lines are not always offered. Details are subject to change.

- Walt Disney Presents is an exhibit dedicated to the man who started it all. Be sure to tour this fascinating gallery. And, if it's presented when you visit, don't miss Walt Disney: One Man's Dream—a 15-minute documentary about Walt himself.

# Hidden Mickeys

These are some of the most popular "Hidden Mickeys" at Disney's Hollywood Studios. How many Mickeys can you find? Check the box when you discover each one.

☐ **FRONT ENTRANCE GATES:** This is an easy one. Simply look for Mr. Mouse in the grillwork of the gates at the park entrance.

☐ **ROCK 'N' ROLLER COASTER:** In the pre-show room, look on the floor on the right side of the room just in front of the guitar stand to see some wire coiled into a Hidden Mickey.

☐ **STAR TOURS—THE ADVENTURES CONTINUE:** Keep an eye on the folks walking past the "window" in the second room you enter while waiting for the attraction. One of the droids sports mouse ears.

☐ There's a Hidden Mickey in the shop at the ride's exit, too—on the front panel of a counter.

☐ **TWILIGHT ZONE™ TOWER OF TERROR:** Take a peek at the balcony in the lobby and you may spot a row of Hidden Mickeys.

☐ Then, as you watch the Tower of Terror pre-show, pay close attention to the "disappearing guests." The little girl is clutching a plush Mickey Mouse toy.

☐ **ALIEN SWIRLING SAUCERS:** Once you've located the Space Ranger mural on the wall, you should have no trouble spotting three buttons that form a multicolored Hidden Mickey.

☐ **TUNE-IN LOUNGE:** There are several tables in the lounge area of 50's Prime Time Cafe. Look at the tabletops to see some Hidden Mickeys!

☐ **TOY STORY MANIA!:** Keep your eyes peeled for a sign that says "Circus Fun!"—the dot in the exclamation point is a pink Hidden Mickey. (The sign is on a wall as the ride vehicle twists into position for the last game.)

☐ **MICKEY & MINNIE'S RUNAWAY RAILWAY:** This happy attraction is Hidden Mickey central. One of the first you will see is on the big screen as you enter. (HINT: It is part of a plant.)

☐ Some H.M.s are visible for just a second or two in Mickey & Minnie's Runaway Railway. Try to spot Mickey-shaped bubbles as Minnie and Mickey dive over a waterfall.

☐ **COVER STORY:** There is a sign in the window of this Hollywood Boulevard shop that says "Melrose." Find it, then look below it for a pattern that creates many Hidden Mickeys in the store's structure.

☐ **THE TROLLEY CAR CAFE:** Look for a number on the building's facade (toward the top, facing Sunset Boulevard). It's not a traditional Hidden Mickey, but it is an especially significant year for the Mouse.

☐ **MUPPET*VISION 3-D:** Mickey first appears in a test pattern in the theater lobby.

☐ Next you may notice Mickey in balloon form during the finale of Muppet*Vision 3-D.

☐ As you exit the Muppets, you'll see a poster detailing Five Reasons to Return Your 3-D Glasses. Study the artwork beside number 2. It sports a Hidden Mickey!

☐ **SID CAHUENGA'S ONE-OF-A-KIND ANTIQUES AND CURIOS:** Visit Sid's front porch and you may see a special Dalmatian statue—it has a Hidden Mickey spot on its left hind leg.

☐ **SLINKY DOG DASH:** Mickey has a tendency to have his head in the clouds. Need proof? Check out the cloud formations on Andy's hand-drawn plans for Slinky Dog Dash. Yep, there's a Hidden Mickey on them.

*Specifics may change during 2024.*

# Where in the World?

All of the photos on this page were taken at Disney's Hollywood Studios. Do you know where? We challenge you to find all the spots where these images were shot and snap a (non-flash) photo for yourself as you discover each one. Happy hunting! (For locations, see page 364.)

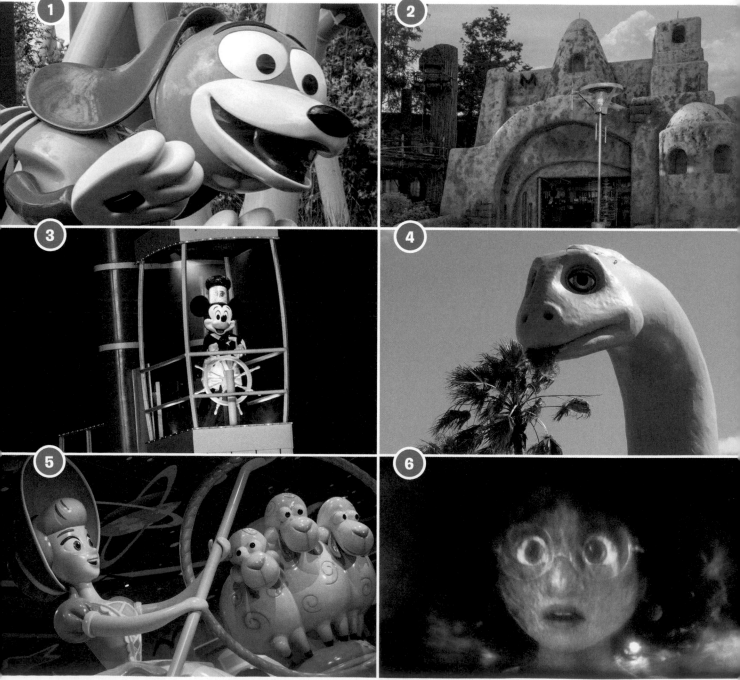

PHOTO NUMBER 4 BY JESSICA WARD

# DISNEY'S ANIMAL KINGDOM

With a mix of lush landscapes, thrilling attractions, and close encounters with exotic animals, this is clearly a theme park raised to a different level of excitement. Here, guests do more than just watch the action—they live it. They become paleontologists, explorers, and students of nature. And if, by doing so, they leave with nothing more than a big smile, Disney will have accomplished one of its major goals. But many guests come away with a little bit more: a renewed sense of respect for our planet and for the life-forms we share it with (not to mention a few boffo souvenirs).

The shows and attractions at Disney's Animal Kingdom theme park are meant to engage, entertain, and inspire. They immerse guests in a tropical landscape and introduce them to creatures from the past and present— as well as a few critters that exist only in our collective imagination. Animal Kingdom opened on Earth Day in 1998 and now offers more opportunities for adventure than ever before. To that end, a fan favorite known as Avatar Flight of Passage has been transporting giddy guests to other-worldly heights since it made its high-flying debut in 2017.

The park, which is accredited by the Association of Zoos and Aquariums, is home to more than 1,800 animals representing 200 different species. Most of the creatures are of the animate variety, as opposed to the Audio-Animatronics kind. Despite that, you won't see beasts behind bars here. Instead, you'll go on safari and see a menagerie of wild critters living in spacious habitats, with remarkably few separations visible to the naked eye.

The following pages will help you get the most out of your visit to Disney's Animal Kingdom. It is, after all, a jungle out there.

> **"The wonders of nature are endless."**
>
> **—Walt Disney**

# DISNEY'S ANIMAL KINGDOM

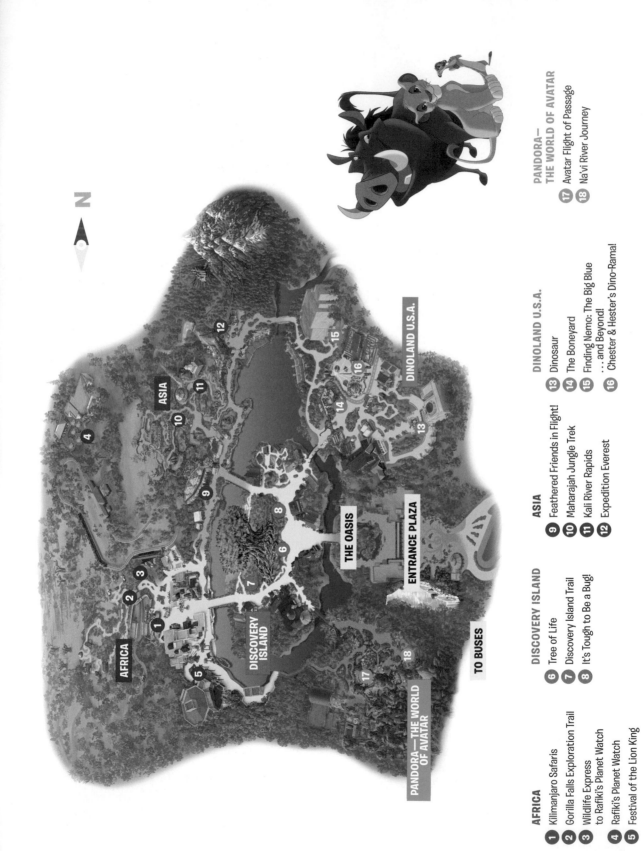

**N**

**AFRICA**

**ASIA**

**DISCOVERY ISLAND**

**DINOLAND U.S.A.**

**THE OASIS**

**ENTRANCE PLAZA**

**PANDORA—THE WORLD OF AVATAR**

**TO BUSES**

## AFRICA
1. Kilimanjaro Safaris
2. Gorilla Falls Exploration Trail
3. Wildlife Express to Rafiki's Planet Watch
4. Rafiki's Planet Watch
5. Festival of the Lion King

## DISCOVERY ISLAND
6. Tree of Life
7. Discovery Island Trail
8. It's Tough to Be a Bug!

## ASIA
9. Feathered Friends in Flight!
10. Maharajah Jungle Trek
11. Kali River Rapids
12. Expedition Everest

## DINOLAND U.S.A.
13. Dinosaur
14. The Boneyard
15. Finding Nemo: The Big Blue . . .and Beyond!
16. Chester & Hester's Dino-Rama!

## PANDORA— THE WORLD OF AVATAR
17. Avatar Flight of Passage
18. Na'vi River Journey

# Getting Oriented

Though Disney's Animal Kingdom park encompasses about five times the area of its Magic Kingdom counterpart, one need not be in training for the Olympics to tackle it. Most of the land is reserved for non-human critters. By all estimates, pedestrians rack up about the same amount of mileage in one day here as they do in a day at EPCOT.

The theme park's layout is relatively simple: a cluster of sections, or "lands," connected to a central hub. In this case, the hub is Discovery Island, an island surrounded by a peaceful river and home to the Tree of Life, the park's icon. Discovery Island is connected by bridges and paths with all other lands: the Oasis, DinoLand U.S.A., Asia, Africa, and Pandora — The World of Avatar.

As you pass through D.A.K.'s entrance plaza, you approach the Oasis. Feel free to meander at a leisurely pace, absorbing the soothing ambience of a thick, elaborate jungle, or you can proceed more quickly and plan to revisit this relaxing region later on. Each of several pathways deposits you at the foot of a bridge leading to Discovery Island. As you emerge from the Oasis, you will see the awe-inspiring Tree of Life, a 14-story Disney-made tree, looming ahead. The massive tree, which stands toward the middle of the island, is surrounded by the Discovery Island Trail. The island is also home to Adventurers Outpost, where Mickey and Minnie mingle with parkgoers.

To the southeast lies DinoLand U.S.A., home of prehistoric animals, a fossil dig, a Broadway-style musical known as Finding Nemo: The Big Blue . . . and Beyond!, and an adrenaline-inducing attraction called Dinosaur. Behind Discovery Island and to the northwest lies Africa, where guests may go on safari, explore a peaceful nature trail, and hop aboard the Wildlife Express train to Rafiki's Planet Watch, the theme park's research and education center. To the southwest lies Pandora — The World of Avatar. Its major draws are the thrilling Flight of Passage and the soothing (and cooling!) Na'vi River Journey. Asia sits northeast of Discovery Island. Here, intrepid travelers come face-to-face with a very angry Yeti (aka the Abominable Snowman) on the Expedition Everest coaster-style ride, encounter real tigers on the Maharajah Jungle Trek, and take a daring journey through the rainforest on a raft at the splashy Kali River Rapids attraction.

## HOW TO GET THERE

If you're driving, take Exit 65 off I-4. Then follow signs to Disney's Animal Kingdom. Trams run between the parking lot and the main entrance.

**By WDW Transportation:** From all Walt Disney World resorts: buses. From Disney Springs: bus to any Walt Disney World resort, then transfer to an Animal Kingdom bus. (If a direct bus is offered, by all means jump on it!) From Magic Kingdom, EPCOT, Disney's Hollywood Studios, and resorts on Hotel Plaza Boulevard (aka Disney Springs area): buses. Lyft, Uber, and taxis are also possibilities (fees apply).

## PARKING

All-day parking at Animal Kingdom starts at $25 for day visitors (preferred parking costs $45–$50); it's free to guests staying in Walt Disney World–owned-and-operated resorts.

Trams circulate through lots regularly, providing transportation from the parking area to the Animal Kingdom entrance. Be sure to take note of the section and aisle in which you park. Best to take a picture *and* jot it down on paper, just in case.

If you plan to "hop" to another park, retain your parking receipt — it'll cover parking for the day. It also allows for same-day re-entry into the Animal Kingdom lot, as well as Walt Disney World's other theme park parking lots.

## ADMISSION PRICES

Restricted to use only in Disney's Animal Kingdom. Prices are for Date-Based tickets. (At press time, sales of Flexible Date tickets were on pause, but they may return.) Prices exclude tax and are likely to rise in the coming year.

|  | ADULT | CHILD** |
|---|---|---|
| **ONE-DAY BASE TICKET*** | $109 - $159 | $104 - $154 |

* 1-Day tickets are valid only on the selected date. This is the cost of a 1-day/1-park-only ticket. Terms are subject to change. For details and updates, visit *disneyworld.disney.go.com/admission/tickets*.

** 3 through 9 years of age; children under age 3 free (no ticket required)

# Park Primer

## HOURS

Hours vary, but the gates are generally open daily from about 9 A.M. until about 6 or 7 P.M. In summer and other periods, hours are extended. It's best to arrive up to a half hour before the posted opening time. For schedules, use the (free) My Disney Experience mobile app or website, visit *disneyworld.com*, or call 407-824-4321.

## BABY FACILITIES

Changing tables and facilities for nursing mothers can be found at the Baby Care Center on Discovery Island, near Creature Comforts. It's also possible to buy certain baby-centric necessities, such as formula, baby food, and diapers, at this facility. Note that Walt Disney World restaurants do not serve baby food, but you are welcome to bring your own.

## DISABILITY INFORMATION

Nearly all Animal Kingdom attractions, shops, and restaurants are accessible to guests using wheelchairs. (Though the park's terrain is a bit bumpy.) Additional services are available for guests with visual or hearing disabilities. The Guide for Guests with Disabilities, available at the park entrance, provides an overview of the services offered, including transportation, parking, and attraction access. (For more information, see *Getting Ready to Go*.)

## FIRST AID

Minor medical problems can be handled at the park's First Aid Center, located on Discovery Island on the northwest side of the Tree of Life, near Creature Comforts (aka Starbucks). *In case of emergency call 911 and alert a cast member (park worker).*

## INFORMATION

Guest Relations, just inside the park entrance, is equipped with (free) guidemaps and a helpful staff. Maps are also available in many shops. Keep an eye out for Tip Boards within the park.

## LOCKERS

Lockers are located just inside the park entrance area, near Guest Relations. Cost is $12 for large lockers, $10 for small lockers, for unlimited use all day (at Disney's Animal Kingdom only).

## LOST & FOUND

Report lost items to Guest Relations, just inside the park entrance and/or visit *disneyworld.disney.go .com/guest-services/lost-and-found*. If you find an item, please hand it to a cast member (aka Disney employee). We recommend adding contact info to all valuables (especially mobile phones).

## LOST CHILDREN

Alert the nearest Disney employee to the matter and report lost children at the Baby Care Center, located on Discovery Island (by Creature Comforts).

## MONEY MATTERS

There is an ATM (automated teller machine) at the park entrance. Currency exchange is done at Guest Relations. In addition to U.S. cash, credit cards (Visa, American Express, Diner's Club, Discover Card, JCB, and MasterCard), Disney gift cards, and Disney resort IDs and MagicBands (backed up with a credit card) are accepted for admission and merchandise, and meals at most restaurants.

## SAME-DAY RE-ENTRY

Planning to return to Disney's Animal Kingdom later in the same day? Wear your MagicBand, use the MagicMobile service via the My Disney Experience app, or retain your park ticket.

## SECURITY CHECK

All guests entering Disney parks are subject to a security check. Bags will be searched before guests may enter the park. A metal detector screens guests. Weapons (including toys) and selfie sticks are among the prohibited items. For a complete listing of Disney Park Rules, visit *disneyworld.com/ParkRules*.

## STROLLERS & WHEELCHAIRS

Strollers, wheelchairs, and Electric Conveyance Vehicles (ECVs) may be rented at Garden Gate Gifts. Cost per day is about $15 for strollers and $12 for wheelchairs (double strollers are $31 a day). Length of Stay rentals for strollers and wheelchairs yield a daily discount. It's about $50 for ECVs, plus a $20 to $100 refundable deposit. Quantities are limited. Flash the receipt for a same-day replacement at any Walt Disney World theme park. Prices subject to change.

# The Oasis

Traditionally, one has to travel across a long, sunbaked stretch of desert in order to experience the soothing atmosphere of a tropical oasis. With that in mind, think of the Animal Kingdom parking lot as a concrete version of the Sahara. Once you've trekked across it, your journey takes you through the park's front gate and entrance plaza. What's that up ahead? Could it be a towering African tree? Here in Central Florida? It must be a mirage.

But, no. Within seconds you arrive at the Oasis, a thriving tropical garden filled with waterfalls, running streams, and lush vegetation. The transition is by no means a subtle one. Guests are immediately enveloped in a world of nature. The peaceful setting is most idyllic.

Though not a full-fledged "land" per se, this small jungle simply oozes atmosphere. It is thick and elaborate, and comes complete with critters. (Some are more difficult to spot than others. When searching for the naturally camouflaged creatures, remember to look up occasionally.) As park visitors walk along the pathways, they may catch glimpses of different kinds of animals, from babirusas and wallabies to giant anteaters and birds. As in the rest of Disney's Animal Kingdom, there is the illusion that guests are walking among the wildlife.

The Oasis is at once an exciting and calming experience. It sets the stage for what's to come. Park guests have several options once they've entered the Oasis. They can continue on a northerly path, making tracks toward the Tree of Life and across a bridge to Discovery Island. They can proceed at a more snail-friendly pace, keeping a tally of the various life-forms that they spot. Or they can simply take time to stop and marvel at what nature—and Disney Imagineers—have created.

**Timing Tip:** Making a trip through the Oasis is the only way to get into (and out of) Disney's Animal Kingdom. Some Oasis paths can become congested during the hours closest to opening and closing times. To avoid the crowds, use the path to the left when you enter the park early in the day.

> "I have learned from the animal world. And what everyone will learn who studies it is a renewed sense of kinship with the Earth and all of its inhabitants."
>
> **—Walt Disney**

# Discovery Island

Once you have passed through the Oasis, you will come to a bridge spanning a peaceful river. The bridge leads to Discovery Island, an area at the center of Disney's Animal Kingdom and the hub from which all other realms of the park may be reached.

Discovery Island is defined by the brilliant colors, tropical surroundings, and equatorial architecture of Africa and the South Pacific. The facades of the buildings are all carved and painted based on the art of nations from around the world. Don't fail to notice all the bright, whimsical folk-art images representing various members of the animal kingdom.

This island is the shopping and dining center of Animal Kingdom. Several of the park's restaurants can be found here, including Tiffins, Pizzafari, and Flame Tree Barbecue. (Reservations are recommended for Tiffins, which is a WDW Signature eatery.)

**Hot Tip!** Take a minute to study a guidemap as you enter Animal Kingdom. It'll give you a sense of the layout. Another good source of information is the park's digital Tip Board. The My Disney Experience app and website provide details about showtimes and character appearances, too. Check *disneyworld.com* for updates.

By far the most striking element standing on Discovery Island is the Tree of Life. It is on the map, but chances are you'll have no trouble finding it. Rising from the middle of the island and as tall as a 14-story building, the Tree of Life is hard to miss.

## Tree of Life

The Tree of Life is the dramatic 145-foot icon of Disney's Animal Kingdom. The imposing tree, with its swaying limbs and gnarled trunk, looks an awful lot like the real thing—from a distance. Up close, it's apparent that this is a most unusual bit of greenery. Covered with more than 325 animal images, it is a swirling tapestry of carved figures, painstakingly assembled by a team of artisans. The tree, though inorganic, stands as a symbol of the connected nature of life on Earth. We think Joyce Kilmer would have approved.

**DISCOVERY ISLAND TRAIL:** The walkway that wraps around the Tree of Life allows guests to get a close-up view of the trunk and even play a game of "spot the animals." (The spiraling animal images go all the way to the top of the tree. You will need binoculars if you hope to see them all.) Scattered about the baobab tree's massive base is a variety of animal habitats. Animals can be seen in a very open, somewhat traditional park-like setting, with lush grass, trees, and other leafy vegetation. Among the creatures you may recognize are kangaroos, storks, vultures, flamingos, and otters. Others to which you may be introduced for the very first time as you meander through the habitats include ring-tailed lemurs (not quite monkeys' uncles — more like cousins).

### BIRNBAUM'S ★BEST★ WINGED ENCOUNTERS—THE KINGDOM TAKES FLIGHT:

This exciting flight features a flock of free-flying macaws. Because of their claws? No, because they're macaws! (Sorry, we couldn't resist a quote from the Enchanted Tiki Room.) Six types of this beautiful bird, some with wingspans of up to 60 inches, are included. Expect them to swoop and soar above your head on Discovery Island (in front of the Tree of Life). It is quite thrilling. If you think you might be spooked by a (very) close encounter with our fine-feathered friends, stand toward the back of the gathered audience. At press time, this short-but-remarkably-sweet show was being presented several times a day. Check a park Tip Board or the My Disney Experience mobile app or website for the current schedule. Details are subject to change.

**THE TREE OF LIFE AWAKENINGS:** The park icon "awakens" each night with a lively projection and music show that features stirring visuals, animal spirits, and enchanted fireflies that combine to reveal stories of wonder and showcase the magic of nature. Projections may be seen from both the front and back of the tree.

**Timing Tip:** The Tree of Life Awakenings experiences begin after dark (on nights when the park is open past dusk), last about 5 minutes, and occur approximately every 10 minutes until the park closes.

### BIRNBAUM'S ★BEST★ IT'S TOUGH TO BE A BUG!:

Beneath the trunk of the Tree of Life is a 430-seat auditorium featuring an enlightening 9-minute animated 3-D film augmented by some surprising "4-D" effects. The stars of the show are the world's most abundant inhabitants — insects. They creep, crawl, and demonstrate why, someday, they just might inherit the Earth. It's a bug's-eye view of the trials and tribulations of their multi-legged world.

As guests enter The Tree of Life Repertory Theater, the orchestra can be heard warming up amid the sounds of chirping crickets. When Flik, the amiable emcee (from *A Bug's Life*), appears, he dubs audience members honorary bugs and instructs them to don their bug eyes (3-D

**Hot Tip!** Attention parents of small children! If you are seeing It's Tough to Be a Bug! for the first time, we recommend grabbing seats by the exit. That way, should your little ones get spooked by Hopper or any of his creepy cohorts, you can make a hasty escape.

glasses). Then the mild-mannered ant introduces some of his less-mild-mannered cronies, including a Chilean tarantula, dung beetles, and "the silent but deadly member of the bug world" — the stink bug. What follows is something of an infestation celebration.

**Note:** The combination of intense effects and frequent darkness tends to terrify tots and young kids. And anyone at all leery of spiders, roaches, and their ilk is advised to skip the performance, or risk being seriously bugged.

## WILDERNESS EXPLORERS

In the movie *UP*, Russell is a very dedicated–and decorated–Wilderness Explorer. He is on a fervent quest to complete his merit badge collection. Now Animal Kingdom guests can become Wilderness Explorers, too. Start by heading to the W.E. Headquarters at the Oasis bridge. After taking the official pledge, guests receive field guides describing a variety of challenges. Successfully complete a challenge and earn a badge! There are about 25 different badges to collect in all. There is no extra charge to be a Wilderness Explorer, and the badges are free. While targeted to the 7- to 10-year-old set, the challenges are fun for everyone.

# Africa

The largest section of Disney's Animal Kingdom, Africa, is bigger than the whole *Magic Kingdom* park. This 110-acre, truer-than-life replica of an African savanna is packed with pachyderms, giraffes, hippos, and other wild critters. All guests enter Africa through Harambe, a village based on a modern East African coastal town. It is the dining and shopping center of Animal Kingdom's version of Africa.

The instant you walk across the bridge to Harambe, you are transported to Africa. Everything here seems authentic, from the architecture to the landscaping to the merchandise in the marketplace. The result was achieved after Disney Imagineers made countless trips to the continent. After seven years of observing, filming, and photographing the real thing, they re-created it here in North America. It even feels a bit warmer here than it does at the other theme parks.

The many animals that live here, however, are not re-creations. They are quite real, most varied, and extremely abundant. In fact, this chunk of land puts the animal in Animal Kingdom.

PHOTO BY JILL SAFRO

## Kilimanjaro Safaris

**BIRNBAUM'S ★BEST★** The Kilimanjaro Safaris experience has something for everyone: lovely landscapes, majestic, free-roaming animals, and a thrilling adventure. It is everything you may expect from an actual trip to the African continent, and (possibly) more.

The 18-minute safari begins with a brief introduction from a guide who does double duty as your driver. Once you climb aboard the ride vehicle, look at the plates above the seat in front of you. They will help you identify the animals you see. And have those phones and cameras ready.

As the vehicle travels along dirt roads, you'll spot free-roaming wild animals: zebras, antelope, hippos, elephants, warthogs, rhinos, lions, and more. Some animals wander near your vehicle, and others cross its path. (Don't worry — only the harmless critters can approach. Others, such as lions and cheetahs, are unable to invade your safe, personal space.)

The majesty of the Serengeti may lull you into a state of serenity, but it's merely the calm before the storm. You will soon be jostled and jolted as the ride vehicle crosses pothole-filled terrain, (seemingly) rickety bridges, and flooded dirt roads.

Good news, safari fans — evening safaris have become a reality. While the Kilimanjaro Safaris attraction is a big draw at any time of day, it's nice to ride before and after the sun sets. It can be a bit challenging to spot distant animals in low light, but the overall experience is pretty cool — and some animals (e.g., lions) are more active in the evening hours. Of course, night-time safaris are only offered on dates when Animal Kingdom stays open after dark.

If you're prone to motion sickness, neck or back issues, or have other physical limitations, sit this one out. The ride is a rather bumpy one.

 **Hot Tip!** There's no need to stampede toward the Kilimanjaro Safaris ride first thing in the morning—the animals are out and active throughout the day. That said, if you do ride early, consider coming back later in the day. The beauty of this attraction is that you tend to see something new each time you ride. And don't let a little rain chase you away—it certainly doesn't bother the animals!

PHOTO BY JILL SAFRO

# Festival of The Lion King

**BIRNBAUM'S ★BEST★** In addition to rustling up grubs in their corner of Disney's Animal Kingdom, the talented cast of *The Lion King* performs a high-energy 30-minute stage show in the Harambe Theatre. Performances take place throughout the day.

Presented in the round, this lavish musical revue is as bright and boisterous as they come. The dramatic opening features a parade of performers in colorful costumes. What follows is an intriguing, energetic interpretation of the beloved film, including familiar songs, dances, and acrobatics. With the exception of Timon, who plays himself, lead characters are portrayed by humans draped in bold African costumes.

Songs include Scar's nasty version of "Be Prepared," as well as "The Circle of Life," and a rousing rendition of "The Lion Sleeps Tonight."

**Timing Tip:** Although this theater accommodates nearly 1,400 guests, plan to arrive at least 30 minutes before a performance time.

"How could this earth of ours, which is only a speck in the heavens, have so much variety of life, so many curious and exciting creatures?"

—Walt Disney

## UP CLOSE WITH RHINOS

Park guests are invited to meet the planet's second-largest land animal—the white rhinoceros—in a 60-minute, guided adventure (fees apply).

During this unique, outdoor experience, guides introduce the park's white rhinos and offer insights into the species' behavior and biology. They also address the challenges that threaten these mighty-but-gentle giants in the wild—and what *you* can do to help.

Guests must be at least 4 years old to participate. Those under age 18 must be accompanied by a paying adult. The cost is about $45 (plus tax) per guest. Park admission is required, but not included. The experience is offered rain or shine (with the exception of severe weather or lightning.) Comfy, closed-toed shoes are recommended. For more information or to make a reservation, use the My Disney Experience app or website, visit *disneyworld.com*, or call 407-939-7529. You can learn about other behind-the-scenes tours from those sources, too—and by turning to page 245 of this book.

# Gorilla Falls Exploration Trail

This self-guided walking trail winds past communities of gorillas and other rare African animals. Access it at the exit of the Kilimanjaro Safaris attraction or by the entrance in Harambe.

The first major stop on the scenic trail (previously referred to as Pangani, which translates to "place of enchantment" in Swahili) is the Research Station. Just outside are a free-flight aviary and an aquarium teeming with colorful fish. Not far away is the hippo habitat, which provides close-up views of hippopotamuses both in and out of water.

Farther along the trail there's a scenic overlook point, where you can get a clear view of the African savanna. This area is also known as the "Timon" zone, featuring a family of perky meerkats. Afterward, you may catch an up-close glimpse (through a glass wall) of a cavorting gorilla or two.

As you reach the end of the suspension bridge, you will find yourself in a beautiful green valley. Congratulations! You've finally reached the gorilla area — an experience well worth the wait. (Note that you may have to wait a bit longer for that first gorilla sighting. Our evolutionary cousins have been known to play hide-and-seek in the lush vegetation.)

# Rafiki's Planet Watch

The Harambe Train Station sits on the east side of the village of Harambe. That's where guests climb aboard the Wildlife Express to experience a rare behind-the-scenes look at a Disney theme park while en route to Rafiki's Planet Watch.

As part of the 5½-minute, narrated trip, you'll glide past buildings where the animals sleep. All guests disembark at the Rafiki's Planet Watch station and cover the remaining distance on foot. (The walk takes about 5 minutes, and you may encounter animal experts en route.) Note that you'll have to re-board the Wildlife Express train to return to Harambe Village.

> ## "Animals have personalities like people and must be studied."
> ### —Walt Disney

While Animal Kingdom's stories often carry a conservation theme, this part really brings the message home. This is the park's conservation headquarters and veterinary lab, as well as the research and education hub. Exhibits are geared to spark curiosity about wildlife and conservation efforts around the world. Here's what you'll find at Rafiki's Planet Watch:

**Habitat Habit!:** An outdoor discovery trail that sports signs with hints on how to share the planet with all members of the animal kingdom.

**Affection Section:** An animal encounter area with critters (mostly goats) to see and touch. Be sure to stop at the hand-washing station before leaving this area.

## GET INVOLVED

When it comes to conservation efforts, the folks at the Walt Disney Company want you to do as they say—and as they do: The Disney Conservation Fund helps nonprofit groups protect and study endangered and threatened animals and habitats. The fund has supported projects from more than 600 nonprofit organizations, protecting more than 1,000 different species. And guests who contribute money while making purchases at many Animal Kingdom shops and restaurants help make a difference, too.

Of course, as a trip to Animal Kingdom makes clear, there are many ways to help our planet's wild inhabitants. Stop by Rafiki's Planet Watch during your visit. There, you can get information about conservation efforts in your neck of the woods. Don't leave your enthusiasm behind when you leave the park.

**Conservation Station:** This is the center of The Walt Disney Company's effort to promote wildlife conservation awareness. Here you'll get an in-depth look at animal habitats around the planet and witness expert veterinary care. Housed within Conservation Station are the Veterinary Treatment Room; Nutrition Center (where you can watch experts prepare meals for the park's animal inhabitants); the Amphibian, Reptile, and Invertebrate Room (home to creatures such as tarantulas, snakes, millipedes, and scorpions), the Science Center, and the Animation Experience. Note that experiences are subject to change without notice.

**Animation Experience:** If you have ever dreamed of being a Disney animator, here's your chance to pursue that dream. In a 25-minute class, taught by an actual animator, you will learn the secrets to bringing Disney characters to life — using real-life animals as inspiration. It's fun for guests of all ages (and skill levels) — and worth visiting more than once. Each session tends to offer something a little different. Check the My Disney Experience mobile app or website for class schedule and availability.

### DID YOU KNOW?
There are 27 million gallons of water flowing in Animal Kingdom's Discovery River. That's enough water to fill about 1,800 average-sized swimming pools!

# Pandora—The World of Avatar

According to the blockbuster film *AVATAR*, Earthlings have a distant, idyllic destination to look forward to in the 22nd century: Pandora, a magnificent moon orbiting the planet Polyphemus about 4.4 light-years from Earth. Pandora, with its lush, bio-luminescent rainforest environment, is home to floating mountains and incredible life-forms, including trees that stand a thousand feet tall and a myriad of infinitely diverse creatures—such as native people known as the Na'vi. These blue humanoids travel via flying mountain banshees and have a sophisticated culture based on a deep connection to each other and all life on Pandora. That connection is rendered possible via the majestic and sacred Tree of Souls.

If Pandora sounds like a place you would like to visit, you're not alone—*AVATAR* was one of the biggest movie sensations of all time. The good news is humans don't have to wait until the 22nd century to visit the wondrous world of Pandora. Thanks to Disney Imagineering magic, it has come to Disney's Animal Kingdom. This land, aka the Valley of Mo'ara, opened in 2017. Note that one need not be familiar with (or a fan of) the film to appreciate a visit here.

## Avatar Flight of Passage

**BIRNBAUM'S ★BEST★** The crown jewel of Disney's Animal Kingdom park, Flight of Passage invites adventurers to take an exuberant trip through Pandora on the back of a flying mountain banshee (aka ikran). The joyful 3-D journey takes place in a cutting-edge, simulator-like environment and offers much more than a thrill a minute. Guests are treated to a bird's-eye view of all the sights, sounds, and smells of the majestic moon that the Na'vi call home.

A high-flying "E-Ticket" attraction, Flight of Passage is an exceptionally realistic, immersive experience. It is not recommended for guests with motion sensitivity, heart conditions, fear of heights, claustrophobia, or any other such concerns. This attraction is perpetually popular—get there as early as you can. Guests must be at least 44 inches tall to experience this ride. Note that the 3-D glasses are one size fits all. If the safety restraints are too tight, alert a ride attendant ASAP. Then sit back, relax, and enjoy the flight.

## Na'vi River Journey

A placid voyage into Pandora's bio-luminescent forest, this trip is calm and family-friendly (though wee ones may be spooked by the large and somewhat daunting Na'vi shaman). The journey begins as guests board canoes and venture along a mysterious, sacred river hidden within the rainforest. The grandeur of Pandora is revealed as canoes float past exotic glowing plants and an array of intriguing creatures, including native humanoids known as Na'vi. The journey culminates in an encounter with a Na'vi shaman, who has a deep connection to the life force of Pandora and sends positive energy into the forest with her music.

The tranquil Na'vi River Journey is generally appreciated by guests of all ages (though timid tykes who are spooked by darkness may find some parts of this expedition a tad unsettling). This indoor attraction provides a nice opportunity to visit the Na'vi world while resting your feet and enjoying a refreshing dose of air-conditioning. If the wait isn't overwhelmingly long (though it often is), by all means give it a whirl.

**DID YOU KNOW?**
The common spirit of Pandora—where all life-forms are constantly connected to each other, the environment, and their host planet—is based on the concept of Gaia, proposed by chemist James Lovelock in 1970 and described in Isaac Asimov's novel *Foundation's Edge* in 1982.

# Asia

PHOTO BY JILL SAFRO

On the far side of a Himalayan-style bridge, beyond an ancient temple, lies the tranquil village of Anandapur (a Sanskrit word meaning "place of delight"). The buildings' design was inspired by structures in Thailand, Indonesia, and other Asian countries known for their rich architectural history.

An impressive product of Disney Imagineering, the village epitomizes the complex, enduring relationship between the animals and ecosystems of the Asian continent. The tiny village borders an elaborate re-creation of a Southeast Asian rainforest. As such, Animal Kingdom's Asia is an ideal location for trekking through the lush jungle, shooting the rapids on a raging river, and gazing upon the multi-hued inhabitants of this treasured terrain.

## Kali River Rapids

Before guests board round rafts at Kali (pronounced *KAH-lee*) River Rapids, a wise voice admonishes that "the river is like life itself, full of mysterious twists and turns." What the voice doesn't say is that this particular river is also full of splashing water and a blazing inferno. This may be business as usual for some daring souls, but for most of us, these elements make for one very dramatic, drenching adventure.

All guests begin the journey in the offices of Kali River Rapids Expeditions, a river rafting company. A slide show offers a look at the sometimes unscrupulous business of logging—how it has ravaged the rainforest and deprived many animals of habitats. But, thanks to ecotourism (among other things), there is hope. Peaceful voyages give people a new appreciation and sense of responsibility for this endangered land.

A 12-seater raft whisks "ecotourists" up a watery ramp and through an arching tunnel of bamboo. It proceeds onward, through a hazy mist and past remnants of an ancient shrine. As the raft careens along

curves of the raging river, guests may enjoy views of undisturbed rainforest.

The tranquility is shattered by a startling sight. A huge chunk of forest has been gutted by loggers. On both sides of the river, the forest has vanished. As guests absorb the image, they are besieged by more disturbing sights and sounds. Straight ahead, the river is choked with a tangled arch of burning logs—and the raft is headed straight for it. Suddenly, the rainforest isn't the only thing endangered.

Kali River Rapids is an especially soggy experience. It is the rare guest who leaves the ride without a thorough soaking. Should you wish to repel as much precipitation as possible, pack a plastic poncho. Stash valuables in a nearby locker while you ride (no charge).

**Note:** This is a very bumpy adventure. In order to experience it, you must be at least 38 inches tall. It is not recommended for pregnant women, guests with heart conditions, people with back or neck problems, or anyone who hopes to stay dry.

## Maharajah Jungle Trek

Welcome to the jungle! The Maharajah Jungle Trek is a self-guided walking tour of a tropical paradise, complete with roaming tigers and dense greenery. Throughout the expedition, trekkers encounter a deluge of flora and fauna typically found in the rainforests of Southeast Asia. Komodo dragons, fruit bats, and a conglomeration of colorful birds call this corner

**Hot Tip!** Everyone and everything gets wet (to varying degrees) on Kali River Rapids. Items that simply must stay dry should be stored in a locker (across the pathway at the attraction's entrance) or with a non-riding member of your party.

of Animal Kingdom home. Majestic Asian tigers can be spotted stalking ancient ruins, strategically separated from would-be prey. Deer and antelope graze and frolic nearby, blissfully oblivious of their fearsome neighbors' proximity.

About midway through the thicket stands a tin-roofed assembly hall. Step inside to witness giant fruit bats showing off their six-foot wingspans. As you gaze upon them through the windows, thinking that the crystal clear glass was cleaned by a super diligent window washer, think again. There is no glass in some of the windows—and, therefore, nothing separating you from the giant creatures hanging about on the other side. What keeps the big bats from getting up close and personal with guests? They're a lot less interested in humans than humans are in them. (Can't say that we blame them.) Note that some viewing areas are fitted with wire mesh or glass barriers—for guests who are more comfortable with a bat buffer.

## Feathered Friends in Flight!

A 1,000-seat, open-air theater, the Anandapur Theatre features performances by actors wearing nothing but feathers and the occasional crown. Members of various avian species have starring roles in this high-flying celebration of the winged wonders of the world. The show is hosted by clever animal behavior specialists who offer an entertaining, behind-the-scenes look at our fine, feathered friends. Each performance runs about 35 minutes. It's a real hoot! Check a park Tip Board or the My Disney Experience app for the day's

schedule. If the thought of up-close encounters with bird kind makes you uneasy, skip this show. (Several of the aforementioned feathered friends fly just above audience members' heads during the performance. Just a heads-up!)

## Expedition Everest

**BIRNBAUM'S ★BEST★** Walt Disney World's mountain range is a bit more intense these days, as the world's tallest mountain—Everest—has risen from the peaceful village of Serka Zong in Animal Kingdom's Asia. Like its sister peaks, Space and Big Thunder, this "E-Ticket" eminence promises "coaster thrills, spills, and chills." Does Expedition Everest deliver on that promise? Boy, does it ever.

The attraction features an old tea train chugging and churning as it climbs up and around snowcapped peaks. Suddenly, the track comes to an end in a gnarled mess of twisted metal. Lurching forward and backward, the train hurtles through caverns and icy canyons before depositing guests in the presence of the legendary Yeti (also known as the Abominable Snowman)—who's most displeased that you've scaled the mountain he so fiercely protects.

Are you feeling up to the challenge of a dramatic, high-speed, out-of-control train ride? If you are free of heart, back, and neck problems, are not pregnant, have no fear of heights (or abominable snowpeople), and are at least 44 inches tall, go for it. As always, never eat right before experiencing an attraction as topsy-turvy as this one.

PHOTO BY JILL SAFRO

# DinoLand U.S.A.

If the look and feel of DinoLand U.S.A. seems familiar, there's a reason: It was designed to capture the flavor of roadside America. It is a mixture of culture and kitsch—the likes of which you might stumble upon during a cross-country road trip. Here, you may ride a flying triceratops, jump into gigantic footprints, and browse through a typically tacky roadside souvenir stand, where you can pick up some mementos for the folks back home.

**Hot Tip!** When the park is open late, Animal Kingdom is a good park to "hop" to. It's always a touch cooler in the evening, the animals are just as active (if not more so) as they are during the day, and the bioluminescent flora and other touches make Pandora—The World of Avatar shine.

This corner of Animal Kingdom comes complete with its own dramatic entrance: a 50-foot (replica) skeleton of a brachiosaurus. As guests stroll beneath the bones, they find themselves smack in the middle of a paleontological dig. Here, guests of all ages (especially little ones) have the chance to play paleontologist as they dig through a fossil-packed pocket of dino discovery.

The dinosaurs that dwell here, though often rather animated, are all of the inanimate variety. But do keep your eyes peeled for prehistoric life-forms that actually live in this land—that is, for living creatures that exist in the here and now, but whose ancestors kept company with the likes of the carnotaurus and its cousins from the Cretaceous era.

## The Boneyard

The Boneyard gives guests—especially very young ones—an opportunity to dig for fossils in a discovery-oriented playground. They will excavate the ancient bones of a mammoth in this re-creation of a paleontological dig (think huge sandbox). They will also unearth clues that may help them solve the mystery of how and when the creature met its untimely demise.

For serious "boneheads" who just aren't satisfied with simple digging, there are plenty of other bone-related activities here. Youngsters can bang out a primitive tune on a bony xylophone (it's located near the car; to make a sound, firmly press on a rib), zip down prehistoric slides, and work their way through a fossil-filled maze. While exploring, be sure to watch your step: If you happen to wander into a giant dinosaur footprint, you might be greeted with a somewhat ominous roar.

While in DinoLand, be sure to check out the Olden-Gate Bridge. It's a gateway structure fashioned from a dinosaur skeleton. The bridge links one end of The Boneyard with the other. This is a good place to take young children while other members of your party ride the Dinosaur attraction.

## Chester & Hester's Dino-Rama!

A colorful land-within-a-land, Chester & Hester's is an area ideally suited for roadside carnival fans. Located just beyond The Boneyard playground, this wild-and-woolly zone features old-fashioned midway games and one family-friendly ride: TriceraTop Spin. Note that the area's other attraction, Primeval Whirl, spun off the map in 2020.

### A DINO NAMED SUE

DinoLand U.S.A. has a celebrity resident: A 67-million-year-old Tyrannosaurus Rex. Named for Sue Hendricksen—the fossil-hunter who discovered her in South Dakota in 1990—Dino-Sue is one of the most famous fossil finds of the 20th century. She's also the most complete, with 90 percent of her bones excavated. You can visit with Animal Kingdom's replica of Sue's 13-foot-high skeleton on your way to the park's Dinosaur attraction. (The real Dino-Sue resides at The Field Museum in Chicago, Illinois.)

PHOTO BY JILL SAFRO

**TRICERATOP SPIN:** The ride is sure to please fans of the Magic Kingdom's Dumbo the Flying Elephant and the Magic Carpets of Aladdin. Guests ride in one of the 16 flying dinos, each of which resembles an oversize tin toy. It's rather tame when compared to its Dinosaur attraction neighbor, but certainly worth checking out—especially for young dinosaur groupies.

**FOSSIL FUN GAMES:** Chester & Hester's Dino-Rama is home to several silly games of skill, including Whac-A-Packycephalosaur (smack mischievous dinos with a mallet), Mammoth Marathon (roll balls into holes to move your woolly mammoth in a race to the finish line), Bronto-Score (basketball toss), Comet Crasher (toss "comets" into moving cups), and Fossil Fueler (a gas-station-themed squirt game). Just like the midway games after which they are modeled, these games come with a fee. Game coupons may be purchased at the souvenir stand in the games area and at Chester & Hester's Dinosaur Treasures. Each game costs about $5 per person. Prizes are awarded to winners.

If you'd rather stick to included-with-the-price-of-admission diversions, we recommend checking out the fun-house mirror for some simple, silly fun.

For a slightly less turbulent experience on the Dinosaur attraction, request an inside seat near the front of the ride vehicle.

Hot Tip!

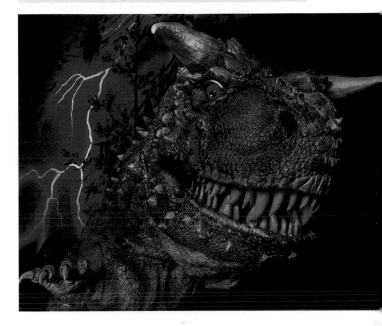

# Dinosaur

**BIRNBAUM'S**
**★BEST★**
This dizzying dino adventure begins with guests being strapped into vehicles and catapulted back in time to complete a dangerous, albeit noble, mission: to rescue the last iguanodon—a 16-foot plant-eating dinosaur—and bring him back to the present. The iguanodon, which lived more than 65 million years ago (during the Cretaceous period), just might hold the answer to the mysterious disappearance of his dino brethren.

Throughout the frenetic quest to locate the elusive iguanodon, you cling to an out-of-control vehicle while dodging blazing meteors and a mix of friendly and ferocious dinosaurs. Soon you'll encounter a carnotaurus — a fearsome, carnivorous dinosaur. The carnotaurus, which has horns like a bull and a face like a toad, is a remarkably unsightly specimen. It and its fellow dinos move as though they were alive. Even their nostrils move as they "breathe."

This 3½-minute attraction offers more than a thrill a minute. You rocket through time, are practically pelted by meteors, and narrowly escape becoming a dino dinner as the carnotaurus suddenly turns the tables and chases after you!

## WHERE TO EAT IN ANIMAL KINGDOM

A complete listing of eateries at Disney's Animal Kingdom—full-service restaurants, fast-food eateries, and snack spots—can be found in the *Good Meals, Great Times* chapter. Refer to the Animal Kingdom section, beginning on page 284.

Guests reach the attraction through the Dino Institute, a museum-like building deep in the heart of DinoLand U.S.A. Here, you will be treated to a pre-show by Bill Nye the Science Guy (audio only) and see a dinosaur skeleton and an assortment of fossils and other artifacts.

This is a very rough (and dark) attraction. Guests must be at least 40 inches tall to ride. It should be skipped if you are pregnant, have a heart condition, back or neck problems, or any other physical limitations. Young kids (and some adults!) will most definitely be frightened.

# Finding Nemo:
# The Big Blue . . . and Beyond!

Fans of an elusive little clownfish known as Nemo will be happy to find him in this dynamic musical production. Like this venue's original show, Finding Nemo—The Musical, which swam off the stage in 2020, this show is based on a familiar set of esteemed aquatic characters (including Marlin, the overprotective clownfish dad; Nemo, his curious son; and Dory, the endearing royal blue tang with the short-term memory issues). It's a "musical retelling of the beloved underwater tale of family, friendship, and kindness."

The 25-minute production, which features nimble narrators (Gill, Peach, Bloat, and Deb), includes original story material and favorite songs such as "Big Blue World" and "Go with the Flow." It made its splashy debut in 2022 at the (completely enclosed and blissfully air-conditioned) Theater in the Wild. For showtimes, check an in-park Tip Board or the *My Disney Experience* mobile app or website, or visit *disneyworld.com*.

## WHERE TO FIND THE CHARACTERS IN DISNEY'S ANIMAL KINGDOM

At press time, many characters were waving to guests from cheery flotillas on the Discovery River. Mickey and Minnie were greeting folks in person at the Adventurers Outpost on Discovery Island. You may discover Chip and Dale mingling in DinoLand U.S.A. Kevin shows up on Discovery Island. Donald and Daisy like to meet park guests in Dinoland, U.S.A., too. Moana is also known to greet guests on Discovery Island. You may spot Pocahontas and Meeko bobbing by on a flotilla. Goofy, Mickey, and other Disney pals like to join Donald Duck for meals at the Tusker House restaurant in Harambe (near the Festival of the Lion King theater). Reservations are required for all Tusker House meals (use the My Disney Experience mobile app or website, or visit *disneyworld.com*). Details are subject to change.

PHOTO BY JESSICA WARD

# Shopping

## ENTRANCE AREA

**GARDEN GATE GIFTS:** Stop here to rent Electric Conveyance Vehicles (ECVs). Wheelchair and stroller rentals are nearby. Stroller accessories may be purchased here. This is also the park's PhotoPass viewing location.

**OUTPOST:** Just outside the park's entrance, Outpost offers character merchandise, snacks, and souvenirs. (This location was "on pause" at press time.)

## PANDORA—THE WORLD OF AVATAR

**WINDTRADERS:** A nice shopper's retreat, Windtraders specializes in Na'vi cultural artifacts (the Na'vi are the native inhabitants of Pandora), plus Alpha Centauri Expeditions (ACE) clothing, toys, and more. Would you like to adopt your own mountain banshee (aka ikran)? Head here.

## DISCOVERY ISLAND

**DISCOVERY TRADING COMPANY:** This is the largest shopping spot in the park. In it, you'll find character merch, clothing, candy, and Disney paraphernalia. Discovery Trading Co. usually stays open about a half hour after the park closes. It's connected to the Riverside Depot, which also sells Disney character-themed items.

**ISLAND MERCANTILE:** This sprawling space is themed as a shipping company that celebrates working animals— camels, elephants, and others. Nature-themed gifts and apparel are the stock-in-trade at this sizable shop. There's an abundance of clothing, plus various items with an animal theme and Disney souvenirs.

## AFRICA

**MOMBASA MARKETPLACE & ZIWANI TRADERS:** An African marketplace and trading company, these shops have animal toys, safari clothing, T-shirts, masks, musical instruments, plus a selection of items featuring *The Lion King*. A wood-carver makes crafts on the spot.

**ZURI'S SWEETS SHOP:** Guests who explore Mombasa Marketplace/Ziwani Traders will discover Zuri's, a treat lover's paradise tucked within the emporium. In addition to sweets with a Disney theme, Zuri proffers a selection of African wine.

## ASIA

**BHAKTAPUR MARKET:** A small shop with a big Asian influence, Bhaktapur sells summer shoes, bags, robes, shirts, teapots and teas, toy dragons and plush animals, chopsticks, and items with a Yak & Yeti theme. Details are subject to change.

**MANDALA GIFTS:** A stone's throw from Royal Anandapur Tea Company, this cozy spot offers Asian-inspired headware, footwear, towels, and more.

**SERKA ZONG BAZAAR:** Located at the exit of Expedition Everest (it can be accessed from the outside for those who prefer to skip the ride), this bustling bazaar sells souvenirs with a Yeti theme, plus a slew of shirts, hats, plush toys, pins, etc., that celebrate the adjacent Expedition Everest attraction.

## DINOLAND U.S.A.

**CHESTER & HESTER'S DINOSAUR TREASURES:** Themed as an American roadside souvenir stand, this shop pays homage to all reptiles and prehistoric animals. Oddly enough, there are no dinosaur treasures to be found— Chester and Hester are more focused on Disney stuff.

**THE DINO INSTITUTE SHOP:** It should come as no surprise that you'll find dino-themed items and other souvenirs here. It's also the spot to view (and buy) that photo of you looking terrified while riding Dinosaur.

### DID YOU KNOW?

Some of the benches in Disney's Animal Kingdom are made of recycled plastic milk jugs. It takes roughly 1,350 jugs to make a single park bench.

# Entertainment

Delightful diversions abound at Disney's Animal Kingdom park—from a stirring flight on the back of a banshee to a serene search for animals on the Tree of Life. The park has also featured live music, lavish stage shows, and lively dance parties. The following is a sample of the park's entertainment slate. For more information and updates, use the My Disney Experience mobile app or website, visit *disneyworld.com*, or check an in-park Tip Board.

**CHAKRANADI:** Listen to the simmering sounds of traditional Indian melodies, performed by a musician deftly playing the sitar (a stringed musical instrument in the lute family). Shows take place in the Asia section of the park and last about 20 minutes.

**DI-VINE:** So convincing is Di-Vine, that many a guest fails to notice she is actually a graceful entertainer and not, well, an actual vine.

**KORA TINGA TINGA:** The kora is a hand-crafted, 21-stringed African harp. Animal Kingdom guests can hear it played several times a day in the park's Africa section, aka Harambe.

**TAM TAM DRUMMERS OF HARAMBE:** Park guests may dance to the beat of the Congo as these spirited musicians dance, drum, and dazzle the crowd. Each 15-minute performance takes place in Harambe Village, in the Africa section of the park.

**VIVA GAIA STREET BAND!:** This exuberant troupe of colorfully clad musicians holds Caribbean street parties on Discovery Island throughout the day. Each performance lasts about 20 to 25 minutes.

## Hot Tips

- Most of Animal Kingdom's attractions take place outdoors. Don't become overheated! Make a point of staying hydrated and slipping into air-conditioned shops and restaurants from time to time to cool off.

- If you arrive at park opening time, enter via the path on the left side of The Oasis. It tends to be less trafficked.

- Rainforest Cafe generally keeps longer hours than the park does. (Buses run until one hour after park closing time.)

- When the weather gets steamy, keep a reusable water bottle with you at all times.

- Narrow, winding paths, grooved pavement, and hilly terrain make this the most challenging Disney theme park in which to navigate a wheelchair or heavy stroller.

- Check the My Disney Experience mobile app or website to get an idea of attraction wait times.

- The line for Kilimanjaro Safaris tends to dwindle a bit by midday. See it then (the experience is enjoyable at any time of day). If the park is open after dark, try to experience the safari ride after the sun sets.

- Bumpy rides aren't for everyone—or for every camera. When it comes to thrill (or wet) rides, it's smart to stash cameras and other electronic equipment in a locker or with a non-riding member of your party.

- Island Mercantile on Discovery Island stays open about a half hour after the park closes.

- If you plan to ride Avatar Flight of Passage (and you should), be prepared for a long wait and a long walk: The distance from the attraction's entrance to the ride itself is more than a quarter-mile. Wear comfortable shoes and be sure to hit the restroom before hitting the queue.

- Disney's Animal Kingdom includes a realistic reproduction of parts of the African continent, right down to the climate. Beat the heat by arriving very early in the morning or "hop" to Animal Kingdom after the sun sets (on days when the park stays open late).

# Hidden Mickeys

These are some of the most popular "Hidden Mickeys" at Animal Kingdom. How many can you find? Check the square when you spot each one!

☐ **TREE OF LIFE:** A Hidden Mickey made of moss is on the front of the Tree of Life just to the right of the tiger and to the left of the buffalo. Although you may be able to spot it from several vantage points, the best place is right when you enter Discovery Island and before the path splits to Africa and DinoLand U.S.A.

☐ **KILIMANJARO SAFARIS:** Pay close attention to the flamingo pond on your left just after you enter elephant country. The center island is shaped like a Hidden Mickey (sit toward the left side of the ride vehicle for the best view).

☐ **MAHARAJAH JUNGLE TREK:** There are more than 10 Hidden Mickeys throughout this jungle trek, but we suggest hunting for these two to start: Inside the first archway near the tiger exhibit, pay attention to the mural on the left and look for three leaves that form a Hidden Mickey underneath the extended arm of a king.

☐ Now walk to the second arch and look at the mural on the right to find a Hidden Mickey image in the clouds.

☐ **GORILLA FALLS EXPLORATION TRAIL:** Okay, while not a Hidden Mickey, the Hidden Jafar (from the animated feature *Aladdin*) found on this trail is well worth searching for. Just past the gorilla viewing area, you will reach a suspension bridge. Look directly to your right and you'll see a huge 3-D head of Jafar carved out of the rock that's covered in moss.

 **RAFIKI'S PLANET WATCH:** Conservation Station is a Hidden Mickey paradise with more than twenty in the entrance mural alone. Two favorites: Just inside the building on the right, find a possum with a Hidden Mickey in its eye.

 Next look above it to find a butterfly with two Hidden Mickeys (one on each wing).

 For good measure, here's a third: Find a frog just to the right of an alligator on the left wall, then locate Mickey's smiling face beneath the frog's right eye.

☐ **HARAMBE MARKET:** There are several H.M.s in this dining zone. The easiest to spot is at the entrance. It's Mickey Mouse waving hello! (Under the picture is the word *fichwa*—that's how to say hello in Swahili.)

☐ Enter Harambe Market and you'll find Mickey enjoying a cup of coffee. (The picture is on a pillar in a seating area.)

☐ **IT'S TOUGH TO BE A BUG!:** This is one of the more challenging Hidden Mickeys to locate at Disney's Animal Kingdom, but cast members are always happy to offer some assistance. After you enter the "underground" room with all the silly musical posters (but before entering the main theater), find the other entrance to the far side of the room. Now look at the far left wall. This well-concealed (but very cool) Hidden Mickey is hiding in the shadows.

☐ **DINOLAND U.S.A.:** First, find the two large dinosaurs holding up a "Chester & Hester's Dino-Rama" sign near the TriceraTop Spin ride. Stand directly underneath the sign and close to the blue dinosaur. Look at the dino's wrist—there's a Hidden Mickey on it!

☐ Next head to the dig site area of The Boneyard playground. Can you spot where two hard hats and a fan combine to form another H.M.?

☐ **DINOSAUR:** Before you travel back in time, your ride vehicle passes a laboratory scene on the left (the vehicle actually stops here for a second to give you an opportunity to look). Search carefully to find a blue Hidden Mickey drawn on the lower left corner of a whiteboard.

☐ **CRETACEOUS TRAIL:** At the end of this short DinoLand trail sits a proud dino. We think he's proud of the Hidden Mickey on his back!

*Specifics may change during 2024.*

# Where in the World?

All of the photos on this page were taken at Disney's Animal Kingdom. Do you know where? We challenge you to find all the spots where these images were shot and snap a (non-flash) photo for yourself as you discover each one. Happy hunting! (For locations, see page 364.)

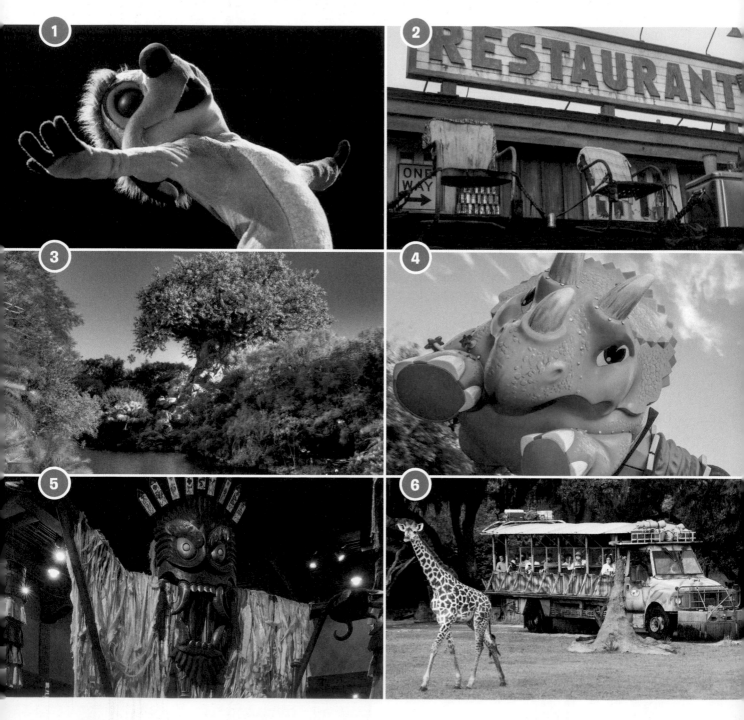

# EVERYTHING ELSE IN THE WORLD

While the total turf of the World encompasses nearly 40 square miles, the theme parks cover a mere fraction of Disney property. Much of the remaining Walt Disney World terrain is crammed with activities of a variety and quality seldom found anywhere else on Earth.

Within WDW's borders you'll find golf and tennis, beaches for strolling, lakes for boating and fishing, canoes to rent and winding streams to paddle along, bicycles for hire, campfire sites, ballooning, horseback riding, nature trails, archery lessons, and picnic grounds. The recreation options continue with Typhoon Lagoon, a lushly landscaped, state-of-the-art water park complete with a surfing lagoon, and Blizzard Beach, a watery wonderland that translates the hallmarks of a ski resort to the realm of swimming.

A lineup of lavish spas and salons provides guests with ample opportunity to pamper themselves silly. Intriguing "backstage" programs invite the curious to slip behind the scenes and learn about the workings of Walt Disney World. Add to all that, Disney Springs—a dynamic dining, shopping, and entertainment district including an eclectic assortment of shops, shows, and eateries. The bustling waterfront zone has more than 200 different venues to discover. It seems this really is a World without end.

> "Laughter is America's most important export."
>
> —**Walt Disney**

225

# Disney Springs

Sprinkled across 120 acres are the shops, lounges, restaurants, and entertainment sites that collectively make up Disney Springs. This timeless place, previously known as Downtown Disney, consists of four neighborhoods interconnected by a flowing spring and vibrant lakefront: the Marketplace, Town Center, The Landing, and West Side. This bustling enclave is a definite hot spot—especially in the evening.

The spirited waterfront zone boasts approximately 200 establishments to discover—all there for your dining, shopping, and playing pleasure. Guests staying at most Disney–owned-and-operated resorts can reach Disney Springs via bus. Water taxis (aka the Sassagoula River Cruise) ferry guests to several nearby resorts from a Marketplace dock: Saratoga Springs, Port Orleans French Quarter, Port Orleans Riverside, and Old Key West. Safe, convenient pedestrian bridges connect the area with the resorts on Hotel Plaza Boulevard (part of the Disney Springs Resort Area).

There is a $20 charge for valet parking. (It's available near the entrance to the Orange garage and Lemon lot from 10 A.M. till 2 A.M. and on the far end of the West Side [near the Cirque du Soleil tent], from 4 P.M. until 2 A.M.). Self parking is free. Plan to arrive at the parking facility at least one hour before a scheduled event. (There is a lot of ground to cover at Disney Springs!)

For updates and additional information, use the (free) My Disney Experience mobile app or website, visit *disneysprings.com* or *disneyworld.com*, or call 407-934-7639. All details are subject to change.

## DISNEY SPRINGS ESSENTIALS

**GUEST RELATIONS:** Inside the Disney Springs Welcome Center in Town Center, Guest Relations is the place to go for information, to make dining reservations, for Lost & Found, and more. Strollers and wheelchairs are available at Sundries Rentals. Details are subject to change.

**HOW TO GET THERE:** If you're driving, take exit 67 off I-4 to access Disney Springs.

**By WDW Transportation:** From Disney's Old Key West, Port Orleans French Quarter and Riverside, and Saratoga Springs: boat or bus. From all other WDW resorts: bus. One-way bus service may be offered from Disney theme parks to Disney Springs after 4 P.M. (There is no return bus service to the parks.) The Marketplace is within walking distance of Saratoga Springs and some resorts on Hotel Plaza Boulevard.

**By Ride-Sharing Service or Taxi:** Guests may use Lyft or Uber to get to and from Disney Springs. Authorized cabs serve the area, too. The cost of cabbing to most WDW resorts is usually $15 to $30 (plus tip). Minnie Vans, which service WDW-owned-and-operated resorts, may be summoned via the Lyft app. The cost depends on the destination.

The Disney Springs address is 1486 Buena Vista Drive, Lake Buena Vista, FL 32830.

**SECURITY CHECK:** All guests entering Disney Springs are subject to a thorough security check. All people, bags, parcels, and other items are subject to screening and search.

# Marketplace

Situated along the shore of Lake Buena Vista, the Marketplace is a relaxing setting for shopping, dining, and much more. The waterside district is sprinkled with gardens featuring whimsical topiaries. Little kids are fond of the Disney Springs carousel (for details, see Marketplace Rides, page 228). While many guests opt to eat at a table-service restaurant, others grab a bite from someplace like the Earl of Sandwich and nosh at outdoor tables. (Refer to the *Good Meals, Great Times* chapter for restaurant details.) After dining, some gravitate toward Dockside Margaritas for live music and a nightcap (or two).

Most shops and eateries within the Disney Springs Marketplace are typically open from about 10 A.M. to 11 or 11:30 P.M. each day. The following pages detail favorite shopping, dining, and entertainment locations. The descriptions suggest the types of wares and cuisine each spot offers. Note that some spots were "on pause" as this book went to press. What will be operating when you visit Disney Springs? Use the My Disney Experience app or website, or visit *disneyworld.com* to find out.

PHOTO BY JILL SAFRO

**ARRIBAS BROS.:** This shop sells handcrafted items from Spanish artisans and designers. Large cut-glass bowls and vases are available, along with mugs, sculptures, and other wares, many of which can be personalized on the spot. Aspiring Cinderellas should appreciate the selection of sparkly tiaras and glass slippers. The store is located between Basin and Marketplace Co-op.

> **Hot Tip!** Disney's Saratoga Springs resort is within walking distance of Disney Springs. It takes about 3 to 10 minutes for most folks to reach the Marketplace. (It's linked by bus and water taxi, too.)

**THE ART CORNER:** The vivid enclave known as The Art Corner offers lovingly crafted works by The Artistic Talent Group. Crafty corners within its walls include **Caricatures** (hand-drawn in traditional and digital formats), **Name Works** (simply provide a name and they'll illustrate it on the spot), and **Artistic Marbling**—where you can learn the ancient art of suminagashi, or "floating ink." There guests work with the in-house experts to create their own customized silk souvenirs. (Artistic Marbling made its WDW debut in 2018, at EPCOT's International Festival of the Arts—and quickly became a fan favorite.)

**THE ART OF DISNEY:** Original Disney art, porcelain figures, ceramics, posters, and other collectibles are available at this engaging gallery. Notable Disney artists often appear at this spot to sign their works.

**BASIN:** Products designed to clean you up and calm you down are the stock-in-trade at this soothing establishment. Candles, soaps, and bath crystals are some of the wares on hand. A sampling area allows shoppers to try before they buy. The bath bombs are the best! To save 15 percent off your total Basin purchase, use the coupon at the back of this book.

**BIBBIDI BOBBIDI BOUTIQUE:** This country parlor–inspired location gives young guests (ages 3 through 12) the royal treatment with the help of Fairy Godmother's apprentices. Youngsters are transformed into princesses and shining knights. Kids can get their faces painted with glitter makeup, do their nails and hair, and don tiaras. The boutique was "temporarily unavailable" as this book went to press. For updates, pricing, and reservations, visit *disneyworld.com*. Details are subject to change.

**DINO-STORE:** Aspiring paleontologists can dig for prehistoric toys and treasures in this corner of T-Rex: A Prehistoric Family Adventure. There is an area in which to custom-build a plush dino, too.

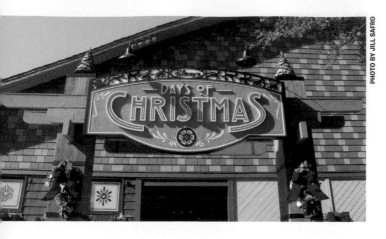

PHOTO BY JILL SAFRO

**DISNEY'S DAYS OF CHRISTMAS:** Ho, ho, ho! Here is the best place for decking the halls Disney style—it is the largest Christmas shop you'll find at Walt Disney World. In addition to character items, the shop has a large assortment of festive ornaments. Other items to look for: Mickey Mouse nutcrackers, stockings, books, and holiday cards. Several of the ornaments can be personalized on the spot.

**DISNEY'S PIN TRADERS:** This shop boasts an assortment of collector pins and pin-collecting accessories, plus hats, MagicBands, and other collectibles.

**DISNEY'S WONDERFUL WORLD OF MEMORIES:** Preserve the memories of your WDW adventure with frames, photo albums, and other merchandise from this shop across from Disney's Days of Christmas. There's a make-your-own Disney charm bracelet station and a wall of mouse ear hats just waiting to be personalized.

## MARKETPLACE RIDES

Disney Springs Marketplace has two genuine kiddie rides for adventurous tykes to enjoy: a carousel and a choo-choo train. The cost for each is $3 per child ($5 to ride twice). Be sure to purchase a token before boarding (payment can be made with Visa, MasterCard, or cash). Parents can accompany kids on the train (no charge for parents, provided they ride in the same car; children under 36 inches tall must be accompanied by a guest over age 14). The train can only accommodate two adults per trip, and grown-ups may not ride in the engine car. For the carousel, kids under 42 inches tall must be accompanied by a guest age 18 or older (who rides for free). The Marketplace rides are between The Earl of Sandwich eatery and Star Wars Trading Post.

**GOOFY'S CANDY COMPANY:** One-stop shopping to satisfy sugary cravings, this shop has a sumptuous selection of chocolates, a dipping kitchen, and more.

On warm days, we gravitate to the corner of this shop known as Goofy's Glaciers for a frozen slushy treat, available in flavors with goofy names such as Razzle Dazzle Pink, Orange You Happy, and Pucker Purple. Another temptation here: the create-your-own specialty-apple station.

PHOTO BY JILL SAFRO

**THE LEGO STORE:** World of Disney's neighbor, this playful emporium is a showcase for larger-than-life LEGO models. It may also invite guests to flaunt their creativity in an interactive outdoor play area. A computer hub lets guests design structures and play games. The store sells a vast selection of LEGO products.

**LEFTY'S:** Step up to southpaw central for scissors, can openers, writing implements, notebooks, mugs, T-shirts, magnets, and more—all made especially for the differently handed. The open-air stand also sells shirts and hats lauding left-handedness.

**MARKETPLACE CO-OP:** A cavernouse retail zone, the Co-op is home to varied specialty shops that may be swapped out from time to time. The following were available as this book went to press: **Wonderground Gallery** is a contemporary art space showcasing unusual collections and emerging artists; **D-Tech on Demand** is the perfect place to personalize and customize electronic accessories; **Centerpiece** showcases home products for folks who dig a dash of Disney in their home furnishings, textiles, and everyday ware; **Bowes Signature Candles** supplies all your aromatic must-haves, including fragrant diffuser oils, wax melts, and natural soy wax candles crafted with eco-friendly wicks (each hand-poured candle burns for a minimum of 72 hours); and **Disney Tails** has whimsically designed products for pets. The sheer variety of merchandise at the Marketplace Co-op puts this diverse destination on the top of many a Disney treasure-hunter's can't-miss list. This ever-evolving marketplace is one of our favorite places to shop in all of Walt Disney World.

**ONCE UPON A TOY:** An oversize toy box, this site features plush toys, action figures, and many other playthings from which to choose.

**THE PEARL FACTORY:** Pick an oyster, any oyster. Then pry it open (with assistance), and *voila*—a pearl! The cost is about $17 per oyster, and you are guaranteed a genuine pearl. The open-air shop proffers pearl earrings and necklaces, too. You'll find it near Lefty's.

**SILHOUETTE PORTRAITS:** A stand staffed by a talented artist, this spot offers single ($10), double ($20), triple ($30), and quadruple silhouettes. There are frames, too (oval and Mickey-shaped).

**THE SPICE & TEA EXCHANGE:** Having taken over the real estate once occupied by Mickey's Pantry, this deliciously fragrant destination offers guests a chance to purchase gourmet spices, salts, peppers, sugars, teas, and more. In all, there are more than 140 spices (including sugars,

peppers, salts, herbs, and spice mixes) and teas from which to choose. There are teapots, cups, pepper mills, and assorted kitchen accoutrements, as well. If you prefer someone else prepare your tea, you're in luck: this spot dispenses freshly brewed beverages from its trusty Tea Bar.

**SWINGS N' THINGS—THE HAMMOCK EXPERTS:** Swing by this leisure-centric kiosk for the things mentioned in its name, plus the appropriate accoutrements.

**TREN-D:** The Mouse is quite a trendsetter. Need proof? Swing by this nifty boutique. It is bursting with quirky Disney merchandise, from loungewear to bejeweled sunglasses and other trendy accessories.

**WORLD OF DISNEY:** A huge, industrial warehouse-like space stuffed with a ginormous selection of Disney merchandise, this is a popular destination for souvenir hunting. Brick walls and dark wood beams provide the backdrop for the vast array of goods. Characters are available on everything from colorful shoes to luggage. (Like at many other WDW merchandise locations, if you're an Annual Passholder, you may receive a discount when you present it at the register.) Reusable bags are available for a small fee.

**STAR WARS TRADING POST:** Here is the place to find a bounty of treasures with a Star Wars theme: shirts, hats, jammies, action figures, toys, mugs, pins, books, and more. There is a special area in which guests may build lightsabers and another that allows them to customize their own droids.

# The Landing

**THE ART OF SHAVING:** A premium shave shop, Art of Shaving offers high-end men's grooming supplies—razors, brushes, creams, shaving sets, and aromatherapy-based products—plus the Barber Spa: a place for guests to relax and get a shave and/or a haircut from a master barber.

**THE BOATHOUSE BOATIQUE:** Adjacent to The Boathouse restaurant, this shop features a bounty of nautically themed treasures. Among the wares here: clothing, jewelry, home accents, and games—plus engravable paddles and life rings.

**CHAPEL HATS:** Fashion-forward headwear for men and women is the stock-in-trade at this hat shop. With shelving made of reclaimed wood, decorative tables made from old shipping container hatch doors, and Arts and Crafts–style mirrors, Chapel Hats has classic appeal. They've got everything from fedoras to fascinators. Fascinating!

**ERIN MCKENNA'S BAKERY NYC:** Folks with dietary restrictions (and those just looking for a freshly made sweet treat) will be in the pink when they visit this bakeshop. In the words of company founder Erin McKenna, the place "focuses on the underserved people with gluten, dairy, egg, and soy sensitivities, the health-minded, and allergic kids who are often unable to indulge. The goal is to make eating vegan and gluten-free fun and delicious." Mission accomplished.

## WHERE TO EAT AT DISNEY SPRINGS

A complete listing of Disney Springs restaurants, bars, and snack spots can be found in the *Good Meals, Great Times* chapter. See the Disney Springs restaurant listings, beginning on page 288. Most of the restaurants here are open from about 11 A.M. until about 11 P.M. or later. Details are subject to change.

**Hot Tip!** Fancy a cruise in a floating car? Head to the Amphicar dock near The Boathouse restaurant (at The Landing). The rare auto/boats drive into the lake and treat guests to a 20-minute guided tour of Disney Springs (for about $125). Each vehicle can accommodate up to 3 to 4 guests. Amphicar tour reservations can only be made in person at the dock podium or inside the Boathouse Boatique.

**THE GANACHERY:** In a fresh take on an old apothecary, the star of the show is the housemade ganache—a luxurious mixture of melted chocolate and cream. The decadent treats aren't cheap, but many a chocolate fanatic finds them more than worthy of a splurge.

**HAPPY HOUND:** Fetch items for Fido at this pup-centric locale. The shop has toys, treats, and accessories meant to make your hound happy.

**HAVAIANAS:** Head here for flip-flops with a Brazilian flair. With more than 300 styles to choose from, this place just may have a flip-flop for every occasion imaginable. Colorful apparel and accessories are also available.

**SANUK:** Retire those pinchy old shoes and replace them with cool and comfy footwear for the whole family at Sanuk. (If we could wear our Sanuks every day, we would!) F.Y.I.: *Sanuk* is the Thai word for fun.

**SAVANNAH BEE COMPANY:** Do luxurious body-care goods made with locally sourced, all-natural honey sound tempting? How about specialty honeys, honeycombs, cookies, candies, and other sweet souvenirs? If so, make a beeline for this honey of a shop. It has it all.
   **Note:** Savannah Bee Company is passionate about bees and advocates for education about the world's vital-but-imperiled pollinators. If you'd like to support your local honeybee, visit *www.thebeecause.org*.

**SHOP FOR IRELAND:** Nestled within Raglan Road (across the esplanade from Morimoto Asia), this quaint boutique lines its shelves with items imported from the Emerald Isle. Among them: Irish clothing, jewelry, family crests, cookbooks, bookmarks, magnets, hats, scarves, and fragrances. You may even harness the luck of the Irish with the purchase of a shamrock. *Sláinte!*

# West Side

**AMC DISNEY SPRINGS 24:** The most popular multi-screen movie theater complex in Florida is also one of the largest. The many screens show a wide selection of current movie releases. The seats are all roomy and comfortable—and some of the theaters offer food and beverage service (see page 288 for details). For current movie schedules, visit *amctheatres.com*.

**SUNSHINE HIGHLINE:** A mini version of Manhattan's High Line (an abandoned elevated roadway converted into a city park), Disney's high line provides much needed shade by day and the possibility of international music by night. Past live performances have featured classic and exotic musical selections.

**CITY WORKS EATERY AND POUR HOUSE:** With its 165 screens (showing the big games of the moment), 80 or so tap beers (including dozens of local and global craft selections), and extensive menu including small bites (Buffalo shrimp, smoked wings, nachos, kung pao cauliflower), salads, burgers, tacos, and entrées such as pan-seared salmon, fish and chips, pork chops, BBQ ribs, etc., this raucous gathering spot aims to please. In addition to the substantial supply of suds, the bar serves specialty drinks, wine, soft drinks, and more. There is a kids' menu, too. You will find City Works directly across from the House of Blues. Theme park annual passholders receive ten-percent off food and non-alcoholic drinks. Details are subject to change.

**EXPOSITION PARK:** Mosey on over to Exposition Park (close to the West Side Starbucks) for live music in a lovely lakeside setting.

**HOUSE OF BLUES:** A combination restaurant/music hall with standing room for 2,000, House of Blues was inspired by one of America's most celebrated musical traditions. There is a lively dose of jazz and country, plus a little bit of R&B and some rock 'n' roll thrown into the music mix. The Southern-inspired cooking lures diners here—especially on Sunday mornings, when the chefs prepare a hearty feast, nicely complemented by live gospel music (and the House of Blues' famous chicken and donuts). Tickets may be purchased through Ticketmaster (call 407-839-3900, or visit *www.ticketmaster.com*) or the House of Blues box office (407-934-2583).

The House of Blues restaurant features a mélange of hearty cuisine, including jambalaya, slow-smoked pulled pork, shrimp and grits, and bread pudding.

**GEAR SHOP:** Gear up with House of Blues hats, shirts, and other apparel at this H.O.B. shop. Art, glassware, musical instruments, and other paraphernalia are sold.

**JALEO BY JOSÉ ANDRÉS:** The flavors of Spain have made their way to Disney Springs. The menu at this expansive eatery features an extensive selection of tapas that celebrate the regional diversity of classic and contemporary Spanish cuisine. Think paella cooked over a wood fire and hand-carved Jamon Iberico de Bellota

## MUSIC TO YOUR EARS

Guests may augment their Disney Springs dining and shopping spree with mellifluous interludes throughout the day. Complimentary live entertainment is presented at a stage near the World of Disney store (in the Marketplace); Riverboat Square and Waterview Park at The Landing; plus Sunshine Highline and Exposition Park on the West Side. Many individual venues supply sweet melodies, too. Among the possible places to take in a live performance are Raglan Road, Paradiso 37, Stargazers (at Planet Hollywood), The Boathouse, Dockside Margaritas, on the porch at House of Blues, and The Edison—just to name a few.

For more information about live entertainment offerings at Disney Springs, visit *www.disneysprings.com*. Keep in mind that all details are subject to change.

(premium ham). The multi-level eatery features a ground-floor grab-and-go section with Spanish-style sandwiches. Reservations are recommended for the table-service restaurant. For further details or to make a reservation, visit *www.disneyworld.com*, or use the My Disney Experience mobile app or website.

**CANDY CAULDRON:** Pop in here for homemade sweets and watch as they are prepared in an open candy kitchen. Among the biggest crowd-pleasers are the specialty apples—fresh, crunchy apples slathered in the candy coating of your choice (for about $11 each). Yum. Kids love to peek through the windows and watch the candy makers at work.

**M&M'S™:** Surround yourself with colorful chocolate in this candy-oriented superstore. Yes, the walls here are lined with tubes of vibrant M&M's—all waiting to melt in your mouth. The shop features several interactive opportunities, including the chance to mingle with larger-than-life-sized M&M's. Can't find the place? Look for the giant red M&M in the sky. (It's next to Splitsville Luxury Lanes.)

**SUPER HERO HEADQUARTERS:** Calling all would-be agents of S.H.I.E.L.D.: You can gear up at this shop, plus snag Super Hero-themed (Spider-Man, Captain America, Guardians of the Galaxy, etc.) shirts, action figures, art, hats, books, mugs, glassware, pins, and other items— all celebrating favorite crime-fighting characters (and the occasional villain).

**DISNEYSTYLE:** Spy the big yellow teacup in the window and you will know you've arrived at the happy place known as DisneyStyle. Brimming with goodies inspired by Disney rides, attractions, animated features, and fun catchphrases, this boutique is paradise for Disney-heads. In the market for a Transportation and Ticket

## UP, UP, AND AWAY!

You can float up to 400 feet above Disney Springs while beneath one behemoth of a balloon. Touted as the "world's largest tethered helium balloon," it carries up to 29 guests at a time in a gondola that measures 19 feet in diameter. Flights last 8 to 10 minutes. Guests board from a platform on the West Side (near Starbucks). Tickets are sold at a nearby window. The cost is about $25 (plus tax) for adults (guests age 10 and up) and $20 for kids ages 3 to 9. Guests under age 3 fly free. Flights begin at 8:30 A.M. daily (weather permitting) and operate on a first-come, first-served basis. It's run by Aerophile—"The World Leader in Balloon Flight."

Center T-shirt? Perhaps a handheld fan shaped like a Mickey ice cream bar? Dumbo socks? Disney Style may have it. We love this shop.

**EVERGLAZED DONUTS & COLD BREW:** "Happiness is glazed daily" at this old-style donut shop. Stop here for warm donuts (classic, funky, and super-funky), donut holes, specialty coffees, sandwiches, and fries.

**SPLITSVILLE LUXURY LANES™:** Come for some casual bowling, stay for some food and live entertainment. This West Side venue features 30 bowling lanes, two high-end kitchens, a full bar, live music—and billiards to boot. This massive 'ville (50,000 square feet) is fun for all ages. However, some areas are restricted to guests over the age of 21 (with legal ID to prove it).

PHOTO BY JILL SAFRO

It's generally open from 11 A.M. to 11 P.M. Sunday through Thursday, 11 A.M. to 11:30 P.M. on Friday and Saturday. (Hours are subject to change.) Shoppers can peruse and purchase merchandise at Memory Lanes, a little shop tucked into a corner on the first floor of the Splitsville building. Look for items such as shirts, pants, hats, glasses, jewelry, and more. For more info, visit *www.splitsvillelanes.com* and refer to page 293.

**STARBUCKS:** That ubiquitous mermaid icon can be spotted on the shore of Lake Buena Vista. Expect all of the Starbucks specialties—from fresh-brewed, free-trade cups of joe to sweet and chilly Frappuccinos. Breakfast sandwiches, fruit, and oatmeal are served. Baked treats include cupcakes, muffins, scones, cookies, and cake pops. Teas, smoothies, veggies, juice, milk, soda, and water are also offered. There are usually several Disney Dining Plan snack options to choose from (subject to change). F.Y.I.: The Green Roof and Living Walls at this location are nourished with compost made from coffee grounds. That's meant to help with recycling and offset greenhouse gases.

**STAR WARS GALACTIC OUTPOST:** The Force is strong with this store. So is its pull on folks strolling the promenade at Disney Springs, West Side. It boasts an impressive bounty of toys, clothes, and accessories inspired by the epic space saga: hats, shirts, dresses (yes, we once spotted a Darth Vader dress), costumes, pins, collectibles, photos, socks, glassware, plush toys, mouse ears, lightsaber key chains, and many more items featuring characters from the Star Wars films. Details are subject to change.

**Hot Tip!** A visit to Disney Springs requires a significant amount of walking stamina. Expect to log a couple of miles per visit—especially if you plan to walk from the Marketplace to the West Side (and back again!). We highly recommend strollers for small children—and very comfortable shoes for all. And make use of the (free) Disney Springs water taxi service—aka the Sassagoula River Cruise—if you're headed to any of the following WDW resort hotels: Saratoga Springs, Old Key West, Port Orleans Riverside, or Port Orleans French Quarter.

**SUNGLASS ICON:** Looking for some super-cool shades? This snazzy shop is full of high-end brands to protect your peepers.

**PELÉ SOCCER:** Fútbol fans, rejoice! You can gather garb to support your favorite club and load up on gear to tackle the game yourself—right here at the well-stocked shop named for one of the greatest soccer players of all time. This spot's goal is to meet all your soccer needs. Score!

**WETZEL'S PRETZELS:** Whether you prefer pretzels on the salty or sweet side, this kiosk has something to satisfy. Also on the menu: hot dogs wrapped in a soft pretzel, pretzel bits, lemonade, frozen lemonade, and frozen granita (a sweet, icy treat).

## DRAWN TO LIFE

Drawn to Life—Presented by Cirque du Soleil® & Disney is an exciting "creative tour-de-force." A lively combination of music, dance, and acrobatic artistry, this production aims to "set your imagination in motion with a love letter to the art of Disney animation."

The dynamic show represents the first-ever collaboration among Cirque du Soleil, Walt Disney Animation Studios, and Walt Disney Imagineering. The result is a fantastic journey into a world where an animator's desk becomes the stage and drawings *come alive*. The artful extravaganza is a celebration of life—accentuated by the mesmerizing movements of Cirque du Soleil's awesome acrobatics.

Drawn to Life, a long-awaited successor to La Nouba (the Cirque du Soleil show that enjoyed a 19-year run in this space), made its debut—to rave reviews—in late 2021. For updates and ticket information, go to *cirquedusoleil.com*, or call 877-924-7783. Advance purchase is recommended.

# Town Center

The architectural design of Town Center's Town Square is "Spanish Revival," drawing from a rich history of explorers who landed in Florida centuries ago. It was ostensibly founded in the 1850s, on the banks of one of the Sunshine State's freshwater springs—where its original homestead stands, having been converted to a restaurant (D-Luxe Burger). The commercial district of Town Center was designed in the Mediterranean Revival style that was popular in 1920s Florida, whereas the Welcome Center area features the American revival architecture that was prevalent in the 1930s. Overall, this sophisticated area has a focus on shopping, but also brings inventive dining opportunities and other pleasant diversions. For details about dining spots, refer to *Good Meals, Great Times*. Here's a sampling of the establishments at which to nosh in Town Center:

## DINING

**AMORETTE'S PATISSERIE:** Classic and contemporary cakes and pastries are the stars in this high-end pastry shop where guests can watch the chefs decorate signature cakes in the on-stage finishing kitchen. Amorette's lovingly packages sweet treats in old-fashioned hat-boxes. Champagne, sparkling wine, soft drinks, pastries, sandwiches, and housemade crepes are also served.

**BLAZE FAST FIRE'D PIZZA:** This eatery lets hungry guests "build their own artisanal pizzas." Custom-made pizzas are prepared in about three minutes—they don't call it "fast fire'd" for nothing. The 5,000-square-foot eatery also serves freshly prepared salads and desserts.

**D-LUXE BURGER:** Come for the burgers, stay for the shakes at this Town Center quick-service location. D-Luxe is a comfy spot for a casual bite. The burgers (most big enough to share) are served on fresh-baked buns. Pair yours with freshly cut fries (which come with a variety of dipping sauces) and (scrumptious) gelato shakes (with rotating flavors such as vanilla, chocolate, raspberry, strawberry, salted caramel, and s'mores). There's a kids' menu, too. Beer, wine, and soft drinks are served. D-Luxe Burger has indoor and outdoor seating (the alfresco area overlooks the water, aka the springs).

**THE POLITE PIG:** A popular quick-service eatery (near the Lime parking structure), The Polite Pig specializes in modern barbecue and Southern sides. The oft-changing menu includes sandwiches such as brisket, fried chicken, smoked turkey BLT, and pulled pork. There are plenty of satisfying salads and sides to mix and match: Caesar, spinach, and Cobb salads, crispy Brussels sprouts, BBQ cauliflower, and sweet potato tots. For dessert, consider the red velvet cake or seasonal pie. There is indoor and outdoor seating and a full bar. Score a free chef's appetizer (with the purchase of an adult entrée) by using the coupon at the back of this book!

**SPRINKLES CUPCAKES:** "The world's first cupcake bakery," as dubbed by Food Network, the Beverly Hills-based Sprinkles now serves said signature cakes, slow-churned ice cream, and cookies here at Town Center.

**FRONTERA COCINA:** Six-time James Beard winner Chef Rick Bayless has brought his signature gourmet Mexican cuisine to Disney Springs' Frontera Cocina. The eatery features Mexican specialties such as handcrafted tortas, tacos, salads, and classic Mexican braised meat entrées, all lovingly prepared with locally sourced ingredients. Margaritas, specialty cocktails, craft beers, wine, and soft drinks are served.

## RETAIL ROUNDUP

Disney Springs, Town Center may appear retro-elegant, but the shopping opportunities here are markedly *au courant*. Treasure-seekers may peruse wares at these retail locations:

ALEX AND ANI • American Threads • Anthropologie • Coach • Coca-Cola Store • Columbia Sportswear • Edward Beiner • Ever After Jewelry Co. & Accessories • Everything But Water • Fabletics • Fit2Run • francesca's • Free People • Harley-Davidson • Jo Malone London • JOHNNY WAS • Johnston & Murphy • kate spade new york • Kendra Scott • LACOSTE • Levis • Lilly Pulitzer • L'Occitane En Provence • lovepop • lululemon • Luxury of Time by Diamonds International • M·A·C Cosmetics • Melissa Clube • Na Hoku • PANDORA • Ron Jon Surf Shop • Rustic Cuff • Sephora • Shore • Sperry • Stance • Sugarboo & Co. • Superdry • Tommy Bahama • Under Armour • UNIQLO • UNOde50 • Vera Bradley • Volcom • Zara

For details about these and other Town Center shopping destinations, visit *disneysprings.com*.

# BoardWalk

A stroll along Disney's BoardWalk Resort is a journey back in time. Inspired by the Middle Atlantic seaside attractions of the early 1900s, BoardWalk recaptures the carefree atmosphere of that bygone era. The resort is surrounded by restaurants, clubs, and amusements similar to those enjoyed by beach-goers of yesteryear. It's bordered by a wood-planked walkway that hugs the shore of Crescent Lake. By day, BoardWalk is a peaceful place to soak up sun, enjoy lunch, or simply walk the boards. After dark, the place turns into a twinkling center of nighttime activity—some of it elegant, some of it downright raucous.

Classic midway games of the BoardWalk challenge onlookers to test their luck and skill, while strolling performers enchant passersby of all ages with magic shows, balloon tricks, or other antics.

BoardWalk is open to everyone. Although there is no admission price, individual venues may charge a cover. There is a $33 charge for valet parking (even for guests staying at a Walt Disney World–owned and operated resort). Self-parking was free at press time, but subject to change. For dining details, refer to this book's *Good Meals, Great Times* chapter.

## CLUBS

**ATLANTIC DANCE HALL:** This is a lovely atmosphere in which to dance the night away. A deejay cranks up tunes, tempting guests to twist and shout on the dance floor. Request your favorite music videos and bust a move while they play on the big screen.

In addition to traditional cocktails, the club serves specialty drinks. Sample one in the "big room" or on the waterfront balcony.

Guests must be 21 or older, with a legal photo ID, to enter. There was no cover charge at press time, but

that could change. Hours are generally 8 P.M. until 1 A.M., Tuesday through Saturday.

**JELLYROLLS:** You might want to warm up your vocal cords before crossing the threshold. They don't call it a sing-along bar for nothing: Guests are expected to sing, clap, and join in the fun at this warehouse home of dueling pianos. You'll hear everything from Gershwin to *Grease*. The piano players take requests, so plan ahead. Write the request—a cocktail napkin will do—and slip it onto the piano. (Although it's not required, we recommend slipping a tip along, too. It'll increase the chances of your hearing the request and help the musicians pay their rent.)

Jellyrolls opens at 7 P.M. Thursday through Sunday. Entertainment begins at 8 P.M. and continues until closing at about 1:45 A.M. There is an $18 cover charge to enter. (Note that the cover charge and hours may vary.) To enter, you must be at least 21 years old and willing to prove it (with a government-issued photo ID). It's often quite chilly in this venue (year-round). Bring a sweater—you won't regret it. Details are subject to change. For updates, visit *disneyworld.com*.

**Hot Tip!** The BoardWalk real estate long occupied by ESPN Club (sports bar/restaurant) is now home to a lovely new eatery: The Cake Bake Shop by Gwendolyn Rogers (see *disneyworld.com* for details). Fortunately, folks can still root, root, root for their home team while staying with the Mouse. City Works Eatery & Pour House (at Disney Springs) is a sports fans paradise, as is the nearby Miller's Ale House. (The latter is located just off Disney property at 12371 Winter Garden Vineland Road, Orlando, FL 32836). Go team!

# Water Parks

# Typhoon Lagoon

This splashy playground was inspired by an imagined legend: A powerful typhoon hit a resort village many years ago, and the storm left the village in ruins. The locals, however, were quite resourceful and rebuilt their town as this fanciful "wateropolis."

The centerpiece of Typhoon Lagoon is a huge watershed mountain known to the locals as Mount Mayday. Proudly perched atop its peak is the *Miss Tilly*, a long-marooned shrimp boat originally from Safen Sound, Florida. *Miss Tilly's* smokestack blows every half hour, shooting a 50-foot spray of water into the air.

The surf lagoon is huge: Giant slides snake through caves, tamer ones offer twisting journeys, and tiny slides delight small kids. Guests under age 14 must be accompanied by someone over age 14.

**SURF POOL:** The main swimming area holds nearly three million gallons of water, making it one of the largest wave pools in the world. The sprawling, blue lagoon

is surrounded by a white-sand beach, and its main attraction is the waves that come crashing onto the shore every 90 seconds. Less adventurous swimmers can loll about in two relatively calm tide pools, Whitecap Cove and Blustery Bay. Life jackets (of varying sizes) may be borrowed for free.

**CASTAWAY CREEK:** The "creek" is a 2,100-foot circular river that winds through the park and offers a lazy, relaxing orientation to Typhoon Lagoon. Tubes are the best way to make the trip along the three-foot-deep waterway. Guests pass through a rainforest,

**Hot Tip!** Guests entering Disney's Typhoon Lagoon water park are subject to a thorough security check. Expect all people, bags, and other items to be screened. Weapons—including toys—are prohibited.

where they are cooled by mists and spray; through caves and grottoes that provide welcome shade on hot summer days; and through an area where "broken" pipes from a water tower unleash refreshing showers. There are several exits along the way. It takes 20 to 35 minutes to ride around the whole park.

**CRUSH 'N' GUSHER:** This "water coaster" thrill ride is one of a kind. In it, daredevils are whisked along a series of flumes and tossed and turned as they weave through an abandoned tropical fruit factory. There are three spillways to choose from: Banana Blaster, Coconut Crusher, and Pineapple Plunger. Guests must be at least 48 inches tall to ride Crush 'n' Gusher.

**GANGPLANK FALLS, KEELHAUL FALLS, AND MAYDAY FALLS:** These white-water rides offer guests a variety of slippery trips, two of them in inner tubes. All of the slides course through caves and waterfalls and past rock work, making the scenery an attraction in itself. Gangplank Falls gives families a chance to ride together in a two- to four-passenger craft.

**Hot Tip!** Early birds get the lounge chairs in these parts. If you want to snag a chair at either of Disney's water parks, arrive as close to park opening time as possible. (Be sure to build in extra time for the commute via Disney Motor Coach.)

**HUMUNGA KOWABUNGA:** These 3 speed slides, reported to have been carved into the landscape by the historic earthquake, will send guests zooming through caverns at speeds of 30 miles per hour. The 214-foot slides each offer a 51-foot drop, and the view from the top is a little scary. But it's over before you know it, and once-wary guests hurry back for another try. Guests must be at least 48 inches tall and free of back and neck trouble, heart conditions, and other physical limitations to take the trip. Pregnant women are not permitted to ride Humunga Kowabunga.

**KETCHAKIDDEE CREEK:** Open only to those children 48 inches tall or under (and their adult guardians), this area has small rides for pint-size visitors. All children must be accompanied by an adult. There are splashy slides, fountains, waterfalls, squirting sea life, a mini-rapids ride, an interactive tugboat, and a grotto with an inviting veil of water.

**MISS ADVENTURE FALLS:** A family-friendly raft ride near Crush 'n' Gusher, this attraction takes guests on a tour of treasures and artifacts left behind by Captain Mary Oceaneer, an adventurous treasure hunter who became stranded at Typhoon Lagoon after a big storm. Each watery voyage takes about two minutes. Kids under the age of 7 must be accompanied by an adult.

**STORM SLIDES:** The Jib Jammer, Rudder Buster, and Stern Burner body slides send guests zooming down winding slides, in and out of rock formations and caves, and through waterfalls. It's a somewhat tamer ride than Humunga Kowabunga, but still offers a speedy descent. The slides are about 300 feet long, and each offers a different view and experience.

## ADMISSION PRICES

Prices do not include sales tax and are subject to change in 2024. **NOTE:** Water Park admission is an option with a date-based theme park ticket that includes a Park Hopper Plus add-on. Water park annual passes were not available at press time.

| | ADULT | CHILDREN* |
|---|---|---|
| One-Day Ticket | $69 | $63 |
| Annual Pass | N/A | N/A |

\* 3 through 9 years of age; children under age 3 free. All tickets allow for park-hopping, provided both water parks are open on day of admission.

## ESSENTIALS

**WHEN TO GO:** Typhoon Lagoon gets very crowded early in the day. Hours vary seasonally, but the water park is generally open from 10 A.M. to 5 P.M., with extended hours in the summer months. All of the park's pools are heated in the winter. Note that this water park is usually closed for refurbishment during certain winter months. The park may also close due to bad weather (including lightning and chilly temperatures). Selfie sticks are not permitted at Typhoon Lagoon. For more information, use the *My Disney Experience* mobile app or website, visit *disneyworld.com*, or call 407-824-4321.

**HOW TO GET THERE:** Complimentary bus service is offered to Walt Disney World resort guests, but it's not direct—so build in extra time for the commute. Guests should board a bus to Disney Springs then switch to a Typhoon Lagoon-bound motor coach. Disney Springs bus service to Typhoon Lagoon runs

**Hot Tip!** Premium cabana-like spaces referred to as Beachcomber Shacks are available for rental. They include an attendant, beverages, towels, and more. Shacks can accommodate up to six guests (with the option of adding up to 4 guests for a per-person fee) and cost about $340–$450 per day (price varies seasonally). For details or to make a reservation, call 407-939-7529.

It's also possible to reserve premium umbrella chair space (including 2 lounge chairs, an umbrella, table, and 2 towels) at Typhoon Lagoon. They're available on a same-day, walk-up basis. Guests may stop at High and Dry Rentals to check availability. Cost is about $40–$70, plus tax. Prices are subject to change.

from 9 A.M. to 6 P.M. There is no charge to park here. Details are subject to change. For updates, check the *My Disney Experience* mobile app or website.

**DRESS CODE:** Proper swim attire is required—and must be free of buckles, rivets, zippers, or exposed metal. String back and thong suits are not permitted. For safety, guests who use diapers must wear plastic pants and/or swim diapers in all pool areas.

**GUESTS WITH DISABILITIES:** Disney is committed to providing access and accommodation for as many guests as possible. For specifics about Typhoon Lagoon, visit *disneyworld.com*.

**FIRST AID:** A first aid station capable of handling minor medical problems is located just to the left of Leaning Palms. For medical emergencies, call 911.

**LOCKER ROOMS:** Restrooms with showers and lockers can be found near the park entrance. Small lockers cost $10 to rent for the day, while large ones cost $15 a day. Towels can be rented for about $2 (it's okay to bring your own); life jackets and tubes are free.

**SMOKING POLICY:** Smoking (including e-cigarettes and vaping) is prohibited in all Disney parks. Typhoon Lagoon guests may smoke in a designated area outside the water park's entrance.

**WHERE TO EAT:** Typhoon Lagoon's two quick-service eateries offer similar fare and outdoor seating. Leaning Palms has burgers, pizza, salads, and snacks. Typhoon Tilly's (open seasonally) serves fish & chips, fish tacos, salad, fruit, and cookies. Let's Go Slurpin' has frozen drinks and spirits. Guests may bring their own food and drink to enjoy in designated picnic areas. Alcoholic beverages and glass containers may not be brought into the water park. Coolers are allowed. Ice packs are permitted, but loose ice and dry ice are not. Refillable Mugs (about $12 each) come with a day's worth of soft drink refills. Mugs may be reactivated for about $9 each day for the length of your Walt Disney World stay. For dining details, turn to page 287.

**WHERE TO SHOP:** Singapore Sal's is set in a ramshackle building left a bit battered by the typhoon. Swimsuits, sunglasses, hats, beach towels, sunscreen, souvenirs, water shoes, snacks, and Typhoon Lagoon logo products are among the available wares.

# Blizzard Beach

A wintry, watery wonderland, Blizzard Beach is said to be the result of a surprise storm that dumped a mountain of snow on Walt Disney World, prompting the construction of Florida's first ski resort. When temperatures soared and the snow began to melt, designers prepared to close the resort. But when they spotted an animal sliding down the slopes, they realized that they had created an exciting water adventure park! The slalom and bobsled runs became downhill waterslides. The ski jump is one of the world's tallest (120 feet) and fastest (60 miles per hour) free-fall speed slides.

The centerpiece of Blizzard Beach is the snowcapped Mount Gushmore and its dramatic Summit Plummet. Most of the runs are on the slopes of this mighty mountain, which tops out at 90 feet. At the summit, swimmers have a choice of speed slides, flumes, a white-water raft ride, and an inner-tube run. Most guests choose to reach the top of Mount Gushmore via chairlift. The chairlift has a gondola that's equipped for guests with disabilities. There are stairs, too. Kids under 14 must be accompanied by a guest over age 14. One-piece bathing suits are highly recommended.

**Hot Tip!** Guests entering Disney's Blizzard Beach water park are subject to a thorough security check. All people and bags are checked and a metal detector is used. Weapons—including the toy variety—are prohibited.

**CROSS COUNTRY CREEK:** This meandering 3,000-foot waterway circles the entire park. A slow current keeps visitors moving merrily along. Inner tubes, which are free, are the most pleasant way to travel. The ride includes a trip through a bone-chilling ice cave, where guests are splashed with the "melting ice" from overhead.

**DOWNHILL DOUBLE DIPPER:** Guests travel down these two parallel 230-foot-long racing slides at speeds of up to 25 miles per hour. The partially enclosed water runs feature ski-racing graphics, flags, and time clocks. You must be 48 inches tall to ride.

**MELT-AWAY BAY:** A one-acre pool at the base of Mount Gushmore, the "bay" has its own wave machine. There are no tsunamis here, however, just pleasant, bobbing waves—perfect for leisurely floating and body surfing.

**RUNOFF RAPIDS:** On this thrilling inner-tube run, guests careen down three twisting, turning flumes. Note that the center slide is completely enclosed. Just a heads up!

**SKI PATROL TRAINING CAMP:** An area designed for preteens, Frozen Pipe Springs looks like an old pipe and drops sliders into eight feet of water. The Thin Ice Training Course tests agility as kids try to walk along broken "icebergs." At the Ski Patrol Shelter, guests under 60 inches grab on to a T-bar for an airborne trip. At any point in the ride they can drop into the

**Hot Tip!** Premium cabana-like spaces known as Polar Patios are available for rental. They include an attendant, beverages, towels, and more. Patios accommodate up to six guests and cost about $340–$450 per day. Premium umbrella spaces are available, too. For more information or to make reservations, call 407-939-7529. Note that prices vary seasonally.

water below. Ski patrol participants also experience Cool Runners, where riders can count on hurtling and whirling over lots of moguls on twin inner-tube slides. No bunny slopes for these brave daredevils.

**SLUSH GUSHER:** This double-humped waterslide offers a brisk journey through a snowbanked mountain gully. Topping out at 90 feet, Slush Gusher is the tallest slide of its kind. You will find it on Mount Gushmore, next to Summit Plummet. Guests must be at least 48 inches tall to take the plunge.

**SNOW STORMERS:** A trio of flumes descends from the top of the mountain. Guests race down (headfirst while lying on a mat) on a switchback course that includes ski-type slalom gates.

**SUMMIT PLUMMET:** This thrilling ride begins 120 feet in the air on a platform 30 feet above the top of Mount Gushmore. Brave souls (who are at least 48 inches tall) hurtle down a 350-foot slide at a rate of about 60 miles per hour. (We find it quite terrifying.)

**THE CHAIRLIFT:** Guests may ascend to the top of Mount Gushmore via chairlift, provided they are at least 32 inches tall and acrophobia-free. The alternate way to reach the top is by using the stairs. Once at the summit,

adventurers can access Slush Gusher, Teamboat Springs, and Summit Plummet. There is a gondola available for guests with disabilities. Just ask a cast member (park employee) for assistance.

**TEAMBOAT SPRINGS:** One of the longest group white-water raft rides in the world, Teamboat Springs sends guests down 1,200 feet of splashy twists and turns. The gravity-fueled propulsion sends rafts careening down the slide, rotating randomly as they move along. Each raft accommodates 4 to 6 passengers. If you have fewer than 4 guests in your party, you may be asked to share a raft with other people.

**TIKE'S PEAK:** A watery winter wonderland inspired by *Frozen*, Tike's Peak offers tame thrills for young guests: wading pools, snow chutes, slides, water jets, and more. Adults must be accompanied by a child to enter this zone. Kids must be under 48 inches to enjoy most attractions in this area.

**Hot Tip!** Early birds get the lounge chairs around these parts. If you want to snag a chair at either of Disney's water parks, arrive as close to park opening as possible.

**TOBOGGAN RACERS:** An 8-lane waterslide sends brave guests racing over several hills and dips. They lie on their stomachs on a mat and zoom headfirst down the 250-foot route.

## ESSENTIALS

**WHEN TO GO:** As a guest favorite, Blizzard Beach gets very crowded early in the day. Hours vary seasonally, but the park is generally open from 10 A.M. to 5 P.M., with extended hours in summer.

All pools are heated in winter. The park is often closed for refurbishment during certain winter months. Know that it may also close due to inclement weather (including lightning and chilly temperatures). For schedules, call 407-WDW-PLAY (939-7529).

PHOTO BY JILL SAFRO

**HOW TO GET THERE:** Blizzard Beach may be reached via motor coach (bus) from all Walt Disney World resorts. A transfer may be required. Parking is free.

**DRESS CODE:** Proper swim attire is required — and must be free of buckles, rivets, zippers, or exposed metal. String back and thong suits are not permitted. For safety, guests who use diapers must wear plastic pants and/or swim diapers in all pool areas.

**GUESTS WITH DISABILITIES:** The Walt Disney Company is committed to providing access and accommodation for as many guests as possible. WDW water parks offer wheelchairs at Guest Relations. There's no charge to borrow one, but valid government-issued photo ID must be presented to do so. Quantities are limited and subject to availability. For details about services provided at Blizzard Beach, visit *disneyworld.com.*

**LOCKER ROOMS:** There are restrooms with showers near the main entrance. Other restrooms and dressing rooms are located around the park. Small lockers cost $10 for the day, while large lockers cost $15. Towels rent for $2 (outside towels are permitted), and life jackets and tubes may be used for free.

**FIRST AID:** Minor medical problems are handled at this station near the main entrance (between Beach Haus and Lottawata Lodge).

**WHERE TO EAT:** Burgers, flatbreads, rice bowls (tofu or chicken), salads, and drinks are sold at Lottawatta Lodge. Kids' selections include chicken strips and rice bowls with chicken. Avalunch offers items such as hot dogs (with assorted toppings) and loaded nachos, while The Warming Hut stand has sandwiches and loaded potato barrels. Polar Pub proffers soft drinks and adult

beverages. Frosty the Joe Man Coffee Shack serves coffee drinks. Frostbite Freddy's has beer and frozen drinks (with or without alcohol). There are picnic areas for those who prefer to pack their own sustenance. Alcohol and glass containers may not be brought into the water park. Coolers (smaller than 24 inches long, 18 inches high, and 15 inches wide) are allowed. Ice packs are permitted, but loose ice and dry ice are not. All-Day Refillable Mugs (approximately $12 each) come with a day's worth of soft drink refills. Mugs may be reactivated for about $8.50 a day for the length of your Walt Disney World stay. For dining details, see page 287.

**SMOKING POLICY:** Smoking (including e-cigarettes and vaping) is prohibited in all Disney parks. Guests may smoke in a designated area outside the park entrance.

**WHERE TO SHOP:** Beach Haus usually stocks swimsuits, T-shirts, shorts, sunglasses, hats, sunscreen, beach towels, snacks, and more. It's also the place to inquire about same-day Polar Patio rental (refer to the Hot Tip on page 240 for details).

## ADMISSION PRICES

Prices do not include sales tax and are subject to change in 2024.
**NOTE:** Water Park admission is an option with a date-based theme park ticket that includes a Park Hopper Plus add-on. Water park annual passes were not available at press time.

|  | ADULT | CHILDREN* |
|---|---|---|
| One-Day Ticket | $69 | $63 |
| Annual Pass | N/A | N/A |

* 3 through 9 years of age; children under age 3 free. All tickets allow for park-hopping, provided both water parks are open on day of admission.

# Fort Wilderness

In a part of Florida where campgrounds tend to look like dried pastures—barren and drab—the Fort Wilderness Resort and Campground, located almost due east of Disney's Contemporary resort, is quite an anomaly—a lushly forested, 750-acre wonder of tall slash pines, white-flowering bay trees, and ancient cypresses hung with Spanish moss. Native Americans from the Seminole tribe of Florida once hunted and fished in this area.

There are more than 800 campsites arranged in several campground loops (including sites that are big-rig ready). There are more than 300 Wilderness Cabins (currently under refurbishment as part of the Disney Vacation Club) available for rent, completely furnished and fitted with all the comforts of home. For additional information about the cabins, refer to the *Transportation & Accommodations* chapter of this book.

Scattered throughout the campground loops are sporting facilities, including two tennis courts and many small playgrounds, basketball, tetherball, and volleyball courts. Fort Wilderness has horse stables (with rather mellow steeds available for trail rides), two swimming pools, canoes, kayaks, bikes and golf carts for rent, and a scenic nature trail. Some facilities are available to Fort Wilderness guests only (including, but not limited to, swimming pools); some are open to everyone.

There's a working ranch that serves as home to the massive horses that pull the Magic Kingdom's Main Street trolleys. The barn houses a small museum that celebrates horses and the cherished role they have played in Disney history.

Two stores—the Settlement Trading Post and the Meadow Trading Post—stock campers' necessities, a small supply of groceries, and souvenirs. And then there's Pioneer Hall, the home of the Hoop-Dee-Doo Musical Revue dinner show (described in this book's *Good Meals, Great Times* chapter). This rustic structure (made of white pine shipped from Montana) also has

a new quick-service, marketplace-style eatery. For details, use the My Disney Experience mobile app or website, or check *disneyworld.com*.

**ARCHERY:** It takes a steady hand to hit the bullseye at the Fort Wilderness Archery Experience. After a brief training session led by a skilled guide, participants (age 7 and up) get to shoot for that coveted bullseye. The cost is about $45. To book the Fort Wilderness Archery Experience, call 407-WDW-PLAY (939-7529).

**BIKE RENTALS:** Bicycles may be rented from the Bike Barn for trips along the paths at Fort Wilderness—or just for getting around. Bikes cost about $20 for the day. Helmets are included at no extra charge. Florida law mandates that all guests age 16 and under wear helmets when biking.

**BOATING:** Fort Wilderness is ribboned with tranquil canals that make for peaceful canoe and kayak trips of one to three hours. Rentals are available at the Bike Barn for about $13 per hour. Sun Tracker pontoon boats are available for rent at the nearby Contemporary resort marina. They cost about $45 per hour (plus tax) and may be used for cruising on Bay Lake and Seven Seas Lagoon. (Refer to the *Sports & Recreation* chapter for additional information.)

**CAMPFIRE SING-ALONG:** Held Wednesday through Sunday nights (weather permitting) near the Meadow Trading Post at the center of the campground, this event features Disney movies, a sing-along, and a marshmallow roast. Chip and Dale may put in an appearance. It's open to Walt Disney World resort guests only. There is no charge to attend, but marshmallows and s'mores kits come with a small fee. You may roast your own marshmallows for free. (They are available for purchase at the Meadow and Settlement Trading Posts.)

**Hot Tip!** Festive, horse-drawn "sleigh rides" may be offered at Fort Wilderness Resort & Campground from Thanksgiving week through December. For details or reservations, visit *disneyworld.com*, or call 407-939-7529.

**CARRIAGE RIDES:** Guests may enjoy a relaxing carriage ride through the picturesque grounds of Fort Wilderness or the Port Orleans Riverside resort. The rate for each 25-minute ride is $55.

Carriages can hold up to 4 adults, or 2 adults and up to 3 small kids. Reservations are recommended. Rides are offered nightly. For information or to make a reservation, use the My Disney Experience mobile app or website, or call 407-WDW-PLAY (939-7529). Walk-up reservations are sometimes possible. Ask the driver about buying tickets. If they're available, expect to pay with cash or a MagicBand. (Disney resort ID and credit cards are not accepted.) Rides may be canceled due to inclement weather. Cancellations must be made at least 24 hours ahead to avoid paying full price.

Guests are picked up in front of Crockett's Tavern at Pioneer Hall or by the marina at Port Orleans Riverside. Feel free to bring your own liquid refreshments.

**ELECTRIC CART RENTALS:** Available at Reception Outpost (for about $67 per night) for sightseeing or transportation. Renters must be at least 18 years old and have a valid driver's license. Reservations are recommended for electric cart rentals (and can be made up to one year in advance); call 407-824-2742.

**ELECTRICAL WATER PAGEANT:** Originally presented for the dedication of the Polynesian Luau dinner show in 1971, this cavalcade of lights is presented nightly on the waters of Bay Lake and the Seven Seas Lagoon. The pageant consists of two strings of seven barges, each carrying a 25-foot-tall screen of lights featuring King Neptune and creatures of the sea. And it's all set to music. The show can be seen from the beach at Fort Wilderness, as well as from the Contemporary, Grand Floridian, and Polynesian Village resorts. (We've caught it while waiting for the monorail at the Magic Kingdom,

too.) Ask for the day's schedule at your resort's Lobby Concierge desk. Details are subject to change.

**FISHING EXCURSIONS:** Walt Disney World's restrictive fishing policy has resulted in plenty of angling action—largemouth bass weighing between two and eight pounds, mainly for fishing excursion participants.

The price ranges from approximately $235 to $270 for up to five people for a 2-hour trip and about $455 for a 4-hour excursion. Cost includes gear, a guide, and soft drinks (guests may not bring food on WDW fishing excursions); no license is required. Life jackets will be provided and are required at all times for guests age 13 and under. It is recommended that adults wear life jackets, too. The price varies based on time of day, with the early-morning trips commanding the highest rate. Solo anglers may be able to book an afternoon excursion at a reduced rate.

All WDW fishing is strictly catch-and-release. Call 407-WDW-FISH (939-3474) for exact times and to make reservations. Guests may use their own equipment on a fishing excursion, but the price is the same.

**DOCKSIDE FISHING:** Fort Wilderness is the only place on Walt Disney World property where dockside lake fishing is allowed. In addition to bass, catfish and panfish can be caught here. Those without their own gear will find rods and reels for rent at the Bike Barn. No license is required. Fort Wilderness resort guests may toss their lines in right from the shore in authorized areas only. All WDW fishing is strictly catch-and-release.

**PLAYGROUNDS, VOLLEYBALL, TETHERBALL, AND BASKETBALL COURTS:** There are courts scattered throughout the camping loops. There is no charge to use them.

**PONY RIDES:** A rustic ranch near Pioneer Hall is home to some very friendly ponies. Rides are available between 10 A.M. and 3 P.M. for $8. Riders must be at least 2 years old, and under 48 inches tall. The weight limit is 80 pounds. Kids must be able to hold on by themselves. A parent or guardian leads the pony. The ranch is a good place to visit before enjoying Hoop-Dee-Doo Musical Revue (for details, see page 316).

**RETURN TO SLEEPY HOLLOW:** This spooky experience takes place on select nights (in late September and throughout October) inside the resort's historic Tri-Circle D Ranch. It features an outdoor viewing of Disney's 1949 animated classic *The Legend of Sleepy Hollow*, galloping ghosts, and (possibly) a photo op with the Headless Horseman himself. The film is generally shown twice each evening, with a dessert party between screenings. For pricing, dates, reservations, and other information, visit *disneyworld.com*, or call 407-WDW-TOUR (939-8687). All details are subject to change.

**SWIMMING:** There are two pools for campers' use. The Meadows Pool complex has a twisting slide and water play area. Note that the pools are open to Fort Wilderness guests only. Swimming and wading are not allowed at the beach (due to a naturally occurring bacteria found in many Florida lakes, and the presence of native wildlife such as alligators and snakes).

**TENNIS:** Two tennis courts are available; play is on a first-come, first-served basis.

**TRAIL RIDES:** Guided horseback trips depart five times daily from the Trail Blaze Corral and take riders on a leisurely, meandering ride through the Florida wilderness, where it is not uncommon to see birds, deer, and even an occasional armadillo. Galloping is not part of the experience, so you don't need riding know-how to sign up. The cost is about $55 per person. Guests age 9 years or older and at least 48 inches tall are allowed to ride. Parents must sign consent forms for kids under the age of 18. The weight limit is 250 pounds. Sturdy footwear with defined heels is recommended; open-toed shoes are not permitted. Reservations are necessary; call 407-WDW-PLAY (939-7529).

**TRI-CIRCLE-D RANCH:** This corner of Fort Wilderness is the place that the world champion Percherons and draft horses that pull trolleys down Main Street in the Magic Kingdom call home. WDW guests are welcome to stop in and say hello. The Tri-Circle-D insignia above the barn door—two small circles atop a large one with a letter D inside—is the WDW brand. The barn is also the site of a museum that pays tribute to horses and their role in Disney history. The laid-back ranch is also home to the remarkable Dragon Calliope—the horse-drawn

musical instrument that Walt Disney purchased for the Mickey Mouse Club Circus Parade at Disneyland Park in the 1950s. It's quite impressive.

**WAGON RIDES:** When offered, the wagon departs from Pioneer Hall at 6 P.M. and 8:30 P.M. and carries guests on a trip through wooded areas near Bay Lake. Rides last about 25 minutes and conclude at Pioneer Hall. Buy tickets from the wagon ride host/driver: $12 for adults, $8 for kids ages 3 through 9. Kids under age 12 must be accompanied by an adult. (Prices are subject to change.) Reservations are not accepted, so get there early.

Group wagon rides are available by calling 407-824-2832 (at least 24 hours in advance). The price is about $300 per hour. Note that wagon rides may be canceled due to inclement weather. Though they were on pause at press time, wagon rides are expected to return. For updates, visit *disneyworld.com*.

**WILDERNESS BACK TRAIL ADVENTURE:** A 2-hour "off-road" Segway tour of Fort Wilderness, this experience costs about $90 per person. Guests must be at least 16 years old, with valid photo ID. For details, see page 248, visit *disneyworld.com*, or call 407-WDW-TOUR (939-8687).

## ESSENTIALS

**HOW TO GET THERE:** From outside Walt Disney World, take Magic Kingdom Exit 64B off I-4 onto U.S. 192 and follow signs for Fort Wilderness Resort & Campground. This is the most expedient way to go, even for Walt Disney World resort guests.

**By WDW Transportation:** Buses or boats. Buses can get you just about anywhere, but allow yourself plenty of travel time—the transportation system, while quite efficient, can be time-consuming.

Water taxis are also available to and from the Magic Kingdom. It's about a 30-minute ride to the park, give or take—not including the time spent waiting to board the boat. Details are subject to change.

**WHERE TO EAT:** For a description of the new marketplace eatery at Pioneer Hall, refer to the *Good Meals, Great Times* chapter.

The Settlement Trading Post, located near the beach at the north end of the campground, and the Meadow Trading Post, near the center of Fort Wilderness, offer a small supply of food staples. For serious grocery shopping, visit a nearby supermarket or order the requisite supplies from your go-to delivery service.

# Tours and Programs

Here's your chance to experience Walt Disney World from the inside out. Adults may be required to carry a photo ID when attending backstage programs. Tours and prices are subject to change at any time. For details or to make reservations, use the My Disney Experience app, visit *disneyworld.com*, or call 407-939-8687 between 8 A.M. and 8 P.M. (daily) and have your credit card handy. Cell phone use and photography are not permitted in "backstage" areas of Walt Disney World. Prices quoted don't include tax. Plan to arrive at least 15 minutes prior to the scheduled start time—or risk being left behind.

At press time, some tours and backstage programs were on pause. What will be offered during your WDW trip? For updates, visit *disneyworld.com*, or use the My Disney Experience mobile app or website.

**AMORETTE'S PATISSERIE CAKE DECORATING EXPERIENCE** (Select mornings starting at 9:30 A.M.): Fans of Amorette's famous character dome cakes (which describes just about everybody!) can master the technique used to create those edible works of art in this special 90-minute class. During each small-group lesson, a talented instructor shares stories and tips while describing the process of cake decorating—from design to completion. Guests learn the proper way to pour glaçage (shiny glaze) and coat Mickey Mouse's sculpted ears, tail, belt, and buttons with edible paint. The finished product will be neatly packaged (complete with a surprise from Amorette's Patisserie.) You can take it with you, or pick it up later in the day. (Amorette will take good care of your cake while you explore Disney Springs!)

The cost for this 90-minute experience is about $199 and covers up to two participants, liquid refreshments (coffee, tea, and select spirited beverages), plus one cake. A second cake can be added for an extra $50, plus tax. (Requests for a second cake can be made up to 48 hours prior to the class reservation by calling 407-934-3500.) Guests must be at least 5 years old to participate. Alcohol may be served to guests who are at least 21 years old with government-issued photo ID. There is a two-day cancellation policy. The full price of the experience will be charged for no-shows or cancellations within 48 hours of the reservation.

**BEHIND THE SEEDS** (Daily; every hour between 10:30 A.M. and 4:30 P.M.): An opportunity for guests of all ages to get a closer look at the greenhouses and fish farm that are part of The Land pavilion at EPCOT. During the tour, guests will have close encounters with insects

and plants. A guide shares knowledge of hydroponics growing systems and crops from around the globe. Expect to be on your feet for the full hour of this experience. The cost is about $35 per person (ages 3 and up). This tour is best enjoyed by sturdy adults and older kids. Advance reservations may be made via *disneyworld.com* or the My Disney Experience app. Same-day reservations or walk-ups may be available at the tour desk on the lower level of The Land (near the entrance to the Soarin' attraction). Theme park admission is required.

**CARING FOR GIANTS** (Daily; groups depart between 10 A.M. and 4:30 P.M.): Guests of all ages are introduced to the majestic world of African elephants in this one-hour backstage experience. The elephant experts share strategies for day-to-day care of the gentle giants, plus a host of fascinating facts. African cultural representatives are also on hand to share stories about Disney's conservation efforts in their homeland. All the while, guests observe Animal Kingdom's elephants from a distance of just 80 to 100 feet. Cost is about $35 per person. Please check in at least 15 minutes prior to the scheduled start of the tour. Park admission is required, but not included with the cost of the tour.

**COLORS OF CORONADO PAINTING EXPERIENCE** (Friday; 1 P.M.): Participants take in breathtaking views as they create a masterpiece at the top of Gran Destino Tower in Disney's Coronado Springs resort. Taught by local artists, each two-hour class yields original works of art.

Cost is about $35 per person, plus tax. The experience is recommended for guests ages 12 and older. Kids under age 12 must be accompanied by an adult. Please arrive at the Toledo—Tapas, Steak & Seafood

podium at least 15 minutes before the class is scheduled to begin. Note that there is a one-day cancellation policy. Guests who cancel within 24 hours or fail to show up for the class will be charged full price. Same-day walk-ups may be available, but space is limited—reservations are recommended. For more information or to make a reservation, visit *disneyworld.com*, or use the My Disney Experience app. Details are subject to change.

**DIVEQUEST** (Daily; 2 P.M. and 5 P.M.): The highlight of the 2-hour program is a 40-minute underwater adventure—complete with sharks, turtles, rays, and lots of other fish—in The Seas with Nemo & Friends aquarium. Participants must show proof of current scuba certification and be at least 10 years old. Cost is about $219. Guests ages 10 to 15 must dive with a parent or guardian. Gear is provided. EPCOT admission is not required or included.

**DOLPHINS IN DEPTH** (Tuesday–Saturday; 10:30 A.M.): This 2-hour EPCOT program (about 30 minutes of it takes place in the water) teaches guests about dolphin behavior as they interact with the social sea creatures and observe researchers and trainers working with them. The cost is about $199 per person. Participants must be at least 44 inches tall. Guests under age 18 must be accompanied by a paying adult. Wet suits are provided; you must wear your own swimsuit underneath the wet suit. EPCOT admission is not required or included.

**Hot Tip!** Are you a WDW Annual Passholder? Perhaps you are a member of the Disney Vacation Club (DVC) or the Automobile Association of America (AAA), or have a Disney Visa card? If so, you may be able to save on some tours described on these pages. Be sure to ask about discounts when you call 407-WDW-TOUR (939-8687).

PHOTO BY MIKE CARROLL

## WILD AFRICA TREK

A thrilling, 3-hour adventure, the Wild Africa Trek is not for the faint of heart or those with any trepidation about teetering high in the air on a rickety rope bridge.

The guided tour, which is offered several times a day at Disney's Animal Kingdom park, is a VIP safari adventure for groups of 12 or fewer. It includes walking along a forest path and riding over the savanna in a rugged safari vehicle—plus up-close encounters of the creature kind (including giraffes, rhinos, crocodiles, and hippos). Along your journey, a knowledgeable tour guide shares insights about the majestic animals on view, as well as details about the park's dedication to animal conservation.

Available to guests age 8 and above, the trek takes place rain or shine (with the exception of lightning or severe weather). The cost (about $199) includes African-inspired snacks (you can't bring outside food), a special souvenir, and an access code to view and download photos. Theme park admission is required but not included. This is a very active experience—be sure to wear comfortable shoes and attire. You must be in good health to participate. Guests seeking a less strenuous or wheelchair-accessible trek should contact Wild Africa Trek operations at 407-938-1373 for alternative programs. For additional information or to make a reservation, use the My Disney Experience app or website, visit *disneyworld.com*, or call 407-939-8687.

**KEYS TO THE KINGDOM** (Daily; departing at 8, 8:30, 9, 9:30, and 10 A.M.): A 5-hour tour, it offers an on-site orientation to the history and workings of Walt Disney World's original theme park, the *Magic Kingdom*. Guests visit an attraction (waiting in the regular attraction line) and take a peek at the Utilidors (the legendary tunnels underneath the park). Cost is about $114, plus theme park admission. Lunch is included. Guests must be at least 16 years old to participate. Keys to the Kingdom Tour is an outdoor walking tour, so check the weather forecast and dress appropriately.

**SAVOR THE SAVANNA** (Daily; times vary): A private, guided journey, this experience is limited to 12 guests per excursion. The evening safari adventure begins with a journey deep in the heart of Harambe Wildlife Preserve. It offers secluded viewing areas of the savanna, plus a sampling of African-inspired, tapas-style nibbles and regional wines, beer, and soft drinks.

Cost is approximately $174 per person, plus tax. (The price includes food, drinks, and a keepsake.) Guests must be at least 8 years old to participate in this program. Note that Animal Kingdom park admission is required but is not included in the tour price.

**SPANISH MOSAIC ART** (Monday, Wednesday, and Saturday; 1 P.M.): A 2-hour experience that immerses guests in a Spanish art tradition as they create their own colorful mosaic keepsakes. Classes are held in the 16th-floor Dahlia Lounge in the Gran Destino Tower at Disney's Coronado Springs resort.

Cost is about $25 per person, plus tax. (The price includes all materials and a carrying case for the finished artwork.) It is recommended for guests ages 12 and older. Kids under age 12 must be accompanied by an adult. Please arrive at the Dahlia lounge 15 minutes before the class is scheduled to begin. Note that there is a one-day cancellation policy. Guests who cancel within 24 hours or fail to show up for the class will be charged full price. Same-day walk-ups may be available, but space is limited—reservations are recommended. For more information or to make a reservation, visit *disneyworld.com*, or use the My Disney Experience app. Details are subject to change.

**STARLIGHT SAFARI AT DISNEY'S ANIMAL KINGDOM LODGE** (Nightly; 8:30 P.M. and 10 P.M.): When the sun goes away, the animals come out to play. This nighttime adventure happens on the African savanna at Disney's Animal Kingdom Lodge, but it's available to all guests ages 8 and up. The adventure takes place in a rugged, open-sided safari vehicle. Thanks to a nifty night-vision device, guests can observe about 30 different species of African wildlife—including zebras, giraffes, gazelles, wildebeest, and antelopes—during the approximately one-hour tour.

The cost is about $89 per person. Guests under the age of 18 must be accompanied by a paying adult. For your safety, you should be in good health and free from high blood pressure; heart, back or neck problems; motion sickness; or other physical conditions that could be aggravated by this adventure. Expectant mothers should not participate. The safari vehicles are equipped for rain, but the Starlight Safari may be canceled due to inclement weather. The adventure takes place at the Kidani Village part of Disney's Animal Kingdom Lodge.

**UP CLOSE WITH RHINOS** (Daily; 11 A.M.): Guests over age 4 may enjoy a close-up encounter with the world's second-largest land mammal in this one-hour back-stage experience at Disney's Animal Kingdom theme park. In it, knowledgeable guides introduce the park's white rhinos, offer fascinating insights into the species' behavior and biology, and discuss the challenges that threaten populations in the wild. The cost is about $45 per person. Animal Kingdom park admission is required, but not included with the tour. Check in at 10:45 A.M. at the Curiosity Animal Tours kiosk, across from the Kilimanjaro Safaris entrance.

**WILDERNESS BACK TRAIL ADVENTURE** (Usually offered Tuesday–Saturday at 8:30 A.M. and 11:30 A.M.): A 2-hour experience, this adventure lets guests explore the Fort Wilderness area while aboard a Segway personal transporter. (It's a special model with off-road-type tires.) The first half hour is devoted to training (it's not as easy as it looks), with the remainder spent exploring with a storytelling guide. Guests must be at least 16 years old and in good health. (You will be on your feet the whole time, and operating the Segway requires more muscle than one might expect.) Helmets are required (and provided). Cost is about $90 per person. The experience takes place outdoors—dress accordingly. Note that part of the adventure may be canceled due to inclement weather.

# DAREDEVIL DISNEY

You've catapulted through the galaxy on Space Mountain, braved an encounter with an angry Yeti at Expedition Everest, and become something of a human yo-yo on the Tower of Terror. Now what? Believe it or not, there are plenty of thrills awaiting you outside the theme park gates. Several of them, such as the wedgie-inducing slides at the water parks, are well known. Others may be lower key, but they're definitely high octane. Here are a couple of our favorite theme-park-alternative thrills. All details are subject to change at any time. Visit *disneyworld.com* for updates.

**BALLOONING:** Going up! A huge, tethered, helium balloon (run by Aerophile—"The World Leader in Balloon Flight") lifts guests 400 feet high into the sky. Moored to a landing at Disney Springs West Side, the balloon can accommodate up to 29 guests at a time—treating all to sweeping panoramic views of Walt Disney World and beyond. It operates on a first-come, first-served basis from 8:30 A.M. until 11 P.M. Adults pay about $25 per flight, while kids (ages 3 through 9) pay about $20. Expect to be airborne for about 8 to 10 minutes. This high-flying attraction does not operate during windy or inclement weather. Spooked by heights and/or enclosed places? Sit this one out.

**SURFING:** Traditionally, when the sun comes up, so does the surf at Disney's Typhoon Lagoon water park. Experienced riders can shoot the curl before the park opens and/or after it closes for the day. It's a great opportunity to spend quality time on the water—just you, your crew, and the waves (which have been known to give Mother Nature a run for her money!)

For details or to book a private surf event, call 407-560-7873, or send an email inquiry to WDPR.Surfing.Programs@Disney.com.

# Fun for Kids

Walt Disney World may appeal to the kid in all of us, but some activities are especially appealing to or specifically tailored to the actual young—not just the young at heart. With the exceptions of pony rides, the following activities are not exclusive to guests who can't remember life before Elsa froze Arendelle—grown-ups can join in the fun or relax while their kids are entertained.

**Note:** Some kid-centric WDW adventures were "on pause" at press time. Will they return? We sure hope so! For updates, go to *disneyworld.com,* or use the My Disney Experience app or website. Details are subject to change.

**BIKING:** Bicycles—including those sized especially for young pedalers (some equipped with training wheels)—are available to rent at several Walt Disney World resorts, including Caribbean Beach, Old Key West, Port Orleans French Quarter, Saratoga Springs, and Fort Wilderness. All kids under age 16 are required to wear a helmet. They're provided for free and available for guests of all ages. It costs about $9 to rent a bike for an hour; about $20 to rent one for the day.

**POLE FISHING:** There's an old fashioned fishin' hole at Disney's Port Orleans Riverside resort. Located at Ol' Man Island, aka the hotel's recreation hub, the water's teeming with bass, bluegills, and catfish. Kids of all ages can pull a big fish from this small pond—just drop the line from your cane pole and wait for a finned friend to take a nibble. Reservations are not required for this activity. Expect to pay about $7 per pole, per hour (including pole and bait) or $17 for a family of four. While this is one of the more youngster-friendly WDW experiences, there are several other ways to angle in the House of Mouse. For details, see page 257. Note that all Walt Disney World fishing is strictly catch-and-release. You can catch it, but you can't keep it!

**PONY RIDES:** Young cowpokes can ride petite ponies at the Tri-Circle-D Ranch at Disney's Fort Wilderness Resort and Campground. Guests must be at least 2 years old, under 80 pounds, no taller than 48 inches, and able to hold on by themselves. Closed-toe shoes are a must. A parent or guardian must lead the pony at all times. Rides are offered from 10 A.M. until about 3 or 4 P.M. daily. Cost is $8 per child (cash, credit, or MagicBand linked to credit card). Currently, pony rides are available on a walk-up basis only. Details are subject to change.

**RESORT ARCADES:** Most Walt Disney World resort hotels boast an arcade stuffed with games featuring modern and classic bells and whistles. With more than 1,500 games in all, WDW arcades offer something for just about everyone. To play, you'll need to purchase a game card. Points may be added (with a credit card or U.S. cash) at a kiosk inside the arcade. Game cards can be used at all WDW resort arcades.

**SCAVENGER HUNTS AND INTERACTIVE QUESTS:** All WDW theme parks feature special in-park scavenger hunts and/or interactive quests—and there's no extra charge to join the fun! Would-be pirates head to Adventureland for Magic Kingdom's A Pirate's Adventure—Treasures of the Seven Seas. At EPCOT's World Showcase, guests join Scrooge McDuck and pals in Disney's DuckTales World Showcase Adventure. Kids of all ages can become official Wilderness Explorers at Disney's Animal Kingdom. And everyone can enjoy out-of-this-world adventures in Star Wars: Galaxy's Edge at Disney's Hollywood Studios. (You'll need to turn a smartphone into a "datapad" via the free Play Disney Parks app to play.) For details about these daring quests, visit *disneyworld.com.*

# WDW Spas

For many guests, a day at the theme parks is an exciting test of physical endurance—complete with sprinting (say, from Dumbo to Big Thunder Mountain before a dinner reservation), weightlifting (toting tired toddlers), and long-distance hiking (covering more than a mile to reach the American Adventure from EPCOT's front gate—and back again!). Fortunately, there are many ways to rest and rejuvenate weary bones, throbbing feet, and noise-addled noggins. Chief among them is a visit to a soothing spa (aah). There are several such spots on Walt Disney World property, open to everyone. Details are subject to change. For updates, visit *disneyworld.com*, or use the My Disney Experience mobile app or website. Here are some highlights:

**THE GRAND FLORIDIAN SPA:** You don't need a magic wand to make your stress disappear—not if you can pay a visit to this Grand Floridian pampering palace. In addition to a relaxation room that features light snacks and soothing music, this place offers a selection of treatments. Among them: facials (including one for the back and self-care facial instruction); revitalizing body therapies, and foot therapy. Massage options include: The Grand Massage ("a customized massage incorporating botanical lotions and other elements to release tension, pain, and fatigue, while replenishing the mind, body, and spirit"), warm stone massage, and one specially designed for expectant mothers. Manicures, pedicures, and additional hand and foot treatments may also be available. At press time, a single spa package was offered: The 2-hour Just the Two of Us experience includes massage and The Grand Pedicure for two. Cost is about $260 plus tax and gratuity.

## SPA TIPS

- Reserve treatments far in advance and be sure to confirm all appointments.
- If you'll feel more comfortable with either a male or a female spa therapist, let your preference be known when you make your reservation. The spas will accommodate such requests whenever possible.
- Plan to arrive 30 minutes prior to your appointment. That'll give you time to change and relax. (Arriving late will reduce your treatment time.) If you're traveling via WDW transportation (buses, boats, monorails, etc.), get an early start on the commute.
- To maintain a peaceful environment, silence your cell phone as you arrive at the spa. Guests are required to keep phones and electronic devices turned off at all times.
- For the privacy of others, photographs, videos, or other social media recording must not be taken inside any spa.
- Leave all valuables in your resort-room safe.
- Drink plenty of water after your spa visit. It will counter any post-treatment dehydration.
- The consumption of alcohol is not recommended before, during, or immediately after a spa treatment.
- Guests under age 18 must be accompanied by an adult to enjoy a spa treatment.
- If you're scheduled for a body treatment, leave your clothes in a locker. Robes and slippers are provided.
- Like most spas in the real world, Walt Disney World spas add a 20 percent gratuity with each spa service. Extra tip may be added at your discretion.
- It's always smart to take a shower before a treatment—especially if you have been at the beach or running around theme parks.
- Appointment cancellations or changes must be made more than 24 hours in advance for The Grand Floridian Spa, and within four hours at Mandara Spa to avoid paying full price. The Spa at Four Seasons Orlando charges 50 percent for appointments that are changed or canceled within 4 hours of the treatment. Details are subject to change.
- Build time into your schedule to enjoy post-treatment relaxation time at the spa. You'll want to hold on to that glow as long as possible! Bathing suits are required for whirlpools, steamrooms, and other areas.
- For spa updates and pricing info, visit *disneyworld.com*.

Hours are usually 9 A.M. to 6 P.M. daily. Prices start at about $175 for a 50-minute massage, $120 for a facial, $70 for a "back facial," $50 for an "express" manicure, and $70 for a pedicure, plus 20 percent gratuity. For additional information, or to book an appointment at the Grand Floridian Spa, visit *https://na.spatime.com/wdpr32875/55247827/home*, or call 407-939-7727.

**BIRNBAUM'S ★BEST★** **MANDARA SPA AT THE DOLPHIN:** As exotic as it is peaceful, Mandara Spa is on the must-do list for all guests eager to swap their stress for a big, relaxed smile.

Mandara specializes in treatments meant to reflect the "beauty, spirit, and traditions of both Eastern and Western cultures." The spa menu showcases Balinese massage, a variation of Swedish massage. It incorporates stretching, "vigorous yet relaxing" movements, and elements of acupressure. Of course, that's just one of many services offered here—all of which emphasize physical wellness and spiritual well-being. Other popular treatments include the Mandara customized massage, Hot Stone Therapy massage, and the Mandara Deep Tissue Muscle massage. The Elemis Superfood Pro-Radiance Facial ($170 for 60 minutes) is a nutrition boost for stressed skin. And the exotic Musclease Aroma Spa Ocean Wrap ($175 for 60 minutes) envelops the body in an aromatic seaweed mask to relieve stiff joints and muscular tension. Prices do not include 20-percent gratuity.

In addition to Balinese-inspired architecture, two interior gardens provide retreats before guests begin the spa ritual. The goal here is to provide a place for guests to rejuvenate their minds as well as those aching "I can't believe I covered four theme parks in two days!" muscles. For more information, call 800-227-1500 or 407-934-4772, or visit *www.swandolphin.com*.

## INTERNET ACCESS AT WDW

We are happy to report that all Walt Disney World resorts offer free in-room, wireless Internet access. (The signal isn't always strong, but the price is right.) Of course, you'll need to supply the hardware. Complimentary Wi-Fi (wireless fidelity) is also offered at all Walt Disney World theme parks, water parks, and Disney Springs. Naturally, your phone, tablet, or computer, must be Wi-Fi ready. Note that in-room, wireless Internet service is also available at the Four Seasons Orlando and the Walt Disney World Swan and Dolphin resorts.

If you'd like to access a computer but didn't pack your own, ask your Lobby Concierge to direct you to the nearest resort business center. There you can email, upload, download, and print to your heart's content. Fees vary—be sure to inquire before you start using business center services.

**THE SPA AT FOUR SEASONS RESORT ORLANDO:** The luxe, serene spa at the sprawling Four Seasons Resort Orlando evokes the natural sanctuary of Florida's Everglades. Expect to be revitalized with spa pleasures like the Hyper-customized facial (starting at $215) and the exclusive Sticks and Stones therapy that massages and relaxes with sculpted basalt stones and birchwood massage sticks. This spa oasis in the midst of Disney's exclusive Golden Oak enclave features 18 tranquil treatment rooms, including couples' rooms and bungalows.

A truly special warm Healing Honey Treatment (50 minutes) uses local, raw, pure honey for a luxurious massage and immune booster; the 80-minute version adds head-to-toe exfoliation with Himalayan salt and organic tea leaves. Complimentary spa extras include an outdoor whirlpool and the unique-to-Florida Experience Shower with settings such as "arctic mist," "island storm," and "tropical rain," plus thunder and lightning effects.

Magical Moments experiences for girls and boys offer choices ranging from the Shining Knight salon grooming with "royal crown, sword of truth, and shield of courage" ($40) to the Princess & Queen "Mommy & Me" salon and makeup extravaganza ($475). Yes, a princess dress and fairy dust are part of the package.

Hours are 9 A.M. to 8 P.M. daily. Prices start at about $175 for a 50-minute facial and $170 for a massage (plus 20 percent gratuity). Note that pool access is not included for spa patrons who are not registered guests of the resort. For details and to make reservations, visit *www.fourseasons.com/orlando/spa*, or call 407-313-6160 or 407-313-7777. All details are subject to change.

# WDW Specialty Cruises

Every Walt Disney World evening ends with a bang—which usually comes in the form of pyrotechnic spectaculars. Two such presentations, the Magic Kingdom's Happily Ever After fireworks show and EPCOT's after-dark extravaganza, are seen by scores of park-goers on a nightly basis. However, these joyful displays are also enjoyed by a subset of guests, far removed from the hubbub of the parks yet close enough to marvel at the subtleties of each brilliant burst. These are the guests who opt for a specialty cruise. The vintage vantage points are available to all, provided they are within budget and reservations are made. Of course, there is the other extreme: a quiet, moonlit, fireworks-free cruise on the waterways of the World.

Guests are advised to make reservations as far in advance as possible. The following is an indication of Disney's specialty cruise offerings. Details are subject to change at any time.

**FERRYTALE FIREWORKS: A SPARKLING DESSERT CRUISE:** Guests are invited to climb aboard a ferry boat and enjoy a memorable evening on the Seven Seas Lagoon. They're welcomed with a beverage as the crew regales them with the backstory of the vessel's magic. Once the boat casts off, it's time to bring on the treats: bite-sized cupcakes, tarts, pies, and popcorn push-ups, to name a few. Enjoy them with a specialty beverage (with or sans alcohol). There's a Hidden Mickey scavenger hunt, too. Before it's time for Happily Ever After to light up the sky, find a spot along the railing and get those "Mickey Vision" glasses ready—they'll enhance the viewing experience in a fun way. (The vessel has an audio feed that plays the show's soundtrack.)

The Ferrytale Fireworks: A Sparkling Dessert Cruise is offered on select Wednesday and Saturday nights. Admission is $130 for adults and $100 for children ages 3 to 9 (tax and gratuity included) and includes a small takeaway treat. The boat departs from the Ferry terminal

## PIRATES & PYROTECHNICS

Avast, ye hearties! There's a pirate-themed adventure at Walt Disney World: The Pirates & Pals Fireworks Voyage. Though it was "on pause" at press time, the hope is that it will return at some point. In it, brave buccaneers board a pirate ship–conveniently moored at the Contemporary Resort marina–and set sail on Bay Lake and Seven Seas Lagoon. Before weighing anchor, participating pirates enjoy unlimited snacks and soft drinks at the Contemporary. They can mingle with Captain Hook and Mr. Smee, who are eager to meet the recruits. After a pirate parade, guests board Captain Patch's ship and set sail. The captain will test your knowledge of Disney trivia, sing sea shanties, and position your vessel in a perfect location to view the Magic Kingdom's fireworks show, Happily Ever After. For updates on the status of this adventure, use the My Disney Experience app or website, visit *disneyworld.com*, or call 407-939-7529.

at the Transportation and Ticket Center. For updates or to make a reservation, visit *disneyworld.com*, or call 407-WDW-PLAY (939-7529). Same-day reservations may be made before 5 P.M., pending availability. Note that there are very few seats on the boat.

**PONTOON BOAT CRUISES:** More practical than luxurious, Disney's fleet of pontoon boats still delivers a crowd-pleasing cruise experience. Voyages are accompanied by a captain, and include assorted snacks and soft drinks. Each boat takes up to 10 guests on tours of the Seven Seas Lagoon and Bay Lake, near the Magic Kingdom park, as well as Crescent Lake by Disney's EPCOT-area resorts (just outside EPCOT's International Gateway entrance). Those in the Magic Kingdom area are treated to VIP viewing of the fireworks show (as well as the synchronized music), while EPCOT-area cruisers take in that park's nighttime extravaganza.

Pontoon cruises last about one hour. Magic Kingdom fireworks excursions depart from the Polynesian Village, Grand Floridian, Contemporary, Wilderness Lodge, and Fort Wilderness marinas. EPCOT cruises leave from the Yacht Club marina. Cost for a pontoon boat fireworks cruise starts at about $399, plus tax, per boatload. Call 407-WDW-PLAY (939-7529) for additional information or to make reservations.

# SPORTS & RECREATION

First-time visitors may not realize that Disney provides a plethora of sporting opportunities. Within WDW's nearly 40 square miles, there are more tennis courts than at most tennis resorts and more holes of championship-caliber golf than at most golf centers, plus so many other diversions—from fishing and golf to biking, boating, and horseback riding—that the quantity and variety are matched by few other vacation destinations.

So while the family golfers are pursuing a perfect swing on one of several first-rate, 18-hole courses, tennis buffs can be wearing themselves out on the courts, and anglers can be casting away in hopes of hooking a big bass. Those who like to spectate as well as participate can visit a veritable sports mecca at ESPN Wide World of Sports, an enormous, state-of-the-art facility that hosts a diverse array of sporting events, both amateur and professional. And those who prefer the sedate can treat themselves to a poolside nap or a soothing spa treatment.

Instruction, as well as guides, drivers, and assorted supervisors, makes every recreational activity as much fun for beginners as for hard-core aficionados. Moreover, the ready accessibility of Walt Disney World sporting and recreational activities—via an extensive system of (free) public transportation (refer to the *Transportation & Accommodations* chapter)—means that no family member needs to give up precious playtime to chauffeur others around.

> "Family fun is as necessary to modern living as a kitchen refrigerator."
>
> **—Walt Disney**

# WDW Golf

Most people don't immediately think of Walt Disney World for a golf outing. Yet there are several superb 18-hole courses here: The Magnolia and the Palm golf courses are across the road from the Polynesian Village resort. Nearby is the Lake Buena Vista course. Its fairways are framed by Disney's Saratoga Springs and Old Key West resorts. And the Four Seasons resort boasts a stellar course, too. While the Walt Disney World courses won't set anyone's knees to knocking, they are demanding enough to have merited the status of a stop on the PGA Tour tournament trail.

**PALM & MAGNOLIA COURSES:** The wide-open, tree-dotted Magnolia measures 5,127 yards from the front tees, 6,558 from the middle, and 7,516 from the back. The Palm is tighter, with more wooded fairways and nine water hazards; it measures 5,213 yards from the front, 6,339 from the middle, and 6,870 from the back. Both courses have received a four-star ("outstanding") rating from *Golf Digest*. The Magnolia and Palm courses share two driving ranges and putting greens.

**Oak Trail Course:** This nine-hole, 2,913-yard layout is a walking course tucked into a corner within the Magnolia. It was designed for beginners and junior golfers, but it's home to some tough holes, including two par 5s. Many moderate and accomplished golfers enjoy the opportunity to tune up or play a quick 9.

FootGolf enthusiasts will be pleased to know that Disney's Oak Trail is also home to an 18-hole Foot-Golf course. The family-friendly game—a mix of golf and soccer—requires minimal experience to play. If you can you kick a soccer ball, you're probably ready for FootGolf. You may rent a ball or bring your own.

For additional information and to reserve tee times, visit *www.golfwdw.com/footgolf*, or call 407-939-4653.

**LAKE BUENA VISTA COURSE:** Joe Lee's design measures 5,177 yards from the front tees, 6,281 from the middle, and 6,745 from the rearmost markers. Among the shortest of the 18-hole, par-72 courses, it has a fair amount of water, and its tree-lined fairways are WDW's narrowest. The course is well suited for beginners but challenges experienced players. A driving range and putting green are also available.

## ESSENTIALS

**WHEN TO GO:** January through April is considered peak golfing season (though enthusiastic WDW guests have been known to hit the links year-round). To avoid the biggest crowds, play on a Monday or Tuesday, and tee off in the late afternoons (mornings are very busy when the mercury rises). Summer discounts may apply. From June through late September, guests pay as little as $79 after 11 A.M. After 3 P.M., the price may drop as low as $49. Theme Park Annual Passholder, Military, and Disney Vacation Club member specials may be offered. Annual golf memberships are also a possibility. For additional information, call 407-939-4653.

**RESERVATIONS:** Call 407-WDW-GOLF (939-4653), or visit *www.golfwdw.com*, to confirm rates and to secure tee times. From January through April, morning and early afternoon tee times should be reserved well in advance; starting times after 3 P.M. are often available at the last minute. Reservations must be made with a major credit card. Cancellations must be made at least 24 hours ahead to avoid penalties.

**FEES:** At the 18-hole courses, greens fees (including a required cart) vary with the course and season. Rates range from about $79 to $149 for day visitors.

Mid-afternoon rates, known as "twilight rates," may yield discounts. Available throughout the year, twilight rates run about $39 to $69.

The cost for adults to play Oak Trail is $25 to $39 for 9 holes; juniors (17 and under) net a 40 percent discount for 9 holes. Prices don't include tax and are likely to change.

**Hot Tip!** Single-rider, adaptive golf carts and clubhouse accommodations are available for guests with disabilities at all Walt Disney World golf courses. For additional information, visit *www.golfwdw.com*, or call 407-WDW-GOLF (939-4653).

**INSTRUCTION:** A staff of PGA professionals at the Palm and Magnolia courses offers private 45-minute lessons costing $90 for adults and $60 for juniors (up to age 17). Lessons are customized to all experience levels. Video analysis may be used. Prices are subject to change. WDW resort guests may make reservations up to 90 days in advance; call 407-WDW-GOLF (939-4653).

**DRESS:** Proper golf attire is required. Collared shirts or golf-style collarless shirts are necessary, and any shorts must be Bermuda length.

**EQUIPMENT RENTAL:** Equipment can be rented at all Walt Disney World golf courses; all guests pay $49 (plus tax) for clubs and two sleeves of golf balls. Shoes rent for $10 a pair. Range balls are among available items. They cost approximately $8 to $12 per basket. Photo ID is required for rentals.

**TRANSPORTATION:** Transportation to and from the golf courses is available with complimentary taxi vouchers from Walt Disney World–owned-and-operated resort hotels. (Swan, Dolphin, Four Seasons, and resorts on Hotel Plaza Boulevard are not included in this transportation program—but taxis may be summoned from these properties, too.) Call or go to your resort's Guest Services desk at least 30 minutes prior to your desired

pickup time and a Cast Member will call for your taxi. That should give you enough time to get to the course, check in at the pro shop, and spend some time at the range and practice putting green before your round. Complimentary transportation is for regular play only. Vouchers include a gratuity for the taxi driver.

# WDW Tennis

Saratoga Springs Resort & Spa has two clay courts. All other Walt Disney World tennis is played on hard courts. The Yacht and the Beach Club share one court; Fort Wilderness, Saratoga Springs, Bay Lake Tower (at Contemporary), Animal Kingdom Lodge's Kidani Village, and BoardWalk each have two; and Old Key West has three. Courts are free to guests staying at a WDW-owned-and-operated resort. For details or to make tennis lesson reservations, call 321-228-1146.

## ESSENTIALS

**WHEN TO GO:** Tennis courts are often open from about 8 A.M. to 7 P.M. daily. Weather-wise, January, October, and November are prime months for playing tennis in Florida. All courts are available on a first-come, first-served basis. During busy periods, the length of time a single group of players can occupy a court is restricted to 2 hours on any morning, afternoon, or evening.

Equipment rental is limited at Walt Disney World. Call 407-WDW-PLAY (939-7529) for details.

**DRESS:** Tennis whites are appropriate, but not required, for play on Walt Disney World's courts. Tennis shoes are a must.

# Waters of the World

PHOTO BY AMY HENNING

## BOATING

Disney World is the home of an impressive fleet of pleasure boats. Cruising on Bay Lake and the Seven Seas Lagoon can be a most relaxing sport, and a number of pontoon boats are available for rent at two Magic Kingdom area resorts: the Contemporary (from its Bay Lake marina) and Grand Floridian (which sends boaters out from its marina on the shore of Seven Seas Lagoon. The Yacht & Beach Club and BoardWalk resorts share a lovely boating haven in 25-acre Crescent Lake.

To rent, guests must show a valid driver's license or passport. Rental of certain watercraft may carry other requirements. No privately owned boats are permitted on Walt Disney World waters.

Some WDW boat experiences were on pause as this book went to press. For status and pricing updates, use the My Disney Experience mobile app or website, or visit *disneyworld.com*.

**AMPHICARS:** It's a car! It's a boat! It's a nautical blast from America's motoring past (the 1960s, to be precise). Yep, the amphibious Amphicar is back. Disney has brought nine of these classic vehicles out of retirement and put them back to work at Disney Springs. Doing double duty as artwork/water taxi, Amphicars are next to The Boathouse eatery. Up to three guests may enjoy a 20-minute tour of Disney Springs waterways for about $125 (captain included). Tours are offered from 10 A.M. until 10 P.M. daily, weather permitting.

**CANOEING AND KAYAKING:** A long paddle down the Fort Wilderness canals is such a tranquil way to pass a misty morning that it's hard to remember that the bustle of the Magic Kingdom is not far away. Canoes and kayaks may be rented at the Bike Barn in the Fort Wilderness Meadow Recreation area. Cost is about $13 per hour. These watercraft are for use on Fort Wilderness canals only, not for Bay Lake or Seven Seas Lagoon. Complimentary life jackets must be worn at all times. Rentals are available on a first-come, first served basis.

**PADDLE BOATS:** These swan-shaped watercraft are exclusively for guests registered at the WDW Swan, Dolphin, and Swan Reserve. Included with the daily resort service fee, they're available at the Dolphin marina. The pedal-powered vessels are available daily from 11 A.M. until 5 P.M. Details are subject to change.

**PONTOON BOATS:** Motorized, canopied platforms on pontoons are perfect for small groups, families, and visitors more interested in serenity than in speed. Available at select WDW resort marinas, the 21-foot craft hold up to ten passengers and cost about $45, plus tax, per half hour. Guests must be at least 18 years old (with a valid driver's license) to pilot a pontoon boat. The maximum weight per boat is 1,900 pounds.

## SWIMMING

Although the beachfronts are strictly for strolling, sun-bathing, and sand castle construction, swimmers may splash in one of WDW's elaborately themed pools—which come in every shape and size imaginable. The water parks (Typhoon Lagoon and Blizzard Beach) only add to the fun.

Walt Disney World resorts have at least one pool apiece. With the exception of sister resorts (Yacht & Beach Club; Port Orleans French Quarter and River-side; All-Star Movies, All-Star Music, and All-Star Sports; and Swan and Dolphin), which share some of their recreational facilities, Disney's hotel pools are open exclusively to guests staying at the respective resort. This policy was initiated to prevent overcrowding. All pools are heated in winter. Resort guests may borrow life jackets at no cost. Guests who cannot swim should wear life jackets at all times while in or near a pool. WDW resort guests of all ages, but especially the little ones, may partake in engaging pool activities throughout the day. For schedules, check at your resort's front desk or at the pool itself.

Featuring one pool each are Animal Kingdom Lodge and Port Orleans French Quarter. The Grand Floridian, Contemporary, Polynesian, Fort Wilderness Resort & Campground, Wilderness Lodge, and the All-Stars have two pools each. BoardWalk, Pop Century, and Art of Animation have three pools; Coronado Springs and Old Key West feature four swimming holes; Saratoga Springs has five (including one by the Treehouse villas) Port Orleans Riverside and Caribbean Beach have six. The Yacht & Beach Club resorts share three unguarded pools, plus a small water park known as Stormalong Bay. It features slides, a sand-bottomed wading area, and a lazy river. The Swan, Dolphin, and Swan Reserve share 6 pools, including a grotto pool with a slide. In addition, each of the resorts on Hotel Plaza Boulevard has its own pool, too.

Lifeguards are on duty during posted hours at each resort's main pool. Even so, be sure to keep an eye on youngsters at all times and borrow life jackets for little ones and weak swimmers.

**Hot Tip!** Swimming and wading are not permitted in any of Walt Disney World's lakes. The rule is meant to protect guests from unguarded water and from exposure to naturally occurring bacteria and dangerous wildlife, such as snakes and alligators, common to Florida lakes.

## FISHING

The 70,000 bass with which Bay Lake was stocked in the mid-1960s have grown and multiplied as a result of WDW's restrictive fishing policy. (It's strictly catch-and-release.) No angling is permitted on Bay Lake or the Seven Seas Lagoon, except on the guided fishing expeditions. Largemouth bass weighing two to eight pounds are the most common catch.

Bay Lake excursions depart daily; call 407-WDW-FISH (939-3474) for more details. Fishing trips last about two or four hours, accommodate up to three anglers (in a bass fishing boat) and up to five in a pontoon boat, and include guide, gear (rods, reels, lures, and bait), and non-alcoholic beverages. Guides will pick up guests at the Contemporary, Grand Floridian, Polynesian Village, Fort Wilderness, and Wilderness Lodge. Guests can enjoy guided fishing excursions at Old Key West, Saratoga Springs, Port Orleans Riverside, and Caribbean Beach, too. Kids under age 16 must be accompanied by an adult (over age 18).

Anglers might also consider two-hour tours that depart from Yacht & Beach Club at 7 A.M., 10 A.M., and 1:30 P.M. Trips accommodate up to 3 or 5 people (depending on boat type). A guide, gear, and soft drinks are included.

The Magic Kingdom–area resorts also offer two-hour excursions on pontoon boats that accommodate one or two guests. They depart from the resort marinas at 7 A.M., 10 A.M., and 1:30 P.M. daily. The $170 to $455 price includes equipment and a guide. (Prices may vary.)

Reservations can be made at least 24 hours to 60 days in advance and should be booked as far ahead as possible; call 407-WDW-FISH (939-3473). Excursions may be canceled or cut short if the weather is stormy or there is lightning in the vicinity of Walt Disney World. Life jackets are provided and are required for all guests age 13 and under. Don't forget to wear sun protection: hats, sunglasses, sunscreen, etc.

Fishing on your own—remember, it is strictly catch-and-release—is permitted at Fort Wilderness. Fort Wilderness guests may toss in lines from authorized dockside locations. Fishing licenses are not required. Rods and reels ($10 for the first 30 minutes; or $16 for the day) and are available for rent at the Fort Wilderness Bike Barn. Live bait (worms or wigglers) may be purchased for about $5.

Guests staying at either of Disney's Port Orleans resorts may enjoy dock-side fishing at Port Orleans Riverside. Equipment should be rented from Fishin' Hole at Ole Man Island. And remember: All WDW fishing is catch-and-release only.

# ESPN Wide World of Sports

Variety is the name of the game at ESPN Wide World of Sports. The multimillion-dollar sports complex invites athletes and spectators alike to dive into more than 60 types of sporting experiences. It's a grand slam for die-hard sports fans.

Designed as a modern vision of old-time Floridian building styles, the architecture harks back to days when sports facilities were convenient extensions of their neighborhoods. The versatile 220-acre facility—which has teamed up with ESPN—hosts events in everything from jump rope to wrestling.

The sprawling site boasts a wide variety of world-class venues, including a baseball stadium; a field house that accommodates basketball, wrestling, and volleyball; a track-and-field complex; and multipurpose fields fit for soccer, football, and a whole lot more.

A general-admission ticket costs about $20 for adults and $15 for children ages 3 through 9. Tickets may be purchased at the front gate and allow guests to watch all "nonpremium" events. Guests are only admitted on days when events are scheduled. For premium event ticketing information, visit *www.espnwwos.com*. Note that tickets to premium events include general admission to the complex.

Premium-event tickets may also be purchased at the Wide World of Sports Complex box office on the day of an event, depending on availability. Ticket prices vary from event to event.

## ESSENTIALS

**HOW TO GET THERE:** During select sporting events, Walt Disney World Resort transportation may be available from host resorts to ESPN Wide World of Sports Complex. Dedicated bus service is provided for some events and is dependent upon event times. Rideshare and guest drop-off lanes are also available.

If you are driving, take Exit 65 off I-4 to Victory Way. ESPN Wide World of Sports is between U.S. 192 and Osceola Parkway. Parking is free but limited. If you plan to attend a premium event, arrive as early as possible—or risk a last-minute scramble for a parking spot in a remote, unpaved, auxiliary lot.

**PARKING:** Free "general" parking is available at ESPN Wide World of Sports Complex. Premium parking is available on select event dates for a fee. In the event the Sports Complex parking lots fill to capacity, guests will be directed to alternate parking locations (including the aforementioned auxiliary areas).

**ADDRESS FOR THE GPS:** The address for the ESPN Wide World of Sports Complex is 700 South Victory Way, Kissimmee, FL 34747.

**WHERE TO EAT:** The big-ticket eatery here is ESPN Wide World of Sports Grill. It is open on most days.

There are a number of concession stands for sports fans seeking a somewhat lighter bite. They offer hot dogs, burgers, snacks, soft drinks, and beer, as well as a few more substantial—yet just as portable—snack selections. Food trucks will be available for many outdoor events, too. For more information, visit *www.espnwwos.com*, or call 407-939-2026.

## TOUCH BASE

Get the full scoop on all the scheduled action at the ESPN Wide World of Sports Complex by visiting *www.espnwwos.com*, or calling 407-939-1500.

# More Ways to Have Fun

**ARCHERY:** Channel your inner Robin Hood at a Fort Wilderness program known as the Archery Experience. The 90-minute experience includes a quick but thorough lesson and lots of shooting time. It takes place every Tuesday through Saturday at 11:30 A.M. and 2:45 P.M. Available to guests age 7 and older, the Archery Experience costs about $45 per person (plus tax). It should be booked as far in advance as possible (60 days) by calling 407-WDW-PLAY (939-7529).

**BASKETBALL:** Guests may shoot hoops at 6 basketball courts at Walt Disney World resorts. There's no fee to play, and equipment may be borrowed by WDW resort guests (with valid ID). Courts, which range in size from quarter- to full-size, may be found at the following resorts: Animal Kingdom Lodge—Kidani Village (half-court), Contemporary, Grand Floridian Resort & Spa (half-court), Disney's Old Key West, Saratoga Springs Resort & Spa, and the Fort Wilderness Resort & Campground (quarter-size court).

**BIKING:** Bicycles may be rented year-round at Disney's Fort Wilderness, Old Key West, Port Orleans, Caribbean Beach, and Saratoga Springs. The cost is about $18 per day. Bikes equipped with training wheels or baby seats are available. Helmets are mandatory for guests up to age 16 (and recommended for everyone) and may be borrowed for free. Details are subject to change.

**MINIATURE GOLF:** The Fantasia Gardens Miniature Golf complex, located near the Swan and Dolphin resorts, offers players two 18-hole courses themed to the Disney film *Fantasia*. The Fantasia Fairways course offers a difficult layout sure to tantalize serious golfers. It has traditional golf obstacles, such as water hazards, doglegs, and roughs. Don't be fooled by the small size of the Fantasia Fairways course—its challenges are big. (The record for the par-72 course is 47.)

Fantasia Gardens, on the other hand, is all in fun, with clever things (a dancing hippo, xylophone stairs, brooms dumping buckets of water) at every hole. The degree of difficulty varies from hole to hole, but this is an easy course to conquer. There are some serious challenges out there, however. Hole number 15, for example, is one of the trickier ones. Here, golfers aim through mini-geysers that randomly squirt water into the air. Good luck with that!

Disney's Winter Summerland miniature golf course is a mere stone's throw from the Blizzard Beach water park. (They share a bus stop; buses run during Blizzard Beach operating hours). Designed as a vacation retreat for Santa and his elves, the two 18-hole courses boast a festive atmosphere, complete with Christmas carol soundtracks. The sandy-surface course is a bit more challenging than its snowy-surface counterpart.

A round on any course costs about $14 for adults, $12 for kids ages 3 through 9. The second round is 25 percent off. Typical playing time is about an hour. Operating hours are generally 10 A.M. to 10 P.M. but vary seasonally. You can book tee times in advance by calling 407-WDW-PLAY (939-7529).

**MOVIES UNDER THE STARS:** Let's all go to the movies! Walt Disney World–owned-and-operated resort hotels offer free screenings of favorite Disney flicks several nights a week. With the exception of Fort Wilderness Resort & Campground, which presents films in a mini amphitheater setting, movies are presented on a big screen in an outdoor space. While snacks are typically not provided, feel free to bring your own. The fun may move indoors should the weather be rainy or otherwise inclement. Each WDW resort features its own weekly

movie lineup. The schedule may be posted near the screening location. If not, inquire at your resort's front desk. There is no cost to partake, but all guests must be registered at a WDW-owned-and-operated resort.

**SPAS AND HEALTH CLUBS:** WDW health clubs include the Contemporary's Olympiad Fitness Center, Sturdy Branches at Wilderness Lodge, Zahanati at Animal Kingdom Lodge and Survival of the Fittest at Kidani Village, Fitness Center at Gran Destino and La Vida at Coronado Springs, Muscles and Bustles at BoardWalk, Health Club at the Dolphin, Grand Floridian, and Saratoga Springs, Resort Fitness Center at Old Key West, Ship Shape at Yacht & Beach Club, Athlétique Fitness Center at Riviera, and Fitness Center at the Swan and Swan Reserve. Registered guests may use their respective resort's facility for free.

In addition to fitness centers, there are full-service spas at the Grand Floridian, Dolphin, Four Seasons Orlando, and Buena Vista Palace resorts. There may be special packages available at each location. (See pages 250–251 for details on WDW resort spas.)

PHOTO BY CHRIS HENNING

**SURREY BIKES:** Go four-wheelin' around Crescent Lake, along the Sassagoula River, or through pastoral paved pathways on a canopied surrey bike built for 2 to 4 (possibly more). Surreys may be rented at the following Walt Disney World resorts: BoardWalk, Port Orleans Riverside, Old Key West, and Saratoga Springs Resort & Spa. Each half-hour rental session runs about $20 for a 2-person bike; $22 for a 4-person bike.

**RUNNING:** Except from late fall to early spring, the weather is usually much too steamy in Central Florida for jogging. If you run very early in the morning in warm seasons, the heat is somewhat less daunting. The 1.2-mile promenade around the lake at Caribbean Beach resort is ideal for running, as is the three-quarter-mile promenade that surrounds Crescent Lake (a waterway that's bordered by the Swan and Dolphin, Yacht and Beach Club, and BoardWalk resorts), and the nearly mile-long path circling Coronado Springs' Lago Dorado. Old Key West also has scenic routes, averaging about a mile in length. There are trails at Disney's All-Stars, Grand Floridian, Contemporary, Art of Animation, Port Orleans, and Pop Century resorts, too.

**TRAIL RIDES:** Guided horseback rides into pine woods and palmetto country set off from the front of Fort Wilderness four times daily. This trip is not meant for seasoned gallopers—you can't wander off on your own. All of the horses have been culled for gentleness, so trips are suitable for novices. Cost is about $55 per person for a 45-minute tour. Kids under the age of 9 are not allowed to ride, and there's a weight limit of 250 pounds. (Younger kids can saddle up on ponies at the Tri-Circle-D Pony Farm for about $8.) Reservations are necessary and should be made up to 60 days in advance by calling 407-WDW-PLAY (939-7529).

**VOLLEYBALL:** There are white-sand volleyball courts at the following WDW resorts: Caribbean Beach, Contemporary, Coronado Springs, Disney's Old Key West, Polynesian Village, Yacht & Beach Club, Fort Wilderness Resort & Campground, and Swan & Dolphin.

# GOOD MEALS, GREAT TIMES

Although quick-service food is in great supply, it is hardly the entire Walt Disney World dining story. EPCOT adds international flavors to the WDW menu. Tempting options at the other theme parks, BoardWalk resort, and Disney Springs—not to mention new dining frontiers in the ever-growing brood of WDW resorts—make deciding where to eat a mouth-watering dilemma. Disney's ongoing effort to expand its culinary horizons has certainly been quite successful, producing prominent palate-pleasers such as The Boathouse, Sanaa, California Grill, Chef Art Smith's Homecomin', and Flying Fish, plus family favorites such as The Crystal Palace and 50's Prime Time Cafe.

The sheer number and variety of eateries around the World can be a tad overwhelming (at last count, there were well over 200 from which to choose). So we've endeavored to present WDW restaurant information in an easily digested format. The eatery descriptions in this chapter were crafted to help you choose dining experiences that will make for happy bellies all around. Comprehensive coverage of food purveyors, including sample menu options, should prove valuable as you book advance reservations and when hunger pangs strike in any given corner of the World.

In the chapter's latter section, we offer a guide to the varied bars and lounge spots of Walt Disney World, along with a briefing about Disney's (ever-evolving) reservations system and dinner show options—and assurance that great times are destined to follow.

Finally, we must reiterate that some of the Disney dynamic dining scene was in flux as this book went to press. Menu selections, meals served, Disney Dining Plan specifics (it's back for 2024!), general procedures, and other details are certain to change throughout the year. For updates, use the My Disney Experience app or website, or visit *disneyworld.com*. Cheers!

# The Restaurants of WDW
## In the Magic Kingdom

A lot has changed since Walt Disney World's original theme park opened in 1971. In those days, when it came to quelling hunger pangs, it was pretty much burger or bust. Nowadays, the options are a lot more diverse—with everything from spring rolls to cinnamon rolls, smoked turkey legs to lamb stew, and fried shrimp

**Hot Tip!** Thanks to a new feature in the My Disney Experience app, WDW guests may have a shot at snagging a spot at a table-service eatery without an advance reservation. Simply open the app and click Check Dining Availability. Then plug in the date, search by preferred time, and see what pops up. Of course, if your heart's set on a particular restaurant and time, book it as far ahead as possible!

## FIRST THINGS FIRST

The red letters at the end of each restaurant entry refer to the meals served: breakfast (**B**), lunch (**L**), dinner (**D**), and snacks (**S**).
- When you see a 🐭 at the end of an entry, it means the eatery is a Disney Dining Plan participant. Eateries may be added or dropped at any time. For updates, check *disneyworld.com*.
- **SR** means the eatery is a Disney Dining Plan Signature Restaurant. As such, it requires two table-service meal credits per person, per meal. For information such as **SR** dress code requirements, visit *disneyworld.com*.
- **MO** means the eatery offers Mobile Ordering (see page 310 for details). Should you decide to use Mobile Ordering, place your order before you're starving. It's best to plan ahead.
- Eateries have been designated inexpensive (under $15 per person), moderate ($15 to $36), expensive ($36 to $60), and very expensive ($60 and up). Prices are based on an adult-sized meal consisting of a soft drink, an entrée, and choice of one appetizer, side, or dessert, not including tax and tip. (Some snack spot totals are based on one snack and a drink.) Classifications are reflected by dollar symbols at the end of each entry. Note that breakfast and lunch may cost a bit less than dinner at some spots.
- Reservations must be modified or canceled at least 2 hours in advance to avoid fees. For details, visit *disneyworld.com*.
- All Disney table-service restaurants and fast-food locations are smoke-free. (All WDW smoking areas are outdoors and outside theme park borders.)
- Reservations for Walt Disney World's table-service restaurants (and dinner shows) can (and should) be made 60 days in advance (up to 70 for guests with a confirmed reservation at select Walt Disney World hotels); visit *disneyworld.com/dining*, or use the My Disney Experience app or website. (The website may accept reservations as early as 5:45 A.M. Eastern Time. Set two alarms!).
- The Disney Dining Plan is available as of January 9, 2024. For updates, visit *disneyworld.com/dining*.

to escargot de Bourgogne. And yes, you can still sink your teeth into a burger—beef or plant-based. Regardless of tastes or budget, the six themed "lands" in the Magic Kingdom boast a bounty of palate-pleasers for everyone in your party. Menu specifics and other details are subject to change.

# Adventureland
## TABLE SERVICE

**JUNGLE NAVIGATION CO. LTD. SKIPPER CANTEEN:** Known to many as "The Jungle Cruise Restaurant," this jovial joint is run by off-duty Jungle Cruise skippers—and the spirit of the ride permeates the place in a most amusing manner. The menu, which is infused with Asian, African, and South American influences, has starters such as Lost and Found soup, Falls Family falafel, and the appropriately corny Orinoco Ida's cachapas (corn pancakes with braised pork). Entrées include sustainable fish, fried chicken ("It tastes like chicken because it is!"), and grilled steak. Soft drinks, beer, wine, and specialty drinks are served. The eatery starts serving at about 11:30 A.M. This spot sits on our not-so-hidden gems list. **LD/$$$/🐭**

## FAST FOOD & SNACKS

**ALOHA ISLE:** After you sing with the birdies in the nearby Enchanted Tiki Room, stop here for all things pineapple—juice, floats, and the ever-popular Dole Whip® frozen pineapple soft-serve dessert. This spot has been around forever—they're definitely doing something right. **S/$**

**SUNSHINE TREE TERRACE:** This sublime snack stand, across from the Swiss Family Treehouse, lets you take a break with a refreshing soft-serve in a cup or a float (with soda). Choose from orange, strawberry, vanilla, chocolate, or a classic swirl (vanilla soft-serve swirled with orange Dole Whip®). Also served: fountain beverages, coffee, and hot cocoa. Sunshine Tree Terrace has been dishing out treats for as long as we can remember. **S/$**

**TORTUGA TAVERN:** The mostly covered casual spot across from the Pirates of the Caribbean offers teriyaki burgers (with red onion and pineapple), chicken strips (tossed in a sweet, orange-soy glaze), all-beef hot dogs (served with house-made chips), and assorted soft drinks. This tavern tends to operate on a seasonal basis. **LS/$$/🐭**

# Fantasyland
## TABLE SERVICE

**BE OUR GUEST RESTAURANT:** Nestled beneath Beast's castle, this (somewhat overrated) eatery transports guests into the realm of Disney's *Beauty and the Beast*. Guests are seated in one of three dining rooms—the cavernous Grand Ballroom, the mysterious (and rather dark) West Wing, or the Rose Gallery—and enjoy a fixed-price table-service lunch or dinner. (Reservations are recommended for all meals.) Note that all dining rooms offer the same fixed price menu.

Last we checked, the menu offerings were the same for lunch and dinner (subject to change). Adults choose an appetizer such as salad, french onion soup, potato leek soup, escargots, or duck and pork terrine.

Entrées include pork chop, center-cut filet mignon, roasted chicken, trout amandine, and Valdouvan spiced vegetables. Specialty drinks, beer, hard cider, wine, and Champagne are offered (for an extra charge).

Youngsters choose an appetizer from among fruit and cheese plate, salad, or applesauce. Their entrée selection includes beef tenderloin, pan-seared chicken, and mac and cheese. Each comes with 2 sides such as zucchini, rice, sweet potatoes, and green beans.

The decadent finale is presented as a dessert trio: a chocolate tart with "Grey Stuff," crisp pearls, and a white chocolate wafer; dark chocolate truffle, and lemon macaron. Kids may choose fruit with yogurt dip or a dessert trio.

Details are apt to change in 2024. To learn if breakfast will be served during your visit to Magic Kingdom, go to *disneyworld.com.* **LD/$$$$/🐭/SR/MO**

**CINDERELLA'S ROYAL TABLE:** You don't have to be a royal to dine like one. At least, not in the Magic Kingdom. This regal eatery, tucked inside Cinderella Castle, is a high-ceilinged, majestic banquet hall. It's tiny as Disney spots go, but there's no feeling cramped—thanks to a small number of tables and towering windows. Hosts and hostesses wear Renaissance-inspired garb and address guests as "my lady" or "my lord."

Cinderella invites "Fairytale Dining" guests into her regal home each day—and traditionally greets them in the Castle lobby. Her princess friends interact with guests in the upstairs dining room. Breakfast favorites have included shrimp and grits, baked quiche, and caramel apple-stuffed french toast, along with traditional fare. The lunch and dinner menus showcase seasonal ingredients, with items such as beef tenderloin, Parisian gnocchi, braised chicken and pasta, and sustainable catch of the day. Wine, beer, Champagne, and sparkling wines are available, but come with an additional charge.

Cost for the fixed-price breakfast starts at about $65 for adults and about $39 for kids ages 3 to 9. Lunch and dinner are offered as 3-course, fixed-price meals and cost about $79 for adults and $47 for kids. Prices quoted here do not include tax and gratuity and may differ depending on the date. Reservations are a must for Cinderella's regal restaurant. Potential diners who

are registered at a Walt Disney World–owned-and-operated resort should note the Hot Tip on page 266.

Cancellations must be made at least 24 hours ahead to avoid paying full price. Cinderella's is an extremely difficult table to reserve (see below)—don't get little ones' hopes up until you actually book it. Good luck! **BLD/$$$–$$$$/❤/SR**

### FAST FOOD & SNACKS

**BIG TOP TREATS:** Inside the Big Top Souvenirs tent, this counter offers character apples, caramel apples, cake pops, caramel corn, brownies, cookies, crispy treats, and Goofy's Glaciers (slushy treats). **S/$**

## ONE TOUGH TICKET

Cinderella's Royal Table is consistently one of the most difficult restaurant reservations to secure at Walt Disney World. Why? For starters, Cinderella is one popular princess. And there's the allure of dining in the castle—the most famous landmark in the world's most popular theme park.

Potential guests may make a reservation via the My Disney Experience mobile app or website, or by visiting *disneyworld .com/dining.* The official booking window opens at 6 A.M., but it may open sooner (possibly as early as 5:45 A.M.) Eastern Standard Time, 60 days in advance. The meal must be paid for in full when the reservation is made. There is no charge for children under age 3, but they must be included in your reservation.

Expect your credit card to be charged immediately upon making the reservation. Cancellations or changes to the reservation must be made at least 24 hours ahead to receive a full refund. The only one who can change or cancel a reservation is the one whose name is on the credit card. Reservations cannot be transferred. Guests using the Disney Dining Plan must also book the table with a credit card, but it will not be charged. However, two table-service credits are required for all meals eaten here, as Cinderella's Table is designated a "Signature" restaurant. Details are subject to change.

Whew! That's a lot of work for one dining experience. Is it worth it? Judging by all the smiles we see day in and day out, we have to say yes.

**CHESHIRE CAFE:** This small stand is a good spot to cool off with a themed slushie, orange juice, coffee (hot or cold-brew), hot tea, and water. The cafe also serves pastries and pepper jack pretzels. The cold-brew coffee makes us smile like the Cheshire Cat. **S/$**

**THE FRIAR'S NOOK:** This window sells breakfast sandwiches, hot dogs, bratwurst, plant-based bratwurst (dogs and brats are served with tots), bacon mac and cheese, bacon mac and cheese tots, and soft drinks. Menu items are subject to change. **BLS/$–$$/❤**

**GASTON'S TAVERN:** A cozy little lodge nestled in Fantasyland's Enchanted Forest, Gaston's serves (huge) warm cinnamon rolls, Grey Stuff cupcakes, ham and cheese sandwiches, and soft drinks. What's the specialty drink at this teetotaling tavern? LeFou's Brew—a refreshing, not-overly-sweet concoction made from frozen apple juice with a hint of toasted marshmallow and topped with all-natural passion fruit-mango foam. It tends to please palates of all ages. And, yes, Gaston really does use antlers in all of his decorating. **LDS/$–$$/❤**

**PINOCCHIO VILLAGE HAUS:** One of the better spots to target with kids in tow, Pinocchio Village Haus is also a good place to take picky adult eaters. It may seem small from the outside, but there are many dining rooms through that door. One room boasts picture windows that overlook the It's a Small World loading area. It's fun to watch the boats bob by as you munch on lunch. Pinocchio offers flatbreads (aka pizza)—including a plant-based variety, chicken strips, tomato basil soup, Caesar salad with chicken, fries, bread sticks served with marinara sauce, and soft drinks. For dessert, there's a seasonal selection and sweet slushies. Kids' picks include packaged PB&J sandwiches, flatbreads (pepperoni or plain), and chicken strips—all served with a choice of two sides, and a beverage. **LDS/$$/❤/MO**

**PRINCE ERIC'S VILLAGE MARKET:** Appropriately anchored across from The Little Mermaid attraction, this alfresco snack spot sells grapes, pickles, turkey legs (served with chips), and soft pretzels (with or without beer cheese sauce). The prince also proffers bottled beverages and frozen soft drinks. This snack location may operate on a seasonal basis. **S/$$**

**STORYBOOK TREATS:** Ice cream fans enjoy this window near the Many Adventures of Winnie the Pooh attraction. It offers creamy soft-serve in cups (vanilla, chocolate, and swirl); hot fudge and strawberry sundaes; plus ice cream floats. Fountain beverages and bottled water are also served. **S/$**

# Frontierland
## FAST FOOD & SNACKS

**GOLDEN OAK OUTPOST:** This wagon offers chicken strips (served plain or "loaded"), french fries (topped with chili cheese), warm fresh-baked chocolate chip cookies, sweet tea slushies, and assorted soft drinks. The outpost operates on a seasonal basis. **LDS/$–$$/❤**

**PECOS BILL TALL TALE INN & CAFE:** Pecos Bill has been feeding hungry cowpokes for more than 40 years. The look has changed over time, as have the offerings (the prices have gone up a bit, too). These days, Pecos Bill is serving cheeseburgers, fajita platters, salad (served with chicken or pork), vegetable rice bowl, and nachos (topped with ground beef, chicken, or pork). Churros

PHOTO BY JILL SAFRO

and yogurt are available, too. Options for the young'uns include cheeseburgers, chicken rice bowl, tacos, or mac and cheese, and come with a choice of two sides and low-fat milk or bottled water. Soft drinks such as soda pop, chocolate milk, coffee, tea, cocoa, and orange juice are served. **LDS/$$/❤/MO**

**WESTWARD HO!:** Amble on over to Westward Ho! for nibbles such as breakfast sandwiches, corn dog nuggets, candied bacon skewer, jalapeño poppers, bear claws, frozen lemonade, coffee, and other soft drinks. It is across from Prairie Outpost & Supply. **BLDS/$**

# Liberty Square
## TABLE SERVICE

**THE DIAMOND HORSESHOE:** An "all-you-care-to-enjoy" Saloon Feast is served for lunch and dinner (about $39 per adult/$21 per child). The bountiful vittles have included roast turkey breast, pot roast, and oven-roasted pork with mashed potatoes, stuffing, mac and cheese, and seasonal vegetables. A sweet ending to the meal may come in the form of "Ooey Gooey Toffee Cake" (vanilla toffee cake with chocolate sauce and vanilla ice cream). There's a plant-based option, too. Beer, wine, cocktails, and soft drinks are served. This location may operate on a seasonal basis. **LD/$$$/❤**

**LIBERTY TREE TAVERN:** Step back in time at this Early American tavern where the detailed decor has a tendency to out-dazzle the fare. Here, wallpaper looks as if it might have come from Colonial Williamsburg, curtains hang from cloth loops, and the rooms are filled with mementos that might have been found in the homes of Thomas Jefferson, George Washington, and Ben Franklin. The restaurant is aptly located across the square from the Hall of Presidents attraction.

Meals are served family style (platters are delivered to your table until you say "when"). The all-you-care-to-eat feast features salad, oven-roasted pork, roast turkey, pot roast, mac and cheese, a plant-based option, stuffing, toffee cake, and more (at press time, the menu here was similar to that at the Diamond Horseshoe). Liberty Tree also offers beer, wine, sangria, mimosas, and hard cider. The cost for lunch and dinner is about $39 for adults and $21 for kids ages 3 through 9. Some drinks—including those of the spirited variety—cost extra. Reservations are recommended (arrive about 20 minutes early). Disney characters do not visit here. **LD/$$$/❤**

**Hot Tip!** Perk alert! If you have a confirmed reservation at a Disney-owned-and-operated resort hotel, you can book—starting 60 days prior to your check-in date—dining reservations for up to 10 days of your resort stay. That amounts to getting a 1- to 10-day head start on everyone else. Check the My Disney Experience mobile app or website, or visit *disneyworld.com* for updates.

## FAST FOOD & SNACKS

**COLUMBIA HARBOUR HOUSE:** This lively spot adds some interesting (and healthier) options to the quick-service lineup, including grilled salmon with rice and steamed green beans; grilled shrimp skewers with green beans; lobster roll with fries; and "Hail to the Leaf!" mixed green salad (with apples, cranberries, onions, cheese, and chicken strips). The menu also offers a New England shrimp boil, "trio platter" (fried shrimp, chicken strips, and battered fish served with hushpuppies), plant-based burgers, battered-fish sandwiches, and New England clam chowder. The kids' menu includes fried or grilled shrimp, grilled salmon, and chicken strips. Fountain beverages, plus milk, coffee, tea, cocoa, juice, shakes, and lemonade slushies are available.

Disney has done up this food emporium with style—with antiques, model ships, harpoons, nautical instruments, and lace tieback curtains. In addition to the chowder, we savor the salmon and lean toward the grilled shrimp skewers. Upstairs dining rooms may be less busy than those on the first floor. **LDS/$$/😋**

**SLEEPY HOLLOW:** Often missed by guests rushing toward park hot spots, this window has a lot to offer. Breakfast (including a fresh fruit waffle sandwich with chocolate-hazelnut spread) is served until 11 A.M. After that, look for sweet and spicy chicken waffle sandwiches, hand-dipped corn dogs served with housemade potato chips,

waffles with heavenly toppings (fresh fruit, chocolate-hazelnut spread, strawberries and whipped cream, etc.), and freshly made funnel cakes (topped with powdered sugar or strawberries and powdered sugar). Drinks include fountain beverages, cold brew coffee, hot tea, hot coffee, cocoa, milk, and juice (apple and orange). Sleepy Hollow is near the Liberty Square bridge. Eat on the patio and get a stunning view of Cinderella Castle at no extra charge. **BLDS/$–$$/😋**

# Main Street, U.S.A.

## TABLE SERVICE

**THE CRYSTAL PALACE:** One of the Magic Kingdom's cherished landmarks, this spot takes its architectural cues from a similar structure that once stood in New York and from San Francisco's Conservatory of Flowers, which still graces that city's Golden Gate Park. The place is spacious, with tables scattered amid a Victorian-style indoor garden complete with flowers and hanging greenery. Tables in the front look out on flower beds, while those toward the east end offer views of a courtyard. What's the big draw here? Winnie the Pooh and his pals from the Hundred Acre Wood visit diners during all meals!

A bountiful buffet features American favorites prepared before you in the onstage kitchen. In the early hours, expect a variety of hearty breakfast selections (pancakes, waffles, biscuits & gravy, freshly prepared eggs, fresh fruit, pastries, etc.) For lunch and dinner, choose from selections such as roasted carved meats, fried chicken, pastas, shrimp creole, veggies, mashed potatoes, and more. Dessert options may include warm seasonal cobbler, pudding, strawberry shortcake, pastries, cookies, and soft-serve ice cream.

All menu items are subject to change without notice. The cost for lunch and dinner runs about $59 for adults and $38 for kids ages 3 through 9. Alcoholic beverages (wine, beer, white sangria, mimosas, and hard cider) are available for an additional fee. The breakfast meal runs about $45 for adults and $29 for kids (ages 3 to 9). Reservations are a must. **BLD/$$$/**🐭

**PLAZA RESTAURANT:** This windowed establishment next to the Plaza Ice Cream Parlor is done up in mirrors with sinuous Art Nouveau frames. Lunch and dinner choices include BLT salad, seared crab cakes, seasonal soup, burgers (meat and plant-based), home-style meatloaf, and hot and cold sandwiches such as fried chicken or Plaza Reuben—plus superb sundaes, heavenly hand-dipped milk shakes, and dark chocolate banana bread pudding. Soft drinks, coffee and tea (hot and cold), beer, wine, sangria, and specialty drinks are offered. Reservations are recommended. Breakfast was not offered at press time, but may return. **LD/$$$/**🐭

**TONY'S TOWN SQUARE:** Tony's decor was inspired by Walt Disney's feature *Lady and the Tramp* (which can be viewed in the waiting area). The menu offers Italian specialties, including Caesar salad, spaghetti (with meat-balls or plant-based meatballs), and garlic bread. Entrées include fettuccine Alfredo (with shrimp or chicken), chicken parmigiana, sustainable fish of the day, shrimp scampi, orecchiette with spicy house-made Italian sausage, and marinated hanger steak. If you require allergy-friendly pasta, just ask—Tony is happy to accommodate. Beer, wine, and specialty soft drinks are offered, too. Top it off with an Italian sweet (gelato, spumoni tart, Italian strawberry short cake, and/or foamy cappuccino). If you time it right, you can fold your napkin, pay the bill, and mosey out to Main Street U.S.A., to enjoy the fireworks from one of the best vantage points in the park. While this doesn't make our must-do list, Tony's Town Square is a very popular destination—reservations are highly recommended. **LD/$$$/**🐭

PHOTO BY JILL SAFRO

## MAGIC KINGDOM RESORTS

Is the Magic Kingdom open late when you plan to visit? If so, consider heading over to the Contemporary, Polynesian Village, Grand Floridian, or Wilderness Lodge to have an early dinner, and then return to finish the day at the park. Each of the aforementioned resorts is reachable by monorail and/or water taxi. (Illuminated pathways connect the Magic Kingdom with Contemporary, Grand Floridian, and Polynesian. The trek takes 8 to 12 minutes to reach Contemporary, about 15 to 20 minutes for the Grand Floridian, and 20 to 25 minutes for the Poly.) Remember to keep sporting that MagicBand if you used it for admission or keep your ticket handy for re-entry into the Magic Kingdom. (You will have to pass through a security check to re-enter the park.) Transportation generally runs for about one hour after the park's posted closing time for the day. Note that, as with most Walt Disney World table-service eateries, reservations are necessary at resort restaurants. Don't forget to book that table!

## FAST FOOD & SNACKS

**CASEY'S CORNER:** Casey's is a grand slam for baseball fans—and those who just happen to love the food associated with "America's pastime," hot dogs. This old-fashioned stop is on the west side of Main Street (near Crystal Palace restaurant). Tables line the sidewalk, where a ragtime pianist often tickles the ivories. There's a room with indoor seating. The fare retains the baseball game mood—hot dogs (plain, chili cheese, plant-based, and more), corn dog nuggets, fries (with or without chili or chili and cheese), fresh fruit, coffee (regular and decaf), hot cocoa, and soft drinks (including the possibility of frozen "Mint Julep" lemonade). Hot dogs come in regular-size and the foot-long variety. Casey's is a Magic Kingdom classic. **LDS/$$/**🐭**/MO**

**MAIN STREET BAKERY:** This festive Main Street landmark resembles a turn-of-the-twentieth-century bakery and coffee shop. If the sight of this old-fashioned storefront doesn't lure you in, the aroma most certainly will. The Main Street Bakery is a nice choice for a light breakfast, salads, sandwiches, or coffee break. The vast array of juice, tea, and coffee concoctions comes courtesy of Starbucks. Assorted pastries, fresh-baked cookies, fruit and veggies, Frappuccinos®, and other snack items are also served. **BLDS/$–$$/🐭**

**PLAZA ICE CREAM PARLOR:** The Plaza boasts the Magic Kingdom's largest variety of hand-scooped ice cream, including mint chocolate chip, vanilla, strawberry, and cookies & cream. There's also no-sugar-added raspberry sorbet and plant-based treats. This locale is perfect for a before-the-parade or an on-the-way-out-of-the-park nosh. Little ones dig the Mickey Mouse kids' cone. (To keep things moving, select your flavors and desired number of scoops before jumping in line.) They have sundaes, too—including those served in a waffle bowl—and (if you're lucky) the Mickey's Kitchen Sink for two (a seasonal offering which is a sink-like version of the Mouse's classic red trousers). **S/$**

# Tomorrowland
## FAST FOOD & SNACKS

**AUNTIE GRAVITY'S GALACTIC GOODIES:** Ice cream may not seem futuristic, but chances are it'll be around at least another billion years, give or take. Auntie G's offers

## HEALTHIER OPTIONS

Health-conscious folks need not abandon all restraint for want of suitable sustenance. Most WDW restaurants can accommodate requests for low-fat, low-cholesterol, low-salt, low-carb, and plant-based entrées. Fast-food stands may feature healthier fare such as salads, grilled chicken or fish sandwiches, fresh fruit, fresh veggies, and no-sugar-added desserts. The Walt Disney World trend toward healthier dining options extends to kids' meals, too. Many come with a beverage choice of low-fat milk or water, and a side dish such as unsweetened applesauce, carrots, or fresh fruit. These healthier selections are easy to find on menus throughout Walt Disney World. Just look for a Disney Check or Leaf symbol.

(plant-based) strawberry smoothies, cups of soft-serve ice cream (chocolate, vanilla, or swirl), sundaes, and floats. Chocolate shakes and soft drinks are served, too. There's virtually no atmosphere in this corner of the galaxy, but we still gravitate toward the frozen goodies. **S/$–$$**

**COOL SHIP:** This (seasonal) spaceship/snack stand is cool for two reasons. First, the water spray it provides during steamy months is beyond refreshing, and second: It serves ice cream novelties, popcorn, cotton candy, and cinnamon-glazed nuts. Fountain and bottled drinks are sold, too. There's no seating, but Cosmic Ray's has plenty and it's just a hop, skip, and a jump away. **S/$**

# MAGIC KINGDOM MEALTIME TIPS

- The hours from about 11 A.M. to 2 P.M. and 5 P.M. to 7 P.M. are the mealtime rush hours in Magic Kingdom. Try to eat a bit earlier or later whenever possible.
- When visiting a fast-food spot, know that queues farthest from an entrance may have a shorter wait. And consider the (ideally) queue-free Mobile Ordering option (see page 310 for details.)
- It is virtually impossible to snag same-day reservations for Magic Kingdom table-service restaurants (with the possible exception of Jungle Navigation Co. Ltd. Skipper Canteen in Adventureland). Be sure to book your desired eatery well in advance.
- Dining reservations may be made via *disneyworld.com/dining* and by using the My Disney Experience app or website. Book your table as far in advance as possible. At press time, that was up to 60 days before your scheduled visit to the Magic Kingdom. Guests with a confirmed reservation at most WDW resorts can book up to 10 days' worth of restaurant reservations, starting 60 days before their check-in date.
- Consider taking the monorail or a water taxi (or walking) to the Contemporary, Polynesian, or Grand Floridian to have dinner in a resort restaurant, and then return to the Magic Kingdom after you eat. Reservations are recommended. Allow plenty of extra time. And remember to keep your ticket or MagicBand handy for re-entry to the park.

**COSMIC RAY'S STARLIGHT CAFE:** Head straight to Ray's for chopped vegetable with crispy noodle salad (plain or with shrimp or chicken), chicken strips, plant-based patty melts, bacon cheeseburgers, grilled chicken sandwiches, fries, fruit, and chocolate cake. Kids choose from chicken strips and mac and cheese. An Audio-Animatronics lounge lizard known as Sonny Eclipse (see above) entertains in the indoor dining room. There are several counters from which to order, but they all serve the same fare. There's lots of indoor and outdoor seating. **LDS/$–$$/☙/MO**

**ENERGY BYTES:** Positioned near the entrance of TRON Lightcycle/Run, this kiosk specializes in **NEW** sweet and spicy small bites. Gracing the menu are beef and broccoli digital dumplings, chocolate cake doughnut holes (with mocha sauce and popping candy), strawberry ice-O-forms (ice cream mochi topped with carmelized graham cracker crumbs and a cheesecake foam), watermelon refreshers (sweet slushie beverages), and cold brew with mocha milk. **S/$–$$/MO**

> **Hot Tip!** To help reduce your time spent waiting in line, dozens of WDW's quick-service spots accept mobile orders. Simply place your order via the (free) My Disney Experience app. As you arrive at the eatery, click the "I'm here" button (in the app) and the kitchen will prepare your order. When your food's ready, you'll get a notification to fetch it by the Mobile Pickup sign at the counter.

**LUNCHING PAD AT ROCKETTOWER PLAZA:** If it's a snack or simple meal you're after, stop at the base of the Astro Orbiter, located in the center of Tomorrowland's concrete plaza. This window dispenses hot dogs, warm stuffed pretzels (filled with sweet cream cheese), churros, Mickey-shaped pretzels (with warm cheese sauce), soda slushies, hot cocoa, and soft drinks. **LDS/$–$$/☙/MO**

**TOMORROWLAND TERRACE:** This stark location has been known to operate seasonally and serve uncomplicated fare. Some tables afford stunning views of Cinderella Castle. Traditionally, this is the site of the theme park's fireworks dessert party. For dessert-party details, visit *disneyworld.com.* **S/$$$$**

## BABY NEEDS

Babies. They're a needy lot. Fortunately, most of the requisite supplies can be found somewhere at Walt Disney World—if you know where to look. Formula and jarred food are sold at Baby Care Centers in the theme parks and all WDW resorts. Most restaurants offer kids' menus with toddler-friendly food (mac and cheese, chicken strips, and the like).

If your baby is partial to a specific formula or food, consider shipping a box of it to your hotel before you leave home. (Note that a $6 delivery fee will be charged to your room for each parcel handled by Front Desk personnel.) Keep in mind that there are several grocery stores near Disney property. If you have a car, it is worth the trip (a Guest Relations clerk can help with directions). Selections are more varied, as are the prices. Stash items in an in-room beverage cooler—they're standard in all Disney-owned-and-operated resorts. Some additional points of interest regarding baby diners at Walt Disney World:

- Most table-service eateries have high chairs and booster seats for little ones. Request them when you make your restaurant reservation. Quick-service spots offer high chairs on a first-come, first-served basis. Ask a cast member for assistance if you need help finding or transporting one to a table.

- Stroller use inside restaurants is not permitted due to fire safety codes. Kindly park it outside the eatery.

- WDW eateries can be chilly. Take a sweater or blanket.

- Be it a fast-food or table-service restaurant, take (quiet) toys to keep youngsters busy.

- The following resorts have snack bars that keep long hours: Grand Floridian, Polynesian, Dolphin, Wyndham, and Hilton Buena Vista Palace. The late-night pickings may be slim, but milk and cereal are served all day long.

- If you'd like a comfortable spot to nurse your tot, head to a Baby Care Center in any of the theme parks. They all have rooms with rocking chairs.

- If you're headed for a long day in a theme park, pack simple, healthy snacks for hungry toddlers. And look for the Disney check symbol on menus (it marks healthier options).

- To make your dining experience a little less harried, consider feeding your baby before you arrive at a restaurant.

- If you prefer organic milk (and more) for your kids, consider ordering from a service such as *gardengrocer.com,* Amazon Fresh, or Instacart, or swinging by a local grocery store (for details, see page 49).

# In EPCOT

The eclectic, international lineup of fare offered here threatens to overshadow the attractions themselves. With no fewer than 11 different countries permanently represented in the World Showcase section of the park, EPCOT provides guests with the opportunity to eat their way around the world without leaving Central Florida. Less ambitious diners will likely have all their taste needs met here, too—there's a bountiful food court in World Nature's Land pavilion, as well as a smattering of satiating snack spots and quick-service eateries. Reservations are an important factor in the Disney dining equation, and EPCOT is no exception; be sure to book tables as far in advance as possible.

## World Celebration
### FAST FOOD & SNACKS

**CONNECTIONS CAFE** (near Spaceship Earth): Housed in the same modern space as Connections Eatery, this cafe is EPCOT's resident Starbucks. As such, it's an ideal spot for a satisfying java jolt, a light meal, or a sweet snack. Pastries, fruit, and cookies are available—as are teas, specialty drinks, and more. **BLDS/$–$$/❤**

**CONNECTIONS EATERY** (near Spaceship Earth): Connect with flavors from around the world at this expansive new eatery. The menu offers burgers (including classic American, French Bistro, and Southwestern), pizza, and salads. There are several selections tailored to tots, too. Be sure to check out the majestic mural as you enjoy your meal. **LD/$$/❤/MO**

## World Nature
### TABLE SERVICE

**CORAL REEF** (The Seas with Nemo & Friends): This peaceful, water-themed restaurant is all about nibbling on creatively prepared fish under the watchful eyes of their brethren. The place is decorated in cool greens and blues to complement its surroundings, and every table has a panoramic view of a living coral reef; some are right up against the glass. (Don't worry: You are not actually eating EPCOT residents—most of Walt Disney World's catches come fresh from fishing boats each day.) Menu items can run the gamut from fish and shellfish, including shrimp and mahi mahi, to slow-roasted prime rib and seasonal chicken dishes (such as Harissa chicken) for those who are satisfied by simply spying on the sea life. The menu tends to vary seasonally. Reservations are recommended. **LD/$$$/❤**

**GARDEN GRILL** (The Land): Garden Grill diners are often so distracted by the sights and the jovial hosts (Chip, Dale, and other Disney pals) that they may not realize the restaurant is actually moving. As the eatery slowly revolves, it moves past scenery featured in the Living with the Land boat ride. The view was designed with diners in mind, and provides them with a peek into a farmhouse window that's out of viewing range of the waterborne passengers.

Breakfast (it's back!) has included cinnamon breakfast loaf, seasonal fruit, scrambled eggs, cheesy potato casserole, grilled flank steak with ranchero sauce, and Mickey-shaped waffles. For lunch and dinner, the Grill serves garden salad, BBQ-roasted chicken, grilled beef with chimichurri, mac and cheese, mashed potatoes, Southern-style spoon bread, veggies (some of which are grown in The Land Pavilion), and shortcake. The cost for breakfast runs about $42 for adults, $27 for kids; lunch and dinner cost about $55 for adults, $36 for kids. Soft drinks are included—beer, wine, and specialty drinks come with an extra charge. Meals are served family style (shared platters for the table; there's no kids' menu). It's not an especially kid-friendly presentation, as items touch and overlap. Reservations are recommended.

**To recap:** This character-hosted, family-style eatery moves in a circle. It's imperceptible to most, but if you are highly sensitive to motion, it may be best to dine in a more stationary environment. **BLD/$$$/❤**

# World Discovery

## TABLE SERVICE

**SPACE 220** (near Mission: SPACE): "Orbiting Earth" at an altitude of 220 miles, this space station/family restaurant promises an out-of-this-world dining experience. Hovering about 20 miles above the International Space Station (ISS), this stellar spot serves up modern American cuisine (the menu features salads, pastas, burgers, fish, chicken, and steaks) and dramatic, panoramic views of the big, blue marble we all call home. The fixed price dining experience offers two courses for lunch and three for dinner. In addition to the celestial eats, Space 220 boasts a top-notch wine and craft beer list—with no fewer than 1,000 bottles from which to choose. The lounge area offers beverages and "flight bites" (small plates).

Guests travel to this 350-seat eatery by boarding a special spaceship/elevator near the entrance (the restaurant is actually located on terra firma, not far from the Mission: SPACE attraction). Reservations are required, though a handful of bar stools may be available on a first-come, first-served basis. Inquire at the entrance. **LD/$$$–$$$$**

## FAST FOOD & SNACKS

**JOFFREY'S COFFEE & TEA COMPANY** (near the EPCOT monorail station): Stop here for a java jolt on your way into or out of the park. This beverage stand specializes in coffee and tea, but it offers other drinks and baked treats. **S/$**

PHOTO BY JILL SAFRO

**SUNSHINE SEASONS** (The Land): It's the closest thing to a food court you'll find in a WDW park, but a bit more upscale. Located near the entrance to Soarin' Around the World on the pavilion's lower level, Sunshine Seasons is an ideal destination for parties who can't quite agree on any one type of fare—there's bound to be something for everyone. Tables are scattered in several seating areas, beneath colorful hot-air balloons. Snagging a

## HOLIDAY HOOPLA

During the Christmas holiday season, EPCOT's World Showcase usually hosts a special Candlelight Processional. The show features a stirring choral concert and a reading of the Nativity story by a celebrity narrator. The event is free (with park admission), but the general admission seating fills up as early as two hours before showtime. Rather than wait in line, we prefer to book a dining package—one that combines a meal at an EPCOT eatery with guaranteed seating at the Processional—the star attraction of EPCOT's International Festival of the Holidays celebration (see page 12). For details, use the My Disney Experience website or app, or visit *disneyworld.com/dining*. We whole-heartedly recommend this package—sure, it's a luxury, but consider it an early Christmas present for yourself!

table can be a challenge during peak mealtimes. (There can be a bit of pedestrian congestion, too, thanks to the popularity of the Soarin' attraction.)

Offerings at Sunshine Seasons may include veggie sandwiches, cheese or pepperoni pizza rolls, stir-fried shrimp, oak-grilled rotisserie chicken, oak-grilled salmon, spicy fish tacos, roast beef sandwich, Mongolian beef, Caesar salad, Asian vegetable noodle salad, and power salad (with chicken, quinoa, almonds, and honey vinaigrette). In addition to the seasonally inspired desserts, expect brownies, chocolate chip cookies, cupcakes, and other sweet treats. A grab-and-go area is stocked with wraps, fruit and cheese plates, veggies and hummus, and assorted snacks. Details are subject to change.

It's a good idea to split up your party and stand in several lines at the same time (when multiple serving stations are open). That will increase your chances of actually eating together. Before you separate, select a table. That way, everyone in the group will know where to meet after they forage for their meals. It's also a nice spot to take a load off your feet before you jump in the line for Soarin' Around the World. Note that this food court does not offer the Mobile Ordering option. Just a heads up. **LDS/$–$$/❤**

### DID YOU KNOW?

More than 30 tons of fruits and vegetables have been grown at The Land pavilion in EPCOT and served to guests dining in Walt Disney World restaurants.

# World Showcase
## TABLE SERVICE

**AKERSHUS ROYAL BANQUET HALL** (Norway): The castle of Akershus dominates Oslo's harbor and is considered the most impressive of all Norway's medieval fortresses. It is actually half fortress and half palace, and many of its grand halls continue to be used for elaborate state banquets. Inside EPCOT's castle-like Akershus, hungry guests are treated to authentic royal Norwegian cuisine. They also get to dine with royalty—as Disney princesses interact with guests throughout the meal.

An all-inclusive price entitles lunch and dinner guests to an all-you-care-to-eat feast of American fare (corn dog nuggets, mac & cheese, etc.), and dishes that don't often leave Scandinavia: field green salad with lingonberry vinaigrette, traditional Norwegian meatballs, and *lefse* (potato flatbread) with cardamom-cinnamon butter. Entrées of note: grilled salmon with herbed butter and *Kylling og Melboller* (chicken and dumplings). Sides, soft drinks, and Norwegian-inspired desserts are included— as are visits by Disney princesses.

For breakfast, guests may enjoy all-you-care-to-eat fare (bacon, scrambled eggs, Norwegian waffles, potato casserole, and sausage are brought to the table) as Disney royals mingle with diners. Ariel, Jasmine, Snow White, and Sleeping Beauty have all popped in for a visit. The character appearance schedule varies. Coffee, tea, and soft drinks are included. Reservations are necessary. Cancellations must be made at least 2 hours in advance to avoid the $10 per-person penalty. Breakfast costs about $53 for adults (age 10 and up) and $34 for kids (ages 3 to 9); lunch and dinner run about $63 (adults) and $41 (kids). Prices don't include tax or gratuity. **BLD/$$$$/❤/SR**

**BIERGARTEN** (Germany): Situated in the back of the St. Georgsplatz in the Germany pavilion, this tiered eatery is a jolly stop on the EPCOT world dining tour. This is partly because the meticulous theming makes it feel like an actual Bavarian village. But equal credit for the *gemütlich* (pleasant) atmosphere goes to the spot's spirited entertainment.

There are appearances by Bavarian musicians—each wearing traditional lederhosen or a dirndl—who play accordions, cowbells, a musical saw, and a harp-like stringed instrument known as the "wooden laughter." The entertaining shows take place on a stage in the dining hall throughout the day.

The fare is hearty and presented as an all-you-care-to-enjoy buffet feast. Highlights include bratwurst, sausage, chicken, späetzle, seasonal fish, schnitzel, assorted cold dishes, salads, pretzel rolls, kid-friendly selections, and desserts (cheesecake, apple strudel, cookies, fruit salad, etc.). Entertainment is intermittent and there's plenty of time to enjoy the pleasant setting. Reservations are recommended. **LD/$$$/❤**

**CHEFS DE FRANCE** (France): "Bright lights, big dining room" describes this inviting Parisian brasserie. With some of France's best chefs responsible for this kitchen, the results are usually rewarding. The menu features fresh ingredients readily available from Florida purveyors, though the restaurant imports as many key ingredients from France as possible.

The offerings are in the nouvelle French cuisine style, which involves lighter sauces using less cream and butter than in classic French cooking. Menu selections include sustainable salmon, beef tenderloin, and boeuf bourguignon. Soups and appetizers such as French onion soup (topped with gooey Gruyère cheese) and escargots are all-day staples. Valrhona chocolate tart with white chocolate mousse and vanilla crème brûlée are dessert specialties of note. Chefs de France is one of the most popular (and pricey) World Showcase eateries. Reservations are highly recommended (book your table as far in advance as possible). **LD/$$$–$$$$**

**LE CELLIER STEAKHOUSE** (Canada): This wine-cellar-like spot is a popular dining destination. The atmospheric eatery has low slung ceilings, stone walls, and flickers

**Hot Tip!** Do you plan to see the park's nighttime spectacular at EPCOT's World Showcase? Be sure to check the schedule before booking your dinner reservation. (You can use the My Disney Experience app or website.) Try to time it so your evening meal winds up no later than 20 minutes before the show starts—and tell your server when you arrive at the restaurant.

of candlelight. Designated as a Signature restaurant for both lunch and dinner, Le Cellier Steakhouse costs a bit more than many other Walt Disney World (and real world) eateries. The steakhouse, unsurprisingly, specializes in quality beef entrées. To start, there is a (complimentary) basket of warm bread, that includes a pretzel roll, plus sourdough and whole-grain creations. The filet mignon with mushroom risotto is a perennial fan favorite. Other main course selections on the somewhat abbreviated menu include New York strip steak, bison strip loin, grilled scallops, and dry-aged pork chop with goat cheese polenta. Many choose to start with the creamy cheddar cheese soup made with Moosehead beer and smoked bacon, but the citrus seafood medley, slow-roasted pork belly, heirloom beets with goat cheese, and cheese & charcuterie plate are appetizer options, too. Canadian beers and wines make for pairing possibilities. Reservations are a must—this is a popular and relatively tiny Walt Disney World restaurant. **LD/$$$$/🐭/SR**

**LA HACIENDA DE SAN ANGEL** (Mexico): Open for dinner or a late lunch (starting at about 3 or 4 P.M.), this festive facility fits nicely on the shore of the World Showcase Lagoon. The menu has starters such as *queso fundido* (melted cheese with chorizo, peppers, and onions with flour tortillas); *flautas* (fried tortillas with potato, chipotle chicken, and cheese), guacamole, tostadas de camaron, and ensalada hacienda. Entrées include short ribs with whipped boniato, carrots, and asparagus, ancho agave-marinated New York strip steak, fried-shrimp tacos, roasted chicken breast with poblano cream sauce, braised duck tacos, and chile relleno. We highly recommend the *parrillada del mar* (a bountiful seafood platter for two). For dessert, there's a sorbet trio, chocolate bread pudding, sweet corn ice cream, *tres leches* (milk-soaked

## LET 'EM EAT CAKE!

What could possibly make celebrating a special occasion at Walt Disney World even more special? How about a custom-made, personalized cake? You can have one delivered to just about any table-service eatery on Disney property. Simply add the cake to your reservation via the My Disney Experience app or website or *disneyworld.com/dining* at least 4 days in advance.

If you miss the ordering deadline, don't despair—no one has to go cake-less at Walt Disney World (perish the thought!). Spontaneous cake delivery is possible, provided you request one at the podium when you check in at a restaurant. At meal's end, you will get a small, non-personalized cake (which serves 4 to 6 guests). It will add about $35, plus tax, to the total tab.

sponge cake with meringue), and more. Among the many handcrafted margaritas that grace the menu are El Diablo, Blood Orange, and La Cava Avocado.

If you book a table for about 8:30 P.M., you may be treated to prime seats for EPCOT's nightly pyrotechnic extravaganza. While window side tables cannot be guaranteed, there's always standing room. As an added bonus, the show's soundtrack is pumped into the eatery. It's quite impressive. **D/$$$–$$$$/🐭**

**MONSIEUR PAUL** (France): Ah, France, where the heralded Gastronomic Meal of the French—an essential element of French culture inscribed on UNESCO's Intangible Cultural Heritage of Humanity list—is a festive meal of culinary excellence celebrating special moments in a life. But if you can't be in Paris, indulge your Francophile cravings at Monsieur Paul.

Just one flight above Chefs de France, overlooking the promenade and World Showcase Lagoon, this elegant bistro is a splurge worthy of any excuse for a celebration. As your host leads you to a table, you'll pass the restaurant's stellar wine collection and framed mementos of the late legendary nouvelle cuisine pioneer Chef Paul Bocuse. His extraordinary honors include being named "Chef of the Century" in 2011 by the Culinary Institute of America.

The seven-course fixed-price menu, $195 per person (plus tax and gratuity), begins with the chef's amuse-bouche served with Monsieur Paul's cocktail—often a specialty French martini—and features gourmet delights such as the sumptuous saffron mussels soup, escargot cassolette, and Maine lobster salad with passion fruit vinaigrette. A sublime fish course offers snapper encrusted in potato "scales" with rosemary sauce, seared scallops, or sea bass in a puff pastry (for two). Meat course entrées such as grilled beef tenderloin and roasted rack of lamb may include seasonal tweaks.

An impressive, *très* French wine list includes pairing options for every palate. This extraordinary experience also features an imported cheese course before a dessert finale such as the decadent chocolate almond cake with warm chocolate Cognac sauce, apple tart with almond cream, or other sweet ending. *Magnifique!*

Though a bit less formal than its predecessor, Bistro de Paris, Monsieur Paul does have a "resort casual" dress code—no tank tops or tattered attire, please. Reservations are recommended. A $100 per-person fee will apply for no-shows or cancellations within 72 hours of the reservation. **D/$$$$**

**NINE DRAGONS** (China): This stop on EPCOT's restaurant tour transports guests to modern China when seated in the palatial dining room. À la carte selections allow guests to sample provincial cuisines. The menu includes starters such as crispy duck bao buns, spicy chicken dumplings, veggie spring rolls, and potstickers. Entrées range from salt and pepper shrimp to Kung Pao shrimp and chicken, vegetable and tofu stir-fry, crispy duck fried rice, and Canton pepper beef. (No MSG is used in any dish.) For dessert, consider caramel-ginger or strawberry red bean ice cream. Chinese teas, beers, and wines are served. The menu features specialty cocktails and non-alcoholic sips such as the Shangri-La (strawberry-mango) slushy and hot Jasmine tea. The childrens' menu offers honey chicken nuggets, sweet and sour shrimp with lo mein noodles, and a combo platter (shrimp and chicken with vegetable fried rice, carrots, and broccoli). Reservations are recommended. **LD/$$–$$$/🐭**

## SPECIAL DIETARY REQUESTS

All WDW table-service eateries that accept reservations strive to accommodate food allergies and intolerances such as gluten, salt, wheat, shellfish, lactose, peanuts, etc. Please indicate all allergies and intolerances at the time of booking and notify your server when you arrive.

Kosher meals may be pre-ordered up to a day ahead at many table-service eateries. Note that 48 hours' notice is needed for restaurants at the Swan and Dolphin hotels, Yak & Yeti restaurant, and Rainforest Cafe. (Kosher meals are not offered at Garden View Afternoon Tea [Grand Floridian resort] and EPCOT's Teppan Edo.) Make your request when you book your table. Note that kosher requests require a credit card guarantee and must be canceled more than 24 hours before the reservation to avoid a penalty. For more information, visit *disneyworld.disney.go .com/guest-services/special-dietary-requests.*

**ROSE & CROWN PUB AND DINING ROOM** (United Kingdom): Don't let the word "pub" throw you. While this place serves up some excellent brews, its Dining Room is also known for such crowd-pleasing dishes as traditional fish and chips, shepherd's pie, and bangers and mash (sausages with mashed potatoes). Appetizers include a Scotch Egg and salad. For dessert, try the sticky toffee pudding or plant-based vanilla gelato. Boddington's ale from England, Harp lager, Guinness stout from Ireland, and more are on tap. Wine, whisky, specialty drinks (with or without alcohol), coffee, tea, and soft drinks may be sipped and swigged, too.

The decor is pretty—mainly polished woods, etched glass, and brass accents. In pleasant weather, it's nice to lunch under a canopy on the terrace outside and watch the FriendShip water taxis cross the lagoon.

The pub's architecture incorporates three distinct styles. The wall facing World Showcase promenade is reminiscent of urban establishments popular in Britain

PHOTO BY JILL SAFRO

since the 1890s, while that on the south side evokes London's seventeenth-century Ye Olde Cheshire Cheese pub, with its brick-walled flagstone terrace, slate roof, and half-timbered exterior. The canal facade, with its stone wall and clay-tile roof, reminds visitors of the charming pubs so common in the English countryside.

The pub region of the Rose & Crown serves all the brews noted earlier and traditional British mixed drinks such as shandies (Harp lager and Sprite) and half-and-halfs (Harp lager and Guinness stout). The pub is quite popular, so it may be necessary to queue up at the door. Note that the pub area spills onto the World Showcase promenade—where the handful of first-come, first-served waterside tables make for a nice spot to sip and, possibly, enjoy some fish and chips from a nearby stand. Reservations are not available in the pub areas, but are necessary for the table-service dining room and the waterside patio. **D/$$$/🐭**

## FOOD & WINE FESTIVAL

Every year, EPCOT's hopping dining scene expands exponentially in what's known as the International Food & Wine Festival. The event, which usually runs from mid-summer through mid-November, is a celebration of the flavors of dozens of nations. Countries without permanent pavilions at World Showcase set up temporary displays from which authentic samples of food, wine, and other spirits are sold. Said samples range in price from about $3 to $12. It is possible to eat and drink your way around the world for about the same price as some table-service restaurants.

The festival has featured special ticket events such as the Party for the Senses, hands-on workshops, and cheese seminars. For details and ticket info, visit *disneyworld.com*. Make reservations as early as you can—this is a mighty popular festival.

**SAN ANGEL INN** (Mexico): The food, or *la comida*, at this moody establishment may come as a surprise to most visitors. Although tacos, tortillas, and other specialties that usually fall under the broad umbrella of Mexican food are available, the menu also offers a wide variety of more subtly flavored fish, poultry, and meat dishes.

For starters, the menu offers *totopos con queso* (corn tortillas with sides of white cheddar cheese and salsa), traditional tortilla soup, guacamole, and more. Entrées include *carne asada* (New York strip steak), *pescado a la Veracruzano* (red snapper atop potatoes with a cilantro-lime vinaigrette), and tacos (ribeye or beer-battered cod).

PHOTO BY JILL SAFRO

Dessert can come as sweet corn ice cream, a brownie sundae, or a sorbet trio. *Bebidas* (drinks) such as Dos Equis, Sol, and Tecate beer, margaritas, juice, and other soft drinks make excellent accompaniments.

The restaurant, which is located to the back of the plaza inside the Mexico pyramid, is a corporate cousin of the famous Mexico City restaurant of the same name. Unsurprisingly, some of the zestier dishes here have a bit of a kick—though not in an overwhelming way. In fact, some diners may be accustomed to a little more heat. Youngsters home in on the kid-friendly section of the menu, with cheese quesadillas, grilled chicken breast, chicken tenders, mac and cheese, and tacos. Reservations are recommended. **LD/$$–$$$$/🐭**

**SPICE ROAD TABLE** (Morocco): Built along the shore of World Showcase Lagoon, this restaurant's style was inspired by outdoor cafes found along the scenic shores of the Mediterranean. Popular for its stunning views of the nighttime pyrotechnic spectacular and its freshly prepared, palate-pleasing fare, Spice Road Table has made its way onto many an EPCOT diner's must-do list. The eatery's whitewashed facade is accented in icy shades of blue from the famous "Blue City of Chefchaouen" in Morocco's Rif Mountains.

**Hot Tip!** Spice Road Table (in Morocco) and the U.K.'s Rose & Crown offer "Dining and Fireworks" packages. Each include sweet and savory nibbles and unlimited drinks, plus lakeside views of EPCOT's nighttime spectacular. For additional information and to make reservations, use the My Disney Experience mobile app or website, or visit *disneyworld.com/dining*.

Spice Road's menu offers Mediterranean small plates such as pomegranate-chili crispy cauliflower, spicy shrimp, fried calamari, hummus fries, grilled lamb kefta, Spice Road sampler, and more. The dessert platter offers a pastry selection. Soft drinks, specialty drinks (Hibiscus Mimosa, Sahara Spritz, and Medina Mixer, to name a few), wine, Mediterranean beer, and sangria are served. Reservations are recommended. **LDS/$$–$$$/**

**TEPPAN EDO** (Japan): Shiki-Sai: Sushi Izakaya's neighbor, Teppan Edo offers a dinner-as-show experience. Guests sit around a large teppan grill and watch as a nimble chef demonstrates just how quickly enough chicken, beef, seafood, and veggies can be chopped, seasoned, and stir-fried. Teppan Edo entrées are sizzling and satisfying. Soups, salads, sushi, desserts, and cocktails (including Japanese beer and sake) are also on the menu. Don't wear your finest attire: There's always potential for a little splattering. Reservations are recommended. Teppan Edo's check-in desk is at the bottom of the eatery's front steps. **LD/$$$–$$$$/**

**TAKUMI-TEI** (Japan): The name of this elegant (relatively new) World Showcase spot translates to "house of the artisan." Specializing in Wagyu beef selections, this upscale eatery features a multi-course tasting menu (omnivorous or plant-based). Signature cocktails and premium sake are served, as are wine and craft beers. The satisfying splurge known as the Omakase Tasting Menu starts at about $250 per adult ($150 for the plant-based dinner), plus tax and 18 percent gratuity. Kids'

prices start at $100. Dishes include Japanese A5 Wagyu steak, lobster tempura, seasonal sashimi, and strawberry yuzu sorbet.

The dress code is resort casual. Reservations are recommended, but a limited number of walk-ins may be accommodated. Details are subject to change. For updates, use the My Disney Experience mobile app or website, or visit *disneyworld.com/dining*. **D/$$$$**

**SHIKI-SAI: SUSHI IZAKAYA** (Japan): Every month, **NEW** a new Japanese festival celebrates seasonal flavors and moments of cultural significance in the relaxed dining atmosphere of this new table-service restaurant. In September, for instance, your chopsticks may deliver the taste of "moon-viewing dumplings" to celebrate the ancient and still-popular Tsukimi harvest moon-viewing festival. Served in the casual Izakaya style, tasty small plates from the grill include savory Karaage Chicken and standouts like Okonomiyaki, a savory pancake filled with shredded cabbage and bacon topped with tangy sauce and pickled ginger. Sushi bar offerings are delightful indulgences—the Tokyo Negi Roll with green onion tempura, tuna tataki, jalapeño aioli, and shredded carrot among them. There's a kids' menu, too. The eatery offers views of World Showcase Lagoon. Evocative décor including hand-painted artwork and traditional lanterns sets the mood for these seasonal celebrations. Reservations are recommended. **LD/$$$–$$$$**

**TUTTO GUSTO WINE CELLAR** (Italy): A welcome retreat for grown-ups, Tutto Gusto is a wine bar that transports guests to an ancient Italian wine cellar. Tutto Italia's next-door neighbor offers more than 200 wines, including grappa; Italian beers and specialty drinks; coffee concoctions; and a marvelous menu. Nibble on starters such as imported Italian cheeses, fried calamari, and Caprese salad. Entrée options include ravioli, lasagna, pan-seared salmon, chicken parm, and grilled steak. For dessert, try the lemon ricotta cheesecake, cannoli, or tiramisú. Reservations are not accepted at Tutto Gusto Wine Cellar—come in the afternoon for the smallest crowds. *Salute!* **LDS/$$$–$$$$/**

**TUTTO ITALIA RISTORANTE** (Italy): There's an impressive menu at one of the most popular (and expensive) World Showcase destinations, and its indoor and outdoor tables make it one of the more appealing spots for an EPCOT meal. Traditional starters such as fried calamari, charred Wagyu beef carpaccio, charcuterie board, and Caesar salad can actually make a meal in and of themselves.

Entrée selections extend toward pastas—fettuccini, gnocchi, spaghetti, and lasagna. The menu also includes fish, steak, and chicken. For dessert, choose from gelato, cannoli, tiramisú, and more. Wine, beer, teas, coffees, and cocktails are served. A children's menu is available. Reservations are recommended. **LD/$$$–$$$$/❤**

**VIA NAPOLI RISTORANTE E PIZZERIA** (Italy): EPCOT's pizza-centric restaurant is tucked into the back of the Italy pavilion. Via Napoli has a casual atmosphere and seating for about 300. How serious are they about the pizza? They import the flour from Italy and select water so the crust tastes as authentically Neapolitan as possible. In addition to the famous wood-fired pizza, house specialties include pastas, salads, fish, chicken parmesan, beef medallions, and Italian wines and signature cocktails. The Acqua Fresca (seasonal fruit cooler) is most refreshing. Dessert offerings may include panna cotta, cheesecake, cannoli, and tiramisú. Reservations are recommended. **LD/$$$–$$$$/❤**

## FAST FOOD & SNACKS

**BLOCK & HANS** (American Adventure): Mickey-shaped soft pretzels, anyone? You can get them here, along with cheese-y dipping sauce. Wash them down with a seasonal craft beer, hard cider, or bottled water. **S/$**

**FUNNEL CAKE CART** (American Adventure): The sweet, doughy treat known as the funnel cake wasn't born in the U.S.A., but it was Kutztown, Pennsylvania, that put it on the map. So it's fitting that funnel cakes are served at a kiosk in the American Adventure pavilion. Toppings include sugar, whipped cream, vanilla ice cream. **S/$**

**LA CANTINA DE SAN ANGEL** (Mexico): Across the promenade from the entrance to Mexico's pyramid, this eatery serves arroz con pollo (grilled chicken over rice); beef tacos (on fresh corn tortillas); nachos (tortilla chips topped with cheese, ground beef, beans, jalapeños, sour cream,

and tomatoes); cheese empanadas; guacamole with tortilla chips; Mickey-shaped ice cream bars; slushies; and churros with chocolate hazelnut spread. Mexican beer, sangria, margaritas (frozen and on the rocks), and soft drinks are available. Kids' picks may include chicken tacos, chicken tenders, and cheese empanadas (served with tortilla chips and fruit). **LDS/$$/❤**

**LA CAVA DEL TEQUILA** (Mexico): Mexico's national drink is the star of this show—there are more than 200 varieties to choose from. Also served: sangria, mezcal, beer, wine, and specialty drinks (the avocado margaritas are uniquely refreshing). Snacks may be offered. It's tiny, so expect a wait to get in. **S/$$**

**REFRESHMENT OUTPOST** (between Germany and China): Stop here for a snack and drink (soft drinks and adult beverages are served). Snacks include all-beef hot dogs with chips, chilly Dole Whip served in a waffle cone (pineapple, watermelon, or swirl), and frozen cola or lemonade slushies. Fountain beverages and water are served, as are beer and specialty drinks—including the Mango Starr (mango purée and African rum) and Outpost Lemonade (frozen lemonade with vodka). **LDS/$–$$/❤**

**FIFE & DRUM TAVERN** (American Adventure): Located on the World Showcase promenade, this small brick edifice proffers American favorites. Among the options: jumbo turkey legs, popcorn, ice cream in a waffle cone, slushies, soft drinks, and beer. Souvenir popcorn buckets cost about $10–$20 each and may be refilled for about $2–3 a pop for the length of your WDW stay. **LDS/$–$$/❤**

**GELATERIA TOSCANA** (Italy): For those who scream for Italian ice cream (and who doesn't?), cravings may be satisfied at this sweet spot. It specializes in creamy gelati, gelati floats, and sorbetti. Other temptations include cannoli, zeppole, and tiramisú. Beer, wine, cocktails, and no-alcohol specialty drinks are served. **S/$–$$**

**JOFFREY'S COFFEE & TEA COMPANY** (American Adventure): One of five Joffrey's outposts at EPCOT, this beverage-based stand proffers coffees, teas, hot cocoa, bottled water, spirited drinks, and baked treats.
    **F.Y.I.:** The other Joffrey's Coffee & Tea Co. locations at this park are on the World Showcase Promenade (near Mexico and between the Canada and United Kingdom pavilions), not far from the Guardians of the Galaxy: Cosmic Rewind attraction (in World Discovery), and at the main entrance (near the monorail station). **S/$**

**KABUKI CAFE** (Japan): Step up to cool down at this kiosk, where the specialty is *kakigori* (shaved ice). Flavors include melon, tangerine, rainbow, strawberry, and blue raspberry. Kabuki also offers edamame, sushi (California rolls, spicy rolls, and sushi combo), Japanese beer (including frozen Kirin), plum wine, sake (hot and cold), Sake Mist (alcoholic shaved ice in coconut-pineapple, blood orange, or blackberry), and soft drinks. **LDS/$–$$**

**KATSURA GRILL** (Japan): The exterior of this restaurant, on the pavilion's left side, was inspired by the historic 16th-century Katsura Imperial Villa near Kyoto, Japan.

Among the fare here is Japanese chicken cutlet curry (a peppery sauce over rice with a panko-breaded chicken breast). That, along with teriyaki chicken, shrimp, and beef (basted with soy sauce and sesame oil as it broils), sushi, pork and veggie ramen, miso soup, udon noodles (veggie or shrimp tempura), edamame, and yuzu (citrus fruit) cheesecake typify the offerings. Beverage choices include sake, plum wine, green tea, beer, and soft drinks. The garden serves as a lovely respite for those who seek a break from the hustle and bustle of a busy EPCOT day. Kids dig the koi pond. **LDS/$$/**🐭

**KRINGLA BAKERI OG KAFE** (Norway): Nestled between the Norway pavilion's wooden church and The Fjording shop, this sweet spot serves *kringlas* (sweet pretzels reserved for special occasions in Norway) and *lefse* (soft flatbread rolled with cinnamon, sugar, and butter). It also has Norwegian school bread (sweet roll filled with custard and dipped in coconut), triple chocolate chip cookies, *epelkake* (apple cake with caramel drizzle), vanilla cake with custard and almond-meringue topping, and creamy rice pudding with strawberry sauce. Soft drinks and spirits (Viking coffee and Nordic draft beer) are available. Many of the menu items work quite well for breakfast—perfect for early visits to Norway's wildly popular Frozen Ever After attraction. **BLDS/$/**🐭

## ONE-STOP SWEET SHOP

A yummy destination on the World Showcase landscape, the Germany pavilion's Karamell-Küche is sure to satisfy your sweet tooth—provided you are a fan of fresh, gooey caramel draped or drizzled over chocolate, cookies, crunchy apples, and much more. The line is often long, but it's worth the wait. Better yet, take advantage of Mobile Ordering (see page 310).

**L'ARTISAN DES GLACES** (France): An artisanal ice cream and sorbet shop, this satisfying spot fills cones and cups with ice cream and sorbets—all crafted in-house. The ingredients are simple and fresh: milk, sugar, cream, eggs, and fruit. There are usually more than a dozen flavors from which to choose. Specials include macaron ice cream sandwiches, iced cappuccino with ice cream, and sundaes in homemade waffle bowls. Guests over age 21 may indulge in an "ice cream martini"—two scoops with a shot of Grand Marnier, whipped cream-flavored vodka, or rum. **S/$**

**LA CRÊPERIE DE PARIS** (France): A sweet quick- and table-service hybrid, La Crêperie draws inspiration from France's famed Brittany region. Its menu, created by world-renowned chef Jérôme Bocuse, includes both sweet and savory crêpes, soups, salads, beer, wine, and soft drinks. **BLDS/$$–$$$**

**LES HALLES BOULANGERIE PATISSERIE** (France): The pastry shop in the France pavilion is not too hard to find: Just follow the wonderful aroma, then watch as the crowds line up to enjoy the fresh baguettes (standard and mini), quiche, croissants, cheese plates, ham and cheese or turkey sandwiches, soups, éclairs, fruit tarts, beignets, macarons, chocolate mousse, and more. Beer, wine, mimosas, lemonade, coffee, and other beverages are served. The popular patisserie is located at the back of the pavilion's left side and is a favorite snack spot among EPCOT veterans. There's always a line to order the treats, but it moves quickly. **LDS/$–$$**

**LOTUS BLOSSOM CAFE** (China): The counter-service cafe is adjacent to the House of Good Fortune shopping gallery in the China pavilion. It offers orange chicken with steamed rice, stir-fried veggies, Mongolian beef, and chicken fried rice, plus chicken potstickers, pork egg rolls, and kid-oriented selections such as sweet-and-sour chicken served with steamed rice. Caramel-ginger or lychee ice cream are dessert possibilities. Coffee, Chinese tea (hot or iced), fountain beverages, Chinese beer, and plum wine round out the menu. There is a small, covered seating section. **LDS/$$/**❤

**REFRESHMENT PORT** (Canada): A good spot for a thirst quencher and/or a quick snack. Stop here for seasonal sweets and beverages, plus traditional *poutine* (fries with beef gravy and cheese curds) and chicken nuggets. It's located on the World Showcase promenade, next to Canada. Drinks include fountain beverages and light beer. **LDS/$-$$/**❤

**REGAL EAGLE SMOKEHOUSE: CRAFT DRAFTS & BARBECUE** (American Adventure): EPCOT continues a proud American tradition at this patriotically appointed quick service bastion of BBQ. The Regal Eagle is a modern barbecue smokehouse with all the accompanying sights, sounds, smells, and savory flavors many Americans have come to know and crave. Craft beers and soft drinks pair nicely with the vittles. There's indoor and outdoor seating. This satisfying spot is situated on the left side of the American Adventure pavilion. **LDS/$$/**❤**/MO**

**SOMMERFEST** (Germany): Bratwurst served on a fresh-baked roll with sauerkraut and house-made paprika chips is the specialty of the haus. Also served: jumbo pretzels and pretzel bread pudding. Assorted fountain soft drinks, bottled water, and German beers are offered at this covered spot near the Biergarten restaurant. There is limited outdoor seating in the area. **LDS/$$/**❤**/MO**

**YORKSHIRE COUNTY FISH SHOP** (United Kingdom): A great choice for a simple meal, this stand offers classic fish and chips. Don't forget the malt vinegar! It makes the tasty fried fish all the more yummy. Soda, iced tea, light lemonade, coffee, and hot tea are served. Bombardier Amber and Harp lager are available on draft. Dessert can come in the form of seasonal fruit. **LDS/$$/**❤**/MO**

# EPCOT MEALTIME TIPS

- The international restaurants of World Showcase offer some of the best dining on the property. It's wise to arrange advance reservations for all table-service restaurants. However, it's important to note that some tables may be available for same-day seating. To make arrangements, head to Guest Relations first thing in the morning, use the My Disney Experience website or mobile app, or visit *disneyworld.com*.
- Don't dismiss the idea of an early seating if you can get it: A 5 P.M. dinner may not only be welcome, but may provide an opportunity to spend more time enjoying the pleasant evening hours at EPCOT's World Showcase.
- Lunch provides guests with another chance to enjoy the most popular EPCOT restaurants. It also has an additional appeal: With reservations for 1 P.M., it's possible to spend some of the busiest hours in the park consuming a pleasant meal while other visitors wait in some of the longest lines of the day.
- If you aren't able to secure reservations for a table-service eatery, don't despair. There are several satisfying alternatives to a traditional sit-down restaurant. Tutto Gusto (Italian wine bar) offers satisfying vittles. Spice Road Table (lagoonside cafe in Morocco) accepts reservations, but often has walk-up availability. Japan has Katsura Grill, good for sushi and chicken curry. Mexican lunch specialties may be sampled at La Cantina. We recommend the brisket sandwich at the Regal Eagle Smokehouse in the American Adventure, fish and chips in the United Kingdom pavilion (at Yorkshire County Fish Shop), or Germany's bratwurst with paprika chips (served at Sommerfest). Last, but not least, do not overlook the heavenly offerings of France's Les Halles Boulangerie Patisserie. *Bon appétit!*
- Sunshine Seasons (food court), in The Land pavilion, offers a bit of everything. However, it can get extremely congested at mealtime rush hours. The situation is similar for Connections Cafe. Don't wait until you're starving to stop and grab a bite.
- The most timid of eaters can still find something pleasing—even in the restaurants of World Showcase. If you're undecided, check the menus via *disneyworld.com/dining* or the My Disney Experience app. Most eateries have menus for kids.

# In Disney's Hollywood Studios

Lights, camera, lunch! This theme park, which was designed to resemble a working Hollywood backlot circa the 1940s, tackles the role of feeding guests with style and whimsy. Here you can sit in a classic car and enjoy a meal at a drive-in, rub elbows with the beautiful people at a reproduction of the Hollywood Brown Derby, enjoy a grilled cheese sandwich in Andy's backyard, and play the part of a sitcom kid as you are served by "Mom" or "Dad" at the 50's Prime Time Cafe (no elbows on the table, please!). While the attention to theming is obvious, it does not upstage the fare. The eateries at Disney's Hollywood Studios are a breed apart. Some feature decor that returns guests to a bygone era; others recapture memorable moments from the big or small screen. The Studios has six full-service restaurants, whose atmospheres and menus are so distinct, they satisfy altogether different moods and whims. Reservations are necessary. Now grab a napkin, and get ready for your close-up.

## TABLE SERVICE

**50's PRIME TIME CAFE:** This retreat is an amusing amalgam of comfort food, kitschy 1950s-style kitchen nooks, and attentive servers of the "No talking with your mouth full" ilk. Nostalgia abounds, meant to bring guests back to the childhood of yesteryear; and TVs broadcast black-and-white clips from favorite fifties comedies (all related to food). Guests are waited on by "Mom" (and other family members) with considerable enthusiasm: They encourage everyone to keep their elbows off the table, eat all of their vegetables, and clean their plates (or no dessert!). Misbehave and you may have to stand in the corner for a few minutes (the 1950s version of the "time-out").

Adding to the appeal is the menu, which is packed with comfort foods. To start, consider the fried herb and garlic cheese, onion rings, or roasted tomato soup. Notable specialties of the house include meatloaf served with mashed potatoes and veggies, fried chicken, and old-fashioned pot roast. Wedge salads, Caesar salad (with chicken or salmon), and a seasonal vegetable dish are served, too. Can't commit to one entrée? Try the sampler platter! Ice cream sodas, root beer floats, and milk shakes are sweet accompaniments. Clean your plate and you may order dessert! Standouts include chocolate-peanut butter layer cake (plain or à la mode), lemon meringue pie, and warm apple crisp. A full bar is available. Guests of all ages get a kick out of this place. Reservations are highly recommended. **LD/$$–$$$/🐭**

**HOLLYWOOD & VINE:** The distinctive Art Deco facade ushers guests into a contemporary version of a 1950s diner—with lots of shiny stainless steel. An elaborate 42-by-8-foot wall mural depicts notable Hollywood landmarks, including the Disney Studios, Columbia Ranch, and Warner Bros. (back when they were the only film studios in the San Fernando Valley). At the center of the mural is the Carthay Circle Theatre, where *Snow White and the Seven Dwarfs* premiered in 1937.

The buffet breakfast—known as Disney Junior Play 'n Dine—is a character affair featuring Roadster Goofy, Doc McStuffins, Fancy Nancy, and Vampirina (details are subject to change). The morning meal includes eggs, salmon and bagel casserole, yogurt, breakfast potatoes, french toast, chicken and waffles, bread pudding, and plant-based frittatas with tomato jam.

Minnie Mouse hosts lunch and dinner, along with Mickey Mouse, Goofy, and Pluto (characters are subject to change at any time). Minnie's Seasonal Dine buffet includes salad, roasted mushroom farro risotto, slow-roasted crispy pork belly, steak tenderloin, and shrimp and bacon mac & cheese. The dessert section includes Mississippi mud pie, soft-serve ice cream, and peanut butter and jelly tarts. Soft drinks are included. Beer, wine, and specialty drinks are served at an extra cost.

Reservations are an absolute must. For pricing and menu updates, use the My Disney Experience app or website, or visit *disneyworld.com.* **BLD/$$$/🐭**

PHOTO BY JILL SAFRO

**HOLLYWOOD BROWN DERBY:** The home of the world-famous Cobb salad is alive and well. This re-creation of the former Vine Street mainstay is quite faithful, right down to the caricatures (reproduced from the original Derby collection) that cover the walls. Old-time gossip queen rivals Louella Parsons and Hedda Hopper would fit right in here, just as they did in the heyday of the original Brown Derby. The place is decorated predominantly in teak and mahogany, and the elegant chandeliers and perimeter lamps (shaped like miniature derbies) are reminiscent of those in the original eatery.

The menu features the famed Cobb salad, created by owner Bob Cobb in the 1930s. It's a mixture of finely chopped fresh greens, tomato, bacon, turkey, egg, blue cheese, and avocado.

Desserts are tempting—particularly the crème brûlée and the legendary grapefruit cake, a Brown Derby institution. (If you'd like to sip your dessert, the Grapefruit Cake Martini fits the bill—it's sweeter than the cake!) Some selections are a bit highbrow (and high-priced) for the theme park crowd, but if you are up for a splurge, this spot should rise to the occasion. Highlights include crab Louie, corn bisque, free-range chicken and dumplings, cioppino, lamb shank, and filet mignon.

The slightly formal atmosphere is not apt to enchant most children, but youngster-friendly fare is available. The New World wine list is excellent. Reservations are recommended. **LD/$$$–$$$$/☙/SR**

**HOLLYWOOD BROWN DERBY LOUNGE:** An alfresco extension of the restaurant with the same name, this is a lovely spot in which to enjoy a beverage and a bite. Guests may order from the Hollywood Brown Derby menu—which includes filet mignon, sustainable fish, Cobb Salad, and grapefruit cake. The drink menu offers beer, wine, scotch, bourbon, and specialty drinks. Signature drinks of note: Grapefruit Cake Martini, Absinthe Minded, sangria (red and white), and margarita flights. Seating is limited and reservations are not accepted, so there may be a wait for a table. All cocktails may be made to go, but must be consumed in the park. **S/$$–$$$$/☙/SR**

**MAMA MELROSE'S RISTORANTE ITALIANO:** This pleasant Italian restaurant (with a California twist) is set inside a warehouse that has been converted into a large dining room. Flatbreads are freshly prepared in a wood-burning oven. The menu also features Caesar salad, housemade pasta, sustainable fish, soup, and crispy calamari. Favorite dishes have included grilled pork chop, charred strip steak, shrimp campanelle, and chicken parmesan. Mama's dessert menu tempts with cannoli, gelato (chocolate or vanilla), tiramisú, and chocolate and cherry cake. Reservations are recommended. **LD/$$$/☙**

**SCI-FI DINE-IN THEATER:** A convincing re-creation of a drive-in theater, the atmosphere here is completely absorbing. The tables are actually flashy, 1950s-era cars, complete with fins and whitewalls. Stars twinkle overhead in the "night sky," and drive-in theater speakers are mounted beside each car. Most seats are within cars, with most featuring front- and backseat counters facing front—not terribly conducive to meaningful table talk, but ideal for viewing the large movie screen, where a 45-minute compilation of the best (and worst) science-fiction trailers and cartoons plays in a continuous loop. There are a couple of traditional tables. If this is your preference, make that known when you book the table and expect to wait a bit when you arrive.

Choose from items such as juicy burgers (served five different ways, including plant-based), grilled chicken citrus salad, chicken salad sandwich, pan-seared salmon pasta, and more. Kids choose from beef skewers, chicken strips, mac and cheese, and cheeseburgers. Delightful desserts include shakes, sundaes, cheesecake, and fresh fruit salad. Reservations are recommended. Warning: Some of the movie trailers feature monsters and may frighten very young diners. **LD/$$$/☙**

**ROUNDUP RODEO BBQ:** Andy from *Toy Story* built a rootin' tootin' rodeo arena in his backyard — and Disney Imagineers turned it into a fixed-price, table-service restaurant for honorary **NEW** toys. Diners may chow down on cheddar biscuits, salads (three types), platters of ribs, brisket, sausage, and BBQ chicken (or a plant-based option); plus four sides that can include potato salad, mac & cheese, roasted veggies, baked beans, and corn on the cob. Each guest chooses one dessert (chocolate silk pie, apple pie, cheesecake, or chocolate cupcake.) Yee-ha! Reservations are recommended. **LD/$$$/**❦

## FAST FOOD & SNACKS

**ABC COMMISSARY:** Located on Commissary Lane, this spot has featured chicken club sandwiches, shrimp tacos, Buffalo-chicken grilled cheese sandwiches, Mediterranean salads, plant-based burgers, and more. Youngsters may choose pork tacos, grilled ham and cheese sandwich, or chicken salad sandwich. For dessert, consider cheesecake or a tropical tart. Beer, wine, sangria, specialty cocktails, slushes, and soft drinks are served. The eatery resembles an actual studio commissary. Memorabilia from ABC shows is on display. Neat! **LDS/$$/**❦**/MO**

**BACKLOT EXPRESS:** Resembling a crafts shop on a studio backlot, this eatery is near Star Tours—The Adventures Continue. The indoor seating areas carry out the prop-shop theme, with paint-speckled floors, car engines, and various spare prop parts. Typical menu offerings include burgers, cheeseburgers, chicken strips, Cuban sandwiches, Southwest salad (with or without chicken), teriyaki tofu bowl, and french fries. There is usually at least one dessert to sample. On our last visit, it was a Star Wars-themed oatmeal cookie sandwich. Soft drinks, beer, wine, margaritas, and daiquiris are served. **LDS/$$/**❦**/MO**

**BASELINE TAP HOUSE:** Housed in a red-brick building by Sci-Fi Dine-In Theater, this wonderful watering hole pays homage to the Golden State with Disneyland touches, Sonoma Valley wines, and California craft beers. Pair 'em with cheese and charcuterie, Bavarian soft pretzels with beer cheese fondue and spicy mustard, coffee-rubbed ribeye beef puff with olive salad, and/or spiced almonds. Or wash them down with a sweet soft drink: Strawberry hibiscus soda and wild strawberry lemonade are house specialties. In tribute to the building's former tenant, a silvery set of letters spells out Writer's Stop. **S/$$**

**DINOSAUR GERTIE'S ICE CREAM OF EXTINCTION:** Gertie serves soft-serve ice cream (vanilla, chocolate, or swirl) in a cup or cone, plus Mickey ice cream bars and cookies-and-cream sandwiches. **S/$**

**DOCKSIDE DINER:** When the lunch or dinner bell rings, stop here for hot dogs (pretzel, bacon mac & cheese, plain, and more), housemade potato chips, milkshakes (chocolate or vanilla), banana splits, frozen lemonade (straight or spiked), soft drinks, beer, and a selection of cocktails (including a chocolate or vanilla Kahlúa and Bailey's Irish Cream milkshake). **LDS/$$/**❦

**DOCKING BAY 7 FOOD AND CARGO:** Chef Strono "Cookie" Tuggs has docked a food freighter loaded with fresh supplies, and he appeases appetites with an array of offerings. His flavors, while a bit unusual, are palate-pleasing. Try the Batuuan beef stir fry, Kaadu pork ribs, or Endorian chicken salad. Kids enjoy Ithorian pasta rings. **LDS/$$/**❦**/MO**

**EPIC EATS:** A tin shack near the theater housing the Indiana Jones Epic Stunt Spectacular, this simple spot dispenses funnel cakes topped with various toppings; soft-serve ice cream (chocolate, vanilla, or twist) in waffle cones; root beer floats; bottled water; fountain beverages; and draft beer. Spirited ice cream floats are also available. **S/$**

**HOLLYWOOD HILLS AMPHITHEATER:** If your stomach starts to growl while waiting for Fantasmic! to begin, consider this snack shack. Menu items include nachos, corn dog nuggets, soft pretzels, cookies, chips, and more. Enjoy your snack with a soft drink, beer, wine, or "wild strawberry lemonade" spiked with rum. **S/$–$$**

**ICE COLD MAIN ENTRANCE CART:** Need to cool off on a hot day? Swing by this stand near the park entrance.

**Hot Tip!** Hollywood Brown Derby, Mama Melrose's Ristorante Italiano, Sci-fi Dine-In Theater, 50's Prime Time Cafe, and Hollywood & Vine offer a "meal and a show" combo. Seating for Fantasmic! is included as part of the package (though tax, gratuities, and alcoholic beverages carry an extra charge). For pricing or reservations, call 407-939-3463 and request the Fantasmic! dining package (lunch or dinner). Guests should arrive at the amphitheater 30 to 45 minutes before showtime to claim their seats.

It sells ice cream bars, cookies, chips, slushies, juices, and fizzy drinks. **S/$**

**JOFFREY'S COFFEE & TEA COMPANY:** There are two Joffrey's stands at Disney's Hollywood Studios: near the entrance to Toy Story Land and by the Tower of Terror exit. These kiosks specialize in (hot and cold) tea and coffee beverages, plus drinks of the frozen and/or spirited style. The pastry board may include fresh-made doughnuts, cookies, and muffins. **S/$**

**KAT SAKA'S KETTLE:** Pop over to this snack counter for some Outpost Mix—a popcorn-based treat—and cold brew topped with sweet cream cheese and chocolate puffs (a fan-favorite). **S/$**

**KRNR: THE ROCK STATION:** In the shadow of Rock 'n' Roller Coaster's gargantuan guitar, KRNR serves chips, nachos with cheese sauce, ice cream in a waffle cone, cookies, ice cream floats, frozen cola, frozen lemonade, soft drinks, and specialty drinks. **LDS/$**

**MILK STAND:** This stall offers parched travelers a drink that's enjoyed by locals—and Luke Skywalker himself. The fruity plant-based (non-dairy) frosty beverage comes in blue or green, spiked or alcohol-free. (For some, the "milk" is an acquired taste.) **S/$–$$/MO**

**PIZZERIZZO:** The Studios' Muppet-themed eatery sells kid-friendly pizza, plus meatball subs, antipasto salad, and cannoli. Also on the menu: Caesar side salads and whole fruit. Assorted soft drinks, beer, wine, sangria, and margaritas are served. Pizzerizzo is located across from Muppet*Vision 3-D. **LDS/$$/☺/MO**

**RONTO ROASTERS:** To find this stand, follow your nose— the aromas of spit-roasted specialties fill the air. The breakfast menu offers oatmeal and the Ronto Morning Wrap. The lunch and dinner Ronto Wrap is stuffed with grilled sausage and roasted pork. Also offered: zucchini wrap, seasoned pork rinds, Tatooine Sunsets, and soft drinks. The aforementioned spit, incidentally, is operated by a pit-master droid. **BLDS/$–$$/☺/MO**

**SUNSET RANCH MARKET:** A salute to California's outdoor lifestyle, this cluster of snack stands has something for just about everyone. **Rosie's All-American** (☺) serves foot-long hot dogs, cheeseburgers, plant-based lobster rolls, chicken nuggets, and desserts. **Catalina Eddie's** (☺) has plain and pepperoni pizzas, chicken Caesar salads, bread-sticks with marinara, and desserts. Vegetables, fresh fruit, juice, churros, chips, and soft drinks are sold at **Anaheim Produce**. **Hollywood Scoops** serves waffle platters (with blueberries and whipped cream) for breakfast and ice cream treats later in the day. Go to **Fairfax Fare** (☺) for waffle bowls filled with chicken, pork, or brisket with tasty toppings, plus plant-based bowls. Soft drinks are served, as are beer and specialty drinks. **BLDS/$–$$/MO**

**THE TROLLEY CAR CAFE:** Step into this jolly trolley station/Starbucks for coffee-based beverages, breakfast sandwiches, whole fruit, sweet treats, savory snacks, bottled soft drinks, and more. The cheery red building is on Hollywood Boulevard. Guests may purchase cups with designs unique to the park, too. **BLDS/$–$$/☺**

**WOODY'S LUNCH BOX:** Hunger pangs may be quelled at Woody's Lunch Box, a stand that serves tasty vittles all day. For a hearty breakfast, there is a potato barrel breakfast bowl. Later in the day, the menu offers BBQ brisket melts, smoked turkey sandwiches, grilled three-cheese sandwiches, potato barrels, and fresh-baked tarts. Beer, wine, hard lemonade, hard cider, and soft drinks are also served. **BLDS/$$/☺/MO**

## STUDIOS MEALTIME TIPS

• To avoid traffic jams at fast-food spots, consider eating at a restaurant that offers advance table-service reservations. The list includes Hollywood Brown Derby, 50's Prime Time Cafe, Sci-fi Dine-In Theater, Hollywood & Vine, Roundup Rodeo BBQ, and Mama Melrose's Ristorante Italiano.

• To make reservations, use the My Disney Experience mobile app or website or visit *www.disneyworld.com/dining*. Keep in mind that same-day seating is nearly impossible at Disney's Hollywood Studios' table-service eateries. Plan ahead.

# In Disney's Animal Kingdom

Whether you eat like a horse or more like a bird, you will have no trouble finding something to sink your teeth into at one of D.A.K.'s eateries. Disney's nature-oriented park has four table-service spots and takes "quick service" seriously—there are plenty of places to keep stomachs from growling like the beasts over at the Kilimanjaro Safaris attraction.

**Note:** The information on these pages was accurate at press time, but details are subject to change.

## TABLE SERVICE

**RAINFOREST CAFE:** Like the Oasis, the region it borders, this cafe is a lush, soothing jungle. Unlike the Oasis, a quiet moment here is merely a calm before the storm—as brief thunderstorms happen frequently. Waterfalls, twisting tree trunks, and colorful fish add to the ambience. The menu has a bit of everything—breakfast items, fish tacos, burgers, sandwiches, flatbreads, pasta dishes, steak, soup, and salads. Dessert can be a brownie sundae (for four), cheesecake, or Key lime pie. Reservations are recommended for all meals. **BLDS/$$-$$$/**🐭

**TIFFINS RESTAURANT:** An inviting escape, Tiffins boasts a globe-trotting menu of artfully prepared fare fit for a weary traveler. The exotic menu features cuisine from the many areas that inspired the creation of Disney's Animal Kingdom. The menu has included selections such as spiced chickpea falafel, charred octopus, plant-based taco, seasonal soup, tamarind-braised short rib, lobster mac and cheese, shrimp & grits, North African spiced tofu, and whole-fried sustainable fish. Kid-oriented menu selections are offered (including grilled beef skewers and grilled teriyaki chicken). For dessert, expect treats such as chocolate brownie (with strawberry-mango sauce and caramel mousse) and tropical trifle (coconut panna cotta with caramelized pineapple and passion fruit tapioca). Reservations are recommended. **LD/$$$-$$$$/**🐭**/SR**

**TUSKER HOUSE:** Harambe Village sets the stage for a dining adventure at this popular buffet spot. The all-you-care-to-enjoy selection is bountiful and satisfying to most palates. All meals are hosted by Disney characters. Breakfast includes pastries, eggs, Mickey waffles, Simba waffles, bacon, sausage, fruit, yogurt, and granola. Lunch and dinner offerings extend to breads and dips, salads, tandoori chicken, marinated pork, curry shrimp, beef, salmon, jasmine rice, roasted veggies, mashed potatoes, and green beans. Kids may choose chicken legs, mac and cheese, and corn dog nuggets. Nature-inspired desserts such as zebra cookies and flamingo cupcakes provide a sweet ending to the meal. Specialty cocktails, beer, wine, and mocktails come at an extra cost. At press time, those scheduled to attend were Donald, Daisy, Mickey, and Goofy (the latter three are subject to change at any time). Reservations are highly recommended for all meals. Book as far in advance as possible. Tusker House may start serving before the park opens for the day. **BLD/$$$/**🐭

**YAK & YETI:** Found in the park's Asia section, Yak & Yeti opens for lunch at 10:30 A.M. It specializes in Asian fusion cuisine. The all-day menu includes chicken tikka masala, coconut-crusted shrimp, kobe beef burger, Korean BBQ ribs, lo mein, and seared miso salmon. For dessert, try fried (sweet) wontons or mango cheesecake. Soft drinks and cocktails are served. **LDS/$$$/**🐭

## FAST FOOD & SNACKS

**ANANDAPUR ICE CREAM TRUCK:** Cool off with soft-serve (chocolate, vanilla, and swirl) from Asia's local ice cream truck. The snack is served in a waffle cone, cup, or soda float. Bottled water and soft drinks are also offered. **S/$**

**CREATURE COMFORTS:** This cozy locale is a home fit for a mermaid. Yep, the sippers' sanctum known as Starbucks is open for business on Discovery Island. It currently comforts creatures with coffee concoctions, pastries, sandwiches, and snacks. **BLDS/$-$$/**🐭

**DINO-BITE SNACKS:** Restaurantosaurus's neighbor, this snack shack proffers hand-scooped ice cream, frosty floats, ice-cream cookie sandwiches, hot fudge sundaes, cookies, plus Mickey pretzels, and chips. **S/$-$$**

**DRINKWALLAH:** While trekking through Asia, intrepid explorers may stop here for a refreshing pit stop: frozen soft drinks, bottled water, and other thirst-quenchers. In addition to beverages, snacks are served (ice cream bars, cinnamon-glazed nuts, and chips). Sausage-and-egg biscuits are offered for breakfast. **BS/$**

**EIGHT SPOON CAFE:** Discovery Island's mac and cheese purveyor, this kiosk serves it plain or with pulled pork. Jelly doughnuts stuffed with pulled pork (yes, you read that right), churros, Mickey pretzels (with cheese sauce), chips, and soft drinks round out the offerings. **S/$**

**FLAME TREE BARBECUE:** A reliable fan-favorite, Flame Tree serves a fragrant selection of wood-roasted sandwiches and platters. Sample the signature barbecue sauce with your chicken, pulled pork, or house-smoked St. Louis ribs. Also served: smoked pulled pork sandwiches, plant-based sausage sandwiches, baked mac & cheese with pulled pork, mixed green salad with chicken, fries, onion rings, and cupcakes. Most platters come with sides of beans and coleslaw. Beer, wine, and assorted soft drinks are served. Youngsters may enjoy baked chicken drumsticks, pulled pork platters, PB&J sandwiches, or hot dogs. There is shaded seating along the river. Please don't feed the wildlife. **LDS/$$/☺/MO**

**HARAMBE FRUIT MARKET:** Sometimes a crunchy apple is just what the doctor—or hungry park guest—ordered. Apples (and other fruits) are sold at this stand near the Kilimanjaro Safaris. It has grilled corn, hot dogs, churros (with chocolate sauce), Mickey pretzels, cheese snack packs, chips, and assorted soft drinks, too. **S/$**

**HARAMBE MARKET:** Enshrined within an old train station, the palate-pleasing Harambe Market features several proprietors offering African takes on American favorites: ribs and grilled chicken topped with salsa and served with cilantro rice and mixed greens, plant-based sausage bowl with rice and greens, and salad. Dessert may come in the form of a cupcake. You'll find the Harambe-style street fare near Mombasa Marketplace. **LDS/$$/☺/MO**

**ISLE OF JAVA:** The "isle" is actually a Discovery Island kiosk specializing in coffees and treats for guests on the go. Among the snack selections offered by Flame Tree Barbecue's next-door neighbor are breakfast biscuits, Mickey-shaped soft pretzels served with cheese sauce, and assorted pastries. Soft drinks, specialty coffees, and spirited beverages are also served. **BS/$**

**KUSAFIRI COFFEE SHOP & BAKERY:** Mornings at this Tusker House-adjacent bakery bring breakfast sandwiches, muffins, cookies, colossal cinnamon rolls, fruit cups, croissants, soft drinks, and specialty coffees (including African coffee with Amarula). Later on, the menu includes flatbreads (marinated pork or chicken), plant-based empanadas, and seasoned house-made chips. There are tables nearby. **BLDS/$–$$**

**MAHINDI:** A swell-smelling snack shack, Mahindi sells fresh-popped popcorn (about $6). If you buy a refillable bucket (about $13), you're entitled to unlimited, discounted refills for the length of your WDW stay. (Refills cost about $2.25 a pop.) Mahindi also serves chips, fountain drinks, bottled water, and beer. **S/$**

**PIZZAFARI:** This colorful dining area offers freshly made, individual pizzas: cheese, pepperoni, or sausage and pepperoni. The menu also features chicken parmesan sandwiches, salads (with or without chicken), breadsticks (served with marinara sauce), Caesar salads (side or entrée), cupcakes, fresh fruit, and bug-shaped graham crackers. Young diners may enjoy pasta with turkey marinara sauce, PB&J sandwich, mac & cheese, and kid-friendly cheese pizza. Soft drinks, beer, wine, and specialty beverages are served. Lively animal murals decorate the walls. **LDS/$$/☺/MO**

## ANIMAL KINGDOM MEALTIME TIPS

• Satu'li Canteen, Pizzafari, Restaurantosaurus, Flame Tree Barbecue, and Harambe Market accept advance orders via the My Disney Experience app. Mobile Order payments must be made through the aforementioned app with a credit card, debit card, Disney Gift Card, Disney Rewards Redemption Card, Apple Pay, or a Disney Dining Plan.

• Tusker House and Rainforest Cafe are table-service places offering breakfast; a few spots, including Creature Comforts, Tamu Tamu, Pongu Pongu, and Yak & Yeti Local Food Cafes, have light breakfast options.

• Restaurants that accept reservations are Tusker House, Rainforest Cafe, Yak & Yeti, and Tiffins. Reservations are recommended and can be made via the My Disney Experience mobile app or website, or by visiting *disneyworld.com/dining*.

• Rainforest Cafe may keep longer hours than Disney's Animal Kingdom park—plan your exit transportation accordingly.

**PONGU PONGU:** Hike through the other-worldly terrain of Pandora—The World of Avatar, and you'll discover this refreshing outpost (next to the Windtraders shop). Na'vi for "Party Party," Pongu Pongu welcomes weary travelers with breakfast offerings such as sausage and egg biscuits, cinnamon rolls, and pineapple cream cheese sweet spring rolls, plus milk, juice, and specialty drinks. Later in the day, this window offers colossal soft pretzels with beer cheese dipping sauce (perfect for sharing), the aforementioned sweet spring rolls, cocktails, and soft drinks. **BS/$–$$**

**RESTAURANTOSAURUS:** This DinoLand spot is a fishing lodge turned commissary for student paleontologists. It offers bacon cheeseburgers, breaded shrimp, fried chicken sandwiches, chicken nuggets, spicy plant-based burgers, Cobb salad with chicken—plus fries, fresh fruit, soft drinks, beer, and margaritas. The kids' menu includes cheeseburgers, mac & cheese, and chicken strips. The jovial joint is jammed with fossils, dinosaur bones, and such; class notes line the walls. **LDS/$$/☺/MO**

**ROYAL ANANDAPUR TEA COMPANY:** After hiking to Asia, park guests can build up quite a thirst. That's where this tea stand comes in handy. Near the Yak & Yeti in the village of Serka Zong, the hut sells iced and hot teas, specialty coffees, and baked treats. **S/$**

**SATU'LI CANTEEN:** Look for familiar dishes with a twist at this exotic canteen, featuring bowls for diners to customize. Each bowl starts with a base of rice and black beans; red and sweet potato hash; noodles; or hearty salad. It's finished by adding wood-grilled chicken, sliced grilled beef, chili-garlic shrimp, or chili-spiced tofu, and a sauce of your choice. Kids' menu selections include sliced grilled beef or chopped chicken bowls and crispy fried tofu (tasty, but not ideal for picky eaters), plus cheeseburger steamed pods, quesadillas, and hot dogs. For dessert, choose blueberry cream cheese mousse with passion fruit curd or flourless chocolate cake with chocolate mousse and raspberry gelée. Soft drinks, beer, wine, and sangria are served. **LDS/$$/☺/MO**

**SMILING CROCODILE:** This handy stand serves street tacos (pulled pork, chicken, or street corn). Soft drinks and beer are also offered, as is a signature beverage dubbed the Island Sunrise (tequila with pineapple-orange-guava juice and a hint of watermelon). **LDS/$**

PHOTO BY JILL SAFRO

**TAMU TAMU REFRESHMENTS:** Stop by this corner spot in Africa's Harambe for a sweet treat. You can choose a breakfast biscuit, pastry, cup of pineapple, warm brownie sundae, churros served with chocolate sauce, or the wildly popular frozen pineapple treat known as Dole Whip (with or without rum). Coffee, soft drinks, and beer also grace the menu. **BLDS/$**

**THIRSTY RIVER BAR & TREK SNACKS:** Best enjoyed *after* tackling the Expedition Everest attraction, the offerings here include fountain drinks, coffee, cocoa, beer, wine, and specialty cocktails. **S/$**

**TRILO-BITES:** Just inside the entrance to DinoLand U.S.A. (not far from the dinosaur skeleton bridge), this kiosk sells Buffalo chicken chips, churros with chocolate sauce, waffle cones (filled with soft-serve chocolate, vanilla, or twist), floats, and orange Dole Whip and vanilla soft serve twist, plus soft drinks, beer, and cocktails. **LDS/$**

**YAK & YETI LOCAL FOOD CAFES:** Next to the Yak & Yeti, this window specializes in items with pan-Asian influences. The morning menu has breakfast bowls and egg muffins—plus fruit and hash brown bites. Lunch and dinner entrées include honey sesame chicken, vegetable tikka masala, veggie burgers, Korean fried chicken sandwich, cheeseburgers, sweet-and-sour tempura shrimp, and teriyaki chicken salad. Egg rolls, fries, and chicken fried rice are also served. For dessert, look for items such as frozen lemonade, and mini chocolate cake. The kids' menu features cheeseburgers, chicken strips, and PB&J sandwiches. **BLDS/$$/☺**

# Water Park Dining

Disney's water parks have plenty of satisfying quick-service spots at which to nosh. (You may B.Y.O. food and soft drinks only). Alcohol and glass containers may not be brought into the water parks. Coolers (smaller than 24 inches long, 18 inches high, and 15 inches wide) are allowed. Ice packs are permitted, but loose ice and dry ice are not. Prefer to have someone else do the work? Read on to learn about your dining options.

**Note**: Water parks are subject to refurbishments and seasonal closures, so it's always a good idea to check in advance to see which one will be open during your visit.

## Typhoon Lagoon

**HAPPY LANDINGS ICE CREAM:** Tucked beside Castaway Creek, this hut serves ice cream in sand pails, soft-serve sundaes, cones, and other chilly treats. S/$–$$

**LEANING PALMS:** Pop over to Leaning Palms for cheeseburgers, chicken wraps, flatbreads (plain or pepperoni), rice bowls, breaded chicken sandwiches, hot dogs, and Caribbean-spiced salad. Chips, cookies, fries, and fruit are also available. Wash it all down with a milk shake, soft drink, beer, wine, sangria, hard cider, or a non-alcoholic piña colada. Kids' meals are offered. LDS/$–$$/🐭

**LOWTIDE LOU'S:** Lou quells hunger pangs with shrimp Louie lettuce wraps, chicken wraps, and cauliflower tabbouleh—all served with chips. Also on the menu: soft pretzels (stuffed with cream cheese or with cheese sauce), kids' sandwiches, ice cream, and frozen lemonade. Soft drinks, shakes, beer, wine, sangria, and specialty drinks are served. Operates seasonally. LDS/$$/🐭

**SNACK SHACK:** Relaxing in the surf pool can really work up an appetite. Fortunately, this nearby shack offers substantial snack selections. Among the possibilities:

**Hot Tip!** All-Day Refillable Mugs (about $13 each) come with a day's worth of soft drink refills at the water parks. Mugs may be reactivated for about $9 a day for the length of your WDW stay. Not to be confused with Disney's resort mugs, the water park vessels are bigger and may only be filled at Typhoon Lagoon and Blizzard Beach.

loaded nachos with chili, Hei Hei cones (pineapple and raspberry non-dairy soft serve; aka Dole Whip), Motunui Island Twist (lime Dole Whip), and chocolate chip cookies. The menu includes assorted soft drinks, bottled water, light beer, piña coladas, and Dole Whip served with rum or tequila. LDS/$–$$/🐭

**TYPHOON TILLY'S:** A shipwreck-turned-snack bar, T.T.'s serves battered fish tacos, lettuce wraps with shrimp, beer-battered fish baskets, chicken strips, plant-based "crab-less" crab cakes, cookies, fruit cups, soft drinks, and spirited beverages. All-day refillable mugs may be purchased for about $13 each. LDS/$–$$/🐭

## Blizzard Beach

**AVALUNCH:** Slide on over to this window for quarter-pound hot dogs (plain or with various toppings, served with chips), Caesar salad with chicken, plus kids' meals, soft drinks, beer, and sangria. LDS/$–$$/🐭

**COOLING HUT:** Strut to this hut for pretzels with cheese, popcorn, yogurt, fresh fruit cups, chips, cheese, frozen treats, and more. LDS/$–$$/🐭

**FROSTBITE FREDDY'S FROZEN FRESHMENTS:** Our frosty friend serves beer, Meltaway Margaritas, passion fruit piña coladas, Bloody Marys, and bottled water. He has also offered savory items such loaded beef nachos and chicken quesadillas. S/$–$$

**I.C. EXPEDITIONS:** Cool off with an I.C. (get it?) sundae, waffle cone, ice cream novelty, or root beer float. S/$–$$

**LOTTAWATTA LODGE:** The lodge offers burgers, chicken strips, flatbreads, chicken rice bowl, Caesar (with shrimp or chicken) salad, and plant-based selections such as roasted tofu rice bowl and "bratwurst" sandwich. Desserts include chocolate chip cookies, Mickey Mouse ice cream bars, and a variety of milkshakes. LDS/$–$$/🐭

**WARMING HUT:** Despite the name, most of the fare is cool. Hit the hut for items such as tuna sandwiches, shrimp lettuce wraps, plant-based tabbouleh, loaded nachos, Mickey-shaped pretzels, waffle cones, brownie sundaes, cookies, and assorted drinks. LDS/$–$$/🐭

# In Disney Springs

Disney Springs encompasses four distinct neighborhoods: the Marketplace, the West Side, Town Center, and The Landing. Eateries tend to operate from about 11 A.M. to about midnight; most snack spots are open from about 11 A.M. to late into the night. For updates, use the My Disney Experience mobile app or website, or visit *disneyworld.com*.

**AMC DINE-IN THEATRES:** (West Side): Popcorn and soda are upstaged by selections such as chipotle chicken melts, flatbreads, and mango margaritas at this in-theater dining experience. Seat-side service allows moviegoers to enjoy dinner before a screening. The menu includes appetizers, entrées, desserts, soft drinks, and spirited beverages—plus classic movie munchies. Simply place your order at the kiosk and take your seat in the theater. Seating is reserved (and is assigned when you purchase the movie ticket). Guests under the age of 18 must be accompanied by a paying adult (age 18 or older). All details are subject to change. **LDS/$$**

**THE BASKET AT WINE BAR GEORGE** (The Landing): Three words of note: *Frosé all day*. Wine Bar George's quick-service window serves this refreshingly chilly libation along with an impressive selection of wine, beer, hard cider, and soft drinks. In addition to the frosé (frozen rosé with vodka and strawberry), frozen drinks include Frozcato (frozen Moscato with vodka and pineapple Dole Whip). Beverages may be paired with crispy mac & cheese bites, cheese, charcuterie, hummus and naan bread, french fries (with cheese or Buffalo topping), landjäger (German-style jerky), Spanish cheese plate, and half baguette. **LDS/$$–$$$**

**B.B. WOLF'S SAUSAGE CO.** (Marketplace): Head to this stand for hot dogs, sausages (bratwurst, Italian, plant-based, and Andouille), and chips. Wash it down with a fountain drink, bottled water, frozen lemonade, frozen sweet tea, or seasonal beer. **LDS/$$/☙ MO**

**BLAZE FAST FIRE'D PIZZA** (Town Center): If you fancy a freshly custom-made pizza, make a beeline for Blaze. The 5,000-square-foot eatery fires made-to-order (aka "build your own") pizzas in just three minutes with the help of super-hot pizza ovens. Guests may customize their 11-inch pies with a vast array of toppings (included in the price), as well as pick their own cheese and sauce. Gluten-free crusts are an option. The menu boasts eight signature pizzas, plus salads and desserts. S'more pie, please! **LDS/$–$$/☙**

**THE BOATHOUSE** (The Landing): An upscale and convivial waterfront destination, The Boathouse serves delightful delicacies from land and sea for lunch and dinner. The raw bar offers oysters on the half shell, wild caught shrimp, and tuna poke. The Dockside Classics collection features a satisfying shrimp boil, grilled fish tacos, and lump crab cakes (large enough to share, though you won't want to). Entrée selections have included coriander-seared Ahi tuna, cedar-planked salmon, shrimp and andouille mac & cheese, and baked crab-stuffed lobster with Béarnaise sauce. Chicken, pasta, and a large lineup of steak dishes tempt, too. A children's menu is available. Guests may enjoy drinks and a full menu at any of the three bar settings. Reservations are highly recommended for tables at this Signature Restaurant, but a number of bar stools are designated for walk-ins. **BRUNCH** (weekend) **LDS/$$–$$$$/☙/SR**

**CHICKEN GUY!** (Town Center): This hoppin' destination boasts no fewer than 22 signature sauces in which to dip chicken tenders. Honey mustard? Check. Garlic parmesan? Check. Sweet sriracha BBQ? Well, you get the picture. Chicken sandwiches and salads are served, as are seasoned fries, loaded fries, coleslaw, mac and cheese, and fried pickle chips. Save room for a whipped cream-topped hand-spun shake: chocolate, vanilla, strawberry, triple double mint, and more. **LDS/$/☙**

**COOKES OF DUBLIN** (The Landing): Raglan Road's delectable quick-service neighbor, this is the place to go for some of the best fish and chips in the World. And don't ask for the recipe—it's a Cooke family secret! Other choices include burgers, chicken tenders, house-made pie of the day, grilled chicken sandwiches, and hog in a box (slow-roasted pork shoulder with potatoes, sage and sweet onion stuffing, caramelized onions, and apple sauce). Save room for a "lovely" dessert. **LDS/$$/**

**CITY WORKS EATERY AND POUR HOUSE** (West Side): A sports fan's dream, City Works sits across from House of Blues. With its 165 screens, more than 90 tap beers, a lunch/dinner menu including shareable plates (spicy shrimp, smoked wings, Kung Pao cauliflower, duck nachos, etc.), soups, salads, burgers, and tacos, plus entrées such as pan-seared salmon, fish and chips, pork chops, BBQ ribs, Cajun linguine etc., this boisterous locale aims to please. In addition to the substantial supply of suds, the bar serves specialty drinks, wine, soft drinks, and more. There's a menu for kids, too. Brunch (Saturday and Sunday) brings breakfast flatbreads and chimichangas, avocado toast, breakfast BLT, grits, and steak and eggs. Reservations are accepted. Care to save some cash at City Works? Use the coupon at the back of this book. **BRUNCH** (weekend) **LDS/$$–$$$/**

**THE DAILY POUTINE** (Town Center): Poutine—a decadent combination of french fries and cheese curds, topped with beef gravy—comes from the Canadian province of Quebec. (Thank you, Canada!) Five different varieties of this savory snack are sold at this Disney Springs stand: Canadian (beef poutine gravy and cheddar cheese curds), Loaded (queso blanco, pico de gallo, and bacon), Italian (mozzarella and turkey bolognese sauce), Korean BBQ (pulled pork, kimchi, and sriracha aioli) and Butter Chicken (chicken, paneer cheese, and tomato curry). Soft drinks (including watermelon lemonade), beer, and Canadian apple slushies are also served. **S/$$/**

**D-LUXE BURGER** (Town Center): D-Luxe is a sweet spot for a quick bite. The burgers (big enough to share) are served on fresh-baked buns. The freshly cut french fries

(which come with dipping sauces) and (scrumptious) artisanal gelato shakes are sure to please. Place your order at the counter and grab a seat while your meal is prepared—it will be delivered to your table. There's indoor and outdoor seating. **LDS/$$//MO**

**EARL OF SANDWICH** (Marketplace): This counter-service spot is brimming with possibilities. Among the fare are hot sandwiches (on warm bread), wraps, salads, and desserts. Sandwich selections such as Holiday Turkey (turkey, cornbread stuffing, gravy, cranberry sauce, and mayo), The Original 1762 (warm roast beef sandwich with horseradish sauce and cheddar cheese), Cuban, pizza, ham & cheese, tuna melt, and veggie sandwiches are served. Breakfast features hot sandwiches, burritos, oatmeal, and assorted muffins. There are soups, salads, brownies, cookies, and grab-and-go items, too. Kids' meals are offered for lunch and dinner. Seating is available inside and out. **BLDS/$–$$/**

**EVERGLAZED DONUTS & COLD BREW** (West Side): "Florida born and glazed," this sweet spot specializes in circular sweets (aka donuts), cold-brewed coffee, and savory bites. Made-from-scratch donuts fall into two categories: classic and funky—with varieties ranging from traditional glazed to Brooklyn Blackout and S'mores Galore.

The mouth-watering menu also features donut holes, sandwiches (including egg and cheese, fried chicken, grilled cheese), burgers, and waffle-style fries (plain, spicy, and loaded). Sandwiches come on sweet buns—which can be swapped out for a griddled glazed donut for an extra buck. The beverage lineup has cold-brewed coffees, hot coffee, lemonade (regular or strawberry), iced tea, hand-crafted flavored milks, and fountain drinks (the latter come with free refills!) **BLDS/$–$$**

**Hot Tip!** Is that gift card burning a hole in your pocket? Disney gift cards may be redeemed at all Disney-owned-and-operated dining, shopping, and recreation locations where credit cards are accepted. They may be used to pay for all (or part) of the bill at a Disney resort, too. If you lose track of what's left on your gift card, simply call the number on the back to find out.

**FOOD TRUCKS** (West Side): **The Mac & Cheese** truck serves (surprise!) mac & cheese with six cheeses and topped with crispy cheese puffs. Other choices include chicken parmesan and barbecued beef. **4 Rivers Cantina Barbacoa** sells street tacos, burrito bowls, quesadillas, taco cones, margarita dessert bars, beer, and soft drinks. **Hot Diggity Dogs** offers Texas chili-, Reuben-, BLT-, and other spiced-up hot dogs (with chips). Newcomer **Local Green Orlando** has shrimp burgers, kale & quinoa wraps, plant-based burgers, and pulled pork BBQ sandwiches. Trucks, menus, and location are subject to change. The trucks usually open between 4 and 5 P.M. **DS**/$–$$/🐭

**GHIRARDELLI ICE CREAM & SODA SHOP** (Marketplace): What is it about an old-fashioned ice cream parlor that makes just about everybody giddy? Oh, yes, the ice cream. This spot does it one better and throws in its world-famous chocolate, to boot. Stop in for a chocolaty treat, root beer float, or a malt. And there's always a possibility of a free sample. How sweet is that?! **S**/$$

**GIDEON'S BAKE HOUSE:** (The Landing): Gideon's has raised milk and cookies to a whole new level. We're talking stratosphere, folks. One such special treat is a hand-made, small-batch chocolate chip cookie that weighs in at nearly half a pound and takes about 24 hours to create! This sweet sensation shares the spotlight with varieties such as peanut butter crunch, pistachio toffee chocolate chip, coffee cake, and cookies & cream. For those not ready to commit to such a colossal confection, smaller versions are offered, as are cake slices, cold-brew coffee specialty drinks, and locally sourced milk. Doors usually open at 10 A.M., but folks start lining up long before that. Get there early. **S**/$–$$

**CHEF ART SMITH'S HOMECOMIN'** (The Landing): "Florida heritage meets New Southern cuisine" at this gustatory homage to the Sunshine State. Created by Chef Art Smith, the menu focuses on Southern favorites such as fried green tomatoes with local greens, Church Lady deviled eggs (which, ironically, are quite heavenly), hushpuppies, chicken & dumpling soup, Brunswick stew, Art's famous fried chicken, shrimp & grits, fried chicken & doughnuts, and chopped pork BBQ plate. Specialty desserts such as Hummingbird Cake, chocolate pecan pie, and fresh doughnuts make for a sweet finish.

A family-friendly destination, Homecomin' has a design inspired by Florida architecture of the late 1800s and pays homage to the Sunshine State's rich agricultural heritage by highlighting local ingredients and farm-to-table cuisine. Reservations are recommended for all meals. Score a free dessert by using the coupon at the back of this book! **BRUNCH** (weekend) **LDS**/$$–$$$/🐭

**THE EDISON** (The Landing): A lavish "Industrial Gothic"–style venue, The Edison (modeled after the original Los Angeles version) is a 1920s-themed restaurant, bar, and nighttime destination. Designed to resemble a power plant, it recalls a robust era of invention and imagination. In addition to classic American food and drink, The Edison supplies electrifying entertainment, starting at about 7 P.M. every evening. Expect a lineup of unique acts, including contortionists, aerialists, live cabaret, and deejays.

The menu tempts with appetizers such as candied bacon, electri-fries, flatbreads, and fried calamari. Entrée selections include St. Louis ribs, grilled salmon, short rib, blackened mahi mahi, burgers (including a plant-based option), chicken sandwich, and grilled cheese served with organic tomato soup. For dessert, choose cheesecake, triple chocolate cake, or housemade gelato. Reservations are highly recommended. All details are subject to change. For additional information, visit *theedisonfla.com*. **DS**/$$–$$$$/🐭

**ENZO'S HIDEAWAY** (The Landing): A combination tunnel bar and restaurant, Enzo's evokes a speakeasy atmosphere. Inspired by Florida's "rum-running" past, this watering hole specializing in barrel-aged cocktails has a selection of rums and scotches, plus beer, wine, and specialty drinks (some served family style).

When you're ready for some solid sustenance, choose from imported meats and cheeses, calamari, rustic pasta dishes, and Italian-inspired entrée selections (grilled salmon, eggplant parmigiana, grilled ribeye steak, etc.). Complete the meal with a sweet treat such as cannoli, tiramisú, or gelato. Advance reservations are strongly recommended, but same-day reservations (and walk-ups) may be available. **LDS**/$$–$$$$/🐭

**FRONTERA COCINA** (Town Center): The brainchild of six-time James Beard Foundation winner Chef Rick Bayless, this spot showcases gourmet Mexican cuisine. Select from items such as salads, chipotle chicken flautas, tacos, grilled mahi mahi, slow-roasted pork, pan-roasted shrimp, freshly made guacamole, and tortilla soup—all prepared with locally sourced ingredients. Pair your Mexican meal with a marvelous margarita (the selection is vast). Beer, wine, cocktails, and soft drinks are served, too. Reservations are recommended. **LDS**/$$–$$$$

**HOUSE OF BLUES** (West Side): Thanks to the combination of its menu and rustic, folk-art-studded design, House of Blues does not disappoint. Menu favorites include smoked brisket sandwiches, shrimp po' boys, baby back ribs, shrimp and grits, jalapeño cornbread, gumbo, and jambalaya. Cap off the meal with a slice of Key lime pie or a bread pudding with bourbon butter and toffee sauce. House of Blues is a solid choice for a meal or a late-night bite. Live music is presented in the eatery and on the front porch on select days. Brunch is offered on Saturday and Sunday (from 10 A.M. to 2 P.M., with a full menu available after noon). Reservations are recommended for lunch and dinner (and downright necessary for brunch). To reserve a table, go to *disneyworld.com/dining*, or call 407-934-2583. **BRUNCH** (weekend) LDS/$$–$$$/☙

**HOUSE OF BLUES SMOKEHOUSE** (West Side): This walk-up window at House of Blues offers savory sandwiches (pulled pork or BBQ brisket), smoked turkey legs, BBQ chicken salad, nachos, jumbo footlong hot dogs, soft pretzels, baked beans, coleslaw, and more. Also available: beer, wine, soft drinks, cookies, chips, and candy. LDS/$–$$/☙

**JALEO BY JOSÉ ANDRÉS** (West Side): The flavors of Spain have found a home in Disney Springs, thanks to Chef José Andrés. The tapas (small plates) menu highlights classic and contemporary España. Savory selections include hand-carved Jamon Iberico de Bellota, grilled Iberico pork, rack of lamb, grilled steak, cheese plates, salads, chicken fritters, house-made chorizo, seared fish of the day, and traditional paella (cooked over a wood fire). Reservations are recommended. The multi-level eatery also has a quick-service area called Pepe. It offers Spanish-style sandwiches, snacks, Spanish sangria, and other drinks. LDS/$$–$$$$/☙/SR

**MARIA AND ENZO'S RISTORANTE** (The Landing): Up, up, and away! Ostensibly set in a storied airline terminal from the 1930s, the edifice morphed into an elegant eatery, thanks to a duo of enterprising immigrants named Maria and Enzo. Vintage maps and artifacts enhance the aviation theme. After checking in, passengers (aka diners) descend the grand, spiral staircase to reach an Art Deco–accented dining room. (Guests may also nosh in the cozy "First Class Lounge," on the top floor.)

The Southern Italian–inspired menu includes braised meatball with whipped ricotta and parmesan, crispy calamari, Caesar salad, burrata Caprese, charcuterie (for two), chicken parmesan, cheese ravioli, fresh fish, grilled ribeye steak, braised beef short rib, and rigatoni Bolognese. Maria and Enzo offer tempting desserts such as tiramisú, cannoli, gelato, and Grandma's custard tart. A kids' menu is available. Reservations are recommended. **BRUNCH** (weekend) LDS/$$–$$$$/☙

**MORIMOTO ASIA** (The Landing): Brought to Walt Disney World by Japanese master chef Masaharu Morimoto—TV's original Iron Chef—this modern eatery features dishes from across Asia. The two-story venue offers Pan-Asian cuisine prepared in show kitchens. The menu features sushi and sashimi (including "towers" that serve 2 to 3 hungry guests); small plates (edamame, miso soup, crispy popcorn shrimp tempura, pork egg roll,

and more); noodle and rice dishes; meat and poultry selections including orange chicken, Mongolian filet mignon, spare ribs, and Morimoto Peking duck for two. Kids' selections include egg fried rice and lo mein. Reservations are recommended. **LDS/$$–$$$$/🐭/SR**

**MORIMOTO ASIA—STREET FOOD** (The Landing): This quick-service window, located on Morimoto Asia's patio, serves ramen (spicy kimchee or ginger chicken), pork ribs, *takoyaki* (octopus fritters), pork egg rolls, soft drinks, Japanese beers, and a no-alcohol specialty cocktail known as South Seas Slush. **LDS/$$/🐭**

**PADDLEFISH** (The Landing): Originally known as the *Empress Lilly* (after Walt Disney's wife, Lillian), and more recently as Fulton's, this spot has been beautifully reinvented and given a new identity. Paddlefish may look as if it might set sail at any moment, but the sleek replica of a boat that houses the seafood-centric eatery is permanently docked at the edge of Lake Buena Vista. The classic Walt Disney World space features a modern interior, roof-top lounge, and two interior bars.

Paddlefish boasts an elaborate selection of appetizers and entrées featuring the day's arrivals. Look for offerings such as fried green tomatoes, clam chowder, calamari, crab cakes, catfish, crab ceviche, salmon, stuffed cod, scallops with cauliflower purée, and whole Maine lobster. And a selection of seafood boils are sure to please. The menu offers plenty for landlubbers, too: beef skewers, filet mignon, pork chop, chicken breast, 16-ounce ribeye, salads, and vegetarian pasta. Youngsters appreciate the more-extensive-than-usual kids' menu.

The meal can come to a sweet finish with a piece of Key lime pie. If you prefer to sip your dessert, consider a refreshing drink such as Lili's Steamboat Breeze or the Captain Handsome. Reservations are recommended. To save cash at Paddlefish, use the coupon at the back of this book. **BRUNCH** (Sunday) **LDS/$$–$$$$/🐭/SR**

**PARADISO 37** (The Landing): A lively (and lovely) waterfront restaurant and bar (with indoor and outdoor seating, plus a live-performance stage), Paradiso 37 specializes in "swirl margaritas," stocks more than 100 different kinds of tequila, and offers the "coldest beer in the world." Oh, and food is served, too!

Paradiso's tapas-oriented menu focuses on "the taste" of the Americas. Starters include fire-roasted "crazy" corn on the cob, quesadillas, nachos, and poutine. Entrées range from Argentinian skirt steak with chimichurri sauce to Patagonian seared salmon. **LDS/$$$/🐭**

**PEPE BY JOSÉ ANDRÉS** (West Side): Tucked within the same dynamic structure as the restaurant Jaleo, Pepe features hot and cold Spanish-style sandwiches showcasing the best of José's native Spain. Options include *pepito ternera*, *bikini 3 quesos*, and *super flauta*. The menu includes hot dogs, salads, gazpacho, chips, and soft-serve treats. Beer, wine, sangria, and soft drinks are served. The counter-service eatery was designed by the acclaimed Juli Capella and features decor representing the colorful culture of Spain. **LDS/$–$$/🐭**

**PLANET HOLLYWOOD** (Town Center): The Hollywood-themed eatery has indoor and outdoor seating and a bar called Stargazers, featuring live entertainment. The menu has salads, sandwiches, pasta, burgers, and desserts. Reservations are recommended. **LDS/$$–$$$/🐭**

**PIZZA PONTE** (The Landing): Adjacent to Maria and Enzo's Ristorante, Pizza Ponte is a satisfying, quick-service dining experience. Step up to the counter and order pizza by the slice (tomato, artichoke, 4-cheese, forest mushroom, etc.), sandwiches (tomato mozzarella; ham and cheese; and mortadella), and desserts such as tiramisú, cookies, or cannoli. Beer, wine, espresso, and soft drinks are served. **LDS/$–$$/🐭**

**THE POLITE PIG** (Town Center): Created by award-winning Orlando chefs Julie and James Petrakis, this quick-service destination features "modern barbecue" and Southern sides. The menu includes sandwiches (brisket, smoked turkey BLT, pulled pork, and fried chicken), and entrées such as chicken, pork shoulder, BBQ brats, ribs, brisket, and salmon. Among the satisfying salads and sides are Caesar and Cobb salads, crispy Brussels sprouts, BBQ cauliflower, and sweet potato tots. For dessert, try red velvet cake or pecan pie. Beer and wine are served—and the bourbon menu is extensive. There's indoor and outdoor seating and a full bar. **LD/$$–$$$/🐭**

**RAGLAN ROAD** (The Landing): As authentically Irish as you can get on this side of the Atlantic, this warm and spirited establishment blends fresh ingredients to create traditional Irish fare with a modern flair. Entrées such as fish and chips, shepherd's pie, 12-hour braised beef sandwich, bangers and mash, seafood dishes, and plant-based offerings are complemented by the welcoming atmosphere, complete with antiques and bric-a-brac, spirits, and live Irish music and traditional dance (starting at 5 P.M. on most days). Whistles may be wet with craft beers, whiskeys, wines, cocktails, and soft drinks. Beer and whiskey flights are an option. Brunch (with live entertainment) is served on Saturday and Sunday. Reservations are recommended. To save money on food and merchandise at Raglan Road, use the coupons at the back of this book. **BRUNCH** (weekend) **LDS/$$–$$$/**

**RAINFOREST CAFE** (Marketplace): This Amazon-emulating eatery transports diners to a makeshift rainforest, complete with banyan trees, tropical fish, waterfalls, singing birds, and trumpeting elephants.

Special effects envelop diners in tropical storms with flashes of lightning and thunder claps. American-style eats (with exotic names) have included the Beastly Burger, Anaconda Pasta, Mojo Bones, and Jungle Turkey Wrap. Reservations may be made via the My Disney Experience mobile app or website, or by calling 407-827-8500. **LDS/$$–$$$/**

**SPLITSVILLE** (West Side): Some go expecting just to bowl, not realizing that Splitsville's two kitchens turn out impressive casual fare such as freshly rolled sushi, grilled salmon with mango chutney, and sliders. They also have pizzas, cheeseburgers, sandwiches, entrée salads, taco bowls, fish 'n' chips, and more. Desserts include sundaes, floats, and brownie à la mode. Food is delivered lane-side or at "non-bowling" tables. Live music is played on the patio each evening. For more information, visit *www.splitsvillelanes.com*. To save ten percent off bowling, use the coupon at the back of this book. **LDS/$$–$$$/**

**STARBUCKS** (West Side and Marketplace): The Disney Springs links of the famous coffee chain serve up all the usual Starbucks specialties all day long: fresh-brewed coffee (hot or iced), blended drinks, teas, smoothies, and kids' drinks, plus sweet and savory snack items—breakfast sandwiches, oatmeal, sandwiches, protein boxes, and pastries. **BLDS/$–$$**

**STK ORLANDO** (The Landing): Steak is the obvious star here, but this modern restaurant has much more to offer. Specializing in American cuisine, STK pleases most palates. This modern-steakhouse-meets-sleek-lounge features a tempting raw bar, salads, appetizers (crispy calamari, tuna tartare, mini burgers), and entrées such as pasta, chicken, fish, and all manner of steak. Enjoy your meal with sides such as sweet corn pudding, lump crab cakes, Brussels sprouts with bacon-cider glaze, lobster mac and cheese, or parmesan truffle fries. Finish with a bag o' donuts, cheesecake, chocolate cake, or apple pie. There's a full bar and impressive wine list. Guests may dine on the rooftop or in the modern main dining area. Brunch is offered on Saturday and Sunday. Reservations are recommended. **BRUNCH** (weekend) **LDS/$$$–$$$$**

**SWIRLS ON THE WATER** (Marketplace): Disney has been doling out Dole Whip to the delight of park-goers for nearly four decades. And now there's a Disney Springs destination dedicated to the beloved frozen, non-dairy dessert. Housed in the waterside space once occupied by Aristocrépes, Swirls serves a variety of Dole Whip flavors in cups, cones, and floats. There's a rum-spiked selection, too. **S/$/**

**SUMMER HOUSE ON THE LAKE** (West Side): Touted as "the place where summer never ends," this lovely lakeside spot showcases garden-fresh foods **NEW** and Florida-sourced ingredients. While menu items change seasonally, expect a steady stream of flavorful salads, sandwiches, pizzas, and more. Desserts come fresh from the in-house bakery: cookies, brownies, and other sweet treats. Beer, wine, cocktails, and zero-proof specialty drinks are served—as is an array of rosé. Meals may be enjoyed inside the "house" or *al fresco* on a lakeside patio. Reservations are recommended. For additional information, visit *disneyworld.com*, or use the *My Disney Experience* mobile app or website. **BRUNCH** (weekend) **LDS/$$–$$$$**

**JOFFREY'S COFFEE & TEA COMPANY** (The Landing): A pleasant counter-service spot, Joffrey's emphasizes the visual beauty and taste of artisan-roasted coffee and loose-leaf teas prepared in a variety of ways: hot, iced, frozen, spirited, etc. Scones, cookies, and doughnuts are at the ready. There are outdoor tables nearby. **S/$**

**TERRALINA CRAFTED ITALIAN** (The Landing): This water-side eatery serves as a flavorful escape inspired by Italy's famed Lake District. The menu boasts genuine Italian cuisine cooked in the eatery's signature olive oil—and a selection of hand-tossed pizzas and vegetable dishes prepared in the wood-burning oven. Appetizers of note: Italian fries (with cheese sauce and salami), mussels (in a spicy lemon-tomato broth), and mozzarella-stuffed rice balls. The menu also features salads, sandwiches, and entrées such as artichoke chicken, eggplant parmesan, pork gnocchi, rigatoni Calabrese, seafood fettuccine, steak, and catch of the day. With 11 choices on the kids' menu, youngsters should have no trouble pleasing their palates. For dessert, try the seasonal bread pudding or chocolate cake. **BRUNCH** (Sunday) **LDS/$$–$$$$/**

PHOTO BY JILL SAFRO

**T-REX CAFE: A PREHISTORIC FAMILY ADVENTURE** (Market-place): Dinosaurs throw one heck of a dinner party. See for yourself at this dino-themed feasting facility.

When you enter, take note of hosts we were all led to believe were extinct. Okay, they're mechanical dinosaurs, but they're still pretty cool. As are the waterfalls, bubbling geysers, and fossil dig site. Appease hunger pangs with anything from Jurassic Salad to Prehistoric Pasta with Shrimp. With soup, sandwiches, pasta, steaks, seafood, and desserts, this place aims to please one and all. Reservations are recommended. **LD/$$$/**

**VIVOLI IL GELATO** (The Landing): A 94-year-old, family-run establishment, Vivoli il Gelato comes to you from Florence, Italy. Creamy gelato is offered in more than a dozen flavors. The list could include chocolate hazelnut, dulce de leche, coffee, peanut butter, cannoli, vanilla, cake batter, and more. Baked treats and milkshakes are available, too. There are a few outdoor tables at this sweet spot across from The Boathouse. **LDS/$–$$**

**WINE BAR GEORGE** (The Landing): The masterpiece of Master Sommelier George Miliotes, this 200-seat eatery resembles a winemaker's estate. It's a cozy yet elegant environment in which to savor sips from acclaimed wineries and promising up-and-comers. There are more than 200 selections on the list, all served by the ounce, glass, or bottle (ask about pricing before you order). They pair beautifully with small-plate offerings—meatballs with triple cheese polenta, crispy mac & cheese bites, a meat and cheese board, chicken breast, grilled ribeye, etc.—plus family-style entrées. Brunch is offered on Saturday and Sunday. Reservations are recommended. **BRUNCH** (weekend) **LDS/$$–$$$$**

**WOLFGANG PUCK BAR & GRILL** (Town Center): "Elegant farmhouse" is the theme behind Chef Puck's latest contribution to the Disney dining scene. Capturing the essence of laid-back California, the eatery features fresh takes on comfort classics, signature dishes with Mediterranean influences, and handcrafted specialty drinks. The menu tempts with crab cakes, pasta, pizza, salads, and entrées such as chicken wienerschnitzel, pork tenderloin, roasted fish, and steak. Cap off the meal with a sweet treat such as Spanish cheesecake, carrot cake, warm chocolate chip cookies, and gelato or sorbet tastings. The kids menu is extensive. A full bar offers beer, wine, handcrafted cocktails, and non-alcoholic selections. A walk-up gelato bar sells sorbet, gelato, beer, wine, and specialty drinks. Frozen treats come in a cone or a cup and may be topped with everything from cookie crumbs to blueberries. Reservations are recommended for the restaurant. **BRUNCH** (weekend) **LDS/$–$$$$**

# In WDW Resorts

Each of the dozens of resorts at Walt Disney World offers its own set of specially themed eateries. You'll find seafood buffets at the Beach Club, sumptuous sushi at the Swan, stellar steak at the Contemporary, and warm beignets at Port Orleans French Quarter. Meals may be served buffet, family, or traditional table-service or fast-food style. Disney characters are often on hand, especially for breakfast, and some snack spots may stay open into the wee hours. In fact, the resort dining scene has expanded and been upgraded so much that the (occasionally arduous) task of resort-hopping is a more worthwhile experience than ever before.

Advance reservations are a key part of the Disney dining circuit (use the My Disney Experience mobile app or website, or visit *www.disneyworld.com/dining*). Note that some of the spots on the following pages were not operating at press time. For updates, refer to the aforementioned app and websites.

## All-Star Resorts

There are three All-Star resorts, each with a themed food court. All-Star Sports has the **End Zone** food court in Stadium Hall. The **Intermission** food court is in Melody Hall at the All-Star Music resort. And All-Star Movies has the **World Premiere** food court in Cinema Hall. All food courts offer similar dining experiences. The selections may include pasta, pizza, cheeseburgers, seafood, hot dogs, sandwiches, salads, ice cream novelties, a reliable variety of breakfast and baked goods, plus a number of grab-and-go selections. Expect to find more than a few kid-pleasers, too. **BLDS/$–$$/❤/MO**

## Animal Kingdom Lodge

**BOMA—FLAVORS OF AFRICA:** Designed to resemble an African marketplace, Boma offers an impressively diverse selection—the fare served represents the continent of Africa. It's one sprawling buffet with multiple stations, and the food is every bit as good as what you would expect in a fine dining place.

The all-you-care-to-eat buffet provides an excellent bang for your Disney dining buck. Breakfast features omelets, fresh fruit, sausage, Simba-shaped waffles,

### FILL 'ER UP—REFILLABLE MUGS*

Buy one cup and get unlimited refills for your entire Disney vacation? It sounds too good to be true. Yet any guest staying at a WDW-owned-and-operated resort may buy a plastic mug—for about $22, plus tax—and refill it with coffee, tea, lemonade, and other soft drinks for the length of their stay.* (Guests who purchase a Disney Dining Plan may receive a mug.) The following resorts offer the WDW "refillable" mug program (filling stations can be found at the spots noted in parentheses below):

All-Star resorts (food courts); Animal Kingdom Lodge (The Mara and Maji pool bar); Art of Animation (Landscape of Flavors and Drop Off pool bar); BoardWalk (BoardWalk Deli and Leaping Horse Libations); Caribbean Beach (Centertown Market); Contemporary (Contempo Cafe and Cove Bar); Coronado Springs (El Mercado de Coronado and Siesta pool bar); Fort Wilderness (P.&J.'s Southern Takeout); Grand Floridian (Gasparilla Island Grill and Beaches Pool Bar); Old Key West (Good's Food To Go and Turtle Shack); Polynesian Village (Capt. Cook's); Pop Century (food court and Petals bar); Port Orleans French Quarter and Riverside (food courts); Saratoga Springs (Artist's Palette, Paddock Grill, Backstretch bar, and On the Rocks bar); Wilderness Lodge (Roaring Fork snack bar); and Yacht & Beach Club (Beaches & Cream, Beach Club Marketplace, Hurricane Hanna's Grill, and Marketplace at Ale & Compass). If your resort is not listed here, inquire about refills at the Front Desk. Note that details are subject to change.

* Refills may be made at any Disney-owned-and-operated resort hotel, but not at any theme park or water park. Note that Typhoon Lagoon and Blizzard Beach water parks offer their own refillable mug program. See page 287 for details.

ham, pancakes, deviled eggs with smoked salmon, and more. At dinner, expect to fill your plate with items such as salads; an assortment of breads, pasta dishes, seafood; roasted meats; and a nice assortment of plant-based selections. For dessert, do sample the decadent zebra domes—you'll regret it if you don't. It's tempting to overeat at a bounteous feast such as this, so consider taking tiny portions of everything. You can go back for seconds of your favorites. Note that Boma's menu tends to change a bit throughout the year. The wine list includes eclectic selections from African vineyards. Even if you're not staying at Disney's Animal Kingdom Lodge, it's definitely worth the trip. Reservations are required. **BD/$$$/❤**

**JIKO—THE COOKING PLACE:** Jiko offers one of the more unusual—and enjoyable—Disney dining experiences. Its cuisine is inspired by the tastes of Africa, with influences from around the globe. Start with a paper-thin flatbread, roasted wild boar tenderloin, seared scallops, or seasonal salads. Entrées may include Moroccan lamb shank, seasonal plant-based stews, sustainable fish, and the guest favorite oak-grilled filet mignon on a bed of mac and cheese. Finish your meal with sweets such as the South African classic, Melktert or African drum "beets." You can also indulge in a heavenly dessert made with single-origin African chocolates.

The wine list is exclusively South African, one of the most extensive collections in the U.S. It's a nice spot for a grown-up splurge. Though it's not exactly a kid favorite, there are picky-eater-friendly offerings. Reservations are recommended. The small lounge area offers the full menu. Incidentally, the word *jiko* is Swahili for "the cooking place." **D/$$$-$$$$/☙/SR**

**THE MARA:** An impressive quick-service restaurant, The Mara has something for everyone—including a small grab-and-go section for those in a hurry. Look for freshly prepared entrées such as (excellent) flatbreads and burgers. Among the prepackaged selections are sandwiches, salads, fruit, yogurt, and baked goods.

**F.Y.I.:** The eatery is named for a river that flows through Kenya and Tanzania. **BLDS/$-$$/☙/MO**

**SANAA:** Pronounced *sa-NAH*, the name of this eatery means "artwork" in Swahili. The Kidani Village spot has a family-friendly menu featuring Disney's take on African-Indian cuisine. The Indian-style bread service, perfect for sharing and served with a choice of three accompaniments, is a satisfying way to start the meal. Past offerings have included samosas, salad sampler, Zanzibari vegetable curry (served plain or with chicken

PHOTO BY MIKE CARROLL

or shrimp), soup, lamb kefta, tumeric-marinated fish, and New York strip steak. At lunchtime, consider the tandoori chicken. Even the burgers have an Indian touch, served on soft, warm naan bread. Dessert introduces butterscotch pudding, coconut rice pudding, and triple chocolate mousse. Breakfast selections such as eggs Benedict, french toast, scrambled-egg sandwiches, fruit, yogurt parfait, and banana bread are available in the morning. (Reservations are not accepted for the casual breakfast experience.) Reservations are recommended for lunch and dinner. **BLD/$$-$$$$/☙**

# Art of Animation

**LANDSCAPE OF FLAVORS:** "Better for you" options is the theme of this vividly adorned food court, where everything is made fresh once it is ordered. Breakfast offerings include fruit, plant-based frittatas, egg and cheese sandwiches, omelets, character-shaped waffles, oatmeal, sausage, potato barrels, yogurt, and pastries. Later in the day, this spot offers salads, pizza, chicken sandwiches, burgers, pasta, and entrées such as seared salmon, shrimp with grits, and tandoori chicken. Sweet treats include cookies, muffins, doughnuts, and cupcakes. There is a selection of grab-and-go items, too. Made-to-order beverage options include cappuccino and other specialty coffees. Also available: milk, juice, tea, beer, hard cider, wine, and soft drinks. Landscape of Flavors promises something for everyone. **BLDS/$-$$/☙/MO**

# BoardWalk

**BIG RIVER GRILLE & BREWING WORKS:** Guests may watch (and sample) as the brewmaster creates flagship ales and two seasonal brews at this working brew pub. The simple but satisfying menu usually includes pasta, steaks, and salads. Sandwiches are a cut above. Other menu favorites: baby back ribs, Cajun pasta, blackened fish tacos, and blackened Creole salmon. The interior has a nice, pubby feel—but we prefer the outdoor tables on the boardwalk (especially at night). Seating is available on a first-come, first-served basis. **LDS/$$-$$$/☙**

**BOARDWALK DELI:** In the morning, Trattoria al Forno's neighbor has bagel sandwiches, baked **NEW** goods, specialty coffees, tea, and snacks. Later on it serves subs, reubens, and other assorted sandwiches, plus salads, soft drinks, and beer. **BLDS/$-$$/☙/MO**

**BOARDWALK ICE CREAM:** The treats served at this cheery ice cream parlor are sure to please. Nearly a dozen flavors are served in cups, cones, or creatively crafted sundaes. They serve shakes, too. **S/$**

**BOARDWALK JOE'S MARVELOUS MARGARITAS:** Step up to Joe's window to order Mickey-shaped pretzels, jalapeño-stuffed pretzels, cheese nachos, and assorted snacks. The beverage menu boasts beer (draft, bottle, and can), piña coladas, margaritas, and soft drinks. **S/$**

**BOARDWALK PIZZA WINDOW:** Nestled into the building that houses Trattoria al Forno is a place to enjoy a nice slice of pizza. Side salads, mini cannolis, wine, sangria, and soft drinks are offered, too. The quick-service spot is usually open from noon until at least 10 P.M. **LDS/$$/☒/MO**

**THE CAKE BAKE SHOP:** Brought to BoardWalk by award-winning baker, entrepreneur, and proud **NEW** mom Gwendolyn Rogers, The Cake Bake Shop is awash with classic charm and homey elegance. The extensive menu offers something for everyone. Savory selections may include gumbo poutine, chicken velvet soup, salads, sandwiches, quiche, roasted salmon, pasta, burgers, crab cakes, steak, and chicken piccata. There are kid-tailored dishes, too (buttered noodles, grilled cheese, sliders, etc.) Among the lovingly prepared sweet treats: cakes, pies, pastries, cookies, ice cream, and heavenly hot chocolate. The beverage lineup features wine, beer, champagne drinks, New Orleans–inspired cocktails, no-alcohol specialty drinks, plus coffee and tea. Speaking of tea, The C.B.S. offers traditional tea service—complete with fresh-baked scones and finger sandwiches. The fixed-price, reservations-required tea is offered at select times. For details, visit *disneyworld.com*. **LDS/$$–$$$$**

**CAROUSEL COFFEE:** This jumpin' java joint is a popular pit stop for guests on the go. It features **NEW** fresh-brewed coffee and specialty brews, hot cocoa, tea, juice, and a slew of soft drinks. Food-wise, expect to find bagels, banana bread, croissants, muffins, coffee cake, assorted pastries, yogurt parfait, cereal with milk, wraps, sandwiches, and fresh fruit. Operating hours are usually 7 A.M. to 4 P.M. daily. **BLS/$–$$/☒**

**LEAPING HORSE LIBATIONS:** This poolside venue offers much more than liquid refreshments. Spotted on a recent menu: Greek salad sandwiches, salads, pizza (plain or pepperoni), pretzel dogs, Mickey ice cream bars, and Mickey-shaped pretzels. **LDS/$–$$/☒**

**FLYING FISH:** The sophisticated decor elevates the appeal of this upscale dining destination, which has been given a thorough and dramatic refurbishment. Look up during the meal—the flying fish chandelier is a sight to behold. As always, this elegant eatery gives most fine, big-city spots a run for their money. (The tab tends to rival said hotspots, too—but we find it reliably splurge-worthy.)

The menu changes often, but the stars of the show are creatively prepared sustainable seafood dishes. You can usually find organic chicken and several beefy items from the grill, too—think filet mignon and char-crusted New York strip steak. We're always impressed by the service and find the menu worthy of the price tag. Reservations are highly recommended. As far as the Disney Dining Plan goes, Flying Fish is designated as a Signature restaurant. **D/$$$–$$$$/☒/SR**

**THE SCREEN DOOR:** Okay, it may not be a restaurant—but this shop is a good place for a nice nosh. Sweet treats include hand-dipped apples, fresh-baked cookies, crispy treats, fudge, and slushes. There's a substantial grab-and-go selection, too. Expect to find milk, juice, eggs, bread, fruit, soft drinks, packaged snacks, beer, wine, and more. **BLDS/$–$$**

**TRATTORIA AL FORNO:** Taste buds take a tour of Italy with Trattoria's tempting array of regional specialties and crowd-pleasing classics. Signature standouts include wood-fired pizzas and pastas prepared al forno (baked in an oven). The family-friendly establishment celebrates the diversity of Italian cuisine with housemade mozzarella atop Neapolitan-style pizzas, hand-rolled pastas, seasonal seafood, and vegetables. Beverage selections include Italian wines by the bottle and the glass. Draft and bottle beers, cocktails, grappa, and soft drinks round out the drink menu. For dessert, consider tiramisú, panna cotta, or house-made gelato. The morning meal comes complete with a side of Disney characters! Expect to see favorite friends from classic films such as *Tangled* and *The Little Mermaid* at the "Bon Voyage Breakfast." The impressive menu tempts with selections such as omelets, steak and eggs, pancakes with seasonal compote, avocado toast, breakfast pizza, tiramisú bread pudding, and more. The Bon Voyage Breakfast is an extremely popular character meal—book your table as far in advance as possible. All details are subject to change. For updates, visit *disneyworld.com*, or use the My Disney Experience app or website. **BD/$$–$$$/❦**

# Caribbean Beach

**CENTERTOWN MARKET:** There's a lot to choose from at this sleek quick-service spot. For breakfast, there are omelets, Mickey-shaped waffles, scrambled eggs, steel-cut oatmeal, avocado toast, yogurt, pastries, and fresh fruit. The lunch/dinner menu includes salads, burgers, sandwiches, pizza, pasta, chicken bowls, and fish tacos. The children's menu includes cheeseburgers, chicken strips, mac and cheese, and PB&J. Enjoy a sweet treat in the form of a cupcake, ice cream bar, fresh fruit, or Key lime tart. The vast beverage selection includes soft drinks, specialty coffees, and bottles of beer, wine, and assorted cocktails. **BLDS/$–$$/❦/MO**

## SNACKS AT SEA

To experience a sea-faring snack-and-show splurge, consider a Walt Disney World fireworks cruise. You and up to nine lucky invitees can enjoy a private tour of the lakes near the Magic Kingdom capped with a viewing of Happily Ever After or a cruise on Crescent Lake followed by EPCOT's nighttime spectacular—all the while enjoying an assortment of snacks and soft drinks. Each 25-foot boat broadcasts each show's respective soundtrack, thus making for a rather immersive experience.

The price (about $400, plus tax) includes the aforementioned refreshments, a captain, festive banners, and balloons. You can take your own snacks and drinks, too (no glass containers, please). To book, call 407-WDW-PLAY (939-7529) at least 24 hours and up to 90 days ahead. For EPCOT, cruises leave from the Yacht Club marina. Magic Kingdom fireworks cruises depart from The Contemporary, Polynesian Village, Grand Floridian, Fort Wilderness Resort & Campground, and Wilderness Lodge marinas.

Cancellations must be made at least two days in advance of the reservation to avoid paying full price. For additional details, visit *disneyworld.com*. Note that, in rare instances, WDW fireworks presentations may be canceled or rescheduled.

**Hot Tip!** Would you like to watch the Magic Kingdom's fireworks from an exclusive perch at the Contemporary resort's California Grill? You'll need to dine at the Grill, of course—but it doesn't have to be during the show. If you eat early, return to the second-floor check-in desk later that day, present your receipt, and you'll be escorted to the eatery via private express elevator.

**CENTERTOWN MARKET GRAB & GO:** A convenient place to grab a cuppa joe and go about your day, this corner of the Centertown Market has a selection of specialty coffees, plus juice, smoothies, beer, wine, hard cider, milk (including soy and almond), and soft drinks. The menu includes hot breakfast bagel sandwiches, cereals, fruit, yogurt, pastries, salads, smoked turkey sandwiches, assorted chips, and ice cream novelties. **BS/$–$$/❦**

**SEBASTIAN'S BISTRO:** The crafty crustacean who managed to evade the big silver pot in Disney's *The Little Mermaid* has loaned his name to this under-the-sea-inspired eatery. Guests of the waterside bistro indulge in a Caribbean feast. The fixed-price meal begins with buttery pull-apart rolls (served with guava butter and caramelized onion jam). Guests may enjoy a salad of mixed greens with kale, candied pumpkin seeds, and Key lime dressing before diving into the main event: the "Taste of the Caribbean" feast. The ample sampler platter offers a selection of the kitchen's favorite dishes, including oven-roasted citrus chicken, slow-cooked Mojo pork, and grilled chili-rubbed beef with mojito relish served with cilantro rice and beans and grilled seasonal veggies. There are plant-based and allergy-friendly platters, too. The sweet finale is a coconut-pineapple bread pudding with caramel sauce and vanilla ice cream. All manner of beverages are served, including pressed-pot coffee, beer, wine, sangria, and specialty drinks. In the mood for some bacon-y booze? Order the Marooned Pig Old-fashioned. Reservations are recommended. Note that Sebastian's Bistro does not offer a kids' menu. **D/$$/❦**

**SPYGLASS GRILL:** A walk-up counter in the Trinidad pool area, this grill sits on a patio overlooking Barefoot Bay. Head there for American fare with Caribbean flair. Start the day with a breakfast Cuban sandwich, Trinidad Sunrise Crispy Yuca Bowl, and more traditional selections. For lunch or dinner, consider chopped jerk chicken or shrimp salad, Mojo pork tacos, Cuban sandwiches, pastries, and fruit. Beer, wine, cocktails, soft drinks, and specialty coffees are also served. **BLDS/$$/❦/MO**

# Contemporary

**CALIFORNIA GRILL:** Delighting diners for decades, the World-famous California Grill still graces most guests' must-do lists. The West Coast theme shines through in dishes prepared with the freshest seasonal and local produce available.

Dinner is a 3-course, fixed-price meal. The menu may feature Sonoma goat cheese raviolo, braised beef short rib wonton, black truffle pizza, sushi rolls, and salad. Entrées include grilled pork tenderloin; black sea bass; oak-fired filet of beef; saffron risotto; Wagyu strip loin; pan seared chicken; and fire-roasted venison. The kids' menu offers chicken noodle soup, green salad with ranch dressing, beef tenderloin, grilled citrus-glazed chicken, seared sustainable salmon, and housemade shells & cheese.

The encyclopedic wine list—which includes about 300 selections, 50 of which are available by the glass—is a nice mix of greatest hits and good finds. There is a full bar with premium spirits, specialty cocktails, craft beers, and hard cider. Housemade desserts (crème brûlée, Valhrona ganache tart, lemon torte, peanut and banana torte, and a cheese plate) add finishing touches, and there are sweeping views of the Magic Kingdom and Seven Seas Lagoon (from select seats).

California Grill is always busy and the fare is first-rate. Reservations are a must. Changes or cancellations should be made at least 24 hours ahead to avoid the $10 per-person fee. This is a Disney Dining Plan Signature restaurant. (It requires two table-service credits per meal, per diner. And, yes—the Dining Plan is back!)

An outdoor perch (exclusively available to California Grill patrons) affords dramatic bird's-eye views of the Magic Kingdom and its fireworks presentations (complete with the Happily Ever After show's soundtrack). All guests check in on the hotel's second floor and are escorted to an express elevator. Dinner service begins at 5 P.M. The cost to enjoy Cali Grill's fixed-price meal is $89 for adults and $39 for kids (ages 3 to 9), plus tax and gratuity. **D/$$$$**

**CHEF MICKEY'S:** Chef Mickey and his Disney pals host this "all-you-care-to-enjoy," buffet-style meal, with striking views of the Walt Disney World monorail passing above. The eatery serves family-friendly fare for breakfast and dinner. The ever-changing menu takes advantage of seasonal offerings and traditional favorites. At some point during the dining experience, Chef Mickey and friends will swing through the dining room to say hello.

This is an exceptionally popular eatery with a very loyal following. Kids simply adore the experience. It's a fun place to celebrate a child's birthday, too. Reservations are an absolute must for both meals. At press time, breakfast cost about $51 for adults and $33 for kids (ages 3 through 9) and dinner ran about $62 for adults and $39 for kids. It's a bit of a splurge, but Chef Mickey's consistently delivers some of the best character interactions on WDW property—so well worth it. **BD/$$$/🐭**

**CONTEMPO CAFE:** The Contemporary snack bar can be found on the fourth floor, beside Chef Mickey's. This underrated spot serves impressive made-to-order fare throughout the day: egg sandwiches, scrambled-egg platters, waffles, and other breakfast selections are served in the morning, while cheeseburgers, hot sandwiches, tofu bowls, and salads are offered for lunch and dinner. Other offerings include drinks (milk, juice, beer, wine, etc.), soup, yogurt, fruit, desserts, and more. (Orders may be placed via Mobile Ordering. Refer to page 310 for details.) If you buy a refillable resort mug, this is the place to make it happy. **BLDS/$–$$/🐭/MO**

**STEAKHOUSE 71:** In late 2021, we waved goodbye to The Wave . . . of American Flavors—and said hello to its successor, Steakhouse 71. The instant favorite was named for the year the Contemporary opened (1971). A classic steakhouse with entrees ranging from filet mignon and pork bone-in rib chop to sustainable fish "en papillote" and vegetable "Wellington," this cozy dining spot with a subtle '70s vibe serves three meals daily. In the Steakhouse 71 Lounge, between-meal bites such as loaded mac & cheese with bacon and jalapeño, the signature (and fan-favorite) Stack Burger, and even PB&J wings keep hunger pangs at bay.

Breakfast specialties include Walt's Prime Rib Hash—a contemporary spin on a favorite of Walt Disney's, plus seasonally inspired pancakes and avocado toast with caramelized onion jam. For lunch, lump crab cake sliders and gourmet grilled cheese tempt diners. Kids' menus are offered at every meal.

Libations like the Citrus Grove Cocktail and the refillable breakfast mimosa give a nod to Florida's orange industry. Pair dinner with a selection from the Disney Family of Wines, then toast the occasion with a real treat—The Iron Horse Fairy Tale Cuvée from Sonoma. Reservations are recommended. **BLD/$$–$$$$/**❤

# Coronado Springs

**CAFE RIX:** Stop here for cereals, muffins and croissants, salads (chicken Caesar, blue cheese wedge, chef's, and house), tuna salad wraps, sandwiches, gelato, specialty coffees, and more. Other snacks may include fresh fruit, candy, cupcakes, donuts, and cronuts. **BS/$–$$/**❤

**EL MERCADO DE CORONADO:** Formerly known as Pepper Market, this busy, casual food court has a large seating area and a variety of food stations. Choose from nachos, burgers, flatbreads, pasta dishes, and rotating entrées such as BBQ pulled pork, bacon-wrapped meatloaf, and chicken parmesan—all freshly prepared. For breakfast, there are egg sandwiches, Mickey-shaped waffles, fruit, breakfast bowls, pastries, and buttermilk pancakes. All selections may be packaged to go. Given this resort's popularity with the convention set, expect a proliferation of hungry humans during traditional weekday breakfast and lunch times. **BLDS/$$/**❤

**RIX SPORTS BAR & GRILL:** A chic but cozy environment in which to root, root, root for your home team, Rix serves breakfast, lunch, and dinner in addition to pubby appetizers "with a unique spin." The morning meal features breakfast burritos, buttermilk pancakes, omelets, bagel with lox, and avocado toast. Later in the day, items such as burgers, wings, soups, salads, seafood, and hot sandwiches grace the menu. Desserts include bourbon pecan pie, seasonal sherbet, and berry mascarpone cake. There are child-friendly menu choices, but the atmosphere is unlikely to enchant most young diners. Reservations are recommended. **BLDS/$$–$$$/**❤

**MAYA GRILL:** Guests here dine inside a Mayan pyramid, beside a volcano (dormant, of course). The menu offers a bit of everything: seafood, meat, and poultry, with a touch of Latin spices added to some of the creations. Entrées range from sizzling steak fajitas to Baja fish tacos or Adobo roasted half chicken. Desserts include sorbet and fried baby churros. Dinner is served from 5 P.M. to 10 P.M. Reservations are recommended. **D/$$$/**❤

**THREE BRIDGES BAR & GRILL AT VILLA DEL LAGO:** This pleasant, table-service locale sits atop an island on a 14-acre lake (Lago Dorado) and is accessed exclusively by bridges. The menu tempts with Szechuan-peppercorn wings, tortilla chips with roasted corn dip, poke bowls, pork tacos, Harissa lamb chops, steak frites, coconut curry chicken, six different salads, and desserts (such as warm churros and sorbet). Spirited and non-alcoholic drinks are served. **DS/$$–$$$/**❤

**TOLEDO—TAPAS, STEAK, & SEAFOOD:** Surrealist Spanish art and 1930s avant-garde were the inspiration for this distinctive rooftop destination. The eatery, which sits atop the resort's 16-story Gran Destino Tower, features vaulted ceilings and panoramic views of Walt Disney World. The show-kitchen serves small plates, charcuterie, and cheeses, as well as entreés such as aged, hand-cut Spanish *chuletón* for two (28-ounce bone-in ribeye steak), red wine-braised chicken, lamb, and seafood offerings. The expansive wine list includes Spanish and California highlights hand-selected by a Master Sommelier, as well as beer, cider, and cocktails. Reservations are recommended. **D/$$$–$$$$/**❤

# Disney's Old Key West

**GOOD'S FOOD TO GO:** A window with simple yet satisfying offerings throughout the day: Burgers, hot dogs, sandwiches, salads, and breakfast items are among the offerings at Good's. **BLDS/$–$$/**❤

**GURGLING SUITCASE:** This pocket-sized lounge packs a powerful punch. In addition to a full bar, the Suitcase serves nibbles such as shrimp fritters, cheeseburgers, BBQ pulled-pork nachos, fried chicken, Caesar salads, and deep-fried pickle chips (aka "frickles"). Many items may be ordered to go. **LDS/$$–$$$/**❤

**OLIVIA'S CAFE:** We thoroughly enjoy the Key West manner with which Olivia's approaches its theme. The laid-back setting and menu convey the spirit of the leisure-centric locale. Kick off your day with brunch selections such as pancakes and eggs, fried chicken, tofu hash, SPAM®-cheddar biscuits, omelets, banana bread pudding, shrimp & grits, bacon cheeseburgers, salads, and more. The dinner menu has shrimp fritters, soup, salad, catch of the day, crab cakes, prime rib, burgers, and fried chicken. Finish with a Key lime tart, coconut panna cotta, or chocolate lava cake. The menu changes seasonally. Wine, beer, and specialty drinks (with or without alcohol) are served. Reservations are recommended. **BRUNCH D/$$–$$$/🐭/MO**

# Fort Wilderness

Many folks choose to cook their own meals here. Supplies are sold at the Meadow and Settlement Trading Posts; others may be delivered by a local grocery store (see page 244). P&J's Southern Takeout offers breakfast, lunch, and dinner selections and the Chuck Wagon serves dinner vittles and snacks.

**THE CHUCK WAGON:** A retro-style camper, this Fort Wilderness wagon serves cheeseburgers, mac & cheese burgers, corn dog nuggets, hot dogs, chicken nuggets, and salads. The side order/snack menu features jalapeño poppers, fried mac & cheese, mozzarella sticks, onion rings, fresh fruit, popcorn, and ice cream novelties. Children's meals include ham sandwiches and chicken nuggets. Quench thirsts with a bottled soft drink, beer, wine, or an Old Smoky Moonshine cocktail. **DS/$/🐭**

**P&J'S SOUTHERN TAKEOUT:** Mosey on over to this marketplace spot for a hearty breakfast featuring bounty platters, biscuits and gravy, french toast sticks, and a bonanza of freshly baked pastries. Later in the day, P&J's proffers family-sized packages of fried chicken, pecan-smoked ribs, pizza (by the slice or the pie), and southern sides and snacks, including first-rate strawberry shortcake. After the meal, you can relax in a rocking chair on the front porch. **BLDS/$$–$$$**

**TRAIL'S END:** This recently re-imagined Fort Wilderness favorite now features a variety of quick-service vittles for the whole family to enjoy. **BLDS/$$–$$$/🐭/MO**

# Grand Floridian

**CÍTRICOS:** From the heavenly aromas wafting from the show kitchen, it's clear that the chef aims to wow you in this delightful dining destination. In an homage to the whimsy and elegance of *Mary Poppins Returns*, guests relish meals in a fanciful garden-like setting. The fare varies seasonally, but may include savory selections such as spectacular sweet corn bisque, butter-poached mahi mahi, and guava BBQ short ribs. For a sweet finish, try a warm apple rose or chocolate torte. The wine list ensures that pairings are practically perfect (in every way!).

You can take the wine and dine experience to a new level in the exclusive new Sommelier room, where boutique wines pair perfectly with the chef's unique creations. Reservations are recommended. A small lounge within Cítricos is nice for solo diners and those caught without reservations. The dress code is business casual. **D/$$$–$$$$/☙/SR**

**GASPARILLA ISLAND GRILL:** Gasparilla is your go-to spot for top notch, casual fare. Breakfast items along the lines of egg sandwiches, Mickey waffles, oatmeal, yogurt, and cereal are served until 11 A.M. After that, made-to-order selections such as sandwiches, burgers, pizza, and salads are available. There's a specialty coffee station and a pastry counter. Grab-and-go options such as pasta salad, fresh fruit, yogurt, ice cream novelties, and other snacks are on hand in this quick-service spot near the marina. There is indoor and outdoor seating. If you purchase a refillable mug, this is one place to make it happy. (Note that Rapid Fill mugs may also be filled at the Beaches Pool Bar & Grill.) **BLDS/$–$$/☙/MO**

**GRAND FLORIDIAN CAFE:** A pleasant spot, the cafe is a relatively reasonably priced, low-key way to enjoy one of Disney's poshest resorts.

Breakfast extends a bit beyond the usual fare and is available until 2 P.M. Lunch and dinner menus may vary seasonally but always offer traditional American dishes: onion soup, salad, buttermilk-fried chicken, miso-glazed salmon, and creatively prepared burgers. The wine selection is impressive. Reservations are recommended, but it may be possible to get a table without one if you are willing to wait. **BLD/$$–$$$/☙**

**NARCOOSSEE'S:** Named for a nearby Florida town, this spot has long specialized in fresh sustainable seafood—with several entrées making surf-and-turf combinations a decadent possibility. Having recently undergone a thorough refurbishment, this WDW classic offers a fresh new menu, while retaining some fan-favorites. It features upscale selections (and prices) in a relaxed atmosphere. A lovely view of the Seven Seas Lagoon and Cinderella Castle completes the experience.

The kitchen presents sublime starters such as lobster bisque, an ocean-inspired charcuterie plate, and sweet potato gnocchi. The entrée lineup includes sustainable seafood offerings such as blackened redfish, yuzu-ginger salmon, seared scallops, New York strip steak, roasted vegetable paella, dry-aged ribeye pork chop, and gulf shrimp bucatini. The eatery's signature dish is a surf and turf (7-ounce filet mignon and butter-poached lobster tail). For dessert, the classic almond-crusted cheesecake is a mainstay. It's joined by berry pavlova, pineapple bavarois, hazelnut-chocolate bar, and an artisanal cheese plate. A menu for the 9 and under set features grilled steak, seasonal fish, and chicken. The beverage menu boasts an array of wines, beers, cocktails (with and without alcohol), and soft drinks.

Reservations are recommended for Narcoossee's dining room. If you find yourself hungry sans reservations, fear not. The lounge here offers tasty bites (and does not require a reservation), as well as a full bar and a bounty of wines by the bottle or the glass. Guests are expected to dress in attire that respects the restaurant's sophisticated and upscale aesthetic. Think business casual. No swimwear, please. **D/$$$–$$$$/☙/SR**

**1900 PARK FARE:** This eatery was "on pause" and in the midst of a thorough refurbishment as this book went to press. In years past, the atmosphere was reminiscent of an old-fashioned amusement park, with a sophisticated family-style menu and subtle decor. Guests could meet Mary Poppins, Alice in Wonderland, the Mad Hatter, Tigger, and Winnie the Pooh during the bountiful breakfast. Cinderella and members of her royal family visited the dining room during dinner hours.

Dinner has featured seafood, salads, pastas, carved meats, veggie sides, and housemade desserts, plus plenty of kid-friendly offerings. The fan-favorite restaurant's focal point has traditionally been Big Bertha, a band organ built in Paris nearly a century ago. Note that all details are subject to change. Reservations are highly recommended. **B BRUNCH** (seasonal) **D/$$$–$$$$/☙**

**Note:** 1900 Park Fare is expected to be open in 2024. For updates (including menu items and meals served) and reservations, use the My Disney Experience mobile app or website, or visit *disneyworld.com*.

**VICTORIA & ALBERT'S:** Walt Disney World proudly presents the one and only AAA five-diamond restaurant in Central Florida! This elegant gem can accommodate up to 48 gracious guests at a time: 34 in the main dining room, 8 in Queen Victoria's room, and 6 at the highly coveted Chef's Table. The appetizing odyssey is indulgent without being too haute to handle (although the steep prices may curb some folks' enthusiasm) and is considered by many to be the grand dame of the Disney dining scene. As such, it's a popular destination for many a special celebration.

The Chef's Tasting Menu, offered in the main room and the Queen Victoria room, changes seasonally and always offers a delectable selection of fish, poultry, meats, and plant-based dishes. But the beauty of this high-end experience is all the little tastes as you make your way through the adventure (which starts at $295 per person, plus tax and gratuity). You might start with caviar or quail, then move on to seared wild turbot or pork tenderloin. Perfect portion sizes keep the many courses surprisingly manageable. And please save room for the indulgent selection of desserts. The cheese course alone is worth every calorie. Strains of a harp provide a romantic backdrop. The wine list is encyclopedic—and pairings are available for about $150 per person. (Be sure to let your servers know about any personal wine preferences—they aim to please.)

For an extra-special (and extra-splurge-y) experience, book the Chef's Table (for up to 6 guests; starting at $425 per person, plus tax and tip). There, you'll have a front-row seat while the Victoria & Albert's culinary team lovingly crafts your feast. Wine-pairing may be added (starting at $200 per person). With just one table, this is the restaurant's most exclusive, luxurious setting.

At meal's end, all guests receive a special souvenir menu to commemorate the occasion. In sum, though the dining experience is an extremely extravagant one, for many it is also exceptionally special. Guests must be at least 10 years old to dine. (There is no children's menu.) Reservations are a must. For reservations, go to *www.victoria-alberts.com*. **D/$$$$**

# Polynesian Village

**CAPT. COOK'S:** The captain serves snacks and light fare throughout the day. It's a good spot for made-to-order breakfast items such as breakfast flatbreads and burritos, eggs, Mickey-shaped waffles, or the ever-popular fried, banana-stuffed Tonga toast. Lunch and dinner bring cheeseburgers, plant-based burgers, pulled pork sandwiches, chicken nuggets, pulled pork nachos, Pan-Asian noodles and vegetables, Thai coconut meatballs, salads, and grab-and-go items such as yogurt, fruit, pastries, and snacks. Milk, beer, wine, and soft drinks are available. Stop at Capt. Cook's to purchase and fill a refillable resort mug. **BLDS/$-$$/❤/MO**

**KONA CAFE:** Warm colors and South Seas decor render the crisp, fluid design of this open dining space cozy and casual. Lunch and dinner menus feature Asian-influenced entrées. Possibilities include market-fresh fish, crispy pork-vegetable potstickers, steak salad, poke bowls, mahi BLT, seasonal soup, (sensational) sushi, Kona-coffee-braised short rib, and desserts such as coconut tapioca pudding or Key lime pie. The morning meal usually offers crowd-pleasing Tonga toast (banana-stuffed, fried sourdough bread coated with cinnamon sugar), and spice-rubbed salmon plate, plus many traditional breakfast items. There is a solid wine list, and islands-inspired cocktails (and mocktails) are served. The pressed-pot coffee is a fan favorite. Kona Cafe is on the second floor of the Polynesian's Great Ceremonial House, around the corner from 'Ohana. Reservations are recommended. **BLDS/$$-$$$/❤**

**KONA ISLAND:** A perky coffee bar, this is a super spot for a quick sip of freshly brewed Kona blend on your way to the monorail. In addition to the aforementioned (heavenly) coffee, light breakfast items such as bacon-cheddar-egg croissants, fresh fruit, banana nut muffins, and other treats are available.

Later in the day, some sushi selections may join the menu courtesy of the adjacent Kona Cafe. Recently, those offerings included California rolls (with real crab meat) and spicy tuna rolls. There is a small amount of counter seating, but all items may be prepared to go. Reservations are not accepted. Details are subject to change. Once folks discover this not-so-hidden gem, it quickly joins their list of happy places. **BLDS/$-$$$**

**'OHANA:** On the second floor of the resort's Great Ceremonial House, this restaurant is a meticulously themed, family-friendly eatery, complete with entertainment. An interesting twist of note: 'Ohana's family-style dinner experience—a South Pacific feast prepared in the restaurant's open-fire cooking pit—does not come with a menu, so no decisions have to be made. The oak-grilled chicken, teriyaki beef, and shrimp just keep coming. Honey-coriander chicken wings, pork dumplings, green salad, pineapple-coconut bread, pan-Asian noodles tossed in teriyaki sauce, and roasted broccolini are among the accompaniments, and dessert is bread pudding served à la mode with warm caramel sauce. Soft drinks are included. Beer, wine, and cocktails are extra.

'Ohana's setting, which features wood carvings under a vast thatched roof, is rather festive. So much so that a singer serenades with song and ukulele rhythms.

Breakfast is also a family affair—make that extended family, as Lilo, Stitch, and their good friends Mickey Mouse and Pluto traditionally host the morning meal. Breakfast fare is basic and presented family style. Keep in mind that the character lineup does change from time to time. Reservations are necessary—book as early as possible. **BD/$$$/**

**OASIS GRILL:** The laid-back Oasis Grill is situated next to the Polynesian's Oasis pool. It serves up items such as cheeseburgers, grilled fish tacos, sashimi, chicken avocado wraps, salads, wings, and more. The O.G. is adjacent to the Oasis Bar. **LDS/$$/**

**PINEAPPLE LANAI:** This sweet stop offers Walt Disney World's classic Dole Whip frozen pineapple dessert—served plain, twisted with vanilla soft-serve, or as a float with pineapple juice. It's possible to get a coconut-rum-drenched serving, too. It may be possible to order yours in a souvenir sipper. Seasonal flavors may be available. You'll find the Lanai on the Poly's ground level, just outside the back door. **S/$**

**TRADER SAM'S GROG GROTTO:** It's virtually impossible to be grouchy at this spot—Trader Sam will make sure of that. With a theme inspired by the Jungle Cruise and Enchanted Tiki Room attractions, Trader Sam's features drinks (tropical and otherwise) and small plates such as pan-fried dumplings, chicken lettuce wraps, and sushi rolls. Patio seating is relatively easy to snag, but securing indoor seats often requires a bit of patience. (It's worth the wait!) Doors usually open at 3 P.M. and close around midnight (food is served till 10 P.M.). Note that enthusiastic folks may start lining up for seats at 2 P.M. **S/$$**

# Pop Century

**EVERYTHING POP!:** The varied selection at this colorful food court in Classic Hall features omelets, waffle platters, bagel sandwiches, yogurt, oatmeal, pastries, and fresh fruit for breakfast. Later in the day, guests may enjoy pizza, pasta, fried chicken, cheeseburgers, plant-based burgers, shrimp & grits, chicken strips, seared salmon, braised beef, salads, sandwiches (including tuna, turkey, or honey BBQ pulled pork), ice cream, a vast selection of baked goods, fresh fruit, and assorted snacks. Feel free to join the jolly cast members as they dance the Hustle at 1:30 P.M. and the Twist at 6 P.M. Details are subject to change. **BLDS/$-$$//MO**

# Port Orleans French Quarter

**RIVER ROOST:** Enjoy bites such as Mardi Gras Fritters and Bayou Wings and classic cocktails like the Southern Hurricane and French 75—plus the live—and lively!—musical stylings of Yeeha Bob (Wednesday through Saturday evenings). **S/$-$$/**

**SASSAGOULA FLOATWORKS & FOOD FACTORY:** A food court with a Mardi Gras theme, this spot serves breakfast staples, pizza, pasta, burgers, sandwiches, salads, ice cream, and bakery treats. The Big Easy is represented with menu items such as classic gumbo, jambalaya, and Mardi Gras cake. Soft drinks, specialty cocktails, beer, and wine are served. **BLDS/$-$$//MO**

**SCAT CAT'S CLUB—CAFE:** Y'all have a hankering for some N'awlins-style beignets? If so, make a beeline for Scat Cat's! There you can enjoy the Mickey-shaped, powdery treats plain, as part of an ice cream sundae, or with a dipping sauce. Baton Rouge beignets come with a choice of spirited infusion. Soft drinks, tea, and specialty coffees are sold, too. Hours are usually about 7 A.M. to 11 P.M. The adjoining Scat Cat's Lounge menu also has beignets, fritters, po'boys, and other fixin's from 5 P.M. to 10 P.M. **S/$-$$**

# Port Orleans Riverside

**BOATWRIGHT'S DINING HALL:** Southern specialties and American comfort food are the big draws in these parts: Mardi Gras fritters, Boudin balls, crispy Cajun chicken, blackened prime rib or salmon, jambalaya, red beans & rice, shrimp & grits, and more. Dessert can be Mississippi mud crème brûlée, Bananas Foster bread pudding, or cheesecake. Beer, wine, and cocktails are available, as are soft drinks. Reservations are recommended. Walk-ups may be admitted when the eatery opens at 5 P.M. **D/$$$/**

**RIVERSIDE MILL:** This high-ceilinged food court styled in the image of a cotton mill (complete with working waterwheel) offers a half dozen food counters. At breakfast, they dispense bagel sandwiches, omelets, waffles, and more. Later on, they serve pizza; pasta; chicken strips; cheeseburgers; salads; entrées such as seared salmon, gumbo, and shrimp & grits; BBQ pulled pork sandwiches; French dips, ice cream; and baked goods. There is ample seating, so it's usually easy to get a table. All items may be packaged to go. **BLDS/$-$$//MO**

# Disney's Riviera Resort

**BAR RIVA:** Mediterranean and European-inspired beverages and bites are served at this poolside locale. Expect selections such as grilled veggie skewers, salmon with orzo, baked brie, and Greek salads. **S/$-$$/❤**

**LE PETIT CAFÉ:** Quench your thirst in an elegant manner at this chic lobby locale. A coffee bar by day and wine bar/lounge by night, Le Petit also features nibbles and sweet treats. **S/$-$$**

**PRIMO PIATTO:** This quick-service trattoria serves up tasty offerings throughout the day: breakfast items such as blueberry-lemon pancakes or scrambled eggs over polenta, plus lunch and dinner choices including house-made pizza, grilled veggie skewers, hot and cold sandwiches, cheeseburgers, salads, soups, and sweets—as well as grab-and-go items. **BLDS/$-$$/MO**

**TOPOLINO'S TERRACE—FLAVORS OF THE RIVIERA:** You just may feel like you're on top of the World at this rooftop restaurant, perched on top of Disney's Riviera resort. While eyes take in the stunning vistas of Walt Disney World, palates take a tasty tour of the Italian and French Riviera with dishes prepared in a modern exposition kitchen.

Breakfast features a fixed-price menu and appearances by favorite Disney characters. The evening meal comes with an à la carte menu brimming with possibilities—including burrata, escargot, house-made ricotta with epi bread, classic sole meunière, filet mignon, bouillabaisse, and the opportunity to enjoy a bird's-eye view of a nearby nighttime spectacular, courtesy of EPCOT. **BD/$$$-$$$$/❤/SR** (dinner)

# Saratoga Springs

**THE ARTIST'S PALETTE:** Set inside a converted artist's loft within Walt Disney World's sprawling resort, this spot offers breakfast, lunch, and dinner. On the menu you'll find Mickey waffles, quiche, salads, made-to-order sandwiches, roasted chicken, pizza, meatballs, baked goods, and more. There are some grocery items, plus a variety of grab-and-go selections. **BLDS/$-$$/❤/MO**

**THE PADDOCK GRILL:** Head to this handy window for breakfast items such as yogurt parfait, quiche, croissant sandwich, bagel with cream cheese, and fruit cups. The lunch and dinner menu offers Cobb salad, shrimp tacos, fried chicken sandwiches, bacon cheeseburgers, and housemade potato chips (which were actually invented in Saratoga Springs, New York). Kid-friendly selections include chicken strips and burgers (served with one side and a beverage). Beer, wine, soft drinks, and ice cream novelties are offered, too. **BLDS/$-$$/❤**

**THE TURF CLUB BAR & GRILL:** A satisfying restaurant with an old-fashioned horse-racing theme, this table-service eatery serves french onion soup, slow-roasted prime rib, pan-seared salmon, steak, pasta, and chopped salads, plus a sweet selection of seasonal desserts. **D/$$$/❤**

# Swan, Dolphin, & Swan Reserve

**AMARE:** The restaurant's name translates "to love" in Italian, and if you love fine Mediterranean fare, head to this signature Swan Reserve casual/upscale destination. Lunch and dinner are served a la carte; breakfast offers a buffet option, as well. Olive oil and citrus play prominent culinary roles with dinner starters like Hearth Fired Tiger Prawns. Sea bass, chicken, beef, and lamb entrées are prepared with Mediterranean flair. Shareable flatbreads like The Amare—leek, potato, roasted black pepper, and Gruyere—showcase the kitchen's versatility. The $29 breakfast buffet is loaded with egg options, biscuits and gravy, buttermilk pancakes, waffles, fruit, and more; à la carte dishes may include avocado toast, frittatas, Belgian waffles, oatmeal, and egg white omelets. Kids' menus are available for all meals, with Mickey-shaped waffles a breakfast highlight. To make reservations for Amare, go to *disneyworld.com/dining*, or call 407-934-1609. **BLD/$$$-$$$$**

**CHILL:** Rich with sips (with or without alcohol), Chill also supplies assorted sandwiches, salads, and snacks such as hummus, chips, and sweet treats. Note that some drinks are available in a refillable cup (discounts apply to refills). Chill is located in the lobby of the Swan hotel. **S/$–$$**

**CABANA BAR & BEACH CLUB:** An elegant poolside destination, the Dolphin's Cabana serves a sophisticated selection of starters, salads, and entrées. Appetizer options include chicken wings and crispy calamari. The main bites menu offers grilled-chicken BLT, fish tacos, shawarma kebob, buttermilk-battered chicken crisps, burgers, pizza, and charred octopus. Among

PHOTO BY JILL SAFRO

# RESORT TO RESORT

If you're staying in one resort and dining in another, you need to plan ahead—even if the resorts are linked by monorail or water taxi. Why? The transportation may be operating before dinner, but if you're out late enough you'll have to get yourself home another way.

The good news is you will never be stranded. Bus transportation may run as late as 1 A.M.—but it's not direct. If the theme parks are closed, you'll have to take a bus to Disney Springs and transfer to a bus to your hotel. If the theme parks are open, you can take a bus to any park and transfer to one that's headed to your resort. Know that the journey can take up to 90 minutes in either direction. If that thought is unpleasant or you're running short on time, do what we sometimes do: splurge on a Minnie Van (if it is offered), Lyft, or Uber ride, or a trip in a taxicab. Taxis should run between $15 and $35 (before tip), depending on the destination and traffic. Minnie Vans start with a base charge of about $15 per trip. (The final cost depends on the distance covered—check *disneyworld.com* for current pricing.) Note that Uber rides are subject to surge pricing. All Walt Disney World resort Bell Services desks can arrange for a taxi pickup.

the many signature cocktails are the Original Mai Tai, Solstice Margarita, and Hibiscus Cooler. Kids choose from pizza (plain or pepperoni), cheeseburgers, hot dogs, grilled cheese, and chicken fingers. **LDS/$$**

**THE FOUNTAIN:** A Dolphin-based soda fountain with grown-up appeal, this is an ideal spot for a sweet snack or a satisfying meal. Housemade ice cream is the house specialty (soft-serve or hand-scooped). Be it served in a simple cone or in an elaborate sundae, the chilly treat is sure to please. Among the entrées from which to choose are cheeseburgers, hot dogs, and sandwiches. Soups and salads can augment the meal, as can fries, onion rings, and soft pretzels. Save room for the inventive shakes. Beer and wine are served. A nearby walk-up window, known as Sweet Treats, has ice cream and shakes for snackers on the go. **LDS/$–$$**

**ROSA MEXICANO:** Just say, "*Sí, por favor,*" to a margarita (or two) and prepare for some Mexican eats at the Dolphin resort's new restaurant featuring **NEW** a fiesta-like dining experience. The morning meal can come via buffet or à la carte menu. The latter has traditional A.M. selections, plus *huevos rancheros*, churro waffles, and *Chilaquiles Divorciados*. Lunch and dinner feature classic dishes with a modern twist. Begin with a starter such as the restaurant's *Guacamole en Molcajete* with warm tortilla chips and tomato salsa, quesadilla, chicken tortilla soup, or salad. Entrées to consider: pork carnitas, salmon *pipian*, mushroom *huarache*, tacos, steak (ribeye or NY Strip), and Rosa's signature "cracklin' pork chop for two." Soft drinks, beer, wine, and specialty drinks are served. As guests soak up the Mexican ambiance, they may feel inspired to sample one of more than 100 varieties of tequila and agave-based spirits. *Olé!* **BLD/$$–$$$$**

**FUEL:** Hungry guests may fuel up at this snack bar/grab-and-go market off the Dolphin lobby. **BLDS/$–$$**

**GARDEN GROVE:** This Swan eatery means to transport guests to the gardens of New York's Central Park (the real-looking 25-foot oak tree is a nice touch). It offers a full, à la carte breakfast menu and the possibility of a visit by Disney characters. Look for morning starters such as oatmeal, fresh fruit, yogurt parfaits, and creamy grits with butter and salt. The next course can be a 3-egg omelet, buttermilk pancakes, Belgian waffle, or french toast. Kids choose from Mickey-shaped Belgian waffles, pancakes (chocolate chip, blueberry, or banana), and an egg platter. Lunch and dinner were on pause at press time, but may return. Reservations are recommended. **B/$$$**

**GROUNDS:** Stop here for an invigorating java jolt (this place brews a slew of specialty coffees, including latte, macchiatto, café Americano, cold brew, nitro brew, and frappes), plus breakfast selections (egg muffin, Mickey waffles, bagels, etc.), sandwiches, desserts, and items to "grab and go." You'll find this quick-service snack bar/market at the Swan Reserve. **BLDS/$-$$**

**IL MULINO NEW YORK TRATTORIA:** A swank Swan dining destination, Il Mulino offers fine Italian cuisine in a vibrant trattoria-like setting. Featuring *piatti per il tavolo*, or family-style dining, the spot is perfect for groups. Signature items include *gamberi al Mulino* (shrimp with spicy cocktail sauce), *gnocchi bolognese* (potato dumplings with meat sauce), *pollo fra diavolo* (chicken in a spicy red sauce with sausage), and *salmone* (sautéed salmon in garlic and olive oil with wild mushrooms and broccoli rabe). *Mangia!*

Dinner might begin with an antipasti tasting (the meatballs and Italian rice balls are divine). Savor your starter while perusing the wine list's 250 or so varietals. The children's menu offers pizza, fettuccine Alfredo, spaghetti marinara, and chicken parmigiana. Live entertainment may be offered on select evenings. To make reservations, visit *disneyworld.com/dining*, call 407-934-1199, or visit *swandolphin.com*. **D/$$$-$$$$**

**JAVA:** Specializing in coffee and tea drinks, this Swan snack spot also offers breakfast sandwiches, Mickey waffles, pastries, sandwiches, salads, fresh-pressed juices, and soft drinks. **BLDS/$-$$**

**KIMONOS:** Are you in the mood for sushi with a side of karaoke? You've come to the right place! This Swan spot is an honest-to-goodness karaoke bar (the only one within Walt Disney World's borders). Some guests come

to croon, while others are drawn to the sushi, sashimi, and tempura. It's also possible to order miso soup, salad, edamame, tempura udon, gyoza, and Wagyu beef satay, among other selections. There's a full bar featuring beer, wine, sake, and specialty cocktails. This spot is usually open from 5:30 P.M. until midnight. The singing generally gets going by 9 P.M. If you would like some sustenance to go, simply place your order with the bartender (in the back of the dining room.) **DS/$$-$$$**

**PHINS:** The sleek lobby lounge serves custom-crafted cocktails, beer, wine, and soft drinks. In the past, Phins served small plates. Until snack service returns, guests can enjoy nibbles they procure from Fuel (conveniently located off the Dolphin lobby). **S/$-$$**

**PICABU:** This Dolphin cafeteria/convenience store serves standard breakfast platters (though many items may be ordered à la carte), chicken dinners, tacos, burritos, nachos, and pizza. Kids meals are available. The house coffee is Starbucks (free refills during your meal). The shop sells snacks and sundries. **BLDS/$$**

**SHULA'S:** This Dolphin spot specializes in generous portions of certified Angus beef, plus soups, salads, and chicken and fish dishes. For dessert, choose from crème brûlée, vanilla cheesecake, molten chocolate lava cake, and more. The upscale eatery pays tribute to the 1972 Miami Dolphins—the year coach Don Shula led his team to a perfect (and historic!) NFL season. Though the interior celebrates the sport of football, this is not a casual spot. The dress code is business or resort casual. Reservations are recommended. There is a menu for little ones, too. **D/$$$$**

**STIR:** There's always something stirring at this lobby lounge at the Swan Reserve. Guests may enjoy beer, wine, and a specialty drinks. Liquid refreshments pair nicely with savory offerings, including charcuterie, crispy calamari, Mediterranean dips (with pita), char-grilled pepper crostino, flatbreads, Angus burgers, grilled fish, and souvlaki. **LDS/$$–$$$**

**TANGERINE:** Vacation memories are delicious when dining poolside beneath a sapphire umbrella. This al fresco bar and grill will serve a Niçoise salad or char-grilled beef burger paired with citrus-infused cocktail specialties like the Orange Crush and Tangerine Whip. At this relaxed Swan Reserve spot, you can't go wrong with savory flatbreads, salads, and handhelds like the grilled mahi-mahi sandwich with arugula, tomato, onion, and caper emulsion on a toasted roll. Cocktails, wine, beer, and soft drinks round out the menu. At 4 P.M., servers may offer a free treat to guests on the pool deck—a signature tangerine popsicle. Say "ahh!" **LD/$$**

**TODD ENGLISH'S BLUEZOO:** A sophisticated member of the Disney dining scene, this Dolphin spot features coastal cuisine, incorporating an innovative selection of fresh seafood with international and New American culinary influences. Popular starters include the signature clam chowder (with salt-cured bacon and oyster crackers), crab nachos, seared sea scallops, tuna poke tacos, Caesar salad, Tuscan kale salad, and flatbreads. All of the entrées are tempting: from linguine with clams and chorizo to grilled steak with black bean puree or steamed pumpkin nudi.

Landlubbers should also consider barbecue roasted half-chicken or filet of beef. Side dishes of note include roasted Brussels sprouts with bacon, risotto tots, and sweet corn. The dessert menu tempts with treats such as strawberry angel food cake, root beer floats, chocolate chip cookie s'mores, and banana splits. Reservations are recommended. It's possible to order food at the bar, a plus for solo diners. Live entertainment may be offered on select nights. **DS/$$$–$$$$**

# Wilderness Lodge

**GEYSER POINT BAR & GRILL:** A rustic yet modern open-air oasis, Geyser Point Bar & Grill rests in the heart of the Wilderness Lodge resort near the shores of Bay Lake. The eatery offers "rustic fare" in a delightful table-service lounge. The all-day menu has featured (scrumptious) lump crab cake, crispy salmon croquettes, bison cheeseburgers, portobello salads, smoked turkey sandwiches, fruit plate, apple cider sorbet with berries, and seasonal pie. A full bar stands at the ready with cocktails, soft drinks, and non-alcoholic specialty drinks. **LDS/$$/🐭**

**ROARING FORK:** Set in a stone-walled area (a bit dungeon-like, but in a cool way), this snack bar serves three meals a day. Breakfast (served from 7 A.M. till 11 A.M.) features a "roaring breakfast platter" (scrambled eggs, potato hash, sausage, bacon, and a cheddar biscuit), Mickey-shaped waffles, croissant sandwiches, vegetable-lovers quiche, plus pastries. Later in the day, feast on burgers, sandwiches, barbecued brisket, salads, and several snacks. Beer, wine, and soft drinks are served. This is the spot to top off Rapid Fill (refillable) resort mugs. **BLDS/$–$$/🐭/MO**

**STORYBOOK DINING AT ARTIST POINT:** The Enchanted Forest theme of this eatery is announced in evergreen touches and landscape murals, while tall red-framed windows look out on Bay Lake. The dining room is cavernous, but not without charm. Part of the appeal comes courtesy of Disney characters. This engaging dinner experience, dubbed "Storybook Dining," invites guests to see Snow White, Dopey, Grumpy, and—if they dare—the Queen!

The meal includes shared appetizers: seasonal soup, shrimp cocktail, and Hunter's Pie. Each guest selects a main course such as Cottage Beef Stroganoff, Royal Prime Rib Roast, Sorceress Spell of "Tricken" Chicken, Magic Mirror Slow-braised Pork Shank, and Bashful's

Butter-poached Sustainable Fish. For dessert, there's gooseberry tart, cookies and cream panna cotta and chocolate gems, and "poison" apple mousse. There are child-friendly selections for several courses. Soft drinks are included. Beer, wine, and specialty drinks (spirited and non-alcoholic) come with an additional fee. The wine list includes many selections from the Pacific Northwest. Reservations are necessary. **D/$$$$/❤/SR**

**WHISPERING CANYON CAFE:** Come and get it! A long-time family favorite, Whispering Canyon is one of the more boisterous WDW restaurants. Meals are offered à la carte and "all you care to eat" style. The latter means heaping plates keep coming until you say "when."

The morning air is filled with aromas of bacon and potatoes and other breakfast fare (omelets, oatmeal, waffles, etc.). Lunch offers skillet platters, pulled-pork sandwiches, bison burgers, salads, and more. For supper, expect skillets to share (BBQ, land and sea, and plant-based), plus char-crusted New York strip steak, cedar plank salmon, and pan-fried quinoa cakes. Kid-friendly selections are offered (burgers, chicken strips, etc.).

Desserts such as apple pie à la mode and Whispering Canyon Pioneer Chocolate Cake tend to garner raves. Reservations are recommended. **BLD/$$–$$$/❤**

# Yacht & Beach Club

**ALE & COMPASS RESTAURANT:** Capturing the breezy essence of an off-shore lighthouse, this Yacht Club spot serves New England comfort food for breakfast, lunch, and dinner. Guests can observe as chefs prepare flatbreads and other items in the onstage open-hearth oven, the focal point of the nautically themed dining area. Morning highlights include salted caramel apple french toast, dark chocolate waffle, and crab cake Benedict. There is a breakfast buffet option, too. Later on, look for crab bisque, roasted garlic shrimp, salad, flatbreads, New England seafood pot pie, and pan-fried sustainable catch of the day—plus beef, chicken, pasta, plant-based dishes, and desserts. **BLD/$$–$$$/❤**

**BEACH CLUB MARKETPLACE:** The resort's beachy setting extends to this newly renovated snack bar/convenience store. There are baked goods, egg sandwiches, Mickey waffles, grocery items, sandwiches, footlong chili dogs, baked pasta dishes, soups, salads, fresh fruit, and many grab-and-go items. There is limited indoor seating. If you purchase a refillable resort mug, this is one place to fill 'er up. **BLDS/$–$$/❤/MO**

**BEACHES & CREAM SODA SHOP:** This recently expanded classic soda fountain is near the pool at the Beach Club. Cheeseburgers, plant-based burgers, Reuben sandwiches, french dip sandwiches, potato tots, onion rings, and chili are served for lunch and dinner. Of course, the star of the show is ice cream! Seven specialty sundaes are offered, including the ever-popular Kitchen Sink. Cups, cones, shakes, and floats round out the menu.

## CHECK, PLEASE!

Paying for a meal at Walt Disney World is a piece of cake—especially if you have a MagicBand or Disney resort ID (and load it with your Disney Dining Plan [available starting on January 9, 2024] or back it up with a credit card). Both are accepted by most restaurants on Walt Disney World property. Notable exceptions: eateries at the Swan and Dolphin resorts, Four Seasons, and the resorts on Hotel Plaza Boulevard, and some snack carts. Simply scan your MagicBand or resort ID when the bill arrives (don't forget to add a gratuity where appropriate), and the charge will appear on your final hotel statement when you check out. (If you are not staying at a WDW-owned-and-operated resort, visit *disneyworld.com* to learn how you can get the most from MagicBand service.)

Of course, there are many ways to pay the piper. In addition to U.S. currency, traveler's checks and most major credit cards are accepted in most locations. Non-U.S. currency is a no-no. Disney gift cards and Disney Visa Rewards Redemption Cards are accepted at most of the aforementioned locations, as well. (If you plan to pay with a Disney gift card or rewards card, tell your server when you place your order.)

Guests who use Disney's Mobile Order service for quick-service meals may pay with a major credit card, Disney gift card, Disney visa Redemption card, or Apple Pay.

Grown-up floats of note: Grasshopper, Tropical Sunrise, and Guinness Stout. Reservations are recommended. Select desserts may be ordered to go. **LDS/$-$$$/❦**

**CAPE MAY CAFE:** Minnie and her friends greet visitors each morning at this whimsical dining area. The stellar morning meal includes all the standards, plus a few specialties. The breakfast buffet—complete with visits from Minnie Mouse and friends—is quite impressive, but dinner doesn't disappoint. It's an all-you-care-to-eat New England–style surf-and-turf dinner, and it's one of WDW's most popular meals and better values. The evening lineup includes a classic seafood boil (steamed clams, mussels, shrimp, corn, and potatoes), carved meat, salads, paella, and desserts. It's possible to order crab legs, too. (They come by the pound for an extra $29.) Soft drinks are included, but cocktails and specialty drinks are not. Note that Disney characters are not in attendance for dinner. Reservations are recommended. **BD/$$$/❦**

**HURRICANE HANNA'S WATERSIDE BAR & GRILL:** Hanna's serves garden salad, Caesar salad with chicken, seafood roll, cheddar cheeseburgers, onion rings, hummus (with crudité), and breaded chicken tenders with fries—plus cocktails, soft drinks, and frozen concoctions. Eat at the bar or have your order delivered poolside. This is also a refillable resort mug station (though it keeps shorter hours than Beach Club Marketplace). **LDS/$-$$/❦**

**THE MARKET AT ALE & COMPASS:** This upscale quick-service spot serves specialty coffees and morning selections such as turkey, egg, and cheese breakfast sandwiches; egg white wraps; oatmeal; breakfast bowls; and Mickey-shaped waffles. The rest of the day brings sandwiches (ham and cheese on a pretzel roll, grilled chicken, roast beef, and more), paninis, hot dogs, and salads (Greek and chicken Caesar). There is a selection of grab-and-go

items, too. Do you have a refillable resort mug? Here's a place to make it happy. **BLDS/$-$$/❦/MO**

**YACHTSMAN STEAKHOUSE:** You know you're in for a serious steak experience the moment you walk through the door. There's a butcher shop here! Meals begin with fresh-baked onion rolls and may continue with a savory appetizer such as lobster bisque or french onion soup. There's no skimping on the expertly crafted entrées, so good luck finding room for strawberry shortcake! In addition to beef (which is house-aged and prepared on an oak-fired grill), the menu includes chicken, pasta, and seafood. One could feast on side dishes alone, with braised mushrooms, creamed spinach, and truffle mac & cheese all vying for your attention. Favorite selections from the dessert menu have included the aforementioned strawberry shortcake, plus carrot cake, brûléed cheese-cake, and chocolate ganache cake. Reservations are recommended. **D/$$$–$$$$/❦/SR**

## MOBILE ORDER MAGIC

Quietly introduced a few years back, Mobile Ordering has surged in popularity of late and many a Walt Disney World eatery has jumped aboard the bandwagon. While you can still place an order with a cheery cast member, you may opt to order and pre-pay for your vittles with the Mobile Order feature in the (free) My Disney Experience mobile app.

If you've made it this far in this book, chances are you have already downloaded the app and set up your profile. If not, be sure to do so *before* you find yourself exploring Walt Disney World with your stomach growling.

When it's time for a meal or snack, open the My Disney Experience app on your smartphone. Hit the plus sign (+) on the home page. Then tap "Order Food." (You will be asked to sign in at some point, so make sure you know your user name and password for the app.)

After you hit Order Food, a list of available restaurants will pop up, along with possible pick-up times. Choose your eatery and select a pick-up time. Now it's time to place your order! You can even customize certain menu items to your taste. After you've reviewed your details, pay for your order using a credit card, debit card, Disney Gift Card, Disney Rewards Redemption Card, Apple Pay, or a Disney Dining Plan (when available).

Restaurants that offered mobile ordering at press time have **MO** at the end of their descriptions in this chapter. Of course, details are apt to change this year—and new places will likely add the mobile order option. For updates, check the My Disney Experience app or website, or visit *disneyworld.com/dining*.

# Reservations Explained

Disney's restaurant reservation system covers most full-service restaurants on Walt Disney World property. It was designed to provide the assurance of a reservation without delays caused by no-shows and latecomers. Here's how it works: Book your preferred seating time; you and your party arrive about 5 to 15 minutes before the assigned time and check in with your mobile device or at the podium; you'll receive the next available table that can accommodate your party.

**Hot Tip!** The Walt Disney World Dining scene is ever-evolving. For updates, visit *disneyworld.com/dining*, or use the My Disney Experience mobile app or website.

It is virtually impossible to walk into a table service eatery without a reservation—secure yours as far in advance as possible. Seating times can be reserved up to 60 days ahead for most Disney eateries by visiting *disneyworld.com/dining*, or via the My Disney Experience app or website. If you are unable to book in advance, check for same-day availability via the My Disney Experience app. A fee of $10 per person will be charged for guests who don't show up or cancel a reservation within two hours of the reservation time (for most places that accept advance reservations—be sure to note the eatery's cancellation policy when you book your table).

Once at the theme parks, reservations can be made via the My Disney Experience mobile app or website or *disneyworld.com/dining*. In-person inquiries may be

## FOR DISNEY RESORT GUESTS ONLY

Do you have a confirmed reservation at a Disney-owned-and-operated resort? If so, you are entitled to a special perk: Book 60 days prior to the first day of your hotel reservation and you can make dining reservations for up to 10 days of your stay. That's like getting a 1- to 10-day jump on everyone else! (For Walt Disney World stays of longer than 10 days, call 407-939-3463.) Before you can book via the app or web site, you'll need to link your resort reservation to your My Disney Experience profile. If you pop for a Disney Dining Plan, know that your meals are pre-paid, but not pre-booked. Be sure to reserve table-service eateries as far in advance as possible. For updates, use the My Disney Experience app or website, or visit *disneyworld.com/dining*.

**Hot Tip!** At most Disney World table-service restaurants, reservations are scheduled in five- or ten-minute intervals. If they don't have a 6 P.M. availability, check for 6:10 P.M. It's worth a try!

made at City Hall in the Magic Kingdom; in EPCOT at Guest Relations by Spaceship Earth; near Hollywood Junction in Disney's Hollywood Studios; and at Guest Relations in Animal Kingdom. Bookings can also be made at Guest Relations at the Welcome Center in Town Center. Last, but not least, many table service eateries offer a "walk-up wait list" via the My Disney Experience mobile app. (We love this addition to the reservation system.)

While the Disney reservation system is often quite efficient, there are times when the wait for a table can be unexpectedly long. This is most likely to occur during peak mealtimes at places that offer buffet or family-style meals, where patrons may opt for seconds (or thirds). For this reason, be sure to check in well ahead of your reservation time (especially for meals that are hosted by Disney characters).

Reservations are necessary for the Hoop-Dee-Doo Musical Revue dinner show (presented at Pioneer Hall at Disney's Fort Wilderness resort); they can be made via the My Disney Experience mobile app or website and *disneyworld.com/dining*. Reservations can (and should) be booked up to 60 days ahead. If you can't snag a table for an early performance, don't rule out a later one (they are usually less heavily booked).

Keep in mind that, with the exception of dinner shows, a reserved Walt Disney World seating time does vary from a traditional reservation—you may have to wait a bit when you arrive at your assigned time. Your party will be given the first table that opens up.

Note that parties of 6 or more may require multiple reservations and being seated together is not guaranteed.

**Hot Tip!** The most expedient way to book a WDW dining reservation is to visit *disneyworld.com/dining*, or use the My Disney Experience app or website. If you have questions about your reservation or need additional assistance, call 407-WDW DINE (939-3463). It's also possible to make a reservation via this number (though there may be a lengthy wait time).

# WALT DISNEY WORLD CHARACTER DINING

| NAME & LOCATION | MEALS | STYLE* | PRICE** | CHARACTERS | THEME |
|---|---|---|---|---|---|
| **Artist Point**<br>Wilderness Lodge<br>(page 308) | Dinner | Fixed-price menu (three courses) | D: $65/39 | **Snow White, Dopey, Grumpy, and the Queen** | Storybook fantasy |
| **Akershus**<br>Norway Pavilion, EPCOT<br>(page 272) | Breakfast<br>Lunch<br>Dinner | Family-style | B: $53/34<br>L/D: $63/41 | **Belle, Jasmine, Snow White, and Aurora** | Fourteenth-century Norwegian castle |
| **Cape May Cafe**<br>Beach Club resort<br>(page 310) | Breakfast | Buffet | B: $45/29 | **Goofy, Minnie, and Donald Duck** | Seaside picnic |
| **Chef Mickey's**<br>Contemporary resort<br>(page 299) | Breakfast<br>Dinner | Buffet | B: $51/33<br>D: $62/39 | **Mickey, Minnie, Donald, Goofy, and Pluto** | A family celebration |
| **Cinderella's Royal Table**<br>Magic Kingdom<br>(page 263) | Breakfast<br>Lunch<br>Dinner | Fixed-price menu | B: $65/39<br>L/D: $79/47 | **B, L, D: Princesses**<br>**B, L, D: Cinderella greets guests in the Castle lobby** | Medieval banquet |
| **The Crystal Palace**<br>Magic Kingdom<br>(page 266) | Breakfast<br>Lunch<br>Dinner | Buffet | B: $45/29<br>L/D: $59/38 | **Pooh, Eeyore, Tigger, and Piglet** | Sunlit conservatory |
| **Garden Grill**<br>EPCOT<br>(page 270) | Breakfast<br>Lunch<br>Dinner | Family-style | B: $42/27<br>L/D: $55/36 | **Mickey, Pluto, Chip, and Dale** | Home-style country cooking |

* Family-style and buffet meals are all-you-care to enjoy experiences. Family-style features a set menu and table service; buffet-style meals usually present more dining options and are mostly self-service.

** Adult prices are followed by children's prices (diners ages 3 through 9). Details and prices are subject to change.

| FEATURED ITEMS | FOR DESSERT | TIP | WINS FOR . . . |
|---|---|---|---|
| Prime rib roast, herb chicken, soup, shrimp cocktail, butter-poached sustainable fish, and pork shank | Gooseberry tart, cookies and cream panna cotta, "poison" dark chocolate/apple mousse | Meeting the Queen is optional—so if your kids aren't ready, they can easily skip an encounter with the Disney villain. | **Best Place to Mingle with Characters from the Enchanted Forest** (It's also the only place to meet the evil Queen.) |
| B: Scrambled eggs, potato casserole, dill salmon gravlax, bacon, sausage, cheese, fruit<br><br>L/D: Norwegian fare (meatballs, chicken & dumplings, fish, and *lefse*), and kid-friendly selections | Chocolate cake and traditional Norwegian rice cream topped with strawberry sauce | The eatery is about a half-mile from EPCOT's front entrance—allow extra time for travel. | **It's Not Cinderella's Castle, but It's Still Pretty Cool** (It's easier to score a reservation here, too.) |
| Omelets, scrambled eggs, french toast, Mickey and Minnie waffles, bacon, sausage, fruit, oatmeal, grits, and potato barrels | Salted caramel "beach buns" served with vanilla cream, fresh fruit | For guests staying in the EPCOT area, Cape May is one of the best breakfast options. | **Best Chance of Getting a Table without Reservations** (But make the arrangements, anyway—there's usually a wait to get in.) |
| B: Eggs, slow-roasted beef brisket, fruit, pancakes, Mickey waffles, banana bread french toast, yogurt parfaits, tofu scramble<br><br>D: Carved meats, shrimp & grits, mac & cheese, veggies, salads | B: Fresh fried sweet fritters, harvest sweet rolls with cream cheese icing<br><br>D: Warm apple crisp, Mickey Mouse dome, strawberry cream cake | A celebration happens every 45 minutes. Be sure to have your camera ready. | **Best All-Around Character Meal** (It has a fun and festive setting and a kid-pleasing menu.) |
| B: Quiche, avocado toast, french toast, beef tenderloin with egg, "traditional breakfast," yogurt<br><br>L/D: Parisian gnocchi, spice-crusted pork, beef tenderloin, pasta with braised chicken, salad | B: Assortment of breakfast pastries<br><br>L/D: Seasonal cheesecake, dark chocolate mousse, and coffee pots de crème | Payment in full is required at time of booking for all meals. | **Best Setting** (The restaurant is inside Cinderella Castle!) |
| B: Breakfast meats, potatoes, eggs, pancakes, waffles, biscuits & gravy, seasonal fruit, grits, yogurt<br><br>L/D: Peel-and-eat shrimp, fried chicken, prime rib, pasta, shrimp creole, ravioli, soup, salads | B: Freshly baked pastries<br><br>L/D: Cake, cookies, panna cotta, chocolate pudding, soft serve ice cream | Don't be put off by the size of this eatery—the characters tend to make the rounds surprisingly quickly. | **Best Theme Park Buffet** (Crystal Palace scores points for its lovely setting, convenient location, and appetizing menu.) |
| B: Cheesy potato casserole, flank steak, Mickey waffles, eggs, fruit<br><br>L/D: Grilled beef with chimichurri, BBQ chicken, seasonal vegetables, Southern-style spoon bread, creamy mashed potatoes, mac and cheese | Short cake topped with berry compote and whipped cream | The room rotates very slowly throughout the meal. It's hardly noticeable to most, but may be disorienting to those highly sensitive to motion. | **Best Character Interaction** (Thanks to a relatively small dining area, guests enjoy lots of attention from Disney pals.) |

# WALT DISNEY WORLD CHARACTER DINING

| NAME & LOCATION | MEALS | STYLE* | PRICE** | CHARACTERS | THEME |
|---|---|---|---|---|---|
| **Hollywood & Vine** Disney's Hollywood Studios (page 280) | Breakfast Lunch Dinner | Buffet | B: $42/27 L/D: $59/38 | **B: Doc McStuffins, Sofia the First, Vampirina, and Roadster Racer Goofy** **L and D: Minnie and friends** | A salute to Playhouse Disney or a seasonal celebration |
| **Trattoria al Forno** Bon Voyage Breakfast at BoardWalk resort (page 297) | Breakfast | À la carte | $38/22 | **Rapunzel, Flynn Rider (aka Eugene Fitzherbert), Ariel, and Prince Eric** | Pre-adventure party |
| **Topolino's Terrace** Disney's Riviera resort (page 305) | Breakfast | Fixed-price à la carte menu | $45/29 | **Mickey Mouse and friends such as Minnie Mouse, Donald Duck, and Daisy Duck** | Elegant rooftop dining |
| **'Ohana** Polynesian Village resort (page 303) | Breakfast | Family-style | $45/29 | **Lilo, Stitch, and others, such as Pluto and Mickey** | Polynesian family feast |
| **1900 Park Fare*** Grand Floridian resort (page 302; details subject to change) | Breakfast Dinner | Buffet | B: $45/29 D: $60/39 | **B: Stars like Mary Poppins and Alice** **D: Cinderella and friends** | Turn-of-the-twentieth-century circus |
| **Tusker House** Donald's Dining Safari at Animal Kingdom (page 284) | Breakfast Lunch Dinner | Buffet | B: $45/29 L/D: $59/38 | **Donald, Daisy, Goofy, and Mickey** | Safari feast |

\* Family-style and buffet meals are all-you-care to enjoy experiences. Family-style features a set menu and table service; buffet-style meals usually present more dining options and are mostly self-service.

\*\* Adult prices are followed by children's prices (diners ages 3 through 9). Details and prices are subject to change.

| FEATURED ITEMS | FOR DESSERT | TIP | WINS FOR . . . |
|---|---|---|---|
| B: Brioche french toast, omelets, chicken & waffles, frittatas, fruit<br><br>L/D: Salads, slow-roasted pork belly, roasted mushroom farro risotto, seared salmon, shrimp and bacon mac & cheese | B: Assorted pastries, soft-serve ice cream<br><br>L/D: Mississippi mud pie, PB&J tarts, ice cream | When making your reservation, remember that breakfast is called Play 'N Dine (with Disney Junior friends), while lunch and dinner are known as Minnie's Seasonal Dine (Minnie and pals). | **Most Tot-Pleasing**<br>(Little ones love to dine along with Doc McStuffins, who appears at breakfast.) |
| Scrambled eggs, frittatas, pancakes, caprese omelet, oak-grilled steak, breakfast pizza, avocado toast | Cherry turnovers, clam shells, fruit, vanilla and blueberry muffins | Expect lots of photo ops, but no PhotoPass photographers. Be sure to bring your camera or smartphone to capture magical moments. | **Best Place to Meet Flynn Rider and Prince Eric**<br>(It's also the only place to meet these gents.) |
| Wild mushroom scramble, sour cream waffles, quiche, smoked salmon, two eggs any style, french toast, wood-fired butcher's steak, fruit plate, avocado toast | Not offered | This eatery is a Disney Dining Plan Signature Restaurant for dinner, while breakfast requires only one table-service credit per person. (Disney characters visit during breakfast, but not dinner.) | **Best Views**<br>(Perched atop the Riviera resort, Topolino's Terrace offers majestic bird's-eye views of the World below.) |
| Mickey-shaped waffles, scrambled eggs, biscuits, fruit, Hawaiian-style ham topped with pineapple, fried potatoes, pork sausage links | Pineapple-coconut breakfast bread, fruit | Don't forget your autograph book and camera. Characters spend a good amount of quality time at each table. | **Speediest Service**<br>(Servers keep those family-style platters coming fast and frequently.) |
| B: Pancakes, eggs, waffles<br><br>D: Prime rib, pasta, seafood | B: Sticky buns, muffins, Danish<br><br>D: Key lime pie, bread pudding, cheesecake | Breakfast here is a nice way to start a Magic Kingdom day. The theme park is just one monorail stop away. | **Fanciest Foods**<br>(The quality is superior to many buffets, and there's plenty to please the kids.) |
| B: Simba- and Mickey-shaped waffles, eggs, fruit salad, potatoes<br><br>L/D: Spit-roasted chicken, shrimp curry, salmon, pork, African-inspired salads, housemade breads and dips | B: coffee cake, cinnamon buns, chocolate danish<br><br>L/D: Animal-inspired mini desserts, chocolate mousse | This spot is just steps from the Kilimanjaro Safaris attraction, making it an ideal location for a pre-safari breakfast or post-safari lunch. | **Best Place to Dine with Donald Duck**<br>(The Duck and his pals greet guests at breakfast, lunch, and dinner.) |

**All characters, menu items, and prices are subject to change. Prices are rounded to the nearest dollar. Prices do not include tax or gratuity. This listing is not comprehensive. Call 407-WDW-DINE (939-3463), or visit** *www.disneyworld.com/dining* **for updates or to make reservations.**

# Special Dining Experiences

Walt Disney World offers skads of special dining opportunities throughout the year. Many are cooked up for events such as EPCOT's International Food & Wine Festival, summer celebrations, and certain holiday periods. Others are available year-round. Here are a few gustatory experiences that can add an extra layer to the Disney dining adventure:

**HOOP-DEE-DOO MUSICAL REVUE:** The fact that Disney is expert in family entertainment is nowhere more readily apparent than amid the whooping and hollering troupe of singers and dancers who race toward the stage at the Fort Wilderness resort's Pioneer Hall. As guests plow through platters of "all-you-care-to-enjoy" fare: barbecue vittles (ribs, fried chicken, strawberry short-cake, beer, wine, and soft drinks), these enthusiastic performers sing, dance, and joke up a storm.

Most of the gags are groaners, but the audience eats 'em up day in and day out. It's all in the course of an evening at the Hoop-Dee-Doo Musical Revue. The cost is about $66 per adult and $39 for kids (ages 3 through 9) for Category 3 seating; about $69 for adults, $40 for kids in Category 2; and about $74 and $44 for Category 1. (With seating on the main floor, Category 1 offers the best views of the show.) Categories 1 and 2 are wheel-chair accessible. Prices include tax and gratuity and are subject to change. Shows are usually presented several times nightly. The show is the equivalent of a Signature Restaurant for folks using the Disney Dining Plan. 🐭

**Reservations:** At press time, the Hoop-Dee-Doo was bookable up to 60 days in advance. For reservations, use the My Disney Experience app or website, or call 407-WDW-939-3463. Reservations must be made using a credit card. Full payment is required upon booking.

The dining room inside Pioneer Hall tends to be chilly year-round. Bring a sweater to combat the sometimes intense air-conditioning.

**Notes:** Cancellations must be made at least 24 hours prior to showtime to avoid paying full price. Special occasions may be acknowledged (no charge)—be sure to tell your server what you're celebrating. Cakes are available for an additional charge and can be added to your reservation (see page 273).

**LA CAVA EXPERIENCE:** Rich in culture and tradition, this gustatory journey is lead by a certified Tequila Ambas-sador at La Cava in EPCOT's Mexico pavilion. Participants, who must be at least 21 years of age, are guided through a selection of rare and unique agave spirits. Each drink is paired with a flavor meant to enhance its essence.

The experience costs $150 per person (plus tax and service charge). Chips and guacamole are included, but a full meal is not. Parties of up to 6 guests can be booked via *disneyworld.com/dining*. If your party is larger than 6 people, groups of up to 14 people can be accommodated by sending an email request to the La Cava del Tequila team at *lacava@palmasrestaurants.com*. To check for same-day availability, stop at the La Cava del Tequila host stand.

**SANGRIA UNIVERSITY:** A 90-minute lesson reveals the history of sangria and four recipes that are served at Three Bridges Bar & Grill at Disney's Coronado Springs resort. As the lesson concludes, students (who must be age 21 or over) sample all four recipes and a light appetizer. Guests younger than 21 can sip a flight of no-alcohol beverages throughout the experience. The class, which is taught at Three Bridges, is held on Satur-day and Sunday afternoons. It costs $59 per person (including tax and gratuity) and may be canceled due to inclement weather. For more information or to make reservations, go to *disneyworld.com/dining*.

**SAVOR THE SAVANNA:** A privately guided African journey, Savor the Savanna takes place at Disney's Animal King-dom park. While drinking in the safari scenery, guests indulge in a sampling of African-inspired cuisine, paired with a selection of regional beer and wine offerings. The tour is available to guests age 8 and older. Guests under age 18 must be accompanied by a participating adult (18 years of age or older). The 2-hour adventure costs about $174 (plus tax) per person and may vary by date. Valid admission to Disney's Animal Kingdom is required for the day of the tour (as is a park reservation if you're an Annual Passholder and the tour is before 2 P.M.) To book this experience, go to *disneyworld.com/dining*.

# Where to Find . . .

From french fries to filet mignon, fried chicken to seared scallops with black truffle spaghettini, Disney dishes truly run the gamut. To help you zero in on the eateries that best fit your needs, we've created a handy index of specialized lists:

## BAKERIES/PASTRY SHOPS
**Amorette's Patisserie** (Disney Springs, Town Center)
**Beach Club Marketplace** (Beach Club resort)
**Big Top Treats** (Magic Kingdom, Fantasyland)
**Cake Bake Shop, The** (BoardWalk resort)
**Everglazed Donuts & Cold Brew** (Disney Springs, West Side)
**Gelateria Toscana** (EPCOT, World Showcase)
**Gideon's Bakehouse** (Disney Springs, The Landing)
**Goofy's Candy Co.** (Disney Springs, Marketplace)
**Karamell-Küche** (EPCOT, World Showcase)
**Kringla Bakeri og Kafe** (EPCOT, World Showcase)
**Kusafiri Coffee Shop & Bakery** (Animal Kingdom, Harambe)
**Les Halles Boulangerie Patisserie** (EPCOT, World Showcase)
**Main Street Bakery** (Magic Kingdom, Main Street, U.S.A.)
**Sunshine Seasons** (EPCOT, The Land)
**Trolley Car Café** (Disney's Hollywood Studios)

## BARBECUE
**City Works Eatery & Pour House** (Disney Springs, West Side)
**Flame Tree Barbecue** (Animal Kingdom, Discovery Island)
**Hoop-Dee-Doo Musical Revue** (Fort Wilderness resort)
**House of Blues Smokehouse** (Disney Springs, West Side)
**Polite Pig, The** (Disney Springs, Town Center)
**Regal Eagle Smokehouse** (EPCOT, World Showcase)
**Roundup Rodeo BBQ** (Disney's Hollywood Studios)
**Whispering Canyon Cafe** (Wilderness Lodge resort)

## BEST BANG FOR THE BUFFET BUCK (all-you-care-to-eat)
**Biergarten** (EPCOT, World Showcase)
**Boma—Flavors of Africa** (Animal Kingdom Lodge)
**Cape May Cafe** (Beach Club resort)

## BEST WITH BABIES (table service)
**Akershus Royal Banquet Hall** (EPCOT, World Showcase)
**Biergarten** (EPCOT, World Showcase)
**Chef Mickey's** (Contemporary resort)
**Crystal Palace, The** (Magic Kingdom, Main Street, U.S.A.)
**Hollywood & Vine** (Disney's Hollywood Studios)
**'Ohana** (Polynesian Village resort)
**Olivia's Cafe** (Disney's Old Key West resort)
**Rainforest Cafe** (Animal Kingdom and Disney Springs)
**Roundup Rodeo BBQ** (Disney's Hollywood Studios)
**Tony's Town Square** (Magic Kingdom, Main Street, U.S.A.)
**Tusker House** (Animal Kingdom, Harambe)

## BRUNCH
**The Boathouse** (Disney Springs, The Landing; weekend)
**Chef Art Smith's Homecomin'** (Disney Springs, The Landing; weekend)
**City Works Eatery & Pour House** (Disney Springs, West Side; weekend)
**House of Blues** (Disney Springs, West Side; weekend)
**Maria & Enzo's** (Disney Springs; weekend)
**Olivia's Cafe** (Old Key West resort; every day)
**Paddlefish** (Disney Springs, The Landing; Sunday)
**Raglan Road** (Disney Springs, The Landing; weekend)
**STK Orlando** (Disney Springs, The Landing; weekend)
**Summer House on the Lake** (Disney Springs, West Side; weekend)
**Terralina Crafted Italian** (Disney Springs, The Landing; Sunday)
**Wine Bar George** (Disney Springs, The Landing; weekend)
**Wolfgang Puck Bar & Grill** (Disney Springs, Town Center; weekend)

**BUFFET** (all-you-care-to-eat)

**Akershus Royal Banquet Hall** (EPCOT, World Showcase—appetizers only)

**Biergarten** (EPCOT, World Showcase)

**Boma—Flavors of Africa** (Animal Kingdom Lodge)

**Cape May Cafe** (Beach Club resort)

**Chef Mickey's** (Contemporary resort)

**Crystal Palace, The** (Magic Kingdom, Main Street, U.S.A.)

**Hollywood & Vine** (Disney's Hollywood Studios)

**1900 Park Fare** (Grand Floridian resort)

**Tusker House** (Animal Kingdom, Harambe)

**BURGERS**

**Backlot Express** (Disney's Hollywood Studios)

**Beaches & Cream Soda Shop** (Beach Club resort)

**Cabana Bar & Beach Club** (Dolphin resort)

**Capt. Cook's** (Polynesian Village resort)

**Cosmic Ray's Starlight Cafe** (Magic Kingdom, Tomorrowland)

**City Works Eatery & Pour House** (Disney Springs, West Side)

**Contempo Cafe** (Contemporary resort)

**D-Luxe Burger** (Disney Springs, Town Center)

**Edison, The** (Disney Springs, The Landing)

**Food Courts** (All-Star resorts)

**Fountain, The** (Dolphin resort)

**Geyser Point Bar & Grill** (Wilderness Lodge resort)

**Pecos Bill Tall Tale Inn & Cafe** (Magic Kingdom, Frontierland)

**Raglan Road** (Disney Springs, The Landing)

**Restaurantosaurus** (Animal Kingdom, DinoLand)

**Riverside Mill** (Port Orleans Riverside resort)

**Sassagoula Floatworks & Food Factory** (Port Orleans French Quarter resort)

**Sci-Fi Dine-In Theater** (Disney's Hollywood Studios)

**Steakhouse 71** (Contemporary resort)

**Sunset Ranch Market** (Disney's Hollywood Studios)

**Tangerine** (Swan Reserve resort)

**CHEAP EATS—FAST FOOD**

**Backlot Express** (Disney's Hollywood Studios)

**Columbia Harbour House** (Magic Kingdom, Liberty Square)

**Connections Eatery** (EPCOT, World Celebration)

**D-Luxe Burger** (Disney Springs, Town Center)

**Everything Pop!** (Pop Century resort)

**Flame Tree Barbecue** (Animal Kingdom, Discovery Island)

**Harambe Market** (Animal Kingdom, Harambe)

**House of Blues Smokehouse** (Disney Springs, West Side)

**Katsura Grill** (EPCOT, World Showcase)

**Landscape of Flavors** (Disney's Art of Animation resort)

**Les Halles Boulangerie Patisserie** (EPCOT, World Showcase)

**Main Street Bakery** (Magic Kingdom, Main Street, U.S.A.)

**Pinocchio Village Haus** (Magic Kingdom, Fantasyland)

**Pizzafari** (Animal Kingdom, Discovery Island)

**Polite Pig, The** (Disney Springs, Town Center)

**Restaurantosaurus** (Animal Kingdom, DinoLand)

**Sommerfest** (EPCOT, World Showcase)

**Sunset Ranch Market** (Disney's Hollywood Studios)

**Sunshine Seasons** (EPCOT, World Nature)

**Woody's Lunch Box** (Disney's Hollywood Studios)

**Yorkshire County Fish Shop** (EPCOT, World Showcase)

**CHEAP EATS** (relatively speaking)

**Table Service**

**Beaches & Cream Soda Shop** (Beach Club resort)

**Big River Grille & Brewing Works** (BoardWalk resort)

**Cape May Cafe** (Beach Club resort)

**Geyser Point Bar & Grill** (Wilderness Lodge resort; lounge)

**Kimonos** (Swan resort)

**Kona Cafe** (Polynesian Village resort)

**Olivia's Cafe** (Disney's Old Key West resort)

**Planet Hollywood** (Disney Springs, West Side)

**Plaza Restaurant** (Magic Kingdom, Main Street, U.S.A.)

**Rainforest Cafe** (Animal Kingdom and Disney Springs, Marketplace)

**Spice Road Table** (EPCOT, World Showcase)

**T-Rex Cafe: A Prehistoric Family Adventure** (Disney Springs, Marketplace)

**Tusker House** (Animal Kingdom, Harambe)

**Via Napoli** (EPCOT, World Showcase)

**Yak & Yeti** (Animal Kingdom, Asia)

**DISNEY CHARACTERS** (dining with)
(see pages 312-315)

## INTERNATIONAL EATERIES
### African
**Boma—Flavors of Africa** (Animal Kingdom Lodge)
**Harambe Market** (Animal Kingdom, Harambe)
**Jiko—The Cooking Place**
   (Animal Kingdom Lodge)
**Sanaa** (Animal Kingdom Lodge, Kidani Village)
**Spice Road Table** (EPCOT, World Showcase)

**Tiffins Restaurant** (also serves Indian cuisine; Animal
   Kingdom, Discovery Island)
**Tusker House** (Animal Kingdom, Harambe)

### American
**Big River Grille & Brewing Works**
   (BoardWalk resort)
**Boathouse, The** (Disney Springs, The Landing)
**Boatwright's Dining Hall** (Port Orleans Riverside resort)
**California Grill** (Contemporary resort)
**Chef Art Smith's Homecomin'** (Disney Springs, The Landing)
**Edison, The** (Disney Springs, The Landing)
**Fife & Drum Tavern** (EPCOT, World Showcase)
**50's Prime Time Cafe** (Disney's Hollywood Studios)
**Flying Fish** (BoardWalk resort)
**Funnel Cake** (EPCOT, World Showcase)
**Garden Grill** (EPCOT, World Nature)
**Grand Floridian Cafe** (Grand Floridian resort)
**Hollywood Brown Derby** (Disney's Hollywood Studios)
**House of Blues** (Disney Springs, West Side)
**Liberty Tree Tavern** (Magic Kingdom, Liberty Square)
**Narcoossee's** (Grand Floridian resort)
**1900 Park Fare** (Grand Floridian resort)

**Olivia's Cafe** (Old Key West resort)
**Regal Eagle Smokehouse** (EPCOT, World Showcase)
**Roundup Rodeo BBQ** (Disney's Hollywood Studios)
**Sci-Fi Dine-In Theater** (Disney's Hollywood Studios)
**Storybook Dining at Artist Point** (Wilderness Lodge)

### British
**Earl of Sandwich** (Disney Springs, Marketplace)
**Rose & Crown Pub & Dining Room** (EPCOT,
   World Showcase)
**Yorkshire County Fish Shop** (EPCOT, World Showcase)

### Canadian
**The Daily Poutine** (Disney Springs, Town Center)
**Le Cellier Steakhouse** (EPCOT, World Showcase)

### Chinese and Southeast Asian
**Jungle Navigation Co. Ltd. Skipper Canteen** (Magic
   Kingdom, Adventureland)
**Lotus Blossom Cafe** (EPCOT, World Showcase)
**Nine Dragons** (EPCOT, World Showcase)
**Yak & Yeti** (Animal Kingdom, Asia)

### French
**Be Our Guest Restaurant** (Magic Kingdom, Fantasyland)
**Chefs de France** (EPCOT, World Showcase)
**La Crêperie de Paris** (EPCOT, World Showcase)
**Les Halles Boulangerie Patisserie** (EPCOT, World Showcase)
**Monsieur Paul** (EPCOT, World Showcase)

### German
**Biergarten** (EPCOT, World Showcase)
**Sommerfest** (EPCOT, World Showcase)

### Irish
**Cookes of Dublin** (Disney Springs, The Landing)
**Raglan Road** (Disney Springs, The Landing)

### Italian/Mediterranean
**Amare** (Swan Reserve resort)
**Blaze Fast Fire'd Pizza** (Disney Springs)
**Il Mulino New York Trattoria** (Swan resort)
**Mama Melrose's Ristorante Italiano**
   (Disney's Hollywood Studios)
**Maria & Enzo's Ristorante** (Disney Springs, The Landing)
**Spice Road Table** (EPCOT, World Showcase)

Tony's Town Square (Magic Kingdom, Main Street, U.S.A.)
Terralina Crafted Italian (Disney Springs, The Landing)
Trattoria al Forno (Disney's BoardWalk)
Tutto Gusto (EPCOT, World Showcase)
Tutto Italia (EPCOT, World Showcase)
Via Napoli (EPCOT, World Showcase)

Japanese
Kabuki Cafe (EPCOT, World Showcase)
Katsura Grill (EPCOT, World Showcase)
Kimonos (Swan resort)
Morimoto Asia (Disney Springs, The Landing)
Shiki-Sai: Sushi Izakaya (EPCOT, World Showcase)
Takumi—Tei (EPCOT, World Showcase)
Teppan Edo (EPCOT, World Showcase)

Mexican/Latin American
Frontera Cocina (Disney Springs, Town Center)
La Cantina de San Angel (EPCOT, World Showcase)
La Hacienda de San Angel (EPCOT, World Showcase)
Maya Grill (Coronado Springs resort)
Paradiso 37 (Disney Springs, The Landing)
Pecos Bill Tall Tale Inn (Magic Kingdom, Frontierland)
Rosa Mexicano (Dolphin resort)
San Angel Inn (EPCOT, World Showcase)

Norwegian
Akershus Royal Banquet Hall (EPCOT,
   World Showcase)
Kringla Bakeri og Kafe (EPCOT, World Showcase)

FAMILY-STYLE (all-you-care-to-eat)
Akershus Royal Banquet Hall (EPCOT, World Showcase)
Diamond Horseshoe (Magic Kingdom, Liberty Square)
Garden Grill (EPCOT, World Nature)

Hoop-Dee-Doo Musical Revue (see page 316)
Liberty Tree Tavern (Magic Kingdom, Liberty Square)
'Ohana (Polynesian Village resort)
Whispering Canyon Cafe (Wilderness Lodge)

FRUIT
Aloha Isle (Magic Kingdom, Adventureland)
Harambe Fruit Market (Animal Kingdom, Harambe)
Liberty Square Market (Magic Kingdom, Liberty Square)
Prince Eric's Village Market (Magic Kingdom, Fantasyland)
Sunset Ranch Market (Disney's Hollywood Studios)
Sunshine Seasons (EPCOT, World Nature)

GOOD FOR GROUPS
Biergarten (EPCOT, World Showcase)
Boathouse, The (Disney Springs, The Landing)
Boma—Flavors of Africa (Animal Kingdom Lodge)
California Grill (Contemporary resort)
Cape May Cafe (Beach Club resort)
Crystal Palace, The (Magic Kingdom,
   Main Street, U.S.A.)
Enzo's Hideaway (Disney Springs, The Landing)
Flame Tree Barbecue (Animal Kingdom, Discovery Island)
Flying Fish (BoardWalk resort)
Hollywood & Vine (Disney's Hollywood Studios)
House of Blues (Disney Springs, West Side)
'Ohana (Polynesian Village resort)
Paddlefish (Disney Springs, The Landing)
Raglan Road (Disney Springs, The Landing)
Rosa Mexicano (Dolphin resort)
Sebastian's Bistro (Caribbean Beach Resort)
Steakhouse 71 (Contemporary resort)
Sunshine Seasons (EPCOT, World Nature)
Teppan Edo (EPCOT, World Showcase)

**Todd English's bluezoo** (Dolphin resort)
**Tusker House** (Animal Kingdom, Harambe)
**Via Napoli** (EPCOT, World Showcase)
**Wine Bar George** (Disney Springs, The Landing)
**Wolfgang Puck Bar & Grill** (Disney Springs, Town Center)

## HOT DOGS
**Backlot Express** (Disney's Hollywood Studios)
**B.B. Wolf's Sausage Co.** (Disney Springs, Marketplace)
**Casey's Corner** (Magic Kingdom, Main Street, U.S.A.)
**Dockside Diner** (Disney's Hollywood Studios)
**Fairfax Fare** (Disney's Hollywood Studios)
**Hot Diggity Dogs** (Disney Springs; food truck)
**Lunching Pad, The** (Magic Kingdom, Tomorrowland)
**Sommerfest** (EPCOT, World Showcase)
**Sunset Ranch Market** (Disney's Hollywood Studios)
**Wetzel's Pretzels** (Disney Springs, Marketplace)

## ICE CREAM AND FROZEN TREATS
**Aloha Isle** (Magic Kingdom, Adventureland)
**Anandapur Ice Cream Truck** (Animal Kingdom, Asia)
**Beaches & Cream Soda Shop** (Beach Club resort)
**BoardWalk Ice Cream** (BoardWalk resort)
**Dino-Bite Snacks** (Animal Kingdom, DinoLand)
**Fife & Drum Tavern** (EPCOT, World Showcase)
**The Fountain** (Dolphin resort)
**Gaston's Tavern** (Magic Kingdom, Fantasyland)
**Gelateria Toscana** (EPCOT, World Showcase)
**Ghirardelli Ice Cream & Chocolate Shop**
   (Disney Springs, Marketplace)
**Golden Oak Outpost** (Magic Kingdom, Frontierland)
**Hollywood Scoops** (Disney's Hollywood Studios)
**L'Artisan's des Glace** (EPCOT, World Showcase)

**Pineapple Lanai** (Polynesian Village resort)
**Plaza Ice Cream Parlor** (Magic Kingdom, Main Street, U.S.A.)
**Plaza Restaurant** (Magic Kingdom, Main Street, U.S.A.)
**Refreshment Outpost** (EPCOT, World Showcase)
**Salt & Straw** (Disney Springs, West Side)
**Storybook Treats** (Magic Kingdom, Fantasyland)
**Sunshine Tree Terrace** (Magic Kingdom, Adventureland)
**Swirls on the Water** (Disney Springs, Marketplace)
**Tamu Tamu Refreshments** (Animal Kingdom, Harambe)
**Vivoli il Gelato** (Disney Springs, The Landing)

## KIDS' FAVORITES
**Akershus Royal Banquet Hall** (EPCOT, World Showcase)
**Cape May Cafe** (breakfast; Beach Club resort)
**Casey's Corner** (Magic Kingdom, Main Street)
**Chef Mickey's** (Contemporary resort)
**Cinderella's Royal Table** (Magic Kingdom, Fantasyland)
**Cosmic Ray's Starlight Cafe** (Magic Kingdom,
   Tomorrowland)
**Crystal Palace, The** (Magic Kingdom, Main Street)
**50's Prime Time Cafe** (Disney's Hollywood Studios)
**Hollywood & Vine** (Disney's Hollywood Studios)
**Hoop-Dee-Doo Musical Revue** (Fort Wilderness;
   see page 316)
**'Ohana** (Polynesian Village resort)
**Pinocchio Village Haus** (Magic Kingdom, Fantasyland)
**Pizzafari** (Animal Kingdom, Discovery Island)
**Rainforest Cafe** (Animal Kingdom and
   Disney Springs, Marketplace)
**Restaurantosaurus** (Animal Kingdom, Dinoland)
**Roundup Rodeo BBQ** (Disney's Hollywood Studios)
**Space 220** (EPCOT, World Discovery)
**Sunset Ranch Market** (Disney's Hollywood Studios)
**Sunshine Seasons** (EPCOT, World Nature)
**T-Rex Cafe: A Prehistoric Family Adventure**
   (Disney Springs, Marketplace)
**Tusker House** (Animal Kingdom, Harambe)
**Whispering Canyon Cafe** (Wilderness Lodge)
**Woody's Lunch Box** (Disney's Hollywood Studios)

## KNOCKOUT VIEWS
**Big River Grille & Brewing Works** (outdoor seating;
   BoardWalk)
**Boathouse, The** (Disney Springs, The Landing)
**California Grill** (Contemporary resort)
**Coral Reef** (EPCOT, World Nature)

**Jock Lindsey's Hangar Bar** (Disney Springs, The Landing)
**La Hacienda de San Angel** (EPCOT, World Showcase)
**Paddlefish** (Disney Springs, The Landing)
**Sanaa** (Animal Kingdom Lodge; select seats)

**Space 220** (EPCOT, World Discovery)
**Terralina Crafted Italian** (Disney Springs, The Landing)
**Topolino's Terrace—Flavors of the Riviera** (Riviera resort)

**KOSHER** (menu selections)
**ABC Commissary** (Disney's Hollywood Studios)
**Artist's Palette, The** (Saratoga Springs resort)
**Cosmic Ray's Starlight Cafe** (Magic Kingdom, Tomorrowland)
**Everything Pop!** (Pop Century resort)
**Food Courts** (All-Star and Port Orleans Riverside resorts)
**Gasparilla Island Grill** (Grand Floridian resort)
**Kusafiri Coffee Shop & Bakery** (Animal Kingdom, Harambe)
**Landscape of Flavors** (Art of Animation resort)
**Mara, The** (Animal Kingdom Lodge)
**Pizzafari** (Animal Kingdom, Discovery Island)
**Satu'li Canteen** (Animal Kingdom, Pandora—World of AVATAR)
**Space 220** (EPCOT, World Discovery)
**Toledo—Tapas, Steak & Seafood** (Coronado Springs resort)
**Topolino's Terrace—Flavors of the Riviera** (Riviera resort)
**Roaring Fork** (Wilderness Lodge)

**LOUNGES AND BARS** (with food)
**Barcelona Lounge** (Coronado Springs resort)
**Bar Riva** (Riviera resort)
**Big River Grille & Brewing Works** (BoardWalk resort)
**Boathouse, The** (Disney Springs, The Landing)
**Cabana Bar & Beach Club** (Dolphin resort)
**California Grill Lounge** (Contemporary resort)
**Cítricos Lounge** (Grand Floridian resort)
**Crew's Cup Lounge** (Yacht Club resort)

**Dahlia Lounge** (Coronado Springs resort)
**Edison, The** (Disney Springs, The Landing)
**Enchanted Rose** (Grand Floridian resort)
**Gurgling Suitcase** (Old Key West resort)
**Il Mulino New York Trattoria Lounge** (Swan resort)
**Jock Lindsey's Hangar Bar** (Disney Springs, The Landing)
**Kimonos** (Swan resort)
**Leaping Horse Libations** (BoardWalk resort)
**Mardi Grogs** (Port Orleans French Quarter resort)
**Martha's Vineyard** (Beach Club resort)
**Muddy Rivers** (Port Orleans Riverside resort)
**Narcoossee's** (Grand Floridian resort)
**Nomad Lounge** (Animal Kingdom, Discovery Island)
**Paddlefish** (Disney Springs, The Landing)
**Paradiso 37** (Disney Springs, The Landing)
**Raglan Road** (Disney Springs, The Landing)
**Rainforest Cafe** (Magic Mushroom bar; Animal Kingdom and Disney Springs, Marketplace)
**River Roost** (Port Orleans Riverside resort)
**Rix Sports Bar & Grill** (Coronado Springs resort)
**Sanaa Lounge** (Animal Kingdom Lodge)
**Scat Cat's Club—Lounge** (Port Orleans French Quarter resort)
**Shark Bar at T-Rex Cafe** (Disney Springs, Marketplace)
**Sommerfest** (inside Germany; EPCOT, World Showcase)
**Splash Terrace** (Swan resort)
**Tambu Lounge** (Polynesian Village resort)
**Territory Lounge** (Wilderness Lodge)
**Trader Sam's Grog Grotto** (Polynesian resort)
**Turf Club Bar & Grill, The** (Saratoga Springs Resort & Spa)
**Turtle Shack** (Disney's Old Key West resort)
**Tutto Gusto** (EPCOT, World Showcase)
**Uzima Springs** (Animal Kingdom Lodge)
**Yak & Yeti Lounge** (Animal Kingdom, Asia)

**OPEN LATE**
**BoardWalk Pizza Window** (BoardWalk resort)
**Il Mulino New York Trattoria** (Swan resort)
**Kimonos** (Swan resort)
**Market at Ale & Compass, The** (Yacht Club resort)
**Sundial Cafe 24-7** (Wyndham hotel)
**Trader Sam's Grog Grotto** (Polynesian Village resort)

**PIZZA**
**Blaze Fast Fire'd Pizza** (Disney Springs, Town Center)
**BoardWalk Pizza Window** (BoardWalk resort)
**California Grill** (Contemporary resort)

**Capt. Cook's** (Polynesian Village resort)
**Everything Pop!** (Pop Century resort)
**Food Courts** (All-Star resorts)
**Gasparilla Island Grill** (Grand Floridian resort)
**Mama Melrose's Ristorante Italiano**
   (Disney's Hollywood Studios)
**Pinocchio Village Haus** (Magic Kingdom, Fantasyland)

**Pizzafari** (Animal Kingdom, Discovery Island)
**Pizza Ponte** (Disney Springs, The Landing)
**PizzeRizzo** (Disney's Hollywood Studios)
**Riverside Mill** (Port Orleans Riverside resort)
**Roaring Fork** (Wilderness Lodge)
**Sassagoula Floatworks & Food Factory**
   (Port Orleans French Quarter resort)
**Sunset Ranch Market** (Disney's Hollywood Studios)
**Trattoria al Forno** (Boardwalk resort)
**Via Napoli** (EPCOT, World Showcase)
**Wolfgang Puck Bar & Grill** (Disney Springs, Town Center)

## PLANT-BASED SELECTIONS
**Boma—Flavors of Africa** (Animal Kingdom Lodge)
**Columbia Harbour House** (Magic Kingdom, Liberty Square)
**Cosmic Ray's Starlight Cafe** (Magic Kingdom, Tomorrowland)
**Everything Pop!** (Pop Century resort)
**Food Courts** (All-Star resorts)
**Jiko—The Cooking Place** (Animal Kingdom Lodge)
**La Hacienda de San Angel** (EPCOT, World Showcase)
**Les Halles Boulangerie Patisserie** (EPCOT, World Showcase)
**Mama Melrose's Ristorante Italiano**
   (Disney's Hollywood Studios)
**Pinocchio Village Haus** (Magic Kingdom, Fantasyland)
**Pizzafari** (Animal Kingdom, Discovery Island)
**PizzeRizzo** (Disney's Hollywood Studios)

**Rainforest Cafe** (Animal Kingdom and
   Disney Springs, Marketplace)
**Sanaa** (Animal Kingdom Lodge)
**Sunset Ranch Market** (Disney's Hollywood Studios)
**Sunshine Seasons** (EPCOT, World Nature)
**Tony's Town Square** (Magic Kingdom, Main Street, U.S.A.)
**Tusker House** (Animal Kingdom, Harambe)
**Tutto Italia** (EPCOT, World Showcase)
**Via Napoli** (EPCOT, World Showcase)

## SALADS
**ABC Commissary** (Disney's Hollywood Studios)
**Amare** (Swan Reserve resort)
**Artist's Palette, The** (Saratoga Springs resort)
**Big River Grille & Brewing Works** (BoardWalk resort)
**Boathouse, The** (Disney Springs, The Landing)
**Boma—Flavors of Africa** (Animal Kingdom Lodge)
**Chef Art Smith's Homecomin'** (Disney Springs, The Landing)

**Cítrico's** (Grand Floridian resort)
**Columbia Harbour House**
   (Magic Kingdom, Liberty Square)
**Earl of Sandwich** (Disney Springs, Marketplace)
**El Mercado de Coronado** (Coronado Springs resort)
**Gasparilla Island Grill** (Grand Floridian resort)
**Hollywood Brown Derby** (Disney's Hollywood Studios)
**Il Mulino New York Trattoria** (Swan resort)
**The Market at Ale & Compass** (Yacht Club resort)
**Pinocchio Village Haus** (Magic Kingdom, Fantasyland)
**Plaza Restaurant** (Magic Kingdom, Main Street, U.S.A.)
**Rainforest Cafe** (Animal Kingdom and Disney Springs,
   Marketplace)
**Sunshine Seasons** (EPCOT, World Nature)

**Steakhouse 71** (Contemporary resort)
**Wolfgang Puck Bar & Grill** (Disney Springs, Town Center)
**Yak & Yeti** (Animal Kingdom, Asia)

## SEAFOOD

**Ale & Compass Restaurant** (Yacht Club resort)
**Amare** (Swan Reserve resort)
**Artist Point** (Wilderness Lodge)
**Boathouse, The** (Disney Springs, The Landing)
**California Grill** (Contemporary resort)
**Cape May Cafe** (Beach Club resort)
**Columbia Harbour House** (Magic Kingdom, Liberty Square)
**Coral Reef** (EPCOT, World Nature)
**Flying Fish** (BoardWalk resort)
**Kimonos** (Swan resort)
**Kona Cafe** (Polynesian Village resort)
**Monsieur Paul** (EPCOT, World Showcase)

**Narcoossee's** (Grand Floridian resort)
**Paddlefish** (Disney Springs, The Landing)
**Sebastian's Bistro** (Carribbean Beach resort)
**Shiki-Sai: Sushi Izakaya** (EPCOT, World Showcase)
**Todd English's bluezoo** (Dolphin resort)
**Victoria & Albert's** (Grand Floridian resort)

## SNACK BARS (at the resorts)

**Beach Club Marketplace** (Beach Club resort)
**Cabana Bar & Beach Club** (Dolphin resort)
**Capt. Cook's** (Polynesian Village resort)
**Contempo Café** (Contemporary resort)
**Fuel** (Dolphin resort)
**Gasparilla Island Grill** (Grand Floridian resort)
**Mara, The** (Animal Kingdom Lodge)
**Market at Ale & Compass** (Yacht Club resort)
**Picabu** (Dolphin resort)
**Roaring Fork** (Wilderness Lodge)

## SOLO DINERS

**Boathouse, The** (Disney Springs, The Landing)
**California Grill Lounge** (Contemporary resort)
**Cítricos Lounge** (Grand Floridian resort)
**Crew's Cup Lounge** (Yacht Club resort)
**Enzo's Hideaway** (Disney Springs, The Landing)
**Flying Fish** (BoardWalk resort)
**Il Mulino New York Trattoria** (Swan resort)
**Jiko—The Cooking Place Lounge** (Animal Kingdom Lodge)
**Narcoossee's Lounge** (Grand Floridian resort)
**Nomad Lounge** (Disney's Animal Kingdom, Discovery Island)
**Paddlefish** (Disney Springs, The Landing)
**Raglan Road** (Disney Springs, The Landing)
**Tune-In Lounge** (Disney's Hollywood Studios)
**Wine Bar George** (Disney Springs, The Landing)

## STEAK

**California Grill** (Contemporary resort)
**Flying Fish** (BoardWalk resort)
**Jiko—The Cooking Place** (Animal Kingdom Lodge resort)
**Kona Cafe** (Polynesian Village resort)
**La Hacienda de San Angel** (EPCOT, World Showcase)
**Le Cellier Steakhouse** (EPCOT, World Showcase)
**Monsieur Paul** (EPCOT, World Showcase)
**Paddlefish** (Disney Springs, The Landing)
**Narcoossee's** (Grand Floridian resort)
**Shula's** (Swan resort)
**Steakhouse 71** (Contemporary resort)
**STK Orlando** (Disney Springs, The Landing)
**Teppan Edo** (EPCOT, World Showcase)
**Toledo—Tapas, Steak & Seafood** (Coronado Springs resort)
**Yachtsman Steakhouse** (Yacht Club resort)

## SUPER SPLURGES (for grown-ups)

**Boathouse, The** (Disney Springs, The Landing)
**California Grill** (Contemporary resort)
**Chefs de France** (EPCOT, World Showcase)
**Cinderella's Royal Table** (Magic Kingdom)
**Enzo's Hideaway** (Disney Springs, The Landing)
**Flying Fish** (BoardWalk resort)
**Hollywood Brown Derby** (Disney's Hollywood Studios)
**Il Mulino** (Swan resort)
**Jiko—The Cooking Place** (Animal Kingdom Lodge)
**Le Cellier Steakhouse** (EPCOT, World Showcase)
**Monsieur Paul** (EPCOT, World Showcase)
**Morimoto Asia** (Disney Springs, The Landing)

**Narcoossee's** (Grand Floridian resort)
**Paddlefish** (Disney Springs, The Landing)
**Sanaa** (Animal Kingdom Lodge)
**Takumi-Tei** (EPCOT, World Showcase)
**Tiffins Restaurant** (Animal Kingdom, Discovery Island)
**Toledo—Tapas, Steak & Seafood** (Coronado Springs resort)
**Topolino's Terrace—Flavors of the Riviera** (Riviera resort)
**Victoria & Albert's** (Grand Floridian resort)
**Wine Bar George** (Disney Springs, The Landing)
**Yachtsman Steakhouse** (Yacht Club resort)

## SUSHI
**Benihana Steakhouse and Sushi**
    (Hilton Lake Buena Vista hotel)
**California Grill** (Contemporary resort)
**Kabuki Cafe** (EPCOT, World Showcase)
**Katsura Grill** (EPCOT, World Showcase)
**Kimonos** (lounge; Swan resort)
**Kona Cafe** (Polynesian Village resort)
**Kona Island** (after 5 P.M.; Polynesian Village resort)
**Morimoto Asia** (Disney Springs, The Landing)
**Shiki-Sai: Sushi Izakaya** (EPCOT, World Showcase)
**Splitsville** (Disney Springs, West Side)

## TERRIFIC THEMING
**Akershus Royal Banquet Hall** (EPCOT, World Showcase)
**Be Our Guest Restaurant** (Magic Kingdom, Fantasyland)
**Biergarten** (EPCOT, World Showcase)
**Boathouse, The** (Disney Springs, The Landing)
**Cinderella's Royal Table** (Magic Kingdom, Fantasyland)
**Edison, The** (Disney Springs, The Landing)
**Enzo's Hideaway** (Disney Springs, The Landing)
**50's Prime Time Cafe** (Disney's Hollywood Studios)
**Jungle Navigation Co. Ltd. Skipper Canteen** (Magic Kingdom, Adventureland)
**Liberty Tree Tavern** (Magic Kingdom, Liberty Square)

**Maria & Enzo's Ristorante** (Disney Springs, The Landing)
**'Ohana** (Polynesian Village resort)
**Rainforest Cafe** (Animal Kingdom and Disney Springs, Marketplace)
**Roundup Rodeo BBQ** (Disney's Hollywood Studios)
**Sanaa** (Animal Kingdom Lodge)
**Sci-Fi Dine-In Theater** (Disney's Hollywood Studios)
**T-Rex Cafe: A Prehistoric Family Adventure** (Disney Springs, Marketplace)
**Tusker House** (Animal Kingdom, Harambe)

## WINE AND DINE (great wine lists)
**Boathouse, The** (Disney Springs, The Landing)
**Boma—Flavors of Africa** (Animal Kingdom Lodge)
**California Grill** (Contemporary resort)
**Chefs de France** (EPCOT, World Showcase)
**Cítricos** (Grand Floridian resort)
**Enzo's Hideaway** (Disney Springs, The Landing)
**Flying Fish** (BoardWalk resort)
**Hollywood Brown Derby** (Disney's Hollywood Studios)
**Il Mulino New York Trattoria** (Swan resort)
**Jiko—The Cooking Place** (Animal Kingdom Lodge)
**Monsieur Paul** (EPCOT, World Showcase)
**Morimoto Asia** (Disney Springs, The Landing)
**Narcoossee's** (Grand Floridian resort)
**Paddlefish** (Disney Springs, The Landing)
**Sanaa** (Animal Kingdom Lodge)
**Shula's Steak House** (Dolphin resort)
**Steakhouse 71** (Contemporary resort)
**Storybook Dining at Artist Point** (Wilderness Lodge)
**Tiffins Restaurant** (Animal Kingdom, Discovery Island)
**Victoria & Albert's** (Grand Floridian resort)
**Wine Bar George** (Disney Springs, The Landing)
**Wolfgang Puck Bar & Grill** (Disney Springs, Town Center)
**Yachtsman Steakhouse** (Yacht Club resort)

# Bars & Lounges of WDW

What distinguishes Walt Disney World pubs and lounges from many bars in the real world? Well, in addition to over-the-top theming, you can almost always get a savory nibble to accompany that cocktail. Most Disney lounges serve food, be it from their own menu or from that of a neighboring restaurant.

Hours vary, but theme park watering holes (at EPCOT, Disney's Hollywood Studios, and Animal Kingdom) shut their doors at park closing time. Pool bars at the resorts generally keep daytime pool hours. Last call at resort lounges can be anywhere from about 10 P.M. to midnight. Disney Springs Marketplace spots stay open till the shops close, usually 11 P.M. Other lounges may keep things going until about 1 A.M.

## All-Star Movies, All-Star Music, & All-Star Sports

**POOL BARS:** There are small poolside oases in All-Star Movies, All-Star Music, and All-Star Sports: Silver Screen Spirits, Singing Spirits, and Grandstand Spirits, respectively. Each serves a selection of beer, wine, traditional cocktails, and specialty drinks. 🐭

## Animal Kingdom Park

**DAWA BAR:** A shaded spot in a busy neighborhood, Dawa is a pleasant place to take a load off weary feet and sip Safari Amber beer and other cocktails. It's next to Tusker House, on Kivulini Terrace. There may be occasional live music, too.

**NOMAD LOUNGE:** Thirsty adventurers can take a load off and relish a savory snack and/or frosty beverage at this atmospheric Animal Kingdom destination. The lounge proffers libations from the world over. The cuisine includes tuna poke bowls (with rice, red cabbage, kimchi, ginger-scallion oil, and edamame), plant-based sliders (with shoestring potatoes and yuca fries), Tiffins bread service (with three dipping sauces), honey-chile glazed pork belly, chicken bowls, and churros with vanilla ice cream. Festive banners pose questions about world travel and the thrill of discovery. Jot your answers on a decorative (free) tag and cast members will post them to a chandelier for all the world to see. This escapist oasis owns a spot on our favorites list. 🐭

**RAINFOREST CAFE:** The Magic Mushroom bar serves, among other things, fruit blends and specialty drinks. Bar stools resemble animal legs (hooves and all). Guests may order from the restaurant's menu, too. The bar is in the Rainforest Cafe. Admission to Disney's Animal Kingdom park is not necessary to enter. Note that Rainforest Cafe may keep longer hours than the park.

**THIRSTY RIVER BAR & TREK SNACKS:** Standing in the shadows of Expedition Everest, this casual outdoor oasis offers many spirited selections, including specialty drinks known as Himalayan Ghost, Durbar Margarita, and Khumbu Icefall. Savory snacks may be available too. The menu has featured light snacks such as popcorn, chips, and pretzels.

**YAK & YETI LOUNGE:** A small but satisfying space inside one of the restaurant's themed dining areas, the Yak & Yeti lounge has a fully stocked bar and seating for six. (There's standing room, too.) House specialties include the Yak Attack, Rickshaw Ricky, Big Bamboo, and Pink Himalayan. Beer, wine, sake, and assorted soft drinks are also served.

🐭 Disney Dining Plan participant at press time

# Animal Kingdom Lodge

**CAPE TOWN LOUNGE AND WINE BAR:** Sip African wines at this intimate space adjacent to Jiko—The Cooking Place. In addition to a full menu, it boasts an impressive selection of African wines. ❤/SR

**MAJI:** A poolside bar (*maji* means "water" in Swahili) serves drinks, hot dogs, nachos, salads, and more when the Samawati Springs pool is open (in Kidani Village). ❤

**SANAA LOUNGE:** In the resort's Kidani Village area, this lounge is within the restaurant of the same name. South African beers and wines, cocktails, and soft drinks may accompany snacks such as samosas, salad samplers, and Sanaa's famous Indian-style bread service. ❤

**UZIMA SPRINGS:** The bar near the main swimming pool serves salads, sandwiches, beer, wine, and specialty drinks during pool hours. The (alcohol-free) Lava smoothie is an excellent antidote to the steamy Florida heat.

**VICTORIA FALLS:** On the mezzanine level overlooking Boma—Flavors of Africa, this lounge offers coffee and spirits, plus the soothing sounds of the falls. (The actual Victoria Falls are located in Africa, between Zambia and Zimbabwe, and are nearly a mile wide.) Snacks (served from 5 P.M. to 10 P.M.) include burgers, goat cheese dip with bread and crackers, and olives with almonds. ❤

# Art of Animation

**DROP OFF BAR:** Open from noon until about midnight, this poolside location offers a variety of cocktails (with and without alcohol), soft drinks, and smoothies—plus salad, sandwiches, soft pretzels, and chips. ❤

# BoardWalk

**ABRACADABAR:** A "curious cocktail lounge," adjoining Flying Fish, AbracadaBAR merges the Golden Age of Magic with the magic of the Mouse. The sophisticated social club, once frequented by famous magicians and boardwalk illusionists, is back in the spotlight and it's open to all. Concoctions of note: The Magic Hattan, The Conjurita, Pepper's Ghost, and Hoodunit's Punch. Snacks (served from 5 P.M. until 10 P.M.) include Abra

fries with truffle cheese sauce, margherita pizza, and charcuterie (assorted meats and cheeses).

**ATLANTIC DANCE:** This club has music, videos, and a deejay. The design is Art Deco, but the tunes are more current. It's open Tuesday through Saturday nights, and guests must be at least 21 (with government-issued photo ID) to enter. Details are subject to change.

**BELLE VUE LOUNGE:** A full bar accompanies old-time tunes from antique radios in this casual space. Board games are usually available for on-site use (free of charge). There's limited seating at the bar, but there are plenty of tables and comfy chairs to relax on. Hours vary, but often run from about 5 P.M. until 11 P.M.

**BIG RIVER GRILLE & BREWING WORKS:** Big River patrons may order appetizers at the bar and sample the brewmaster's flagship ales and specialty beers. They may even get to watch as a new batch is brewed. In addition to fresh-brewed beer, drink selections include freshly squeezed lemonade, strawberry lemonade, pomegranate lemonade, and more. Note that Big River Grille & Brewing Works does not accept reservations and can get crowded during mealtimes (and right after EPCOT closes for the evening). ❤

**JELLYROLLS:** Dueling pianos and lively sing-alongs are the draw at this club, serving beer, wine, and other drinks. There is a cover charge in the neighborhood of $18, and guests must be at least 21 years old to enter. (Government-issued photo ID is required.) Requests are encouraged. And don't forget to tip the piano players before you leave. Note that it can be exceptionally cool here: Bring a sweater.

PHOTO BY JILL SAFRO

**LEAPING HORSE LIBATIONS:** The pool bar—designed to resemble a carousel (hence, the leaping horses)—offers cocktails, hot dogs, sandwiches, pizza, salad, soft drinks, and snacks during pool hours. ❤

# Caribbean Beach

**BANANA CABANA:** In the running for best pool bar, the open-air lounge offers a relaxing respite from the real world. It features a full bar and nummy nibbles. 🐭

# Contemporary

**CALIFORNIA GRILL BAR:** Perched atop the Contemporary resort, this small space tops many a "must-visit" list. Tucked within the acclaimed restaurant, the small bar offers an appealing menu and shares access to California Grill's exquisite wine selection.

In addition to wine, the lounge features sake, craft beers and ciders, mixed drinks, alcohol-free signature drinks, and more. Guests seated at the bar may order light bites such as sushi, pizza, or goat cheese raviolo, or opt for the 3-course, fixed-price menu offered by the restaurant itself. Guests who wish to visit the California Grill bar must check in at a desk on the Contemporary's second floor. When seats open up, they'll be notified by text and escorted to an express elevator.

**COVE BAR:** Set beside the pool in the resort's Bay Lake Tower, Cove Bar serves fruit, frozen desserts, Mickey pretzels, and lunch items (turkey BLT wrap, nachos

## GOT ID?

The legal drinking age in the state of Florida is 21. However, just being 21 isn't enough to get served—you have to prove it. To do so, present a government-issued photo ID. If your driver's license doesn't have a photo, bring it and an official photo ID (a passport is ideal). Otherwise, you'll have to stick to soft drinks.

with cheese, Caesar salad with chicken, and hot dogs). Wash it down with one of their specialty drinks, such as a Banana Cabana or Poolside Plunge.

**OUTER RIM:** Located on the resort's fourth floor across from Contempo Cafe, this stark lounge has a few bar stools and an abundance of tables with beverage service. The main draw here is not the view of the big TV, but rather the sweeping views of Bay Lake and the natural wonder of Fort Wilderness (on the lake's far shore). Beer, wine, sangria, specialty drinks, and no-alcohol sips are served from about 11:30 A.M. till 10 P.M.

**SAND BAR:** A full bar is offered poolside at the Contemporary (weather permitting). Quick-service snacks, salads, cheeseburgers, hot dogs, sandwiches, and soft drinks are served at an adjacent counter. 🐭

# Coronado Springs

**BARCELONA LOUNGE:** In addition to lovely lake views, the sophisticated Barcelona Lounge serves specialty coffees (spirited or sans alcohol), signature gin drinks, wines, craft beers, soft drinks, and small plates (charcuterie, hummus and vegetables, marinated olives, and more). Breakfast selections are available in the A.M. 🐭

**DAHLIA LOUNGE:** If a Spanish rooftop lounge in the heart of Walt Disney World sounds surreal, well, it is! Inspired by Spanish surrealism, Dahlia invites you to snack on tapas (citrus-poached shrimp cocktail, smoked paprika chips, crispy artichokes, Spanish charcuterie, etc.) and enjoy sublime sips of beer, wine, sherry, and specialty cocktails (Epumoso Punch, *por favor*, and zero-proof potables such as refreshing hibiscus-mint *limonada*). 🐭

**RIX SPORTS BAR & GRILL:** Located in the resort's main building, this upscale, eye- and palate-pleasing lounge serves hand-crafted specialty drinks, beer, wine, soft drinks, and a full menu. In addition to traditional sports bar fare, Rix offers soup, grilled cheese sticks, BBQ rib tips, fried green beans, calamari, salads, and french fries. Desserts may include cake, pie, and seasonal sherbet. The 300-seat venue features about 40 TVs—ensuring that you will catch the big game—and a Mediterranean-inspired atmosphere. 🐭

**SIESTAS CANTINA:** Swimmers can take time out for fried shrimp, salads, cheeseburgers, hummus platters, soft drinks, and spirits at this pool bar in the Dig Site area. 🐭

**THREE BRIDGES BAR & GRILL:** Alluring for its location (on top of a lake called Lago Dorado), this bar serves signature sangria pitchers, beer, wine, and specialty cocktails, no alcohol specialty drinks, and soft drinks. Dine on burgers, steak frites, poke bowls, lamb chops, tortilla chips (with guac or cheese dip), and more. 🐭

## Disney's Hollywood Studios

**BASELINE TAP HOUSE:** California wines and craft beers are specialties of this house. Pair them with cheese and charcuterie, soft pretzels with beer cheese fondue and spicy mustard, coffee-rubbed ribeye beef puff with olive salad, and spiced almonds. Or wash them down with a sweet soft drink: black cherry soda or wild strawberry lemonade.

**THE HOLLYWOOD BROWN DERBY LOUNGE:** An alfresco enclave, the Derby Lounge serves as an extension of the elegant eatery to which it is attached. The full menu touts creative cocktails (including the Grapefruit Cake Martini), non-alcoholic specialty drinks, appetizers, entrées, and desserts. Choose items such as Cobb salad, shrimp cocktail, BLT sliders, escargot, spoon bread, charcuterie board, filet mignon, lamb shank, grapefruit cake, and crème brûlée. 🐭/**SR**

**OGA'S CANTINA:** Come to the cantina to quench your thirst and rub elbows (or not!) with bounty hunters, smugglers, and travelers of all ages. As guests quaff spirited beverages such as the Jedi Mind Trick, Bad Motivator IPA, or Toniray wine, they're treated to bold musical entertainment courtesy of droid DJ R-3X, a former Starspeeder 3000 pilot. (He was the original Star Tours pilot.) Non-alcoholic specialty drinks and light snacks are also served throughout the day. Guests of all ages are welcome to enjoy Oga's hospitality, but valid ID is required for alcohol.

**TUNE-IN LOUNGE:** A sitcom living-room setting with comfy stools and couches characterizes this lounge next to the 50's Prime Time Cafe. Old TV sets play scenes from beloved sitcoms (all of which feature food). Specialty cocktails, beer, wine, and soft drinks are served. This joint is always jumpin'.

## Disney's Old Key West

**GURGLING SUITCASE:** This friendly, pocket-size lounge on the Turtle Krawl boardwalk serves an assortment of Key West specialties, along with traditional cocktails, beer, and wine—plus an unexpectedly large selection of sustenance, including fried chicken, BBQ pulled-pork nachos, burgers, shrimp fritters, and fried pickles.🐭

**TURTLE SHACK:** Refreshments at this poolside counter include frozen drinks, beer, and edibles such as nachos, pizza, salads, fried chicken, and sandwiches. 🐭

**Hot Tip!** At some Walt Disney World lounges, you may order food from a neighboring or nearby restaurant's menu. It can't hurt to ask!

# Disney Springs

**DOCKSIDE MARGARITAS:** Get "a taste of the Sunshine State" at this casual, waterside bar at the Marketplace. In addition to blended margaritas, this breezy spot serves rum runners, and a selection of seasonal beers, wines, and zero-proof cocktails. Live entertainment may be provided in the evening.

**ENZO'S HIDEAWAY TUNNEL BAR:** This sprawling, underground speakeasy has a marble-topped bar and an impressively massive menu of potent potables. In addition to beer, wine, cocktails, and specialty drinks, Enzo offers a vast array of scotches and "antique" specialty rums. The bar is set within a restaurant and is accessed via tunnel. (Hence, the name.)

**HOLE IN THE WALL:** Blink and you'll miss it. This tiny establishment is bookended (and dwarfed) by Raglan Road on the left and Cookes of Dublin on the right. A full bar is available, but the Irish stout stands out. In addition to the outstanding nibbles (whipped up over at Raglan Road), this diminutive spot boasts something that is beyond rare at Walt Disney World: Happy Hour specials!

**HOUSE OF BLUES BAR:** Set in the back of the dining section of H.O.B., this bar serves drinks that are as cool as the atmosphere. It's also possible to have drinks in the enclosed Voodoo Garden (table-service only). Guests may order from the restaurant menu.

**JOCK LINDSEY'S HANGAR BAR:** A waterside lounge with an aviation theme, Jock Lindsey's appeals to adventurous guests of all kinds (with seating both in- and outdoors). Visitors may savor beer, wine, cocktails, or specialty drinks and nibble small-plate treats such as Snake-bite Sliders, Nona's home-style meatballs, Doctor Astorga's Queso Dip (with tortilla chips), hot wings, and Air Pirates Cargo Loaded Pretzels (with spicy mustard and beer cheese fondue). You'll find the exotic dive bar on The Landing, between The Boathouse and Paradiso 37. 🐭

**F.Y.I.:** Jock Lindsey is Indiana Jones' frequent pilot and the proud owner of a pet snake named Reggie. (Reggie also happens to be the name of the boat that sits outside the lounge. And, yes, guests may sit inside Reggie. The boat, not the snake.)

**MAGIC MUSHROOM BAR:** When Downtown Disney's Rainforest Cafe is mobbed, we recommend taking in the thunderstorms and waterfalls from this central bar. You can sip a beverage and order a snack from the restaurant's menu. Note that there is another *Magic Mushroom Bar* inside the Rainforest Cafe at Disney's Animal Kingdom park. Details are subject to change.

**PADDLEFISH ROOFTOP LOUNGE:** One of three lounges on this regal riverboat (it was originally known as the *Empress Lilly* to honor Walt's wife, Lillian Disney), the Rooftop Lounge is a must-visit for many Disney Springs devotees. Guests may sip their drinks while drinking in panoramic views of Disney Springs and Lake Buena Vista. Libation highlights at this alfresco oasis include a well-rounded wine list and specialty drinks such as the Captain Handsome, Mayan Empress, and Lilly Spritz. The menu extends to savory nibbles, too. Plan to sample palate-pleasers such as crab cakes, calamari, fried green tomatoes, oysters, and lobster guacamole with chips (prepared tableside).

🐭 Disney Dining Plan participant at press time

**PARADISO 37:** The bar at Paradiso 37 has an international wine list, a selection of tequilas, frozen margaritas, and the "coldest beer in the world." This spot offers indoor and outdoor seating. It is possible to order items from the restaurant's menu, too.

**PLANET HOLLYWOOD OBSERVATORY:** The Planet Hollywood lounge space includes an inviting outdoor terrace—perfect for sipping cocktails under the stars.

**RAGLAN ROAD:** Top o' the evening to you! This jovial joint is an authentic Irish pub and simply oozes Irish charm. The polished interior is a meticulously decorated Emerald Isle oasis—complete with divine Irish cuisine and live entertainment (the latter starting at about 5 P.M. on weekdays, noon on weekends). Oh, and of course, Raglan Road serves pints of Irish stout and other spirited beverages—including 75 whiskeys, 7 whiskey flights, and 6 whiskey cocktails. This place is quite popular and can get rather crowded on weekend evenings—get there early if you can.

**SHARK BAR:** This space, inside the T-Rex Cafe, puts the water in watering hole. Anchored under the belly of a giant Technicolor squid, the aqueous area serves all kinds of cocktails, plus items from the restaurant's menu. (One of our favorite things to order here is the tomato soup. Your taste may differ.) Guests must be at least 21 years of age to sit at the bar.

**WINE BAR GEORGE:** The brainchild of Master Sommelier George Miliotes, this 200-seat establishment resembles a winemaker's estate. It's a cozy yet elegant setting in which to savor sublime sips from acclaimed wineries and promising up-and-comers. They pair perfectly with George's small plate offerings and family-style entrées. Some highlights: crispy mac & cheese bites, house-made meatballs, roasted beets, and charcuterie board. There are more than 140 wines at any given time—available to enjoy by the glass, bottle, or ounce. Reservations are not required to sit at the bar, but there may be a bit of a wait (and it's well worth waiting for!)

    **F.Y.I.:** George Miliotes is one of just 273 Master Sommeliers in the world. It is the highest achievable level for a wine professional. Impressive!

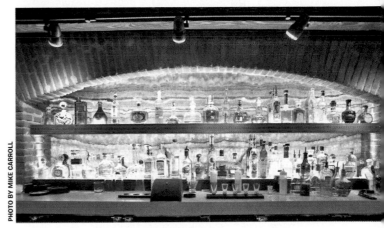

PHOTO BY MIKE CARROLL

# EPCOT

Most dining locations, including several fast-food spots, serve alcoholic beverages. A few other EPCOT locales actually specialize in liquid refreshments.

**LA CAVA DEL TEQUILA:** A warm glow envelops guests in this little lounge in the big pyramid at the Mexico pavilion—and that's before they sample any of the 70-plus tequilas on the menu. In addition to blended margaritas (many made with fresh fruit and spices), guests may sip Mexican beer, wine, cocktails, and soft drinks. Snacks have included chips and salsa.

**ROSE & CROWN PUB:** This classic EPCOT pub—a veritable symphony of polished woods, brass, and etched glass—adjoins the Rose & Crown Dining Room in the United Kingdom pavilion. English, Scottish, and Irish beers are available on tap, along with a score of specialty drinks

PHOTO BY MIKE CARROLL

imported from the other side of the Atlantic. Feel free to B.Y.O. snacks (we highly recommend the fish and chips from the nearby Yorkshire County Fish Shop). Seating indoors and out is limited and available on a first-come, first-served basis.

**SOMMERFEST:** Just outside the Biergarten in Germany, there's a window serving bratwurst (served on a roll with sauerkraut and housemade paprika chips) and jumbo pretzels. Wash 'em down with a cold German beer. Sommerfest also dispenses German Riesling and Pinot Noir, bottled water, and fountain drinks. ❦

**SPACE 220 LOUNGE:** In the center of the Space 220 eatery, the tiny out-of-this-world lounge is extremely popular—expect to spend some time in the standby line before touching down on a bar stool. In addition to eye-popping views of Earth (from 220 miles up), guests drink in beer, wine, champagne, and "atmospheric spirits" along the lines of Planetary Punch, Astrospritz, and The Big Tang. On the solid sustenance menu you'll find selections such as Starry Calamari, Astro Deviled Eggs, Blue Moon Cauliflower, short rib sliders, chicken on a waffle, and shrimp cocktail. The only way to snag a barstool is to belly up to that standby line. Reservations are not accepted for this micro off-world hotspot.

**TUTTO GUSTO WINE CELLAR:** Tucked into the heart of the Italy pavilion, this rustic room offers about 200 wines (including grappa), beers from Italy, Italian specialty drinks, coffee drinks, and a bountiful menu. Afternoon is a good time to visit Tutto Gusto (that's when crowds tend to be the lightest). Reservations are not available.

**WEINKELLER:** An aptly named establishment, there's a lovely little tasting counter tucked in the back of this Bavarian wine cellar. Belly up to the bar to order a glass of German wine—red, white, or sparkling—plus beer, and cocktails. Wine flights are always an option. Cheese plates may grace the menu, too. There are no seats, but there are benches and tables nearby.

**Hot Tip!** In addition to a few traditional bars and lounges, the international pavilions of World Showcase feature a multitude of snack and beverage stands. Highlights include Block and Hans in the American Adventure, Joy of Tea in China, Choza de Margarita in Mexico, Sake Bar (inside the Mitsukoshi Department Store at the Japan pavilion), Les Vins de France, and the Via Napoli Donkey Cart (in Italy)—just to name a few!

# Fort Wilderness

**CROCKETT'S TAVERN:** You needn't brandish a coonskin cap to order a spirited beverage in Pioneer Hall's rustic saloon, merely a government issued photo ID to prove you're not a young'un. (Guests must be at least 21 years of age to consume spirits of any kind.) ❦

# Grand Floridian

**CÍTRICOS LOUNGE:** As inviting as any lounge gracing Disney property, this elegant establishment has excellent eats and a stellar wine list. Old World, New World, red, white, sparkling . . . you name it, they got it (by the glass or the bottle). Beer, port, sherry, and creative cocktails (212 Manhattan, Passion Margarita, Purple Penguin, etc.) are available, too.

Orders may be placed until about 10 P.M. (If it's very busy, the bar may continue to serve drinks until the

crowd dwindles.) Menu selections include smoked duck breast, salad, (simply superb) sweet corn bisque, Berkshire pork belly, butter-poached mahi-mahi, guava BBQ beef short ribs, filet mignon, truffle mac & cheese, and chocolate torte. There are a handful of seats at the bar and roughly ten tables in the lounge. If you sit at a table, be sure to place your order with the bartender before grabbing a seat. 🐭/SR

**ENCHANTED ROSE:** Disney's poshest resort invites you to be its guest at this lounge located on the second floor overlooking the grand lobby. Celebrating the live action version of the film *Beauty and the Beast*, this elegant locale has indoor and outdoor seating, a full bar (with specialty drinks such as the Lavender Fog and the Island Rose) and a menu with "small bites" that are ample enough to share. You can't go wrong with the smoked trout and crab dip. It's delicious! 🐭

**NARCOOSSEE'S LOUNGE:** This upscale bar-within-a-restaurant offers a little bit of everything: a small bites menu, hand-crafted cocktails, and a premium wine list, by the bottle and by the glass. How serious are they about wine here? Our last bartender was a certified sommelier. A large selection of bottled craft beers is available, too. Note that the dress code for this lounge is "business casual." 🐭

**POOL BARS:** Relax by the pool while sipping a specialty cocktail, beer, wine, or soft drink. The Courtyard Bar, near the big pool, also serves light snacks. Beaches Bar & Grill (by the zero-depth-entry pool) stands by with a satisfying grill menu and a Rapid Fill Mug station. 🐭

# Polynesian Village

**BAREFOOT BAR:** Adjacent to the Lava pool (close to the beach), this unassuming bar serves beer, wine, frozen tropical drinks (with and without alcohol), and soft drinks. Items of note: margaritas with lime Dole Whip and The Lava Flow (a delightful mix of frozen strawberry daiquiri and piña colada). It shares a food menu with the Oasis Bar & Grill. See below for details.

**OASIS BAR & GRILL:** Set beside the resort's unguarded "quiet" pool, Oasis B&G offers nibbles (grilled fish tacos, chicken wings, salads, cheeseburgers, wonton chips, and more), a full bar, and a number of specialty cocktails. Spirited drinks of note: Blueberry Lemonade, Banana Cabana, and the refreshing Frosty Pineapple. It's exclusively for guests of the Polynesian Village resort. 🐭

**TAMBU LOUNGE:** Adjoining 'Ohana, this tiki bar offers cocktails and specialty drinks in a tropical setting. Snack selections include potstickers, BBQ ribs, hot wings, and California rolls. The table section serves as the waiting area for guests dining at 'Ohana, so it gets busy at mealtimes. Libation of note: the Lapu Lapu. The rum and fruit juice mixture is served in a real pineapple! 🐭 (dinner)

**TRADER SAM'S GROG GROTTO:** There's so much to see in this festive first-floor lounge that folks may not notice there is a world beyond Sam's walls. Guests may enjoy tropical drinks and savory small plates in the richly themed locale (think Jungle Cruise meets the Enchanted Tiki Room). Drink favorites include the Krakatoa Punch, Nautilus, and Dark & Topical Stormy.

Sam's doors may open at 3 P.M. Guests under 21 are not admitted after 8 P.M. Seats on the outdoor patio, aka Sam's Tiki Terrace, tend to be easier to come by than those inside. If you simply must infiltrate the grotto, arrive at about 2:30 P.M. and wait for the doors to open. (Don't be shocked if there is already a line when you arrive early.) You can also place your name on Trader Sam's waiting list and be contacted when real estate opens up in the Grotto.

# Pop Century

**PETALS:** In addition to sandwiches, salads, and soft pretzels, this cheery poolside watering hole serves beer, wine, cocktails, and soft drinks. Specialties of note: Captain's Mai Tai, Bourbon Breeze, and Pina CoLAVA. Petals is located near the resort's main pool area. 🐭

# Port Orleans French Quarter

**MARDI GROGS:** Beer, specialty drinks, sandwiches, salads, chips, and soft pretzels with cheese sauce are among the offerings at this pool spot. 🐭

**SCAT CAT'S CLUB—LOUNGE:** Next to the Sassagoula Float-works & Food Factory, this casual spot pays tribute to the uniquely American music that is jazz. In addition to the usual brews and blends, this happening locale specializes in Southern drinks—including Hurricanes. There's an appetizer menu—including warm beignets, sandwiches, fritters, and spicy BBQ wings. A live jazz band plays Wednesday through Sunday nights. 🐭

# Port Orleans Riverside

**MUDDY RIVERS:** Situated on Ol' Man Island, the poolside bar serves beer, wine, soft drinks, and specialty drinks—including several of the frozen variety. Sandwiches, salads, and soft pretzels are options, too. 🐭

**RIVER ROOST:** Set in an airy room designed as a cotton exchange, this spacious lounge features specialty drinks, as well as light hors d'oeuvres. Sink into a comfy chair

beside the warm glow of the fireplace, and sip specialty beverages (with or sans alcohol). There are stools at the bar and table service, too. Among the appetizer choices are potato puffs, spinach artichoke dip with cornbread crostini, spicy wings, and a charcuterie board. Live entertainment—courtesy of local legend Yeeha Bob—is offered Wednesday through Saturday nights. 🐭

# Riviera Resort

**BAR RIVA:** Meander to this poolside oasis for European- and Mediterranean-style fare, plus specialty beverages, soft drinks, and snacks. 🐭

**LE PETIT CAFE:** The grand lobby of the Riviera is filled with the soothing scent of coffee concoctions and the sounds of clinking glasses. A popular coffee and wine bar destination, this lobby locale also dispenses beer, cocktails, soft drinks, pastries, and snacks.

# Saratoga Springs

**THE TURF CLUB LOUNGE:** This casual, frill-free corner of the resort serves all manner of spirits (from a walk-up window). Lounge fare is usually available from 5 P.M. until 9:30 P.M. Look for items such as pizza (plain or pepperoni), cheeseburgers, and house-cut fries. There's a pool table, too. (No charge to play. Sweet!) 🐭

# Swan, Dolphin & Swan Reserve

**CABANA BAR & BEACH CLUB:** Come for the food, stay for drinks. This Dolphin spot's sophisticated air and edgy design is a definite draw for the grown-up set, yet the

place doesn't take itself so seriously that it fails to please little ones (think pizza, hot dogs, grilled cheese, and lemonade). Grown-up pleasers include flatbreads, crispy calamari, fish tacos, salad, burgers, bowls (tuna poke or fried rock shrimp), grilled hanger steak, and fresh Gulf catch of the day.

Classic cocktails share the spotlight with creative, original creations (The Astronaut, Mountains in Florida, Hibiscus Cooler, Strawberry Basil Lemonade Jar, etc.). Frozen libations abound, as do beer (micro- and macro-brews), rum, tequila, and more. Wine, scotch, cognac, and soft drinks are served, too.

**IL MULINO NEW YORK TRATTORIA LOUNGE:** A lovely spot (at the Swan) to sip wine, cognac, single malt scotch, cocktails, and soft drinks, and/or enjoy the bar menu, this lounge may feature live music on Friday and Saturday evenings. There are lots of seats at the bar, plus bar tables and comfy couches. It is usually open for business starting in the late afternoon.

**KIMONOS:** This Swan lounge, attractively decorated in Japanese style, has a full bar, as well as sushi and other culinary treats. It opens in late afternoon/early evening, and last call is usually between 10:30 P.M. and 1 A.M. The karaoke traditionally starts cranking at about 9:30 P.M.

**PHINS:** The edgy Dolphin lobby bar serves beer, wine, cocktails, and soft drinks. (Snack service was suspended at press time, but it may return.) Phins' operating hours are generally 3 P.M. until about 10 P.M.

**SHULA'S LOUNGE:** This small, austere Dolphin saloon within Shula's Steak House features rich wood tones and plush seating—the perfect place to sip a cocktail while enjoying savory and/or sweet items from the extensive menu. Look for New Orleans style shrimp, herb-crusted prime rib, and everything in-between.

**SPLASH POOL BAR & GRILL:** A poolside oasis near the Swan hotel, Splash serves soft drinks, beer, wine, cocktails, and specialty drinks. It operates seasonally.

**STIR:** A lobby lounge with a tropical air, the sleek Stir offers specialty drinks and a tempting selection of light bites. Look for items such as spiced almonds, hummus with pita, marinated olives, fried calamari, cured meats from Spain and Italy (aka Salumi), assorted flatbreads, burgers, mahi mahi, and souvlaki. It's on the second floor of the Swan Reserve hotel.

**TANGERINE:** Named for this spot's signature snack— a tangerine-flavored popsicle—the pool bar serves casual fare including several flatbreads, tiger prawns, char-grilled pepper crostino, chips with housemade salsa and guacamole, burgers, salads, sandwiches, soft drinks, beer, wine, and cocktails.

**F.Y.I.:** Tangerine and other Swan Reserve dining/drinking venues feature citrus-inspired menu items as a nod to Florida's rich citrus history.

**TODD ENGLISH'S BLUEZOO BAR:** The underwater mojo of Todd's bluezoo restaurant extends to the lounge area (booths and tables augment the ample bar seating, easily

accommodating large parties). In addition to the liquid refreshments, this is a genuine raw bar—many guests order a cocktail with a side of something ocean-y.

Last call varies, depending on how crowded the place is at any given moment. Figure on getting the boot at any time between 9 P.M. and 11 P.M.

# Wilderness Lodge

**GEYSER POINT BAR & GRILL:** A truly delightful lakeside watering hole, the Geyser Point lounge menu offers selections such as a cheese and charcuterie plate for two, edamame, cheesy BBQ brisket, teriyaki wings, crispy salmon croquettes, bison cheeseburgers, hand-crafted crab cakes, roasted salmon, and sandwiches. A full bar stands at the ready, with beer, wine, specialty drinks (many without alcohol), and soft drinks. 🐭

**TERRITORY LOUNGE:** Tucked between Artist Point and the Whispering Canyon Cafe, this rustic homage to the explorers of the Great West is an ideal spot for a savory snack or a pre-dinner treat. Shareable appetizers of note: candied bacon (aka Bacon on the Wire), flatbread (salmon or loaded baked potato), artisanal cheese and charcuterie plate, and popcorn sampler, just to name a few. Soft drinks, beer, wine, and specialty drinks are served. 🐭

# Yacht & Beach Club

**ALE & COMPASS LOUNGE:** The boisterous, nautically themed Yacht Club lobby lounge offers a full drink menu with premium spirits and appetizers (blue crab bisque, seasonal flatbreads, garlic shrimp, bacon cheddar burgers, and more). Ale & Compass Lounge is usually open until at least midnight. 🐭

**CREW'S CUP LOUNGE:** Styled after a New England waterfront pub, this casual lounge has a seafaring feel to it. This is one of our favorite places to relax after a long day in the parks. In addition to spirits (served every evening), dinner is served Thursday through Monday from 5 P.M. to 9:30 P.M. daily. Menu items to consider: lobster bisque, prime rib, truffle fries, and Yachtsman Steakhouse signature bread (sourdough onion pull-apart rolls with roasted garlic and butter). 🐭

**HURRICANE HANNA'S WATERSIDE BAR & GRILL:** A poolside destination, Hanna's is a sophisticated yet casual place to sip a beverage and enjoy a bite (until about 10 P.M.). The ever-changing menu may include items such as garden salad, Caesar salad with chicken, onion rings, hummus with crudité, seafood roll, breaded chicken strips, and cheeseburgers (the last three come with fries). This is also a Rapid Fill mug refilling station. 🐭

**MARTHA'S VINEYARD:** While a full bar is available, a small but satisfying selection of wines from Martha's Vineyard (and other areas) is this Beach Club bar's specialty. Light appetizers are served, too—usually from about 5 P.M. until 10 P.M. Savory snack selections may include artisanal cheese plate, loaded potato barrels, New England clam chowder, mussels sautéed in white wine with garlic broth, and Buffalo-glazed chicken wings. 🐭

# DISNEY CRUISE LINE

Walt Disney World, home to one of the planet's largest fleets of watercraft, has an inimitable nautical neighbor: Disney Cruise Line. And two of its majestic ocean liners—the award-winning *Disney Fantasy* and the new *Disney Wish*—set sail from Central Florida's Port Canaveral. That's a mere 50 miles from Walt Disney World, making the prospect of pairing a visit to WDW with a Disney cruise a rather convenient temptation for many a World traveler.

A voyage with Disney Cruise Line, however, is atypical in many ways. First, there's the simultaneous catering to families with kids and grown-ups sans offspring in tow. In fact, each ship has programming designed to draw young and old, and those in between, to entirely different recreational areas. Then there's the innovative "rotational dining system," a lineup of Broadway-style musical productions, delightful deck parties, fireworks at sea, and, of course, the possibility of a unique grand finale: a full day of fun in the sun at Castaway Cay or Lighthouse Point—Disney's tropical hideaways in the Bahamas. (The latter is on the island of Eleuthera.)

Like swaying in a hammock in the aforementioned retreats, the process of selecting a cruise package and combining it with a stay at Walt Disney World should be as carefree as possible. Within this Birnbaum bonus chapter, you will find information meant to ensure that planning a "land and sea" holiday is smooth sailing. *Bon voyage!*

# Land & Sea Vacations
## Pairing a Disney Cruise with a Walt Disney World Vacation

It's the ultimate surf-and-turf experience for Disney fans—a Walt Disney World vacation that's paired with a Disney cruise. (What better way to chase the Pirates of the Caribbean attraction than by visiting the Caribbean?! Minus real pirates, of course.) And with two Disney ships sailing out of Port Canaveral, Florida, throughout the year, "land and sea" opportunities abound. The pages that follow describe how Land and Sea vacations work and give a brief overview of the Disney Cruise Line fleet.

If you have been to Disney's world before (or read the first 300 or so pages of this book), you know that it is not a small one. In fact, it covers 40 square miles—and with about as many attractions, restaurants, and places to stay as one might expect from an area that size. There are four theme parks, two water parks, more than two dozen resort hotels, a dynamic dining, shopping, and entertainment district, championship golf courses, boating, fishing, tennis, and more. Add a cruise to the mix, and even the most seasoned Disney veterans run the risk of becoming overwhelmed when it comes to planning the vacation.

The good news is that a customized vacation package can include just about everything you would ever want. That frees you up to focus on a very important goal: having fun.

## Surf & Turf

Folks dreaming of a "land and sea" escape can customize that dream vacation with (or without) a little help from Disney Cruise Line or a travel agent. In addition to settling on a budget, there are decisions to be made:

1. Do you want to cruise before or after you visit Walt Disney World?
2. How long do you wish to play on land and on sea?
3. Where do you want to stay while you're on land?
4. Which sailing itinerary is best for you? (See page 340 for a sampling of popular itineraries that depart from Central Florida's Port Canaveral, about an hour's drive from Walt Disney World.) Note that the *Disney Magic* sails out of Fort Lauderdale, Florida, in the summer of 2024.

**Hot Tip!** Disney Cruise Line can assist with adding a resort stay before and/or after your cruise. For additional information or to add a hotel stay to your vacation, call 800-951-3532 or contact your travel agent.

## DISNEY CRUISE LINE AIR PROGRAM

If you plan to fly to the port, consider allowing the Disney Cruise Line Air Program to help you make the arrangements. In addition to lining up round-trip airfare for your whole party, the service includes pre-travel and day-of-travel flight monitoring. (Guests may choose between restricted and flexible fares.) It's also possible to add ground transportation and/or a hotel stay. For more information about the Disney Cruise Line Air Program, call 800-951-3532, or contact a travel agent. Details are subject to change at any time.

To pair a visit to Walt Disney World with a Disney cruise, contact a travel agent or call 800-951-3532. (That's the number to call if you'd like help finding a hotel near Disney Cruise Line's other home ports, too.)

**Hot Tip!** While many folks enjoy "Sea and Land" vacations (starting with a cruise), we prefer to begin with a visit to Walt Disney World. That way we are already in the vicinity of the port on sail-away day, thus alleviating any anxiety about flight delays or late arrivals.

## COMBINATION VACATION

Walt Disney World/Disney Cruise Line combination vacations can include accommodations on land (at a WDW resort) and a stateroom on a Disney ship. In addition to accommodations, shipboard meals, snacks, soft drinks, and entertainment are included with all Disney Cruise Line packages.

What's *not* included in a "Land and Sea" combination vacation? Meals and drinks at Walt Disney World (unless a Walt Disney World Dining Plan is purchased in advance), transfers to Port Canaveral (these may also be purchased in advance), airfare, excursions, meals ashore in ports of call—with the exception of Castaway Cay, where food and soft drinks are included (refer to page 351)—extra gratuities, laundry or valet services, parking at the port, or any other items not specifically included.

What can be added to the adventure? Just about everything. Options include tickets to Walt Disney World theme parks, water parks, a dinner show, and more. For more information, visit *disneycruise.com*, or call 800-951-3532.

## WALT DISNEY WORLD RESORT OPTIONS

The following is a comprehensive list of Walt Disney World-owned-and-operated resort hotels. Many guests choose to visit WDW before they cruise, while others enjoy a post-cruise visit with the Mouse. As an extra-special treat, there's the option of sandwiching a cruise between two WDW resort stays—if time and budget allow, of course! For details on these resorts and other hotels at Walt Disney World, turn to our *Transportation & Accommodations* chapter. For updates, use the My Disney Experience mobile app or website, or visit *disneyworld.com*.

# Sample Itineraries

Two Disney ships—the *Disney Wish* and *Disney Fantasy*—are scheduled to cruise out of Port Canaveral, Florida, in 2024. The *Disney Wonder, Disney Dream,* and *Disney Magic* will sail from various ports around the world. (The *Magic* will sail from Fort Lauderdale, Florida, in the summer of 2024.) What follows is a sampling of the itineraries offered from Port Canaveral, the port closest to Walt Disney World—and most logically paired with a WDW vacation. Note that most DCL cruises include a stop at one of Disney's tropical island hideaways: Castaway Cay or Lighthouse Point. Of course, new itineraries are sure to be added when the new *Disney Treasure* joins the fleet. For a complete list of this year's ports of call and Disney Cruise Line itineraries, visit *disneycruise.com.*

## 3-NIGHT BAHAMIAN CRUISE • *DISNEY WISH*

| DAY | ITINERARY |
|-----|-----------|
| DAY 1 | **Check in at Port Canaveral Terminal. Aboard by 3:45 P.M.** |
| DAY 2 | **Ashore at Nassau at 9:30 A.M. Aboard by 5:15 P.M.** |
| DAY 3 | **Ashore at Disney Castaway Cay at 8:30 A.M. Aboard by 4:45 P.M.** |
| DAY 4 | **Ship at Port Canaveral. Disembarkment beginning at 7:30 A.M.** |

## 4-NIGHT BAHAMIAN CRUISE • *DISNEY WISH*

| DAY | ITINERARY |
|-----|-----------|
| DAY 1 | **Check in at Port Canaveral Terminal. Aboard by 3:45 P.M.** |
| DAY 2 | **Ashore at Nassau at 9:30 A.M. Aboard by 5:15 P.M.** |
| DAY 3 | **Ashore at Disney Castaway Cay at 8:30 A.M. Aboard by 4:45 P.M.** |
| DAY 4 | **Full day at sea.** |
| DAY 5 | **Ship at Port Canaveral. Disembarkment begins at 7:30 A.M.** |

## 4-NIGHT BAHAMIAN CRUISE • *DISNEY WISH*

| DAY | ITINERARY |
| --- | --- |
| DAY 1 | Check in at Port Canaveral Terminal. Aboard by 3:45 P.M. |
| DAY 2 | Ashore at Disney Castaway Cay at 9:30 A.M. Aboard by 5:15 P.M. |
| DAY 3 | Ashore at Nassau at 8:30 A.M. Aboard by 4:45 P.M. |
| DAY 4 | Full day at sea. |
| DAY 5 | Ship at Port Canaveral. Disembarkment begins at 7:30 A.M. |

## 7-NIGHT EASTERN CARIBBEAN CRUISE • *DISNEY FANTASY*

| DAY | ITINERARY |
| --- | --- |
| DAY 1 | Check in at Port Canaveral Terminal. Aboard by 3:45 P.M. |
| DAY 2 | Full day at sea. |
| DAY 3 | Full day at sea. |
| DAY 4 | Ashore at Tortola, British Virgin Islands, at 7:30 A.M. Aboard by 5:45 P.M. |
| DAY 5 | Ashore at St. Thomas, U.S. Virgin Islands, at 7:45 A.M. Aboard by 3:45 P.M. |
| DAY 6 | Full day at sea. |
| DAY 7 | Ashore at Disney Castaway Cay at 10 A.M. Aboard by 4:45 P.M. |
| DAY 8 | Ship at Port Canaveral. Disembarkment begins at 7:30 A.M. |

## 7-NIGHT WESTERN CARIBBEAN CRUISE • *DISNEY FANTASY*

| DAY | ITINERARY |
| --- | --- |
| DAY 1 | Check in at Port Canaveral Terminal. Aboard by 3:45 P.M. |
| DAY 2 | Full day at sea. |
| DAY 3 | Ashore at Cozumel, Mexico, at 8:30 A.M. Aboard by 4:45 P.M. |
| DAY 4 | Ashore at George Town, Grand Cayman, at 10:30 A.M. Aboard by 5:30 P.M. (This port requires tendering.) |
| DAY 5 | Ashore at Falmouth, Jamaica, at 7:30 A.M. Aboard by 4:45 P.M. |
| DAY 6 | Full day at sea. |
| DAY 7 | Ashore at Castaway Cay at 8:30 A.M. Aboard by 4:45 P.M. |
| DAY 8 | Ship at Port Canaveral. Disembarkment begins at 7:30 A.M. |

# Before You Sail

What to do, what to do. There are many factors to consider when pairing a cruise package with a stay at Walt Disney World. Among the most important are destination, budget, time available, stateroom needs, and preferred itinerary. If you want to take the most inexpensive cruise possible, then a shorter cruise in a standard inside stateroom is probably a good choice. If money is no object, do consider a high seas adventure in the super-deluxe Royal Suite. Of course, there are plenty of options in between.

## Check Your Calendar

Determining the ideal length of your cruise depends on several things—the first, how much time do you have in your busy schedule to devote to leisure? If your answer is only four days, don't despair: Disney has short cruises to the Bahamas (most of which include a stop at Disney's private island, Castaway Cay). If you have at least a week to sail, you may choose a 7-night cruise to the Caribbean. For additional information, call 800-951-3532, or visit *www.disneycruise.com*.

### www.disneycruise.com

We've done our best to provide an accurate, current overview of the Disney Cruise Line experience. But you'll likely need more info to book your dream cruise. For that, we respectfully direct you to *www.disneycruise.com*. It's chock-full of details to help you select an itinerary, accommodations, shore excursions, and much more. It's one of the most user-friendly websites we have ever seen.

## Check Your Checkbook

The cost of your Disney cruise is the next issue on the planning board. Budget constraints can be eased in several ways: taking one of the shorter cruises, choosing a less-expensive stateroom class, and limiting the number of excursions (aka Port Adventures) you take at ports of call. (We often forgo pricey excursions because the ships themselves have so much to offer.) Plan to eat aboard the ship, too—meals and snacks are included in the vacation package, as are many extras, such as stage shows, movies, lectures, games, bands, fun with Disney characters, and much more.

## Selecting a Stateroom

Sure, you would like the largest suite on the ship. No question, you want the biggest verandah. And, of course, you absolutely must have a fabulous view. But if these don't fit your budget, there are other appealing options. Consider this: Every stateroom boasts nautical decor, and has ample closet space, a television, and a small safe. Inside staterooms can be a bit less expensive and not much smaller than their outside counterparts; on the *Dream* and the *Fantasy* they have virtual portholes (aka "magical" portholes, these high-tech wonders have high-def digital screens). On the other hand, should you decide to splurge, know that there are concierge rooms and larger suites with private verandahs where you can savor a beverage and read the newest page-turner, periodically taking a moment to gaze out at the sea.

Certainly, there are other factors to ponder when choosing a stateroom. How many people are in your party? Are you traveling with kids? Perhaps a Deluxe Stateroom would suit your family's needs. Most of these accommodations have queen-size beds, bunk beds for the young'uns, and a split bath (one room with a sink and a toilet and another with a sink and a shower/tub). A curtained divider provides a bit of privacy.

Of course, there's always the Walter E. Disney Suite and the Roy O. Disney Suite—so if money is no object, treat your crew to one of the thousand-plus-square-foot Royal Suite/homes away from home. No matter what your requirements, chances are pretty good that Disney Cruise Line can meet them.

# WHAT'S NOT INCLUDED WITH A DISNEY CRUISE?

Rest assured that all basic vacation needs are covered by the "all-inclusive" price of the cruise. However, there are always "extras" for which you may want to ante up a little cash. Here's a list of some items and services that carry an extra charge while sailing with Disney Cruise Line:

- Child care for tots ages 6 months to 3 years
- Port Adventures (aka shore excursions)
- Expenses incurred while on land in ports of call (with the exception of food and most soft drinks at Castaway Cay)
- Alcoholic beverages and Royal Court Tea
- Palo, Remy, Enchanté by Chef Arnaud Lallement, and Palo Steakhouse restaurants. (These optional, reservations-necessary, grown-ups-only restaurants carry an extra charge: starting at about $45 per person for dinner and brunch at Palo; about $75 per person for brunch and $125 for dinner at Remy. Prices do not include gratuity and are subject to change.)
- Vanellope's Sweets & Treats (on the *Dream*)
- Refreshments at any bar
- Sweet on You Sweets & Treats (on the *Fantasy*)

- Spas, salons, and Bibbidi Bobbidi Boutique services
- Joyful Sweets and Olaf's Royal Picnic (on the *Wish*)
- Merchandise purchased onboard
- Sports simulators
- Private cabanas at Castaway Cay and Lighthouse Point
- Portraits and snapshots taken by the ship's photographers
- Internet usage
- Telephone usage (see page 351)
- Ship-to-shore telephone calls (There is a sizable fee for all calls, incoming and outgoing. Calls within the ship are free.)

With the exception of non-Disney ports of call, all incidental charges will be billed to your stateroom, provided that you leave a credit card number upon check-in. It's a good idea to have some cash on hand, but there are few chances to use it. Except for tips, cash is not accepted on the ships. Same goes for Castaway Cay, with the exception of the post office—stamps must be purchased with cash. Most of the shops at non-Disney ports accept major credit cards, and the majority accept U.S. currency.

# How to Book a Cruise

In addition to using *www.disneycruise.com* or calling Disney Cruise Line (800-951-3532), many guests book (and cancel) through travel agents.

**PAYMENT METHODS:** Cruise packages, as well as incidentals, gratuities, hotel bills, and deposits, may be paid with a major credit card (Visa, MasterCard, Discover, American Express, Diners Club, and Japanese Credit Bureau), Disney gift cards, Disney Rewards Redemption cards, cashier's check, money order, or personal check. Personal checks must bear the guest's name and address, and be drawn on a United States bank. The reservation

number must be written on the face of the check. Note that checks will not be accepted within 21 days prior to vacation commencement date. Depending on the itinerary and category, final payment for a package is usually due between 90 and 150 days prior to the cruise. (Specifics are subject to change at any time. Check *www.disneycruise.com* for updates.)

Payments that are sent via traditional mail should be addressed to: Disney Cruise Line, P.O. Box 277763, Atlanta, GA 30384-7763.

Payments that are sent via courier service (e.g., UPS or FedEx) should be addressed to: Disney Cruise Line, Bank of America, Lockbox Services, Lockbox 277763, 6000 Feldwood Road, College Park, GA 30349 (407-566-3500).

**DEPOSIT AND FINAL PAYMENT REQUIREMENTS:** When you book a Disney cruise, you will be given a "due date" for a deposit. Reservations will be canceled if a deposit is not received by the deadline. Final payment for a cruise is typically due between 90 and 150 days prior to the cruise, depending on the itinerary and category. (Cruise packages that are booked within the final payment due date or in categories IGT, OGT, and VGT come with special instructions.) Visit *www.disneycruise.com,* or call 800-951-3532 for details.

## GROUND TRANSFERS

Disney Cruise Line provides reliable, friendly service aboard its trusty fleet of motor coaches. Getting to the buses is relatively easy. Upon arrival at Orlando International Airport, take a shuttle to the Main Terminal. Once there, proceed to baggage claim to retrieve your checked luggage. Make sure that you have affixed your DCL tags to all bags *before* you give them to a Disney Cruise Line rep. Said rep can direct you to the motor coach. (For guests with transfers included in their package, instructions come with their pre-arrival package and will be specific to the type of transfers purchased.) Transfers from the airport run continuously, starting at about 9 A.M.

Note that the next time you will see your luggage will be in your stateroom, likely by 6 P.M. Pack essential items such as medication and baby supplies in a carry-on bag.

From the airport, a bus will take you to Port Canaveral. (Buses to Port Canaveral depart from select Walt Disney World resorts. Guests with resort-to-port transfers can expect a letter with bus departure specifics to be delivered once they arrive at their Walt Disney World resort.) Here is pricing for Orlando ground transfers:

| TRANSFER TRIP | PRICE* |
|---|---|
| Select WDW resorts to Port Canaveral | $39 |
| Round-trip from Orlando International Airport (MCO) to Port Canaveral | $78 |
| Port Canaveral to Walt Disney World resorts | $39 |

*Prices are per person, were correct at press time, and are subject to change. For pricing details about transfers to and from other locations, call 800-951-3532.

**CANCELLATION POLICY:** Cancellations may be made by phone or in writing (we prefer phone). To avoid a cancellation fee, we recommend insuring your trip.

Fees paid for canceling a cruise depend on when that cancellation is made. The policy for suites and concierge rooms are as follows:

• Canceling 90 or more days prior to sailing costs the entire deposit.

• Canceling within 89 to 56 days prior to sailing costs 50 percent of the voyage fare.

• Canceling 55 to 30 days prior costs 75 percent of the voyage fare.

• Canceling 29 days or less prior to the cruise costs the entire voyage fare.

For cruises of 1 to 5 nights, the cancellation fees for non-suite and non-concierge guests are as follows:

• Canceling 89 to 45 days before sailing costs the whole deposit.

• Canceling 44 to 30 days costs half the voyage fare.

• Canceling 29 to 15 days costs 75 percent of the fare.

• Canceling 14 days or less costs the entire fare.

The cancellation policy for cruises of 6 nights or longer, for non-suite and non-concierge guests are as follows:

• Canceling within 119 to 56 days before the sailing costs the whole deposit.

• Canceling within 55 to 30 days costs 50 percent of the cruise fare.

• Canceling within 29 to 15 days costs 75 percent of the voyage fare.

• Canceling less than 14 days ahead means you will pay 100 percent of the voyage fare.

## What to Pack

"Cruise Casual" is the operative phrase with Disney. Shorts, T-shirts, sundresses, and the like are fine daytime wear. At dinnertime, casual takes on a more formal meaning: Set aside flip-flops and plan on nice slacks (jeans are okay, as long as they're in good condition) and a collared shirt for men, with real shoes, as opposed to the tennis kind. The same goes for women, while dresses are fine, too. There is an optional dress-up night, too. On 7-night-or-longer cruises, there is a semi-formal and a formal night. While some folks don black tie and sequins, it's fine to sport a less formal look.

**Hot Tip!** Guests who plan to arrive at Port Canaveral the night before setting sail might consider staying at one of these resorts on nearby Astronaut Boulevard:

Country Inn & Suites by Radisson. Rates range from about $151-$415, and there is a shuttle to the cruise terminal; 321-784-8500 or 800-333-3333.

Residence Inn by Marriott. Rates range from about $278-$461; 321-323-1100 or 800-331-3131.

## IDENTIFICATION PAPERS

Unlike a visit to EPCOT, where it only feels as if you leave the country, in the case of a Disney Cruise Line vacation, you usually do. Given that, you will need a passport to provide proper proof of citizenship when passing through Customs for most cruises. (There are some itineraries for which U.S. citizens may use other forms of proof of citizenship such as a state-issued birth certificate.) U.S. government regulations related to passport requirements are subject to change at any time. Therefore, all guests are advised to have a valid passport for all cruises. Visit *travel.state.gov*, or call 877-487-2778 for current requirements. Non-U.S. citizens must travel with valid government-issued passports and appropriate travel visas at all times.

The Disney Cruise Line Navigator app (see page 354) will tip you off as to the appropriate attire. Many guests travel with their own pirate garb, too, in anticipation of a pirate-themed party night—don't forget to pack your puffy shirt and eye patch. (The pirate party takes place on most sailings.)

Bathing suits are a must, as are beach shoes, wraps, sunscreen, sunglasses, and hats. Some sundries, such as shampoo and body lotion, are provided. Others are available for purchase, but the prices are steep, and the shops aren't always open (U.S. Customs sets limits on operating hours). Be sure to pack your valid government-issued passports and appropriate travel visas in a day bag (and in a spot that can be accessed easily).

**PACK A DAY BAG:** Guests may check in at the port and board the ship when their boarding number is called. Your checked luggage may not arrive until 6 P.M (though it usually shows up much earlier). Keep in mind that you can enjoy most shipboard amenities as soon as you board, including all pools, so pack your swimsuit in a day bag. This should serve as, or fit in, a carry-on, as checked bags will be out of your hands once you surrender them. (Day bags can't be larger than 9 inches by 14 inches by 22 inches and do not count as part of

the two-bags-per-passenger quota.) The bag should also include your passports, visas, valuables, breakable items, and anything else you might need during those first hours on board. Note that most airlines require that carried-on liquids be in 3.4-ounce (or smaller) containers and fit into one quart-size, clear, plastic zip-top bag.

## Booking Port Adventures

Port Adventures, aka shore excursions, can fill up quickly. To reserve yours, visit *www.disneycruise.com*. To make last-minute arrangements, visit your ship's Port Adventures desk. Port Adventures are not operated by The Walt Disney Company—not even those on Castaway Cay (see page 351 for more on Disney's private island).

For descriptions of all of the excursions offered in more than 70 destinations around the world, including Castaway Cay, visit *www.disneycruise.com*. (We considered including all of the shore excursion possibilities here, but that would have added about 600 pages to this book!)

Cancellations or changes to shore excursion reservations must be made at least 3 days before a cruise starts to receive a refund. Certain restrictions apply.

### WHAT'S IN A NAME?

A whole lot, when it comes to Disney Cruise Line accommodations. Here's a sampling of the types of rooms available on Disney ships. Note that it is possible to request side-by-side staterooms, but it can't be guaranteed.

- Standard Inside Stateroom
- Deluxe Inside Stateroom (*Dream, Fantasy, Magic, Wonder*)
- Deluxe Ocean-view Stateroom
- Deluxe Family Ocean-view Stateroom (*Dream* and *Fantasy*)
- Deluxe Ocean-view Stateroom with White Wall Verandah (*Magic* and *Wonder*)
- Deluxe Ocean-view Stateroom with Verandah
- Deluxe Family Ocean-view Stateroom with Verandah
- Concierge Family Ocean-view Stateroom with Verandah
- Concierge 1-Bedroom Suite with Verandah
- Concierge 2-Bedroom Suite with Verandah (*Magic* and *Wonder*)
- Concierge Royal Suite with Verandah
- Concierge Family Ocean-view Stateroom (*Wish*)
- Concierge 1 Story Royal Suite (*Wish*)
- Concierge *Wish* Tower Suite (*Wish*)

**Hot Tip!** You must show your "Key to the World" card (stateroom key and ID) when disembarking or boarding the ship. Adults also need a government-issued photo ID (a passport is ideal). Your Walt Disney World MagicBand or hotel key won't work on the ship.

# How to Get to Port Canaveral

**BY PLANE:** Fly to Orlando International Airport (MCO). We prefer to arrive the night before or take a flight that is scheduled to arrive in the early morning hours. (That helps avoid potential travel delays.) If you get there on the early side, you can make a day of it (but be sure to note your port arrival time. You can't board before the designated time). And, if your flight's delayed, you'll still have a shot at making it to the port before the ship sails. (When you book your cruise, ask about the check-in cutoff time. Don't be late!)

**FROM THE AIRPORT:** If you purchased airport transfers (which we highly recommend), follow the directions printed on your cruise documents. (A limited number of same-day transfers may be available, but there is no guarantee.) After you collect your bags at baggage claim, you'll give them to a Disney Cruise Line rep. Make sure you have affixed your DCL luggage tags to all bags. (The tags are included with your cruise documents.) The next time you see your luggage will be inside your stateroom. Note that each guest may carry one personal item and one carry-on bag on to the ship.

Guests without DCL transfers may pre-book transportation via towncar or Mears Connect (see page 16), or take a taxi (ask an Orlando airport representative to direct you to the taxi stand), car-sharing services Lyft or Uber (make sure you download the appropriate app and set up an account before leaving home), or your own vehicle (parking fees apply).

The following details apply specifically to Disney cruises departing from Port Canaveral, Florida. For details about departure ports in other cities (such as Fort Lauderdale, New Orleans, Galveston, and others), visit *www.disneycruise.com*, or call 800-951-3532.

**DISNEY MOTOR COACH:** The bus journey from Orlando International Airport or a Walt Disney World resort to Port Canaveral takes about 90 minutes (without traffic). While on board, you can fill out paperwork (though it is best to do this online in advance). There's a restroom onboard. Motor coach transportation may be purchased with a cruise package.

**CAR SERVICE:** Ride-sharing services Lyft and Uber may drop guests at the port. Noris Limousine and Florida Towncar also offer service between Orlando International Airport (MCO) and Port Canaveral. For rates, info, or to make a reservation with Noris Limousine, call 407-240-4533, or visit the Noris Facebook page. For Florida Towncar, go to *www.floridatowncar.com*, or call 407-277-5466. Reservations are necessary, and cancellations must be made at least 24 to 48 hours in advance. Disney Cruise Line's reservations department can handle most car service requests, as well.

**AUTOMOBILE:** Disney Cruise Line's Port Canaveral Terminal is located at Cruise Terminal 8 (CT8); 9155 Charles M. Rowland Drive, Port Canaveral, Florida 32920. It's approximately a 90-minute drive from Orlando International Airport (MCO) and from Walt Disney World. The parking facility, which is operated by the Canaveral Port Authority, accepts American Express, Visa, Discovercard, and MasterCard only. (Cash, traveler's checks, and personal checks are not accepted.) Parking costs about $17 per day.

From Orlando International Airport, take State Road (S.R.) 528 East (Beachline Expressway). Continue over the Indian River and the Banana River. Turn right onto S.R. 401, which will loop and head north over the channel locks. Stay in the right-hand lane and follow signs to the "A" Cruise Terminals. S.R. 528 is a toll road.

If you are driving from Walt Disney World, take State Road 536 East to 417 (the GreeneWay). Follow 417 to S.R. 528 East (Beachline Expressway). When you come to a fork in the road, veer right to stay on S.R. 528. Continue over the Indian and Banana rivers. Turn right onto S.R. 401. Stay in the right lane and follow signs leading to the "A" Cruise Terminals. Note that 417 and 528 are toll roads.

Guests who are driving from North Florida should take I-95 South exit number 205 for S.R. 528 East (Beachline Expressway). Continue over the Indian and Banana rivers. Turn right onto S.R. 401. Stay in the right lane and follow signs to "A" Cruise Terminals.

Drivers originating in South Florida should take I-95 North. Exit at number 205 for S.R. 528 East (aka the Beachline). Take S.R. 528 to S.R. 401. Keep to the right and follow the signs to "A" Cruise Terminals.

**GETTING TO PORT CANAVERAL FROM WALT DISNEY WORLD WITHOUT A CAR:** Disney Cruise Line offers convenient motor coach service (aka buses) to take guests directly from most Disney resorts. One-way transfers cost $39 per person, while $78 will cover the round-trip. Guests with transfers will get a letter in their resort room with departure details. Bell Services will automatically pick up your luggage when Disney Cruise Line transfers have been prearranged. (Car services and Mears Connect make the trip to and from Port Canaveral, too. Refer to pages 16 and 346 for more information.)

## Customized Travel Tips

**TRAVELING WITH BABIES:**

**Cribs:** If you are traveling with a baby, it is possible to have a playpen-like, foldaway crib sent to your stateroom. (The cribs are 39.8 inches long, 28.25 inches wide, and 31.25 inches high.) Request one when you make a reservation, and confirm it before leaving home. Supplies are limited. Bring your own blanket, as the cribs come with fitted sheets only.

**Diaper Service:** It is possible to have a disposable diaper system sent to your stateroom. You can request it when you make a reservation, or speak with your Stateroom Host or Hostess upon arrival.

**Food:** Accommodations come with a small fridge, safe for storing formula and food. Homemade baby food is not permitted on any Disney ship. At least one shop on board sells diapers, formula, and a limited selection of baby food. (The shop isn't always open, as U.S. Customs

### TAG YOUR BAGS

Flying to Orlando International Airport for a cruise out of Port Canaveral? After you book your cruise and purchase ground transfers, you'll receive a personalized info packet in the mail. Included in this valuable envelope will be colorful luggage tags. We can't overemphasize the importance of affixing these tags to all bags. Why? They will ensure that your luggage is properly delivered to your stateroom.

Upon arriving at the airport, you will need to proceed to the baggage claim area to claim your luggage. Before giving the bags to a Disney representative, make sure tags are affixed. The next time you'll see your luggage is when it is delivered to your stateroom, typically by 6 P.M. Note that only one personal item and one carry-on bag per guest may be carried on board—the rest must be checked with a stevedore.

If you travel to the port by car or other ground transportation and arrive with luggage, drop your bags with a stevedore at the Disney Cruise terminal. They will be delivered to your stateroom for you. Guests who arrive from Walt Disney World via Disney motor coach (aka bus) need to tag their bags, too. (Tags come with all cruise documents.) The driver will see to it that tagged bags are removed from the motor coach and loaded on the ship.

If you'd rather not haul your bags off the ship, expect to use a similar color-coding/character method at the end of your cruise. A set of tags will be left in your stateroom. Slap them on your bags, make a note of the color/character and place them in the hall on the last night of the cruise. (Be sure to keep items such as pajamas, sundries, and clothes for the morning in a day bag.) Look for them in the designated section of the terminal once you debark the ship.

It's not mandatory to surrender bags on the last night of a cruise—but guests are responsible for removing all luggage from the ship in the morning.

limits its hours.) If you'd like to save money—or if your tot is partial to particular num-nums—pack as many baby rations as possible.

**Nursery:** Onboard baby care is available for tots ages 6 months to 3 years (for most cruises). The cost is $9 an hour for the first child, with a one-hour minimum stay. Each additional child (who must be the first child's sibling) is $8 per hour. The service is offered in the ship's It's a Small World nursery. Reservations for said nursery can be booked via *www.disneycruise.com* or aboard your ship (based on availability). In-room babysitting is not offered by any Disney vessel.

## COLD & FLU ADVISORY

Disney Cruise Line follows extraordinary sanitation efforts to ensure the safety and comfort of all guests. Even so, humans do get sick from time to time. If you or a member of your party experiences any symptoms of illness (cold, flu, stomach flu, etc.) within 72 hours of sailing, you may be assessed by the medical team during the embarkation process. (If necessary, Cruise Line reps will direct you to someone to help your party make alternate plans if you are too ill to sail.) For updates and additional information regarding Disney Cruise Line's current health and safety protocols, visit *disneycruise.com/knowbeforeyougo*.

Once on board, guests are asked to wash their hands frequently and thoroughly, as this is a highly effective barrier to spreading germs. If you or someone in your party becomes ill during your trip, please contact the Health Center. You'll be taken care of, and immediate treatment will help limit the potential impact to others. Note that fees apply at the Health Center.

**Hot Tip!** If you will be using an ECV (Electronic Conveyance Vehicle) during your cruise, be sure to reserve an accessible stateroom (other rooms can't accommodate ECVs). No ECV parking is allowed in the stateroom corridors or on elevator landings. There are ECV parking stations on Deck 6 midship on the *Magic* and *Wonder*, and on Deck 2 midship, outside Enchanted Garden, on the *Dream* and *Fantasy*. The *Wish* and *Treasure* have parking stations for ECVs, too.

**Other Supplies:** Diapers, pacifiers, pool toys, and other items can be purchased on board. The ships' shops are not always open, so take inventory and plan ahead to avoid being caught short. If it's an emergency, inquire at Guest Services. They can help with just about any onboard crisis involving supplies.

Bottle sterilizers and warmers are available; inquire at the Guest Services desk.

**TRAVELERS WITH DISABILITIES:** Measures have been taken to make your stay as comfortable and effortless as possible. Disney Cruise Line offers special equipment and facilities for guests with disabilities. Each ship has staterooms that are equipped for guests using wheelchairs. They have ramped bathroom thresholds, open bed frames, bathroom and shower grab bars, fold-down shower seats, handheld showerheads, and lowered towel and closet bars. Captioning is available for stateroom televisions, and for some onboard video monitors and movies. Stateroom communication kits may be reserved upon request. They include door-knock and phone alerts, bed shaker notification, and a strobe light smoke detector; a text typewriter (aka TTY) may also be requested. There is no charge for the kit, but supplies are limited. Please make your needs known when you make your reservation and confirm them prior to sailing. Wheelchair-accessible restrooms are available in several common areas on board. There are pool lifts on all Disney Cruise Line ships.

A limited number of sand wheelchairs are available on Castaway Cay. American Sign Language (ASL) interpretation is available for many onboard performances for various cruise dates. (The service is not available on every cruise, so be sure to start planning your trip far in advance.) For further details or to make special requests, ask your reservationist. To get information via TTY (text typewriter), please call 407-566-7455.

**TRAVELERS WITHOUT CHILDREN:** This being a Disney cruise, one could argue that you—the footloose, fancy-free folks—are on their turf. And, as such, you might expect to have youngsters underfoot at all times. This is simply not the case. The Disney ships were designed with three specific types of vacationers in mind: families, children, and grown-ups cruising without kids. On board, there is an adults-only deck area, complete with its own swimming pool and whirlpool spas. There's at least one gourmet restaurant and a cozy coffee bar on each ship. It goes without saying that many of those places, as well as several lounges, are strictly for the grown-up set (as in adults with legal proof of age). Plus, there are countless other ways to enjoy a grown-up getaway in various ports of call. With that in mind, Castaway Cay (Disney's private island) guarantees you and your ilk a piece of prime beachfront real estate where you can

## NEW SHIPS ON THE HORIZON

Ahoy! Disney Cruise Line's family is growing—in addition to the *Disney Treasure*, which is expected to set sail in 2024, two new ships will be joining the DCL fleet in the not-too-distant future. At press time, Disney Cruise Line's 7th and 8th ships were still being built and had not yet been named. What do you think they'll be called? It's fun to speculate.

you will be responsible for paying any charges that are incurred while on board prior to debarkation. The Health Center will provide you with the paperwork you'll need to process any claim through your health insurance provider.

If you get sick while on shore, your guide should direct you to your ship's tour director at the dock, who will help you get medical care at the nearest treatment facility.

Regarding younger passengers, know that any child exhibiting symptoms of illness will not be allowed to participate in youth activities or be cared for in the ship's nursery until medical clearance is given. No exceptions.

# Fingertip Reference Guide

**BUSINESS SERVICES:** Wait a minute, aren't you here to relax? For those of you who simply must get a little bit of work done while at sea, there are some business services available to you for an additional charge. Among them are fax transmission, copy-making, and Audio Visual equipment. Wireless Internet service is available throughout the ships (including staterooms) for a fee. Guests access the Internet via cell phone and various personal computing devices. Note that the ship's Wi-Fi service at sea can best be described as "low speed." As you sail, you will likely experience repeated instances of buffering and many dropped connections. Internet connectivity can be intermittent based on the strength

bask in the sun or read a novel in the shade without the fear of sand being kicked in your face. You can even have a massage in a cabana overlooking the ocean. Can you manage to spend days on end without encountering any of the wee ones of our species? No way. But who'd want to?

**MEDICAL MATTERS:** The ship's Health Center, located forward on Deck 1, is open daily to provide non-emergency medical care throughout each cruise. All Disney Cruise Line ships have a physician and nurse on call 24 hours a day (even while in port) for conditions that require immediate attention. All medical services are provided by a company independent of Disney Cruise Line, and standard prevailing fees will be charged for all medical services. Any fees incurred will be charged to your stateroom account.

In serious cases, Disney Cruise Line will arrange to have a passenger taken to the nearest port to receive medical care. The cost of this varies with the location of the ship and the nearest port. Because all health care provided qualifies as "care outside the United States,"

## DISNEY CRUISE LINE GIFTS

Whether you will be celebrating a special occasion or simply consider a cruise to be a special occasion in and of itself, you may want to have a gift delivered to your stateroom. Among the items that can be pre-ordered by calling 800-601-8455 or visiting *disneycruise.disney.go.com/gifts-and-amenities* are floral arrangements, food and beverage packages, wine packages, cakes, and Disney Cruise Line merchandise. Specialty cakes must be ordered at least 7 days in advance. Other orders must be placed at least 72 business hours before the sail date for your Disney cruise.

## A TENDER SUBJECT

Some ports of call require a process known as "tendering." This means, rather than pulling right up to a dock, the ship will pull close to port and drop anchor. Ferries take guests back and forth to shore. It's an efficient system, but it could knock you for a loop if you're not expecting it—especially if you have an early excursion booked. In this case, you may have to leave a bit earlier than you anticipated. That is accounted for in the "meet time" for shore excursions.

of the satellite connection. All staterooms have phones (ship-to-shore rates apply), and electrical outlets are laptop friendly. Note that the ships' computers do not accept uploads and do not run any Microsoft Office applications (so attachments from associated email accounts cannot be opened).

**CAMERA NEEDS:** By all means, bring a camera. There are also roving photographers capturing moments throughout the day. You'll find shots taken at "static locations" (e.g., character sets in the lobby) are available for viewing at photo kiosks at Shutters (the photo store on all Disney ships). These photos may be viewed and purchased during the cruise. (Some photo packages may be purchased in advance, with special promotions.) It's possible to purchase an all-inclusive digital package, individual prints, and/or a Photo Book, which lets you select photos that will be printed directly into its pages. Photos can be downloaded instantly while onboard or after your cruise is over. You will have 45 days after you depart to download your purchased cruise photos. Otherwise, all photos will expire at that time.

**DRINKING LAWS:** The drinking age on Disney's ships is 21 and is strictly enforced. Valid government-issued photo ID is required. Disney Cruise Line reserves the right to refuse alcohol sales to anyone. On cruises departing from European countries where the legal age is lower than 21, a legal guardian who is sailing with a passenger between the ages of 18 and 20 may sign a waiver allowing their charge to imbibe.

**MAIL:** Letters and postcards may be mailed from the post office at Disney's private tropical island, Castaway Cay. Stamps are the only thing available for purchase here (cash only). It is also possible to mail items from other ports—it's just less convenient. Postcards and stamps may be purchased on the ship. If you plan to buy stamps from the Castaway Cay post office, do so early. The office is operated by Bahamian authorities and may not be open late in the day. Even if it's closed, you can still mail letters from the post office, and items will be stamped with a Castaway Cay postmark.

**MONEY MATTERS:** There's no need for cash aboard the ship. You'll apply a credit card to your account during check-in. (Most major credit cards, including Master-Card, JCB, Visa, and American Express, are accepted.) From then on, all you'll need to do is sign for extras you want (including excursions booked on the ship), and these amounts will be charged to that card.

Cash or credit cards will be necessary for meals, taxis, and other purchases made in ports and during some port adventures. Purchases made at Castaway Cay and Lighthouse Point, however, are covered with a stateroom key (except for stamps, which must be bought with cash). A few hundred dollars should suffice for port purchases. Standard gratuities are automatically attached to your cruise folio if you do not get a chance to pre-pay before boarding the ship. (Once aboard the ship, you can adjust the amount of pre-paid gratuities at Guest Services.) Extra gratuities may be charged to a stateroom

**Hot Tip!** If you plan to use your cell phone during your cruise, be sure to check with your wireless provider before leaving home. Ask if you will be able to get cell service through them while on board and how much voice, data, and text service costs—including roaming rates.

or paid in cash. Special envelopes will be delivered to your stateroom. They may be used to present extra gratuities and/or receipts for prepaid tips.

Automated teller machines may be available in ports of call, but there are none on the ship. Be sure the ATM dispenses U.S. currency before you use it. It's a good idea to alert your bank and credit card company to the fact that you will be using cards while traveling.

**SMOKING:** All Disney cruise ships are, for the most part, smoke-free zones. Smoking (including pipes, cigars, e-cigarettes, and vaping) is prohibited in all staterooms and verandahs. (Guests who violate this policy are subject to a $250 deep cleaning fee.) There are designated smoking areas on every Disney ship.

**TELEPHONE CALLS:** All staterooms have telephones with ship-to-shore capability. Rates range from at least $7 to $9.50 per minute (rates are subject to change). Toll-free and collect calls can't be placed from ship phones. Wireless mobile service is available on the ship (fees apply). Be sure to check with your mobile carrier (before you leave home) for talk and text rates and roaming fees. Some ports have pay phones (you will need an international calling card to use them).

**TIPPING:** Some servers, such as bartenders, receive an automatic 15 percent gratuity each time you call upon their services, while spa services have an automatic 18 percent tip. That said, folks such as your dining room servers and stateroom host or hostess rely on guests to tip them appropriately. Suggested gratuity amounts will be posted to your account during the cruise (it's okay to leave more if you deem the service to be outstanding). If you prefer to pay in cash, inform Guest Services at the beginning of the cruise. For those dining at Palo, Palo Steakhouse, Remy, and Enchanté the total gratuity amount is at the discretion of the guest.

**WEDDINGS:** Whether you're planning to wed for the first time or wish to renew your vows, Disney Cruise Line has the means to make the occasion exceptionally

## TROPICAL ISLAND RETREATS

If you've ever dreamed of getting away to a tranquil, tropical island, the folks at Disney Cruise Line have made it easy to fulfill that fantasy. Many Disney cruises wrap up with a visit to Castaway Cay (pronounced *key*), a tiny island in the Abacos, one in the string of Bahamian isles. This patch of paradise was secured for the sole use of passengers cruising on Disney ships. It's small—only 3.1 miles long by 2.2 miles wide—and most of it was left undeveloped so that nature lovers may enjoy the still-unspoiled terrain.

Here you can take a ride in a glass-bottom boat, go back to nature on a kayak adventure, try your wings at parasailing, or go snorkeling offshore—and then return to a barbecue feast. Of course if you'd prefer to loll about in a palm-tree-shaded, beach-side hammock, refreshing beverage in hand, well, that can be arranged.

Other island amenities include biking, beach games, organized activities for kids and teens; a shaded pavilion complete with billiards, table tennis, basketball, shuffleboard, and more; Disney character meet-and-greets; beaches designated for families and teens, dozens of private cabanas (available for rent), plus a secluded grown-ups-only stretch of beach (complete with a bar and casual BBQ joint).

Lighthouse Point is similarly appointed, with tropical diversions for the whole family. Disney's newest island destination, which occupies the southernmost tip of the **NEW** island of Eleuthera, is on course to welcome its first DCL visitors in June 2024. A vibrant celebration of nature and Bahamian culture, Lighthouse Point offers something for everyone. For more information or to book port adventures, visit *www.disneycruise.com*.

memorable. Ceremonies may be performed aboard the ship or on the pristine sands of a tropical hideaway. Some couples invite guests along for the occasion, while others prefer to have this time to themselves.

For additional information, visit *disneycruise.disney.go.com/featured/weddings-honeymoons-vows*, call 800-951-3532, or contact your travel agent. Make your plans as far in advance as possible.

# All Aboard!

The moment you cross the gangway, you'll realize this vessel is no ordinary home away from home. Step into the grand, multi-story atrium, and, amidst the happy hubbub, your presence is made known in dramatic fashion—with a heartfelt announcement for all to hear. And so begins your high-seas adventure.

Disney's ships rank among the world's finest ocean-going vessels. They are casually elegant and designed to capture the majesty of early ocean liners. They're equipped to satisfy most cruisers, with a mix of traditional seafaring diversions and classic Disney touches. Though some theming and entertainment vary from ship to ship, the accommodations and amenities are similar. As is the service, which is expertly provided by a crew of thousands (representing dozens of countries). All staterooms aboard the Disney ships are a cut above normal cruising quarters—with an average of about 25 percent more space than the industry standard. The ships were designed to draw families and grown-ups sans offspring to entirely different recreational areas. So, please cast aside any preconceived notions you may have about cruising, and expect the unexpected. All details are subject to change.

## At the Port Terminal

No matter where it is they call home—be it Bangkok or Boca—all Disney Cruise Line guests begin their respective journeys at a port terminal. Most Bahamas- and Caribbean-bound guests leaving from Florida's Port Canaveral will board their ship at Cruise Terminal 8 (CT8). Guests who have not completed their check-in online (which is recommended) may do so at the aforementioned DCL terminal. (For information about other ports the Disney ships may sail from in 2024, call 800-951-3532, or go to *www.disneycruise.com*.) Note that the online check-in process must be completed one day before setting sail.

Guests should arrive at the port terminal during their pre-assigned arrival time (selected during online check-in via *disneycruise.com* or the Disney Cruise Line Navigator App). After dropping off luggage (and parking if you arrived in your own vehicle), head to the terminal entrance. There you will be asked to scan the QR code from the Port Arrival Form. (This can be done digitally with a mobile device or by using a printout. Keep the QR code handy, as you'll need it again soon.) Once scanned, cast members will let you enter the terminal where you will visit the check-in station. Be prepared to show your government-issued identification (i.e., passport or birth certificate; refer to page 345) and your cruise QR code. Congratulations, you're officially checked in!

Before you can enter the main part of the terminal, all members of your party must go through the security checkpoint. It's a lot like airport security, so save the holey socks for the second day of your trip (you may be asked to remove your shoes, along with jackets, glasses, belts, etc.). Since children must go through the security check, too, we recommend having snacks and games to entertain them while you wait (in case the line is more than a few minutes long). Once you've cleared security, your party can go up a flight and relax in the waiting area while listening for your boarding group to be called. If you have any questions or concerns, fear not—Disney Cruise Line cast members are available to help you out at any time.

The terminal has restrooms and ample seating. (At Port Canaveral, Florida, there's also a nifty model of the ship to give you a preview of the real thing.) And,

## GUEST SERVICES DESK

If you have any questions or concerns while on board, head to the Guest Services Desk (Deck 3, midship). This is also the place to go to secure printed copies of the day's schedule of events, color-coded luggage tags (for use on the last day of the cruise), and postage stamps. Should you have any type of question or problem while on board, bring it to their attention. More often than not, they will resolve the issue in a matter of minutes.

if little ones get antsy, there's lots of room for them to roam (while closely supervised), plus a TV that runs a loop of Disney cartoons. Mickey Mouse and his friends occasionally greet guests in the terminal, too.

What happens when your boarding group is called? First, be sure you have all the documents you submitted when you booked your cruise. Then, grab the kids and your day bags, file through the Mickey-shaped portal, and head for the gangway. All aboard!

## The Boarding Experience

After you slip through the entry portal, you'll enter a subdued hallway. This is where you may have "pre-cruise" photos taken by a Cruise Line photographer. If so, try to look as stressed out as possible. That'll make the post-boarding shots that much more enjoyable. (You can view/buy the photo on the ship later on. Just stop by the ship's photography shop.)

Beyond the photo-op area, there's a portal leading to a gangway. Cross that gangway and you'll be deposited into the ship's grand atrium—a dramatic backdrop for a dramatic entrance.

Depending on the time (staterooms are usually ready by 1:30 P.M.) and your hunger level, you may want to make a quick stop, change, and head out for lunch or a snack. Ships' pools are usually open all afternoon. After

that, it's safety drill time! Once the mandatory drill is complete, you may head back to your room to prepare for the sailing away party. If you have an early dinner seating, this is the ideal time to change into your evening attire. If you haven't already downloaded the Disney Cruise Line Navigator app, do so before you sail away.

Finally, we can't overemphasize the importance of making reservations for spa and salon treatments, and for Palo, Remy, and Enchanté (upscale restaurants) as far in advance as possible. Palo begins accepting reservations at about 1 P.M. on day one of the cruise. Note that reservations for an upscale dining experience may also be made at an eatery itself (pending availability), but it's best to reserve in advance via *disneycruise.com*. Make last-minute spa appointments at the spa itself. If you haven't already registered kids for onboard youth activities via *disneycruise.com*, do so soon after boarding.

## Key to the World

Once the cruise begins, you will use your stateroom key—aka Key to the World card—to make purchases and to open your stateroom door. The card also serves as a form of identification for debarking and reboarding purposes (though all ports of call also require a photo ID such as a driver's license for guests over age 18). If you prefer that a member of your party not have charging privileges, indicate your preference when checking in, or at the ship's Guest Services Desk. You'll get your Key to the World card upon arrival at your stateroom.

## The Disney Ships

The Disney ships are equipped to satisfy even the most savvy of cruisers, with a mix of traditional seafaring diversions and Disney touches. The ships' classic exteriors recall the impressive majesty of early ocean liners. Guests enter a three-story atrium, where traditional definitions of elegance expand to include bronze Disney character statues and subtle cutout character silhouettes along a grand staircase. Various recreation areas are designed to draw families and kid-free adults to different parts of the ship. By day, fun in the sun alternates with touring, lunching, indoor distractions, snoozing, and perhaps even a little bingo action. Evenings give way to sunset sail-away celebrations, themed dining experiences, drinks under the stars, and live theatrical extravaganzas.

# Staterooms

The accommodations on Disney's ships range from standard inside rooms to suites with verandahs. All staterooms are a cut above the standard cruising cabin. On average, Disney's staterooms offer more space; most have a split bath (one room with a sink and toilet and another with a sink and a shower/tub), and the majority of them are outside rooms with ocean vistas—many with verandahs.

Staterooms aboard the *Wonder*, *Magic*, *Dream*, and *Fantasy* are decorated in a nautical theme with natural woods and subtle Disney touches, while rooms on the *Wish* celebrate iconic moments in classic Disney films. Universal amenities include a TV, phone with voicemail (and ship-to-shore capability), USB charging outlets, safe, room service menu, and lots of drawer space. Staterooms also come with a small fridge/beverage cooler. After that, different types of accommodations—which are labeled by category—offer different amenities.

# The Navigator App

Disney Cruise Line offers a handy app to help you make the most of every day. Updated daily, the (free) Disney Cruise Line Navigator app offers a comprehensive listing of a day's onboard activities, events, and entertainment. The app should be downloaded prior to the sail away. No access to a smart phone or other app-compatible device? Head to your ship's Guest Services desk for a printed schedule of the day's events.

The Navigator app is an indispensable tool. Check it thoroughly. In addition to listing activities, it provides handy bits of info such as the suggested evening attire for that day. It changes from day to day, so be sure to take note. The app also gives the time and location of character appearances, any points of interest the ship

> **Hot Tip!** If you or a member of your party misplaces their Key to the World card while on board, head to the Guest Services desk on Deck 3. They can issue a new one on the spot (free of charge).

may have scheduled, and a notification of any time zone changes, as well as any special offers or promotions for merchandise, events, or services aboard the ship.

Additional features of the DCL Navigator mobile app include the ability to chat with other cruisers (that you connect with), port information, menus, and account balance (charges made to your onboard account).

# Dining

A Disney cruise is not the place where you'll want to count calories—although most special dietary needs can be accommodated upon request. There's no shortage of rations on these ships.  If your tastes are simple (say, a hot dog) or sublime (how does a juicy beef tenderloin, prepared at Palo, sound?), rest assured you'll never be hungry. Or under-stimulated, for that matter, as many of the ships' restaurants are downright entertaining. And, thanks to a system called "rotational dining," you will get to experience three restaurants, all the while being made to feel like a VIP by your serving staff. That means you will eat at a different one of the three main restaurants each evening, often with the same table guests, and enjoy the services of the same waitstaff. Your serving team gets to know you, as well as your likes and dislikes, very well. The system, unique to Disney Cruise Line, tends to get an enthusiastic thumbs-up from newcomers and cruise veterans alike. The exceptions to the rotational dining scene are Palo, Remy, and Enchanté. (They are reservations-necessary restaurants.)

How do you know where to go on which night? Easy. Your dining rotation is printed on your Key to the World card. And be sure to refer to the Navigator app to note the style of attire for the evening.

# Entertainment

For some folks, a deck chair, a good book, and a steady stream of sunshine are all the entertainment required. Others may delight in an evening of dancing or a bingo-filled afternoon. And some are satisfied with nothing short of a Broadway-style stage show. Fortunately, Disney Cruise Line has it all, plus first-run movies, game shows, variety acts, and more.

## Deck Parties

When it comes to on-deck celebrations, the area surrounding the family pool is party central. Starting with a sailing away celebration and continuing with daily dance fests with Disney characters present, live bands, and fireworks (on most itineraries), it seems like there is always a reason to party. Deck parties are traditionally offered on all sailings—but details may change.

## Just for Kids

The wildly popular kids' programs and activities tend to elicit raves from participants and parents alike. For starters, adults who leave their kids at supervised facilities can be assured that the watchword here is safety. There are plenty of counselors on hand, and the secured programming ensures that they know where every child is at any given time. Kids are checked in with Youth Activities when entering and signed out when exiting with an authorized guardian. Upon check-in, each child is given an Oceaneer wrist band. (It assists with the check-in and checkout process and adds an additional level of security to all youth venues.)

Parents can be contacted via the Disney Cruise Line app if their child has a problem or wants to see them. (It has been our experience that youngsters rarely, if ever, want to leave the kids' programming areas.)

Kids' programs are concentrated on Deck 5 on all ships but the *Wish*, where they're focused on Deck 2. The specially tailored programming is open to kids ages 3 through 12 who are completely potty-trained, able to interact comfortably within the counselor-to-child ratio groups and mix well with peers. There is no extra charge for youth activities. (Non-potty-trained tykes, ages 6 months to 3 years, may go to a cheery nursery. Fees apply.) Cleanliness is a priority.

Kids between ages 3 and 12 can choose to play in the Oceaneer Club or Oceaneer Lab based on what interests them. Siblings and friends between the ages of 3 and 12 can play together regardless, as kids are not segregated by age group. And don't worry about little ones ever being dominated by bigger kids—participants are closely monitored at all times.

Kids who show symptoms of illness are not allowed to participate without approval from the ship's medical center. When it comes to kids' behavior, Disney Cruise Line has a zero tolerance policy for the inappropriate kind, including scratching, biting, and bullying. If your child (or children) displays inappropriate behavior, the Youth Activities team will get in touch with you to discuss the best plan of action.

Except for the nursery, there is no fee for youth activities on any Disney ship.

## ALL GOOD THINGS

How time flies when you're having fun. You blink and it's time to go home! Here are a few tips about the Disney Cruise Line debarkation process.

The day before your return to the debarkation terminal, you will receive an information packet that includes a set of character luggage tags. The character coding designates the area of the terminal in which you can fetch your bags. Be sure to remove the original tags from the inbound trip before adding new tags to all bags. (Guest Services has extra tags.) You will also receive a U.S. Customs form when applicable. Hand this form in as you leave the terminal (one form per household).

On the night before debarkation, you'll place luggage outside your stateroom. (Bags will be collected and delivered to a color/character-coded area in the port terminal.) Keep all valuables, clothing for debarkation, medications, tickets, passports, and other key documents with you. (You have the option of "express walk off" if you're able to take your own bags off the ship in the morning.) Your waitstaff will tell you about last-morning breakfast options. After breakfast, it's time to leave the ship, taking all your happy memories and, quite possibly, making a promise to return again soon. Of course, guests participating in onboard airline check-in don't have to claim bags until their plane lands at their home airport. Certain restrictions apply.

About to begin the "land" part of your vacation? Fetch your bags in the terminal and make a beeline for the bus depot. Flash your Key to the World card (to show you purchased the transfer) and climb aboard. You're going to Disney World!

# INDEX

## Where in the World?
### (photo locations)

**Magic Kingdom:**
1. Peter Pan's Flight, Fantasyland
2. Magic Carpets of Aladdin, Adventureland
3. Walt Disney World Railroad
4. It's a Small World, Fantasyland
5. Dumbo the Flying Elephant, Fantasyland (Storybook Circus)
6. Under the Sea—Journey of the Little Mermaid, Fantasyland

**EPCOT:**
1. Mission: SPACE, World Discovery
2. Journey Into Imagination with Figment, World Celebration (Imagination! pavilion)
3. American Adventure, World Showcase
4. Vanellope Von Schweetz, World Celebration (Imagination! pavilion)
5. Disney Skyliner and Spaceship Earth
6. Living with the Land, World Nature (Land pavilion)

**Disney's Hollywood Studios:**
1. Slinky Dog Dash, Toy Story Land
2. Tatooine Traders, Echo Lake area
3. Fantasmic!, Sunset Boulevard
4. Dinosaur Gertie, Echo Lake area
5. Roundup BBQ, Toy Story Land
6. Fantasmic!, Sunset Boulevard

**Disney's Animal Kingdom:**
1. Festival of the Lion King, Discovery Island
2. Restaurantosaurus, DinoLand U.S.A.
3. Tree of Life as seen from Asia, Discovery Island
4. TriceraTop Spin, Dinoland U.S.A.
5. Kilimanjaro Safaris, Africa
6. Serka Zong Bazaar, Asia

## WDW Resorts:
1. Caribbean Beach resort
2. Pop Century resort
3. Contemporary resort
4. Animal Kingdom Lodge
5. Port Orleans—French Quarter
6. Fort Wilderness Resort & Campground

# COUPONS

## $25 OFF
### YOUR VINTAGE AMPHICAR TOUR

*Subject to terms and conditions on reverse side.*

## RECEIVE $1 OFF
### ANY 16oz ICED OR HOT TEA TO GO

**Creating & Sharing the Experience of a More Flavorful Life**

*Subject to terms and conditions on reverse side.*

## SAVE WITH THE FAMILY FOUR PACK OFFER

Get four tickets for a special price at one Wednesday or Thursday performance.

*Subject to terms and conditions on reverse side.*

## SUGARBOO & CO.
### DEALER IN WHIMSY

## 10% OFF
### ENTIRE PURCHASE OF REGULAR-PRICED ITEMS

Uplifting art prints, charming home goods & whimsical accessories

*Subject to terms and conditions on reverse side.*

## RECEIVE 10% OFF YOUR PURCHASE

**At House of Blues® Gear Shop located in Disney Springs® West Side**

*Subject to terms and conditions on reverse side.*

## 20% OFF LUNCH OR 10% OFF DINNER
**For up to 8 guests in the HOB Restaurant (discount on food and non-alcoholic beverages only)**

Enjoy distinctive Southern-inspired cuisine in an enjoyable atmosphere filled with creative folk art.

*Subject to terms and conditions on reverse side.*

## TERMS AND CONDITIONS

Offer only available at The Spice & Tea Exchange® located at Disney Springs® Marketplace.

Coupon cannot be combined with any other offers or discounts.

Not valid on previously purchased items.

Coupon not redeemable for cash in whole or part.

Reproductions not accepted.

Coupon must be surrendered at time of purchase.

Some merchandise exclusions may apply.

See store for details.

Offer subject to change without notice.

Expires 12/31/24

## TERMS AND CONDITIONS

Located at Disney Springs® The Landing.

Not valid with any other discount or offer.

Reproductions of coupon not accepted.

No cash value.

Minors must be accompanied by a paying adult.

Tours are from 10 A.M. to 10 P.M. (weather permitting)

Up to 3–4 people per car, per tour.

Offer and hours subject to change without notice.

*http://www.theboathouseorlando.com*

407-939-2628

Expires 12/31/24

## TERMS AND CONDITIONS

Offer valid at Disney Springs® Town Center location only.

Cannot be combined with other offers or discounts.

Not valid on sale items or gift cards.

Some exclusions may apply.

Reproductions of coupon not accepted.

Must surrender coupon at time of purchase.

No cash value in whole or in part.

Offer subject to change without notice.

*www.sugarbooandco.com*

Expires 12/31/24

## TERMS AND CONDITIONS

Offer valid on purchases of sets of 4 adult tickets made 9/1/2023–12/12/2024 for Wednesday & Thursday performances 9/6/2023–12/12/2024 on seat categories C3 & C4.

Limit 8 tickets (2 sets of 4) per customer, per coupon.

Tickets subject to taxes and fees and must be purchased at the Drawn To Life Box Office at Disney Springs® located at Walt Disney World® Resort. Tickets sold by Cirque du Soleil.

Coupon must be relinquished at time of purchase. Tickets are non-refundable and non-exchangeable. Cannot be combined with any other offer.

Number of tickets allocated to this offer is limited and subject to availability. Block out dates apply, including 3/18/24–3/24/24, 3/25/24–4/7/24, 11/25/24–12/1/24.

Full details at *cirk.me/Birnbaum*

Expires 12/12/24

## TERMS AND CONDITIONS

Valid only in the House of Blues Restaurant & Bar at Disney Springs®.

Not valid with any other offers, discounts, or at The Smokehouse.

Excludes alcohol, tax, and gratuity.

Reproductions of coupon not accepted.

One offer per check for up to 8 guests.

Must present coupon to receive offer.

Offer subject to change without notice.

Opens daily at 11:30 A.M.; Lunch hours are 11:30 A.M. to 5 P.M.

For reservations, call 407-934-2583.

*www.houseofblues.com/orlando*

Expires 12/31/24

## TERMS AND CONDITIONS

Valid only in the House of Blues Gear Shop at Disney Springs®.

Not valid with any other offers or discounts.

Excludes art, books, jewelry, and sale items.

Reproductions of coupon not accepted.

Must present coupon to receive offer.

Offer subject to change without notice.

*www.houseofblues.com/orlando*

Expires 12/31/24

# COUPONS

## Splitsville
### LUXURY LANES™

## 10% OFF
## BOWLING

*Subject to terms and conditions on reverse side.*

**A FREE SLICE OF HUMMINGBIRD CAKE
WITH PURCHASE OF
A MEAL OR AN APPETIZER**

Southern Favorites and Comfort Food

*Subject to terms and conditions on reverse side.*

©Disney

## 10% OFF
## FOOD & BEVERAGES

15386-2296-2183

*Subject to terms and conditions on reverse side.*

## planet hollywood®

## 10% OFF
## FOOD & BEVERAGES

19866-4191-9066

*Subject to terms and conditions on reverse side.*

## planet hollywood®

## 10% OFF
## MERCHANDISE

12153-9806-6858

*Subject to terms and conditions on reverse side.*

©Disney

# COUPONS

## 15% OFF
### ENTIRE PURCHASE
(exclusions apply)

*Subject to terms and conditions on reverse side.*

©Disney

## 15% OFF
### ENTIRE PURCHASE
(exclusions apply)

*Subject to terms and conditions on reverse side.*

## 15% OFF
### ENTIRE PURCHASE
at Basin

*Subject to terms and conditions on reverse side.*

## RECEIVE 10% OFF
### YOUR ART SUPPLY PURCHASE

"ART. It's what we do. It's ALL we do."

*Subject to terms and conditions on reverse side.*

## RECEIVE 20% OFF
### A SINGLE ITEM

(Limited to Orlando Harley-Davidson®
licensed products)

*Subject to terms and conditions on reverse side.*

©Disney

# COUPONS

# RAGLAN ROAD
### IRISH PUB AND RESTAURANT

## 15% OFF
## MERCHANDISE

*Subject to terms and conditions on reverse side.*

# RAGLAN ROAD
### IRISH PUB AND RESTAURANT

## 20% OFF
## LUNCH

*Subject to terms and conditions on reverse side.*

# PADDLEFISH

## 10% OFF
## WHEN YOU SPEND $30
### (Discount excludes alcohol)

Enjoy fresh seafood, waterfront dining, and 360-degree rooftop views

*Subject to terms and conditions on reverse side.*

## 10% OFF
## WHEN YOU SPEND $30
### (Discount excludes alcohol)

Authentic Italian dishes and handmade pastas inspired by Italy's Lake District

*Subject to terms and conditions on reverse side.*

*arribas brothers*
CRISTAL ARTS

## 10% OFF
## ENTIRE PURCHASE

Offering authentic Disney collectibles, exquisite crystal mementos, and sparkling hand-blown glass gifts.

*Subject to terms and conditions on reverse side.*

©Disney

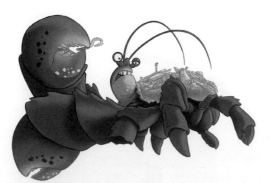

©Disney

# COUPONS

## 20% OFF
### ENTIRE PURCHASE

BRMALLCODE2023

*Subject to terms and conditions on reverse side.*

## 10% OFF
### FOOD & BEVERAGES

*Subject to terms and conditions on reverse side.*

©Disney

## FREE PRETZEL

**When you purchase 2 pretzels
of equal or greater value**

*Subject to terms and conditions on reverse side.*

## 20% OFF
### YOUR ORDER

Enjoy a variety of specialty beverages at Joffrey's,
plus explore the Disney Specialty Coffee Collection
online. Joffrey's Coffee & Tea Co. is the Official
Specialty Coffee of Walt Disney World® Resort.

Use code: JoffreysFan20 to redeem at *Joffreys.com.*

*Subject to terms and conditions on reverse side.*

# CORKCICLE.

## ENJOY 10% OFF
### YOUR ORDER AT CORKCICLE
### AT DISNEY SPRINGS

Corkcicle creates innovative, obsession-worthy
Drinkware, Coolers, and Accessories that
elevate every sip.

*Subject to terms and conditions on reverse side.*

## TERMS AND CONDITIONS

Offer redeemable at Everglazed™ Donuts & Cold Brew.

Valid at Walt Disney World location only.

Must present coupon to receive discount.

Subject to availability.

Limit one coupon per transaction.

Reproductions of coupon not accepted.

Coupon may not be redeemed for cash in whole or in part.

Coupon cannot be combined with any other offer or discount.

Offer subject to change without notice.

*everglazed.com*

Expires 12/31/24

## TERMS AND CONDITIONS

Offer valid for 20% off your entire single purchase (excluding tax and shipping) at participating Columbia Sportswear-owned retail brand store at Disney Springs location only. Limit one discount per household. Must surrender original coupon at time of purchase. Offer is non-transferable and may not be applied to prior purchases, combined with any other offer or discount, used online, redeemed by employees, or applied to gift card purchases, tax or shipping charges. If any portion of the purchase is returned or exchanged, you will be refunded (in the case of a return) or credited (in the case of an exchange) the price paid after discount (prorated per item based on price), and prorated discount amount will be void. All refunds are in the form of the initial payment. Columbia reserves the right to change or cancel this offer at any time. Void if altered or reproduced, and where prohibited, restricted, or taxed.

Valid from 01/01/2023 through 12/31/2024

## TERMS AND CONDITIONS

Valid only at Disney Springs® West Side.

and Marketplace locations.

Coupon not valid with any other offers or discounts.

Limit one per coupon.

Coupon must be surrendered at time of purchase.

Reproductions of coupon not accepted.

Not redeemable for cash in whole or part.

Offer subject to change without notice.

*www.wetzels.com*

Expires 12/31/24

©Disney

## TERMS AND CONDITIONS

Offer is one-time use per customer and valid at Disney Springs only.

Customer must show this coupon to redeem.

Cannot be combined with any other gift cards or discount codes.

Applies to full-price items only.

*corkcicle.com*

1-866-780-0007

Expires 12/31/24

## TERMS AND CONDITIONS

Valid at *Walt Disney World*® Resort locations and *Joffreys.com* only.

Restrictions may apply.

Cannot be combined with any other coupon, offer, or promotion.

Excludes alcoholic beverages.

Limit one coupon per customer.

Coupon must be surrendered at time of purchase.

Reproductions of coupon not accepted.

Not redeemable for cash in whole or part.

Offer subject to change without notice.

Expires 12/31/24

# COUPONS

✂

## FREE CHEF'S APPETIZER
With adult entrée purchase at our
Disney's Animal Kingdom location

*Subject to terms and conditions on reverse side.*

## FREE CHEF'S APPETIZER OF THE DAY
With adult entrée purchase

*Subject to terms and conditions on reverse side.*

## FREE CHEF'S APPETIZER
With adult entrée purchase
at our Disney Springs location

*Subject to terms and conditions on reverse side.*

## 15% OFF DINO STORE PURCHASE
(exclusions apply)

*Subject to terms and conditions on reverse side.*

## 15% OFF RETAIL VILLAGE PURCHASE
(exclusions apply)

*Subject to terms and conditions on reverse side.*

©Disney

# COUPONS

## COMPLIMENTARY GHIRARDELLI® CHOCOLATE BAR

**With purchase of any specialty sundae at Ghirardelli® Soda Fountain & Chocolate Shop**

The world famous chocolatiers, Ghirardelli® Soda Fountain & Chocolate Shop delivers decadent sundaes smothered with hot, house-made fudge, as well as chocolate treats and drinks. Located in the Disney Springs® Marketplace.

*Subject to terms and conditions on reverse side.*

**FAST · FIRE'D®**

## 10% OFF
### ENTIRE PURCHASE
**(exclusions apply)**

*Subject to terms and conditions on reverse side.*

## FREE CHEF'S APPETIZER
### at The Polite Pig

**With a purchase of an adult entrée**

*Subject to terms and conditions on reverse side.*

## RECEIVE A FREE SUITE TREAT
**Of your choice with the booking of any daycare/overnight stay**

Creating Magical Experiences
Bring your pet to stay and play with us — and your best friend will quickly become one of ours, too.

*Subject to terms and conditions on reverse side.*

©Disney

## 10% OFF YOUR IN-STORE PURCHASE OF $50 OR MORE

*Subject to terms and conditions on reverse side.*

# NOTES

# NOTES